英语常用惯用语手册

HANDBOOK OF EVERYDAY ENGLISH IDIOMS

计道宏 编 著

东南大学出版社
SOUTHEAST UNIVERSITY PRESS
·南京·

图书在版编目(CIP)数据

英语常用惯用语手册 / 计道宏编著. -- 南京：东南大学出版社，2025.1. -- ISBN 978-7-5766-2023-8

Ⅰ. H313.3-62

中国国家版本馆 CIP 数据核字第 2025XS9037 号

| 责任编辑：刘　坚(635353748@qq.com) | 责任校对：周　菊 |
| 封面设计：王　玥 | 责任印制：周荣虎 |

英语常用惯用语手册
Yingyu Changyong Guanyongyu Shouce

编　　著	计道宏
出版发行	东南大学出版社
出 版 人	白云飞
社　　址	南京市四牌楼 2 号　邮编：210096
经　　销	全国各地新华书店
印　　刷	广东虎彩云印刷有限公司
开　　本	880 mm×1230 mm　1/16
印　　张	18.125
字　　数	420 千字
版　　次	2025 年 1 月第 1 版
印　　次	2025 年 1 月第 1 次印刷
书　　号	ISBN 978-7-5766-2023-8
定　　价	59.00 元

本社图书若有印装质量问题，请直接与营销部调换。电话(传真)：025-83791830

Contents 目录

A

a	001
aboard	001
about	001
above	002
abroad	003
absence	003
absent	003
abstract	003
accident	003
accidentally	003
according	004
account	004
accounting	004
ace	004
ache	005
acknowledge	005
across	005
act	005
action	006
actual	006
add	006
admit	007
ado	007
advantage	007
adventure	008
affair	008
afraid	008
after	008
against	009
age	009
agree	009
aid	010
aim	010
air	010
alive	011
all	012
alone	017
along	017
another	017
answer	018
any	018
anybody/anyone	018
anyhow	019
anything	019
anywhere	021
AOK	021
apartment	021
ape	021
arm	022
army	022
as	022
ask	024
ass	024
assure	025

目录 Contents

at ……………………… 025	beef ……………………… 039
attention ………………… 026	beer ……………………… 039
aught …………………… 027	before …………………… 040
aunt ……………………… 027	beg ……………………… 040
away …………………… 027	begad …………………… 041
axe ……………………… 028	beget …………………… 041
aye ……………………… 028	beggar ………………… 041
	behave ………………… 041
B	believe ………………… 041
baby …………………… 029	bell ……………………… 042
back …………………… 029	belt ……………………… 043
bad ……………………… 030	Bennett ………………… 044
bag ……………………… 031	beside ………………… 044
bail ……………………… 032	best ……………………… 044
ball ……………………… 032	bet ……………………… 046
bang …………………… 033	better …………………… 047
bargain ………………… 033	between ……………… 047
bark …………………… 034	beware ………………… 048
barn …………………… 034	beyond ………………… 048
bat ……………………… 034	bid ……………………… 050
battle …………………… 035	big ……………………… 050
bawl …………………… 035	bill ……………………… 051
be ……………………… 035	bird ……………………… 052
beam …………………… 037	bit ……………………… 052
bean …………………… 037	bite ……………………… 053
beat …………………… 038	black …………………… 054
bedpost ………………… 039	blame ………………… 054
bee ……………………… 039	blank …………………… 054

Contents 目录

blast	055	box	071
blaze	055	boy	072
bleeding	056	brain	072
bless	056	bread	073
blessing	056	break	073
blind	056	breathe	074
blink	057	breeze	074
block	057	brick	074
blood	057	bridge	075
blow	058	bright	075
blue	060	bring	076
blush	060	broad	076
board	060	broke	077
boat	060	broom	077
bob	061	brother	077
body	061	brown	077
bone	062	brush	077
book	063	bug	078
boom	065	bull	078
boot	066	bully	078
bootstraps	067	bump	079
bore	068	burn	079
born	068	bush	079
bottle	068	business	079
bottom	068	but	081
bounce	070	butter	082
bound	071	button	083
bow	071	buy	083

目录 Contents

buzz	083
by	083

C

Cain	085
cake	085
call	086
can	088
candle	089
candy	089
cap	090
caper	090
card	090
care	091
carpet	093
carry	093
castle	093
cat	093
catch	095
cave	097
ceiling	097
chalk	098
chance	098
change	100
chase	101
cheap	101
cheek	101
cheer	101
cheese	102
chest	103
chew	103
chin	104
chip	105
chuck	106
clear	106
cloud	106
club	107
cobbler	107
cock	107
cod	108
coin	108
cold	108
collar	108
color	108
come	109
comfortable	112
common	112
company	112
complain	113
compliment	113
concern	113
confess	114
cook	114
cookie	114
cool	115
cotton	115

Contents 目录

cough	116	dare	126
could	116	dark	126
count	116	darken	126
country	117	darn	127
course	117	dash	127
cow	117	date	127
crack	117	day	127
crap	119	dead	129
crazy	119	deal	129
creation	119	dear	129
credit	120	death	130
crikey	120	declare	130
crook	120	depend	131
cross	120	deuce	131
crow	121	devil	132
cry	121	diamond	133
cup	122	dice	134
curiosity	122	dickens	134
curse	122	die	134
customer	123	difference	135
cut	123	dirt	135
		discord	136
D		dish	136
daily	124	do	136
damage	124	doctor	139
damn	124	dod	139
dance	125	dog	139
dander	125	doggone	140

目录 Contents

dollar	141		ease	153
door	141		easily	154
dose	142		easy	154
dot	142		eat	155
doubt	143		egg	155
down	143		element	156
dozen	143		elementary	156
drat	144		elephant	156
draw	144		else	156
dream	144		end	157
dress	145		enemy	157
drive	145		enough	157
drop	145		ever	158
drum	147		every	159
dry	147		everything	160
duck	147		exactly	160
dumb	148		excuse	160
dust	148		expect	161
dusty	149		eye	161
Dutch	149		**F**	
Dutchman	149		face	163
duty	150		fact	164
E			fail	164
each	151		fain	164
ear	151		fair	165
earth	153		faith	165
earthly	153		fall	165

Contents 目录

fancy	166	fling	178
far	167	floor	178
fare	167	flume	179
farther	167	flush	179
fast	167	fly	179
fat	168	fob	180
father	168	fog	181
fault	168	foggy	181
favor	169	follow	181
fear	169	food	181
feather	169	fool	181
feed	170	foot	182
feel	170	for	185
feeling	171	forbid	185
fig	171	forget	185
figure	172	forgive	186
find	172	fork	186
finder	172	fortune	186
fine	173	forty	187
finger	173	fox	187
fire	174	fraction	187
first	174	free	187
fish	175	French	188
fist	176	fresh	188
fit	176	friend	188
fix	177	frill	189
flat	177	frog	189
flatter	178	front	190

目录 Contents

fruit	190
fuck	190
full	191
fun	191
funeral	192
funny	192
fur	193
further	193
fuse	193
fuss	193

G

gad	195
gaff	195
game	195
gang	196
garden	197
gas	197
gee	197
George	197
get	197
gift	206
girl	207
give	207
go	212
god	217
golly	219
good	219
goodness	221
Gosh	221
grab	221
grape	221
grasp	221
grass	222
gravy	222
great	222
green	223
grief	223
grin	223
grow	223
guess	223
guest	224
gum	224
gun	224
gut	225

H

habit	226
hail	226
hair	226
half	228
hand	230
handful	232
handle	232
handsome	232
hang	232

Contents 目录

happen ········· 234	honest ········· 261
happy ········· 234	honour ········· 261
hard ········· 235	hook ········· 261
hash ········· 235	hookey/hooky ········· 262
hat ········· 236	hoop ········· 262
hatch ········· 237	hoot ········· 262
haul ········· 237	hop ········· 262
have ········· 237	hope ········· 263
head ········· 243	horn ········· 263
headache ········· 248	horse ········· 264
health ········· 248	hot ········· 265
hear ········· 249	how ········· 266
heart ········· 249	hundred ········· 268
heave ········· 251	**I**
heaven ········· 251	I ········· 269
heck ········· 252	ice ········· 269
heel ········· 253	idea ········· 269
hell ········· 253	if ········· 270
help ········· 256	ill ········· 271
here ········· 257	imagine ········· 271
Hey ········· 258	in ········· 271
high ········· 258	Irish ········· 272
hint ········· 258	iron ········· 272
hip ········· 258	issue ········· 272
hit ········· 259	it ········· 272
hold ········· 259	**J**
Holy ········· 260	Jack ········· 274
home ········· 260	

目录 Contents

jacket 274	kill 286
jam 274	kind 287
jaw 275	kiss 287
jazz 275	kite 288
jeeper 275	knife 288
Jerusalem 275	knock 288
Jesus 275	knot 289
jiffy 276	know 290
jig 276	known 296
jigger 276	**L**
jiminy 276	lady 297
jingo 277	lake 297
job 277	land 297
Joe 278	lap 297
John 278	large 298
joke 278	lark 298
Jove 279	last 299
joy 279	latch 300
judgement 279	late 300
jump 279	lather 301
Jupiter 281	laugh 301
just 281	law 303
K	lay 303
keep 282	lead 305
kettle 283	leaf 306
kick 284	league 306
kid 286	leap 306

Contents 目录

leave	307
leg	308
length	309
less	309
let	310
level	313
liberty	313
lick	313
lid	314
lie	314
life	315
light	317
like	317
likely	318
limit	319
line	319
lip	320
little	322
live	322
lo	323
load	323
loaf	323
lock	323
long	324
look	324
loose	325
loosen	325
lose	325
lost	326
lot	326
louse	326
love	326
luck	327

M

mad	330
made	330
make	331
man	333
marine	334
mark	335
matter	335
mean	335
means	336
mention	336
mercy	337
merry	337
middle	337
might	337
mill	338
million	338
mind	338
mirror	341
mischief	341
miss	341
Missouri	342
mistake	342

目录 Contents

moment	342
money	343
monkey	343
moon	343
more	343
mother	344
motion	344
mouth	344
move	345
much	346
muck	347
mud	347
mum	348
music	348
my	348

N

nail	349
name	349
nature	350
naughty	351
near	351
neck	351
need	352
needle	353
nerve	353
never	354
new	354
news	354
next	355
nice	355
nickel	355
night	355
nip	356
nix	356
no	356
nod	356
noise	357
none	357
nose	358
nosey	360
not	360
note	360
nothing	361
notice	363
now	363
nowhere	364
number	364
nut	365

O

o	366
oar	366
oat	366
oddly	367
odds	367

Contents 目 录

off	367	part	380
offence	369	pass	381
oil	369	passenger	381
old	369	past	381
on	370	pat	382
once	370	patch	382
one	371	path	382
ooh	372	pay	382
oops	372	peace	383
open	372	pecker	383
order	373	peg	383
out	373	penny	384
over	375	pennyworth	385
owe	376	perch	385
own	376	peril	385
		perish	385

P

		person	385
pace	377	phooey	386
pack	377	phrase	386
paddle	378	pick	386
pair	378	pickle	387
palm	378	picnic	387
pan	379	picture	387
panic	379	pie	388
pants	379	piece	388
paper	380	pig	388
par	380	pile	389
pardon	380	pin	390

目录 Contents

pinch ... 390	pour ... 402
pink ... 391	powder ... 402
pip ... 391	power ... 403
pipe ... 391	practice ... 403
piss ... 392	practise ... 404
pitch ... 393	praise ... 404
pity ... 393	preserve ... 404
place ... 394	press ... 404
plague ... 394	price ... 404
plate ... 395	proud ... 404
play ... 395	pull ... 405
please ... 397	pumpkin ... 407
pleasure ... 397	punch ... 407
pocket ... 398	pup ... 408
point ... 398	purse ... 408
poison ... 399	push ... 408
poker ... 399	put ... 409
pole ... 399	
polish ... 399	

Q

quite ... 413

R

pop ... 400	rabbit ... 414
pope ... 400	rack ... 414
possess ... 400	racket ... 414
possum ... 401	rag ... 414
post ... 401	rage ... 414
pot ... 401	rain ... 415
pot-luck ... 402	raise ... 415
potato ... 402	
pound ... 402	

Contents 目录

rake ………… 415	rock ………… 426
ram ………… 416	rocker ………… 426
rap ………… 416	rocket ………… 426
rat ………… 416	roll ………… 426
rate ………… 417	roof ………… 427
rather ………… 418	root ………… 428
rattle ………… 418	rope ………… 428
raw ………… 418	rose ………… 429
read ………… 418	round ………… 429
ready ………… 418	rout ………… 429
really ………… 419	row ………… 430
reason ………… 419	rub ………… 430
red ………… 420	run ………… 431
remedy ………… 420	**S**
remember ………… 420	sail ………… 433
remote ………… 421	sake ………… 433
respect ………… 421	salt ………… 433
rest ………… 421	sam ………… 433
return ………… 421	same ………… 433
rib ………… 421	sand ………… 434
rich ………… 422	sauce ………… 434
ride ………… 422	save ………… 435
riddance ………… 423	say ………… 435
right ………… 423	saying ………… 439
ring ………… 424	scare ………… 439
rip ………… 425	score ………… 439
river ………… 425	Scott ………… 440
road ………… 425	scratch ………… 440

目录 Contents

screw	440		short	454
sea	441		shot	454
seam	441		shoulder	455
search	441		shout	456
second	442		shove	456
see	442		show	456
sell	444		shut	457
send	444		shy	458
sense	444		sick	458
separate	445		side	458
serve	445		sight	459
service	445		sin	459
set	445		sink	459
shade	446		sit	460
shadow	446		six	461
shake	447		size	461
shame	448		skid	461
shape	448		skin	462
share	449		skip	463
sharp	449		sky	463
shell	449		slap	463
shine	450		sleep	463
ship	450		sleeve	464
shirt	450		slip	464
shit	450		smart	464
shoe	451		smile	464
shoot	452		smoke	465
shop	453		snap	465

Contents 目录

snook	466	stake	475
snow	466	stand	476
so	466	star	476
sock	467	start	477
soft	467	stay	477
soldier	467	steady	477
some	467	steam	477
somebody	468	step	478
something	468	stew	478
son	469	stick	479
song	469	stink	481
soon	470	stir	481
sort	470	stone	481
soul	470	stool	481
sound	471	stop	482
soup	471	storm	482
spade	471	story	482
speak	471	stow	483
speed	472	straight	483
spender	472	strain	483
spirit	472	strange	483
spit	472	stranger	484
splash	473	street	484
split	473	strength	484
spot	473	stride	484
spread	474	strike	485
square	474	string	485
stab	475	stroke	486

目录 Contents

strong 486	teach 499
stuff 486	tear 499
stuffing 487	tee 499
stump 488	tell 500
style 488	ten 501
such 488	thank 501
suck 489	that 502
sublime 489	there 503
suffice 489	thick 504
suit 489	thin 505
suppose 490	thing 505
sure 490	think 507
surely 491	this 509
surprise 491	thought 509
sweat 491	throat 509
sweet 492	throw 509
swing 493	thumb 510
system 493	ticket 510
T	tickle 511
tab 494	time 511
tack 494	tip 513
tag 494	toffee 514
take 494	tomorrow 514
tale 497	tongue 514
talk 497	tooth 514
tan 498	top 514
taste 498	toss 515
tea 499	tower 515

Contents 目录

track	516
trade	516
trap	516
tree	516
trick	517
trouble	518
true	518
trump	519
trust	519
truth	519
try	519
tube	520
tuck	520
turkey	520
turn	520
turn-up	521
tut	521
twaddle	521
two	521
twopence	522

U

under	523
understand	523
up	523
upset	525
use	525
usual	525

V

very	526
vest	526
visit	526
vow	527

W

wade	528
wag	528
wagon	528
wait	528
walk	529
want	530
wash	530
watch	531
water	531
wave	532
way	532
wear	533
weather	533
weight	534
welcome	534
well	534
wet	535
whack	535
whale	536
what	536
wheel	538

目录 Contents

where	538	wood	544
whether	539	wool	545
while	539	word	545
whistle	539	work	547
white	539	world	548
whoop	540	worry	550
wick	540	worse	550
will	540	worst	550
win	540	worth	551
wind	541	wrap	551
wipe	541	write	551
wire	542	wrong	552
wise	542		
with	543		
woe	543		
wolf	543		
wonder	544		

Y

year	553
yes	553
you	553
yourself	554

A

a

1 `A 1/one/【美】A number one/No.1` 头等的，极好的，顶呱呱的

Auctioneer：Unique property—an A 1 chance to an A 1 audience. 拍卖商：头等的产业——顶呱呱的机会，只给顶呱呱的顾客。

2 `from A to Z` 从头至尾，彻底地，完全地

Tours knows the subject from A to Z. 图尔斯对这一科目了如指掌。

3 `not know from A to B` 一字不识，什么都不懂

Roland doesn't know from A to B. 罗兰目不识丁。

aboard

1 `all aboard` 请大家上车（或船等）

All aboard! The ship is about to sail. 上船喽！马上就要开船啦。

2 `come/get aboard`【美】加入，入伙

New employees coming aboard in the last six weeks have not been tested. 最近六个星期内来的新雇员没有经过测试。

about

1 `about East` 正确的（方向），对的

Nora found out what was about East and shaped her course accordingly. 诺拉找到了正确的方向，并制定了相应的路线。

2 `how/what about...` ……怎么样，……如何，有……的消息吗，对……打算怎么办，是怎么回事呀

How about the other side beating us last night by three goals? 昨天以一分之差赢了我方的球队打得怎么样？

What about Foster's qualifications for the position? 福斯特担任这个职务够格吗？

3 `how/what about that` 真了不起，真棒（表示惊讶或赞赏的感叹语）

How about that then! Our school's finally beaten yours! 真棒！我们学校终于战胜了你们学校！

4　that's about (the size of) it 就是那么回事，大概如此；大概就是这些了
I like a girl that can make me laugh, I think that's about it. 我喜欢的女孩子要可以逗我笑，我想差不多就这样吧。

5　what you are about 你在做的事情，你自己的事
Mind what you're about. 小心做你自己的事。

above

1　above all 尤其是；最重要的是，首要的是
I should like to rent a house—modern, comfortable and above all in a quiet location. 我想租一幢房子，要求现代化，舒适，尤其是地段要清静。

2　above all things 第一，首先
Above all things, reverence yourself. 最重要的是人要自尊自爱。

3　above and beyond 另外，除此以外
Above and beyond working hard all day, Norton spent his evenings helping in a youth club. 除了整天辛勤工作之外，诺顿每天晚上还在一家青年俱乐部里帮工。

4　above/beyond (all) measure 非常；无可估量；极度，过分
Lowell loves Lucy above measure. 罗威尔非常爱露西。

5　above oneself 趾高气扬，自命不凡，得意忘形；兴高采烈
When Alice gets a bit above herself, she inclines to be a nuisance. 当爱丽丝显得有点儿趾高气扬时，她就会令人厌恶了。

6　above/beyond/without price 无价之宝，珍贵的，千金难买的
This gem is above price. 这块宝石是无价之宝。

7　above the rest 特别，格外
Nancy is head and shoulders above the rest of the class in literature. 在文学方面，南希比班上其他人强得多。

8　above the weather 在高空；无病的
Jack, we wanna fly above the weather. 杰克，我们要在云层之上飞行。

9　above water 水面上的；摆脱困境（麻烦、债务等）
The cost of living is now so high that you need to earn a good income just to keep your head above water. 生活成本现在是如此之高，必须要有很好的收入才能维持。

abroad

1 be all/much abroad 稀里糊涂，莫名其妙；完全离谱，离题万里，大错特错

Your guess is all abroad. 你猜得离题太远。

I am much abroad in my guess. 我猜得大错特错。

2 be all abroad to do anything with 对……一窍不通

I'm all abroad to do anything with philosophy. 我对哲学一窍不通。

absence

absence of mind 心神不定，心不在焉

The driver's absence of mind during driving nearly caused an accident. 司机驾车时心不在焉，差点儿导致意外发生。

Disquietude, absence of mind is on every face. 每个人都显得惶惑不安和心神不定。

absent

absent in one's mind 心不在焉，思想开小差

Newman was absent in his mind then. 当时纽曼心不在焉。

abstract

in the abstract 抽象的，观念上，理论上

The advice, however sound in the abstract, is always dangerous when applied to practice. 这个建议尽管在理论上是无瑕疵的，但在实际运用时却往往是危险的。

accident

have an accident 【委婉】……撒尿喽

Little Jimmy's had an accident! 小吉米撒尿喽！

accidentally

accidentally on purpose 佯装无意，状似巧合实则故意地

The old man used to buy bottles of drink and then accidentally on purpose to get another one. 那个老人出门常常是为了去买酒，可老装成是为了买别的东西而顺便带点儿酒回来。

A

according

1 according to/by 根据，依照

The teacher regraded the students into small groups according to ability. 教师按照能力的高低将学生重新分成若干小组。

2 according to Cocker 正确无误地，严格地

It's all right, according to Cocker. 这按理是不错的。

3 according to Hoyle 根据规定，按照规则；公平地

In quitting without notice, Julius didn't act according to Hoyle. 朱利叶斯没有打声招呼就离开了，这是有悖常理的。

It's not according to Hoyle to hit a man when he's down. 当一个人倒霉时落井下石是有欠公平的。

account

1 be called/go to one's account/【美】hand in one's account 死，被上帝召去

Hyde has gone to his account. 海德已经死了。

2 by all accounts 根据各方面的意见，据大家所说，人人都说

They didn't pass the exam by all accounts. 据说他们没有通过考试。

3 on all accounts/every account 无论如何，总之

It is best to do so on every account. 从哪一方面来看，这样做都是最好的。

On all accounts you must do it. 你无论如何必须做这件事。

4 on no account 决不，无论如何不

On no account do that, you would be wrong. 这件事绝对不要做，你会犯错误的。

On no account should you go. 你绝对不应该去。

accounting

there's no accounting for taste 人各有所好

You may not agree with what she wears; there's no accounting for taste. 你也许不同意她的穿着，但是人各有所好。

ace

1 ace in the hole 秘密的底牌，出奇制胜之术，王牌，备用的有效手段

The lawyer's ace in the hole was a secret witness who had seen the accident. 那个律师手中的王牌是目睹那次事件的一个秘密人证。

2 ace of aces【美】特级王牌飞行员；能手中的能手，强中强

Tom is the ace of aces in the competition. 汤姆是竞赛能手中的能手。

3 have/keep an ace up one's sleeve 手中握有王牌，有应急的妙计

The competition is very keen and all the contestants have an ace up their sleeve. 这次竞赛十分激烈，所有参赛者都会使出他们的看家本领。

4 play one's ace 打出王牌，使出绝招

The general decided to play his ace and send in the tanks. 将军决定使出绝招，派坦克参加战斗。

5 within an ace of 差点儿，险些，几乎

Yes, Paul's better; but he was within an ace of dying/death. 是呀，保罗现在好些了，但前些日子他几乎送了命。

ache

ache to do/for sth. 渴望做某事，渴望得到某物

I'm aching to join in the game. 我渴望参加比赛。

acknowledge

acknowledge the applause 谢幕，答谢

The speaker acknowledged the applause with a small bow. 演讲者微微鞠躬以答谢欢呼。

across

1 be across to 是……的事

It's across to you. 那是你的事。

2 put it across sb. 向某人报仇；欺骗某人

The boss has put it across Mr. White. 老板欺骗了怀特先生。

act

1 act up（机器）运转不正常；（疾病）发作；【美】开玩笑，调皮

The children started to act up as soon as the teacher left the classroom. 老师一离开教室，孩子们就闹起来了。

Every time it rains, our car acts up and stalls at every stop. 每当下雨时，我们的车都出问题，每到一站就抛锚。

2 act one's age【美】行为彬彬有礼；不再调皮捣蛋

A

Act your age, Jim, you're eighteen now! 吉姆，别再孩子气了，你现在已经十八岁了。

You're a big boy now. Act your age. 你现在是个大孩子了，做事要有大孩子的样子。

3 do the... act【美】采取……行动

They did the hospitality act in great shape. 他们殷勤招待客人。

4 do the Dutch act 自杀

Yesterday Dal was found dead in his bed. His father believes he did the Dutch act. 昨天达尔被发现死在床上，他父亲认为他是自杀。

5 get into/in on the act 加入，参与，插一手（为赶时髦或出于利害关系）

If you get in on the act, you wouldn't be short of money for years. 如果你在这中间插一手的话，你会好几年不愁钱花的。

6 put on an act 装腔作势，炫耀，夸夸其谈

George put on an act, pretending he was surprised. 乔治做了一番表演，装出吃惊的样子。

action

1 action stations 各就各位

Action stations, everyone! The royal couple will be here an hour from now! 请大家各就各位！女王夫妇一小时后就到！

2 suit the/one's action to the/one's word 使动作与台词同步；说到就要做到，言行一致

Do talk about your own feelings about others much more, act according to your capability and suit the action to the word. 多谈谈你自己对他人的感受，根据自己的能力行事，做到言行一致。

actual

your actual... 真正合格的（人）；货真价实的（物）

So this is your actual automatic washing-machine! 这才是真正的自动洗衣机！

add

1 add up 加起来得到理想的结果；合乎情理，说得通

Of all my jobs, this adds up. 在我从事的所有职业中，就数这工作报酬

较丰。

It has to be true. It all adds up. 这事一定是真的,从各方面看都说得通。

2 add up to **总括起来意味着,总之就是**

Taylor's sick, but his symptoms don't add up to anything recognizable. 泰勒是病了,但是把各种症状综合起来考虑还看不出来是什么病。

What does all the argument add up to? 所有的论据归根结蒂说明了什么?

3 add fuel to the flame **火上浇油;变本加厉;倍增情感**

By criticizing his son's girl, the father added fuel to the flame of his son's love. 父亲批评了儿子的女友,反而使儿子更加爱她。

Bob was angry with Ted and Ted added fuel to the flame by laughing at him. 鲍勃本来就生特德的气,特德对他的嘲笑更是如同火上浇油。

admit

1 I must admit **我得承认,坦白地说**

I must admit that I'm glad it's all over. 我承认,这一切都过去了,我非常高兴。

I must admit, I'm not as fit as I used to be. 说实话,我身体是不如以前那么结实了。

2 (while) admitting that **虽然承认,但是**

Prudent parents, while admitting that their daughters should marry for love, take care that all the young men they met should be rich. 精明的父母虽然承认女儿应为爱而嫁,但却一定要使女儿遇到的青年男子都是有钱人。

ado

1 much ado about nothing **无事生非,小题大做**

It's just a rumor, a choreographed much ado about nothing. 这只不过是谣言,是有人故意地小题大做、无事生非。

2 without more/further ado **不再啰嗦地,干脆地,立即**

Toby indicated my simple tasks and without more ado set off at an amble. 托比向我交代了几项简单的工作,随即不慌不忙地走了。

advantage

1 gain/get/play/have the/an advantage over **【美】骗人,哄人;胜过**

A

A man who can think will always **have an advantage over** others. 能动脑子的人总是会胜过别人。

Toward the end of the race, I **got the advantage over** Mary. 赛跑接近终点的时候,我超过了玛丽,取得了优势。

2 take advantage of 欺骗,捉弄;占……便宜

Ulysses **took advantage of** his friend's kindness. 尤利塞斯利用他朋友的仁慈来帮他做事。

The little children did not know how much to pay for the candy, and Ralph **took advantage of** them. 小孩子们不知道买糖果得付多少钱,于是拉尔夫就乘机欺骗他们。

adventure

what an adventure 哎呀,真了不起;多么惊险啊

affair

1 mind your own affairs/business 莫管闲事

I wish you would **mind your own business**, and not poke your nose into my affairs. 我希望你还是管管你自己的事,别干涉我的事情。

2 that's my own affairs/business 那是我的私事

That's my own affairs, not yours. 那是我的事,与你无关。

3 none of your affairs/business 不关你的事,与你无关

That's **none of your affairs**. 那不关你的事。

afraid

I'm afraid (that) 恐怕,很遗憾

I'm afraid you are wrong. / You are wrong, **I'm afraid**. 恐怕是你错了。

I'm afraid we can't go on Monday. 恐怕我们星期一去不了。

I'm afraid that it's not going to work out. 恐怕这事不会成功。

I'm afraid that you have not appreciated the urgency of the matter. 恐怕你还没有意识到这件事的紧迫性。

after

1 after a fashion 不高明地,差劲地

Walton played tennis **after a fashion**. 沃尔顿网球打得马马虎虎。

The roof of the house kept the rain after a fashion. 那栋房子的屋顶漏雨。

2 after you 您请（先走）
"After you," the gentleman said, opening the door to the lady standing by. "您先请，"这位先生边说边为站在一边的女士打开房门。

3 after you with 您用过后给我
After you with the salt, Jo. 乔，你用过盐后给我。

against

against a raining/rainy day 未雨绸缪，以备不时之需
We'd better make preparations against a rainy day. 我们最好做好准备以备不时之需。

age

1 age before beauty 年龄比美貌重要（常被青年女子用作对年长男子的戏谑恭维语）；长者先请（常被较貌美的青年人戏谑地用作礼貌用语）
"Age before beauty," the young man said to his mother as he opened the door for her. "长者先请，"这个年轻人边说边为他的母亲打开门。

2 in your old age 你还是……，你到底……（幽默）
"Have one of these apples!" "Thanks—you're getting generous in your old age!" "吃一个苹果吧！""谢谢，你终于变得大方些了。"

3 for ages/an age 好久……
I haven't seen you for ages. 好久不见了。

agree

1 I couldn't agree less 我完全不同意，我绝对不同意
"This government's policies are really helping the country along." "I couldn't agree less; everything seems to have gone wrong for them." "这届政府的政策的确有助于国家的发展。""我完全不同意你的看法：这些政策的实施，恰恰导致一切都乱了套。"

2 I couldn't agree more 我完全同意
"This will satisfy everybody." "I couldn't agree more." "这将会让大家都感到满意。""我的意见和你的完全相同。"

A

aid

in aid of 为了……目的；为了帮助……

What are all these books in aid of? Don't tell me you've finally started your revision! 这些书是做什么用的？不用说你终于开始复习了！

What is the collection in aid of? 这笔募集的捐款是做什么用的？

aim

1 we aim to please 愿为顾客提供最佳服务，保证顾客满意（餐馆、商店、宾馆的服务人员回答管理人员问候时的套语）

"This meal is absolutely delicious!" "We aim to please." "这顿饭真的很可口！""为顾客服务是应该的。"

2 aim at the moon 瞄准月亮；痴心妄想，好高骛远

He who aims at the moon may hit the top of a tree; he who aims at the top of a tree is unlikely to get off the ground. 瞄准月亮，可能打中树梢；瞄准树梢，很可能连地面都离不了。

You are just aiming at the moon. 你简直是痴心妄想。

air

1 get the air 【美俚】被解雇；求爱被拒；被情人抛弃

After Bernard got the air, he moped in a lovesick trance for weeks. 伯纳德求爱碰壁后好几个星期闷闷不乐、精神恍惚。

2 give the air 【美俚】解雇；拒绝；抛弃情人；与……断绝关系

Anthony gives the air too freely to opinions he doesn't happen to agree with. 安东尼往往轻率地拒不接受与自己不同的意见。

3 beat the air/wind 白费力气，徒劳

To argue with Armstrong is like beating the air. 跟阿姆斯特朗辩论无异于白费力气。

4 eat the air 【英古】枉费心机，画饼充饥，想入非非

I don't like the person who always eats the air. 我不喜欢整天想入非非的人。

5 fish in/plough the air 白费力气，水中捞月，缘木求鱼

To ask the boss for help is to fish in the air. 找老板帮忙是缘木求鱼。

6 be up in the air 【美】不肯定；非常生气；很激动，心神不安；感到疑惑；悬而未决

We haven't decided on which restaurant to eat at. It's still up in the air. 我们还没决定去哪一家饭馆吃饭呢,现在仍悬而未决。

7 go up in the air【美】感到疑惑,拿不准;十分恼火;非常激动,异常兴奋
My father went straight up in the air when he heard I damaged the car. 父亲听说我撞坏了汽车,立即火冒三丈。

8 leave sb. (up) in the air 让某人感到如堕五里雾中不知如何是好
What the boss said left us in the air. 老板说的话让我们不知如何是好。

9 leave sb. in the cold 对某人冷酷无情,不理睬某人,冷落某人
Jane left Tom in the cold on purpose. 简故意冷落汤姆。

10 leave sb. in the lurch (在某人需要帮助时)袖手旁观,见死不救
They will not leave you in the lurch. 他们不会在你有困难时袖手旁观的。

11 tread/walk on/upon air 得意洋洋,乐得飘飘欲仙
The execution of this arrangement so thrilled Temple that he felt as though he were walking on air. 这事的安排使坦普尔从心眼儿里乐了起来,觉得浑身轻飘飘的。

12 put on airs 摆架子
That would be putting on too many airs. 那样的话可就是过分摆架子了。

13 assume/give oneself airs 装腔作势,摆架子
Benjamin was in great demand. Consequently, he gave himself airs. 到处都需要本杰明,因此他自以为了不起。

14 off the air 停止广播,不再被播报
We used to watch that show, but it's off the air now. 过去我们常常看那套节目,可现在已经停播。

15 on the air (被)广播;在广播/电视直播中
Viewers of BBC news have been seeing Mr. Harris regularly on the air. 收看BBC电视新闻的观众近来经常在电视中见到哈里斯先生。

alive

1 heart alive 什么,哎呀,我的天哪
Heart alive! That's my lost laptop! 天哪! 这是我丢失的笔记本电脑!

2 man alive 哎哟(表惊讶、不耐烦等)
Man alive! What an exciting ball game! 呦,好紧张的一场球赛!
Why, man alive, I can't do it! 哎呀,我不能做这件事!

A

Man alive! What are you doing here? 哎呀,你在这儿干什么?

3 look alive 赶快,加油,干起来

I say, look alive. We've got only two minutes left. 喂,快点！我们只剩两分钟了。

4 sakes alive 【美】哎呀,吓我一跳,真糟糕,好家伙

"Sakes alive!" ejaculated the American girl. "哎呀,我的天哪!"那个美国女孩儿吃惊地说。

5 skin alive 【美】严厉责罚;彻底击败;痛骂,斥责

Our team will skin the visiting team alive. 我们的球队将把客队打得一败涂地。

You will be skinned alive by your mother. 你准会挨你母亲一顿痛骂。

all

1 after all 毕竟,究竟,归根到底;虽然如此

I don't think we should let Adela go to town by herself. After all, she is ten now. 我认为我们不该让阿德拉独自进城去,要知道,她现在才十岁呀。

After all, facts are facts. 无论如何,事实毕竟是事实。

2 all along 始终,一直,一贯

I thought all along that you two would end up getting married, and you have! 我始终认为你们俩终究会结婚的,现在果然如此。

We know all along that Bach is going to make it. 我们始终认为巴赫会成功的。

3 all in 疲倦极了,精疲力尽

After the marathon, most of the competitors looked all in. 跑完马拉松,大部分参加比赛的人显得疲惫不堪。

4 all in all 总的说来,总之;合计,总共;完全地;最重要的,最宝贵的;最心爱的

All in all, we see things pretty much in the same way, although we do disagree on minor details. 总之,我们的观点大部分是接近的,尽管在一些细节上我们还确实存在分歧。

Study is all in all to me. 对我来说,学习永远排在第一位。

5 all of 足足,整整;不少于,至少

It's all of millions of miles to the stars! 到别的星球上去足足有数百万英里之遥。

Caroline's all of eighty years old, you know. 你看,卡罗琳已整整八十岁了。

6　all of a 完全处于……状态;显然

Field was all of a dither/shake/tremble with cold. 菲尔德冷得浑身发抖。

Mother is all of a flutter because of the thunder and lightning. 由于电闪雷鸣,母亲显然很紧张。

7　all of a doodah/dooda【美俚】非常兴奋,非常激动;焦急不安的

I feel all of a dooda. 我感到非常兴奋。

8　all one can/has 尽自己的一切力量

You must sit still all you can. 你必须规规矩矩坐着别动。

Felix slammed the desk drawer all he had. 费利克斯使劲把书桌抽屉砰地关上。

9　all one knows 自己力所能及的一切

We must try all we know to do it. 我们必须全力去做这件事。

10　all over 到处,浑身;全部结束,完蛋;覆盖着;向……献殷勤

Hansen has lots of money. That's why these people are all over him. 汉森很有钱,所以这帮人老是围着他献殷勤。

Before I noticed what happened, Jacob was all over me. 我还没弄清发生了什么事,雅各布就已经缠上了我。

11　all right 安然无恙的;健康良好的;正确的;好,可以;好啊,没关系(表示讥讽、不耐烦、威胁等);确实,当然(加强语气);正如所料;令人满意的

I was ill for a week, but I'm all right now. 我病了一个星期,但现在好了。

All right, don't take my advice if you don't want to, but don't blame me when you fail. 好吧,你不愿意接受我的建议就算了,可你失败了别怨我。

12　all right for you 算了吧(儿童用语)

All right for you! I'm not playing with you any more. 算了吧,我再也不跟你玩了!

13　all round/【美】**all around** 周围,处处;广博的,全面的;多才多艺的

Things looked a bit more promising all round. 看来各方面情况都有所好转。

Silence all around, if you please! 请大家全体肃静!

14 all serene【俚】好的，行；一切正常，平安无事

"You'll meet me tonight at the railway station and bring me the money." "All serene." "今晚你到火车站来见我，并且把钱带来。""好的。"

15 all that 那么，如此

Thinking back, I feel it wasn't all that bad. 回想起来，我觉得事情还没有糟到那般地步。

I never knew the child was all that good at painting. 我从不知道那个孩子画画竟那么出色。

16 all the 仅有的；更，甚至

A hut was all the home O'Neil ever had. 一间茅屋是奥尼尔仅有的栖身之所。

A touch of the iron is all the care this dress needs. 这衣服只需熨斗稍微一熨就行。

17 all the more 更加，越发；反而更好

If you don't eat your dessert, all the more for us. 你若不吃那份甜食，我们会有更多好吃的。

18 all there 神志正常的，头脑清醒的（常用于否定句或疑问句）

Do you think Occam is all there? 你认为奥卡姆神志正常吗？

Joe acted queerly and talked wildly, so we thought he was not all there. 乔的行为怪异，言语狂放，所以我们认为他精神不太正常。

19 all things considered 大体上说，总的来说

All things considered, this is good news for epidemiologists. 总的来说，流行病学家认为这是好消息。

20 all this 这么过分的，如此极度的

Stop all this grumbling. 别这么没完没了地发牢骚。

If you go out in all this rain, you'll get wet. 这么大的雨还出去，你会淋湿的。

21 all through 一直，始终

Piers never uttered a word all through. 皮尔斯始终没说一句话。

I knew that all through. 我自始至终与闻其事。

22 all together 一道，同时，一起

They arrived all together. 他们一起到达。

All together now, children, "All things are bright and beautiful…" 孩子

们,大家一起念:"万物明媚美好……"

23 all told 总共,合计;总之

All told, I attended school less than one year. 我总共上了不到一年学。

Including candy sale profits, we have collected $300 all told. 包括卖糖果的利润,我们总共进账300美元。

24 all up （即将）完蛋,无望

With their ammunition gone, the patrol knew it was all up with them. 弹药打完之后,巡逻队意识到他们快完了。

By night it was all up for the trapped miners. 随着夜幕降临,困在井下的矿工越发感到绝望。

25 all very fine/well 【反】很好,顶好,好倒是好

It's all very well for you to complain, but can you do any better? 你固然可以抱怨,但叫你来做,你能做得更好吗?

It's all very well if Jane comes with us, but how will she get back home? 简跟我们一起来当然好,但她怎么回家呢?

26 and all 及其他一切;等等;连同……一起;以及由此引起的后果;也;当然喽

I went to school regularly, even with mama sick and all. 我按时上学,甚至在妈妈生病的情况下也是如此。

27 and all that 以及其他等等;以及诸如此类的事情（通常用来结束致谢、致歉、问候之类的话）

By cereals we mean wheat, oats, rye, barley, and all that. 我们说谷类,指的是小麦、燕麦、黑麦、大麦以及诸如此类的东西。

The plot is very interesting and all that, but I still don't like it as a play. 这个情节很有趣、很生动什么的,可是作为一个剧本我还是不喜欢它。

28 as all that 果如所料,如预料的那样

Raman's not as clever as all that, considering what his brothers are like. 照他的几个兄弟的情况来看,拉曼不像我们想象的那么聪明。

Oh come now, things aren't as bad as all that. 哦,好啦,情况并不是那么糟。

29 damn all 一点也不,丝毫不

I know damn all about it. 我对此一无所知。

30 for all 虽然,尽管

You might as well never have gone to college, for all the good it's done you. 你本来可以不上大学的,尽管这给你带来了好处。

Sam's been ill for two weeks, but for all that, he must be fit for next week's big match. 山姆已经病了两周了,尽管如此,他还是得尽快恢复健康,以便参加下周的大型比赛。

31 for all I/you, etc. know 不知道;也未可知,说不定与……所知相反

Vincent may be very rich, for all I know. 据我所知,文森特可能很有钱。

They may be dead for all we know. 说不定他们已死亡。

32 for all/what I/you, etc. care 漠不关心;无动于衷;全然不在乎

For all I care, Jim could be at the North Pole for the rest of his life—I'm never speaking to him again. 吉姆可能在北极了此一生,我才不管呢,我再也没有同他说过话。

Her mother may be starving, for all she cares. 她母亲可能在挨饿,她才不管呢。

33 in all 总共,合计;总之,简言之

There were 100 people in all. 总共有 100 人。

In all, this is an interesting textbook. 总之,这是一本有趣的教科书。

34 it's all very well ……好倒是好;……固然不错;好极了,真是太妙了(表示不满、讥讽等)

It's all very well for you to say that, but what can I do? 你说得容易,可我又有什么办法?

35 of all (the) 有的是……;偏偏要……(表示烦恼或惊讶);在……中偏偏

Of all the… someone's taken my bicycle! 偏偏我的自行车被盗了,真倒霉!

Why ask me to help, of all people? 人这么多,为什么偏偏叫我去帮忙?

36 over all 全部地,从一头到一头;总的说来

Over all, the proportion of the population 19 and under may stabilize at about 27 per cent. 总的说来,19 岁及以下的人口比例可能稳定在 27% 左右。

37 that's/it's all right 不值一谢;别客气;不必介意,没关系

"Thank you for your present!" "That's all right!" "谢谢你的礼物!""别客气!"

"Thank you very much for coming to see us!" "That's all right! Any time!" "非常感谢您来看我们!""别客气!别客气!"

38 that's all there's to it 只是这些;就是这么回事

I love him, and he loves me, and that's all there's to it. 我爱他,他也爱我,就是这么回事。

39 when all comes/goes to all 概括一切之后,通盘考虑之后
When all comes to all, nothing was done. 说到底,什么都没有做。

40 when all is said and done 结果,毕竟,终究;归根结蒂
When all is said and done, it's your house. 说到底,这毕竟是你的家。
You've been a pretty good friend, when all is said and done. 归根结蒂一句话,你真是个好朋友。

alone

all alone 独自地;独自一人,孤单的
Each one of us is all alone at some point in our lives. 我们中的每一个人,在人生的某些时候,都是非常孤单的。

along

be along 到达,到场,拜访
I'll be along about three. 三点钟左右我到场。
My relief would be along in a couple of weeks. 两三星期后会有人来接替我。

another

1 ask (me) another 我不知道;问别的吧,我答不上来,我怎么晓得
"Are you fond of birds, Uncle Nic?" "Ask me another, Greta! Well, I suppose so." "你喜欢鸟儿吗,尼克叔叔?""那我可不知道,格里塔!嗯,我想大概喜欢吧。"
"If the government knows how to run the country, why aren't things getting any better?" "Ask me another! I've no idea either!" "如果政府知道如何治理国家,为什么国家形势不见任何好转呢?""你问我算瞎问,我也不知道怎么回事。"

2 you're another 你也不例外! 你也是(用于反驳)
"You're a liar!" "You're another!" "你是个骗子!""你也是!"
"I think Jim's rather a fool!" "Yes, and you're another!" "我看吉姆有点傻!""不错,你也一样!"

A

answer

1 answer back 回嘴，顶嘴
Don't answer back! 不许顶嘴！

2 know all the answers (自以为)什么都精通；老于世故，看透人生
It is better to ask some of the questions than to know all the answers. 还是问些问题好，不要自以为什么都知道。

3 one who knows all the answers 【美俚】万事通，老世故
William thinks he is the only one who knows all the answers and doesn't respect anybody else's opinion. 威廉以为自己什么都懂，不尊重其他人的意见。

4 the answer's a lemon 回答是"柠檬"；你这个可笑的问题无法回答，没有回答的必要（一种无实际意义的俏皮回答，用于回答荒谬的或难答的问题）；无法理解
The answer is a lemon why Mary acted so. 无法理解玛丽为什么要这样做。

any

1 be not having any 不愿参与；不予理会；无法容忍
They wanted me to be in it. But I wasn't having any, thanks. 他们要我参与这件事。但谢天谢地，我才不呢。

2 any old how 【俚】乱糟糟；无论如何
The books were piled up all over the floor any old how. 地板上书堆得乱七八糟的，到处都是。

anybody/anyone

1 anybody's/anyone's game/match/race 【美】（参赛者势均力敌而）无法预测输赢的比赛
The match between the two teams is anybody's game. 两队之间的比赛结局无法预料。

2 anybody's/anyone's guess 大家都拿不准的事
What will happen next is anybody's guess. 下一步会发生什么事，谁也说不准。

anyhow

all anyhow 【美】草率,潦草,马虎
Things are all anyhow. 事事都很马虎。

anything

1 anything but 除了……以外什么都可以;远不是,根本不是,绝不是
(anything but 颇为常用,但不如 not at all 通俗)
Hoover is anything but a scholar. 说胡佛是什么都可以,但绝不是一个学者。
The boys know they had broken the rules and they were anything but happy when they were called to the office. 孩子们知道自己犯了错,所以当他们被叫到办公室时绝对高兴不起来。

2 anything doing 打算干什么,有什么活动吗,能帮帮忙吗
"Anything doing tonight?" "Yes, would you like to come and play football with us?" "今晚有什么活动吗?""有,愿意和我们踢足球吗?"
I'd like a lift into town this morning, anything doing? 今天早晨我想搭车进城去,你能帮帮忙吗?

3 anything like 全然;完全像……
Maggie is anything like as nice as her sister. 玛吉像她姐姐那样可爱。
Winning first prize of \$1,000 still doesn't mean we are anything like near being able to buy a house. 尽管我们获得了头等奖的 1,000 美元奖金,但买一幢房子还是远远不够。

4 anything of 一点儿;一点儿……的味道
I haven't seen anything of Edmund just lately. 近来我连埃德蒙的影子也没有见到过。
Is George anything of a scholar? 乔治有点儿学者气质吗?

5 as... as anything 非常,很;无比地
Gracie is as busy as anything with a new baby, a job, and a house to run! 格雷西忙得什么似的:有了新生儿,有工作,还要料理家务!
Don't worry about it. It isn't final. We'll get a reversal as sure as anything. 别担心,这不是最终结果,我们一定可以转败为胜的。

6 don't do anything I wouldn't do/be good if you can't be good/careful 再见
(友好而幽默的告别用语,有时含有性生活方面的暗示)

"Don't do anything I wouldn't do, Claire!" Sue said, winking at Claire. "OK, cheerio, then!" "再见！克莱尔，"苏说着，向克莱尔使了个眼色。"好吧，再见！"

7 for anything 无论如何；极度地，过分地

Jackson wouldn't travel by air for anything. 杰克逊说什么也不愿意坐飞机旅行。

I will not give up halfway for anything. 我决不半途而废。

8 for anything I care 我管不着，与我无关

Keats may die for anything I care. 基茨的生死关我屁事。

9 for anything I know 据我所知；总之，大概

Lawrence may be an honest person for anything I know. 据我所知，劳伦斯可能是个诚实的人。

Macaulay may be a good man for anything I know. 据我所知，麦考利可能是个好人。

10 if anything 如果稍有区别的话；甚至正相反，甚至还不如说

Nora's family, if anything, was poorer than mine. 如果有区别的话，诺拉家比我家更穷。

I'm not ashamed of Parker. If anything, I'm proud. 我并不为帕克而感到羞耻，正相反，我甚至感到骄傲。

11 like anything 厉害地，很凶地；要命地，拼命地；飞快地

Though the young man ran like anything, he couldn't catch his train. 尽管那个年轻人飞快地跑，但还是没赶上那趟火车。

The thief ran like anything when he saw the policeman. 那个小偷一看见警察就飞快地跑了。

12 not come to anything 落空了

Roy's plan did not come to anything. 罗伊的计划落空了。

13 or anything 或其他什么的

Shelley's not suffering from any peculiar disease or anything. 雪莱没有患任何特殊的疾病，也没有什么其他问题。

If you want to ring me or anything, I'll be at the office all day. 如果你要打电话给我或来找我什么的，我会一整天都在办公室。

anywhere

1 anywhere near 在任何程度上；全然，压根儿；几乎，差不多

Stella isn't anywhere near as kind as Barney is. 斯特拉一点儿也不像巴尼那样和蔼可亲。

Does my answer come anywhere near the correct one? 我的回答是否多少接近正确答案了？

2 get anywhere/any place 进展；成功；吃得开（用于否定句、疑问句、条件从句）

The programme couldn't get anywhere. 计划不可能取得什么进展。

If the talks are to get anywhere, both sides will have to make concessions. 如果谈判要取得进展，双方都必须作出让步。

3 if anywhere 如果有什么地方的话

You will find it in London if anywhere. 如果有什么地方能找到这东西的话，也只有在伦敦了。

4 we can't take you anywhere 真拿你没办法，我们哪儿也不能带你去（当某人做了某些不体面的事或说了某些不合适的话，特别是在会见朋友或在餐馆进餐时的诙谐说法）

That's the sixth cake you've had so far! Honestly, Peter, we can't take you anywhere, can we? 这是你吃完的第六块蛋糕了，彼得，老实说，我们真拿你没办法，真是哪儿也不能带你去！

AOK

AOK/A-OK/A-Okay【美】一切正常，极好的，完美的；一切就绪（源自美国宇航员向发射指挥中心的报告语）

Everything is going to be AOK. 一切都会顺利的。

apartment

apartment to let【俚】头脑空空如也

Walton has got apartment to let. 沃尔顿有点儿傻里傻气的。

ape

go ape over【美】热衷于，迷上，爱上

Yeates goes ape over a girl. 耶茨为一个姑娘神魂颠倒。

A

arm

1 chance one's arm 冒险,做冒险的事;碰碰运气
You must chance your arm if you want to succeed. 要想成功就一定得冒险一搏。

2 would give one's right arm for 愿意为……付出巨大代价
Most of the people would give their right arm for a better education. 大多数人愿付出巨大的代价以求得到更好的教育。

3 talk one's arm/ear/head off【俚】对……唠叨个没完
The old lady talked my arm off. 那个老太太对我唠叨个没完没了。

4 under the arm【俚】低劣的,质量差的
I read no matter how bad the book is and some are right under the arm, stand on me. 不管多烂的书我都读,相信我,有些书实在不怎么样。

5 an arm and a leg【美俚】极高的价格
The house must have cost the couple an arm and a leg. 这房子一定让这对夫妇花了不少钱。

6 be up in arms 大动肝火,非常气愤
The boss is up in arms about the company's poor sales record in the past few months. 由于公司最近几个月的销售业绩不佳,老板正在大动肝火。

army

you and whose army 你算老几,你也配,你敢
"If you don't shut up, I'll come and hit you!" "Yeah—you and whose army?" "你再不闭嘴,看我不揍你!""呸,你敢!"

as

1 as good as 简直是,几乎是;事实上;实际上,实质上
The business is as good as done. 这件事情可以说已经结束。
What MacArthur said has as good as shown his attitude. 麦克阿瑟的话实际上已经表明了他的态度。

2 as well be hanged for a sheep as (for) a lamb 一不做二不休,要干索性大干一场

3 as how 是否
I don't know as how he will be back. 我不知道他是否会回来。

4 as if 别指望……；才不会……（表示不同意的生气说法）；瞎话，骗人

As if you expect me to believe that story! 别指望我会相信那个鬼话！

It isn't as if Norris were poor. 诺里斯不见得穷。

5 as (it) is【美】原样，照原来的样子，按现状（指不再修理或改进）

Leave it as it is. 听其自然。

We bought the table as is. 这张桌子我们买来时就是这个样子。

6 as it is/was 实际上，其实

We hoped things would get better, but as it is, they are getting worse. 我们希望形势会好转，但事实上现在形势正在恶化。

Abe pretended not to know Daisy, as it was, she was his wife. 阿贝假装不认识戴西，其实戴西就是他的妻子。

7 as it were 似乎，仿佛；可以说是；在某种程度上

Cromwell is not equal to the task, as it were. 克伦威尔似乎不能胜任这份工作。

Edward's father is, as it were, his friend. 爱德华的父亲好像是他的朋友。

8 as well 倒不如；还是……的好；最好……；同样；也；不妨；而且

It's nothing very secret, but it's always as well to keep quiet about these things. 这也算不了什么秘密，不过这种事还是不开口的好。

We may as well begin at once. 我们不妨立刻就开始。

9 as well as 既……又，和……一样；也，而且

Our classroom is sunny as well as large. 我们的教室不但大而且阳光充足。

The book tells about the author's life as well as his writings. 这本书讲了作者的作品和他的生平。

10 as you please 随你的便；非常

You may do as you please. 你喜欢做什么就做什么。

There was Tinker, sitting there, cheerful as you please. 廷克坐在那里，非常愉快的样子。

11 as you were 不，不对，我再说一遍（用于纠正说错的话）；原地不动，复原（指恢复原来的姿势）

As you were! （军事口令）原地不动！

I saw Smith—as you were—I mean Brown. 我见到了史密斯，哦，不对，我

指的是布朗。

ask

1 ask for it/trouble 自找麻烦,自讨苦吃

"You were asking for it," Pat said as she hit her child. "你是自作自受,"帕特边打她的孩子边说。

If you turn up late when you promised to be early, you'll really asking for trouble! 如果你答应早点到,而结果却迟到,那就是自找麻烦了。

2 I ask you 请问(表示惊讶、厌恶或其他的强烈感情)

Peter says he's applying for a job as a policeman! I ask you! I know he's had a lot to do with them in the past, but that's been when he's been caught speeding! 彼得说他正在申请一份警察的工作!他过去是同警察打过不少交道,可那是他在开车超速被抓住的时候,请问,这你知道吗?

Now, I ask you, can anybody stand this kind of thing? 请问,有谁忍受得了这种事?

3 if you ask me 我认为,据我看,叫我说,实话说(常用于并未被询问的情况下)

If you ask me, Sally's a fool for going out with Alan—she's not his type at all! 依我看,莎莉真傻,她不该同艾伦一道出去,因为她根本不是艾伦喜欢的那种人。

"I don't think you're as ill as you look, if you ask me." "I wasn't asking you, so shut up!" "照我看,你不像是在生病。" "我又没问你,你给我闭嘴!"

ass

1 act/play the ass 做糊涂事,出洋相

Don't act the ass. 别干傻事。

2 make an ass of oneself 做蠢事

I made a real ass of myself at the meeting. 我在会上出了个大洋相。

You only make an ass of yourself when you meddle in business matters. 你在生意经营方面多管闲事只能让你自己丢脸。

3 make an ass of 捉弄……

Don't make an ass of the honest man. 不要捉弄那个老实人。

4 keep one's ass out of the way 滚开

The boss said, "Keep your ass out of the way or I'll kill you." 老板说："滚开,否则我就宰了你。"

5 break/bust one's (sweet) ass 拼命干
Pearson busts his ass all day to take home 170 bucks a week. 为了每星期挣170美元,皮尔逊整天拼命干活。

6 chew one's ass (out) 【美俚】严厉责骂,训斥,呵斥,申斥
I knew my dad was going to chew my ass out. 我早就知道我爸准会训斥我的。

7 have/get one's ass in a sling 遇到了麻烦,垂头丧气,情绪低落;生气
The members of the team have got their ass in a sling after they were defeated. 比赛输了,全队球员垂头丧气。

8 kiss (one's) ass 拍马屁
It was that everyone would just kiss my ass. 这就是为什么每个人都会来拍我马屁的原因。

9 on one's ass 破产,穷困潦倒,处境艰难,毫无希望
Peter has been on his ass after he was fired. 彼得自从失业以后一直穷困潦倒。

10 stick/shove it up one's ass 关你屁事;关我屁事;收起你那一套

11 work one's ass off 拼命干
I've been working my ass off delivering food for the restaurant! 为了给这家餐馆送外卖,我都快累死了!

assure

(you can/may) rest assured 请放心
You can rest assured that I will do my best. 请放心,我一定尽力而为。
Rest assured, we are doing all we can to find your son. 请放心,我们正竭尽全力找回你的儿子。

at

1 at all 完全,丝毫,绝对(用于否定句);究竟,果然(用于肯定句、疑问句及条件句)
I want to know how long Agnes has been there. I want to know what she's there at all for. 我要知道艾格尼丝在那里待了多久。我要知道她究竟去那里干什么。

A

You must know it if you know anything at all. 如果你当真知情的话，那么这个你应该知道。

2 at all costs/at any cost 无论如何，不惜任何牺牲和代价

I will accomplish my purpose at all costs. 我要不惜一切代价达到我的目的。

I must try to get a computer at all costs. 不论花多少钱，我一定要买一台电脑。

3 at/in all events/in any event/case/at any rate 无论如何，总之，一定

It may rain tomorrow, but we are going home in any case. 明天可能下雨，但无论如何我们要回家。

I may not go to Europe, but in any event, I will visit you during the summer. 我可能不去欧洲，但无论如何我将在夏天拜访你。

4 at all risks/any risk 无论如何；无论如何危险；冒险地

Peggy will go to see Richards at all risks. 佩吉将冒险去看望理查兹。

It must be done at any risk. 不管冒什么风险，这事必须完成。

5 at any price 无论如何；无论价格高低；无论付出多大代价

We wanted to win at any price. 我们要不惜任何代价去争取胜利。

I would not sell this picture at any price. 不论出价多少，我都不愿卖这幅画。

6 at that 而且还是，偏偏又是；即使如此；就照那样

It was in the dead of night, and a cold night at that. 时间在深夜，偏偏又是一个寒冷的夜晚。

Helen's assertion that Tom and she are strangers is absurd; but at that I doubt whether he has known her for more than a few weeks. 海伦说她和汤姆不认识，这是无稽之谈；不过，即使汤姆认识她，最多也不过几个星期罢了。

attention

(your) attention, please （口令）立正；请注意

Attention, please! 立正！

Your attention, please. The train now standing at platform two is the fast service to London Euston. 请注意，现在停在二号站台上的火车是开往伦敦尤斯顿车站的快车。

aught

1　for aught I care 我才不管呢（表示不在乎）

Rossetti may starve, for aught I care. 罗塞蒂饿死也罢，我才不管呢。

I've missed seeing Sophia all these years. She might even have emigrated, for aught I care. 这些年来我一直没有看到过索菲娅。她也可能已经移居国外了，我才不管她呢。

2　for aught I know 亦未可知，也许；据我所知

Sherwood may be rich, for aught I know. 据我所知，舍伍德也许有钱。

For aught I know, Temple might be dead by now. 据我所知，坦普尔现在可能已经死了。

aunt

1　my giddy/sainted aunt/saints alive 哎呀，天哪；【美】哎呀，好家伙，真糟糕（表示惊讶、遗憾等）

My giddy aunt! It's Joe Greenway! I haven't seen him for years! 哎呀，那不是乔·格林韦吗！我多年没见到他了！

My sainted aunt! I haven't heard that song for ages! Didn't we used to dance to it before the war? 天哪，我好多年没听过这首歌了。战前我们不是常常伴着这首歌跳舞吗？

2　my aunt/eye/eyes/hat/stars/【谑】my stars and garters/word/world 哎呀，天哪；好家伙；你看，真要命（表示惊讶、懊丧、赞叹的感叹语）

If my aunt had been a man, she'd have been my uncle. 要是我的婶婶是个男人，她就是我的叔叔了。（表示绝对不可能的事）

3　go and see one's aunt 上厕所，去大便

The boy went and saw his aunt. 那个男孩儿上厕所去了。

away

1　away with 把……拿走，带走；赶走；停止……（表示对……不赞成、不允许）

Away with the old ideas and in with the new! 扫除旧观念，树立新思想！

Away with the universities! 停办这些大学！

2　they're away （赛马、选手等）已经出发；竞赛已经开始

They're away! And it's Magic Bullet in the lead at the first fence! 竞赛已

经开始。现在"魔术子弹"领先跑在第一跑道上。

axe

1 an axe/axes to grind 自私企图,个人打算,别有用心;牢骚满腹,不满

The worker looks like he's got an axe to grind. Better have a talk with him. 那个工人看起来牢骚满腹,你最好找他谈谈。

Like all politicians, the mayor says he wants to do good for people, but I think he has an axe to grind. 像所有政客一样,市长说他要为人民做好事,可是我认为他另有个人打算。

2 get the axe 被斩首;被解雇,被开除;被抛弃;被取消

They will get the axe because of depression. 因为经济萧条,他们将被解雇。

3 give sb. the axe 解雇,开除;撤销(机构、计划等);抛弃

The designers estimate we'll be giving half of our workforce the axe this year. 设计者们预计我们将解雇一半的员工。

aye

aye, aye 是,明白(海员回答上级命令时);啊,原来如此;果真如此(表示惊喜或自己的猜测得到证实)

Aye, aye, sir, I'll see it's done immediately. 是,长官!我会看着它立即执行。

Aye, aye! So Neil and Lynette are together again! 啊,果然尼尔和丽奈特又结合了。

B

baby

1 it's your/his, etc. baby 这是你/他等的事情

"Jack, I need your help in working out the cost of the new centre." "Oh, no, Freda, it's your baby, and you can work it out for yourself." "杰克,请你帮我计算一下新中心的费用。""啊,不行,弗雷达,这本是你的事情,同时你自己也能够计算出来。"

2 carry/hold the baby 做不愿做的事,干推脱不掉的苦差事

"I didn't think she'd want to carry the baby to term," Shannon said. 我原以为她不想承担这份苦差,"莎伦说。

back

1 get off one's back 少啰唆

Get off my back! Can't you see how busy I am? 少啰唆! 你没看见我有多忙吗?

Stop picking on me and get off my back, will you? 别再对我挑剔了,别再找我的麻烦了,好不好?

2 mind your back(s)/out/away 让开,让我通过

Mind your backs, please—Mr. Jones wants to come through with the tea trolley. 请让开,琼斯先生推着茶水车要经过这里。

3 back and fill 【美口】举棋不定,动摇,出尔反尔,反复无常

You shouldn't back and fill. It's time to make your choice. 别犹豫了。是该你做出选择的时候了。

4 (in) back of... 【美】在……的后面,作……的后盾;是……背后的原因

What's back of his proposal? 他提这个建议的动机是什么?

5 back off 【美俚】放慢速度

Hey, back off a little, I don't get you. 喂,说慢点,我没听清楚。

6 get/have one's own back (on sb.) 向某人报复

I'll get my own back on him one day, I swear! 我发誓,我总有一天要报复他。

7 on one's back 找……麻烦,纠缠……

My wife has been on my back for weeks to buy her a new dress. 几星期来,我妻子老缠着我给她买新衣服。

8 the back of beyond【英口】天涯海角;穷乡僻壤

After living in London, this little town seems like the back of beyond. 住在伦敦以后,我才发现这个小镇像是个极偏僻的地方。

9 the back of one's/the hand 斥责;蔑视,轻视

When we have no strength, we get the back of the hand. 我们如果没有实力,就会被人瞧不起。

The back of my hand to you! 去你的吧!

10 back the wrong horse【美】估计错;选错

If you choose Jimmy over Jane, you would back the wrong horse. 如果你选吉米而不选简,那会押错宝的。

bad

1 bad character/actor/egg/halfpenny/hat/lot/penny/sort 没出息的人;坏蛋,歹徒,流氓,二流子

It seems Frank's terribly dissipated—drinks. Yes, sir, like a fish… a bad lot, to say the least. 弗兰克似乎过于放荡——纵饮无度。的确,先生,他总是喝得醉醺醺的。至少可以这么说,他是个没出息的家伙。

2 bad/badly off【美】贫困的;境况不好的;缺少……的

Ford is not so bad off. 福特并没那么穷。

The school was badly off for teachers. 学校缺少教师。

3 go to the bad 堕落;没落

Gilbert's gone to the bad since he got rich. 吉尔伯特发财后就堕落了。

Huggins wept at seeing his son go to the bad. 哈金斯为自己儿子的堕落而痛哭流涕。

4 in a bad way 境况不佳的;不景气;健康可虑

If we don't speak of our achievements, they won't run away. If we don't find out our faults, we'll be in a bad way. 成绩不夸跑不了,缺点不找不得了。

5 in bad【美】倒霉,失宠;遇到麻烦,处于困境

Any time you are in bad, I'm glad to be of service. 不论什么时候你遇到

麻烦,我都愿意帮忙。

It'll put me in bad if you notify the police. 要是你通知警察,那就会使我为难。

6 not (so/too) bad/not half bad 不错,很好

The teacher thought the idea of a class picnic was not bad. 老师认为我们班举行一次野餐的主意不错。

The weather's not half bad for this time of year, is it? 一年中这段时间的气候很不错,是吗?

7 that can't be bad 真不错,太好了;祝贺你,恭喜你

"I've just heard I've won first prize in the competition—a trip to California!" "Well, that can't be bad, can it!" "我刚听说我获得了竞赛的头等奖——去加利福尼亚旅游一次!" "啊,真不错,祝贺你!"

8 (it's) too bad 太不巧了,太糟了;太可惜了,不幸

It's too bad that you've got to go now to catch your bus—still, we've had a good time together. 真是遗憾,你们得搭车回去了,不过我们在一起还是玩得很痛快的。

Too bad you couldn't come to the party—you'd have enjoyed yourself there. 真可惜你没能来参加晚会,你要是来了会玩得很尽兴的。

bag

1 bags I/I bags【英俚】是我的,我有优先权,该让我先……(源自儿童讹用)

I bags that seat! 那个座位是我的!

Bags I first ride on the bike! 该让我先骑这辆自行车!

2 three bags full, sir 是,是,当然可以(幽默地、略显谦卑地表示愿做某事)

"Would you come and help me?" "Yes, sir. Three bags full, sir! Is there anything else I can do for you?" "你能来给我帮帮忙吗?" "当然,愿为您效劳,先生!还有什么事需要我做吗?"

3 bag it【美俚】抛弃,放弃;逃学

Let's bag it for now. 我们现在不要考虑它。

4 bag school【美】逃学

The teacher criticized me for bagging school. 老师因为我逃学批评了我。

5 empty the bag 和盘托出

The accessory criminal could not but empty the bag in face of conclusive evidence. 从犯在确凿证据面前不得不把作案过程一一作了交代。

6 give sb. the bag 解雇……；拒绝……

The manager gave the clerk the bag after she made a serious mistake. 那个办事员犯了一个严重的错误后，经理把她解雇了。

7 hold the bag【美】背黑锅，代人受过；一无所得

Under no circumstances have I made anyone hold the bag for me. 在任何情况下，我从没有让任何人为我背黑锅。

8 in the bag 十拿九稳的，确定无疑的；落入他人手中；被俘的

Judging by the enthusiastic reception given to him everywhere, they felt that his election was in the bag. 看到他到处受欢迎的样子，他们觉得他当选是十拿九稳的。

bail

1 go bail for 保证是真实的

I'll go bail for that. 我保证那是真实的。

2 I'll go bail that 我肯定……

I'll go bail that the contestant will win the competition. 我敢肯定那个选手会赢得比赛。

ball

1 the ball is in your/his, etc. court 该你/他等来了；轮到你/他等了；该你/他等采取行动了

You've heard what he told you about the robbery and now you've got to decide whether to go to the police or not—the ball is in your court. 你已经听他讲过了这件抢劫案，现在该你来决定是否去报警。

2 the ball is with you 下一轮归你，轮到你了；该你发球了（源自法语）

3 have something/nothing/much/a lot on the ball【美】有些/没有/很有些能耐

When it comes to speech eloquence, some under-educated people also have something on the ball. 论到演讲口才，有些没有多少文化的人还真挺能说的。

4 get on the ball【美俚】机灵一点

If you're going with her, you'd better get on the ball. 你若是跟她一起去,最好放机灵点。

5　put balls on【美俚】给……增加生趣
This story is too namby-pamby. Put some balls on it. 这个故事太乏味了。给它掺些有趣的东西。

6　run with the ball【美】赶紧执行命令;尽快完成任务;把……接过来干下去;带球跑
Run with the ball or you'll get fired. 赶紧执行命令,否则你会丢饭碗的。

bang

1　bang on【俚】完全正确;完全符合要求;十分恰当,极好;正中目标
I'd been to Brighton for a holiday, and I think it was bang on. 我去布赖顿度的假,我认为那里极好。
Your answer's bang on and you've won yourself ＄100! 你答对了,你赢了100美元。

2　bang on about【口】喋喋不休
The English like to bang on about the Empire and the glory days. 英国人喜欢吹嘘他们的帝国和辉煌时代。
They have been banging on about education reform for years. 多年来,他们一直在唠叨教育改革的事。

3　bang out/up【美】好极了,好货色;完全;响亮/砰砰地弹奏乐曲
We got a bang out of watching the old movies. 再看昔日的影片使我们激动不已。
The musician is banging out the latest popular tunes. 那个音乐家正在砰砰地弹奏最新的流行曲。

4　bang-up 出色的,好极了的,顶呱呱的,第一流的
The football coach has done a bang-up job this season. 那名足球教练本赛季的工作非常出色。
Sam did a bang-up job on the car. It runs great! 山姆的修车水准真是一流。这车跑起来真棒!

bargain

1　a bargain is a bargain【谚】买卖一言为定,契约就是契约,成议不可妄废

I believe the old saying, "A bargain is a bargain." 我相信那句老话,"君子一言,驷马难追。"

2 it's/that's a bargain 就这么讲定了,一言为定

"You do the washing-up and I'll put the baby to bed!" "Right, it's a bargain!" "你洗碗,我哄宝宝睡觉!" "好的,一言为定!"

3 a real bargain 真便宜

The book is a real bargain at ＄2. 这本书定价两美元,真是够便宜的。

4 no bargain【美】不容易对付的人

His mother-in-law is no bargain. 他的岳母可不是容易对付的人。

bark

1 go bark up another tree【美】少管闲事,用不着你操心

2 one's bark is worse than one's bite/more bark than bite（狗）光吠不咬,并不伤人;有口无心;嘴巴尖刻但心地不坏;说话严厉但并无恶意

The small dog barks savagely, but his bark is worse than his bite. 这只小狗吠得凶,但它光吠不咬人。

The boss sometimes talks roughly to the men, but they knew that his bark is worse than his bite. 老板有时对职员很凶,但他们都知道他是刀子嘴豆腐心。

barn

must have been born in a barn ……真没教养(……一定是出生在马棚里的)

Lawrence must have been born in a barn—he never shuts the door. 劳伦斯真没教养——他从来不知道随手关门。

bat

1 off/on one's own bat 全凭自己的力量;主动地,自己负责地

I didn't invite Malory; he came off his own bat. 我没有邀请马洛里,是他自己主动来的。

2 go to bat against 作出不利于……的证词,反对

John will go to bat against me. 约翰不会支持我的。

3 go to bat for 为……出力(辩护、说项),支持

And Laurie really did go to bat for his client. 劳里确实帮了他的客户一把。

4 (right) off the bat 毫不犹豫地；一下子，马上

I was all prepared to put up a fight, but he gave in right off the bat. 我正准备和他大打一场，但是他马上就服软了。

5 have bats in one's/the belfry 神经有点失常，头脑有点古怪，行为乖张，想法荒诞

When Nicholas talked about going to the moon, he was thought to have bats in his belfry. 当尼古拉斯谈及登月之旅时，大家认为他是异想天开。

6 like a bat out of hell 如飞地；不顾一切地

Oscar drives like a bat out of hell. 奥斯卡横冲直撞地开车。

7 never/not bat/without batting an eye/eyelash/eyelid 泰然自若，毫不流露情感

When I told Sailsbury the price of the car, he never batted an eye. 我告诉索尔兹伯里车子的价格时，他神色泰然。

Bill told his story without batting an eyelash, although not a word of it was true. 比尔面不改色心不跳地讲着他瞎编的故事。

8 sling the bat【军俚】说外国话，说土语

Maria slings the bat like a native. 玛丽亚说起土话来像个当地人。

battle

half the battle 成功的重要条件

Persistence is half the battle. 坚忍不拔是取胜的保证。

When you write an essay for class, making the outline is half the battle. 写报告时完成了大纲即是完成了工作的大半。

bawl

bawl out 把……痛骂一顿，大声训斥

Father bawled me out for cutting/bagging school. 我因逃学被父亲痛骂了一顿。

The teacher bawled us out for not handing in our homework. 老师因为我们没有交作业而批评我们。

be

1 be gone 滚开，走开；离开，消失

Feel it rise with the ashes and smoke and disappear and be gone. 感觉到的

是它与灰烬和烟气一同上升、消失,然后全都不见了。

2 be it so/so be it/let it be so 就这样吧,算了吧,这样也好,别管它了(但愿如此)

If you do not wish my friendship, so be it. 要是你不愿和我交朋友,那就算了。

3 be it that 即使……,也得……

Be it that you are poor, I will still love you. 即使你穷,我也会爱你。

4 be that as it may 即使如此,尽管那样

Be that as it may, you are still wrong. 就算这样,你还是不对。

I know I won't be here on Monday. Be that as it may, I intend that you should do some homework, so I'm setting it today. 我知道我星期一来不了。即使这样,我想你还是应该做点家庭作业,所以我今天给你布置一点。

5 have been (and gone) and 竟然,居然(表示惊讶或恼火)

After all the bother about his injury, Occam has been and gone and won the first prize in the race! 不顾伤痛的折磨,奥卡姆居然赢得了比赛的冠军。

Who's been and gone and bought another block of ice cream when we've still not finished this one. 我们这块冰激凌还没吃完,谁又去买了一块?

6 have been and gone and done it 竟然做出这样的事来

Mike's been and gone and done it now; old Jake must have seen him climbing on the school roof. 迈克竟然做出这样的事来!老杰克肯定看见他爬上了学校的屋顶。

7 I've been there 我是过来人,用不着你来告诉我

And I understand this, because I've been there, most of my life. 其实我也理解,因为之前的大部分人生,我也是如此。

8 if so be 要真是那样的话,如果是这样

"Honor to be hanged, glory to be nailed to a tree and burned, if so be that God has asked," said they. "只要上帝发话,即使被绞死也值得自豪,即使被钉在树上烈火焚身也是一种荣耀,"他们异口同声地说。

9 let... be 由……去,不打扰……,听任……继续下去

At last Raphael stopped searching for words and let silence be. 拉菲尔终于不再没话找话,干脆一声不吭了。

Let it be! 让它去吧!
10 (well,) I'll be blowed 真奇怪,才怪呢(表示惊讶和气愤)
I'll be blowed if I help Roger. He never helps me when I need him. 我要是帮助罗杰才怪呢! 在我需要他帮忙时,他从来没帮助过我。

beam

1 on the beam 对头,正确
Their instruments indicate that their plane is on the beam. 他们的仪表显示,他们的飞机航向是完全正确的。
2 off the beam 不对,错误;步入歧途
Her answer was right off the beam. 她的回答完全不正确。

bean

1 a hill/row of beans【俚】一点儿,丝毫(一般用于否定句)
Robbins doesn't care a hill of beans. 罗宾斯毫不在乎。
Rockefeller doesn't know a hill of beans about foreign policy. 洛克菲勒对外交政策一窍不通。
2 full of beans/prunes【美】兴高采烈;精力旺盛;情绪高涨;无稽之谈,胡说八道
The football team was full of beans after winning the tournament. 足球队在赢了比赛以后兴高采烈。
The children were full of beans as they got ready for a picnic. 孩子们在为野餐做准备工作时情绪高涨。
3 like beans 猛烈地,使劲地,拼命地;有力地,很好地
The thief ran away like beans. 小偷拼命地逃走了。
4 old bean 老兄(熟人间的称呼)
Well, Jim, how are you today, old bean? 啊,吉姆,今天过得怎么样,老兄?
5 spill the beans【美】泄密;破坏计划;陷入窘境
John's friends were going to have a surprise party for him, but Tom spilled the beans. 约翰的朋友们正在悄悄地为他筹办舞会,想给他一个惊喜,不料汤姆走漏了风声。
6 use one's bean/brain/head/noodle/noggin【美俚】用脑筋,动动脑子,想一想,该有点常识(常用于命令口气)
If you used your bean, you wouldn't be in trouble now. 如果你肯动动脑

筋,现在就不会惹上麻烦。
Never point a gun at anybody, John. Use your head! 绝对不可拿枪指任何人,约翰,这是常识!

beat

1 beat anything/all (creation)/everything/my grandmother/the devil/the Dutch/cock fighting/【美】hell/the band/the world 真是从来没有的怪事,令人吃惊;压倒一切,超过一切;极其,非常,棒极了

Londoners beat all creation for thinking about themselves. 伦敦人那种只关心自己的劲儿真令人吃惊。

Kelvin's impudence beats everything. 凯尔文的厚颜无耻简直令人难以置信。

2 beat sb./sth. (all) hollow/beat into fits 彻底打败某人/某物;远远胜过某人/某物

This movie beats that one all hollow. 这部影片远远胜过那一部。

There's nothing like real life, after all. Beats the theatre hollow. 究竟还是现实生活有味道,一比就叫戏剧黯然失色了。

3 beat sb./sth. all to pieces/nothing/ribands/sticks 把某人/某物打得一败涂地,把某人/某物打得落花流水,叫某人/某物大吃苦头

I rode a race against Bob Dashwood and beat him all to ribands. 我和鲍勃·达斯伍德进行了一次赛马,我把他完全打败了。

4 beat it 拔腿就跑;滚开

The thugs beat it when the police came. 警察赶到时,暴徒们早已逃之夭夭。

The reporter beat it to the telephone to call in the news. 记者疾步奔向电话机,向报社报告这一消息。

5 beat sb. out of his boots/black and blue/to a mummy/【美】to a frazzle/to a pulp 把某人打得遍体鳞伤,打得半死

I'll beat you to a pulp. 我要把你们揍个稀烂。

6 can you beat it/that 【美】还有比这更妙的吗;哎哟,有这等事;岂非咄咄怪事

"Have you heard Carlos won that trip for two to California?" "Well, can you beat that!" "你听说卡洛斯赢得了去加利福尼亚双人旅游的机会吗?"

"哎哟！有这等事！"

7 if you can't beat them, join them 非此即彼；不进则退；如果不能击败他们，就加入他们

8 that/it beats me 这真叫我糊涂了，这真把我难住了；使我大吃一惊

It beats me that they turned down the invitation. 他们拒绝了邀请使我大吃一惊。

9 beat the band/hell/devil 起劲地；又快又狠地

They are working to beat the band. 他们正在拼命干活。

The fire engines were going down the road to beat the band. 救火车一路风驰电掣般地疾驰而去。

bedpost

between you, me, and the bedpost/doorpost/gatepost/post/lamppost/between you and me/ourselves 私下地，秘密地；你知我知，天知地知；不可告诉别人

Between you, me, and the bedpost, I don't want to go with Jack. 咱们私下说说，我实在不愿和杰克一起去。

Between you and me, I think Peter and Sarah's marriage is breaking up. 告诉你，莫对别人说：我觉得彼得和萨拉的婚姻破裂啦。

bee

1 he/she, etc. thinks he's/she's, etc. the bee's knees 他/她等认为他/她等是这儿最了不起的人

Now that Hardy is at university, he thinks he's the bee's knees! 自从哈代上了大学，他就觉得自己高人一等了。

2 put the bee on 【美俚】向……募捐；借钱

Smith put the bee on her yesterday. 史密斯昨天向她借了些钱。

beef

more beef/put your/some beef into it 加油干，使劲儿干

beer

1 beer and skittles 吃喝玩乐，享受

It goes without saying that life is not all beer and skittles. 毋庸置疑，人生

并不全是吃喝玩乐。

2 cry in one's beer【美俚】大恸；因自怜而借酒浇愁

"Come on, Joe! Instead of sitting around in a bar all day crying in your beer about not having any money, why not get off your bottom and go out and look for a job!" "行了,乔! 与其成天闲坐在酒吧里,为了没有钱而借酒浇愁,为什么不振作起来到外面去找个工作呢?"

3 drink one's beer【美】闭嘴

Finally I had to tell Ivan to drink his beer. 最后我不得不叫伊凡住嘴。

4 think small beer of 轻视,小看

Julian thinks small beer of painters. 朱利安瞧不起画家。

5 think no small beer of oneself 妄自尊大,夜郎自大,自命不凡

The student thought no small beer of himself. That was what hindered him from making greater progress. 那个学生很自负,这阻碍了他取得更大的进步。

before

1 before one's very eyes 当着……的面；……亲眼看见

Misfortune is before one's very eyes. 祸在眼前。

2 before one knows where one is 马上就,转瞬间就,突然就

I made a serious mistake before I know where I was. 我突然就犯下了一个严重的错误。

3 before you can say knife/Jack Robinson 一刹那,很快就

Before I could say Jack Robinson, the boy was gone. 我还没有开口说话,那孩子就走开了。

4 our services are before 我们乐于为……服务

Our services are before you, sir! 我们乐于为您服务,先生!

5 would die/choose death before 宁死不……

They would die before surrendering. 他们宁死也不投降。

True men choose death before dishonour. 士可杀不可辱。

beg

beg the question 未定之数；言之过早；避而不答

Laura told Tom that he must believe her argument because she was right; father laughed and told Laura she was begging the question. 劳拉告诉汤

姆他必须相信她的论点,因为她是对的;父亲却笑着告诉劳拉,她未免言之过早。

begad

begad【谑】天哪,老天爷作证;千真万确,的确;完了,糟糕(by God 之委婉语)

beget

1 bad luck begets bad luck 祸不单行
2 money begets money 钱生钱

Because money begets money. They get more good chances. 那是因为钱能生钱。他们得到的好机会更多。

3 like begets like/like father, like son 有其父必有其子

beggar

1 poor beggar 可怜的家伙

The poor beggar looked silly trying to portray the role of Hamlet. 那可怜虫因为拼命想把哈姆雷特的角色演好而大出洋相。

2 a beggar to argue 能言善辩的人
3 a beggar for work 工作积极的人
4 I'll be beggared if 绝不会;如果……让我变成叫花子好了(发誓用语)

I'll be beggared if I tell a lie. 我若撒谎,就叫我没好下场。

behave

do behave/behave yourself 放规矩点(对孩子的口气)

believe

1 believe it or not/would you believe it 信不信由你

They were great fans of the Beatles, so believe it or not, when they had children they called them John, Paul, George and Ringo! 他们都是披头士乐队狂热的崇拜者,信不信由你,他们生了孩子就起名叫约翰、保罗、乔治和林戈。

2 believe me 真的,是真的,请相信我说的话

I feel like the United States president with his finger on the button—believe me, I take the responsibility of this job seriously. 我觉得就像美国

总统把手指放在核按钮上一样,真的,我就是这样全身心地投入这项工作的。

3 ... , I believe 您是……我没说错吧

"Mr. Ronson, I believe?" "Yes." "Then come in." "是朗森先生吗?""正是。""那么,请进!"

4 I believe you, thousands wouldn't 我完全相信,我绝对相信(相当幽默的说法)

"Excuse me, don't think I'm not sitting next to you because I don't like you or anything—it's just that I've seen Ruth over there, and I've not spoken to her for ages!" "I believe you, thousands wouldn't!" "对不起,别以为我没坐在你旁边是因为我不喜欢你或什么别的原因。只不过是因为我看到露丝就在那边,我已有多年没同她说话了。""啊,放心,我绝对相信你说的话。"

5 if you believe that, you'd believe anything 你连这也相信,你竟相信这个

"Here's a racing tip guide in the three o'clock at York." "If you believe that, you'd believe anything!" "这是三点钟约克郡赛马的预测指南!""你连这也相信!"

6 would you believe 请看啦(招呼、引起注意;企图打消别人的疑虑)

"Ladies and gentlemen, this is, would you believe, the last rabbit of its kind in the world," the man at the fair shouted as he held up what looked like an old rag! 集市上一个小贩手上举着一块像是破布的东西大声叫喊:"女士们,先生们,请看啦,这就是世界上这类野兔中的最后一只啦,千真万确!"

7 you'd better believe it【美】你就这样相信吧,你就当它是真的吧

bell

1 ring a bell 引起模糊记忆;激起怀旧情绪

The name *rang a vague bell* somewhere in the back of his mind. 他脑海中依稀记得那个名字。

Patrick Mann, you say? That name *rings a bell*. Ah yes, did you go to Bristol University? 你说什么,帕特里克·曼?这个名字听起来好熟悉呀!啊,对了,你考上布里斯托尔大学了吧?

2 ring the bell 获得成功;取得良好成绩;击中目标;正中下怀;大受欢迎

Well, you've rung the bell on me. I am a sucker. I know it. 好,就算你赢吧,我当了冤大头,这个我晓得。

The book rings the bell with teenagers. 那本书大受青少年的欢迎。

3 with bells on【美】热切期望地,做好准备地;【美俚】十足,确定无疑地

"Will you come to the farewell party I'm giving for Billy?" asked Jerry. "I'll be there with bells on," replied Ed. 杰里问:"你愿意参加我为比利举办的告别晚会吗?"埃德回答说:"乐意之至!"

Joyce went with bells on. 乔伊斯穿戴整齐兴致勃勃地去了。

belt

1 belt out 引吭高歌;扯破嗓门

Louisa belted out ballads and hillbilly songs one after another all evening. 路易莎整晚大唱民谣与乡村歌曲。

Young people enjoy belting out songs. 年轻人喜欢引吭高歌。

2 belt up 住口,安静点;【美】系紧安全带

"Belt up, I'm trying to work!" Pat shouted impatiently. "安静,我要工作了!"帕特焦躁地吼道。

It's as well to belt up about this matter. 关于这个问题还是保持沉默的好。

3 hit/strike/tackle below the belt 体育运动中的犯规行为,使用卑鄙手段;暗箭伤人,有失公允

The sportsman struck the other boy below the belt. 那个运动员犯规打人。

It was hitting below the belt for Mr. Jones's rival to tell people about a crime that Mr. Jones committed when he was a young boy. 琼斯的对手揭发他幼年时的犯罪行为不是正大光明的行为。

4 tighten one's belt 束紧腰带,节衣缩食

Father lost his job and we had to do without many things, but when our savings were all spent, we had to tighten our belts another notch. 父亲失业了,我们只得节衣缩食。但当积蓄花光了的时候,我们必须进一步束紧腰带、节衣缩食。

5 under one's belt 入肚;被获得;掌握或经历

Once he had a good meal under his belt, the man loosened his tie and fell asleep. 佳肴入肚之后,此人宽衣解带随即进入了梦乡。

Jones is talkative when he has a few drinks under his belt. 几杯酒下肚之

后,琼斯话就多了起来。

Bennett

Gordon Bennett 哎呀(戈登·贝内特是美国《纽约先驱报》的创始人,这里用它是为了避免直呼上帝的名字)

Gordon Bennett! It's old Jake—how are you keeping these days? We've not seen each other for years, have we? 哎呀,那不是老杰克吗! 近来好吗? 我们好久没有见面啦,是吗?

beside

1 beside oneself 激动异常,欣喜若狂;精神失常

Sophia was beside herself with fear. 索菲娅吓得要死。

When his wife heard of his death, she was beside herself. 他的妻子听说他死了,几乎发狂。

2 beside the mark/point/question/subject 离题万里,不相干,风马牛不相及

"It's not for me to disagree there," said Jolyon. "But that's all quite beside the mark." "我倒不是反对你,"乔里恩说道,"可是问题不在这里。"
When you meant to do is beside the point; the fact is you didn't do it. 你想要做的是另一回事,问题在于你没有去做。

best

1 (all) for the best (尽管看来不尽如此)完全出于好意;(虽说初时不妙)终于十分圆满地了结;最好;幸运;不错;快乐地

I did it (all) for the best. 我这么做完全是出于好意。

You feel unhappy now because you got sick and couldn't go with your friends, but it will all turn out for the best. 你虽因生病不能与你的朋友外出游玩而闷闷不乐,但这最终会给你带来好处的。

2 all the best 祝一切顺利(祝酒、告别时说)

All the best then, Jean, and we'll see you in three weeks. 祝你顺利,琼! 我们三星期以后再见!

3 at (the) best 就最乐观的一方面看;至多,充其量

It's a gloomy outlook at best. 即使从最乐观的方面看,前景也是暗淡的。

The treasurer had at best been careless with the club's money, but most people thought he had been dishonest. 俱乐部的会计充其量不过是处理金钱不慎，但大多数人却认为他不老实。

4 **at one's/its best** 处于最佳状态，在全盛时期

Professor Gay was at his eloquent best today. 今天盖伊教授把他的口才发挥得淋漓尽致。

Fanny is at her best in short lyrics. 范妮最擅长的是写抒情短诗。

Theodore Dreiser is at his creative best now. 西奥多·德莱塞正处于创作能力的旺盛时期。

5 **get/have the best/better of** 战胜，使屈服；占上风，得便宜；赢得，打败

The sportsman got the best of his opponent. 那个运动员打败了对手。

David's asthma gets the best of him from time to time. 戴维的哮喘病时时发作，使他受不了。

6 **give sb./sth. best** 承认某物优越，向某人认输

So I went to work and gave the schooling best. 因此我就去工作了，自认不是读书的料。

All right, I give you best. 算了，我认输。

7 **had best/better/【美】would best** 应当，最好

I had better leave now or I'll be late. 我应该走了，否则会迟到。

If you want to stay out of trouble, you had best not make any mistakes. 假如你要避开麻烦，最好不要犯错误。

8 **make the best of** 充分利用，善于利用；尽情享受

You should make the best of this valuable opportunity. 你应当充分利用这个宝贵的机会。

9 **make the best of it/things/a bad bargain/a bad job** 在不利的情况下尽力而为，勉为其难；以随遇而安的态度对待不利的情况；善处逆境

The boy did not like to mop the floor, but he made the best of it. 这男孩不喜欢拖地，可他还是乖乖地拖了。

The situation is difficult, but we must make the best of it. 形势很困难，不过我们必须妥善处置。

10 **the best of British luck** 好运气（常作反语，源自二战期间形势发展不利于英国时）

The best of British luck to you! 祝你好运！（愿你倒霉！）

11 **to the best of one's ability/belief/knowledge/power/memory/recollection/**

remembrance 在……的能力/认识/知识/权力/记忆范围内；就……的能力/认识/知识/权力/记忆等所及

Wood has never won a game, to the best of my knowledge. 据我所知，伍德从未赢过比赛。

Of his daughters I will only say that, to the best of my knowledge, they are dutiful young ladies, and take after their father closely. 关于他的女儿,据我所知,她们都是安分守己的淑女,并且很像她们的父亲。

12 try/do one's best 竭尽全力

13 with the best (of them) 做得跟（他们之中的）任何人一样好

Old as Foster is, he can play tennis with the best. 福斯特虽然年纪大了,可是打起网球来不比任何人差。

bet

1 I bet 我确信,我断定；我不信

After swimming across the Channel, you were glad to see the White Cliffs of Dover, I bet. 在游过海峡之后,我敢断定你一定会很高兴地看到多佛白崖。

2 bet one's bottom/last dollar/shirt/boots/life/hat/a cookie/cookey on/【美】you bet/I'll bet my bottom/last dollar 拿一切来打赌,完全有把握；孤注一掷；用一切担保；当然,管保没错

This horse will win. I would bet my bottom dollar on it. 此马必赢,我愿倾囊下注。

Jim said he would bet his boots that he would pass the examination. 吉姆敢以性命担保,他必定通过考试。

3 bet on the wrong horse 估计错误,判断失误

To count on the small family farm as an important thing in the American future now looks like betting on the wrong horse. 现在把小家庭农场当作美国未来的一件大事,看来是估计错了。

Gray expected Stevenson to be elected President in 1952, but as it happened, he bet on the wrong horse. 格雷预计史蒂文森将于1952年当选总统,结果他完全猜错了。

4 what's the betting 真有可能吗；很可能,大概会

What's the betting the bus will turn up late—it has done every day this week so far. 这趟车有可能来得很晚,这个星期以来它一直是这样的。

better

1 for better or/for/or for worse 不论是祸是福;不管是好是歹;不管结果怎样(源自祈祷书,在结婚仪式上的用语)

Harvey has resolved to take Isabel for better or for worse. 不论是祸是福,哈维决心娶伊莎贝尔为妻。

What are you talking about? You took Jenny for better for worse. 你这是什么话?你在结婚时就说过与珍妮苦乐与共、永世不渝的。

2 go sb. one better 比某人更胜一筹,击败某人;出价高于对手

Bill's mother gave the boys in Bill's club hot dogs for refreshments, so Tom's mother said that she would go her one better next time by giving them hot dogs and ice cream. 比尔的母亲为比尔所在的俱乐部的会员们准备热狗当点心,因此汤姆的母亲说,下回她要招待得更好,除给他们热狗外,另加冰激凌。

John made a good dive into the water, but Bob went him one better by diving in backwards. 约翰的跳水动作很棒,但是鲍勃后翻跳水更胜一筹。

3 never better 从来没有这样好,再好不过了(主要指身心健康)

The baby is fine, never better. 婴儿很好,比以往任何时候都好。

4 so much (all) the better 这就更好了,这样做好极了

If the teacher will help us, so much the better. 假如老师肯帮助我们那就更好了。

between

1 between life and death 生死关头,生死攸关

Lawrence held on to the mountainside between life and death while his friends went to get help. 当他的朋友寻求救援时,劳伦斯正紧紧抓住半山腰上的岩石,生死攸关。

The little sick girl lay all night between life and death until her fever was gone. 这个生病的女孩躺在床上,生命垂危,直到后来高烧消退。

2 between the devil and the deep blue sea/two fires/Scylla and Charybdis 进退维谷,两难之间,腹背受敌

The pirates had to fight and be killed or give up and be hanged, they were between the devil and the deep blue sea. 海盗们不是抗拒被杀死,就是投

降被吊死,他们真是进退维谷。
When the man's wife and his mother got together, he was between two fires. 当这个男人的妻子与他的妈妈在一起时,他真是两头受气。

beware

beware of 当心
Beware of the dog/pickpockets/the sharpers at the fair! 当心恶犬/扒手/市场上的骗子!

beyond

1 beyond all hope 完全绝望
That sick man is beyond all hope of recovery. 那个病人已完全没有了恢复健康的希望。

2 beyond all praise 赞不绝口,好极了
His heroism was beyond all praise. 人们对他的英勇行为赞不绝口。

3 beyond all questions/question/without question 毫无疑问,当然,显然,确实
People always believe anything that Mark says; his honest is beyond question. 大家总是相信马克的话,因为他的诚实是无可置疑的。
John's drawing is without question the best in the class. 约翰的画显然是班上最好的。

4 beyond all things 第一,首先;最重要
We should value sincerity beyond all things. 我们应该把诚意看得比什么都重要。

5 beyond comparison/compare 无与伦比,无可比拟

6 beyond comprehension 难以理解,难解

7 beyond dispute 无可争辩的,无疑的
This is beyond dispute the best book on the subject. 这的确是关于这一问题的最好的一本书。

8 beyond (a) doubt/without question/out of question 无可置疑,毫无疑问,一定
I believe beyond doubt that Maggie is honest and diligent. 我毫不怀疑地认为玛吉是诚实和勤勉的。
It is beyond a doubt that Needham will come back. 尼达姆一定会回来的。

9 beyond expectation 出乎预料地,意外地

10 beyond expression/description/words 形容不出的,非言语、笔墨所能形容的

The grand sight of Niagara Falls is beyond description. 尼亚加拉瀑布的壮观非笔墨所能形容。

11 beyond measure 非常,极度;无可估量的

They are delighted, beyond measure, with the prospects of the land. 他们非常喜爱这片土地上的景色。

With her parents reunited and present at her graduation, Mary had happiness beyond measure. 父母和好如初,又双双出席她的毕业典礼,玛丽真是乐不可支。

12 beyond sb. 某人无能为力;某人不能理解

It is beyond me. 这我无能为力。

13 beyond one's depth 难以了解,无法胜任;水深没顶

Jack wasn't a good swimmer, and nearly drowned when he drifted out beyond his depth. 杰克不善游泳,当漂到水深没顶的地方时他几乎淹死。

Bill decided that his big brother's geometry book was beyond his depth. 比尔确认他不能理解大哥的几何书。

14 beyond/out of one's power 力所不及,无能为力

It is beyond my power to help you. 我没有能力帮助你。

15 beyond/out of (one's) reach 在够不着的地方;力所不及的

You must keep poisons beyond the children's reach. 你必须把毒药放在孩子们够不着的地方。

16 beyond the pale 超出范围,离经叛道,为人所不齿

After the outlaw killed a man, he was beyond the pale and not even his old friends would talk to him. 这歹徒杀了人,为人所不齿,甚至连老朋友也不愿搭理他。

Tom's swearing is beyond the pale; no one invites him to dinner any more. 汤姆的污言秽语令人不能容忍,无人再请他赴宴。

17 see beyond (the end of) one's nose 有远见,远见卓识,有先见之明

Gabriel couldn't save money or make plans for the future; he just never saw beyond the end of his nose. 加布里埃尔从不存钱,也不为将来打算,实在无先见之明。

People who always complain about school taxes would stop it if they could see beyond their noses and understand the importance of first-class school. 常抱怨征收教育税的人如果有远见并理解一流学校的重要性,就会停止抱怨了。

bid

bid fair 很有希望,有可能
The negotiations bid fair to be successful. 谈判很有成功的希望。
The effort bids fair to succeed. 这番努力可望成功。

big

1 be big on 喜欢,偏爱
Hobbes is very big on Jack London. 霍布斯很爱读杰克·伦敦的作品。
I am not big on playing cards. 我不爱玩纸牌。

2 be/get/grow too big for one's boots/breeches/trousers/pants 自以为是,摆架子,妄自尊大,目中无人
That boy had grown too big for his breeches. I'll have to put him back in his place. 那男孩儿太骄傲了,我要治治他。
When the teacher made Bob a monitor, he got too big for his boots and she had to warn him. 老师选鲍勃当班长,他就自高自大起来,老师不得不告诫他。

3 big cheese/gun/shot/wheel/wig 老大;要人,领袖;大亨,显贵
Bill had been a big shot in high school. 比尔在中学里曾是个顶尖人物。
Uncle Ferdinand is a big wheel in Washington, maybe he can help you with your problem. 费迪南德叔叔在华盛顿是一位炙手可热的人物。他也许可以帮你解决难题。

4 big card/pot/noise/bug/dog/fish/number 【美俚】要人,大亨
Saxenden is a big noise behind the scenes in military matters. 撒克圣登是幕后掌握军事机要的大亨。

5 big daddy 大亨;翘楚,头儿;同类中最大的、最重要的人或物
The whale is the big daddy of everything that swims in the ocean. 鲸鱼是海洋中最大的动物。
The H-Bomb is the big daddy of all modern weapons. 氢弹是一切现代武器中的翘楚。

6 big boy【美俚】大家伙;大亨,大人物;百元钞票;大学优等生

7 big brother 哥哥;老大哥,充当兄长角色的人

8 big Chief/white Chief【口】要人,大亨

9 big enchilada【美俚】要人,大亨;头儿

10 big guy 官吏;老板;暴徒头子;要人,名人;上帝

11 big name 知名人士,大名鼎鼎的人;众所周知的事情

12 come/go over big【美】取得突出效果,成功;(作品、歌曲等)大受欢迎,(演员等)走红

Newton's humour went over big in the room. 一屋子里的人都十分欣赏牛顿的幽默。

The play will go over big. 这出戏一定会大受欢迎。

13 take sth. big 勇敢地/感情冲动地对待某事

Orlando took his defeat big. 奥兰多虽失败而不气馁。

Now I see why you took it so big when you heard his remark. 现在我明白了为什么你听到他的议论时反应如此强烈。

14 that's big of you 你可真大方呀,真得感谢你呀(常用惊讶的口吻,表示讥讽)

That's big of you to help me wash the car—I thought you were far too busy to care about other people. 哎呀,帮我洗车你可真勤快呀!我还以为你忙得根本顾不上关心别人呢。

bill

1 fill the bill 符合要求,合乎条件;出类拔萃;挂头牌,领衔演出

The boss was worried about hiring a deaf boy, but after he tried Tom out a few weeks, he said that Tom filled the bill. 老板担心雇用到一个耳聋的男孩,但在试用汤姆几周以后,他说汤姆正是合适的人选。

As a teacher, Partridge isn't filling the bill. 作为教师,帕特里奇不称职。

2 foot the bill 负担费用,会账;承担责任

An administration official said the Obamas would foot the bill for the celebrations. 一名政府官员说,奥巴马夫妇要为庆祝活动自掏腰包。

3 sell sb. a bill of goods【美】以花言巧语骗得某人相信或同意

That dishonest salesman sold us a bill of goods. 那个奸商把商品高价卖给了我们。

My friends, my opponent is selling you a bill of goods when he promises to spend more on schools and cut taxes too. You ask him how he can spend more money without raising taxes! 朋友们,我的对手既保证要给学校多拨款,又答应减税,这是花言巧语骗人的话。你们问一下他怎么做到既多花钱又不加税。

bird

1 a little bird told me 消息灵通的人对我说;私下有人对我说;听说
A little bird told me you quarrelled this morning. 一个消息灵通的人对我说今天你们吵架了。

2 birds of a feather 有共同兴趣爱好的人;一丘之貉
Don't be friends with bad boys. People think that birds of a feather flock together. 不要和坏孩子交朋友,人们认为物以类聚,人以群分。

3 the early bird catches/gets the worm 凡事趁早,捷足先登,先下手为强
When Billy's father woke him up for school, he said, "The early bird catches the worm." 当比利的父亲唤醒他去上学时,他说:"早起的鸟儿有虫吃。"
Charles began looking for a summer job in January; he knows that the early bird gets the worm. 查理在一月时便开始找夏天的工作,他深知早做准备早得益的道理。

4 fine feathers do not make fine birds 人不可貌相
Mary is pretty and she wears pretty clothes, but she is very mean. Fine feathers do not make fine birds. 玛丽很美丽,穿着又漂亮,但人却很刻薄。真是人不可貌相!

5 kill two birds with one stone 一石二鸟,一箭双雕,一举两得
You'll save both time and material, and kill two birds with one stone. 你把时间和材料都节省下来了,这不是一举两得吗?

bit

1 a (fair) bit of all right 极好,正好,很不错
This jelly's a bit of all right. 这果冻很不错。
North was a fair bit of all right. 诺思实在不错。

2 every bit 从头到尾,完全,全然;全部
The end was every bit as good as the beginning. 结尾与开头同样圆满。

Patrick wants to get elected *every bit* as much as his brother. 帕特里克一心想当选，完全和他兄弟一模一样。

3 **not a/one bit 一点也不（常用作回答）**

"Do you mind if I read your newspaper?" "*Not a bit.*" "我看看您的报纸，您不介意吧？" "一点也不。"

I don't mind you smoking *one bit*. 您尽管抽烟，我一点也不在乎。

4 **pick up the bits 收拾残局**

It's Tom's mother again who is *picking up the bits*. 又是汤姆的妈妈在收拾残局了。

bite

1 **bite off more than one can chew 好高骛远，承担力所不及的事**

Samuel *bit off more than he could chew* when he agreed to edit the paper alone. 塞缪尔同意独自编辑这份报纸简直是不自量力。

Roosevelt started to repair his car himself, but realized that he *had bitten more than he could chew*. 罗斯福亲自动手修车，但随即发现力不从心。

2 **bite on that 费费脑筋吧，好好想想吧，啃啃这块硬骨头吧**

3 **bite the dust/ground 倒地毙命；一败涂地**

Squire and Gray fired again. Two *had bit the dust*, one had fled. 乡绅与格雷又开火了。两人被打死，一个逃走了。

Captain Jones raised his gun and bang, another Indian *bit the dust*. 琼斯队长举枪砰的一声，又一名印第安人应声倒地。

4 **bite the hand that feeds one 恩将仇报，以怨报德**

Toby *bit the hand that fed him* when he complained against his employer. 托比竟怪起他的老板来，真是恩将仇报。

5 **once bitten/bit twice shy/a burnt child dreads the fire 一次被咬，下次胆小；一次上当，下次小心；吃一次亏，学一回乖；一朝被蛇咬，十年怕井绳**

Once Mary had got lost when her mother took her downtown. But *a burnt child dreads the fire*, so now Mary stays close to her when they are downtown. 玛丽在母亲带她进城时走失过一次，但吃一次亏，学一回乖，所以现在当她们再去城里时，玛丽就紧跟着母亲。

6 **put the bite on【美俚】向……借钱；讹诈……**

Mike just *put the bite on* me. 迈克刚向我借了钱。

7 two bites at/of a/the cherry 婆婆妈妈地，踯躅不前；两次机会

Never make two bites at a cherry. 做事不要拖泥带水。

8 what's biting sb. 某人在为什么事烦恼

What's biting Geoffrey? He seems so nervous today. 杰弗里为什么事烦恼？他今天看上去很焦虑。

black

1 black and white/black-and-white 书写；印刷；黑白的，白纸黑字；黑白分明，非善即恶，绝对化

Wagner insisted on having the agreement down in black and white. 瓦格纳坚持把协议写成文字。

Washington gave me assurance in black and white. 华盛顿给了我书面保证。

2 not so/as black as sb. is painted 某人不像传说的那么坏

The young man is not so black as he is painted. 那个小伙子并不像人们所说的那么坏。

3 put the black on【俚】对……进行讹诈

The criminal put the black on the family. 犯罪分子对这家人进行了讹诈。

4 put up a black【俚】犯重大错误

The student had put up a black when he was giving a speech. 那个学生演讲时犯了一个严重的错误。

blame

1 I don't blame sb./I can't say I blame sb. 某人完全正确

I don't blame Hudson for walking out on Julia—I'd have done the same. 赫德森抛弃朱莉娅是对的，要是我也会这样做的。

2 I'm blamed/blame me【美俚】诅咒

I'm blamed if I go. 我决不去，我死也不去。

3 blame it【美俚】该死，去你的

4 and small blame to him 而这也不能多怪他

blank

draw (a) blank 抽空签；失败，白搭；记不得；认不得

Do you draw a blank trying to think of things to talk about after you've introduced yourself? 你有没有向别人自我介绍后，努力想说些什么的时

候,却感到脑子里一片空白,无话可说?

blast

1 blast it/you/him 该死,活该

I can't get this screw into the wall, blast it! 真该死! 这个螺钉我怎么也钉不进墙里去。

Blast you, can't you shut up while I'm trying to read? 你这个该死的,能不能在我看书的时候闭上你的嘴?

2 (at/in) full blast 开足马力,开足音量;大力地;极响地;完全地

Do you have to have your radio on full blast all the time? 你是不是非得让你的收音机这样大声地一天嚷到晚呢?

The cement plant is going full blast. 水泥厂正大力发展生产。

3 blast off【俚】走开,离开;破口大骂;发火,大发雷霆;发射,升空

Either you come in or blast off. 你要么进来,要么走开。

The coach was blasting off at the poor players. 教练正在大骂球打得糟糕的运动员。

blaze

1 go to blazes/dogs/Bath/Jericho/hell/pot/the devil/【美】go to grass 该死,活该;滚开,见鬼,去你的吧;去巴斯/去杰里哥(滚远一点);完蛋,失败

"You followed us, then?" "What's that to you?" said Jonas, "Go to the devil!" "那么你是跟在我们后面吗?""这与你有什么相干?"乔纳斯说,"去你的吧!"

I drink too much and my work has gone to blazes. 我饮酒过度,工作搞得一塌糊涂。

2 as/like blazes 极度,极端;如烈火般;飞快地;非常;吓人地,猛烈地

Hopkins ran like blazes away from the scene of the explosion. 霍普金斯飞快地逃离了爆炸现场。

The horse went like blazes. 马狂奔而去。

3 old blazes 恶魔

4 what/how/when/where/who/why the blazes 到底……,究竟……

What the blazes is going on here? 这儿到底发生了什么事?

How the blazes did you get here? I thought you were on holiday in Canada! 你怎么突然跑到这儿来了? 我还以为你在加拿大度假呢!

bleeding

bleeding【俚】该诅咒的,该死的;非常的
Hamlet is a bleeding idiot. 哈姆雷特是个该死的傻瓜。

bless

1 bless you 长命百岁(西方习俗在自己或别人打过喷嚏后说的话)
2 bless me/the boy/my life/soul/heart/heart and soul/I'm blest/I'll be blessed 哎呀,我的天哪,好家伙,谢天谢地,完了(表示惊讶、意外、愤怒、庆幸等)
Bless my soul! You've won first prize again—well done! 哎呀,你又得了第一名,干得好!
I'm blest if I know! 哎呀,我一无所知呀!
3 God bless (you) 上帝保佑(用于向亲密的朋友告别时说的祝福语)
As we stood at the gate, we shouted "God bless" to Johnny; he turn round and waved goodbye as he walked slowly down the lane. 我们站在大门口向约翰尼喊道:"上帝保佑你一切顺利!"他回过身来向我们挥手告别,然后沿着小巷慢慢走远了。
God bless you, my children! 愿上帝保佑你们,我的孩子们!
4 (God) bless you/him, etc./bless your/his, etc. heart/(对小孩子说)bless his (little) cotton socks 谢谢你(表示感谢、愉快或良好的祝愿)
Bless you, Martha, you shouldn't have bothered to buy me these flowers, but it really is very kind of you. 谢谢你,玛莎,你真不该费心买这些花给我,真是太感谢你了。

blessing

a blessing in disguise 貌似灾祸,实际使人得福之事;塞翁失马,焉知非福
Not getting that job was actually a blessing in disguise, because I have now got a much better one. 没有得到那份工作,其实是塞翁失马,因为现在我已得到一份好得多的工作。
However, his misfortune soon proved to be a blessing in disguise. 但事实很快证明,他的不幸实际上是变相的幸福。

blind

1 blind me/blimey/blimy【英俚】天哪!哎呀(表示惊愕或轻蔑, God blind

me 的缩略语）

2 the blind leading the blind 盲人领瞎子；半斤八两；由不能胜任的人来帮助别人

Jimmy is trying to show Bill how to skate. The blind are leading the blind. 吉米竟教比尔学滑冰，其实两人半斤八两。

It's a case of the blind leading the blind. 这真是问道于盲。

3 go in blind【美】猜测

I'm not one of those people who go in blind. 我不是那种靠猜测办事的人。

4 go it blind 盲目乱搞；鲁莽从事；蛮干；碰运气

"I don't like to go it blind," he hazarded. "我可不想冒冒失失地胡搞,"他壮起胆子说。

blink

on the blink【俚】发生故障，频繁修理

Bob's car went on the blink, so he rode to school with John. 鲍勃的汽车坏了,所以他与约翰一起骑车上学。

Mother called the repairman because her washing machine was on the blink. 洗衣机坏了,母亲请人来修理。

block

knock one's block off 使……吃苦头，痛击……

Stay out of my yard or I'll knock your block off. 不要待在我的院子里,否则我要揍你。

Jim will knock your block off if he catches you riding his bike. 吉姆若撞见你骑他的自行车,一定会揍你。

blood

1 curdle the blood/make one's blood run cold/creep 使……极度惊恐；使……不寒而栗；使……毛骨悚然

The assault, when it came, curdled the blood. 当进攻真正来临的时候,人们惊恐万分。

Here, Laurie read of dreadful crimes that made the blood run cold. 劳里读到一些令人不寒而栗的罪案。

2 freeze one's blood/make one's blood freeze 使……极度惊恐

What John said made our blood freeze. 约翰说的话让我们极度惊恐。

3　blood freezes/turns to ice 浑身发抖，不寒而栗，毛骨悚然

Oscar's blood turned to ice when he saw the shadow pass by outside the window. 奥斯卡看到窗外掠过的影子时吓得魂飞魄散。

Mary's blood froze when she had to walk through the cemetery at night. 当玛丽不得不在夜间走过公墓时，她吓得浑身发抖。

4　make one's/the blood boil 使……怒火中烧

It used to make my blood boil to think that such things couldn't be prevented. 一想到这类事情不能制止，常常使我怒火中烧。

When someone calls me a liar, it makes my blood boil. 有人说我是骗子时，我会勃然大怒。

5　get/have one's blood up 使……发火，使……生气

His rudeness got my blood up and I hit him in the face. 他的粗暴无礼使我勃然大怒，因而我打了他的脸。

6　move/stir one's blood 使……激动；激起某人的欲望、热情

7　draw blood 伤……感情，惹……生气；造成损失；使遭受痛苦

If you want to draw blood, ask Jim about his last money-making scheme. 如果你要惹吉姆生气，问一问他上次的赚钱计划。

Her sarcastic comments drew blood. 她的冷嘲热讽真伤人感情。

8　one's blood is up 激动起来；动怒，发火，怒火中烧

9　bloody【俚】该死的，该诅咒的；非常的

Of course not, you bloody idiot! 当然不是这样，你这该死的傻瓜！

blow

1　blow it 真该死，真可恼；混蛋，讨厌

Blow it! I just can't get this wallpaper straight! Will someone come and help me, please? 真该死，这张墙纸我怎么也贴不正！来个人给我帮帮忙好吗？

2　blow me (down)【美】真没料到；竟然

Blow me, if it isn't Charlie—I've not seen you for years. How are you, old friend? 哎呀，真想不到，这不是查理吗？我多年没见到你了。怎么样，老朋友，你还好吗？

I asked Lily twice to remember to post the letters, and blow me down if she didn't forget all about it! 我两次提醒莉莉记得寄那些信,可是你看,她竟然还是忘得一干二净。

3 blow me tight 如果我说谎,送我下地狱好啦

4 blow high, blow low 不管发生什么事,不管怎样

The workers were resolved to stand by each other through thick and thin, blow high, blow low. 工人们决心要互相支援,不顾艰难险阻,同甘共苦。

5 blow hot and cold 冷热无常,出尔反尔,摇摆不定,三心二意

The President blows hot and cold about a tax act. 总统对是否提出一项征税法案犹豫不决。

Mary blew hot and cold about going to college; every day she changed her mind. 玛丽上大学的兴致忽冷忽热,天天都在变。

6 blow a fuse/a gasket/one's top/one's stack 【俚】七窍生烟,暴跳如雷

When Mr. McCarthy's son got married against his wishes, he blew a fuse. 麦卡锡先生的儿子未照他的意思结婚,他气得暴跳如雷。

When the umpire called Joe out at first, Joe blew his top and was sent to the showers. 起先裁判要乔出去,他竟粗言相对,结果被禁止参加比赛。

7 blow one's brains out 脑袋开花(举枪自杀);殚精竭虑,绞尽脑汁;努力工作

Mr. Jones lost all his wealth, so he blew his brains out. 琼斯输得倾家荡产,于是举枪自杀。

The boys blew their brains out to get the stage ready for the play. 孩子们想尽一切办法,把舞台布置得十分完美。

8 blow one's mind 开窍;因服药过度而神志不清

Read Lyall Watson's book *Supernature*; it will simply blow your mind! 阅读莱尔·沃森的《超自然》一书,会使你脑子开窍。

Joe is entirely incoherent—he seems to have blown his mind. 乔语无伦次,好像是服药过量而神志不清。

9 blow/toot one's own horn 自吹自擂,自我炫耀,大肆吹牛

People get tired of a man who is always blowing his own horn. 喜欢吹牛的人总是令人讨厌。

A person who does things well does not have to toot his own horn; his abilities will be noticed by others. 一个认真做事的人并不需要自我吹嘘,别人自然会注意到他的能力。

10 blow the cost 价钱真贵

11 blow the whistle on 出卖，供出，告密；反对；取缔

The police caught one of the bank robbers, and he blew the whistle on two more. 警方逮捕了一名银行抢劫犯，他又供出了两名同伙。

The police blew the whistle on hot rodding. 警察严厉制止开快车的人。

blue

1 by all that's blue 糟糕，见鬼（源自法语）

2 be in/have the blues 没精打采，快快不乐，沮丧

John was in the blues on account of his failure in business. 约翰因事业失败而意志消沉。

3 (be) out of the blue 意外地；晴天霹雳，从天而降

In 1998 at age 15, Alina took out the European Championship in Portugal. Her victory was considered by many to be completely "out of the blue". 1998 年在她 15 岁时，阿丽娜在葡萄牙拿到欧洲冠军，她的胜利被认为非常出人意料。

blush

1 put sb. to the blush 使某人受窘脸红

What Peter said put us to the blush. 彼得的话使我们感到难为情。

2 spare one's blushes 不使……受窘脸红

Presumably this was to spare Japanese women their blushes. 或许是为了避免日本女人难为情吧。

board

back to the drawing board 得重新开始（用于设计或发明失败时）

"Have you heard the new car we're working on blew up this afternoon?" "Well, it's back to the drawing board then, I suppose!" "我们正在试制的新车今天下午又发生了爆炸，你听说了吗？""嗯，我想，咱们还得重新开始。"

boat

1 burn one's boats/bridges 背水一战，破釜沉舟，一干到底

Margaret is intelligent, ardent, and ready to burn her boats. 玛格丽特聪明、热情，且随时准备破釜沉舟。

The coach burned his boats in the ninth inning by putting in a pinch hitter for his best pitcher. 教练下决心在第九局时换上一个代打球员，以代替他最好的投球手。

2　in the same boat 处境相同，面临同样危险

If you lose your job, I'll lose mine; so we're both in the same boat. 假使你失业，我也会失业，所以我们是难兄难弟。

When one factory in the town closed and hundreds of people lost their jobs, all the storekeepers were in the same boat. 镇里一家工厂关闭并有数百人失业时，所有的店主也遭遇到同样的不幸。

3　miss the boat/bus 错过机会，坐失良机

Maxwell claims the government is missing the boat. 马克斯韦尔声称，政府正在坐失良机。

Mr. Brown missed the boat when he decided not to buy the house. 布朗先生决定不买这所房子，从而坐失良机。

4　push the boat out 庆祝；想方设法花钱取乐

I really pushed the boat out last Friday. 上星期五我玩得很痛快。

5　rock the boat 破坏现状，捣乱；(发表不同意见)使集体陷入困境

Well, if anyone rocks the boat, it's not gonna be me. 嗯，若有人想破坏此事，那不会是我。

The administration was clearly anxious not to rock the boat in its dealing with the unions. 政府部门显然极力希望不去破坏和工会的交易。

bob

1　Bob's your uncle【俚】一切正常，一切都将顺利解决；易如反掌

You turn left at the roundabout, go straight on for a little way, and, Bob's your uncle, you're at the motorway. 你走到环形路口时向左转，然后再朝前走一段路，那么，一切顺利，你就可以上高速公路了。

2　bob/pop up (like a cork) 突然出现；(失败后)恢复元气，东山再起

The question bobbed up again. 这个问题又突然出现了。

Just when the coach thought he had everything under control, a new problem bobbed up. 教练正以为万事俱备的时候，没想到又出现了新的难题。

body

1　body/heart and soul 全身心地，整个地

The male chauvinist thinks that he owns his wife body and soul. 那个大男子主义者认为妻子整个身心都是他的财产。

The town turned out body and soul for the Democratic candidate. 全城出动竭诚支持民主党候选人。

2 keep body and soul together 苟延残喘，勉强度日，几乎无法生活

The employers' conception was that the workers had no democratic rights whatever, that they were only a somewhat different kind of slave and should work from early morning until late at night for a wage barely enough to keep body and soul together. 雇主们的想法是：工人根本没有任何民主权利可言,他们只是一种变相的奴隶,他们为了一点勉强糊口的工资,就应该从清晨一直工作到深夜。

3 over my/his, etc. dead body 这绝对不行（在……抵死反对的情况下）

You can have this over my dead body. 除非我死,不然你休想得到这东西。

"A wage freeze—over our dead body," the trade union leaders cried. "冻结工资——这绝对办不到！"工会干部们高喊。

bone

1 be/feel/know in one's bones 从内心里感到,凭直觉,有预感,确信

I feel in my bones that tomorrow will be a sunny day. 我凭直觉判断明天是个晴天。

Roger felt in his very bones that his wife was dying. 罗杰确信他的妻子快要断气了。

2 have a bone in one's/the arm/leg【谑】胳膊/腿抬不起来啦

3 have a bone in one's/the throat【谑】不能开口啦,不能说话啦

I have a bone in my throat. 我不能说话了。

4 have a bone to pick with sb. 对某人有不满之处,与某人有需要解决的争端

Ah, there you are, Andrey, I've a bone to pick with you—why didn't you tell me you'd be out all night? I was worried stiff about you! 啊,你在这儿,奥德利,我正要找你算账呢。为什么你在外面过夜不事先告诉我,我为你担心死了！

5 make no bones about/of/to sth. 对某事毫不犹豫；就某事直言不讳；不反对,不顾忌,不掩饰

The squire made no bones about the matter; he despised the captain. 这绅士毫不掩饰,他看不起船长。
Mary made no bones about her love of poetry even after some of her friends laughed at her. 甚至在受到一些朋友的讥笑之后,玛丽仍不讳言她对诗歌的喜爱。

6　make no bones/mistake about it/no bones about it 毫无疑问,当然是真的(用于加强许诺的语气或表示坦白与直率)

Make no bones about it, my boy, I'm going to see you're punished properly this time! 没错,孩子,这次我会看到你受到应有的惩罚的。
I shall be coming back, make no mistake about it! 我会回来的,绝对没错!
Baseball is the national pastime in the U. S. and no bones about it. 棒球是美国全国性的娱乐,这一点毫无疑问。

7　no bones broken 没有什么,没事

"What happened to you?" "No bones broken!" "出什么事了?""没事儿!"

8　not make old bones 活不到老,活不长

Morgan has always been delicate from a child; I'm afraid he won't make old bones. 摩根自小身体羸弱,我怕他活不长。

9　a bone of contention 争论的起因,争执所在

The Chinese currency has long been a bone of contention at G20 summits. 中国货币一直是G20峰会的争论焦点。

book

1　a closed book 秘密,不为人知;一窍不通

The man's early life is a closed book. 那人早年的生活是一个谜。
The history of the town is a closed book. 这个小镇的历史没人知道。

2　an open book 昭然若揭的事情;极坦率的人

Your life in this town has been an open book—perhaps too open. 你在本镇的生活一直是公开的——也许太公开了。
Rose is an open book. 罗丝是个坦率的人。

3　a sealed book 天书般难懂的文字;奥博的学问(原为英国国教祈祷书的标准版本之一)

I can manage a little French, but this is a sealed book to me. 我略知一点法语,可这个对我来说犹如天书一般。

You are a sealed book to me; I have always found so; what you really think and do I shall never know. 你对我是个谜,我常有这种感觉,我将永远不会知道你真正在想什么、做什么。

4　be in one's good/bad books 得到/失去……好感,得/失宠于……

Parker is in the boss's bad books. 帕克不得头儿的欢心。

5　by/according to the book 一丝不苟地照规则办事,依照惯例

Pearson always goes by the book. 皮尔逊一贯照章办事。

Jonathan always goes by the book; I doubt if he will let you do what you want. 乔纳森总是循规蹈矩;我怀疑他是否让你干你想干的事情。

6　cook the book 伪造账目

Harrison was fired for cooking the books. 哈里森因为篡改公司的账本而被开除了。

7　hit the/one's books【美】做功课,用功

Jack broke away from his friends, saying, "I've got to hit the books." 杰克突然撇下朋友走了,说道:"我做功课去了。"

8　in one's book【美】按……一己之见

In my book, Oscar is an okay guy. 按我个人看法,奥斯卡这人不错。

9　not in the book 按规定不允许的

This is not in the book. 照规定这是不允许的。

10　know/read sb. like a book 通晓,对某人了如指掌,对某人的心思洞若观火

After all these years I can read you like a book. 这么多年以来,我对你了如指掌。

Clothes or no clothes, I can read you like a book. 不管你怎么伪装,我都能看透你。

11　one for the books 很不平常

The newspaper reporter turned in a story that was one for the books. 报社记者写了一篇很不平常的报道。

Their trip through the Rocky Mountains was one for the books. 他们的横穿洛基山脉之行很不寻常。

12　a turn-up for the book 出乎意料的事,意想不到的事

It was a turn-up for the book when I was offered the job. 我被录用做这件工作实在是意想不到的事。

Well, Jim's here early for a change—that's a turn-up for the book! 噢,吉姆今儿一反常态来早了,这真是个奇迹!

13 speak by the book 引经据典,说话正确,说话有根据

I can't speak by the book, but I know this is wrong. 我记不清原话,但我知道这句话是错的。

14 speak/talk like a book 说话文绉绉的,咬文嚼字

"I wish I could talk like that," said Cashel, "—like a book, I mean." "我很希望能那样讲话,"克沙勒说,"我是说,说话文绉绉的。"

15 speak/talk without the book 信口开河,任意乱说,说话无根据;不了解情况

You're talking without the book, things have travelled past you. 你是毫无根据地乱说,你已经落于形势了。

16 throw the book at/throw...the book 严惩

Because it was the third time he had been caught speeding that month, the judge threw the book at him. 因为他是那个月第三次超速被捕,法官予以严惩。

If I didn't plead guilty, they would throw me the book. 假使我不认罪,他们将从严判我。

17 beware of a man of one book 不要与一个有专业知识的人争论

The teacher advised us, "Beware of a man of one book." 老师忠告我们:"不要与一个有专业知识的人争论。"

18 I'm booked (for it) 【俚】我逃不了啦,我要倒霉了

boom

1 lower the boom 【美】严惩,禁止;采取严厉措施

The mayor lowered the boom on outside jobs for city firemen. 市长禁止消防队员在外兼职。

The police lowered the boom on open gambling. 警察严惩公开赌博行为。

2 top one's boom 【俚】溜之大吉,匆忙走开

We kept a good lookout, too—but Rossetti topped his boom directly he was outside the court. 我们倒也小心提防着,可是罗塞蒂一走出法庭,就溜之大吉了。

boot

1 boots and all【澳新】拳打脚踢起来；彻底地，全力以赴地
The next thing Saul will do is counter-attack, boots and all. 索尔计划下一步展开彻底的反击。

2 get the boot/the order of the boot 被解雇
Bill got the boot after fourteen years and had to find a new job. 比尔工作了14年后竟然被解雇了，只好另谋职业。

3 give sb. the boot/the order of the boot 解雇某人，开除某人
Eric's company gave him the boot. 埃里克被公司开除了。

4 go down in one's boot【美口】吓得魂不附体，吓坏了
The boy went down in his boot when he saw the tiger. 看到老虎，那个男孩儿吓坏了。

5 go it boots 迅速地干，起劲地干，加油干
The coach yelled to the runner to go it boots. 教练大喊着给赛跑选手加油。

6 go to bed in one's boots 酒醉上床，酩酊大醉
Macaulay went to bed in his boots after the evening party. 麦考利晚上聚会之后喝得酩酊大醉没脱衣服就上床睡觉了。

7 have one's boots laced【美】保持警觉

8 lick one's boots/feet/shoes/lick the boots of 奉承……；拍……的马屁
Thomson looks for courtesy from his subordinates, but he doesn't expect them to lick his boots. 汤姆森希望他的部属对他谦恭有礼，但不愿意他们拍马奉承。
A wise king would not want his friends and officials to lick his boots. 贤明的国王不会希望他的朋友和官员一味奉承自己。

9 lick the boots off 使……惨败
Victor licked the boots off me. 维克多把我打得惨败。

10 like/as old boots 彻底地，猛烈地；拼命地，劲头十足地，竭力，尽量
I was working like old boots. 我竭尽全力拼命干活儿。
It's rainning like old boots. 大雨倾盆。

11 make one boot serve for either leg 说话模棱两可，言语自相矛盾
The professor always makes one boot serve for either leg. 那个教授说话老是模棱两可、似是而非。

12 move/start one's boots【美】动身，出发，离开

The police started their boots as soon as they got the news. 警察一得到消息马上就动身出发了。

13 over shoes, over boots 将错就错，一不做二不休

The old saying goes,"Over shoes, over boots." 老话说得好，"一不做，二不休。"

14 put the boot in（通常在对方倒地后）再踢上一脚；落井下石；做出过分的残酷行为（尤指在橄榄球赛中）；做危险动作

The presidential aide decided to put the boot in—to tell the true story. 总统助理决定落井下石——把真实情况和盘托出。

15 put the boot on the wrong leg 错爱；错怪，毁誉不当

You will put the boot on the wrong leg if you think they deserve the credit. 如果你认为他们值得称赞，那你就看错人了。

16 quiver/shake/shiver in one's boots/shoes 吓得发抖

The robber shook in his boots when the police knocked on his door. 警察敲门时，强盗吓得瑟瑟发抖。

17 the boot/shoe is on the other leg/foot 情况正相反；这应由其他方面负责

Everyone knows that the boot is on the other foot. 每一个人都知道形势已经完全不同了。

18 to boot 更加，加之，况且，而且

Wilson not only got fifty dollars, but they bought him dinner to boot. 威尔逊不仅得了五十美元，而且他们还请他吃了饭。

The fellow is drunk and he's a bad driver to boot. 这家伙不仅喝醉了，而且他还是个不高明的司机。

19 wipe one's boots on 侮辱……

Don't wipe your boots on our guests. 不要侮辱我们的客人。

20 with one's heart in one's mouth 提心吊胆；紧张

Our monitor got up to make his first speech with his heart in his mouth. 我们班长站起来发表他的第一次演讲时紧张得心都要跳出来了。

bootstraps

pull/raise/lift oneself up by one's (own) bootstraps 靠自己的力量出人头地，独立自主地，自力更生地

Wright had to pull himself up by his bootstraps. 赖特必须自立自强。

bore

bore (sb.) to death/tears 令人厌烦

The party was dull, and Roger showed plainly that he was bored to tears. 这宴会没啥意思,罗杰坦然表示他极为厌烦。

Mary loved cooking, but sewing bores her to tears. 玛丽喜欢烹调,但讨厌缝纫。

born

1 born and bred 在……长大的,地地道道的,本地的

Mr. Evans is a Londoner born and bred. 埃文斯先生是个地道的伦敦人。

The great writer was born and bred in Yorkshire. 那个著名作家自幼在约克郡长大。

2 born yesterday 初出茅庐,少不更事,幼稚可欺

I wasn't born yesterday. 我又不是不懂。

When Bill started the new job, the other workers teased him a little, but he soon proved to everyone that he wasn't born yesterday. 比尔开始做新工作时,其他工人都揶揄他,但不久他就向所有人证明了他不是个嫩小子。

3 in all one's born days 一生中,有生以来(常用于否定句或疑问句)

In all my born days I've never seen such a fool as you are. 我有生以来还从未见过像你这样的傻子。

I've never heard such nonsense in all my born days. 我有生以来从未听过这样的废话。

4 there's one born every minute 竟然到处都有这样的笨蛋

We were trying to sell our house for a long time and then suddenly someone came up and offered us thousands more than it's really worth; there's one born every minute! 我们早就打算卖掉我们的房子,后来忽然来了一个人愿以高出实际房价几千元的价格买下它;真没想到到处都有这样的笨蛋。

bottle

bottle it【美俚】不要吵了,静一静,住嘴

bottom

1 bottoms up 干杯

Bottoms up to you! 为您的健康干杯!

Webster drank his whiskey almost bottoms up. 韦伯斯特把杯中的威士忌一饮而尽。

2 at (the) bottom 内心里，实际上，本质上

I am a pretty bad fellow at bottom and I find the pretence of virtues very irksome. 实际上，我是个很坏的家伙，我认为种种美德的伪装是十分令人厌烦的。

At bottom, Tracy is convinced that their ways are the best. 特雷西打心底里相信他们的方法是最好的。

3 at the bottom of one's heart 在……内心深处

Sophia put on a show of indifference, but at the bottom of her heart she was bitterly disappointed. 索菲娅装出一副满不在乎的样子，但在内心深处却感到极度失望。

4 at the bottom of fortune's wheel 时乖命舛，倒霉透顶

Faulkner is at the bottom of fortune's wheel. 福克纳时运极差。

5 be/lie at the bottom of 是……的真正起因或根源

Who is at the bottom of all this trouble? 这些麻烦归根到底是谁引起的?

The increase of the population is at the bottom of it all. 这一切的根源在于人口增长。

6 bet one's bottom dollar 参见 bet 2

7 from the bottom/ground of one's/the heart/soul 打心眼里，衷心地，诚心诚意地

I wish you happiness from the bottom of my heart. 我衷心祝你幸福。

If a book comes from the bottom of the heart, it will contrive to reach other hearts. 一本用心写出来的书是会感动别人的。

8 from the bottom up 从头，从一开始；完全

The job will have to be done all over again from the bottom up. 这件工作还得从头再干。

Learn something from the bottom up. 从头学起。

9 touch bottom/search to the bottom/get to the bottom of/get down at the bottom of/get down to rock bottom 追根究底，彻底查明

It is much better to touch bottom at once and know the whole truth than to remain in suspense. 立刻探明究竟并知道全部实情比起老是悬而不决要

好得多。

The superintendent talked with several students to get to the bottom of the trouble. 教育主管与几位同学谈话,以查明骚乱的真相。

No one has ever really got to the bottom of this problem. 不曾有人把这个问题弄个水落石出。

10 start at the bottom (of the ladder) 从最基层做起;始于卑微

Shaw started at the bottom of the ladder and worked his way up to success. 肖从最基层的工作做起,发奋努力,一路升迁,取得了成功。

11 stand on one's own bottom 独立自主,自力更生

Every tub must stand on its own bottom. 桶须自立,人贵自助。

Don't ask me to do your work for you. You should learn to stand on your own bottom. 别叫我替你干活了,你应该学会自立。

bounce

1 get the bounce/sack/hook/gate/air/axe/bird【美】被解雇;被(学校)开除;失恋,失去心爱的人,与女友分手

Joe is sad because he just got the gate from his girl. 乔很伤心,因为他失恋了。

Shirley was afraid she might get the air from her boyfriend if she went out with other boys while he was away. 莎莉很怕失去男友——如果她趁他不在的时候与其他的男孩子约会的话。

2 give sb. the bounce/gate/sack/hook/air/ax【美】解雇,开除;断交,决裂;告吹

The ball team gave Joe the gate because he never came to practice. 球队开除了约翰,因为他从不参加训练。

Mary gave John the bounce after she saw him dating another girl. 玛丽看见约翰与别的女孩约会,就与他分手了。

3 bounce back 很快恢复元气,迅速挽回败局

Although he was disappointed about not getting the job, Jack soon bounced back. 虽然杰克没找到工作很失望,但他很快就重新振作起来了。

4 bounce off【俚】向……作试探;向……兜售自己的想法,了解……对……的看法

They bounced their ideas off each other. 他们相互交换彼此的想法。

5 give it to them upon the bounce 【英俚】虚张声势逃脱警察追捕

bound

I'll be bound/I dare bound 我敢肯定；我能担保
The bus will be late again, I'll be bound. 这趟车又晚点了，我敢肯定。
Marjory will have some good reasons for being late, I'll be bound. 我敢肯定，马乔里一定会为迟到找到一些冠冕堂皇的理由。

bow

1 bow and scrape 打躬作揖，奴颜婢膝，巴结奉承
The old servant bowed and scraped before them, too obedient and eager to please. 这个老仆人在他们面前卑躬屈膝，极尽巴结谄媚之能事。

2 make one's bow 进入，初次在公众前露面；向观众、听众致意
His new novel will make its bow next year. 他的新小说将于明年与读者见面。
This pianist made his bow and sat down to play. 钢琴家向观众致意，然后坐下演奏。

3 draw/bend/pull a/the long bow 夸口，吹牛，说大话；说谎
What is it makes him pull the long bow in that wonderful manner? 是什么让他那样大吹特吹呢？

4 draw a bow at a venture 突然袭击；盲目评论；瞎碰，乱猜
Tina drew a bow at a venture for the numbers of lottery. She did not expect to win anything and was surprised to win the first prize. 蒂娜胡乱猜测了彩票号码。她并不抱有任何希望，对于能赢得头奖感到相当惊讶。

box

1 in a (tight) box/bind 身处困境，左右为难
Sam is in a box because if he carries home his aunt's groceries, his teacher will be angry because he is late, and if he doesn't, his aunt will complain. 山姆真为难，假如他把姑妈的杂货先拿回家，老师会因为他迟到而生气；倘若不这样，姑妈又会埋怨。

2 in the same box 【口】处于同样的困境，面临同样的狼狈局面
Jim always told himself that all the members of the staff were in the same box. 吉姆常常对自己说，所有职工的处境都同样艰难。

3 in the wrong box 格格不入,处于窘境;出错
The woman who entered the smoking car soon discovered that she was in the wrong box. 走进吸烟车厢的那位妇女很快就发现自己走错了地方。

boy

1 (oh) boy/good boy 好家伙(表示惊喜、惊奇、兴奋等)
Good boy, Willy! 好样儿的,威利!
Oh, boy, our team's going to win! How fantastic! 好家伙,我们队要赢了,真了不起!

2 there's/that's my/the boy 好啊,好样的(表示鼓励、赞成、兴奋、欣喜等)
There's my boy! First again! Well done! 好家伙,又得了第一,真棒!

3 (a) boy's play 容易的事,儿戏
The work is not a boy's play. 这工作可不容易做。

4 boys will be boys 孩子总是孩子嘛(意为青少年的不当行为可以宽恕)
Boys will be boys and make a lot of noise, so John's mother told him and his friends to play in the park instead of the backyard. 男孩子总归是男孩子,免不了大吵大闹,所以约翰的母亲叫他和他的朋友们别在后院而是到公园去玩。

5 old boy/chap/cock/fellow/man/ship/bean/egg/fruit/thing/top 老朋友;老兄;老家伙;老人,老头;老同学,校友
Every year we have a gathering of old boys. 我们年年举行校友联欢会。
Well, Jim, how are you today, old boy? 喂,吉姆,今天怎么样,老伙计?
The old man's just gone out. 我们老头子刚出去。

6 big boy 老弟(对男子的亲热称呼)

brain

1 beat/cudgel/rack/pound/puzzle/busy/drag one's brains (out/about/with) 绞尽脑汁,苦苦思索,殚精竭虑
It was too hard for him and he beat his brains out trying to get the answer. 这对他来说太难了,因而他苦苦思索以求答案。
Some students are lazy, but others beat their brains and succeed. 有些学生懒惰,而有些学生则肯动脑筋,因而功课很好。

2 crack one's brain(s) 发狂

3 go off one's brain 【口】(因欢喜、生气、焦急等)发狂(尤指狂喜)

4 have one's brain on ice【口】保持头脑冷静
Have your brain on ice! Don't jump to conclusions. 保持头脑清醒,不要轻易下结论。

5 have/get sb./sth. on the brain 念念不忘某人/某事,热衷于某人/某事
Even since the house was burgled, the old man has had burglars on the brain. 自打房子遭盗窃以来,那个老人脑子里总摆脱不了盗贼。
I've (got) that new tune on the brain. 那支新曲子一直萦绕在我的脑中。

6 pick/suck one's brains 窃取……脑力劳动的成果
His real reason for coming was to pick Michael's brains and pump him for information. 他前来的真正原因是窃取迈克尔脑力劳动的成果,并从他那儿刺探情报。

7 turn one's/the brain/head 冲昏……的头脑,使精神错乱
The loss of her boy has turned her brain. 失去儿子使她精神错乱。

bread

1 as I live by bread 说实话,一点不假
Why, it's Bill, as I live by bread! 哎呀,的确是比尔!

2 bread and butter/bread-and-butter 生活资料,生活来源,日常所需,主要收入来源;吉星高照,老天保佑,阿弥陀佛;感谢款待的,例行道谢的;谋生需要的,有实际用处的;年轻的,十六七岁的
Ed earned his bread and butter as a bookkeeper, but added a little jam by working with a dance band on weekends. 埃德当会计以维持生计,同时利用周末为舞厅伴奏赚些外快。
Jim was a plumber's apprentice whose weak chin and hedonistic temperament, coupled with a certain nervous stupidity, promised to take him nowhere in the race for bread and butter. 吉姆是个水暖工学徒,不善言辞,贪图享受,还有某些神经过敏的傻气,在抢饭碗的竞争中前途暗淡。

break

1 break it up【澳】别胡扯了,给我住口;【美】停止扭打或争吵;住手;住口
"Break it up! Move along there," the police called out to the rival gangs of teenagers milling around in the town square. "住手!统统给我离开这里!"警察向聚集在城市广场上斗殴的一群少年喊道。
The boys were fighting and a passing policeman ordered them to break it

up. 一些孩子在打架,路过的警察命令他们住手。

2 give me a break/【口】gimme a break 【美】得了吧！收起你那一套,别以为我那么笨

3 give sb. a break 给某人一个机会,给某人一次优待

Give me a break and pass me, or else I'll have to be a freshman again. 帮帮忙给我个及格分,不然我就得重读一年级了。

breathe

1 as I live and breathe 【口】只要我还有口气（用来表示态度坚决）；使我非常吃惊,竟然是,原来是（表示出乎意料）

You will never enter this house again, as I live and breathe! 你永远别再进这个家！听到没有！

As I live and breathe, Thodore is here again after 20 years! 真让人意外,西奥多又在这儿待了二十年。

2 breathe again/freely/easily/easy 如释重负,松了一口气

Take a moment to calm down, breathe easy, concentrate, let your heartbeat slow, and get in the zone. 花点时间让自己平静下来,放松地呼吸,全神贯注,让心跳放缓,然后进入拍摄状态。

breeze

1 bat/fan/shoot the breeze/bull 【美】聊天

Father shot the breeze with his neighbor while the children were playing. 孩子们在玩耍时,父亲与邻居聊天。

The women were shooting the breeze about Jim's latest trouble with the police. 女人们在谈论吉姆最近与警察的争执。

2 breeze off 【美俚】走开；住嘴

3 get/have/put the breeze up 【俚】使紧张,使惊慌；惊慌,害怕；紧张不安

4 hit/split/take the breeze 【俚】上路；离去,走开,溜掉

5 win in a breeze/walk 轻松获胜

Joe ran for class president and won in a walk. 乔竞选班长轻松当选。

Our team won the game in a breeze. 我们的球队轻松赢了比赛。

brick

1 like a brick/like a load/ton/carload/thousand of bricks 猛烈地,充满活力

地,劲头十足地,势不可当地,以泰山压顶之势(常与 to come down 连用)
Before North could defend himself, they were (had come) down upon him like a ton of bricks. 诺思还来不及防卫,他们就以泰山压顶之势向他扑来。
The outside left was hit a bit too hard and he went down like a ton of bricks. 左边锋狠狠地挨了一下,重重地倒了下去。

2 make bricks with straw 做无米之炊,做极为困难而又无功的事
John could not go to a library, and writing the report was a job of making bricks with straw. 约翰不能去图书馆,因此这篇报告就是在缺乏资料的情况下写成的。

3 shit bricks/a brick 十分忧虑,非常担心
Occam was shitting bricks while his wife was having her first baby. 妻子生头胎时,奥卡姆真是担心得要命。

4 have/wear a brick in one's head/hat 有醉意

5 hit the bricks【美俚】走上人行道;上街巡逻;上街行乞;罢工;释放出狱

bridge

burn one's bridges (behind one) 自断退路,义无反顾,破釜沉舟
Japan had burned its bridges with America during the Second World War. 二战期间日本采取破釜沉舟的态度,断绝了与美国的关系。

bright

1 (as) bright as a button 机灵到极点

2 (as) bright as a new penny/pin 光可鉴人,打扮得漂漂亮亮的;聪明伶俐
I knew that Will loved that boy of his—red-haired, bright as a new penny, full of life. 我知道威尔爱他那个孩子——红头发、聪明活泼、充满朝气。

3 bright and early 一大早;兴高采烈、满面春风地准时到来
Get up bright and early. 一大早起身。
Peggy arrived bright and early for the appointment. 佩吉满面春风地准时赴约。

4 bright in the eye 微醉,有醉意

bring

1 bring down/come about/around one's ears 毁灭；落空

They planned to have factories all over the world, but the war brought their plans down about their ears. 他们计划在世界各地建厂,但战争使他们的计划成为泡影。

John hoped to go to college and become a great scientist some day, but when his father died he had to get a job, and John's dreams brought down around his ears. 约翰希望上大学,将来成为一个伟大的科学家。但父亲去世了,他只得去工作,他的希望也随之破灭。

2 bring down the house 赢得满堂喝彩；引起哄堂大笑

The principal's story was funny in itself and also touched their loyalties, so it brought down the house. 校长说的故事滑稽有趣,同时也触及了忠诚问题,所以引起了大家热烈的掌声。

A young girl brought the house down with a ballet dance. 一个年轻的姑娘跳了一段芭蕾舞博得全场喝彩。

3 bring home 清楚到极点,十分明白,昭然若揭

The accident caused a death in his family and it brought home to him the evil of drinking while driving. 车祸使他失去了一个家人,这使他对酒后开车的危害一清二楚。

A parent or a teacher should bring home to children the value and pleasure of reading. 父母或老师应该让孩子们了解读书的价值与乐趣。

4 bring home the bacon 供养家庭；成功,获胜；完成任务

Kennedy was a steady fellow, who always brought home the bacon. 肯尼迪是一个可靠的人,总是妥善地照顾家庭。

The football team brought home the bacon. 这支足球队赢得了比赛。

broad

as broad as it is long 横竖一样,反正一样,半斤八两；无关紧要

Whether we travel south first down the main road and then east along the motorway or east along the main road and south down the motorway is just the same; it's as broad as it is long. 我们是先沿着大街向南开然后再向东上高速公路,还是先沿着大街向东开然后再向南上高速公路都是一样的,结果都一样。

broke

1 be broke to the world (wide)/go broke/be clean/dead/flat/stone/stony broke 完全破产的,不名一文的;彻底破产;不名一文

Jill wanted to go to the movies but he *was stone broke*. 吉尔想看电影,但他身无分文。

The inventor *went broke* because nobody would buy his machine. 因为没有人买他的机器,这位发明人遂债台高筑。

2 go for broke【美俚】破釜沉舟,孤注一掷;尽力而为

The racing car driver decided to *go for broke* in the biggest race of the year. 赛车者决定为一年中最大的一次比赛孤注一掷。

broom

1 a new broom sweeps clean/new brooms sweep clean 新官上任三把火

The new superintendent has changed many of the school rules. *A new broom sweeps clean*. 新校监大肆修改校规,真是新官上任三把火。

2 get/have a broom in/up one's tail/ass【美俚】卖力大干

brother

Oh brother 啊,老兄;啊,天哪(表示极为烦躁、不耐烦或惊讶)

Oh brother, the phone's ringing again! That's the tenth time this morning—who can it be now? 啊,天哪!电话铃又响了。这是今天早上第十次电话了——又可能是谁呢?

brown

1 do (it) up brown【美】把……彻底搞好,把……做得尽善尽美,把……干得十全十美

When she gives a dinner party, Alma always *does it up brown*. 当阿尔玛举行晚宴时,她总是办得尽善尽美。

2 do sb. brown【俚】使某人上当

brush

be/get tarred with the same brush/stick 被看成一丘之貉

When you fraternize with people like Adolph, you *get tarred with the same brush*. 跟阿道夫这一类人交往,你就同他们是一路货色了。

They are all tarred with the same brush—all stuffed with a heap of lies. 他们都是一丘之貉,只会满口胡扯。

bug

1 bug off【美俚】逃跑;撤离;(停止干扰而)走开

Don't bother me again. Bug off or I will call the police. 不要再骚扰我了,走开,不然我就报警。

2 bug out【美俚】逃跑;撤离;(眼睛)突出

Jim decided to bug out, the concert was just too noisy. 吉姆决定开溜,这音乐会太吵了。

3 bug up【美俚】激动;迷惑

4 put/drop a bug in one's ear【美】事先给人暗示;私下叮嘱

The young man wants to put a bug in his girlfriend's ear. 那个男青年想给他的女朋友暗示一下。

bull

1 shoot/throw (the) bull【美俚】闲谈;瞎扯,吹牛

Rebecca likes to shoot the bull, she can talk with her friends over the phone for hours and hours. 丽贝卡很喜欢闲聊,她可以跟她的朋友在电话中聊几个小时。

2 take the bull by the horns 大胆对付困难或危险;明知山有虎,偏向虎山行

Those who take the bull by the horns at difficult times are really brave men. 那些面对困难采取行动的人是真正勇敢的人。

bully

bully for you/him 干得好;妙啊;好极了,妙极了;那好啊(用于回答别人的夸耀,带忌妒和讥讽的口吻)

"We're flying to America for a month next week." "Oh, bully for you. I suppose I've got to stay here and work all the time you're away." "下星期我们要飞往美国待一个月。""啊,你真走运! 我想这段时间我只好在这儿工作了。"

bump

like a bump on a log 呆头呆脑，一声不吭
Don't sit there like a bump on a log. 别坐在那里像一根木头似的。

burn

1 feel one's ears burning 觉得有人说自己的闲话
Someone may be talking about me. I feel my ears burning. 可能有人正在议论我，我觉得耳朵发烧。

2 burn you 该死的

3 there you burn 我可抓住你了（玩捉迷藏游戏）；答案快找到了
There you burn! （捉迷藏）我可抓到你了！

bush

1 beat about/around the bush 闪烁其词，东拉西扯，转弯抹角
Jasper would not answer yes or no, but beat about the bush. 贾斯珀顾左右而言他，不做正面回答。
Keats beat about the bush for half an hour without coming to the point. 基茨东拉西扯地讲了半小时，不得要领。

2 beat the bushes to/for 【美】寻觅，到处寻找
Lena beat the bushes to find a good job. 莉娜为寻找一份好工作而到处奔波。
They beat the bushes for people who are eligible to vote but don't. 他们到处寻找那些有资格投票但不投票的人。

business

1 business as usual 照常营业；一切照常
Schulte says now is not the time for business as usual. 舒尔特说，现在不是进行正常贸易的时候。

2 business before pleasure 正事当先，正事要紧
"Business before pleasure," as the man said when he kissed his own wife. 男的给了自己的妻子一个吻，说道："先干活而后再去享乐吧。"

3 business is business 公事公办
We shouldn't let the fact that we've just got engaged affect our relationship at work—business is business, you know. 我们不能因为我们刚订婚这一

事实影响我们之间的工作关系。你看,公事公办嘛。

4　do sb. business/do the business for sb. 够某人受的;要某人的命

If you eat any more pudding, it will do the business for you. 你要是再吃布丁,就会撑死的。

That much will be enough to do his business. 那些就足够要他的命了。

5　do the business 完成工作;解决问题,把事办成

The boys had trouble in rolling the stone, but four of them did the business. 男孩们推不动那块石头,但其中四个人做到了。

When the little boy cut his finger, a bandage did the business. 小男孩割破了手指,缠上绷带就没事啦。

6　get down/come to business 动手做事

It's time we got down to business. 我们该认真办事了。

7　get the business 受到训斥;受到惩罚

Fred got the business when Tom caught him with his bicycle. 汤姆抓到弗雷德偷他的自行车,于是狠狠地揍了他一顿。

Mike thought he was the star of the team until he got the business from the coach. 迈克认为自己是队里的尖子,结果挨了教练的一顿痛骂。

8　give sb. the business 把某人收拾一顿,把某人揍一顿;杀害某人;欺骗某人,戏弄某人;尽最大努力

The teacher gave Malan the business when he came to school late. 马伦迟到了,老师把他训斥了一顿。

Nelson has been giving his partner the business for years. 几年来纳尔逊一直在欺骗他的同伙。

9　go about your business 走开,去你的吧;干你自己的事去

Just go about your business and don't keep looking out of the window. 干你自己的事,别老望着窗外。

10　good business 干得好,妙极了

11　have no business 无权;没有理由;不该

You have no business to say such a thing. 你无权说这样的话。

Such kind of architecture has no business with rich ornament. 这种建筑不应有华美的装饰。

12　know one's own business 熟悉自己的事情;不过问别人分内事;胜任本职工作

13 (like) nobody's business 非常地，特别地

Edison plays the piano like nobody's business. 爱迪生钢琴弹得非常好。

My head this morning is nobody's business. 今天早晨我感觉很不舒服。

14 make it one's business 把这事当作自己的任务或本分；特别注意某事；负责办某事

Edward never makes it his business to inquire whether you are rich or poor. 爱德华从不打听你是富还是穷。

I will make it my business to see that the money is paid promptly. 我将负责督促迅速付款。

15 mean business 认真地；说到做到

They convinced the enemy that they mean business. 他们使敌人相信他们是说到做到的。

The boss said he would fire us if we didn't work harder and he means business. 老板说如果我们不更加卖力，他就会解雇我们，他是说到做到的。

16 mind your own/none of your business/affairs 莫管闲事，与你无关
参见 affair 1、3

17 on business 因公

George visited Africa on official business. 乔治因公访问了非洲。

No admittance except on business. 非公莫入，闲人免进。

18 a pretty business【讽】干的好事，真糟糕

19 send sb. about his business 把某人打发走；解雇某人；叫某人不要多管闲事

20 what's your business 有何贵干，你来干什么

but

1 but/except for 要不是，倘若没有；除……以外

But for the doctor's skill, Guy would have died. 要不是医生医术高明，盖伊早就死了。

But for your interference, things would have looked very black indeed. 如果不是你来干预，事情可就惨了。

2 but good【美】狠狠地，有力地；彻底地

Jack insulted Tom, and Tom hit him, but good. 杰克侮辱了汤姆，于是汤

姆狠狠地揍了他一顿。

Jack called Charles a bad name, and Charles hit him, but good. 杰克骂查尔斯,查尔斯因此狠狠地揍了他一顿。

3 but me no buts 别老对我说"但是"了;不要一直反对和解释

But me no buts this time, just do what I tell you and do it at once! 这次别给我啰唆了,立刻照我说的去办!

4 but then 但是,然而,可是

Johnny is a good fellow, but then he is so erratic. 约翰尼是个好人,但是另一方面,他又是那样乖僻。

The villa is beautiful, but then, I expected nothing less. 这别墅很美,不过话说回来,这也是意料中的事。

5 but too 很遗憾

It was but too true. 很遗憾,那是真实的。

6 (there are) no buts (about it) 这是毫无疑问的;没有但是,不接受反驳

I saw you steal the money from the drawer. There are no buts about it. You can't defend yourself because I caught you in the act. 我看见你从抽屉里偷了钱,这是毫无疑问的。你无法为你自己辩护,因为我当场抓住了你。

Do as I tell you, no buts about it. 就照我说的办,不要有二话。

butter

1 butter to butter is no relish 千篇一律的东西,令人生厌

2 butter up (to) sb./lay on/spread butter【口】阿谀奉承,巴结,讨好

Harry is working hard to butter up the boss to get that promotion. 哈里为了得到提升,正在想方设法地巴结讨好老板。

3 fair/fine words butter no parsnips 花言巧语是不中用的;画饼充饥

Mr. Carter reminded everybody at the so-called "summit-meeting" in London that fine words butter no parsnips. 在伦敦所谓的"高峰会议"上,卡特先生提醒大家高谈阔论是无济于事的。

4 (look as if) butter would not melt in one's mouth 假装天真无邪;表面老实,实则不然

Kingsley looks as if butter wouldn't melt in his mouth, but he's not so harmless really! 金斯利表面上装得很老实,可事实上并非那么善良。

The new secretary was rude to the other workers, but when she talked to the boss, butter wouldn't melt in her mouth. 这位新秘书对其他工人态度很粗暴,但在老板面前她总是毕恭毕敬。

button

1 button up one's face/lip/keep one's lip buttoned 住嘴;不吭声;守口如瓶
Button up your face! 别讲了,安静!
John wanted to talk, but Dan told him to keep his lip buttoned. 约翰想说出去,但丹要他守口如瓶。
2 be a button short/not have (got) all one's buttons (on)【口】略有痴呆,头脑不正常
3 have a button/a few buttons missing【俚】行为古怪,精神失常

buy

I'll buy it 我不知道,我放弃回答(回答谜语或问题时)
"What did the gum say to the glue?" "Go on, I'll buy it." "橡胶对胶水说了些什么?""问下一个吧,这个我不知道。"

buzz

1 buzz off 走开!
Buzz off, I'm trying to work. 走开,我要干活了!
2 go with a buzz 进行得很顺利

by

1 by and by 一会儿;以后,后来;迟早
Roger said he would do his homework by and by. 罗杰说过一会儿再做功课。
The mother knew her baby would be a man by and by and do a man's work. 母亲知道孩子迟早会长大成人,承担起一个男子汉的责任。
2 by and large 大部分地;通常地,一般地
There were bad days, but it was a pleasant summer by and large. 今夏虽有恶劣天气,但大体上还是个令人愉快的季节。
Taking it by and large, we had a pleasant ten days' run. 总的说来,我们进行了一次为期十天的愉快旅行。

3 by the by/by the way 顺便说一下

We shall expect you, by the by, dinner will be at eight. 我们等你,还有,晚饭是八点开始。

I was reading when the earthquake occurred, and by the way, it was *The Last Days of Pompeii* that I was reading. 地震发生时我正在看书,顺便说一句,我读的是《庞贝城的末日》。

C

Cain

raise Cain/hell/hell's delight/the devil/the mischief/a big smoke/the roof 生气，吵闹，闹事，闹乱子；制造麻烦；大叫大嚷；破口大骂

When John couldn't go on the basketball trip with the team, he raised Cain. 约翰不能随球队参加篮球巡回赛，这使他十分生气。

The children raised Cain in the living room. 孩子们在客厅里大喊大叫。

cake

1 a piece of cake 轻松愉快的事；容易做的事

This job is anything but a piece of cake. 这份差事绝不轻松。

2 a slice of the cake （分享的）一份利益

The unions tried to secure a bigger slice of the cake of economic prosperity for the working populations. 工会尽力为工人们争取更多的经济繁荣带来的利益。

3 cakes and ale 吃喝玩乐，生活上的享受，人生的乐事

Life is not all cakes and ale. (Life is not all beer and skittles.) 人生并不总是吃喝玩乐。

4 cannot have one's cake and eat it (too)/cannot eat one's cake and have it (too) 两者不可兼得

Roger can't make up his mind whether to go to college or get a full-time job. You can't eat your cake and have it too. 去上大学还是找个全职工作，罗杰还是拿不定主意，鱼与熊掌不可兼得。

We won't let you work shorter hours and get more money—you can't have your cake and eat it. 我们不能让你少干活，多拿钱，两者不可兼得嘛。

5 go/sell like hot cakes 畅销

We hope this dictionary sells like hot cakes. 我们希望这本词典畅销。

6 go off like hot cakes 畅销；迅速处置

Our dictionaries go off like hot cakes. 我们的字典很畅销。

7 one's cake is dough 希望落空，计划失败

My cake is dough. 我的计划失败了。

8 take the cake/bun/biscuit/chromo 得第一，位列榜首；达到极限；最糟的；胆大妄为；真是妙极了（一般用于讽刺）

Jones takes the cake as a storyteller. 琼斯讲故事，无人能望其项背。

I let Jack borrow my baseball and he never gave it back. Doesn't that take the cake. 我让杰克借用我的棒球，但他却有借无还。真是岂有此理。

call

1 at (one's) call/on call 随时可以支取的；随时可供使用的；随时听命的

There are thousands of men at his call. 有好几千人听命于他。

The company car is always on call to take you to our meetings. 公司的汽车可随时来接你出席会议。

2 at one's beck and call/at beck (and call) of 任人使唤

The Queen had a large household of servants at her beck and call. 女王有很多仆人供她使唤。

Lena came at beck (and call) of a youth when she had known him for only one month. 一个莉娜才结识了一个月的男子一招呼，她就来了。

3 call a pikestaff a pikestaff/a spade a spade/things by their proper names 据实而言，直言不讳，实事求是

They were a little frightened at this young fellow, and the awing and smash of his words, and his dreadful trait of calling a spade a spade. 他们对这个年轻人都有点害怕，怕他那泼辣而尖锐的言论，怕他那可怕的直言不讳的脾气。

A boy took some money from Dick's desk and said he borrowed it, but I told him he stole it; I believe in calling a spade a spade. 一个男孩从迪克的抽屉里拿了钱，他说是借的，但我说这是偷的，我认为应该实事求是。

4 call it a day 今天结束吧，休息；终止

Bob studied hard till 10 p.m., and then decided to call it a day and went to bed. 鲍勃用功学习到晚上十点，然后决定休息，就上床睡觉了。

Johnson painted his house all morning, then he called it a day and went to the ball game. 约翰逊整个早晨都在刷房子，然后他停下工作去看球赛。

5 call it quits 罢休，决定停止；收工；双方扯平，对等

When Tom had painted half the garage, he called it quits. 汤姆将车库刷

了一半,就决定罢手不干了。

Peter called Tom a bad name, and they fought till Tom gave Peter a bloody nose; then they called it quits. 彼得骂了汤姆,两人大打出手,直到彼得把汤姆打得鼻青脸肿,双方才罢手。

6 call sb. names/a bad name 骂某人

Bill got so mad that he started calling Frank names. 比尔愤怒不已,破口大骂弗兰克。

7 call one's bluff 当面证实,立刻对证

Tom said he could jump twenty feet and so Dick called his bluff and said "Let's see you do it!" 汤姆说它能够跳 20 英尺远,迪克不信,要他当面证实,说"让我们看你的表演吧。"

8 call the/one's turn/shots(射击时)知其命中何处;预测未来

An expert rifleman can call his shots regularly. 一个优秀的射手能知道他命中何处。

Mary won three games in a row, just as she said she could. She called her shots well. 玛丽说她能连胜三场,果然不差。

9 call (sb.) on the carpet 叫去当面斥责

The worker was called on the carpet by the boss for sleeping on the job. 这个工人被老板叫进办公室当面训斥了一顿,因为他上班时间睡觉。

The principal called Tom on the carpet and warned him to stop coming to school late. 校长把汤姆叫进去当面训斥,警告他不得再迟到。

10 call the shots 颁布命令;发号施令;指挥有方

Bob is a first-rate leader who knows how to call the shots. 鲍勃是一流的领导者,他知道如何指挥一切。

The quarterback called the shots well, and the team gained twenty yards in five plays. 四分卫指挥有方,在球队进攻五次后就攻下了 20 码。

11 call the tune 发号施令,指挥一切;操纵一切

Bill was president of the club, but Jim was secretary and called the tune. 比尔是俱乐部主席,但吉姆是秘书,一切是吉姆说了算。

The people supported the mayor, so he could call the tune in city matters. 人民支持市长,所以他才能放心大胆地开展工作。

12 call sb. to account 要求澄清,说明,解释;责骂,斥责

The principal called Bellamy to account after she left school without permission. 校长要贝拉米说明未经允许擅自早退的原因。

The father *called his son to account* for disobeying him. 这位父亲训斥他的儿子不听自己的话。

13 call sb. to order 正式开幕,会议开始;命令遵守秩序

The chairman *called the committee to order*. 主席要求委员们肃静,以便正式开会。

The judge *called the people in the courtroom to order* when they talked too loud. 法官警告法庭上喧哗的人群遵守秩序。

14 a close call 幸免于难,死里逃生

Why, Lawrence might near be starved, so he learnt the trade, and then he was all right—but it was *a close call*. 劳伦斯当时险些饿死,因此他才学了这个行当,然后才活了下来——但已经是死里逃生了。

15 don't call us, we'll call you/don't ring us, we'll ring you 别来找我,我会通知你的;少安毋躁,静候佳音

"I've been trying to get work from that firm for a long time, but they don't seem to like me." "*Don't call us, we'll call you*, you mean?" "I suppose so." "我尽力设法在这家公司谋一份工作已经很长时间了,可是看来他们并不喜欢我。""你是说他们让你'静候佳音'喽?""我想是这样。"

16 (now) that's what I call 哎呀,真是……极了(高度赞赏……,常用惊叹语调)

Now that's what I call a meal! It was delicious, dear! 啊呀,真是一顿丰盛的美餐,好吃极了,亲爱的!

Just look at that sunset! *That's what I call* beautiful! 看那落日,真是美极了!

can

1 can do 可以,可行

"One hundred kilometres an hour." "*Can do*." "每小时100千米。""可以。"

I've tried everything to make Jasper talk and no *can do*. 我想尽了办法让贾斯珀开口,但是没成功。

2 can but/only 只能,只好,充其量不过

With no key on us, we *can but* wait outside the door. 我们没带钥匙,只好

在门外等。

3 cannot but（后接动词原形）不得不，不能不，不禁

Whenever I think of the exam, I *cannot but* feel nervous. 每当我想到考试，我就忍不住感到紧张。

4 cannot... enough/sufficiently/cannot... too/can never... too 无论……也不过分；越……越好

You *cannot* be *too* careful. 你要特别小心。

candle

1 burn the candle at both ends 浪费精力；浪费钱财；过荒唐放荡的生活；劳累过度

Hardy had, in fact, *burned the candle at both ends*; but he had never been unready to do his fellows a good turn. 哈代确实生活放荡，但他对朋友却总是很讲义气。

Herbert worked hard every day as a lawyer and went to parties and dances every night; he *was burning the candle at both ends*. 作为一名律师，赫伯特每天工作劳累，每晚又参加宴会及舞会，这简直是在玩命。

2 cannot/is not fit to hold a candle to 远远不如，不能与……相提并论

Henry thought that no modern ball club *could hold a candle to* those of 50 years ago. 亨利认为现在的舞会俱乐部无法与50年前的相比。

There's no one in the business who *can hold a candle to* Jonathan. 在这一行里没有人能比得上乔纳森。

3 (the game is) not worth the candle 不值得；划不来，不合算

I don't want to walk so far on such a hot day. *The game is not worth the candle*. 我真不愿意在这么热的天走这么远的路，不值得。

candy

take a candy from a baby 【美】抢夺；贪婪，卑鄙；不费力气

Lynch would *take a candy from a baby*. 林奇连娃娃的糖也抢。（林奇是个贪婪卑鄙的人。）

That's like *taking a candy from a baby*. 那等于从娃娃手里抢糖吃。（不费吹灰之力。）

cap

1　(with) cap/hat in hand【口】恭敬地，卑躬屈膝地，毕恭毕敬地

Thailand, Indonesia and South Korea were humiliatingly forced cap in hand to the IMF. 泰国、印尼和韩国被迫低三下四地哀求国际货币基金组织给予帮助。

The students are listening to the master's speech cap in hand. 学生们正在毕恭毕敬地聆听大师的演说。

2　put on one's considering/thinking cap 认真考虑，仔细想想

Miss Stone told her pupils to put on their thinking caps before answering the question. 斯通小姐叫学生们在回答问题前仔细想想。

3　set one's cap at/for/on sb.（女子）追求，挑逗，企图赢得男子的爱情

The young girl set her cap for the new town doctor, who was a bachelor. 镇里的新医生是个单身汉，这个年轻的女孩子企图赢得他的爱情。

Have a care, Joe, that girl is setting her cap on you. 乔，留心点，那女孩子看上你了。

4　to cap it all 更有甚者；更糟糕的是；更使人高兴的是

It was raining, the bus was late, and to cap it all, I had not coat. 天在下雨，公共汽车又晚了点，更糟糕的是，我没有穿外套。

To cap it all, in 2007 the state squashed consumer demands by increasing added tax. 更有甚者，2007年政府提高了增值税率，从而进一步遏制了消费需求。

caper

1　cut a caper/capers 开玩笑，恶作剧；蹦跳；做怪相

Somebody could cut a caper seriously, but be serious in fun. 有一种人认真时开玩笑，开玩笑时却很认真。

2　cut one's caper/capers 滚开；让……后悔

I'll make him cut his capers! 我会叫他后悔的。

card

1　keep/have a/that/this card up one's sleeve 袖中王牌；留有一手；别有妙计，锦囊妙计

John knew his mother would lend him money if necessary, but he kept that card up his sleeve. 约翰知道必要时母亲会借钱给他,但他暂时还没有利用这一点。

Bill always has a card up his sleeve, so when his first plan failed he tried another. 比尔心里早有打算,所以第一个计划失败后,他就尝试第二个。

2 go through the (whole) card 【口】考虑或尝试一切可能性

3 have/hold all the cards (in one's hands)/hold the trump card 手中有王牌,有把握,有必胜之策

Morris did not attempt to answer. He felt that Mary held all the cards, and not unnaturally, was in a mood to play them. 莫里斯不打算回答。他感到所有的王牌都在玛丽手上,而她不至于不想把它们打出来。

Well, what else is there for me to do? You hold all the cards in your hands. 好吧,我还有什么别的法子呢?所有的王牌都捏在你手里。

4 in/on the cards 很可能的,可能发生的;意料之中的;既定的

I must think over this. I have known for years past that it was on the cards. 我得再想一想。许多年来,我就知道这在意料之中。

I believe it wasn't on the cards for me to stay there. 看来我命中注定不该留在那儿。

5 lay/place/put/throw one's cards on the table 摊牌;公开意图;坦诚表示

In talking about buying the property, Peterson laid his cards on the table about his plans for it. 彼得森在谈到置产时坦率表明了他的计划。

Some of the graduates of the school were unfriendly toward the new superintendent, but he put his cards on the table and won their support. 该校若干毕业生对新任校监颇不友好,但他却以坦诚的态度赢得了大家的支持。

6 show one's cards/colours 摊牌;公开自己的计划;吐露自己的真实意图

It's not the proper time to show our cards. 还不到我们摊牌的时候。

7 that's the card 正合要求;正对路;正是这个

That's the card for it. 这事就该那么办。

care

1 a (fat) lot you/I, etc. care 你/我等才不管呢,你/我等才不关心呢

A fat lot you care about whether I've got a job or not—you don't help me to find one. 我找得到找不到工作你才不关心呢!反正你又不会帮我找

一个。

2 could/couldn't care less 【美】不在乎；不注意
I could care less what happens. 不管发生什么事我都不在乎。
I couldn't care less what you do with those old boxes. They've been there for months. Just get them out of here. 我才不管你到底用那些旧箱子干什么哩！它们在那儿放了几个月了。立即把它们弄走。

3 have a care/take care 当心，小心
Have a care, James, you nearly knocked over that pile of books! 小心，詹姆斯，你差一点把那堆书碰倒了。
The judge told the accused to have a care what he said in court. 法官叫被告注意在法庭上的陈述。
Take care that you don't spill that coffee! 小心别把咖啡弄洒了。
We must take care to let nobody hear about this. 我们要谨慎，别让人听见。

4 I don't care if I do 我愿意；我不反对
"Would you like to come along with us?" "I don't care if I do." "跟我们一起去好吗？""也好。"

5 not care a bean/bit/brass farthing/button/cent/curse/damn/darn/rap/straw/not give a hang/damn 对……不感兴趣，不在乎，不在意
Up Scrooge went, not caring a button for its being dark. 斯克鲁奇往前走着，对于天黑毫不在意。
I see you don't care a brass farthing for me. 我知道，你一点也不爱我。

6 take care of 照顾，供应；对付；处理
Kitty stayed home to take care of the baby. 基蒂留在家里照顾婴儿。
The coach told Jim to take care of the opposite player. 教练叫吉姆对付对方球员。

7 that's more than I care for 对……我无所谓

8 who cares 管它呢，没关系，无所谓
"This is the problem, Sue—if you don't apply for college by January, you won't have a chance of a place!" "Who cares? I'm not really interested in studying anyway!" "问题是你如果不在1月份前提出入学申请，苏，你就会失去上大学的机会！""管它呢！反正我并不是真正对上学感兴趣。"

carpet

1 call (sb.) on the carpet 参见 call 9

2 sweep/push/shove sth. under the carpet 掩盖或无视某事

It would be self-deception to think that unemployment could be pushed under the carpet. 认为失业问题可以被掩盖起来,那是自欺欺人。

Irving wanted to sweep his years in prison under the carpet. 欧文想把自己那段铁窗生涯隐瞒起来。

3 walk the carpet 被……训斥;哄劝;为……困扰

We walked the carpet with Julia all night. 我们哄劝了朱莉娅一晚上。

I walked the carpet over it for hours. 我一连好几个钟头对这事一筹莫展。

carry

1 carry all/everything/the world before 势如破竹,大获全胜

Jenny carried all before her in the athletic field. 珍妮在运动场上大获全胜。

Her zeal carried everything before it. 她的热心克服了一切障碍。

2 carry me out 哪有这种事,我才不信呢

Carry me out! Are you kidding me? 哪有这种事! 你开玩笑吧?

3 carry the baby/be left holding the baby 承担麻烦的工作,担负不愿担当的工作

"I didn't think she'd want to carry the baby to term," Shannon said. "我原以为她不想承担这份苦差,"莎伦说。

4 carry the can 单独承担全部风险;代人受过;背黑锅

While Green will inevitably carry the can for this disappointment, in truth it was not a great England performance, just a great start. 英格兰不孚众望,格林难辞其咎,事实上英格兰的表现称不上漂亮,只是开局不错罢了。

castle

castle in Spain 空中楼阁;空想

My Shanghai mansion may prove to be a castle in Spain after all. 我在上海买套宅子的梦想只不过是座空中楼阁而已。

cat

1 dog my cats【美】见鬼;我可以赌咒;畜生,该死的

Dog my cats if it isn't all I can do. 我敢赌咒,除了我,谁也别想。

I began to feel sorry for Hubby, dog my cats if I didn't. 我敢赌咒,我开始替哈贝感到难过。

2 enough to make a cat laugh (事情)真可笑

3 enough to make a cat speak (事情)真离奇

4 has the cat got your tongue【美】你为什么不吭声

What's the matter, Ronny? Has the cat got your tongue? 罗尼,出了什么事,你怎么不说话?

5 holy cats/cow/smoke/mackerel/Moses 啊,哎呀(表示惊讶、愤慨等)

"Holy cats! That's a good pie!" said Dick. "啊,这馅饼真不错!"迪克说。

"Holy cow! They can't do that!" Mary said when she saw the boys hurting a much smaller boy. 玛丽看到众多孩子打一个很小的孩子时叫道:"老天,他们不能这样!"

6 let the cat out of the bag/the cat is out of the bag 说走了嘴,泄露秘密,露了马脚

I've let the cat out of the bag already, Mr. Corthell, and I might as well tell the whole thing now. 我已经泄露了秘密,科塞先生,干脆现在就把一切都告诉你吧。

We wanted to surprise Mary with a birthday gift, but Allen let the cat out of the bag by asking her what she would like. 我们打算送玛丽一件生日礼物给她惊喜,可是因为埃伦去问她喜欢什么而泄露了秘密。

7 see/watch how/which way the cat jumps/wait for the cat to jump 观望形势,然后行动;见风使舵

There's nothing for it but to wait and see how the cat jumps. 目前只有等待,看看事情如何变化。

Harvey wants to see which way the cat will jump before he acts. 哈维想先观望一下形势再行动。

8 that cat won't jump/【美】fight 这个办法行不通,这一手不行;问题不是这样

"They talk of suicide here." "That cat won't jump." "他们在这里谈论自杀。""那可不行。"

9 a cat's paw 傀儡;上当,被人利用

10 make a cat's paw of 利用某人作为工具、爪牙

I don't want to make a cat's paw of him. 我不想拿他当傀儡。

11 live under the cat's paw/foot【口】惧内,怕老婆,受老婆虐待

catch

1 catch/get it 挨骂;受责备,受罚

Anne will catch it for breaking that vase. 安妮打破了那个花瓶,这下她可要挨骂了。

You'll catch it if your father finds you trampling on his flower beds. 要是你父亲发现你踩他的花坛,你可要挨骂了。

2 catch/get it in the neck 受严厉的惩罚或责备

Tom got it in the neck because he forgot to close the windows when it rained. 汤姆因为下雨时忘了关窗户而受到严厉惩罚。

Students get it in the neck when they lose library books. 学生丢失了图书馆的书时,会受到严厉惩罚。

3 catch me (at it/doing) 我决不会……

Catch me making the same error again. 我决不犯同样的错误。

Catch me ever telling him anything again! 下次再不告诉他了!

4 catch/grasp/clutch at a straw/straws 饥不择食,慌不择路,溺水的人拼命抓住救命稻草

To depend on your memory without studying for a test is to catch at straws. 应付考试光凭记忆而不学习是靠不住的。

The robber caught at straws to make excuses. He said he wasn't in the country when the robbery happened. 盗贼枉费心机地找借口说劫案发生时他不在国内。

5 catch sb. cold 遇到未准备的事情或意外

I had not studied my lesson carefully, and the teacher's question caught me cold. 我未仔细研读课文,老师的问题正好难倒了我。

The opposing team was big and sure of winning, and they were caught cold by the fast, hard playing of our smaller players. 对方队员个个人高体壮,理当获胜,不料却被我们这些矮小精悍选手的凌厉攻势所打败。

6 catch dead 看人受窘,看人好戏;(由于尴尬)死也不肯做的事

You won't catch Bill dead taking his sister to the movies. 比尔不会让人看到他带妹妹去看电影的窘事。

John wouldn't be caught dead in the necktie he got for Christmas. 约翰再

也不想用那条圣诞节用过的领带。

7 catch fire 燃烧；激动，异常兴奋

The audience caught fire at the speaker's words and began to cheer. 听众因演说者的演讲而激动，开始欢呼。

His imagination caught fire as he read. 他阅读的时候，他的想象力便开始燃烧。

8 catch one's breath 因恐惧或兴奋而屏息；喘喘气以恢复正常呼吸；放松一会儿

The beauty of the scene made him catch his breath. 风景之美使他凝神静气。

After the day's work we sat down over coffee to catch our breath. 一天辛劳工作后，我们坐下来喝杯咖啡，放松一会儿。

9 catch/take one's death 病入膏肓，(因受冷)得致命的感冒，患重感冒

Johnny fell in the icy water and almost took his death of cold. 约翰尼掉入冰水中，得了重感冒几乎送命。

Come right in here and put your coat and hat on. You'll catch your death! 过来穿衣戴帽，否则你会得那要命的重感冒。

10 catch one's eye 耀眼；引人注意

I caught his eye as he moved through the crowd and waved at him to come over. 当他走过人群时注意到了我，我挥手叫他过来。

The dress in the window caught her eye when she passed the store. 路过商店时橱窗里的衣服引起了她的注意。

11 catch some Z's 稍睡片刻

I want to hit the sack and catch some Z's. 我想上床小睡片刻。

12 catch sb. bending/napping/off guard/off one's guard/on the hop 使某人措手不及

Hamilton did not propose to be caught napping. 汉密尔顿不打算被弄得措手不及。

13 catch sb. in the act (doing sth.)/catch sb. red-handed 当场捕获，当场发觉

Hansom flushed, looking as guilty as though he had been caught red-handed in some dreadful crime. 汉萨脸一红，好像犯了什么可怕的罪行给人当场抓住似的。

14 catch sb. tripping 发现某人的过失，查出某人的错处或失策

15 catch with one's pants down 突陷窘境，十分尴尬

They thought they could succeed in the robbery, but they got caught with their pants down. 他们以为可以抢劫成功，却出人意料地被警察抓获。

When the weather turned hot in May, the drive-in restaurant was caught with its pants down and ran out of ice cream before noon. 五月天气变热时，汽车饭店突陷窘境，中午以前冰激凌就卖完了。

16 no catch/not much of a catch 不值得买的物品，不合算的东西

Geoffrey is welcome to the job; it's no catch. 欢迎杰弗里来干这项工作，反正不是什么好差事。

Being a games mistress in a third-class school isn't much of a catch. 在三流学校里当一名体育女教师不值得。

17 there's a catch in 当中有圈套

Be careful! There is a catch in the question. 当心，这个问题听起来很容易，一不小心就会答错。

18 be caught with chaff 易上当受骗

Mr. Smith is a shrewd man, he is not to be caught with chaff. 史密斯先生是个精明的人，不会轻易上当。

cave

1 cave【俚】当心（老师走近时的报警语）

Cave the dog! 当心狗！

2 cave in 让步，屈服，投降

The children begged their father to take them to the circus until he caved in. 孩子们一直请求父亲带他们去看马戏，直到他答应了为止。

When I argued, Bobby caved in and was silent. 我一和鲍比理论，他就缩回去，不敢吭声。

3 keep cave【俚】把风，望风

I shall keep cave from the classroom window. 我会在教室窗口把风。

ceiling

hit the ceiling/roof【美】勃然大怒，大发雷霆

When Emily came home at three in the morning, her father hit the ceiling. 当艾米丽凌晨三点回家时，她父亲大发雷霆。

Bob hit the roof when Joe teased him. 乔戏弄鲍勃时,鲍勃怒不可遏。

chalk

1 as different as chalk and/from cheese/as like as chalk to cheese/as alike as chalk and cheese 本质上完全不同,截然不同;外貌相似,实质不同

The music of Strauss is as different from Bach's as chalk from cheese. 施特劳斯的乐曲同巴赫的乐曲是截然不同的。

The two brothers resembled each other physically, but were as different in their natures as chalk from cheese. 这兄弟俩外表长得很像,但性情却迥然不同。

2 by a long chalk/long chalks/a long way/a long shot/long odds/(all) odds 相差很远,相差很大;远远地,在很大程度上

You are a more decent chap than I am, Jeremy, by a long chalk. 你为人比我好,杰里米,比我好得多。

3 not by a long chalk/shot 一点也不,完全没有

I've not given up my hopes of becoming a famous footballer, not by a long shot. 我没有放弃成为一个著名的足球运动员的愿望,绝对不会!

I've lived in Oakland all my life, but I'm not going to live in Oakland the rest of my life, not by a long shot. 我已在奥克兰住了一辈子,以后的日子,我决不想待在奥克兰了。

4 walk the chalk/the/a chalk line/the chalk mark【美】举止得体;顺从,循规蹈矩

In some classes the students play and talk, but Mr. Parker makes them walk the chalk. 一些班级的学生吵吵嚷嚷,但帕克先生能使他们乖乖听话。

That theater owner wants his place to be orderly, and if boys and girls don't walk the chalk, he puts them out. 戏院主人希望戏院内秩序井然,如有男女不安分,他便将他们赶出去。

5 walk/stump one's chalks 走掉,逃走

The prisoner has walked his chalks, and is off to London. 那囚犯逃走了,逃到伦敦去了。

chance

1 (a) fat chance/some hope(s)/not a hope【讽、反】良机;希望渺茫,可能

C

性很小

Some hopes of playing games today—it's been raining since early morning! 看来今天没希望进行球赛了,一清早就下雨,一直到现在。

"I want to sail around the world one day!" "Some hope!" "我想有朝一日环球旅行!""做梦去吧!"

"Are you scared?" "Fat chance." "你受惊了吧?""才没呢!"

2 as chance would have it 凑巧

As chance would have it, I met my old friend at a dinner party. 我凑巧在一次宴会上碰到我的老朋友。

3 as it may chance 要看当时情况,事先不能预料

The man will come by train or by air as it may chance. 那人是坐火车还是乘飞机来要视情况而定。

4 by chance 偶然地,意外地

I met my English teacher only by chance. 我只是偶然遇到了我的英语老师。

5 by any chance 万一,也许

If by any chance somebody comes to see me, ask him to leave a message. 万一有人找我,就请他留个言。

Do you by any chance have a pen with you? 你身边也许带着钢笔吧?

6 chance it 冒险一试,碰碰运气

I wonder if you can get back the lost watch, but let's chance it. 我不知道你能不能找回那块丢失的表,不过让我们碰碰运气吧。

7 give sb. a chance 给某人一个机会;让某人喘口气;饶某人这一回

"Have you done the washing-up yet?" "Give me a chance—I've only just finished my meal." "你把餐具洗完了吗?""行行好,让我喘口气吧,我才刚吃完饭呢!"

8 not (even) a dog's/day's chance 一点儿机会也没有,没有任何可能

However, not even a dog's chance you are unwilling to give me. 你却连一点儿机会都不肯给我。

9 on the chance of/that 对……怀有希望

I'll call at his office on the chance of seeing him before he leaves. 我要到他办公室去拜访,希望能在他离开之前见到他。

Go ahead with the printing on the chance that no major correction may prove necessary. 开印吧,也许将来不会有重大的勘误。

10 on the off chance (of/that) 对……抱有微小的希望;万一某事发生的话

I was lucky to find Barrie at the airfield, I only went on the off chance. 我在飞机场找到巴里真是运气。我是抱着万分之一的希望去的。

11 stand a chance 有希望,有机会

When they got together, I didn't stand a chance. 当他们站在同一阵营的时候,我根本没有希望胜过他们。

12 stand no chance 没有希望,可能性不大

With his lack of experience, Baldwin stands no chance of getting this job. 由于缺少经验,鲍德温没有获得这个工作的可能性。

13 stand/take one's chance 听天由命,碰碰运气

Mrs. Long and her nieces must stand their chance. 朗格太太和她的侄女一定会去试试运气的。

change

1 all change 全体下车(终点站已到,全体下车或换乘)

"All change!" the guard shouted as the train drew into Amersham station. "全体下车!"乘警在火车驶进埃莫森车站时喊道。

2 get no change out of 从……得不到什么好处;从……打听不到什么消息

We plied the stranger with questions but got no change out of him. 我们不停地问那个陌生人这样那样的问题,可没有探听出什么消息。

For all Mary complained about her misfortunes, she got no change out of anybody. 尽管玛丽大谈她的不幸,她还是得不到任何人的同情。

3 give sb. change【口】为某人尽力;【讽】给某人相当的赏罚

4 give sb. no change【口】不让某人知道,对某人秘而不宣

5 make a change 换换口味,感到新鲜

Having pizzas is nice! It makes a change from the usual pie and chips! 吃比萨真不错! 天天吃普通馅饼和煎土豆片真得换换口味!

We went to Bournemouth for our holidays. The sea air made a welcome change for Ruth and myself. 我们到伯恩茅斯去度假,那儿的海上空气使我和露丝都感到新鲜。

6 take your change out of that 这就是回答,自食其果,自作自受(还嘴、报复时)

C

chase

(go) chase oneself 走开，别捣乱

John's father was busy and told him to go chase himself. 约翰的父亲工作很忙，叫他走开别去打扰。

Go chase yourself, you are too small to play with us. 别捣乱，你太小，不能跟我们一块玩。

cheap

1 on the cheap 便宜地，经济地

Don't try to get things on the cheap. 别贪便宜。

2 feel cheap 【俚】觉得身体不适；觉得惭愧

The teacher made the girl feel cheap by making her stand in front of the class. 老师罚那个女生站在全班同学面前，这令她感到羞耻。

3 make oneself cheap 干出降低自己声誉的事

4 make oneself too cheap 过分自卑，过分迁就别人

cheek

1 cheek by jowl 紧靠着；非常亲昵；非常接近

All sorts and conditions of men and women and he cheeked by jowl with them—like sardines in a box and he didn't mind. 他跟各种各样的男女挤在一起，像罐子里的沙丁鱼一样，可是他并不在乎。

You never get through that crowd of people; they're packed in there cheek by jowl. 你无法通过那堆人群，他们挤得水泄不通。

2 I like your/his cheek 你/他倒是不怕难为情

You say you love her? I like your cheek. 你说你爱她？我真佩服你的厚脸皮。

3 to one's own cheek 只供个人使用，不与他人分享

Let Tim keep his earnings to his own cheek. 让蒂姆把他挣的钱留着自己用吧。

4 none/no more of your cheek 别说了，没脸没皮的；别吹牛；别无礼

Put it down, and none of your cheek. 把它放下，不得无礼。

cheer

1 cheer up 振作起来，别泄气

Cheer up, Peter, we're winning by three goals, and there's only ten minutes left! 别泄气,彼得,我们赢了三个球,现在还有十分钟,怕什么!
Keynes cheered me up, laughed at my dejection. 凯恩斯用话鼓舞我,笑我垂头丧气。

2 three cheers 欢呼三声(Hip, hip, hurrah! 一人领呼Hip, hip, 众人随之高呼 hurrah, 如此反复三遍);为……三呼万岁
Three cheers for the cricket team! 来,大家为板球队加油!
Orville Mason, you deserve the thanks of the country! Three cheers for Orville Mason! 奥维尔·梅森,你应该得到全国人民的感谢! 为奥维尔·梅森三呼万岁!

3 two cheers 得了吧,算了吧,让……靠边吧(对做的事不积极、不热情)
Two cheers for your plan to go to the National Park on a coach outing—we'd much rather watch the football on television! 让你打算乘长途汽车去国家公园郊游的计划靠边吧! 我们倒是更愿意在电视上看足球赛。

4 what cheer (with you) 你好呀
My friend, what cheer? 老朋友,你好吗?

cheese

1 cut/cry the cheese【美俚】放屁
Weasel cut the cheese when it is in hazard. 黄鼠狼一遇到危险就会放屁。

2 get the cheese 碰钉子,失望
You would get the cheese if you know the truth. 如果你知道真相,你会很失望的。

3 hard cheese 恶运,倒霉
"I failed my driving test again." "Oh, hard cheese—what went wrong this time?" "我驾照考试又没通过。""啊,真是的,这回是哪儿出了问题?"
It's hard cheese for Jacob if he can't go to the cinema with us. 雅各布要是不能同我们一道去看电影,那真是不幸。

4 say cheese/watch the birdie 笑一笑(照相时摄影师招呼用语)

5 that's (quite) the cheese 很对头,十分得体(指言谈、品行等)

6 the whole cheese/show【美】自命不凡,自以为了不起
Joe thought he was the whole cheese in the game because he owned the ball. 乔因为拥有球就认为自己是球赛的核心人物。

You're not the whole show just because you got all A's. 并不是因为你的成绩全是优等,你就是学校里的顶尖人物。

7 make the cheese more binding【美俚】使事情更加复杂困难

Father had intended to help them. But unfortunately he made the cheese more binding. 父亲本来想帮他们,但是不幸的是他把事情弄得更糟了。

8 cheese it 快逃,快溜,当心;停下,住手,安静下来

Cheese it, the cops are coming! 快逃呀,警察来了!

Come on, cheese it, Jack. 嗨,得了吧,杰克!

chest

1 get sth. off one's chest 把心里话讲出来

It's good to get the annoyance off your chest. 把你心里的烦恼说出来是件好事。

2 on one's chest 郁积在胸

You look sad. What's on your chest? 你看上去闷闷不乐,有啥心事吗?

Jane looks unhappy because she has the quarrel with Susan on her chest. 简因同苏珊争吵而心中不快。

3 play sth. close to one's/the chest 把某事隐藏在心里;对某事小心谨慎

You have to play these things close to your chest. 对这类事你得保守秘密。

4 throw a chest 挺起胸膛,振作精神

I'm a proud fox. In my daily life, I always bridle and throw a chest. I am congenital eutrapelia so that I am haughtiness. 我是一只骄傲的狐狸,生活中我永远昂首挺胸,天生机智让我傲气冲天!

chew

1 bite off more than one can chew 参见 bite 1

2 chew out【美】责骂,痛骂,训斥

The boy's father chewed him out for staying up late. 男孩的父亲因他熬夜而责骂他。

The coach chews out lazy players. 教练训斥懒惰的队员。

3 chew the fat/rag 闲聊,聊天

We used to meet after work, and chew the fat over coffee and doughnuts. 我们过去常常在下班后聚到一起边喝咖啡、吃甜甜圈,边聊天。

The old man would *chew the rag* for hours with anyone who would join him. 这个老人能和愿同他交谈的人一聊就是几个小时。

chin

1 chin-chin 你好，再见；为健康干杯

Going on your way, and you? Well, *chin-chin*! 走了吗? 那么,再见!
Chin-chin—to you and yours. 为你和你们一家的健康干杯。

2 (keep one's) chin up/keep one's pecker up 不要灰心，振作起来

Peter didn't think that he would ever got out of the jungle alive, but he *kept his chin up*. 彼得虽然想到他可能不会活着走出丛林,但他仍然不灰心。

Chin up, Freddie, it's not far to go now—we're almost home. 别灰心,弗雷迪,没有多远了。我们就快到家了。

Things may be bad at the moment but *keep your pecker up* and I'm sure they will get better. 目前情况也许不好,但你不要灰心,我相信一切都会好起来的。

3 stick one's chin/neck out 甘冒风险，自惹麻烦

When I was in trouble, Paul was the only one who would *stick his neck out* to help me. 当我遇到困难时,保罗是唯一不顾危险来帮我的人。

John is always *sticking his chin out* by saying something he shouldn't. 约翰总是说些不该说的话,自找麻烦。

Halifax has been fired for *sticking his* ignorant *neck out* too far. 哈利法克斯遇事不知高低太逞强,结果被解雇了。

4 take it on the chin 挨揍；受伤或受挫；忍受痛苦、失败等

Our football team really *took it on the chin* today. They are all bumps and bruises. 我们的足球队今天可吃够了苦头,个个都是鼻青眼肿的。

A good football player can *take it on the chin* when his team loses. 好的足球队员能够接受任何失败。

5 up to the/one's chin/ears/elbows/eyes/knees in 位居要津；有罪于；知情的；深陷于；忙于,从事；大大地,满满地

Mr. Johnson is *up to the eyes in* debt. 约翰逊先生债台高筑。

They are *up to their elbows in* business before Christmas. 圣诞节前他们的生意很红火。

chip

1 carry/go about with/have/wear/get a chip on one's shoulder 以挑衅的姿态出现；摆出打架的架势；傲慢地；易被激怒的

Jackson has got a chip on his shoulder because he can't read or write. 杰克逊因为没有文化而表现得十分横蛮粗暴。

Charles often gets into fights because he goes about with a chip on his shoulder. 查尔斯脾气很坏，常跟人争吵。

2 cash/hand/pass in one's chips 【美】算账，以筹码换现款；死亡；关门歇业；辞工不干

When the card game ended，the players cashed in their chips and went home. 牌局结束时，客人把筹码换成现金，各自回家。

Small businessmen were forced to cash in their chips. 做小生意的人只好关门大吉。

3 chip/kick in 同心协力地；贡献，捐助；插入

The pupils chipped in a dime apiece for the teacher's Christmas present. 学生们每人捐一毛钱给老师买圣诞礼物。

All the neighbors kicked in to help after the fire. 所有的邻居都捐助火灾受难的人们。

4 in the chips/money 富裕；赚钱

After his rich uncle died，Richard was in the chips. 理查德有钱的叔父死了以后，他富了起来。

You're in the chips and you can give me back the money. 你发财啦，可以还我钱了吧。

5 let the chips fall where they may/might 不顾后果

The Senator decided to vote against the bill and let the chips fall where they might. 参议员决定投票反对此案，对别人的不满置之不理。

The police chief told his men to give tickets to all speeders and let the chips fall where they might. 警长叫属下给所有超速者开罚单，不管产生什么后果。

6 when the chips are down 紧要关头，关键时刻

Tom hit a home run in the last inning of the game when the chips were down. 在最后一局比赛的紧要关头，汤姆击出一记本垒打。

When the chips are down，John will go to any length to save his own neck.

关键时刻为了保全自己，约翰什么事都干得出来。

chuck

chuck it (in) 住手，停止，别闹了；认输，甩手不干

Chuck it in, Ted, or I'll go and tell your dad. 别闹了，特德，不然我要告诉你爸爸了。

Oh, chuck it, I never was any good at arithmetic. 啊，够了，我的算术从来就不行。

clear

1　all clear 警报解除；道路畅通

The teachers have all gone now. All clear! We can climb over the fence! 老师们都走了，警报解除了！我们可以翻过篱笆了。

The signal "All clear" was sounded. "解除警报"声音响过了。

2　clear off/out 走开，离开

You children are not supposed to come into this room—now clear off! 小孩子不准进这间房子，你们快点离开！

Bob cleared out without paying his room rent. 鲍勃未付房租就离开了。

3　clear the air 澄清事实；尽释前嫌

The President's statement that he would run for office again cleared the air of rumors and guessing. 总统宣布竞选连任，澄清了谣言和猜测。

When Bill was angry at Bob, Bob made a joke, and it cleared the air between them. 比尔生鲍勃的气，鲍勃开了个玩笑，于是两人尽释前嫌。

4　the coast is clear 无人注视；毫无危险

The men knew when the night watchman would pass. When he had gone and the coast was clear, they robbed the safe. 那些人知道值夜的人何时来巡逻，他走后便无危险，于是他们便洗劫了保险柜。

The boys waited until the coast was clear before climbing over the wall. 孩子们等到四下没人时才爬过墙头。

cloud

1　on a cloud【美俚】高兴得飘飘欲仙，忘乎所以

I accepted the order and walked out on a cloud of happiness. 我接受了他的订单，兴高采烈地走出了餐厅。

2 on cloud seven/nine 极为幸福,乐不可支

I was on cloud nine after winning the marathon. 赢了那场马拉松比赛后我高兴极了。

club

join the club 大家都一样,彼此彼此

"I've failed the exam!" "Join the club! Lots of us have as well, don't worry!" "我考试没及格!" "我们都一样! 许多人都没及格,别担心!"

cobbler

a load of (old) cobblers 屁话,蠢话,胡说

I've never heard such a load of old cobblers in my whole life! 我一生从来没听说过这种屁话!

"Our car goes much faster than yours!" "What a load of old cobblers! Ours will beat yours any day!" "我们的车比你们的车快得多!" "胡说! 任何时候我们的车都会赢你们的车!"

cock

1 a load of (old) cock 蠢话,屁话

2 that cock won't fight 那行不通;那话讲不通

"Tell that to the marines, Major," replied the valet, "That cock won't fight with me." 仆人回答说:"我可不信,少校,我不吃你这一套。"

3 at full cock 一切准备就绪,一触即发

The commander ordered the soldiers to set their guns at full cock. 指挥官命令士兵们端起枪,准备射击。

4 at half cock/half-cocked 未准备好就行动

Bill often goes off half-cocked. 比尔时常未做好充分准备就着手干一件事。

Mr. Jones was thinking about quitting his job, but his wife told him not to go at half cock. 琼斯先生想要辞职,但他的太太告诉他决定一件事要深思熟虑。

5 talk cock 胡说八道

The young man always talks cock before the children. 那个年轻人经常在孩子们面前胡说八道。

cod

a load of (old) cods 胡说八道，一派胡言
It's all a load of old cods. 那全是胡说八道。

coin

1 coin it (in)/coin money/mint money 一夜暴富，发横财
Fred coined money with many cigarette vending machines and jukeboxes. 弗雷德靠经营香烟自动售货机和自动点唱机发了一笔财。

2 coin a phrase 杜撰一个词语；套用一种说法
To coin a phrase, we could kill two birds with one stone, by visiting friends and doing the shopping when we go there. 正像俗话说的"一箭双雕"：我们去那儿既看了朋友，又买了东西。
Many hands make light work, to coin a phrase. 老话说"人多好办事"。

cold

1 have/get sb. cold 牢牢掌握某人，任意摆布某人

2 leave sb. cold 冷淡某人，不睬某人；未能打动某人，未能激起某人兴趣
His book left me rather cold. 我感到他的作品相当乏味。
The idea of going to the birthday party left him cold. 他对去参加生日宴会的主意不感兴趣。

collar

1 be/go hot under the collar 发怒，生气，火冒三丈
We really go hot under the collar when we saw what those dogs have done to those flowers we worked so hard to grow. 当我们看到这几只狗把我们辛辛苦苦种好的花弄成那个样子的时候，我们非常生气。

2 fill one's collar 尽本分，尽职尽责

3 wear the collar 受束缚，受制于他人，没有行动自由，听人差遣

color

1 change color 变色，脸色变白；脸色泛红
The sight was so horrible that Mary changed color from fear. 这情景如此恐怖，玛丽吓得脸色发白。
Tom got angry at the remark and changed color. 汤姆因一句话而气得

脸红。

2 haul down/strike/lower one's/the colors 投降，屈服，退让，认输

After a long battle, the pirate captain hauled down his colors. 经过持久的激战，海盗船长只得举白旗投降。

About three weeks after the elephant's disappearance I had to strike my colors and retired. 大象失踪大约三周以后，我不得不放弃继续寻找的计划。

3 a horse of a different/another color 两码事，截然不同

Anyone can be broke, but to steal is a horse of a different color. 每个人都可能贫穷，但是偷盗却完全是另一回事。

"Do you mean that the boy with that pretty girl is her brother? I thought he was her boyfriend." "Well, that's a horse of another color." "你说那个男孩是那个漂亮女孩的哥哥吗？我以为是她的男朋友呢！""唉，那真是两码事呀！"

4 nail one's colors to the mast/stick to one's colors/guns/stand by one's guns/stand one's ground/hold one's ground 坚持原则，坚持自己的信念；不后退，不投降；固执己见

During the election campaign, the candidate nailed his colors to the mast on the question of civil rights. 竞选活动中候选人在民权法案问题上固执己见。

But I called to mind that I was speaking for his good and stuck to my colors. 但是我想起来我是为他好而讲话的，因此就坚持了自己的意见。

come

1 as... as they come/make them 极其，非常

Lewis was as clever as they come, but ever he made a mistake. 尽管刘易斯非常聪明，但还是免不了犯了一个错误。

Your new girlfriend's as cheeky as they made them, isn't she? 你新交的女友真厚颜无耻，不是吗？

2 come across 给人深刻印象，看上去似乎是

Malachi came across to voters as (being) honest, sincere and hardworking. 选民们觉得玛拉基似乎是个诚实、真诚和勤奋的人。

3 come/say again 你说什么，请再说一遍

"I hope this diagram is clear." "Come again?" "I said I hope this diagram is clear." "我希望这张图表是清楚的。""你说什么？""我说我希望这张图表是清楚的。"

"Harry has just come into a fortune." My wife said. "Come again?" I asked her, not believing it. 我太太说："哈里又走运了。""你说什么？"我不相信地问道。

4 come and get it 饭菜准备好了，开饭喽（原用于军中）

"Come and get it!" Jo called to the children and they all came running downstairs to the dining-room. "饭好了，开饭喽！"乔对孩子们一叫，孩子们便立刻从楼上跑到了餐厅。

5 come back..., all is forgiven【幽默】好啦，一切都会过去的（当……离开后被怀念时）

If only she were here now... Come back, Freda, all is forgiven! 要是她现在在这儿就好了，好啦，弗里达，一切都会过去的！

6 come, come/come now 喂，注意，得啦，别忙（表示气恼、不耐烦、责备、鼓励等）

Come, come, what were you really doing behind the bicycle sheds? I think you've been telling me lies so far. 喂，你到底在车棚后面干什么来着？我看直到现在你还在说谎话骗我。

Come now, let's not get angry about your results in the exams, but see if we can talk about them calmly. 好啦，好啦，我们先别为这次考试中你的成绩生气，让我们看看我们能不能平心静气地谈谈这次考试。

7 come/get off it 别骗人，别吹牛

Come off it, Henry, we know you're only joking! 别吹牛啦，亨利！我知道你是在开玩笑。

"As I was saying to the President only last week..." Penny began. "Oh, come off it, Penny, you've never even met him," Susie interrupted. "就在上星期我当时正在同总统谈话……"彭妮开始吹起来，苏茜立刻打断了她，"好啦，别吹牛，彭妮，我看你连总统的影子都没有见过。"

8 come off/get down your high horse/perch 放下你的臭架子，不要神气

Come off your high horse and apologize. 放下你的臭架子并道歉。

9 come on/along 来吧，动手吧，别拖了；好啦，求求你啦，帮帮忙吧

"Come on, or we'll be late," said Joe but Lou still waited. "快呀，要不然

就迟到啦,"乔说,可是卢仍在拖延。

Sing us just one song, Jane, come on! 简,给我们唱支歌,来吧!

10 come out flat-footed (for)【美】说话直截了当,打开天窗说亮话

Don't be angry with me because I come out flat-footed like a friend and say what I think instead of tattling behind your back. 我跟你像朋友一样,有话讲在当面,心里有什么说什么,决不背着你嚼舌头,你不要生我的气。

11 come out of that 走开,滚蛋,放手

I saw a long spy glass on a desk… and reached after it… "Ah, ah, hands off! Come out of that!" 我看见桌上有一只长的小望远镜……伸手想去拿……"喂,喂,住手! 不许动!"

12 come right in【美】进来吧

13 come to that/if it comes to that 既然如此;如果那样的话

I remember we didn't have much money at the time. Come to that, none of us did. 我记得当时我们没有很多的钱,说实话,谁也没有许多钱。

I don't think I've seen Jim for ages now. If it comes to that, I've not seen his brother, either. 我想我已有多年没见到吉姆了,这样的话,我也没有见到过他的兄弟。

14 come what may/might 无论发生什么事情,不管怎样,无论如何

Charles has decided to get a college education, come what may. 查尔斯决定无论如何也要上大学。

The editor says we will publish the school paper this week, come what may. 编辑说不管有什么困难,本周一定要出校刊。

15 how come【美】这是为什么,怎么搞的,怎么会

How come Parker told you? 帕克怎么会告诉你?

How come you didn't call me last night? 你昨晚怎么没给我打电话?

16 (now I) come to think of it 想起来了;的确,真的

Come to think of it, Sander has already been given what he needs. 桑德的确已经得到他所需要的东西了。

Come to think of it, I should write to my daughter today. 想起来了,我今天要给女儿写信。

17 what is coming to 会发生什么事,会变成什么样子

Grandfather doesn't like the way young people act today; he says, "I don't know what the world is coming to." 祖父不喜欢现代青年人的行为,他说:

"我不知道这个世界将来会变成什么样子。"

18　where do I come in 我该干什么；给我什么好处，我怎么捞到好处

19　come off with flying colors 大获全胜，凯旋

The young executive's sales presentation came off with flying colors. 那位年轻经理的推销活动极为成功。

comfortable

1　comfortable as an old shoe 逍遥闲散；气量宽宏，平易近人

The stranger was as comfortable as an old shoe, and we soon were talking like old friends. 这个陌生人很随和，我们很快就像老友般开怀畅谈。

2　please make yourself comfortable 请不要客气（招待客人用语）

common

1　common as an old shoe 毫无架子，平易近人；谦虚和善

Although Mr. Jones ran a large business, he was common as an old shoe. 虽然琼斯先生是主持大企业的，但他为人却很谦和。

The most famous people are sometimes as common as an old shoe. 最有名的人有时也最和善。

2　the common touch 平易近人，亲切和善

Voters like a candidate who has the common touch. 选民喜欢平易近人的候选人。

The premier still has not lost the common touch. 这位总理仍然不失平易近人的美德。

company

1　present company excepted 在场的人除外

Present company excepted, I don't think many people realize the full significance of this project. 我认为还有许多人没有认识到这项计划的全部重要意义，当然，在座者除外。

2　two's company, three's a crowd/two is company, (but) three is none 两人成伴，三人不欢

Two is company, three is none.【谚】两人成伴，三人不欢。

3　err in good company/to err is human 人非圣贤，孰能无过

It should be understood that to err is human. 应该理解，人非圣贤，孰能

无过。

4 sin in good company 许多更有地位的人也犯同样的错误,人非圣贤

If John is wrong, he has sinned in good company. 如果约翰错了,许多更有地位的人还不是一样。

complain

can't/mustn't complain/grumble 还好,还可以(回答别人问候)

"How are you, Carol?" "Can't complain, I suppose, but I've got a lot of shopping to do today." "你好吗,卡罗尔?""还好,不过我想我今天还得去买很多东西。"

"How's things?" "Mustn't grumble—I've finished most of my work and I'm just about to go home." "情况如何?""不错,我刚完成大部分工作,现在打算回家去。"

compliment

1 (please present/give) my/our compliments to the chef 这厨师手艺真不错

My compliments to the chef; that fish was very tasty! 感谢厨师,这鱼真好吃!

2 the compliments of the season 谨致以节日的祝贺(往往指圣诞节或新年)

"The compliments of the season to you, Jack!" "Thank you, sir, and I wish you the same." "杰克,祝你节日快乐!""谢谢,祝你同样快乐!"

concern

1 as/so far as I am concerned 就我而言

As far as I'm concerned, you're welcome to come to the lecture, but the Head of the Department may not agree. 就我而言,欢迎你来听讲座,但是系领导恐怕不会同意。

2 I'm not concerned 与我无关

3 that's no concern of yours 这跟你毫无关系

4 mind your own concerns/business 别多管闲事

confess

1 I must confess 我得承认

I must confess I'm glad the holidays are over and the children are back at school. 我得承认,假期结束了,孩子们都上学去了,我真高兴。

2 to confess the truth 说实话

To confess the truth, I began to feel dizzy and then I got palpitations and felt limp. 说实在话,我起初感觉眩晕,然后心悸虚弱无力。

cook

1 cook up 捏造,假造;想出,策划

The absentee cooked up some excuse about having to visit a sick friend. 那个缺席者捏造了一个借口,说他没来是因为要去探望一位生病的朋友。

What plan are they cooking up now? 他们现在搞什么鬼把戏呢?

2 cook one's goose 毁人;泼人冷水;自毁前途

The bank treasurer cooked his own goose when he stole the bank's funds. 这名银行会计挪用公款而自毁前途。

Sophy cooked John's goose by reporting what she knew to the police. 索菲把事情报告了警察而毁了约翰。

3 cook with gas/electricity/radar 如鱼得水,做得很好;想得对路;做时髦的事

4 what's up/cooking/doing 干什么,忙什么,出了什么事

"What's doing tonight at the club? 俱乐部今晚有何活动?

Hello, Bob, what's up? 嗨,鲍勃,最近忙些什么?

cookie

1 that's the way the cookie crumbles/it goes/how the cookie crumbles 事已至此,无可挽救

Sorry to hear you've failed your exam again, Sarah, but that's the way the cookie crumbles. 萨拉,真可惜,听说你考试又不及格,算啦,事已至此,急也无用。

2 toss one's cookies【美俚】呕吐

It turns out that "toss one's cookies" is just "empty one's stomach", and it is not necessarily true that you vomit only after you eat cookies. 原来"toss one's cookies"就是"呕吐"的意思,并不一定指吃了饼干后呕吐。

cool

1 cool it【美】沉住气,冷静下来
Cool it, you two, let's see if we can discuss this more calmly. 你们俩冷静一下,让我们看看能否更冷静地讨论这件事。

2 cool one's heels 苦苦等候,左等右等
Pearson cooled his heels for an hour in another room before the great man would see him. 在另一房间等了一个小时之后,皮尔逊才见到那个大人物。
I was left to cool my heels outside while the others went into the office. 别人都进办公室去了,而我却被留在外面苦等。

3 cool off 沉着,变得冷静
If you have a bad day, cool off before complaining. 如果你某一天过得很糟糕,那么记住发牢骚之前先冷静下来。

4 keep cool 别慌,保持冷静
Keep cool. Don't respond instantly or say yes to everything. 保持冷静,对听到的任何事情不要立刻表态。

5 stay cool【美口】好好休息,慢慢来,别着急
Be prepared to stay cool while facing some tough questions. 准备好在遇到某些棘手的问题时保持冷静。

6 play it cool【美俚】遇事泰然处之,采取从容不迫的态度;耍酷
If things go wrong, don't panic, just play it cool and keep going. 如果遇到问题,不要惊慌。只要冷静下来继续进行下去就好了。
Just can't help wondering why you play it cool. 我忍不住想知道你为什么总是耍酷。

cotton

1 cotton up to 讨好……,巴结……;与……交友
Jack is very friendly and will cotton up to anyone easily. 杰克待人热情友好,跟谁都很容易结为朋友。

2 in tall cotton【美俚】极成功的;非常富足的

3 shit in high cotton【美俚】过富裕生活;暴发

cough

1 cough it up 认罪，供认

Come on, cough it up; we know you're guilty. 快点，供出来吧，我们知道你是有罪的。

2 cough up 勉强付钱，勉强交出；说出，吐露真相；咳出

Rosa's husband coughed up the money for the party with a good deal of grumbling. 罗莎的丈夫满口抱怨地勉强付了宴会的钱。

Richards coughed up the whole story for the police. 理查兹把整个事件的真相告诉了警察。

could

1 could I/you, etc. 我/你等可以……吗（礼貌地请求或要求允许）

Could you open the window slightly, please, it's very hot here. 请你把窗户稍稍开一下好吗？这儿真是太热了。

Could I ask you to help me if you've got time? 要是您有时间的话，可不可以给我帮点忙？

2 how could I 我怎么能（由于做了错事而表示歉意）

How could I have been so stupid? I'm sorry I stepped on your toe! 咳，我怎么这么笨！实在抱歉，踩了您的脚！

3 how/however could/can you 你怎么能……（不该做某事而做了）

How can you speak to her like that? 你怎么能那样对她讲话？

However could you have forgotten my birthday? 你怎么连我的生日都忘了？

4 if you could/would 如果你愿意的话，请……（用于礼貌地请求）

Pass me that glass, if you could. 请把那只杯子递给我好吗？

5 you could 你可以……；你最好……（用于礼貌地建议、邀请等）

You could always try the library to see if they might be able to help you. 你总是可以试着找找图书馆，看他们能否帮你的忙。

You could be cleaning the kitchen while I'm away. 我不在的时候，你可以打扫厨房。

count

count to ten (before you lose your temper) 别发火，冷静一点

Father always told us to count to ten before doing anything when we got angry. 父亲常常告诉我们生气时要冷静一会儿，再做别的事。

Colin looked furious, but Josh tried to calm him down and told him, "Count to ten." 科林看起来很生气，乔希尽力劝慰他，对他说："冷静点！"

country

it's a free country 没有什么不合法，有权这样做（提议的行动）

But it's a free country, Mum, why shouldn't I stay out all night if I want to? 我这样做没有什么不对，妈妈。如果我想的话，为什么就不能在外面过夜呢？

course

1 steer/tread/follow a middle course 采取稳健方针，取中庸之道

It took the three a day's disputation, before they agreed to steer a middle course. 他们三人争论了一整天，最后才决定采取折中方法。

2 steer/tread/follow a steady course 稳步前进

These goals are often enough for some lucky people to steer a steady course. 对于一些比较幸运的人，这些目标足以使他们按照自己的想法稳步前进。

3 steer/tread/follow the right course 按正确方向前进，找到正确途径

I can help steer the right course among competing interests and shield us from undue political influence. 我可以协助在各种相互竞争的利益之间正确地前进并避免过度的政治影响。

cow

1 holy cow/cats/smoke/mackerel/Moses 参见 cat 5

2 salt the cow to catch the calf 【美】用间接手段达到目的

3 till/until/when the cows come home 长时间地，永远地，没完没了地

You could argue with him till the cows come home, but he'll never change his mind. 你可以和他一直争论下去，可是他绝对不会改变主意。

crack

1 a fair crack of the whip 均等的机会

All I want is a fair crack of the whip so that I can demonstrate what I can do. 我所需要的一切是均等的机会，这样我就能表现自己的能力了。

2 crack a book 读书(常用于否定)
John did not crack a book until the night before the exam. 约翰直到考试前才开始读书。
Many students think they can pass without cracking a book. 许多学生认为不读书也能考及格。

3 crack a joke/jokes 开玩笑,讲笑话
The men sat around the stove, smoking and cracking jokes. 男人们围炉而坐,抽烟谈笑。

4 crack a smile 绽开笑容,扑哧一笑
Bob told the whole silly story without even cracking a smile. 鲍勃一脸正经地讲完了那个可笑的故事。
Scrooge was a gloomy man, who never cracked a smile. 斯科鲁奇成天愁眉苦脸,面无笑容。

5 crack back 气冲冲地顶嘴

6 crack down 执法如山,采取严厉手段惩罚
After a speeding driver hit a child, the police cracked down. 超速开车的人撞了一个小孩后,警察将其严办。
Police suddenly cracked down on the selling of liquors to minors. 警方突然开始严厉打击售酒给未成年人的行为。

7 crack on 继续疾走;继续干下去

8 crack up 夸奖,赞美,吹捧;(身体)垮下来;撞毁;(使)捧腹大笑;失声痛哭
The independent writer's life isn't always everything it's cracked up to be. 独立撰稿人的生活并不像人们所说的那么好。
The play is not what it is cracked up to be. 那出戏不像传说的那么好。

9 crack the whip 要挟,采取严厉措施
If the children won't behave when I reason with them, I have to crack the whip. 如果好言相劝,孩子们仍不听话,那我只好采取严厉措施。

10 fall between the cracks 【美俚】不被注意,遗漏,被遗忘
But I know that sometimes things can fall between the cracks, so I'm taking the liberty of calling to follow up. 但是我知道有时候有些东西可能还是会被遗漏,因此我冒昧地打电话跟进。

11 get cracking/weaving/going (使)干起来,快点;开始

C

Get cracking, Mary, you've got all your packing to do by six o'clock and it's five o'clock now. 快点,玛丽,你得在六点钟前将你所有的行李打包,而现在已经五点了。

I'd better get cracking on the painting, as it'll take me a long time. 我最好赶快开始刷油漆,因为这得花我很长时间。

12 give sb. a crack 让某人做一次尝试

13 have/take a crack 做一次尝试

Ford said he had always wanted to take a crack at writing a novel. 福特说,他总怀有一个念头,就是要尝试写本小说。

14 paper/paste/cover over the cracks 草率地掩饰错误或困难,掩盖分歧

The candidate agreed to paper over the cracks for the period of the election. 那个候选人同意在选举期间暂时把分歧掩盖起来。

crap

1 cut that/the crap 别说废话了

Cut the crap! I know what you are up to. 少说废话!我知道你在打什么主意。

2 don't crap an old crapper 别骗到老骗子头上去

3 crap around 【美俚】胡闹,瞎忙活

Moll used to crap around like that. 莫尔以前老是做那样的傻事。

crazy

1 crazy like/as a fox/as sly as a fox 【口】十分精明,非常狡猾

Call me crazy, but I'm crazy like a fox. 你们可以说我疯狂,但我像一只狐狸那样精明。

Don't go there, Mary. He's as sly as a fox. 不要去,玛丽,他狡猾得像只狐狸。

2 like crazy 发狂似地,拼命地

You'll have to work like crazy to get this finished. 你得拼命干才能把这活干完。

creation

1 beat/lick/whip (all) creation 超过一切,胜过一切

That beats creation! 那倒是惊人极了!

2 in (all) creation 【美】究竟，到底

How *in creation* did you manage to do it? 你究竟是怎么做到的？

3 like all creation 【美】猛烈地，拼命地；严重

credit

do sb. credit/do credit to sb. 为某人增光；抬高某人的身价；证明某人有某种才能或品质

These words *do you credit*. 这些话抬高了你的身价。

Mary's painting would *do credit to a real artist*. 玛丽的画作称得上是真正的杰作。

crikey

by crikey 哎呀（表示惊讶或温和地诅咒）

By crikey! That's a big fish you've caught. 哎呀，你逮到的鱼好大呀！

crook

1 a crook in the lot 倒霉时刻，人生坎坷

There is *a crook in the lot* of everyone. 人人都有不如意的时候。

2 on the crook 不正当的，欺骗的，非法的

cross

1 cross one's fingers/keep one's fingers crossed 把中指与食指交叉勾住以求好运，交叉两指以求说谎时心安

Mary *crossed her fingers* during the race so that Tom would win. 在比赛时玛丽两指交叉，希望汤姆会赢。

Keep your fingers crossed while I take the test. 我考试时请你交叉手指祝我好运。

2 cross one's heart (and hope to die) 我发誓（小孩赌咒用语）

Cross my heart, I didn't hide your bicycle. 我发誓，我绝对没有藏你的自行车。

I didn't tell the teacher what you said. *Cross my heart and hope to die*. 我绝对没有把你的事告诉老师，我发誓，否则我不得好死。

3 cross/pass through one's mind 突来念头；领悟过来；想起来，油然而生

At first Bob was puzzled by Virginia's waving, but then it *crossed his mind*

that she was trying to tell him something. 起先鲍勃不明白弗吉尼娅为什么向他挥手,后来他才省悟过来,她有事要对他说。
When Jane did not come home by midnight, many terrible fears passed through mother's mind. 简深夜未归,母亲满脑子可怕的念头,怕她出事。

crow

1 as the crow flies/in a crow line 沿直线,不绕道
It takes half an hour as the crow flies to get to the next village. 到下一个村庄如果直穿过去约需半个小时。
It is not more than thirty miles from London as the crow flies. 从这里到伦敦如果走直线,至多三十英里。

2 eat crow【美】被迫认错,被迫收回说过的话
John had boasted that he would playing the first team; but when the coach did not choose him, he had to eat crow. 约翰本来夸口说他一定会在第一梯队比赛,但教练并未选他,他只得承认自己不行。
Fred said he could beat the new man in boxing, but he lost and had to eat crow. 弗雷德说他可以在拳击赛中击败新手,可是他输了,只好认错。

3 have a crow/bone to pluck/pull/pick with sb. 对某人不满;有事与某人争论不休
I have no crow to pick with him. 我和他没有什么纠葛。

4 stone/stiffen the crows/stone me 啊,哎呀,哎哟(表示惊讶、震惊、厌恶等)
Stone the crows! Do you really expect me to believe that story? 哎呀,你真以为我会相信那种事?
Stone me! I've not seen one of those cars for years! 哎呀,我多年没见过一辆那样的车了!

cry

1 a far/long cry from 远距离,远处;大不相同,相差悬殊
It is a far cry from here to Britain. 这儿离英国很远。
Their house is a far cry from what we expected. 他们的房子和我们原先想象的大不相同。

2 cry/holler (out) before one is hurt 未痛先喊,惊慌过早,杞人忧天;牢骚发得过早

I took up a pistol. You see it is not loaded, and this coward cried out before he was hurt. 我拿起一把手枪。你看它并没有装上子弹,但是这个胆小鬼却惊慌起来。

When Billy went to the barber, he began to cry before the barber cut his hair and his father told him not to cry before he was hurt. 比利去理发,理发师还未开始理,他就哭喊起来,他父亲叫他不要大喊大叫。

3 for crying out loud【美】岂有此理;哎呀,我的天哪(表示生气、愤怒)

For crying out loud, leave me alone! 哎呀,别打扰我吧!

For crying out loud, don't worry about money all the time. 求求你,别老为钱担忧。

4 give sb. sth. to cry for 让某人哭个够(指更严厉地责罚因受责罚而胡闹的人)

5 much cry and little wool/more cry than wool 雷声大,雨点小;徒劳

cup

1 a cup of coffee 一杯咖啡的工夫,很短的一会儿

2 a/one's cup/dish of tea 喜爱的人或事物;特定的人或事物,有某种特点的人

Travelling is just his cup of tea. 旅行正是他所喜爱的。

Onions is a very unpleasant cup of tea. 奥尼恩斯是一个很讨厌的家伙。

curiosity

curiosity killed the cat 好奇伤身,多事伤身;闲事少管

"Curiosity killed the cat," Fred's father said, when he found Fred hunting around in closets just before Christmas. 弗雷德的父亲发现他在圣诞节前翻箱倒柜找东西,就说:"好奇伤身。"

curse

1 curse it/you, etc. 该死的

Curse it, why does the phone always ring just when we're eating our meal? 见鬼,为什么每次我们吃饭的时候电话铃都要响?

2 not care/give a tinker's curse/damn 一点儿不在乎,不介意

I don't give a tinker's curse for what he thinks. 我对于他的想法毫不介意。

C

3 not worth a tinker's curse/damn 毫无价值，一文不值

His ideas are not worth a tinker's curse; they are all borrowed from others. 他的见解毫无价值，都是从别人那里抄来的。

customer

the customer is always right 顾客永远正确，顾客是上帝

cut

1 cut both/two ways 有利有弊，有正反两种效果；两面倒

People who gossip find it cuts both ways. 好说闲话的人既损人又害己。

2 cut it 停止胡说八道，住口；办事有成效，胜任工作

3 cut it/that out【美】停止，住口

"Cut it out, you two, or one of you will get hurt," Adam said, as he tried to stop the fight. "住手，别打啦！不然的话，你们两个总有一个会受伤的，"亚当边说边把他们拉开。

4 cut it too far 做得过分，做得过火

5 cut it short 别说啦，说得简短些；长话短说

To cut it short, I made him pay for this. 长话短说，我已经让他为此付出了代价。

6 cut it up【美】把问题分析后做深入研究，仔细分析某事

7 cut the rough stuff【美俚】矫正粗鲁的行为，停止粗鲁的言行，别无礼

I hope he does cut the rough stuff when I tell him what I've done. 我把我做的事情告诉他，但愿他别发火。

8 cut up rough/nasty/ugly/crusty/stiff【美】大发脾气，大吵大闹

The boss is bound to cut up rough when he hears what happened. 如果老板知道发生的事情，他肯定要发脾气。

9 have a cut/crack at 试着做；努力做

You may be tired but have a crack at finishing the work. 你可能累了，但要努力把工作做完。

10 cut and run 慌忙逃走；急忙离开

It could backfire by emboldening the Taliban and annoying ally Pakistan, which fears Washington will cut and run as the Soviets did in Afghanistan. 这可能会导致相反后果，让塔利班武装分子更为嚣张，并激怒同盟国巴基斯坦，后者担忧华盛顿会重现苏联人逃离阿富汗的一幕。

D

daily

daily dozen 早操,体操

The boys did their *daily dozen* early each morning. 每天清晨孩子们都做早操。

damage

what's the damage 多少钱(代价、费用等)

Thanks for mending the car. *What's the damage*? 谢谢你修好了车,多少钱?

damn

1 as near as damn it 差不多,几乎

2 damn all 完全没有,毫无

You'll see I know *damn all* about it. 你会发现我对此一无所知。

You people sit around all day, doing *damn all* and expect to get paid for it! 你们这些人整天坐在这里什么事也不干,还想拿报酬!

3 damn it/you, etc. 该死,糟了

I can't remember his name, *damn it*! What did you say it was? 我记不得他的名字,真该死! 你刚才说他叫什么来着?

Damn that fool who left his bike in front of the door! 谁把自行车停在门口,真是该死的笨蛋!

4 damn me/I'll be damned/I'm damned if 我决不……;要是……我就不是人

I'll be damned if I'll help him. He never helps me when I need him. 我要是帮他,我就不是人。他在我需要帮助的时候,从来就没有帮助过我。

5 damn me, but I'll 我一定要……;我死也要……

Damn me, but I'll do it! 我一定要干!

6 well, I'll be damned/I'm damned/damn me 我太惊奇了

Well, *damn me*, if it isn't my old schoolmate, Peter; I wonder what he's doing here in California! 哎呀,我真不敢相信,那不是我的老同学彼得吗? 我不知道他到加利福尼亚来干什么。

Well, I'm damned, it's started snowing. 啊,我太惊奇了,居然下起雪来了!

7 be damned to you/God damn you 混账

8 do/try one's damnedest/best 拼命干,尽力干

I tried my damnedest last night. 昨晚我尽了最大的努力。

They are doing their damnedest to win. 他们拼尽全力争取胜利。

9 not care/give a damn 毫不在乎

10 not worth a damn/a tinker's damn/dam/curse 参见 curse 3

11 you damned 混账,该死

dance

1 dance after/to one's pipe/piping/whistle/tune 听从……指挥,跟着……亦步亦趋

Why should I dance to your tune? 为什么我该听命于你?

2 dance to another tune 改变态度,改弦易辙

Johnny refused to do his homework but punishment made him dance to another tune. 约翰尼拒绝做功课,但处罚使他不得不改变态度。

3 dance off 走开;【美俚】死,被处死

Dance off now. I wish to be alone. 走开,别打扰我!

4 lead sb. a pretty/merry dance 把某人引得晕头转向;给某人增加不必要的麻烦

What do you know of the human heart, my boy? A pretty dance the heart will lead you yet! 你哪里懂得别人的心思,孩子。你的心思会给你带来不少的麻烦呢!

dander

get one's dander/back/Irish up 使发火;发火

Finally, David got his dander up and wrote direct to the president. 最后戴维实在气愤,就直接给总统写信。

Fred got his back up when I said he was wrong. 当我批评弗雷德错了时,他竟大发雷霆。

dare

1 how dare you 你怎么敢……；你竟敢……

How dare you speak to me like that! You must apologise at once! 你怎敢这样对我说话！你必须马上道歉！

How dare you be so rude! 你怎么敢如此粗鲁！

2 I dare say（我想）可能，大概，或许

We've run out of sugar, but I dare say there's some in the cupboard. 我们的糖已经吃完了，不过我想食品柜里大概还有一点。

I dare say you're hungry after your long walk. 我想你们走了这么远的路大概很饿了。

3 I dare swear 我确信，我敢断定

4 (just) you dare/don't you dare（只要）你敢（吓唬或劝阻……干某事）

"Can I jump off that tree?" "You dare!" "你看我能从那棵树上跳下来吗？" "你敢！"

"Mummy, look—I'm going to fly through the air!" "Don't you dare!" "妈妈，看哪，我要飞起来喽！" "你敢！"

dark

1 be/keep/leave in the dark (about/on) 完全不知道，被蒙在鼓里

We were putting our heads together over the letter just now; and there certainly were one or two points on which we were a little in the dark. 我们刚才还在一起研究这封信，信中的确有一两处是我们不清楚的。

John was in the dark about the job he was being sent to. 约翰不知道派他去做的是什么工作。

2 in the dark 秘密地，暗中

Mostly such transactions were made in the dark. 这种买卖大都是在暗中进行的。

darken

darken one's/the door 进入……家门；登门造访

If you leave this house now, never darken my door again. 假如你现在离开这所房子，就别再进我的家门了。

After a son shamed his father by having to go to prison, the father told him never to darken his door again. 一个儿子因坐过牢让父亲蒙羞，其父不准他再进家门。

darn

1 darn it【美俚】讨厌

Darn it! I've missed the last bus home! 真可恼！我没赶上回家的末班车！

2 I'll be darned 我决不；如果……我就不是人

It's not me I'm worried about, but I'll be darned if my children have to grow up in such a world of inequality and injustice! 我担心的并不是我自己，可是我决不能让我的孩子生活在这样一个不平等、不公正的环境里！

dash

dash it (all)/my buttons 该死，真见鬼，真糟糕，真可恶，真混账（表示惊讶或愤懑）

Dash it all, old chap, when I say I'll pay you back, I mean it! 真见鬼，老伙计，只要我说了要还你钱，我一定说话算数！

I suddenly discovered, dash it all, that I'd forgotten its name. 真该死，我突然发现，我把它的名字忘了。

date

1 to date 到今天，至今，到现在

Jim is shoveling snow to earn money, but his earnings to date are small. 吉姆靠铲雪挣钱，但现在他的收入仍然很少。

This is his finest achivement to date. 这是他迄今为止最杰出的成就。

2 up/down to date 现代化的；熟悉最新的发展；直到现在，直到最近

Abraham is always right up to date in his information about this subject. 在这方面亚伯拉罕一向掌握最新的情报。

day

1 any day (of the week) 随便哪一天，任何时候；不管怎么说，在任何情况下

I am a better chess player than he is any day of the week. 我的棋艺怎么说也比他高明。

I'd rather be on holiday in Florida any day of the week than stuck in this office all of the time. 不管怎么说,我宁可随便哪天到佛罗里达去度假也比待在办公室里强。

2 all in a/the day's work 难免不愉快的常事,习以为常,不足为奇

Keeping ants away from a picnic lunch is all in the day's work. 野餐时有蚂蚁出现不足为奇。

To anyone working in a hotel, angry complaints from guests are all in a day's work. 对在旅馆里工作的人来说,客人们怒气冲冲地提意见是家常便饭。

3 if a day 不多不少,至少

Carrie was eighty-nine if she was a day. 嘉莉至少有八十九岁了。

That was a good thirty years ago if it was a day. 那至少是整整三十年前的事了。

4 it's one's day 是……非常得意或走运的日子

5 it's not one's day 是……非常倒霉或不走运的日子

I had a quarrel with my boss then lost my money on my way home—it just wasn't my day yesterday. 我同老板吵了一架,回家路上又丢了钱。昨天实在是我倒霉的日子。

The washing-machine flooded this morning; I burnt the dinner; it's just not my day. 早晨洗衣机流了一地的水,饭又烧糊了。真是个倒霉的日子。

6 make one's day 使……非常高兴

You've quite made my day by coming to see me. 承蒙你来看我,使我一天生活生色不少。

It'll really make his day when David hears what I've been through. 戴维听到我所经历的一切以后一定乐不可支。

7 one of these (fine)/some of these days 不日,不久,总有那么一天

I'm going to do that sewing some of these days. 不久我就学会缝纫了。

One of these fine days, I'll get round to decorating the living room. 总有一天我要花点时间把客厅装饰一下。

8 one of those days 倒霉的一天

And "one of those days" never comes. 而"倒霉日"从未到来。

9 that'll be the day 绝不可能,做梦

Joe wanted me to lend him money to take my girl to the movies. That'll be the day! 乔要我借钱给他带我女友去看电影,我绝不干!

Me get married? That'll be the day! 想要我结婚吗？那是做梦！
10 those were the days 那真是好年头啊（亦作反语）
Those were the days when you could buy a big bar of chocolate for half the price it costs now! 那些年的日子才叫好呢，那时候买一大块巧克力是现在价钱的一半。

dead

1 be caught dead 被逮个正着；出洋相；献丑
When you say you wouldn't be "caught dead" doing something, it means that you would never do it, because it would be really embarrassing if someone saw you. 当你说你不愿正在做某事时"被逮个正着"，那意味着你永远不要去做它，因为如果某人看到了你，那你会真的非常尴尬的。
2 dead-and-alive 郁郁不乐，烦闷，无聊
It's a dead-and-alive day today. 今天真无聊！

deal

1 big deal 那有什么了不起的；妙极了（讽刺、反语）；【美俚】好极了
So you became college president—big deal! 你当了大学校长，有啥了不起的！
2 good deal【美】(这主意)好极了
It's a good deal! 这是笔好买卖！
3 it's a deal 一言为定
It's a deal then? You'll pay me two thousand pounds for the car. 那么，就这样决定了？你要付我 2000 英镑的汽车款。
4 make a big deal (out) of 极端重视；对……大惊小怪
Don't make such a big deal out of it please. 请别对这事小题大做。
5 think a great deal of/a lot of 重视，评价甚高
Mary thinks a great deal of Tim. 玛丽对蒂姆的评价很高。

dear

1 dear knows 天晓得，上天为证
2 dear me/oh dear/dearie/deary me 哎呀（表示悲伤、同情、焦急、惊奇等）
Dear me! My purse is lost; what shall I do now? 哎呀，我的钱包丢了，我该什么办？

Oh dear, where can Harry be? He should have been here an hour ago. 哎呀,哈里会跑到哪儿去呢? 他一个小时前就该来的呀。

3 my dear(s) 亲爱的(表示亲切的称呼,也用于较正式、表示关心或讽刺的场合)

How lovely to see you, my dear! 看见你多高兴呀,亲爱的!

My dears, come in and tell me all your news. 亲爱的诸位,请进来把你们的情况告诉我。

4 that's/there's a dear 这才乖呢,这才是个好孩子

5 what dears they are 多么可爱呀

death

1 will be the death of 令人痛苦的经历;使人伤脑筋的(孩子);(笑话)把……笑死;害死……,要……的命;伤透……的心(常用恼怒或讽刺的语调)

Going out without a coat will be the death of you! 外出不穿外套那可真要你好看喽!

Stop joking or you'll be the death of me. 千万别再讲笑话啦,不然你会把我笑死。

2 be death on 善于处理,擅长应付,能手;深恶痛绝,非常苛刻

Joe is death on fast balls. He usually knocks them out of the park. 乔很会应付快速球,他常把球击出场外。

The new teacher is death on students who come late to class. 新来的老师对迟到的学生非常严厉。

3 flog/ride to death 重复谈论某一题目使人厌烦

The joke has been flogged to death. 这个笑话已经说得令人生厌了。

4 like death warmed up 筋疲力尽;不舒服;病重

I still feel like death warmed up after my cold. 伤风感冒过后我仍感觉不舒服。

declare

1 (well,) I (do) declare 哎呀,说真的;哎哟,有这种事;真奇怪,我可真没想到

I declare, it has been a very warm day! 啊,天气可真热呀!

Well, I do declare, this is an awful mess you've got us in! 哎哟,你把我们

搞得一团糟!

2 declare off 宣布作废,声明作废

Sad to say, the engagement was declared off. 说来很遗憾,那婚约已宣布解除。

depend

1 it/that (all) depends 那要看情况

Sometimes I support him, and sometimes he supports me; that depends. 有时我支持他,有时他支持我,这要看情况而定。

It all depends (on) what you mean. 这要看你是什么意思。

2 (you can) depend on/upon it 靠得住,你放心,你看好啦,你相信好啦

We'll be there at six, you can depend on it. 我们六点钟准到那儿,你放心好啦。

Depend upon it, you will succeed. 你准能成功。

deuce

1 a/the deuce of a 非常糟糕的,极麻烦的,异常的

They got into a deuce of a fight. 他们开始了一场恶斗。

Katharine paid a deuce of a price for it. 凯瑟琳为这付出了极大的代价。

2 deuce take it 见鬼,该死,糟了

3 deuce knows 天晓得

4 go to the deuce/bowwows/dogs 见鬼去,去你的;堕落,毁灭

Then she can go to the deuce. 那就叫她见鬼去吧!

5 the deuce 活见鬼;啊呀

The deuce is in them! 他们真是见了鬼啦!

The deuce is in it if I cannot. 我不能做才怪呢。

6 the deuce/devil you/he, etc, will/have, etc. ……才怪呢(表示不以为然的粗鲁回答)

Peter said I'd drive him into town—the devil I will! 彼得说我要带他进城去,我真带他去才怪呢!

7 what/how/when/where/who/why the deuce 到底,究竟(用于加强语气)

Who the deuce is Orlando? 奥兰多到底是谁?

Where the deuce did I put the keys? I can't seem to find them anywhere. 我到底把钥匙放到哪儿去了? 看来我是哪儿也找不到了。

devil

1 a/the devil of a 非常糟糕的，极麻烦的，异常的

We had the devil of a job to get the wardrobe upstairs! 我们费了好大劲才把这个衣柜搬上楼去。

A devil of a poor hand I shall make at the trade, no doubt. 我要是干这行，准定蹩脚得要命。

2 and the devil knows what/when/who, etc. 谁也不知道（什么时候、什么人等）；等等，以及其他种种

This shop sells knives, forks, and the devil knows what. 这个商店出售刀、叉，以及其他种种东西。

3 as the devil 很，极其，非常

Gee, the old man was as mad as the devil. 天哪，这老人气极了。

4 be a devil 勇敢些，鼓起勇气

Come on, Joe, be a devil and have another drink! 来吧，乔，勇敢些，再喝一杯！

Be a devil to eat. 狼吞虎咽。

5 be the devil 非常困难，很棘手，很恼人

My new car is super to drive, but it's so big it's the very devil to find a parking place for it. 我的新车非常好开，就是太大了些，很难给它找到停放的地方。

6 between the devil and the deep blue sea 参见 between 2

7 catch the devil 【口】受到严厉的责备，受到申斥

8 go to the devil 滚开，见鬼去，去你的

Go to the devil, Jo, I'm sick of your questions all the time. 滚开，乔，我讨厌你一个劲地提问题。

George told Bob to go to the devil. 乔治叫鲍勃滚开。

9 play the devil with/play hob/old gooseberry with 搞坏，糟蹋，搅乱，造成巨大混乱

This rough roads can play the devil with the tyres of your car. 这些坎坷不平的道路会损坏汽车的轮胎。

Uncle Bob's unexpected visit played the devil with our own plans to travel. 鲍勃叔叔的意外来访打乱了我们外出旅行的计划。

10 pull devil, pull baker/pull dog, pull cat 双方加油，加油

D

Now you boys, get to it—pull devil, pull baker! 你们这群男孩儿，现在开始，加油！加油！

11 talk/speak of the devil (and he will appear) 说曹操，曹操到

We were just talking about Bill when he came in the door. Speak of the devil and he appears. 我们正谈论比尔时，他就进了门，真是说曹操，曹操到。

12 the devil and all 全部，整个，一股脑儿（特指坏事）；坏透了

I needn't take the devil and all trouble to explain matters to you. 我才不必费那么大的劲儿来对你解释呢！

Someone says Effie is the devil and all. 有人说埃菲坏透了。

13 the devil/deuce to pay 困难局面，严重后果；麻烦事情，倒霉事情

If you do that, there will be the devil to pay. 如果做这件事，你就会遇到很大麻烦。

There'll be the devil to pay if we're caught breaking into the room, you know! 如果我们闯进这间屋子被当场抓住的话，后果是严重的，你知道的！

14 the devil you/he, etc. will/have, etc. 参见 deuce 6

15 to the devil with/of 我对……不感兴趣

To the devil of you all! You amateurs don't know how to run a gardening club at all! 我对你们丝毫不感兴趣。你们这些外行一点也不知道如何管理园艺俱乐部。

16 what/how/when/where/who/why (in) the devil 究竟，到底

How the devil do I know where your book is! When were you last reading it? 我怎么知道你的书放哪儿去了？你最近什么时候读过它？

Where in the devil did Bryan go? 布赖恩究竟上哪儿去了？

diamond

1 a diamond in the rough/a rough diamond 未经琢磨的钻石，可造之才

The boss looks bad-tempered, but he is a diamond in the rough. 这个老板看起来好像脾气很坏，其实他是个很有教养的人。

John looks awkward for a ball player, but he is a rough diamond. 约翰看起来似乎是个笨拙的球员，事实上他是个可造之才。

2 diamond cut diamond 势均力敌，棋逢对手

It was diamond cut diamond when the two men met because they were both so sure their own ideas were right. 那两人一交锋真是棋逢对手,互不相让。因为他们都确信自己的想法是对的。

dice

1 load the dice 事先决定成败,事先注定事情的结果;使用不正当手段
Mr. Smith used his great wealth to load the dice in his favour. 史密斯先生利用他的庞大财富使事情对自己有利。

2 no dice/deal/go/sale/soap 没门,没用,没结果,徒劳无益
Billy wanted to let Bob join the team but I said that was no deal because Bob was too young. 比利想让鲍勃加入球队,但我说不行,因为鲍勃太年轻。
I tried to get him to back us with $1,000. But no dice. He just wasn't interested. 我试图让他在我们这边下1,000美元的赌注,但是他不干。他对此不感兴趣。

dickens

1 as the dickens 真是,实在是
My old hound dog is ugly as sin, but faithful as the dickens. 我的老猎犬虽然长得难看,但它对我却是忠心耿耿。

2 the dickens 哎呀,糟了;混账

3 the dickens of it 最糟的
The dickens of it was that Pollitt had no money. 最糟的是波利特没有钱。

4 what/how/where/who the dickens 究竟是什么/如何/在哪/谁(用于表示惊奇、生气的强烈感情,但又比较委婉、不失体面的一种方式,dickens 是 devil 的一种变体)
What the dickens are you doing here? 你们到底在这儿干什么呀?
What the dickens is Reed? 里德究竟是干什么的?

die

1 as straight as a die 绝对正直,非常诚实
John has been with me 18 years and I know he's as straight as a die in everything. 约翰跟我已经有18年了,我知道他为人正直,对什么事都毫不含糊。

2 never say die 别灰心,别气馁
Never say die. It'll be all over soon. 别灰心,一切都会很快过去的。

Sally spoke to me gently, "Never say die! It won't last forever!" 萨莉轻声对我说:"别灰心,情况不会永远这样。"

3 **the die is cast/thrown** 木已成舟,已成定局,无法挽回

Your choice cannot be dependent on the results you anticipate or hope for, because you will not know those results till after the die is cast. 你不能以你预料或期望的结果为基础做选择,因为你只有在一切都已成定局后才能知道结果。

difference

1 **all the difference (in the world)** 天渊之别,大不相同

Sometimes it's what you don't see that makes all the difference in the world. 有时正是那些你看不到的东西让一切变得不同了。

2 **carry the difference**【美俚】携带枪支

In some countries only the police or soldiers can carry the difference. 有些国家只有警察或士兵才可以携带枪支。

3 **it makes a difference** 那就是另一回事了,那情况就完全不同啦

4 **it makes no difference** 无关紧要,没有关系,没有差别

5 **the same difference**【美俚】同样的东西,一样的

dirt

1 **dish the dirt/dig dirt about sb.**【美俚】论人是非,散播谣言

The journalists like to dish the dirt about television stars. 记者喜欢揭电视明星的疮疤。

2 **do sb. dirt** 恶意中伤某人;欺骗某人

3 **eat dirt/humble pie/one's/the leek/**【美】**eat crow/dog** 卑躬屈膝,忍气吞声

Mr. Johnson was so much afraid of losing his job that he would eat dirt whenever the boss got mean. 约翰逊先生唯恐失去他的工作,所以他卑躬屈膝,忍受老板的欺辱。

Tom told a lie about George and when he was found out, he had to eat humble pie. 汤姆说乔治的坏话,当被识破时,他只得向乔治赔礼道歉。

4 **throw/fling/sling dirt at** 诽谤,中伤

In campaigning many people would throw dirt at their opponents indiscriminatingly. 竞选时,许多人肆意诽谤他们的对手。

discord

an apple of discord 引起争端的不祥之物,争端,祸根

The use of the computer is an apple of discord between the couple. 谁来用电脑,是这对夫妇争吵的原因。

dish

1 **a/one's/dish/cup of tea** 参见 cup 2

2 **dish it out** 辱骂;惩罚;折磨

Harrod likes to dish it out in the newspaper. 哈罗德爱在报纸上骂人。

Jim likes to dish it out, but he hates to take it. 吉姆好骂人,却不愿挨骂。

3 **dish out** 分发,大量提供,给予

They are dishing out the tickets. 他们正在分发票证。

The teacher dished out so much homework that her pupils complained to their parents. 那个老师布置了大量的家庭作业,以至于学生纷纷向家长诉苦。

4 **dish up** 提出事实、论点等;把……说得娓娓动听

The teacher dished up the story in a humorous way. 老师以幽默风趣的语调,把故事讲得娓娓动听。

do

1 **and have/be done with it** 一不做,二不休(常用于幽默地建议)

You've broken four out of the six windows—why don't you smash the other two and be done with it? 六扇窗户你已打碎了四扇,一不做二不休,何不把那两扇也砸了?

You should tell Peggy the truth, and be done with it. 你应该告诉佩吉真相,不要再隐瞒事实了。

2 **did you ever see/hear the like** 真的吗,难道真是这样吗;你真的听说/看到这事了吗

Well, did you ever hear the like? Mary's marrying Dave after all! 玛丽到底还是要嫁给戴夫,你听说这事了吗?

3 **don't... me** 别老是……的(表示说话人对对方话中的某一个词反感)

"Come on, dear!" "Don't 'dear' me, you nasty man!" "来吧,亲爱的!" "别给我一口一个亲爱的,你这个下流胚!"

4 done with you 好吧，就这样，行，同意

5 do oneself well 生活阔绰，养尊处优

6 do the business 奏效；解决问题；把事干成

7 easy does it 别慌，小心点

"*Easy does it*!" Steve said as he and Leslie lifted the wardrobe through the narrow door. 斯蒂夫正同莱斯利把大衣柜抬进这个狭窄的房门，他嘱咐道："别慌，小心点！"

8 fair do's 公平

Fair do's, Jane, I only said I might phone you, not that I definitely would. 请你对我公平点，简，我只是说过我可能给你打电话，并没有说一定会打。

9 have done with 够了，算啦；停止，结束

Have done with it! 把它了结了吧！

10 how are you (doing) 你好

"*How are you*, Paula?" "Very well, thanks, and you?" "OK, thanks." "你好吗，波拉？""很好，谢谢你，你呢？""也好，谢谢。"

How are you doing, Vic? I've not had a chance to talk to you for ages! 你好吗，维克？好久没有机会同你谈谈了。

11 how do you do 你好

12 how do you do it 这是怎么搞的（表示惊讶）

How do you do it, Tony? You travel long distances every day—I just don't know where you get the energy from! 托尼，你这是怎么搞的？你每天走很远的路，我真不明白你从哪儿来的那么多精力！

13 could/can do with 想要，需要；容忍，忍受（用于否定句）

I *could* just *do with* a nice cup of tea. 我只需要喝一杯清茶就行了。

I think the car *could do with* a good clean. 我看这车需要好好清洗一下。

14 it isn't done 没有人这样做；这样做不合适

15 nothing doing 没有什么事或活动；绝对不，当然不；毫无结果，毫无成果

There's *nothing doing* in this town. 这个镇子里的生活平淡无奇。

Nothing doing tonight—there is only an old film on at the cinema, the bowlling alley's closed down, so we're staying at home. 今天晚上没有什么活动，电影院放的是一部老片子，保龄球场也关门了。我们只好待在家里。

16 sure do【美】行，好的

"Do you want an ice-cream?" "Sure do." "给您来一份冰激凌好吗？""好的。"

17 that's/you've done it/that does/did it 这就糟了，这就完蛋了；好了，行了，够了

I guess that does it, gentlemen, unless you have anything further to discuss. 先生们，我想就这样吧！除非你们还有事要讨论。

That does it! You've been rude so many times tonight that I'm sending you straight up to bed! 好了，够了，今天晚上你这么一次又一次地胡闹，我只好把你送上床去睡觉。

18 that will do 够了；好吧，行，同意；得啦，你可以走啦

I think that will do, Mr. Smith. Thank you very much for coming to speak to us. 我想这样就行了，史密斯先生，非常感谢你来告诉我们。

Children, that will do! How many more times do I have to tell you to be quiet? 好啦，够了，孩子们，还要我说多少遍，你们才会安静下来？

19 that won't do 那不行

That won't do the kid any good. 那对孩子没有任何好处。

20 well done 干得好

"Daddy! I came second in history." "Well done, sweetheart!" "爸爸！我历史得了第二名。""做得好，宝贝儿！"

21 what do you do (for a living) 你是干什么（工作）的

"What do you do, Martin?" "I write dictionaries." "马丁，你是干什么的？""我是编辑词典的。"

22 what's... doing 为什么放到……（表示不同意）

What's that coat doing on the floor? 那件外衣为什么放在地板上？

23 what's done is done/what's done cannot be undone 木已成舟，无可挽回

24 why don't 为什么不……（发出请求、邀请）

Why don't you shut up? 你怎么不闭上嘴？

"Why don't you come round for dinner one evening?" "I'd love to, but I'm busy at the moment." "为什么晚上不过来吃饭？""我倒想来，可是近来很忙。"

25 will do 我会的

"Can you go upstairs and get my jacket?" "Will do!" "你能上楼把我的夹克拿来吗？""我会的。"

26 you do that 行,你干吧(表示鼓励、支持);你敢(表示制止)

"Shall I try some of your chicken pie?" "You do that!" "我尝尝你的鸡肉馅饼,好吗?" "行,你吃吧。"

"Mummy, I'm going to turn on the television!" "You just do that!" "妈妈,我要开电视!" "你敢!"

doctor

1 you're the doctor 你是专家,应由你做决定

2 just what the doctor ordered 正是需要、合适或欣赏的东西

After a hard day at work a nice meal at home is just what the doctor ordered. 辛苦工作一天之后,需要的正是在家享受一顿美餐。

dod

dod-rot 见鬼,岂有此理

dog

1 a dog in the manger 占着马槽的狗,占着茅坑不拉屎的人

Marner's a real dog in the manger—even though he doesn't have a car he won't let anyone else use his garage. 马南真是占着茅坑不拉屎,自己没有汽车,还不让别人用车库。

2 dog it 逃避工作或责任,做事拈轻怕重,干活吊儿郎当;【美】摆阔,过寄生生活;溜走

The sponsor of the project dogged it when needed most. 在最需要他们的时候,项目主办方退出了。

3 give/throw/cast/send to the dogs (出于自私)抛弃、牺牲别人,舍车保帅

Why did the old lady give furniture to the dogs? 老太太为什么把家具给扔了?

4 go to the dogs 堕落,完蛋,垮台,毁灭,日趋恶化,日落西山

Norris seems to have gone completely to the dogs and spends all his time in the pub. 诺里斯似乎已完全堕落了,整天泡在酒馆里。

According to some pessimists, the country is going to the dogs. 按照某些悲观者的看法,那个国家正在走向衰亡。

5 hot dog 【美俚】好极啦,好样儿的;热狗

"Hot dog!" Frank exclaimed when he unwrapped a birthday gift of a small

record player. 弗兰克打开生日礼物，发现是一个小型收录机，他叫道：
"哇，好棒啊！"

"Did you have a good time?" "Hot dog!" "你们玩得痛快吗？" "好极了！"

6 shouldn't happen to a dog【美】这事真不该发生，这事真不像话

Echoes of a Summer, a story about a kid dying of a bad heart and her divided parents shouldn't happen to a dog, certainly not to Jodie Foster.《夏日的回声》讲述的是一个女孩患严重的心脏病而濒临死亡之际其父母离异的故事，任何人都不该遭此痛苦，乔迪·福斯特当然就更不该了。

7 keep a dog and bark oneself 用了人还要亲自操劳，做应由下属做的工作

Why keep a dog and bark yourself. 既然请了人，何必事事亲力亲为？

8 let sleeping dogs lie/it is ill to waken sleeping dogs 不要招惹麻烦，莫惹是非

I saw them today, and they seemed to be getting along. Maybe you should let sleeping dogs lie. 我今天看到他们的时候，他们似乎很融洽。或许你最好别去惹麻烦了。

9 like a dog with two tails 高兴得什么似的

Russell was not at all like a dog with two tails. 拉塞尔丝毫没有高兴的样子。

10 put on (the) dog 摆架子，摆阔气，装腔作势

Patrick always puts on a lot of dog about something. 帕特里克总是喜欢虚张声势没事找事。

But what I like about Petty was that she never put on the dog to show off her money. 但是我最欣赏佩蒂的是她从来不炫耀自己有钱。

11 dog-eat-dog 残酷争夺；人吃人的关系，自相残杀的；竞争激烈的

It goes to show that in the dog-eat-dog world of business, it's often not as much about the product as it is about the process. 这也证明了，在竞争激烈的商业世界里，更多的是经营方式而非产品的竞争。

doggone

1 doggone it 去你的，他妈的（God damn 的委婉语）

Because I'm good enough, I'm smart enough, and doggone it, people like me. 我够好了，我够聪明了，真是该死，大家这么喜欢我。

2 doggone your silly ideas 让你的那些蠢念头见鬼去吧

3 I'll be doggoned if I'll go 我要是去就不是人

dollar

1 (bet) dollars to buttons/doughnuts/bet (one's) bottom dollars【美】的确，毫无疑问，十拿九稳

I'd bet dollars to doughnuts that he would win. 我愿打赌，他取胜是十拿九稳的事。

2 feel like a million dollars 精力充沛，精神焕发

Sandy feels like a million dollars today. 今天桑迪自我感觉极好。

3 look like a million dollars 满面春风，气宇轩昂

John, driving a fine new car, looked like a million dollars. 约翰开着一辆漂亮的新车，看上去洋洋得意。

Dressed in the new formal, Betty looked like a million dollars. 贝蒂穿着新礼服显得十分漂亮。

door

1 answer the door （听到敲门声）去开门

Henry took ages to answer the door. 亨利听到有人敲门，隔了很久才去开门。

2 close/bar/shut the door to/on 封锁言行；把……关在门外，拒而不纳；使……没有可能

The president's veto closed the door to any new attempt to pass the bill. 总统的否决使得任何通过此项法案的企图都受到了阻碍。

Their attitude has closed the door to any new agreement. 他们的态度使得任何新协议都无法达成。

If god were to close the door on you, he would leave a window open. 如果上帝为你关了一扇门，他必定会为你打开一扇窗。

3 lay sth. at sb.'s door 把某事归咎于某人

The failure of the plan was laid at his door. 计划的失败归咎于他。

4 lie at sb.'s door （责任）归于……

The blame for his death lies at my door, and I will never be able to forget it. 他的死应归咎于我，我永远不会忘记这件事。

5 open a/the door for/to 使……成为可能；给……办法或机会

It was my teacher who opened the door for me. 是我的老师给我提供了机会。

Rising dependence on imported oil would open the door to higher fuel prices. 越是依赖进口石油，燃料价格就越上涨。

6 show sb. the door 向某人下逐客令

After a long argument, Fielding showed me the door. 争论了好久以后，菲尔丁向我下了逐客令。

7 shut/slam the door in one's face 吃闭门羹，关门不许进入

Geoffrey backed away and in that split second she slammed the door in his face. 杰弗里往后退去，就在那一刹那，她砰地把他关在门外。

The workers asked for only a small increase in pay, but the boss just slammed the door in their faces. 工人们只要求增加少量工资，但老板就是拒绝同他们谈判。

dose

1 give sb. a dose of his own medicine/treat sb. with a dose of his own medicine/dose sb. with his own physic 以其人之道还治其人之身；以牙还牙

Jim was always playing tricks on other boys. Finally they decided to give him a dose of his own medicine. 吉姆总是捉弄其他男孩，最后他们决定对他以牙还牙。

2 get/have a dose/taste of one's own medicine 自食其果，受到报应

Tony has smeared John's reputation. It is now time for Tony to have a dose of his own medicine. 托尼曾经损害了约翰的名誉。现在该是他自食其果的时候了。

dot

1 dot the/one's i's and cross the/one's t's 一丝不苟，重视细节；准确无误

You'll have to make sure you dot your i's and cross your t's if you go to work at that company. 如果你去那家公司工作，你做事得一丝不苟。

2 on the dot/button 准时地；在指定的时间，在指定的空间点上

They must show up promptly on the dot and in good condition for the work every day. 他们必须精神十足地、按照规定时间、分秒不差地上班工作。

Susan arrived at the party at 2:00 p.m. on the dot. 苏珊在下午两点准时

到会。

3 to a/the dot 【美】正确;恰好,丝毫不差的;详详细细地
It suits Adela to a dot. 这对阿德拉正合适。

doubt

beyond/no/without doubt 无疑地,确实地;很可能
His honesty is quite beyond doubt. 他的诚实是确定无疑的。
Without doubt, you have been working very hard. 你确实一直在努力工作。

down

1 be down on 怨恨,厌恶;责骂;迅速发现
Kitty was down on the junior typist. 基蒂厌恶那个年轻的打字员。
They were about to be down on her when she came into the office. 他们正要埋怨她时,她走进了办公室。

2 down in the bushes/mouth 【美】意气消沉,心灰意懒,垂头丧气
If this should happen, the speaker might feel down in the mouth. In other words, he might feel sad for saying the wrong thing. 这种情况发生时,说话的人会觉得心情沮丧,换句话说,他会因为说错话而心情不好。

3 down with 打倒;不要
Down with tyranny! 打倒暴政!
Down with smoking! 不要抽烟!

4 hit/kick sb. when he's down 对某人落井下石

5 down and out 穷困潦倒
The writer was down and out, but he still went on with his writing. 那个作家虽然已经穷困潦倒了,但他还是坚持写作。

dozen

1 at dozens/sixes and sevens 乱七八糟;意见不合
Everything is at dozens and sevens in our house after last night's party. 昨晚舞会之后家中一片狼藉。
The committee is split over the scheme. They are at dozens and sevens. 委员会在这个方案上意见不合,众说纷纭。

2 hit/knock for dozen 打败,完全挫败

The general assured his men that they would hit the enemy for dozen. 将军要士兵们相信,他们一定会彻底打败敌人。

3 six of one and half a dozen of the other/six and two threes 半斤八两,毫无差别,不相上下

"Which coat do you like better, the brown or the blue?" "It's six of one and half a dozen of the other." "你喜欢哪件外衣,褐色的还是蓝色的?" "两件都差不多。"

Johnny says it's six of one and half a dozen of the other whether he does the job tonight or tomorrow night. 约翰尼说他无论今晚还是明晚做那件事都无所谓。

drat

drat sb./sth. 讨厌,见鬼

Drat their interference! 谁要他们管!

Drat this pen, it never write when I want it to! 这讨厌的笔,我一用它就不下水!

draw

1 beat... to the draw/punch 捷足先登,抢先一步

I beat him to the draw and shot him in the leg. 我比他先拨出枪,击中了他的腿部。

Hitler wanted to beat Roosevelt to the draw with his declaration of war. 希特勒想通过宣战抢在罗斯福之前抢得先机。

2 draw it mild 不要吹过头了,不要说过火了,不要吹牛

In speaking of the assault upon him he drew it mild. 讲到他受攻击时,他言辞中肯而不夸张。

dream

1 dream up 凭空想出,虚构出

The raid was dreamed up by the journalists who reported it. 这次袭击是写报道的记者虚构出来的。

2 like a dream 轻而易举地,完美地

The engine starts like a dream. 这台引擎很容易发动。

Everything went like a dream. 一切进展得十分顺利。

dress

1 dress down 训斥；痛打

The manager dressed Isaac down for being late again. 因为艾萨克又迟到，经理狠狠地训了他一顿。

Joel was dressed down till he was black and blue. 乔尔被打得遍体鳞伤。

2 be dressed up to the nines 打扮得华美漂亮，穿得十分考究

Every time she went to a dance, she would always be dressed up to the nines. 每次去参加舞会，她都打扮得特别美丽。

drive

1 drive at 用意所在，意指

I see prefectly what you are driving at. 我完全明白你的意思。

What are you driving at? 你这话是什么意思？

2 drive away at 勤奋地工作，孜孜不倦地干

MacAdam was still driving away at his dictionary. 麦克亚当依旧在孜孜不倦地编写他的词典。

Nora sat at her desk for hours, driving away at her work. 诺拉在桌边一坐就是几个小时，拼命地工作。

3 drive in/into 向……灌输；对……不断强调；反复地教

The speaker tried to drive in his point. 演讲人试图灌输他的观点。

I tried to drive into Moulton that his drinking was harmful to himself and others. 我试图叫莫尔顿明白，喝酒对人对己都有害。

4 drive/force to the wall 【美】陷入绝境，走投无路

John's failing the last test drove him to the wall. 约翰上一次考试失败使他陷入了绝境。

The score was 12—12 in the last minute of play, but a touch down forced the visitors to the wall. 比赛最后一分钟的比分是12比12，但一次触地得分，使客队败北。

drop

1 a drop in the bucket/ocean 沧海一粟，九牛一毛

They were only a drop in the ocean of refugees. 他们仅仅是大批难民中的少数。

2 at the drop of 一听到(或一看到)……就

O'Casey quavered at the drop of his name. 奥凯西一听到他的名字就发抖。

Penn is ready to defend fair language at the drop of a solecism. 佩恩一碰到语法错误,就要站出来维护语言的纯洁。

3 at the drop of a hat 一有信号就……,立即;毫不迟疑地;乐意地

The dog responds at the drop of a hat. 那条狗一见到信号就做出了反应。

MacDonald is willing to cancel the order at the drop of a hat. 麦克唐纳愿意随时取消订单。

4 drop a brick/clanger 说话闯祸;做事出岔子

I knew I had dropped a brick in making that remark. 我知道那句话一出口,我便闯了祸。

The queen's husband had a somewhat caustic tongue, and every now and then he would drop a political brick. 女王的丈夫说话有点刻薄,不时在政治问题上失言。

5 drop across 偶然遇到或发现

Katharine dropped across an old friend in the street yesterday. 凯瑟琳昨天在街上遇见了一位老朋友。

I dropped across this photograph in the drawer. 我在抽屉里无意间翻到了这张照片。

6 drop around/by/in/into/over/up 顺便访问,串门;顺便到

They asked him to drop around. 他们请他去串门。

Jacob travelled from one village to another, dropped in on families and listened to their problems. 雅各布从一个村子到另一个村子串门走户,听取他们的呼声。

7 drop dead 走开,别烦我,去你的

"Drop dead!" Bill told his little sister when she kept begging to help him build his model airplane. 比尔的妹妹一直请求帮比尔制作模型飞机,比尔却对她说:"走开,别烦人!"

When Sally bumped into Kate's desk and spilled ink for the fifth time, Kate told her to drop dead. 当莎莉第五次碰撞凯特的桌子,将墨水碰翻时,凯特叫她滚开。

8 drop it 丢开不谈;停止,不干

Let's drop it, shall we? 我们不谈这个好吗?

I think the boy has been concerned in criminal activity, so I've asked him to drop it. 我认为这孩子参与了犯罪活动,便劝他悬崖勒马。

9 drop off 让……从(交通工具上)下来;途中顺便带人或物;睡着

Joe asked Mrs Jones to drop him off at the library on her way downtown. 乔请琼斯太太在开车进城时顺便带他去图书馆。

The little girl closed her eyes, and soon dropped off. 那个小姑娘合上眼,不久就睡着了。

10 drop on 偶然发现;选中……;突然造访;感到突然

We dropped on it after searching for days. 我们找了几天,后来无意中把它找到了。

Why does the boss always drop on me for the worst job? 老板为什么老是挑我去干最糟的差事?

drum

1 beat the drum(s) 竭力鼓吹或支持

More than once the politicians have beaten the drums for a stronger navy. 政界人士多次竭力主张加强海军建设。

2 drum in 反复强调,强行灌输

The teacher tried to drum in the formula, but the students were not listening. 教师设法反复讲解这个公式,可是学生们听不进去。

dry

dry up 住口,停止发言,安静

I won't dry up; I must say something about it. 我不能停止发言,关于这件事我要发表意见。

You've gone too far, Jimmy. Now dry up! 吉米,你太过分了,住口!

duck

1 does/will/would a duck swim 当然愿意,那还用问

"Perhaps you would not object to drinking his health?" "Would a duck swim?" "你不反对为他的健康祝酒吧?" "那还用问!"

"Will you dine with me?" "Will a duck swim?" "和我一道吃饭好吗?" "那

还用问!"

2 fuck a duck【美】去你的（表示惊讶、不信、拒绝等）

3 take to sth./sb. like a duck to water（像鸭子入水一样）很自然地，轻而易举地

Hardy takes to vice like a duck to water. 哈代坏事儿一学就会。

Jackson took to German like a duck to water. 杰克逊德语一学就会。

dumb

1 don't be so dumb【美】别犯傻了

2 play dumb 装聋作哑

Don't play dumb with me! 别跟我装聋作哑！

dust

1 down with the dust 拿出钱来，现款交易，付现

Here is your bill, down with the dust! 这是你的账单，付钱吧！

2 dust off 把（长期不用的东西）备好待用；重新采用

I'd better dust off the large meat tin for Christmas. 我最好准备好一大罐肉，供圣诞节时吃。

We dusted off a scheme that has been lying on the shelf for years. 我们重新采用搁置多年的一个方案。

3 kick up a dust/row/fuss 吵闹，引起骚乱，惹是生非

The children kicked up a dust when their parents were out. 父母外出时孩子们闹作一团。

When the teacher left the room, two boys kicked up a row. 老师离开时，两个男孩吵了起来。

4 the dust settles 骚乱平息，混乱结束

We can not clearly foresee the outcome until the dust settles. 在事态平息之前，我们无法清楚地预见结果。

5 throw dust in/into one's eyes 迷惑……，蒙蔽……

The information the criminal's wife gave the police only threw dust into their eyes. 罪犯的妻子提供给警方的信息反而转移了他们的视线。

6 watch one's dust/smoke 看……干得多快

I can do it in five minutes. Just watch my dust. 我五分钟就能把它搞好，

你就瞧我的速度吧。
Offer Bill a dollar to shovel your sidewalk and watch his smoke! 给比尔一元钱,叫他铲人行道上的雪,你会看到他干得有多快!

dusty

not/none so dusty【俚】还不错
"What do you think of this?" "Well, it's not so dusty." "你认为这个怎么样?" "嗯,还不错。"
That was none so dusty. 那还不错。

Dutch

1 beat the Dutch/beat all【美】令人吃惊,了不起
It beats the Dutch how Tom always makes a basket. 汤姆投篮百发百中,真了不起。
John found a box full of money buried in his garage. Doesn't that beat all! 约翰发现一个装满钱的盒子埋在他的车库地下,真令人惊喜不已!

2 go Dutch【美】各人付各人的费用,平摊费用,AA 制
Johnny wanted to go Dutch with me at the restaurant last night. 昨晚在饭店吃饭后约翰尼要和我平摊费用。
Sometimes boys and girls go Dutch on dates. 小伙子和姑娘约会有时各付各的账。

3 be in Dutch【美】丢脸,受气,为难,得罪(上司等)
The new director told me if I don't finish on time I'll really be in Dutch. 新主管告诉我,如果我不能及时完成任务,我就有罪受了。

4 the Dutch have taken Holland 荷兰人占领了荷兰(少见多怪,不足为奇)

Dutchman

1 I'm a Dutchman if/or I'm a Dutchman/unless I'm a Dutchman 绝对会这样,否则我就是个笨蛋;要是……我就不是人(温和的发誓用语)
That precious young thing will have something to say about this, or I'm a Dutchman! 我敢担保,那个娇生惯养的小家伙准对这件事有意见。
"Then we've won?" said Flear. "Unless I'm a Dutchman," answered Soames. "那么我们是打赢了?" 芙蕾说。"担保没错,"索米斯回答。

2 well, I'm a Dutchman 没这回事（表示不相信）

"You've passed the examination!" "Well, I'm a Dutchman!" "你已考试及格了！""我可不相信！"

duty

do one's duty【委婉】上厕所，方便，解手

E

each

1 each and all/every 人人都，每个都，通通，没有例外
Each and all have gone to see the play. 大伙都看戏去了。
They bade me a most disconcerting farewell—each and all spat at me. 他们向我告别的方式使我狼狈不堪——所有的人都往我身上吐唾沫。

ear

1 about/around one's ears 彻底地，猛烈地（垮台、崩溃）
All Raman's dreams could be so easily tumbled about his ears by Sophy and because of one false step on his part. 只要拉曼走错一步，他所有的美梦就会被索菲不费吹灰之力地加以破坏。
Palmer saw the illusions tumbling about his ears. 幻想在帕尔默的眼前破灭了。

2 be all ears 全神贯注地听，洗耳恭听

3 bend one's ear 对……喋喋不休
Marion bent my ear for two hours. 马里恩缠住我唠叨了两个小时。
Lily was ready to have her ear bent. 莉莉准备耐心地听。

4 burn one's ear【俚】狠狠责骂……，痛斥……，呵斥……

5 by ear 凭听觉
The children sing by ear. 孩子们凭听觉唱歌。
We dodged people by ear. 我们靠耳朵听动静避开人群。

6 by the ears（动物）相咬，相斗；打架，扭打；争吵
During his short stay, Philip set us all by the ears. 菲利普在短期逗留期间，搬弄是非，搞得大家不得安宁。

7 chew one's ears off【美】教训……，训斥……；唠叨不已；沉闷地与……谈话

8 I would give my ears for/to 我为……不惜任何代价

9 in (at) one ear and out at the other 听了就忘，左耳进右耳出
The teacher's directions to the boy went in one ear and out at the other. 这

孩子把老师的指示当耳边风。

I remember that you said that anything you told your landlady went in at one ear and out at the other. 我记得你说过,你告诉你那房东太太的任何事情,她都是左耳入右耳出。

10 wet/not dry behind the ears 无经验的,不成熟的,少不更事的,初出茅庐的

John had just started working for the company, and was not dry behind the ears yet. 约翰才开始在公司工作,尚无经验。

The new student is still wet behind the ears, he was not yet learned the tricks that the boys play on each other. 这个新同学依然无所适从,他还不知道同学们彼此间玩的是什么把戏。

11 oh, my ears and whiskers 天哪,妈呀

Oh, my ears and whiskers! Why didn't you say so before? 啊,天哪！为什么你早先不说?

12 one's ears burn/feel one's ears burning/one's ears are burning（因被人议论）耳朵发烧

Were your ears burning last night? 你昨晚耳朵发烧吗?

Joan overheard the girls criticizing her and it made her ears burn. 琼听到女生在批评她,觉得很尴尬。

13 pin one's ears back 击败;责骂

After winning three games in a row, the Reds had their ears pinned back by the Blues. 连赢三场后,红队被蓝队打败了。

Mrs. Smith pinned Mary's ears back for not doing her homework. 史密斯太太责骂玛丽不做功课。

14 out on one's ear 被不客气地打发走,被不光彩地解雇

If you ever made that mistake, you went out on your ear. 如果你犯下那种错误,准得滚蛋。

15 play by ear 凭记忆演奏乐器;事先无准备,随机应变

Mary does not know how to read music. She plays the piano by ear. 玛丽不识乐谱,她凭背记乐谱弹钢琴。

Joe doesn't need any music sheets when he plays his guitar, he knows many songs well and can play them by ear. 乔弹吉他时不需要乐谱,他记得很多歌曲,并且弹得很好。

I'll have to play this by ear. 我只得凑合着做了。
16 up to the/one's ears/chin/elbows/eyes/knees/neck/shoulders in 参见 chin 5

earth

1 cost the earth 花一大笔钱
Our new car cost the earth, I can tell you! 我告诉你,我的新车是很昂贵的!

2 mop the earth/floor with sb. 击倒某人,痛击某人,大败某人
The warrior expected to mop the floor with his opponents. 那个勇士期待能彻底击败他的对手。

3 move heaven and earth (to do sth.) 竭尽全力,尽一切努力
Joe moved heaven and earth to be sent to Washington. 乔想尽方法希望被派到华盛顿去。

4 on earth/in the world (用于最高级或否定词的后面以加强语气)世界上,人世间;(用于疑问词后加强语气)究竟,到底;(用于否定句中)一点也不,全然不
Master Edward Waller in soldier suit looked like nothing on earth. 爱德华·沃勒少爷穿上水手服难看死了。
On hearing the news, Jasper felt like nothing on earth. 听到这消息,贾斯帕感到极为尴尬。

earthly

not (have/stand) an earthly (chance/hope/use) 【英口】完全没有成功的可能,没有丝毫的希望
It won't stand an earthly. 此事毫无希望。
"Have you any thoughts on what you'd like to do after you finish college?" "Not an earthly." "你考虑过大学毕业后想干什么吗?""完全没有考虑。"

ease

1 be at ease 轻松
Though still young and with no experience, the little actor can be at ease with the stars who worked with him. 尽管年纪小,没经验,这位小演员却能同一起工作的明星无拘无束地相处。

2 ease nature/oneself 大、小便

3 ease up/off 放慢,放松,缓和

With success and prosperity, Mr. Smith was able to ease off. 随着成功的到来,史密斯先生能够轻松些了。

The rain was easing off at last. 雨势终于减弱了。

4 with (great) ease 轻松,轻而易举

The girl answered all the questions with great ease. 那女孩儿非常轻松地回答了所有问题。

easily

breathe easily/freely 如释重负,轻松自在,心里坦然

Now that the big bills were paid, Stephen breathed more easily. 既然巨债已还,斯蒂芬现在轻松多了。

His mother didn't breathe easily until Temple got home that night. 那天晚上直到坦普尔回家后,他母亲才放下心。

easy

1 be easy 别忙,悠着点

2 easy all (命令语)停划,停桨;冷静

"Easy all, Long John," cried Israel. "Who's acrossing of you?" "得了吧,高个子约翰,"伊斯雷尔嚷了起来,"谁招你惹你啦?"

3 easy does it 参见 do 7

4 go easy on/with 节省着用;小心谨慎地对待,温和地对待

We're short of milk, so go easy with it. 我们的牛奶不多了,所以要省着点。

Children should go easy on candy. 小孩应当少吃糖果。

5 I'm easy 我随便(你们怎么决定都行)

"Francis, would you like to go to the cinema or go out for a meal tonight?" "I'm easy—which would you like to do?" "弗朗西斯,今晚你想去看电影还是外出吃饭?""随便,我怎么都行,你看呢?"

6 stand easy (口令)休息(比 at ease 更随便一点儿)

7 take it/things easy/go easy 小心谨慎,温和地;轻松一下,不要太紧张,不要太劳累;不忧虑,不焦急

Take it easy, the roads are icy. 慢一点,路上有冰。

"Go easy," said Billy to the other boys carrying the table down the stairs. "小心点!"比利对抬桌子下楼的孩子们喊道。

eat

1 eat dirt/humble pie 参见 dirt 3

2 I'll eat my hat/boots/head if 要是……就砍我的头,我就不是人;绝无此事

If ever he returns to this house, sir, I'll eat my head. 他要是再回到这个家来,先生,我就不是人。

If this is true, I'll eat my hat. 这不是真的,我敢用头来担保。

3 what's eating you【美】你有什么苦恼,你怎么啦

What's eating you, Anne? You look so miserable. 你怎么啦,安妮?你看上去那么伤心的样子。

egg

1 good egg/sport/sort/onion/scout 好人,好事,好东西;这太好了

I think it's a very good egg. 我想这是件好事。

Tommy is such a good egg that everybody wants to be his friend. 汤姆真是个好人,大家都想和他交朋友。

2 have/put all one's eggs in one basket 孤注一掷;集中财力干一件事

To buy stock in a single company is to put all your eggs in one basket. 只买一家公司的股票是孤注一掷。

Vincent has decided to specialize in lathe work, although he knows it is risky to put all his eggs in one basket. 文森特决定专攻车床这一行,虽然他知道孤注一掷是危险的。

We didn't want to put all our eggs in one basket. 我们不想冒孤注一掷的风险。

3 lay an egg (常指表演、讲笑话等)完全失败;(表演等)不受欢迎

The investigation laid an egg. 调查完全失败了。

Sometimes Turner is a successful speaker, but sometimes he lays an egg. 有时特纳是成功的演讲者,有时却不受听众欢迎。

4 walk/tread on/upon eggs/eggshells 如履薄冰;战战兢兢;小心翼翼地行动,谨慎行事

To work with our boss, you need to walk on eggshells. 与我们老板共事,

你需极为谨慎地做事。

element

1 be in one's element（源自法语）在适宜的环境，适得其所，如鱼得水
The deep-sea fish is in his element in deep ocean water. 深海中的鱼只能在大洋中生存。
The babysitter was certain in her element taking care of children. 照料小孩那个保姆自然是得心应手。

2 be out of one's element（源自法语）在不适宜的环境，不得其所，不适合于
Wild animals are out of their element in cages. 野生动物不习惯笼中生活。
Chris is out of his element in singing class. 音乐课不适合克里斯的性格。

elementary

elementary, my dear Watson 啊，那太简单了（源自柯南·道尔的《福尔摩斯探案集》一书）
"I can't get this tape recorder to work. Can you help me?" "Ah! You've not plugged it in! There you are—elementary, my dear Watson!" "这个录音机我打不开，你能帮帮我吗？""啊，你没接通电源，这太简单了！"

elephant

1 rain elephants and whales/cats and dogs 倾盆大雨
2 see/get a look at the elephant【美】见世面，开眼界，获得经验

else

1 or else 否则就……（用于威胁、警告）
Hand over the money or else! 把钱交出来，要不就够你受的！
Do what I say or else! 照我说的做，否则我就不客气了！
2 something else【美俚】特别出色的人或物
Janet Hopper is really something else. 珍妮特·霍帕实在出众。
3 something else again 不同的东西，另当别论
I don't care if you borrow my dictionary sometimes, but taking it without asking and keeping it is something else again. 我不介意你偶尔借用我的词典，但是未经允许擅自拿走，用后又不归还，那就另当别论了。

end

1 it isn't/wouldn't be the end of the world 这不是什么灾祸，这没有多大关系

It's not the end of the world, Suzie. You'll soon forget Peter and there are lots of other nice boys around. 这没有什么了不起的，苏西，你会很快忘掉彼得的，而且你周围还有好多好小伙子。

2 no end 极端地，非常；无限的，许多，大量的；不停地

Box at the opera costs no end. 歌剧院里的包厢非常昂贵。

Jim was no end upset because he couldn't go swimming. 吉姆很烦恼，因为他不能去游泳。

3 no end of/to 无止境，很多，非常的，特殊的，美好的，出众的

Valentine has no end of books. 瓦伦丁的书多得不得了。

Bob and Dick became close friends, and had no end of fun together. 鲍勃和迪克成了好朋友，他们在一起玩有许多乐趣。

4 the (absolute) end/limit 糟透了的事物，坏透了的人

This car of mine is the end. I've had nothing but trouble with it since I bought it. 我这个车真是糟透了！自从买了它就给我带来了无穷无尽的烦恼。

That child is the absolute limit! He howls every night and keeps us awake all the time. 这孩子真烦人！他整夜地哭叫，闹得我们睡不成觉。

5 the very end【美】顶呱呱，绝妙，最佳

6 to what end 为什么

To what end are we doing all this? 我们做这一切的目的是什么？

enemy

how goes the enemy 现在几点了

How goes the enemy? It must be nearly lunch time. 现在几点钟了？一定快到吃午饭的时间了吧。

enough

1 cry enough 认输吧

2 enough is enough 够了，行了，适可而止

"I don't mind good clean fun, but enough is enough," the principal said.

校长说:"我并不介意有趣、健康的玩笑,但要适可而止。"

Enough is enough. Can't you talk about anything else but politics? 够了,适可而止吧。你除了政治话题以外,能不能谈点别的?

3 enough of 停止做某事;实在忍受不了某事

Enough of your rudeness! Come here at once and apologize! 你太放肆了!立即过来道歉!

Enough of this folly! 不要干这种傻事了!

4 fair enough 有道理,很好,我赞成

"I'll give Pat and Judy a lift home if you take Charlotte and Margret." "Fair enough." "要是你带夏洛特和玛格丽特回家的话,我就带帕特和朱迪。""很好,我同意。"

5 funnily/curiously/oddly/strangely enough 奇怪的是,说来也怪

Funnily enough, Alan, we just talking about you and here you are! 奇怪呀,埃伦,怎么我们刚谈到你,你就来了!

No one, strangely enough, has ever noticed this mistake before. 奇怪的是,以前谁也没有注意到这个错误。

6 that's enough 够了,停止

That's enough now, children! Stop playing and put your toys away please. 好啦,孩子们,玩够了!现在请把你们的玩具放回原处。

7 well enough 还不错,还可以,够了,别再说了;充分地,完全地

You know well enough. 你明明知道,你心里明白。

ever

1 as ever is/was【口】非常,格外,真是,实在是

Keep your chin up and keep trying, the importance of grades, scores and degrees may vary, but the one thing that remains as rewarding as ever is the "never say die" spirit. 打起精神继续努力,等级、分数、学位的重要性可能会有变化,但是永不言败的精神是终身受益的。

2 ever so 非常,极其,十分,特别,……得多

This road is ever so much shorter. 这条路真的近得多。

Thank you ever so much. 十分感谢你。

3 ever such (a) 非常

Rosa's ever such a nice girl. 罗莎是个非常好的姑娘。

It is ever such a tool. 这个工具很有用。

4 never ever **决不,从不**

Classes were never ever dull. 上那些课从不感到沉闷单调。

5 yours ever/ever yours **你永久的朋友(书信结尾时署名前的套语)**

every

1 at every turn **每次,总是,不断地,无例外地**

Because of his drinking, the man was refused a job at every turn. 因为酗酒,他每次谋职都遭到拒绝。

2 each and every/every single/last （强调）**每一个**

Your choices, each and every one, determine how well you feel and how well you are. 是你自己做出的每一个选择,决定了你自己的感受,造就了现在的你。

Sally dropped the box, and when she opened it, every single glass was broken. 萨莉的盒子掉在地上,当她打开时,每一个玻璃杯都碎了。

3 every inch **十足的,地道的,完完全全的**

Victor was every inch a man. 维克托是个十足的男人。

Herry looked every inch a soldier. 亨利看起来真有十足的军人气质。

4 every last man/every man Jack **每一个人**

I want every last man to be here on time tomorrow morning. 我要每一个人明天早晨都要准时到这儿来。

All the workers want a pay increase, every man Jack of them. 全部工人无一例外地要求增加工资。

5 every now and then/now and again/so often/once in a while **经常,时常,重复地;不时,间或,偶尔**

John comes to visit me every now and then. 约翰经常来看我。

It was hot work, but every so often Susan would bring us something cold to drink. 干这工作真热,但苏珊会不时给我们送来冷饮。

6 every time one turns around **经常**

Mr. Winston must be rich. He buys a new suit every time he turns around. 温斯顿先生一定很有钱,他时常添购新西装。

No, Charles—I can't drive you to the park every time I turn around. 不,查尔斯,我不能常常开车送你去公园。

everything

1　everything in the garden is lovely 一切都尽如人意,一切都十分完美

We've just moved to a lovely house; Roger's settled in his job, and Ruth is doing well at school. Everything in the garden is lovely. 我们刚搬进新居,罗杰找到了工作,露丝在学校取得了优异的成绩,一切都尽如人意。

2　have everything 具有各种吸引力(优点、所需之物等)

George has got a new book in mind. It has everything: rich people, a poor but beautiful girl, romance, adventure, etc. 乔治准备写一部新书,故事里有各种吸引人的内容:富人、一个贫穷但美丽的姑娘、风流韵事、冒险经历等。

3　hold everything/it (常用命令式)停止,站住,别动

The pilot was starting to take off when the control tower ordered, "Hold it!" 驾驶员正准备起飞时,控制台命令道:"暂停起飞!"

Hold it, son, where do you think you're going with that picture under your coat? 站住,儿子,你衣服里藏着那张画想到哪儿去?

4　like everything 拼命地,使劲地,有效地

Gray ran like everything. 格雷拼命地跑。

It shook Harrod up like everything. 那件事使哈罗德大为震惊。

exactly

not exactly 【讽】并不,根本不,并没有

Isabel was not exactly pretty ever then. 即使那时伊莎贝尔也并不见得漂亮。

That's not exactly what I had in mind. 我心里想的并不完全是那样。

excuse

1　can/may I be excused 我可以出去一会儿吗(尤指学生想上厕所时)

"Can I be excused, Miss?" "Yes, Jason." "老师,我可以出去一会儿吗?" "可以,杰森。"

2　excuse me 请原谅(用于与陌生人搭话、打断别人说话、从他人身边挤过、表示异议等场合);【美】对不起(用于道歉或没听清对方的话时)

Excuse me, could I come past? 对不起,请让我过去一下。

Excuse me, but isn't that parking place you've put your car in? 劳驾,难道

不是你把车停在那个停车位上的吗?

3 excuses, excuses 总是找借口

"The bus was late, Mr. Faversham. Honest, sir!" "Excuses, excuses, my boy!" "公共汽车晚点了,法弗沙姆先生。是真的,先生。""借口,借口,你总是有借口,孩子!"

expect

1 expect me when you see me 我不能肯定何时回来,说不准我什么时候回来

Sometimes I travel at an hour's notice. My brothers expect me when they see me. 有时候我接到通知一小时内就要外出,我的兄弟们却不知道我什么时候回来。

2 I/we, etc. shall not expect you till I/we, etc. see you 你愿意什么时候回来都可以

eye

1 all (in) the eye/my eye/(that's) all my eye (and Betty Martin) 瞎说,胡说;胡闹

Their opinions are all my eye. 他们的意见完全是胡说八道。

"I'll have finished my work by seven o'clock." "My eye! You'll still be working at midnight!" "我将在七点钟前完成工作。""胡说,我看你会一直干到半夜。"

2 be all eyes 很注意地看,目不转睛

At the circus the children were all eyes. 看马戏时孩子们全神贯注。

3 clap/lay/set eyes on 看,看见

You never clapped your eyes on him before, didn't you? 你以前从未见到过他,对吗?

"How did you know?" he demanded. "You never laid eyes on me before." "你怎么知道的?"他责问道,"你又未见过我。"

4 damn your eyes 真该死,他妈的,混账

5 eyes down 注意(开始玩牌的一种叫法,或学生看见老师来时的警告语)

6 eyes in the back of one's head 脑后长眼睛,神通广大,无所不知

Mother must have eyes in the back of her head, because she always knows when I do something wrong. 母亲真是神通广大,他总是知道我做错的事情。

"You must have eyes in the back of your head—how did you know I'd come in!" "I just knew you had!" "你真是神通广大,怎么知道我进来过?""我就是知道你来过。"

7 an eye for an eye and a tooth for a tooth 以眼还眼,以牙还牙

In ancient times if a man's eye was put out by his enemy, he might get revenge by putting his enemy's eye out. This was the rule of an eye for an eye and a tooth for a tooth. 古时候,如果谁的眼睛被敌人挖出,他可能会挖出敌人的眼睛作为报复。这就是"以眼还眼,以牙还牙"的来历。

8 if you had half an eye 假如你不是瞎子,如果你有一点点洞察力,如果你稍加注意

If you had half an eye, you could be able to make some money from the new contract. 如果你不是那么笨,你就可以从新合同中赚一些钱。

9 meet the eye 被看到,出现在眼前

There's more to the man than meets the eye, she thought. 她想,那人可比外表看到的要复杂些。

"There's more here, sir, however," he said, "than meets the eye. I don't believe in suicide, nor in pure accident, myself." "不过,先生,"他说,"这是表面现象,事实远不止这么多。我自己并不认为是自杀,也不相信完全出于偶然。"

10 mind one's eye 谨慎,小心

Edward would recommend Frederick to mind his eye for the future. 爱德华劝告弗雷德里克,以后要小心行事。

11 my eye/aunt/hat/stars/word/world 天哪,哎呀;瞎说,胡说

"A diamond, my eye!" "That's glass." "什么,钻石!""那是玻璃。"

"My eyes, how green!" exclaimed the young gentleman. "哎哟,多么幼稚!"年轻绅士喊道。

12 one in the eye 令人失望的事,挫折,失败

If Jessie wins the case, it'll be one in the eye for George. 要是杰西赢了这场官司,这对乔治将是一个打击。

F

face

1 face the music 勇敢地面对麻烦和困难；接受处罚

The boy was caught cheating in an examination and had to face the music. 那孩子考试作弊被捉住，必须接受处罚。

The official who had been taking bribes was exposed by a newspaper and had to face the music. 官员受贿被报纸揭发了，他必定要吃官司。

2 let's face it【美】让我们正视现实，我们实话实说吧；不要退缩，尽力对付

Let's face it, Jim, you never were very good at playing the guitar. 实话实说吧，吉姆，你的吉他弹得并不好。

This country has, let's face it, been going downhill for years. 让我们面对现实吧，这个国家近年来一直在走下坡路。

3 not just a pretty face 可是凭的硬本事，不是一只绣花枕头，真看不出来你有这套本领

Gone to university, got a BA and a doctorate—not just a pretty face, are you! 进了大学，取得了学士和博士学位，还真看不出你有这身本事！

4 save face 保全名声，顾全面子

The policeman was caught accepting a bribe; he tried to save face by claiming it was money owed to him. 警员受贿当场被抓，他为保全面子而说是别人欠他的钱。

Bill would not play in the game because he knew he could not do well and he wanted to save face. 比尔不肯加入游戏，因为他知道自己玩不好，所以想顾全面子。

5 shoot off one's face/mouth 胡扯，瞎说；过分渲染；说出想法

Tom has never been to Florida, but he's always shooting his mouth off about how superior Florida is to California. 汤姆从未到过佛罗里达州，但他常瞎说佛罗里达要比加利福尼亚好。

I was to study the problem before I shoot off my face. 在我说出我的想法

之前,我要研究一下这个问题。

6 fall flat on one's face(彻底)失败,一败涂地

What is terrifying is the risk of humiliation, of metaphorically falling flat on one's face. 人们怕的是丢脸的风险,就好像摔个嘴啃泥那样脸面尽失。

fact

1 (and) that's a fact 事实就是这样(用于强调上述事实的真实性)

2 as a matter of fact/for that matter/in (actual/point of) fact 事实上,其实;事实恰恰相反

I didn't go to the club on Saturday. As a matter of fact, I've not been for months. 星期六我没有到俱乐部去。事实上,近几个月来我都没去那里。

3 the fact (of the matter) is 事实上

The fact of the matter is that Juliet does not like work. 事实上朱丽叶不爱工作。

fail

1 don't fail to 务必,一定

Don't fail to write me! 别忘了给我写信。

Don't fail to ring me up! 别忘了给我打电话。

2 never fail to 必定

Longfellow will never fail to come on Sunday. 朗费罗星期天准来。

3 without fail 必定,务必

Be here at 8 o'clock sharp without fail. 务必在八点整到达这儿。

Malan promised to return the bike at certain time without fail. 马伦答应到时一定归还自行车。

4 words fail me (由于惊奇、愤怒或高兴、激动而)说不出话来

Words failed me at the last minute. 到了最后我说不出话来了。

fain

fain(s) I【儿】别叫我干

Fain I! 我不干!

Fain(s) I keeping goal! 可别叫我守球门!

fair

1 fair and softly 轻些，静些；平心静气
Fair and softly goes far! 宁静致远！

2 fair and square 光明正大地，公平合理地
The player won the game fair and square. 那个选手光明正大地赢了这场比赛。

3 fair's fair 办事要公平合理
Fair's fair, children, Paul can stay up late tonight because I let Roger stay up late last night. 孩子们，办事要公平合理。今天晚上保罗可以晚睡，因为我让罗杰昨晚晚睡了。

4 a fair shake 【美】公平对待，机会均等，公平处理，待人以诚
Joe has always given me a fair shake. 乔总是诚实地对待我。

5 (from) fair to middling（常用于回答问候）还好，还过得去，马马虎虎
"How are you?" "Fair to middling." "近来好吗？""马马虎虎，还过得去。"

6 for fair 【美】完完全全，实实在在，极度
What you say is true, for fair! 你说得对，一点没错。

faith

1 by/upon my faith 我担保，千真万确

2 keep (the) faith 信守诺言，忠于信仰或原则
We're reaffirming our commitment to always keep faith with their families. 我们将永远信守我们对他们家人的承诺。

fall

1 fall about 捧腹大笑
We fell about when we saw the child. 我们看到那个孩子的时候禁不住笑了。

2 fall down 失败，未能符合要求
Harper's plan has fallen down. 哈珀的计划已经失败了。
The boss was disappointed when his workers fell down on the job. 老板看到工人干活不卖力感到很失望。

3 fall flat 失败，告吹
The party fell flat because of the rain. 宴会因下雨而告吹。

Jerry's jokes fell flat upon the audience. 杰里的笑话没有赢得观众的笑声。

4 fall for 信以为真，受骗；爱上，迷恋上

We must not fall for such nonsense. 我们绝不能听信这种胡言乱语。

Dick fell for baseball when he was a little boy. 迪克从小就迷上棒球了。

5 fall over each other/one another 互相竞争，争先恐后

His admirers fell over each other with offers of hospitality. 羡慕他的人都争先恐后要宴请他。

6 fall/bend/lean over themselves/backwards 极力讨人喜欢，尽力使人满意；煞费苦心，不遗余力；手足无措

The hotel manager fell over backwards to give the movie star everything she wanted. 旅馆经理对这位电影明星特别关照。

The boys fell over themselves trying to get the new girl's attention. 这些男孩极力设法引起新来女孩的注意。

7 fall through 失败，泡汤，不能实现，不能践约

Jim's plan to go to college fell through at the last moment. 吉姆上大学的计划最后泡汤了。

Mr. Jones' deal to sell his house fell through. 琼斯先生卖房子的交易没有成功。

8 fall up 落下；散落；上楼梯时跌倒

A shell had fallen and while we waited three others fell up the road. 有颗炮弹刚刚落下，而当我们等待的时候，路上又掉下来三颗炮弹。

The old man fell up the stairs. 那个老人上楼梯时跌倒了。

9 fall on one's ear 被某人听到，传到某人的耳朵

10 fall on dead ear 没有听到；不受重视

It seems that the suggestions have fallen on dead ear. 看来这些建议并未受到重视。

fancy

1 fancy his believing it 谁想到他会相信

2 just (only) fancy/fancy (that) 真想不到，真奇怪

It is really raining. Fancy that! 真的在下雨了！真想不到！

Fancy her saying such rude things! 真想不到她会说出这种粗俗的话来！

far

1 far be it from me 我决不会,决不想,决不敢
Far be it from me to condemn him. 我决不会谴责他。
I am acquainted with my faults. Far be it from me to deny them. 我明白自己的缺点,我决不否认。

2 far from it 远非如此,一点也不,绝不是那样,完全相反
I'm not tired—far from it. 我不累,一点也不累。
"You've done very well." "Far from it!" "你干得很出色。""差得远哩!"

3 far out 【美】真了不起,真奇妙
Far out, man! This music's great! 太妙了,伙计! 这音乐美极了!

4 so far, so good 暂时还不错,到目前为止一切顺利(通常指即将有麻烦降临)
The new president has been in office for a year now—so far, so good; but I don't know whether he'll last another year. 新总统上任已一年了,到目前为止一切平安无事。可是我不知道他能否平安地度过下一年。

fare

1 fare you well 再见,祝你平安

2 how fares it with you 近来怎样,你好吗,你近来过得好吗

3 to a fare-you-well 【美】充分,十足,完全,彻底,尽善尽美
The steak was cooked to a fare-you-well. 那块牛排烧得好极了。
Leighton lies to a fare-you-well. 莱顿撒谎手段很高明。

farther

1 I'll be farther if I do/I'll see you farther first 【口】我决不干,我才不干呢,见你的鬼

2 no farther 够了,到此为止
I approved the amusing one's self with poetry now and then, so far as to improve one's language, but no farther. 我赞成偶而写写诗作为消遣,提高自己的语言水平,但是仅此而已。

fast

not so fast 莫慌,等一下(说话人发现有问题)
Not so fast, young man, let me check your ticket. 等一下,年轻人,让我

看看你的票。

fat

1 cut it (too) fat 做得过分；炫耀，卖弄
2 fry in one's own fat 自作自受
3 live on one's own fat 吃老本
4 the fat is in the fire 闯祸了，大祸将临；完蛋了，事情不可收拾

Martin found out you took it? Well, the fat's in the fire now. 马丁知道你拿了它？那你就闯祸了。

father

1 a miserly father makes a prodigal son 有悭吝的父亲，必有败家的儿子
2 like father, like son 有其父必有其子
3 many a good father has but a bad son 慈父多败儿，棍棒出孝子
4 the father (and mother) of a 非常大的，十分严重

There would be the father and mother of a public fuss about it. 这件事会在公众中引起轩然大波。

fault

1 at fault 负有责任，难辞其咎

The driver who didn't stop at the red light was at fault in the accident. 闯红灯的司机应对车祸负责。

When the engine would not start, the mechanic looked at all the parts to find what was at fault. 引擎不能发动，机械师检查各个部分看毛病出在哪里。

2 find fault with 吹毛求疵，指责，批评

Lily tried to please Malan, but he always finds fault with her. 莉莉尽力使马伦高兴，但他对她总爱吹毛求疵。

They found fault with every box I made. 他们对我做的每个箱子都加以指责。

3 to a fault 过分，苛求

Aunt May wants everything in her house to be exactly right; she is neat to a fault. 梅婶婶要求家中每件东西都要整整齐齐地摆放，她的要求太苛刻了。

Kate acts her part to a fault. 凯特把自己的角色演得用力过度了。

favor

1 curry favor with 奉承，讨好，巴结，献媚

Joe tried to curry favor with the new teacher by doing little services that he didn't really want. 乔为了讨好新老师，做了些其实他并不真正想要做的事。

Jim tried to curry favor with the new girl by telling her she was the prettiest girl in the class. 吉姆想讨好新来的女同学，就跟她说她是班上最漂亮的女生。

2 do me/us a favor 请帮帮忙，行行好；对不起，我不相信

Do us a favor, Ken, go and annoy someone else! 行行好，肯，你去烦别人吧！

Do me a favor, John, sit still and stop messing about! 行行好，约翰，安静地坐一会儿，别胡闹了。

fear

1 never fear/have no fear 不用怕，别担心，放心好了

Never fear, I am here. 不用怕，我在这儿。

Have no fear, I'm not going yet. 别担心，我还没走呢！

2 no fear 肯定不会，没有可能，不必担心；当然不，决不

There's no fear of his coming here. 不必担心他到这儿来。

"You didn't agree to go to the States with him, did you?" "No fear! I'm staying right here in London!" "你不同意和他一道去美国，是吗？" "当然不，我就待在伦敦，哪儿也不去！"

feather

1 a feather in one's cap 值得骄傲的事，荣誉

Being promoted Senior Salesman was a real feather in his cap. 被提升为高级售货员真是他极大的荣誉。

It was a feather in his cap to win first prize. 赢得一等奖对他是很大的光荣。

2 crop one's feather 杀……的威风，使……丢脸

3 in fine/grand/good/high feather 身体健康；精神饱满，情绪极佳

For the moment, the members of the team were in fine feather. 此刻，球

队的队员们情绪高昂。

4 knock sb. down with a feather 使某人十分惊奇,吃惊

You could have knocked me down with a feather. 我感到太惊奇了,我太震惊了。

5 make (the) feathers/sparks fly 【美】工作干得起劲;(用激烈的语言等)引起骚乱、争斗或争论

The decision is sure to make the feathers fly. 该项决定肯定会引起争论。
I don't think Adam will give you a break. He'll make the feathers fly. 我想亚当不会让你有喘息的机会,他会给你制造更多的麻烦。

6 not a feather to fly with 一筹莫展;一贫如洗;破产;【俚】(应试)落选,(考试)不及格

7 fine feathers makes fine birds 【谚】马靠鞍装,人靠衣裳;【讽】好的衣服只能使人外表漂亮

8 birds of a feather flock together 物以类聚,人以群分

The saying that "birds of a feather flock together" is very true. 俗话说"物以类聚,人以群分",这话一点儿不假。

feed

be off (one's) feed 胃口不好,食欲不佳

Jane seems to be slightly off her feed today. 今天简好像有点食欲不佳。
Mary was worried her canary was off feed. 玛丽很担心,因为她的金丝雀不吃东西。

feel

1 feel cheap/mean/small 觉得丢脸,感到惭愧

I felt cheap not being able to return their invitation. 我感到惭愧,因为不能报答他们的邀请。

2 feel free 请自便,悉听尊便

"May I sit down here?" "Feel free." "我可以坐在这儿吗?""您请自便。"
Feel free to come and go as you want. 来去悉听尊便。

3 feel funny/seedy/shaky 感觉不舒服;感到好笑

Every time I look at these people, I feel funny, as well as poor. 每次看这些人,我都会感到好笑,还有可怜。

4 feel like 想要

I don't feel like running today. 今天我不想跑步。

I just don't feel like pancakes this morning. 今天早晨我不想吃煎饼。

5 feel like a boiled rag 觉得非常不舒服，感到浑身虚弱无力

I feel like a boiled rag so I won't go to school. 我觉得非常不舒服，所以不想去上学了。

6 feel like a fighting cock 觉得精力充沛，觉得能胜任

7 feel like a fish out of water 感到不自在，感到不得其所

I feel like a fish out of water among those high-society people. 和那些上流社会的人在一起，我感到很不自在。

8 feel like a million dollars　参见 dollar 1

9 feel like/quite oneself 觉得自在舒畅，觉得身体正常

10 feel up to 觉得可以胜任，觉得可以应付

William doesn't feel up to the job. 威廉觉得胜任不了这项工作。

feeling

1 I know the feeling 我有同感，我有相同的经历

"I realised that the other people being interviewed were more qualified than me." "I know the feeling. It was like that when I went for a job once." "我意识到其他的应征者都比我强。""我有同感，这就像我有一次外出求职时的心情一样。"

2 no hard feelings 我不怪你，我不生你的气（用于比赛后向对手做的友好表示）

At last I've finished in front of you after all these months of running—no hard feelings, are there? 跑了几个月以后，我终于在你前面跑完了全程，你不见怪吧？

fig

1 a fig for 这有什么了不起的

A fig for housework! 家务活算得了什么！

2 not care a fig【口】毫不在乎，丝毫不感兴趣，毫不介意

She does not care a fig more for one creature than for another, and is equally on the side of both, or perhaps it would be better to say she does not care a fig for either. 她不会对一种动物的关注胜过另一种动物，她对谁都是公平的，或者毋宁说她对任何一方都毫不关心。

3 not worth a fig 毫不足取，一文不值

You can forget his offer of help; it's not worth a fig. 你可以把他主动提供帮助的事忘掉，因为那毫无价值。

figure

1 cut/make a (fine/good/brilliant/dashing) figure 崭露头角，引人注目，超群出众

The young soldier cut a fine figure in his smart new uniform. 这名年轻士兵穿上崭新的制服，看起来一表人才。

No doubt he'd been looking forward to the wedding ever since it was announced, as an invaluable chance to cut a figure and do some good public relations work. 毫无疑问，打从婚礼的消息宣布之日起，他就期望这一天的到来，认为这是崭露头角和扩大社会关系的极宝贵的机会。

2 cut/make a poor/sorry/bad figure 出丑，出洋相，显得很不像样

Ronaldo was the typical player you hoped never to face, he could make every defender cut a poor figure. 罗纳尔多是那种典型的你永远不想交手的球员，他能让每一个防守队员丢尽颜面。

3 cut no figure【美】默默无闻

4 do things on the big figure【美俚】大干特干，大规模地干某事

5 go/come the big/whole figure【美】干到底，彻底地干；摆阔气；出风头

If you are getting a new amplifier, why don't you go the big figure and replace everything? 要是你打算买一个新的扬声器，何不干脆将全套设备换成新的？

6 miss a/one's figure【美俚】失算，铸成大错

7 that/it figures【美】不错，有道理，合乎情理；活该，本该这样

I suppose it figures. 我想这是合乎情理的。
Sure, that figures. 没错，那是合乎情理的。

find

1 find what o'clock it is 查明事实真相

2 how do you find yourself 你觉得好吗，你近来怎么样

finder

finders keepers (, losers weepers)【儿语】谁人找到谁人要

I don't have to give it back; it's *finders keepers*. 这是我找到的,谁人找到谁人要嘛。

Finders keepers, losers weepers! It's my knife now! 我找到了小刀,小刀归我啦。

fine

1 all very fine 好倒是好,固然不错

That's *all very fine*, but what about me? 好倒是好,可我怎么办呢?

2 cut/run it fine 做出精确的计算,做出精细的区分;(空间、时间、金钱等)几乎不留余地

These two words have almost the same meaning. Can you *cut it fine*? 这两个词的意思几乎相同。你能区分其中的差异吗?

finger

1 burn one's fingers/get one's fingers burned 吃过亏,有前车之鉴

Jackson *had burned his fingers* in the stock market once, and didn't want to try again. 杰克逊曾在股市吃过亏,所以再也不尝试了。

Some people can't be told; they have to *burn their fingers* to learn. 有些人不听劝告,直到吃了亏才会学乖。

2 have/stick a/one's finger in the/every pie 参与其事,多管闲事;干涉

When the girls got up a Christmas party, I felt sure Alice *had a finger in the pie*. 只要是女孩子们筹备的圣诞舞会,我确信爱丽丝一定会参与其事。

The Jones Company was chosen to build the new hospital and we knew Mr. Smith *had a finger in the pie*. 琼斯公司负责承建医院一事,我们知道史密斯先生个中必有关照。

3 lay a finger on sb./sth. 触碰,干扰(用于否定、疑问句或条件句)

Don't you dare *lay a finger on the vase*! 你敢碰一下这花瓶,我就对你不客气!

If you so much as *lay a finger on my boy*, I'll call the police. 你如果敢动我儿子一根毫毛,我就叫警察来。

4 lay/put one's finger on sth./the right spot 正确了解,准确判断;准确指出,击中要害

The engineers couldn't *put their fingers on the reason* for the rocket's failure to orbit. 工程师们找不出火箭不能进入轨道运行的原因。

We called in a electrician hoping he could put a finger on the cause of the short circuit. 我们找来一位电工,希望他能找出短路的原因。

5 my little finger told me 我当然知道;我有一种预感

My little finger told me that. 我有一种预感。

6 work one's fingers to the bone 不停地干活,竭尽全力

Mary and John worked their fingers to the bone to get the house ready for the party. 玛丽和约翰为张罗举办舞会而竭尽全力。

Mr. Brown worked his fingers to the bone to make enough money to buy a new car. 布朗先生为赚钱买新车而拼命工作。

fire

fire away 说吧,有问题就问吧(常用于祈使句);开始讲,连续地问;口头攻击

Fire away. We're all listening. 开始讲吧,我们都在听。

It's useless to fire away with such trivial details. 喋喋不休地谈这些琐碎的细节是无用的。

first

1 at first sight/blush/at/in/on the first face/gaze/at the first glance 一见就,乍看起来,一见之下

At first blush the offer looked good, but when we studied it, we found things we could not accept. 乍见之下该项建议似乎不错,但经研究才发现我们无法接受。

At first sight, his guess was that the whole trouble between the two men resulted from personalities that did not agree. 一见之下他猜想这两个人的所有问题都源自性格不合。

2 first come, first served 先到者先招待

Get in line for your ice cream, boys. First come, first served. 孩子们,先到者先招待,排队来取你们的冰激凌。

The rule in the restaurant is first come, first served. 餐馆的规矩是先来先招待。

3 first off/first at all/first and foremost 首先,第一

First off, I want you to mow the lawn. 第一件事,我要你去给草坪除草。

I want you to remember to pay that bill first and foremost. 首先我要你们记得付账。

4 first things first 最重要的事先做

Study your lessons before you go out to play. First things first. 在你出去玩之前最重要的是先把功课做好。

Anna was uncapable of putting first things first. 安娜处理事情不分轻重缓急。

5 (the) first thing 首先

First thing in the morning I open the window and let in some fresh air. 早上我首先打开窗户，让新鲜空气进来。

I must do that first thing. 我必须先做那件事。

fish

1 a fine/nice/pretty kettle of fish 真是乱七八糟，真是糟糕透顶

Camilla had two flat tires and no spare on a country road at night, which was certainly a pretty kettle of fish. 在夜间的乡村道路上，卡米拉的两个轮胎都瘪了，又没有备用的，真是糟糕透顶。

This is a fine kettle of fish! I forgot my book. 糟糕透顶，我忘了带书了。

2 have other/bigger fish to fry 另有重要的事要干，另有他图

They wanted John to be the secretary, but he had other fish to fry. 他们要约翰当秘书，但他另有打算。

Mary was invited to the party but she refused because she had other fish to fry. 玛丽虽然被邀请参加舞会，但她不去，因为她另外有事。

3 feel like a fish out of water 参见 feel 7

4 not the only fish in the sea/not the only pebble on the beach 并非仅有，并不稀罕

Benjamin said he could find other girls—she was not the only fish in the sea. 本杰明说他可以找别的女孩——她又不是绝无仅有的。

George was acting pretty self-important, and we finally had to tell him that he wasn't the only pebble on the beach. 乔治相当自满，最后我们只好告诉他，像他这样的人才多得是。

5 there's/there are as good fish in the sea as ever came out of it 有水何患无鱼；机会有的是

Hey, cheer up, there's as good fish in the sea as ever came out of it. 嘿，振作起来，有水何患无鱼，机会有的是。

6 fish in troubled water 浑水摸鱼

A man of good character will not fish in troubled water. 一个高尚的人是不会混水摸鱼的。

Never fish in troubled water. 不要混水摸鱼，趁火打劫。

fist

1 make a good fist at sth. 把某事做得很好

Peter reckoned he should make a better fist at farming than educating. 彼得认为自己搞农业会比教育更成功。

2 make a poor fist at sth. 把某事做得很糟

fit

1 beat/knock sb. into fits 把某人打得落花流水，轻易地打败某人

2 go into fits（因癫痫病等）昏过去

3 by fits and starts 断断续续地；三天打鱼，两天晒网

Anthony had worked on the invention by fits and starts for several years. 安东尼断断续续地从事发明已经很多年了。

You cannot learn a foreign language working by fits and starts. 一曝十寒学不好外语。

4 fit out/up 供给，装备，布置

The soldiers were fitted out with guns and clothing. 这些军人获得了枪支和衣物的供给。

The government fitted out warships and got sailors for them. 政府供给他们战舰和水兵。

5 fit to be tied【美】十分恼火，暴跳如雷；非常，极力地，强烈地，剧烈地

The CEO looked fit to be tied. 那个首席执行官看上去气得要命。

6 fit to kill【美】极度地，大大地，十分显眼地

The girl dresses up fit to kill even to go out shopping. 那个姑娘其至外出购物，也打扮得花枝招展。

7 give sb. a fit/fits 使某人大吃一惊；使某人大发脾气

8 have/throw/take a fit/fits 大吃一惊；大发脾气

Howard will have a fit when he learns that he lost the election. 当霍华德

得知他落选后，他一定会非常生气。

9　see/think fit (to do) 决定，选择

The President has seen fit to let the prisoner go free. 总统已决定释放那名囚犯。

You could do whatever you saw fit. 你想要做什么就可以做什么。

10　survival of the fittest 适者生存

Life in the old West was often a case of survival of the fittest. 昔日西部时代是一种适者生存的世界。

With changes in the world's climate, dinosaurs died but many smaller animals lived on. It was survival of the fittest. 随着世界气候的改变，恐龙灭绝了，但很多小动物仍生存着，这便是适者生存。

fix

1　be in a (pretty) fix/get oneself into a bad fit 处境困难，进退两难

Bless my heart! We are in a fix. 天呀！我们真是进退两难。

2　fix it【美】处理，修复

Then he would introduce me and I'd tell people what we intended to do to fix it. 然后他将我介绍给人们，我将告诉大家我们会采取什么措施来处理这些问题。

3　fix up 修理，修补；安顿，照应；整理，安排；解决，商妥，约定；设法提供；打扮

We were fixed up for the night in a hotal. 我们被安顿在一家旅馆过夜。

I have fixed up with Johnson to meet them at seven o'clock tomorrow evening. 我已和约翰逊约定明晚七点会见他们。

flat

1　(and) that's flat 确定不移，绝对如此

I won't go, and that's flat. 我不会去，那是确定无疑的。

I will not go to your mother-in-law's, and that's flat. 我不会去你岳母家，绝对不去。

2　fall flat 参见 fall 3

3　in nothing flat/no time 迅速地，很快地

When the entire class worked together they finished the project in no time. 全班一起动手，他们很快把这个项目做完了。

The driver got us to the station in nothing flat. 司机很快把我们送到了车站。

flatter

1 feel oneself's highly flattered 得意扬扬，扬扬自得
2 flatter oneself 自信，自以为是，确信
I flatter myself that I am a better swimmer than he is. 我确信我的游泳技术比他高明。
The player flattered herself that she might win the prize. 那个选手自信会获奖。
3 you flatter yourself 你太自信了，你对自己评价过高
"I wonder if they'll invite me to the cocktail party." "You flatter yourself—why should they invite you?" "我不知道他们会不会邀请我参加鸡尾酒会。""你别异想天开，他们为什么要邀请你？"

fling

1 fling/throw oneself at one's head/feet 极力讨好；（女子）勾引某人，接受某人求婚；公开对某人表示爱慕
2 have/take a fling at sb. 嘲笑/讽刺/挖苦某人；尝试；攻击
The excited fans had a fling at the lost team. 情绪激动的球迷们嘲笑输球的球队。
3 have one's/a fling 尽情放荡，花天酒地
We quite often have our fling down at the pub after a hard day's work. 一天劳累之后我们常在小酒馆内尽情寻欢作乐。

floor

1 get/be let in on the ground floor 【美】在有利条件下参加某种事业；以与发起人同样优先的资格入股
Well, now, if you'd have come along here ten or fifteen years ago you might have got in on the ground floor. 哎呀，假使你在十年或者十五年前来到这儿的话，你可能在许多生意上和创办人站在同等地位上了。
2 mop/wipe (up) the floor with 把……打得大败
Our team wiped the floor with the visiting team. 我队大胜客队。
The bully threatened to mop up the floor with Billy. 这个恶棍威胁比利说

要揍扁他。

flume

go/be up the flume【美】垮台；落空
Well, then, that idea's up the flume. 那么，这计划就落空了。

flush

flush it【美】(表示轻蔑、不相信)见鬼去吧；失败，不及格
I started to explain, but the cop told me to flush it. 我刚开始解释，那警察就叫我闭嘴。
I really flushed it in my maths course. 我的数学真的考砸了。

fly

1 a/the fly in the ointment 美中不足之处；使人扫兴的小事；一粒老鼠屎坏一锅汤
I enjoy my job—the fly in the ointment is that I start early in the morning. 我喜欢我的工作，美中不足的是我得很早动身。
We had a lot of fun at the beach, the only fly in the ointment was George's cutting his foot on a piece of glass. 在海滨我们玩得很愉快，美中不足的是乔治被玻璃割伤了脚。

2 a fly on the wheel 狂妄自大的人
Come, confess, both of you! You were only flies on the wheel. 来来，你们两人，自己承认吧，你们都是些狂妄自大的人。

3 don't let flies stick to your heels 快点，别慢腾腾的

4 there are no flies on sb./sth. 机灵，识时务，可靠；(某事)很正当，无可指摘
There are no flies on old Harold. 老哈罗德是个很机灵的人。
You can't get through without showing your ticket to old Parley, you know—there are no flies on him. 你不把票给老帕里看是进不去的，你知道，他可是个机灵鬼。

5 fly around 匆忙地走来走去；四处飞
They'll fly around and drop bombs. 它们到处飞，还会投掷炸弹。

6 fly high/fly at high game 有雄心壮志，野心勃勃；情绪高昂；繁荣昌盛
Aren't you flying high, hoping for a place in the first team? 你希望进甲级

队,这难道不是雄心壮志吗?

Hamilton was *flying high* after his team won the game. 汉密尔顿欢欣鼓舞,因为他的球队大获全胜。

7 fly in the face/teeth of 忽视,罔顾;不屑;反对,反抗,违抗

You can't *fly in the face of* good business rules and expect to be successful. 违反良好的商业规则,你是不会成功的。

Floyd's friends tried to help him, but he *flew in the teeth of* their advice and soon became a drunkard. 弗洛伊德的朋友想帮助他改正错误,但他无视他们的忠告,不久就沦为一个酒鬼。

8 fly low 销声匿迹;谦卑

Those robbers are now *flying low* somewhere in Europe. 那些强盗目前正藏匿在欧洲某处。

9 fly/go off at a tangent 说话离题;突然改变行径

Don't *fly off at a tangent*, stick to the subject. 紧扣主题,不要东拉西扯。

10 fly/go/slip off the handle 勃然大怒,大发雷霆;【俚】死去;十分激动;失去控制

John *flew off the handle* whenever Mary made a mistake. 每当玛丽做错事,约翰便勃然大怒。

The children's noise made the men next door *fly off the handle*. 孩子们的吵闹声惹得邻居们大发脾气。

11 fly the coop 越狱;潜逃;开溜

The robbers *flew the coop* before the police arrived. 劫匪在警察到来之前就逃走了。

His partner *flew the coop* with all the money. 他的同伙卷款而逃。

12 go fly a kite 【美俚】走开,去你的

Harry was tired of John's advice and told him to *go fly a kite*. 哈里厌烦了约翰的唠叨,于是叫他走开。

After Mary stood around telling Sue what was wrong with her dress, Sue told her to *go fly a kite*. 玛丽喋喋不休地挑苏衣服上的毛病,苏气得叫她走开。

fob

fob off(以假充真)骗人;鱼目混珠;搪塞;哄走

It is not right to fob off a worthless article upon a customer. 把劣质货物卖给顾客是不对的。

Herbert fobbed me off with promises that he never intended to keep. 赫伯特用不想兑现的诺言把我搪塞开了。

fog

in a fog/haze 困惑，头脑昏沉

After three pitchers of beer I was in a fog. 三罐啤酒下肚，我头脑昏沉。

I didn't vote for Alice because she always seems to be in a fog. 我没有投爱丽丝的票，因为她看起来总是稀里糊涂的。

foggy

not have the foggiest/faintest/first/remotest (idea) 完全不知道

I haven't the foggiest (idea) why he left so suddenly. 我根本不知道他为什么突然离开。

"How long will it take you to do this work?" "I haven't the faintest." "你干这活得多长时间？""我不知道。"

follow

follow that 真了不起，不可思议；我办不到

"That's the answer to the problem. I'm sure you're all surprised at how easy it all was." "Follow that, Jim!" "这就是这道难题的答案，我想你们一定都会惊讶答案是多么的简单。""吉姆，真了不起！"

food

food for thought 使人担忧；引人深思

The teacher told John that she wanted to talk to his father, and that gave John food for thought. 老师告诉约翰她想和他的父亲谈谈，这使约翰忧心忡忡。

Her lecture gave us much food for thought. 她的演讲给我们提出了许多引人深思的问题。

fool

1 fool/mess/play/monkey around 闲逛，胡混；摆弄；粗心大意；虚度光阴

You don't have any time to fool around. 你没有时间到处闲逛。

If you go to college, you must work, not fool around. 你要是上了大学就得好好用功,不要浪费时间。

2 fool/fritter away 浪费,挥霍;虚度

Paul failed history because he fooled away his time instead of studying. 保罗不好好学习,虚度光阴,因而历史考试不及格。

The man won a lot of money, but he soon frittered it away and was poor again. 这人赢了一大笔钱,但不久他就挥霍干净,再受穷困。

3 fool with 瞎弄;戏弄

Don't fool with that razor. 别玩弄那把剃刀。

4 (the) more fool you/him, etc. 你/他等真傻

More fool you for believing him; you should have known he only wanted your money. 你真傻,竟然相信他,要知道,他只是想要你的钱。

"Darrin's just eaten some strange berries." "More fool him. They could be poisonous!" "达林刚刚吃了一些奇怪的浆果。""他真傻,那可能是有毒的呀!"

foot

1 at one's feet/at the feet of 拜倒在……的脚下(表示钦佩、服从、忠诚或求爱)

Her voice kept audiences at her feet for years. 多年来她的歌声一直使观众为之倾倒。

The country lies at the feet of the dictator. 那个国家受独裁者统治。

2 catch sb. on the wrong foot 使某人措手不及,乘人不备

Tom caught me on the wrong foot—I left all my money at home. 汤姆令我措手不及——我的钱都留在家里。

3 Christ's foot 哎呀,天哪,好家伙,糟糕

4 die on one's feet 垮掉,失败;(非正式)突然死亡,早逝,夭折

It's better to die on one's feet than live on one's knees. 宁可站着死,也不跪着生。

5 fall on one's feet 安然摆脱困境;运气好

You'll fall on your feet all right. 你将会安然摆脱困境。

6 get/have a foot in/into the door 获得机会,参加

Maltz has already got a foot into the door. 马尔兹已经加入进来了。

They tried to get a foot into the theatre's door. 他们试图进入戏剧界。

7　get one's feet wet 开始参加，初试

It's no hard to dance once you get your feet wet. 跳舞不难，一学就会。

8　get/have cold feet 害怕起来，胆怯起来

Newman urged me to go ahead, not to faint or get cold feet. 纽曼催我往前走，别软弱、别胆怯。

Ralph was going to ask Mary to dance with him, but he got cold feet and didn't. 拉尔夫想邀请玛丽同他跳舞，但由于胆怯而最终错失了良机。

9　land on one's/both feet 安然脱离困境；总会成功

No matter what trouble he gets into, Oscar always seems to land on his feet. 奥斯卡无论遇到什么困难，似乎总能克服。

Mary lost her first job because she was always late to work, but she landed on her feet and soon had a better job. 玛丽因为经常迟到而失去了第一份工作，但她未受影响，不久她获得了更好的工作。

10　my foot 那才怪呢，算了吧，去你的吧（不相信对方的话）

"This is glass, isn't it?" "Glass, my foot! It's made of plastic—can't you see?" "这是玻璃的吧？""玻璃的，得了吧，这是塑料的，难道你看不出来？"

Raglan didn't know, my foot! Of course he knew! 拉格伦不知道？去他的吧！他当然知道。

11　off one's feet 躺着；坐着；脚不沾地

The patient has to stay off his feet. 这个病人只能躺着。

I was run off my feet with jobs to do. 我有许多事要做，忙得脚不沾地。

12　on the right foot 开始就顺利，打响头一炮，开张大吉，开门红

It was important for me to get off on the right foot with the Democratic leaders. 对我来说，在与民主党领导人的交往中取得良好的开端是很重要的。

13　(get off) on the wrong foot 出师不利，处于不利地位

When Joe went to his new job, he got off on the wrong foot—on the first morning he upset his new boss by arriving at the store two hours late. 乔找到了一份新的工作，可是他刚开始到那家店里去上班就给人一个坏印象。第一天上班他就迟到了两个小时，让他的老板很不高兴。

14　pull foot 逃走，跑开

The ruffian pulled foot. 那个无赖拔腿就跑。

15 pull/draw one's foot/leg 开玩笑

The college student said,"My roommate said this girl had told him she wouldn't mind going out with me. But when I invited her to a movie, I learned he was just pulling my leg." 这个大学生说:"我的室友说,那个女孩愿意和我一起出去玩。可是,当我请她去看电影的时候,我才发现他是开我的玩笑。"

16 put one's best foot forward/formost 全力以赴;全速前进;尽可能给人以好的印象

When Sam applied for the job, he put his best foot forward. 申请这份工作时山姆尽可能给人以好的印象。

If you put your best foot forward, you'll reach the hotel before the evening. 如果你以最快的速度前进,在天黑前就可以到达旅馆。

17 put one's feet up 双腿平放,休息

If you are feeling tired, come and put your feet up. 如果你感到疲倦,就休息一会儿。

18 put one's foot down 表现坚定,行动果断;坚持不懈

Sophy put her foot down, forcing her family to sanction her engagement. 索菲坚持己见,迫使她的家人同意她的婚约。

This has gone far enough, he's going to put his foot down. 这做得太过火了,他坚决不再让步。

19 put one's foot in/into it/one's mouth 陷入窘境;弄糟,闯祸;中伤,出言不逊

I beg your pardon, I'm always putting my foot in it. 请原谅,我总是闯祸。

Tracy put her foot in her mouth with her joke about that church, not knowing that one of the guests belonged to it. 特雷西拿教堂开玩笑时陷入窘境,她不知道其中一位客人是那所教堂的教友。

20 sweep off one's feet 使人激动不已,令人倾心,令人狂喜

The handsome football captain swept Joan off her feet when he said so many things to her at the dance. 这位英俊潇洒的足球队长在舞会上的一席话赢得了琼的芳心。

The officer swept Mary off her feet. 这位军官使玛丽倾心不已。

21 think on one's feet 思维敏捷;行为果断,行动迅速

A good basketball player can think on his feet. 一个好的篮球运动员能够

当机立断。

Our teacher can think on his feet, he always has an answer ready when we ask him questions. 我们的老师思维敏捷,当我们问他问题时,他总是成竹在胸。

22 with both feet【美】完全,全然,十足,彻底,坚决

A radical is a man with both feet firmly planted in the air. 激进分子就是完全不讲实际的人。

As soon as permission to attack arrived, the company jumped in with both feet. 获准进攻的消息一到,该连队便迅速地行动起来。

for

1 for crying out loud【美】真想不到,有这种事;真见鬼;去你的吧;哎哟

For crying out loud, haven't you finished that book yet? 哎哟,你还没有看完那本书吗?

2 for one 至少

Roy for one will never do such a thing. 至少罗伊不会这样做。

3 Oh/O for 要是能有……该多好啊

Oh for a cold beer! 要是能喝一杯冰啤酒多好啊!

Oh for wings! 要是能展翅高飞该多好啊!

forbid

God/Heaven/the Saints/Lord forbid 但愿别这样,绝不会这样,千万不要这样

God forbid that the dam break and flood the village! 愿上帝保佑堤坝不要溃堤淹没那个村庄。

God forbid that you should ever regret your marriage. 但愿你结婚后永不后悔。

forget

1 forget (about) it【美】不必在意,别提它了;休想,不可能

Forget it, she never did intend to go. 别抱希望,她根本就不打算去。

If you're after the manager's job when you've only been here for two months, forget it! 你刚来这儿才两个月,就想谋求经理这一职位,休想!

2 forget oneself 失态,忘形;先人后己,忘我,不自私;心不在焉

Walter knew he should hold his temper, but because of the trouble he forgot himself and began to shout. 沃尔特知道应当克制自己,可是因为出现了困难而失态,开始大叫起来。

3　not forgetting 包括……在内

This song has been requested for Bill, Maggie, and little Tom, not forgetting Fido the dog. 这首歌送给比尔、玛吉和小汤姆,还有小狗费多。

forgive

1　forgive me/my..., but... 请原谅,可是……

Forgive me, but I think you're wrong. 对不起,可是我想是你错了。

Forgive my ignorance, but just who is it you're talking about? 请原谅我的无知,请问你刚才谈到的那个人到底是谁?

2　forgive and forget 尽释前嫌,不记前仇,既往不咎

After the argument, the boys decided to forgive and forget. 一场争论之后,男孩子们决定不记前仇。

Come on now, forgive and forget. 得啦,别记仇啦。

3　may you be forgiven 这是可原谅的,这没什么关系

"Sheila really is a very nasty piece of work!" "May you be forgiven—she's one of the nicest people I know!" "希拉真是令人讨厌!" "怎么可能,她是我认识的最和善的人之一。"

fork

fork over/out/up (不情愿地)交出,付出,付款

Wesley had to fork over fifty dollars to have the car repaired. 韦斯利得付50美元修车。

You'll have to fork out on payday. 你得在发薪日付款。

fortune

1　a small fortune 一大笔钱

Those jewels must have cost a small fortune. 那些首饰一定值一大笔钱。

2　make a/one's fortune 发财,发迹

No one's ever gone into teaching to make a fortune. 没有人当教师是为了发财的。

3　push one's fortune 力图发迹,设法提高自己的社会地位;拼命赚取财富

4 seek one's fortune （外出）寻找发迹的机会
Tommy left the farm to seek his fortune in the city. 汤米离开农场去城里寻找发迹的机会。
5 try one's fortune 碰运气

forty

like forty 【美】非常猛烈地；非常厉害地
The warder whipped him like forty. 监狱看守狠命地鞭打了他一顿。

fox

1 crazy like/as a fox 参见 crazy 1
2 play the fox 耍滑头，假装；行为狡猾
With foxes, we must play the fox. 遇到狐狸时，我们一定要比狐狸还狡猾。

fraction

to a fraction 地地道道的，百分之百的
Spenser is truthful, faithful and honest to a fraction. 斯宾塞是个地地道道的忠诚、老实、可靠的人。
This place suited him to a fraction. 这地方百分之百地合他的心意。

free

1 be free, white and/over twenty-one 是个行动不受约束的人
2 be free with 滥用；慷慨地给予
Buck's free with his money. 巴克花钱大手大脚。
I would advice you not to be so free with your tongue. 我劝你别那么信口开河。
3 for free/free, gratis, and for nothing 【美】免费（常含幽默意味）
Hey, you guys, look at this balloon! They're for free down at the new store. 喂，小伙子们，来看看这个气球，这是那家新开张的商店免费赠送的。
They got a great lunch for free. 他们没花钱，中午饱餐了一顿。
4 free and easy 不受拘束的，潇洒的，自由散漫的，随便的；不拘形式的聚会，文娱晚会

Davy was a frequenter of free and easies. 戴维经常参加不拘形式的聚会。
They were free and easy with their money and it was soon gone. 他们花钱大手大脚,那笔钱不久便被挥霍殆尽。

5 free hand 行动自由;自主行事
Profitable ones will have a free hand in setting their medical service prices. 营利性医疗机构医疗服务价格放开。
Roy is the expert so they gave him a free hand to sort out the problem. 罗伊是专家,因此他们让他可以不受约束地处理那个问题。

6 freeload 吃白食,寄人篱下,寄生虫;爱占便宜的人
When are you guys going to stop freeloading and do some work? 你们什么时候停止寄人篱下的生活,自己干点儿事?

7 free rein 随心所欲
The king had free rein in his country. 国王在国内可以随心所欲、为所欲为。
Father is strict with the children, but mother gives them free rein. 父亲对孩子很严厉,母亲对他们很宽松。

8 make free with 擅自取用;行动放肆,粗鲁无礼
Bob makes free with his roommate's clothes. 鲍勃擅自穿室友的衣服。
The girls don't like Ted because he makes free with them. 女孩子们不喜欢泰德,因为他对她们粗鲁无礼。

French

pardon my French 请原谅我言语粗鲁
Pardon my French, but can you turn that radio down a bit, please. 对不起,你能不能把收音机声音开小一点?

fresh

be fresh out of【美】刚用完,刚卖完
We were fresh out of tomatoes. 我们刚卖完西红柿。
Fielding was fresh out of words. 菲尔丁无话可说。

friend

1 some of my/your, etc. best friends are... 我的/你的等一些最好的朋友恰好就是……的一种人(用于幽默地回答对某一类型人的无理指责)

"I can't stand Spaniards!" "Some of my best friends are Spaniards!" "我看不惯那些西班牙人!""我的几个最好的朋友正是西班牙人!"

2 (to) absent friends 为远方朋友的健康干杯

At the college reunion, the president called a toast, "To absent friends!" 在学校举行的聚会上,校长举杯说:"为今天未到场的远方朋友的健康干杯!"

3 we're just good friends 我们只是朋友关系

At the airport, as the two film stars flew off to Brazil together, they told the waiting reporters, "We're just good friends!" 在机场上当两位影星同机飞往巴西时,他们对等候在那里的记者们说:"我们只是好朋友而已。"

4 what's... between friends 朋友之间,这算得了什么

"Let me pay for the petrol." "What's a few pounds between friends?" "让我来付汽油钱吧。""朋友之间,这点钱算得了什么?"

frill

1 cut down frills 不摆架子,不装腔作势

2 put on (one's) frills 摆架子,装腔作势

I shouldn't have thought a missionary was such a big bug that he could afford to put on frills. 我以为一个海外传教士不该是这样一位大亨,居然摆出这副臭架子来。

frog

1 a big frog in a small pond 井底之蛙,小地方的要人,小组织的头目

As company president, Ferdinand had been a big frog in a small pond, but he was not so important as a new congressman in Washington. 费迪南德不过是一个小公司的董事长,还比不上华盛顿的新任国会议员重要。

2 a little/small frog in a big pond 无足轻重的人

In a large company, even a fairly successful man is likely to feel like a little frog in a big pond. 在大公司里即使是一个颇有成就的人也会觉得自己微不足道。

When Bill transferred to a large high school, he found himself a small frog in a big pond. 比尔转学到一所较大的中学后发现自己在这里无足轻重。

3 have a frog in one's throat 说话有点沙哑

I'm sorry I've a frog in my throat. It's this cold I've had all week. 对不

起,我说话有点沙哑,是一周来的感冒引起的。

front

1 front and center(口令)出列;(命令……)快去
Front and center, Smith. The boss wants to see you. 史密斯,快去吧,老板要见你。

2 get in front of oneself【美】赶紧,赶快;弄不清楚

3 out front 在门外,在观众中
Freeman sat at the little desk out front of professor Hill's office. 弗里曼坐在希尔教授办公室门外的小桌旁。
My family are out front this evening. 今晚我们全家都去看戏。

4 put a bold front on 勇敢地对待,表现出勇敢的样子,装出大胆的样子
Katharine was a shy girl, but she put a bold front on and went to the party. 凯瑟琳是个害羞的女孩子,然而她却装出一副勇敢的样子去参加聚会。

5 up front 在最前面的位置,在前线;公开地;预先
Grey sat on a seat up front. 格雷坐在最前面的座位上。
The company financed a project up front. 这家公司公开资助一个项目。

fruit

1 eat/swallow the bitter fruit of 自食恶果
They will have to swallow the bitter fruit of the war one day. 将来他们将不得不吞下战争的苦果。

2 forbidden fruit is sweet 禁果分外甜
While forbidden fruit is said to taste sweeter, it usually spoils faster. 虽然禁果据说尝起来更甜,但它烂起来也更快。

3 old fruit 喂,老兄(对好朋友的称呼)

fuck

1 come on, for fuck's sake 行啦,看他妈的老天的份上

2 fuck a duck 去你的(表示惊讶、不信、拒绝等)

3 fuck it 他妈的,算了吧,别啰唆(表示吃惊、讨厌)

4 fuck off 走开,滚开,别惹人讨厌
If you don't like it, you can just fuck off. 如果你不喜欢,就滚吧!

5 fuck you/Charley（表示拒绝）滚你妈的蛋，去你妈的

full

1 as full as an egg is of meat/【美】as full as a tick 吃得酒足饭饱的；喝得酩酊大醉的

Little Billy ate and ate until he was as full as a tick. 小比利吃呀吃，肚皮都快要撑破了。

2 at (the) full 完全的，完整的，充分的

Lancelot recited his own sufferings at full length. 兰斯洛特详尽地叙述了自己的苦处。

3 full of it/the Old Nick/the devil 老惹事的，顽皮的；有满肚子新闻的；胡扯

I think you are full of it! 我想你是在胡说八道。

4 full out/tilt 全速的，快速的

Harry was riding his motorcycle full out. 哈里当时正骑摩托全速前进。
Jordan ran full tilt into the door and broke his arm. 乔丹飞快地冲进门而折断了手臂。

5 in full 全速地，全部地，全文地

The bill was marked "Pay in full". 账单上写着："全部付清。"
The hotel can meet requirements of the guests in full. 这家旅馆能满足客人的全部要求。

6 in full blast/play/swing 正在炽烈之际，正起劲，正在紧张进行，正积极进行中

The meeting was in full swing when Sapir arrived. 当萨皮尔到那里的时候会议开得正热烈。
The Valentine party was in full swing. 情人节庆祝会正热烈进行中。

7 to the full 完全地，充分地，彻底地，非常

Use your abilities to the full. 充分发挥你的才能吧。
We appreciated to the full the teacher's help. 我们非常感谢老师的帮助。

fun

1 for fun/for the fun of it/the thing/in fun/out of fun 闹着玩地，开玩笑似地

Palmer's learning French for fun. 帕尔默学法语是为了好玩。

2 fun and games 嬉戏，寻欢作乐；特别困难的工作

The fun and games are over—now it's time to work. 玩过了，现在该工作了。

I was sick of their fun and games. 我讨厌透了他们的打打闹闹。

3 like fun 奋力地，很快地，非常；【美】决不会，当然不会

The bolts went to like fun. 门闩闩得很紧。

Pearson told us he finished the exam in an hour. Like fun he did! 皮尔逊告诉我们他在一小时内就考完了。他考得完才怪呢！

4 make fun of/poke fun at 拿……开玩笑

Rebecca realized she was being made fun of. 丽贝卡意识到自己正被人取笑。

Don't poke fun at us! 别拿我们开玩笑！

funeral

1 it's/that's his/her/your funeral 这是他/她/你的事，这事由他/她/你负责

If you break into the factory, it's your funeral—don't expect us to help you if you're caught. 你要是闯进这家工厂，你就得倒霉了。一旦被抓住，别指望我们来帮你的忙。

If you get lost in the desert, that's your funeral. 如果你在沙漠里迷了路，那你就要倒霉了。

2 none of our funeral/it's not our funeral 不用我们操心，不关我们的事

funny

1 don't be funny 别出洋相

You don't have to be funny in order to use humor and playfulness in everyday conversations. 在日常谈话中幽默轻松不是说要表现得滑稽可笑。

2 feel funny/go all funny 浑身不舒服

The patient told the doctor that he felt funny all over. 病人对医生说他浑身都不舒服。

3 as funny as a crutch 【美】没什么可笑的

His story is as funny as a crutch. 他讲的故事一点儿都不好笑。

4 get funny with 对……不敬，放肆，对……无礼

Don't get funny with me. 别跟我耍把戏。

fur

1 make the fur/feathers/dust fly 引起骚乱、争论或斗争；惹是生非；暴跳如雷；痛加挞伐；大干一场

The plan has made the fur fly in Parliament. 这项计划在议会中引起了轩然大波。

A man fooled Mr. Black and got his money. Mr. Black will really make the fur fly when he finds the man. 一个人愚弄了布莱克先生并骗了他的钱，布莱克先生一旦发现此人，必然会暴跳如雷狠揍他一顿。

I don't think he'll give you a break. He'll make the feathers fly. 我想他不会让你有喘息的机会，他会给你制造很多的麻烦。

2 rub/stroke one's fur the wrong way 惹恼……

The CEO of our firm is a friendly sort of person so long as you do not rub his fur the wrong way. 我们公司的首席执行官是很友善的，只要你不惹恼他。

further

1 I'll see you further/dead/hanged/in hell first 我绝不干；绝不，也不

2 go further and fare worse 越搞越糟，每况愈下

You may go further and fare worse. 【谚】走得越远，情形越糟。

You can go a lot further and fare a lot worse. 这山望着那山高，到了那山把脚翘。

fuse

1 blow a fuse/a gasket/one's top/one's stack 参见 blow 6

2 have a short fuse【美口】性子急，动辄发怒，脾气暴躁

Boy, that football coach sure has a short fuse. 天哪，那个足球教练真是个脾气暴躁的人。

3 have a slow fuse【美口】性子慢，不易激动

fuss

1 fuss and feathers 大吹大擂，过分夸耀；喜怒无常

Sarah is full of fuss and feathers this morning. 萨拉今早喜怒无常。

2 fuss around/up and down 瞎忙活，忙得团团转

The husband fussed around, preparing the meal. 那个丈夫为这顿饭忙得

团团转。

3 **get into a fuss** 焦急,忙乱

Don't *get into a fuss* about nothing. 别没事找事,自寻烦恼。

4 **kick up a fuss/row/dust** 参见 dust 3

5 **make a fuss of/over** 过分关怀、体贴、溺爱

My mother *makes a fuss of* me every time I come home. 我每次回家,母亲对我总是关怀备至。

Stella *makes a* big *fuss over* her children. 斯特拉百般溺爱孩子。

G

gad

Gad, gad/by gad/by gum（gad 和 gum 都是 God 的委婉语）哎哟，天哪（表示惊奇、厌恶等，或用于发誓）

By Gad, it's time for dinner already! 哎哟，已经到吃饭的时间啦!

gaff

1 get the gaff【美】受到苛刻的待遇；受到严厉的批评
2 give sb. the gaff【美】严厉地对待某人，尖锐地批评某人，刺激某人
3 stand the gaff【美】任劳任怨地忍受困难、辱骂、讥讽等；经得起考验

game

1 ahead of the game【美】有优势，领先，超出；事先，太早；（尤指在赌博中）处于赢家地位

The time you spend studying when you are in school will put you ahead of the game in college. 你现在花在中学里的学习时间，会让你在大学里领先其他的人。

After Tom sold his papers, he was ＄5 ahead of the game. 汤姆卖了废纸后，他比平时多挣五美元。

2 none of your games 别耍花招啦，我不会上你的当
3 play fair/cricket/the game 遵守规定，诚实正直

Your parents want you to play the game in life. 你父母要你一生为人正直。

Harold eats no fish and palys the game. 哈罗德既忠诚又守规矩。

4 (so) that's your/his, etc. little game 原来那就是你的/他的等鬼把戏

So that's your little game, Smith—stealing other boys' textbooks and selling them back to them. Well, we've caught you now! 啊，史密斯，原来这就是你玩的鬼把戏，偷了人家的课本，又去卖给人家。好哇，我们这下可逮住你了!

5 the/a game (at which) two can play 机会均等

Rough football is a game two can play. 粗鲁的足球比赛双方机会均等。
Politics is a game at which two can play. 政治是一种机会均等的竞争。

6 the game is not worth the candle 参见 candle 3

7 the game/jig is up 秘密泄露,一切都完了,没指望了

The game is up; the teacher knows who took her keys. 秘密泄露了,老师已经知道是谁拿了她的钥匙。

The jig's up; the principal knows the boys have been smoking in the basement. 这下完了,校长已发现男孩子们在地下室里抽烟了。

8 the name of the game 事情的要点,真相

Getting medium income families to support the rest of society—that's the name of the game. 由小康家庭支持整个社会——这才是事情的真相。

9 two can play at that game 那一套不只你会,我也会;别跟我来那一套

"Two can play at that game," said Rick as he was tripped up playing football, so later in the game he tackled the boy in the other team viciously. "别跟我来这一套,你等着瞧吧,"当里克在踢足球时被人绊了一跤时,他说道。接着他就死死地缠住了对方的一个队员。

10 what's the game 你在干什么,发生什么事啦

I thought we were all supposed to meet at six, and there's only you and me here. What's the game? 我想我们大家都应当在六点钟碰头,可现在这儿只有你我二人,发生什么事了吗?

11 what's your/his, etc. little game 你/他等在耍什么花样

What's his little game now? How is he going to stop them beating us this time! 他在玩什么花样? 他这次打算怎么阻止他们打败我们?

gang

1 gang up 聚集,会合

The boys would gang up around the corner drugstore. 那些男孩常聚集在街角的杂货店周围。

2 gang up with/on/against 结成一伙,联合起来对付……

Marner ganged up with a group of unruly youths. 马南和一群不守法纪的青年结成团伙。

They ganged up on me. 他们联合起来对付我。

garden

1 everything is nice in your garden 【讽】你家的狗屎都是香的；什么都是你家的好

2 lead sb. up/down the garden path 引诱某人，欺骗某人，把某人引入歧途

Someone posing as a television reporter has been leading us up the garden path. 有人装成电视台记者，一直在骗我们。

The candidate dressed up his statement to lead the voters up the garden path. 那个候选人用花言巧语来欺骗选民。

gas

1 turn off the gas 关煤气；关掉话匣子，停止吹牛

2 turn on the gas 开煤气；打开话匣子，开始吹牛

gee

1 gee up 嘚，驾（吆喝马、牛等向前跑）

I think we got a wee bit of a gee up then, and when the crowd gets up, it makes a difference to our game. 我想我们那时候开始发力了，而球迷们站起来为我们加油对我们的比赛产生了重要影响。

2 gee whiz 【美】天哪，不得了（表示惊讶、热烈或强调等）

Gee whiz, I never thought I'd pass that exam! 哎呀，我没想到居然通过了那次考试！

George

1 by George 啊呀，天哪，好家伙；确实，的确（表示惊奇、赞许或决心，或用于赌咒）

By George, you're right. How amazing! 哎呀，你对了，真稀奇！

I mean what I say, by George I do! 我说话算数，说到做到！

2 let George do it 【美】让别人去干自己该干的事，自己坐享其成

Many people expect to let George do it when they are on a committee. 许多人当了委员以后，就指望别人去干自己职责范围以内的事，自己坐享其成。

get

1 can't get there from here 【美】从这儿到那儿路远难行；难题无法解决

2　don't get me wrong 别误会我的意思

Don't get me wrong, Charles, I wasn't trying to do your job for you. I just worked out some of the figures for last year's trading for the report I'm writing. 别误会，查尔斯，我不打算取代你干这件工作。我只是为我正在撰写的有关去年贸易情况的报告统计几个数字而已。

3　get a load of this 你瞧，你听

Get a load of this—it's the new recorder I've just bought! 你听，这是我刚买的新录音机。

Get a load of this. Alice got married yesterday! 你听这事，爱丽丝昨天结婚了。

4　get a move/wiggle on【美】快点

Get a move on, or you will be late. 快点，否则你会迟到。

Get a move on, or you'll miss the bus! 快点，否则你会赶不上公共汽车。

5　get a rise out of 激怒；戏弄，揶揄

The boys get a rise out of Joe by teasing him about his girlfriend. 男孩儿们开乔女友的玩笑惹得乔生了气。

6　get a word in (edgewise/edgeways)/get in a word 趁空插嘴

The little boy listened to the older students and finally get in a word. 这小孩听高年级学生谈话，最后找到了插嘴的机会。

Mary talked so much that Jack couldn't get a word in edgewise. 玛丽不停地说，杰克无法插嘴。

7　get above oneself 变得自高自大

Grace's been getting a bit above herself since winning her award. 格雷斯获奖以后，渐渐有点骄傲了。

8　get across 使（观点等）被理解，被接受；讲清楚自己的意思；使恼火

The idea got across to the leader. 这主意被领导接受了。

The plan seems quite simple to me, but I just can't get it across. 这计划看起来很简单，可我却没法把它讲清楚。

9　get after 喝斥，责骂；一再催促

Rosa is always getting after the children for one thing or another. 罗莎老是责骂孩子们这也不是那也不是。

Pound gets after her to change her mind. 庞德敦促她改变主意。

10　get along with you/(get) away with you/get on/away 走开，滚开，去你

的吧,别胡扯

Get along with you! I've heard that excuse before and I just don't believe you! 去你的吧,我早就听了你的解释了,可我就是不相信你!

Away with you! What nonsense you do come out with! 去你的吧,你尽胡扯些啥呀!

11 get anywhere/any place　参见 anywhere 2

12 get at 贿赂,买通,以不正当手段施加影响;指责,含沙射影地攻击;纠缠不清

Someone had got at the witness before the trial. 在审判前已经有人买通了证人。

Who are you getting at? 你在攻击谁?

13 get away with 做了坏事或错事未被发觉或未受处罚;偷走

How did Peter get away with cheating? 彼得作弊是如何得逞的?

The thief got away with ＄500. 那个贼偷走了五百美元。

14 get away with murder【美】过关,做了坏事却免受处罚

John is scolded if he is late with his homework, but Robert gets away with murder. 约翰因作业迟交而挨骂,但罗伯特却过了关。

Mrs. Smith lets her children get away with murder. 史密斯夫人从不处罚她的孩子,即使他们做了错事。

15 get back at 报复

John played a joke on Henry, and next day Henry got back at him. 约翰捉弄了亨利,第二天亨利就进行了报复。

16 get behind 查明真相

The police are questioning some people to try and get behind the bank robbery. 警察正在询问一些人,设法查明银行抢劫案的真相。

17 get by 通过,走过

The cars moved to the curb so that the fire engine could get by. 车子开到街边让消防车通过。

The crowd moved aside to let the firemen get by. 人群退到一边让消防人员通过。

18 get couthed up 打扮得很漂亮

What are you getting all couthed up for? 你干吗打扮得这么漂亮?

19 get cracking/going 快点;开始干……

Come on, you guys, let's **get cracking**! 来吧,让我们快点!
The teacher told Walter to **get going** on his history lesson. 老师叫瓦特开始上历史课。
The foreman told the workmen to **get cracking**. 工头叫工人们开始干活。

20 get done with 把……结束掉,做完;与……了结关系,不再同……打交道
Harold managed to **get** the work **done with** very little help. 哈罗德在几乎没有帮助的情况下设法完成了工作。

21 get... down 使……沮丧,使……忧郁
Low grades are **getting** Helen **down**. 考试得了低分,海伦闷闷不乐。
Three straight losses **got** the team **down**. 连输三次使全队气馁。

22 get down on 【美】申斥,唠叨不休地找岔子;对……开始不喜欢
I start to **get down on** the work. 我开始对这项工作生厌。

23 get down to brass tacks/cases 进入正题,言归正传
The man talked about little things and then **got down to brass tacks**. 这些人先谈了些小事,然后才进入正题。

24 get even 报复
Jack is waiting to **get even** with Bill for tearing up his notebook. 杰克伺机报复比尔,因为比尔撕了他的笔记本。
Last April First Mr. Harris got fooled by Joe, and this year he will **get even**. 去年4月1日哈里斯被乔愚弄,因此他想今年报复。

25 get/be in one's hair 一再烦扰,触怒
Johnny **got in father's hair** when he was trying to read the paper by running and shouting. 约翰尼在父亲看报时又跑又叫,父亲实在受不了了。
The grown-ups sent the children out to play so that the children wouldn't **be in their hair** while they were talking. 大人把孩子们赶出去玩,以免他们谈话时受干扰。

26 get into a mess/muddle/scrape 把事情搞糟,陷入困境
How did you **get into** such **a mess**. You great idiot? Nothing between your ears, that's your trouble. 你这个大笨蛋,怎么把事情搞得一团糟?你的问题就在于没脑子。

27 get/catch it 参见 catch 1
28 get it all together 【美】沉着冷静,冷静下来;精打细算
You've sure **got it all together**, haven't you? 你都算准确了,对不对?

A few minutes after the burglars left he *got it all together* and called the police. 小偷走了几分钟之后他冷静下来,报了案。

29 get it hot/get hell 受严厉处罚,受到申斥

Mark will *get hell* for it. 马克会为这事挨一顿臭骂。

30 get/catch it in the neck 参见 catch 2

31 get lost 走开,别烦人

Get lost! I want to study. 走开,我要学习了!

John told Bert to *get lost*. 约翰叫伯特走开。

Get lost, I'm trying to work. 走开,我要开始工作了。

32 get off 逃避;说(笑话)

No one should *get off* paying his tax. 每个人都应该照章纳税。

The governor *got off* several jokes at the beginning of his speech. 州长在演说开始时讲了好几个笑话。

33 get off and milk it 下来加点油吧;下来挤奶去吧(嘲讽某人不配做什么事)

Why is he driving so slowly? Hey buddy, *get off and milk it*! 他为什么开那么慢? 嗨,老兄,下来挤奶算了!

34 get off easy 无甚大碍,幸免;逃脱严厉惩罚

Why does Jessica always *get off easy*? 为什么杰西卡总是可以逃过惩罚?

The children who missed school to go to the exhibition *got off easy*. 逃学去看展览的孩子们没有受到严厉的惩罚。

35 get/come off it 少吹牛;少装样

"So I said to the duchess…" Jimmy began. "Oh, *come off it*!" the other boys sneered. 吉米说:"我对公爵夫人说……"其他男孩嘲笑他:"别吹了!"

Fritz said he had a car of his own. "Oh, *come off it*," said John. "You can't even drive." 弗里茨说他有一部车子。约翰说:"得啦,你连车都不会开。"

36 get off one's back 参见 back 1

37 get off one's tail 动手,着手干

OK, you guys! *Get off your tail* and get cracking! 好啦,各位,干起来吧!

38 get off on the wrong foot 参见 foot 13

39 get off the ground 成功的开端;进行

Our plans for a party didn't *get off the ground* because no one could come.

我们举办舞会的计划一开始就不妙,因为没有人会参加。

40 get on/onto 责骂,斥责
Mrs. Thompson *got on* the girls for not keeping their rooms clean. 汤普森太太责备女孩子们没有保持房间清洁。

The fans *got on* the new shortstop after he made several errors. 球迷们在新游击手出了几次失误以后向他喝倒彩。

41 get on (with) 赶快
Get on, we shall miss the train at this rate. 快点,照这样速度我们会赶不上火车。

Get on with it, we've a train to catch. 快点,我们得去赶火车。

42 get on at 不断指责
My wife is always *getting on at* me for not keeping the rooms clean. 我的妻子老是抱怨我没有保持房间清洁。

43 get on to 觉察,发觉(秘密、不法行为等);要求,请求
Maud tricked people for years until the police *got on to* him. 多年来莫德一直欺骗人们,直到被警方识破。

I'll *get on to* the manufacturers to replace these damaged goods. 我们要求厂方调换这些损坏了的商品。

44 get on one's nerves 使人不安,使人心烦
John's noisy eating habits *get on your nerves*. 约翰大声吃东西的习惯使人心烦。

Children *get on their parents' nerves* by asking so many questions. 孩子们问了太多的问题,令他们的父母心烦。

45 get one's/what's coming to one 【美】善有善报,恶有恶报
Don't worry, the bad guy will *get his*, before all this is over. 别担心,事情还没了结,坏蛋会受到惩罚的。

At the end of the movie the villain *got what was coming to him* and was put in jail. 电影结束时,恶有恶报,坏人被关了起来。

46 get one's dander/back/Irish up 参见 dander

47 get one's ducks in a row 安排就绪,准备妥当
The scoutmaster told the boys to *get their ducks in a row* before they went to camp. 童子军教练叫孩子们在去营地前做好一切准备。

Mr. Brown *got his ducks in a row* for his trip. 布朗先生已将旅行之事准

备妥当。

48 get one's feet wet　参见 foot 7

49 get one's goat 使人生气、厌烦

The boy's laziness all summer got his father's goat. 整个夏天这孩子都是懒懒散散的，这使他父亲很生气。

The slow service at the café got Mr. Robinson's goat. 咖啡店的服务太慢，这使罗宾逊先生很生气。

50 get/have one's number 心中有数；看透……

The boys soon had the new student's number. 男孩子们很快就了解了那个新同学的为人。

The girls got their new roommate's number the first week of school. 女孩子们开学第一周就了解那个新室友的脾气了。

51 get one's rear in gear 赶快

I'm going to have to get my rear in gear. 我得赶快开始。

52 get/sink one's teeth into 投注心力，大费脑筋

After dinner, John got his teeth into the algebra lesson. 晚饭后约翰认真地学习代数。

Frank chose a subject for his report that he could sink his teeth into. 弗兰克选了一个可以让他深入研究的报告题目。

53 get out 走开，滚开，去你的，胡说（用于祈使句）

Oh, get out, you can't mean that! 哎，胡说，你不会是那个意思。

Get out of here! 滚出去！

54 get over 不为……感到惊讶；不相信……是真的

I just can't get over her leaving so suddenly. 我对她的突然离去实在感到难以置信。

We could not get over the speed of Mary's recovery from pneumonia. 我们简直不敢相信玛丽的肺炎康复得这么快。

55 get round 用哄骗/奉承的手段说服……

Nora could always get round him in the end. 最后诺拉总能哄得他顺从自己。

We'll soon get him round to our point of view. 我们会很快说服他接受我们的观点。

56 get set 准备出发，动身，开始

The runners *got set*. 赛跑选手都已各就各位。

The seniors are *getting set* for the commencement. 毕业生正准备动身参加毕业典礼。

57 get sth. on sb. 抓住某人的把柄

58 get somewhere （使）有一些进展；（使）有一些成果

Now we're *getting somewhere*. 这下我们总算有了一些进展。

Your degree should *get* you *somewhere* in the chemical industry. 你的学位可以使你在化学工业方面有些奔头。

59 get the air/axe/bounce/gate/hook/sack/bird 参见 bounce 1

60 get the feel of 熟悉，熟练

John had never driven a big car, and it took a while for him to *get the feel of* it. 约翰从未开过大车子，因此需要费些时间才能熟练。

You'll *get the feel of* the job after you've been there a few weeks. 你上班后几周内就能熟悉你的工作。

61 get/have the goods on 知道内幕；发现问题，得到证据；实话实说

Tell the truth, Johnny, we know who your girl is because we've *got the goods on* you. 实话实说吧，约翰尼，我们早就知道你的女友是谁了，因为我们掌握了证据。

The police *had the goods on* the burglar before he came to trial. 在起诉之前警方已经掌握了那个盗匪的罪行证据。

62 get/have the jump on 占优势，领先，胜过

Don't let the other boys *get the jump on* you at the beginning of the race. 比赛一开始不要让别的男孩占优势。

Our team *got the jump on* their rivals in the first minutes of play, and held the lead to win. 我们队一开始就领先对方，直到最后胜利。

63 get the lead out of one's pants 忙碌，加紧工作

The captain told the sailors to *get the lead out of their pants*. 船长叫水手们加紧工作。

The coach told the players to *get the lead out of their pants*. 教练叫选手们加油。

64 get the message/word 完全了解；理解

The principal talked to the students about being on time, and most of them *got the message*. 校长告诫学生养成守时的习惯，大部分同学都能

理解他的用心。

Mary hinted to her boyfriend that she wanted to break up, but he didn't get the message. 玛丽暗示男友要和他分手,但他居然没有听懂。

65 get the picture 了解情况

After the fight on the playground, the principal talked to the boys who were watching, until he got the whole picture. 操场上一场打斗之后,校长和在场的目击者交谈,最后他了解到了事件的整个过程。

66 get the show on the road 实施计划;开工

It was several years before the scientists got the show on the road. 过了许多年以后科学家们才开始实施这个计划。

67 get it through one's head 使……了解或相信

Jack couldn't get it through his head that his father wouldn't let him get to camp if his grades didn't improve. 杰克不相信如果他的成绩没有进步,他的父亲就不让他参加野营。

I'll get it through his head if it takes all night. 哪怕耗费整夜的时间我也要让他明白事情的真相。

68 get (it) through to 使……了解,使……理解

The little boy could not get through to his housemother. 这小孩儿没法让他的女管家了解他。

When the rich boy's father lost his money, it took a long time for the idea to get through to him that he'd have to work and support himself. 当富家孩子的父亲一旦变穷时,他得经历一段漫长的时间,才能理解他必须努力工作才能维持生计。

69 get to 开始,着手处理;被……理解;对……产生影响;使担心,使沮丧;买通

Let's get to work. 我们干起来吧。

Dorothy gets to worrying over nothing at all. 多萝西无缘无故地担心起来。

70 get together 【美】取得一致意见

They simply couldn't get together on matters of policy. 在政策的问题上他们硬是没法取得一致意见。

Mother says I should finish my arithmetic lesson, and father says I should mow the lawn. Why don't you two get together? 母亲要我做数学功课,父亲要我除草,为什么你们两人不协调一下呢?

71 get up 准备；安排，组织；打扮，装饰；鼓起勇气；增进有关的知识

I have to get up a talk for the club's next meeting. 我得为俱乐部下次会议的讲话做好准备。

Mary got up a picnic for her visitors. 玛丽为她的客人们筹备了野餐。

72 get up and go【美】赶快行动起来

"I didn't have the motivation to get up and go," the girl said. 那个姑娘说："我没有迅速行动起来的动力。"

73 get up to 干坏事，干蠢事

Billy's always getting up to mischief. 比利老是在捣鬼。

74 get you 我才不相信你的瞎吹呢

"I went to America for three months this summer and stayed on a cowboy ranch." "Get you!" "今年夏天我去了美国，在一个牛仔牧场待了三个月。""我才不信你的瞎吹呢！"

75 tell sb. where to get off 严厉斥责某人

The boss was telling the foreman where to get off. 老板正在训斥那个工头。

76 you get/we get/there be 有，存在着

Within the Chinese language you get quite different sounds. 汉语里有种种迥然不同的语音。

77 you've got me there/you have me there/it gets me 你可把我难住了，我不知道

"Why did you decide to put a fifth leg on the table?" "You've got me there, I was hoping you wouldn't ask me that!" "为什么你打算给这张桌子安上五条腿呢？""你可把我问住了，我以为你不会问这个呢。"

78 get the best of 胜过，战胜，打赢

You're a pair of superstitious goats and it's got the best of you. Now, this appears to be no more as we have a stowaway on board. 你们已经迷信到昏头了。看来我们的船上有位不速之客。

gift

1 God's gift 自以为了不起的人

Bloomer thinks he's God's gift to football. 布卢默自以为是个了不起的足球运动员。

Camp thinks he's God's gift to women. 坎普自以为是女人心目中的美男子。

2　gift of (the) gab 口才，辩才

Many men get elected because of their gift of gab. 很多人当选是由于口才好。

Mr. Taylor's gift of gab helped him get a good job. 泰勒先生的口才帮他获得了一份好工作。

girl

1　girl Friday 得力助手（尤指秘书）

Miss Johnson is the manager's girl Friday. 约翰逊小姐是经理的得力助手。

There was an advertisement in the newspaper for a girl Friday. 报上刊出一条招聘优秀女职员的广告。

2　old girl 友好地称呼一个熟悉的女性或雌性动物

Come on, old girl, you can look happier! 来吧，姑娘，你看上去应该更高兴些才是。

give

1　don't give me that 我才不相信你呢

"Would you like to go out for a meal on Saturday?" "Don't give me that! You've been saying you'd take me out for months now, and you've not done so yet!" "星期六我们出去吃顿饭好吗?""我才不相信你的话呢，你答应带我出去吃饭说了好几个月了，可是一次也没去。"

2　give (sb.)/lend (sb.)/bear a hand 帮助

The stage manager asked some of the boys to lend a hand with the scenery. 舞台经理叫男孩子们帮忙移动布景。

Dick saw a woman with a flat tire and offered to give her a hand with it. 迪克看到一个女士的车胎爆了，就主动给她帮忙。

3　give a hang/care a damn/rap/straw 有兴趣；在意（常与否定词连用）

You can quit helping me if you want to, I don't give a hang. 你不想帮我就算了，我根本不在乎。

Bruce never goes to the dances; he does not care a straw about dancing. 布鲁斯从不跳舞，他对舞蹈不感兴趣。

4 give sb. a hard time 惹麻烦，捣蛋；抱怨；逗笑

Jane *gave her mother a hard time* on the bus fighting with her sister and screaming. 简在公共汽车上和妹妹打架，大喊大叫，给她母亲惹了不小的麻烦。

Don't *give me a hard time*, George, I'm doing my best on this job. 乔治，别抱怨我了，这事我已尽了力。

5 give sb. a pain 令人厌烦

Ann's laziness *gives her mother a pain*. 安的懒惰使她母亲烦恼。

John's bad manners *give his teacher a pain*. 约翰的粗鲁行为使老师头疼。

6 give sb. a piece of one's mind 怒斥某人

Mr. Allen *gave the other driver a piece of his mind*. 艾伦先生生气地责备另一个司机。

The sergeant *gave the soldier a piece of his mind* for not cleaning his boots. 士官因为士兵没给他擦亮靴子而责骂他。

7 give sb. a ring/buzz 给某人打电话

Mrs. Jacob promised to *give her husband a ring* in the afternoon. 雅各布太太答应下午给她丈夫打电话。

Alice will *give her friend a buzz* tonight. 爱丽丝将在今晚给她朋友打电话。

8 give... a wide berth 避开，保持距离以求安全

Mary *gave* the barking dog *a wide berth*. 玛丽远远躲开那只吠叫的狗。

After Tom got Bob into trouble, Bob *gave* him *a wide berth*. 汤姆把鲍勃拉下水后，鲍勃便远远地躲开他。

9 give/lend an ear to 听从

Children should *give an ear to* their parents' advice. 小孩应听从父母的劝告。

10 give and take 礼尚往来，公平交换，互相让步；驳斥；互殴

Developing and maintaining healthy friendships involves *give and take*. 发展并维持健康的友谊包括礼尚往来。

11 give as good as one gets 反击；反驳；针锋相对，以牙还牙；防卫得法

The Americans *gave as good as they got* in the war with the English. 美国人在战争中善于反击英军。

George *gave as good as he got* in his fight with the older boy. 乔治毫不示

弱地反击那个年纪较大的孩子。

12 give away 赠送,捐赠;在婚礼上把新娘交给新郎;泄露;告发;分发

Edward *gave away* medals at the sports meeting. 爱德华在运动会上分发奖牌。

Mary was *given away* by her father. 在婚礼上玛丽由她父亲交给新郎。

13 give chase 追逐

The policeman *gave chase* to the man who robbed the bank. 警察追赶抢劫银行的人。

14 give/lend color to 对……加以渲染;使人信服

The boy's torn clothes *gave color to* his story of a fight. 那孩子被撕破的衣服让人相信他说的是实话:他的确与人打了一架。

The way the man ate *lent color to* his story of near starvation. 那人狼吞虎咽的样子使人相信他说的他饿得要死的话。

15 give sb. fits 使人不安、烦恼、生气

The short guard *gave his tall opponent fits*. 这个矮个子后卫使对方的高个子感到烦恼。

Paul's higher grades *give John fits*. 保罗更好的成绩使约翰生气。

16 give gray hair(s) 令人焦虑,伤人脑筋

The traffic problem is enough to *give policemen gray hairs*. 交通问题足以使警察大伤脑筋。

17 give ground 败退,撤退,后退

After fighting for a while the troops slowly began to *give ground*. 打了一阵之后,军队慢慢开始撤退。

Although they were outnumbered by the enemy, the men refused to *give ground*. 虽然敌人数量超过他们,但是大家仍然拒绝撤退。

18 give it (to) sb. 责罚某人,责骂某人;打某人

I'll *give it (to) him* (hot/straight). 我要(狠狠/当面)责骂他。

The crowd yelled for the prizefighter to *give it to his opponent*. 人群喊叫着要拳击手狠揍他的对手。

19 give of oneself 献出时间和精力帮助别人

You should *give of yourself* sometimes. 有时你应当帮助别人。

During World War Ⅱ governer Baldwin *gave of himself* by sweeping the halls of a hospital every afternoon. 二战期间鲍德温州长每天下午帮助一

家医院扫走廊。

20 give sb. an inch and he will take a mile 得寸进尺

I gave Billy a bite of candy and he wanted more and more. If you give him an inch and he'll take a mile. 我给比利咬一口糖果,他还要更多,真是得寸进尺。

21 give one's due 公平对待;有功必赏

The boxer who lost gave the new champion his due. 失败的拳击手衷心地祝贺新拳王。

We should give a good worker his due. 我们对表现好的工人应该有功必赏。

22 give oneself airs 盛气凌人;装腔作势;神气活现

Mary gave herself airs when she wore her new dress. 玛丽因穿了新衣服而扬扬得意。

John gave himself airs when he won the first prize. 约翰得了第一名便神气活现。

23 give oneself away 露马脚;泄露秘密或罪行

The thief gave himself away by spending so much money. 小偷因大量花钱而露了马脚。

Carl played a joke on Bob and gave himself away by laughing. 卡尔跟鲍勃开了个玩笑,但因大笑而露了马脚。

24 give oneself over 放任自己

Jenny gave herself over to laughter before she could go on. 珍妮纵情大笑一阵之后,才能接着讲下去。

25 give oneself up 自首;尽情享受

The thief gave himself up to the police. 小偷向警方自首了。

Mr. Thompson hit another car, and his wife told him to give himself up. 汤普森先生撞了另一辆车,他妻子叫他去自首。

26 give one's right arm 不惜任何代价

Mr. Thomas would give his right arm to be able to travel in Europe. 为了到欧洲旅游,托马斯先生不惜任何代价。

After it is too late, some people would give their right arm for a better education. 为了接受更好的教育,虽然为时已晚,有的人还是愿意付出一切。

27 give or take 相差不到……；出入至多……

I'll be there at one o'clock, give or take ten minutes. 我会在一点钟到那里，前后至多不超过十分钟。

Give or take a few minor mistakes, your essay is very good. 你的文章写得不错，至多有点小错误。

28 give out 停止运转

The engine of the boat suddenly gave out. 船上的发动机突然停止了运转。

The bus gave out halfway up the hill. 公共汽车在半山腰熄火了。

29 give over 停止……；安静下来；抛弃（某种习惯）

Please give over crying. Do give it! 请别哭了！千万别哭了！

It's time you gave over such childish behaviour. 该是你改掉这种幼稚行为的时候了。

30 give pause （使）踌躇，（使）犹豫，（使）考虑

The heavy monthly payments gave Mr. Smith pause in his plans to buy a new car. 数目颇大的款项使史密斯先生对购买新车的计划颇费踌躇。

The bad weather gave Miss Carter pause about driving to New York city. 恶劣的天气使卡特小姐对是否开车去纽约犹豫起来。

31 give sb. to understand/know/believe 暗示；使……明白/知道/相信

Am I given to understand that Gallup is a liar? 这是要告诉我盖洛普是个骗子吗？

Mr. Johnson gave Billy to understand that he would pay him if he helped him clean the yard. 约翰逊先生向比利暗示如果他帮他清扫庭院，他会付工钱给他的。

32 give the ax 忽然决裂；革职，辞退

Judith gave me the ax last night. 朱迪思昨晚忽然跟我绝交了。

John's boss gave him the ax last Friday. 约翰的老板上星期五炒了他的鱿鱼。

33 give the benefit of the doubt 在没有确证前不轻下结论

The money was stolen and John was the only boy who had known where it was, but the teacher gave him the benefit of the doubt. 约翰是唯一知道被盗的钱放在何处的孩子，但老师因没有确切证据而宁愿相信他是无辜的。

George's grade was higher than usual and he might have cheated, but his teacher gave him the benefit of the doubt. 乔治的成绩比平时高,可能有作弊嫌疑,但老师未轻下结论。

34 give the bounce/gate/air/sack/hook 断交,决裂;解雇,开除

Mary gave John the bounce after she saw him dating another girl. 玛丽看到约翰约了别的姑娘,就与他绝交了。

Bill and Jane had an argument and Bill is giving her the gate. 比尔和简发生了口角,就不再理她了。

35 give the shirt off one's back 贡献一切,倾其所有

Kipling would give you the shirt off his back. 基普林会倾其所有地给你一切。

36 give the slip 避开,溜走

Some boys were waiting outside the school to beat up Jack, but he gave them the slip. 几个孩子在校外等着要揍杰克,但他溜走了。

37 give up 不再抱希望;承认(对猜谜、解题等)无能为力;承认失败,认输

You took so long to arrive; we had almost given you up. 你迟迟不来,我们几乎以为你不来了。

The missing climbers were given up for lost. 人们认为失踪的登山者已经遇难了。

38 give up on 对……绝望,无法理解

I give up on you; you'll never be a qualified teacher. 我对你不抱任何希望了,你永远成不了合格的教师。

It's a kind of mystery that one gives up on. 这是你我永远无法理解的那种疑案。

39 what gives 【美】发生什么事了

What gives? What's everyone looking at? 出了什么事?大家都在看什么呀?

go

1 go 居然,竟然(后接动词的-ing 形式,或由 and 连接另一动词表示惊讶等)

Don't go saying that! 别冒失地说那些话!

Lena went and told it to everybody she met. 莉娜竟把这事告诉了每一个

她遇到的人。

2 go 忍受,容忍(常用于否定句)

I simply can't go him any more. 我实在不能容忍他了。

I can't go the price. 我付不起这个价。

3 go (*n*. 复数 goes) 尝试;一举成功;精力;活动频繁;意外的事;时髦的东西;约定;轮到的机会;差点送命

I have a go at painting. 我试着作画。

Locke finished the job at one go. 洛克一下子把工作做完了。

4 as the saying goes 如俗话所说,俗话说,常言道

As the saying goes: the effect of good examples is immense. 常言道:榜样的作用是无穷的。

5 as far as it goes 就一般标准而言,无论如何

Information is information as far as it goes. 无论如何信息永远只是信息。

6 be gone 参见 be 1

7 go a long/good/great way 大有用处,大有帮助;(食物)能存放很久,(钱)经用;叫人受不了;不辞辛劳

Well-chosen wallpaper can go a long way toward making a room look attractive. 墙纸选择得好使房间增色不少。

Helina makes a little money go a long way. 赫莉娜精打细算花很少的钱买很多东西。

8 go about 忙于,从事

Go about your business! 忙你的事去吧! /别管闲事!

If you go about it in the right way, you'll soon get it finished. 假如你用了正确的方法,你很快就会完成任务。

9 go ahead 着手,继续,先行一步

You go ahead and tell him that we're coming. 你先走一步,告诉他我们就来。

Go ahead, what are you waiting for? 朝前走吧,你还等什么?

10 go along (with you) 走开;去你的,别胡扯;进行;支持

Go along, you naughty boy! 走开,你这顽皮的孩子!

11 go away 走开,离开

I think we need to go away and think about this. 我认为我们需要离开,然后考虑这件事。

12 go back to sleep 回去睡觉；不用管……

Go back to sleep, Catherine—it's useless trying to explain things to you when your mind is somewhere else. 好啦,凯瑟琳,随你便吧,既然你心不在焉,对你说什么也没用。

13 go by（过错、侮辱等）不予计较；【美】顺便走访

We'll let the error go by this time. 这一次我们对这一差错不予计较。

All the family were at home when Tom went by yesterday. 汤姆昨天去看他们时,他们全家人都在。

14 go fly a kite 走开，滚开

Harry was tired of John's advice and told him to go fly a kite. 哈里厌烦了约翰的唠叨,于是叫他走开。

After Mary stood around telling Susan what was wrong with her dress, Susan told her to go fly a kite. 玛丽在苏珊身边不断地数落苏珊衣服上的毛病,苏珊叫她走开。

15 go for 袭击；抨击；严厉斥责

Nichols went for me with a dagger. 尼科尔斯手持匕首向我扑来。

The newspapers went for the Prime Minister over the government's tax proposals. 报纸围绕政府的税收提案严厉抨击首相。

16 go hard/ill with 使……大吃苦头；对……不利

It might have gone hard with Henry, had the mistake not been discovered. 要是这错误没被发现,亨利就要倒霉了。

17 go home 死；损坏；（食物）腐败

I'm afraid old Charlie's gone home; he had been ill for years. 老查利患病多年,恐怕他已经到老祖宗那里去了。

The new washing machine's going home already, I shall complain to the makers. 这台新洗衣机已经坏了,我要向厂家投诉。

18 go beyond the veil/go hence/go out of the world/go to glory/go to heaven/go the way/go to one's account/go to one's long rest/go the way of all flesh/go the way of all the earth/go the way of nature/go to a better world/go to one's own place/go to one's last long home/go over to the great majority/go off the hooks/go to grass/go to pot/go west/go up the flume 死去,逝世,长眠,升天,上西天,到老祖宗那里去报到；结束；无法使用；破灭

My new camera has gone west after only three months. 我的新照相机只

用了三个月就坏了。
Our hopes have *gone west*. 我们的希望破灭了。

19 go in 被理解
Nothing much *goes in* if I try to read in the evenings. 如果我在晚上读书，读进去的东西往往不多。

20 go it 使劲干；飞速前进；(在比赛中)加油；生活放荡、挥霍成瘾
The driver is *going it*. 司机没命地开快车。
The coach yelled to the runners to *go it*. 教练向赛跑运动员们大声叫喊，要他们加油。

21 go it alone 独自干；独自生活
Neither of the two consortia has sufficient cash to *go it alone*. 两个国际财团都没有独自经营的资金。
John wants to leave home and *go it alone*. 约翰想离开家庭独自生活。

22 go, man, go 【美】太棒了，干得好
You can beat Perry—*go，man，go*! 你能打败佩里，太棒了!

23 go on 赶紧；唠叨；勉强生活下去；不相信；(用于否定句)喜欢；责骂
Go on! There isn't a moment to lose! 快点，一秒钟也拖延不得!
How Elizabeth does *go on*! 伊丽莎白说话真啰唆!

24 go round and round 旋转；争吵不休

25 go sb. one better 参见 better 2

26 go soak yourself/your head 走开，别烦我
When I asked for a date, Isabel told me to *go soak my head*. 我提出想要跟伊莎贝尔约会时，她却叫我不要烦她。

27 go some 顺利进行；很有成就，收获很大；跑得很快
That's *going some*. 那是很快的速度。
It was a fast freight, and she *went some*. 那是辆货运客车，速度很快。

28 go somewhere 出去一下(指上厕所)

29 go to it 干起来，加油干(用于祈使句)
Go to it, Robert—if you work hard, you'll have it finished by lunchtime! 加油干，罗伯特，要是你努力干，午饭前就能干完它。

30 go without saying 不言而喻
It *goes without saying* that children should not play with guns. 不用说，小孩子不应当玩弄枪支。

31 going, going, gone 拍卖师宣布拍卖品成交用语；描写人或物在视线中逐渐消失

Any more offers for this fine vase, then? Going, to the man in the black suit, going, going, gone! 还有哪位要给这个精致的花瓶加价？要卖了，要卖了，好，那位穿黑礼服的先生买定了。

My little boat's sinking! Going, going, gone; now it's sunk! 我的小船要沉了，看哪，它正在沉下去，沉下去，沉没了。

32 here goes （在做游戏或做某种冒险举动时）我这就开始啦

Here goes then! I'll see you in three hours after the exam! 我这就开始啦，考完这场考试三小时以后，我去见你。

"Here goes," shouted the paratrooper as he jumped. 伞兵往下跳时大喊："我开始跳了。"

33 here we go again 同样不愉快的事又发生了

"Here we go again," muttered Susan as she left the waiting room to go into the dentist's surgery for the sixth time that year. "我又来了，"苏珊轻声咕哝着离开候诊室走进外科医生的诊室，这是她那一年第六次来这个地方了。

34 how's it going/how goes it/how are things going 你好吗，近况如何

"How's it going, Jane?" "OK, thanks. And how are you?" "你好吗，简？" "很好，谢谢。你呢？"

How goes it? 你好吗？近况如何？

35 it's a go 就这样决定了

36 it's no go 不行，没用，办不到，不可能；无价值

It's no go, I'm afraid—that plan will never work. 我怕办不到，那个计划绝对行不通。

You want to trot me out, but it's no go. 你想出我的洋相吧，没门！

37 let it go at that 【美】就这样吧，不用再说了

Bob was not quite satisfied with his haircut but let it go at that. 鲍勃对新理的发型不太满意，但也只能如此了。

38 off we go 我们走吧

"Off we go, then," said Dad as he drove off at the beginning of the family holiday. "好，我们出发啦，"爸爸边说边开动汽车，开始了家庭的假日旅行。

39 one can go hang 管他呢,他爱怎样就怎样吧

40 there it goes 你看,开始了

41 there you go again 你又来这一套

There you go again, chewing your food loudly—I've told you not to do that lots of times, now stop it! 你又犯老毛病了,大声地嚼食物。我已经说过你多少次了。还不停下来!

42 what has gone of/with 发生了什么事,怎么啦

43 where do we go from here/there 下一步怎么办

We've cut all the pieces of card out. Where do we go from here? Do we stick them all together or paint them first? 我们已经把这些小纸片剪好了,下一步怎么办? 是先粘起来呢,还是先涂上颜色?

44 who goes there 谁(哨兵喝问口令)

god

1 by God 凭上帝发誓;实实在在,的的确确

2 God bless me/my soul/my life 天哪

3 God bless you/him, etc. 愿上帝保佑你/他等;一路平安;长命百岁

4 God damn 该死,糟透了

God damn you! 天罚你!

5 God forbid 愿上帝保佑,不要发生这样的事

Someone told the worried mother that her son might have drowned. She said, "God forbid!" 有人告诉这位忧伤的母亲,她的孩子可能淹死了,她说:"上帝保佑,千万别这样!"

6 God grant 但愿,祝愿

God grant you much happiness in your marriage! 祝愿你的婚姻幸福美满!

God grant that I never have to see this essay again once I've finished writing it! 但愿我这篇文章能一次写成,不再看第二遍。

7 God/Heaven help sb. 愿上帝帮助某人

God help us all at this time of national disaster. 愿上帝在此民族危难之际救救我们吧!

Heaven help Mary in this crisis in her life. 愿上帝保佑玛丽度过生活上的难关。

8 God/goodness/Heaven/Lord knows 天晓得;上天为证;说不准

Goodness knows, the poor man needs the money. 老天做证，这穷人真需要钱。

Heaven knows, I have tried hard enough. 上帝做证，我真的尽了最大的努力。

9 God/Saints/Heaven preserve us 天哪（表示惊讶、烦恼、害怕等）

You say you want some more money? Saints preserve us, woman, you'll be asking for every penny I ever earned next! 你说你还要一些钱，天哪，老婆，你会把我挣的每一文钱都榨干的！

10 God willing/please God 如系天意，如上帝许可

I'll see you again Tuesday, God willing. 如果一切顺利的话，我下星期二再来看你。

We'll be married this time next year, please God. 我们将在明年此时结婚，但愿如此。

11 God save 愿上帝保佑

God save the Queen! God save the Prince! 愿上帝保佑王后！愿上帝保佑王子！

12 God save sb. from 上帝保佑某人免受……之苦

I know her approaches are well-meant but may God save me from her constant offers of help! 我知道她的这种亲近表示是出于好意，但是我还是希望上帝保佑我免受她持续不断提供的帮助对我的困扰之苦。

13 Good God/great God/my God/God almighty/oh God 哎呀，天哪，好家伙（表示痛苦、忧伤、愤怒）

Oh God! I wish this pain would stop! 天哪，这疼痛能止住就好了！

14 honest to God/goodness 真的，的确

Honest to God, sir, I wasn't anywhere near the garden at the time of the accident! 真的，先生，事故发生时我根本没到花园附近去过。

When we were in Washington we saw the President, honest to goodness. 我们在华盛顿时的确看到过总统。

15 in God's/heaven's name 到底，究竟（加强语气）

Where in heaven's name did you put my keys? 你到底把我的钥匙放哪儿去了？

16 so help me God 我说的是实话；实在；上帝作证

I really did see a flying-saucer, so help me God! 我真的看见了一个飞碟，

我说的是实话。
I never want to see you again, so help me God! 我真的再也不想见到你了,老天爷作证!

17 Thank God/goodness/heaven(s) 感谢上帝的恩赐,谢天谢地
Thank goodness for life and breath, and everything! 感谢上帝给我们生命、空气和一切!
Thank goodness it's Friday! 谢天谢地,今天是星期五!

18 ye gods 天哪,好家伙,怎么搞的
Ye gods! I didn't expect to see you here—I thought you were on the other side of the world! 天哪,真没想到会在这儿看到你,我还以为你升天了呢!

golly (god 的委婉语)

1 golly/by golly(表示惊奇、高兴或愤怒)啊,天哪,好家伙,糟糕,见鬼
Golly, they fell for it! 天哪,他们受骗了!
By golly, that's Pete Bates over there! 啊,那不是皮特·贝茨吗!

2 golly gumdrops 哎呀,天哪(表示惊奇)
Golly gumdrops! You're back already—that was quick! 啊,你已经回来了,真快呀!

good

1 a good one 令人难以置信的;真笑死人啦
"The bus never turned up, sir!" "That's a good one, Smith—I was on it myself, so where were you?" "公共汽车没来,先生。" "那倒稀奇了,史密斯,我坐在它上面,而你到哪儿去了呢?"
"A good one, Freddie!" they cried, as they bent double with laughter. "真笑死人,弗雷迪!"他们边喊着边笑弯了腰。

2 (and) (it's) a good job/thing 真不错,真好,真走运
"I complained about the broken bag they'd sold me and the shop gave me my money back." "A good job too!" "我投诉这只才买来就破了的皮包,结果商店退了货。" "真不错!"
"Pete's rung to tell me not to come this weekend." "And a good thing too—if you'd driven all that way and found no one there, you'd have been very annoyed." "皮特打电话叫我这个周末不要来。" "真好,幸亏你没有来,要是你开车来了找不着人,那才让人恼火呢。"

3 be good【美】好好干（告别时祝福语），听话；做个好人；【戏谑】规矩点

4 for good or ill 不论好歹

For good or ill, Denise Hyland had sent me a second diary in the spring to chronicle whatever happened next. 无论是好是坏，丹尼斯·海兰已在春天给我寄来了第二个日记本，我可以详细地记录接下来发生的事了。

5 good cop bad cop 一个唱红脸，一个唱白脸；软硬兼施

Successful management requires a variation of the "*good cop bad cop*" routine. 成功的管理需要软硬兼施，恩威并用。

6 good deal【美】适意的处境，惬意的工作；好极了

You have a *good deal* at the bank. Don't blow it. 你在银行干得挺惬意，可别搞砸了。

You made it? *Good deal*! 是你干的？太棒了！

7 good/hurrah for sb. 干得好，说得好，棒极了，好消息（祝贺用语）

"I got three grade A's, you know!" "*Good for you*!" "我考试得了三个'优秀'。""棒极了！"

Good for Peter—I'm glad he's beaten John at the long jump at last! 彼得干得棒极了，我真为他终于在跳远中击败约翰而高兴。

8 good gracious/goodness gracious/gracious me/by heaven/good God/good heavens/good Lord/my goodness 天哪，哎呀（表示惊讶、怀疑、忧虑等）

Good gracious, you should have done your homework by now! It's ten o'clock already! 天哪，你早该做完家庭作业呀，现在已经十点了！

My goodness, have you been expelled? 天哪，你被开除了吗？

9 good/great grief 哎呀，天哪（表示惊讶、慌张等，常带幽默效果）

Good grief! It's Jill Winter—how are you? We've not seen each other for years, have we? 天哪，这不是吉尔·温特吗！你好吗？我们有好几年没见过面了，对吧？

Good grief! How am I going to manage now my wife's left me? 天哪，现在我妻子离开了我，我可怎么办哪？

10 good money 高工资

Peter is earning *good money*. 彼得的工资很高。

11 good night【美】(表示惊讶、恼怒、强调等)哎呀，天哪(good是god的委婉语)

Good night! Must you chew that gum so loud? 天哪，你非得把口香糖嚼得那么响吗？

12 it's a good thing 幸好

It's a good thing these walls are thick, or our neighbours might hear what we're saying! 幸好这些墙厚，否则我们的邻居就把我们说的话全听去了。

It's a good thing we verified the time of the train. 幸好我们核对了火车的行车时刻表。

13 much good may it do you 但愿这对你有好处；【讽】这对你有什么好处

goodness

1 for goodness sake/in the name of goodness 看在老天爷份上，做做好事，求求你

2 wish/hope/surely to goodness 真希望，但愿

I wish to goodness he were here. 我真希望他在这儿。

Surely to goodness you don't expect me to believe that! 老实告诉你，别指望我会相信那件事。

3 thank goodness/God/heaven(s) 参见 god 17

Gosh （God 的委婉语）

(by) gosh 哎呀，天哪，好家伙，糟糕

Gosh, it's cold out today. 哎呀，今天外面好冷！

grab

by grab【美】哎呀，好家伙，糟糕（表示惊讶、谴责、惋惜等）

grape

the grapes are sour/sour grapes 葡萄好酸哟（指得不到想要的东西便说它不好，出自《伊索寓言》）

Belloc said that the book that I wrote is not worth reading, but that is sour grapes, because he'd like to write one himself! 贝洛克说我写的书不值得读，那只不过是吃不到葡萄说葡萄酸罢了，因为他自己想写书却没写成。

grasp

1 grasp/clutch at straws 参见 catch 4

2 grasp the nettle 迎难而上；大胆地抓棘手问题

The nettle will have to be grasped. 那棘手问题非大胆地抓不可。

grass

1 come/keep off the grass 勿践踏草地；别再胡说了；别多管闲事
We need a fence to keep the dogs off the grass. 我们需要个围篱，不让狗践踏草坪。

2 the grass is always greener on the other side of the fence/hill/the grass is greener on the other hill 这山望着那山高
John is always changing his job because the grass is always greener to him on the other side of the fence. 约翰一直在换工作，因为他总是认为到手的工作不如未到手的好。
Almost all people see that the grass is greener on the other hill. They never feel satisfied with what they've already got. 人们总是这山望着那山高，对自己的现状没有满意的时候。

gravy

1 by/good gravy【美】哎呀，糟糕，好家伙（表示惊讶、谴责、惋惜等）
2 gravy train/boat 美差，肥缺
His father believes that the only good reason for going to university is to be able to get on the gravy train. 他父亲认为上学的唯一好处是可以找到容易赚大钱的工作。

great

1 great God/Caesar/Scott/Godfrey/Heavens/Sun/guns/snakes 哎呀，老天爷（表示惊讶、谴责、惋惜等）
Great guns! The lion is out of his cage. 哎哟，狮子跑出笼子啦！
Great Scott! Who stole my watch? 老天爷，谁偷了我的表？

2 great oaks from little acorns grow 万丈高楼平地起，小橡实可能长成参天大树
Many great men were once poor, unimportant boys. Great oaks from little acorns grow. 许多大人物一度都是贫穷、微不足道的，他们的成功是一点一滴的努力积累而成的。

3 no great of【美】不大好的，没有什么了不起的
They have no great opinion of our work. 他们对我们的工作没有多大

意见。

4 no great shakes/things/shucks 没有什么了不起,十分平常,不重要

As Prime Minister, he was no great shakes. He never did anything worthwhile during his whole period of office. 作为首相,他不太在行。他在整个执政期间没有做过任何有价值的事。

green

do you see any green in my eye 你以为我幼稚可欺吗

Lend you 5,000 dollars! Do you see any green in my eye? 借给你五千美元! 你以为我那么容易上当吗?

grief

good/great grief 参见 good 9

grin

1 grin and bear it 苦笑忍受,咬紧牙关

I'm not sure how I'll fit in this extra work when I am so busy already, but I suppose I'll just have to grin and bear it. 我还不能肯定我能否胜任这件分外的工作,我已经够忙的了。但是我想我会咬紧牙关坚持去做。

If you must have a tooth drilled, all you can do is grin and bear it. 如果你要补牙,就得忍受钻牙之苦。

2 take/wipe that grin/smile off your face 别对我嬉皮笑脸

Take that grin off your face for a start, Jones—this is serious. I'm going to find out who broke that window! 你先别对我嬉皮笑脸,琼斯,这是严肃的事。我要查出是谁打碎了那扇窗户。

grow

grow up 别孩子气

Grow up, Michael—when are you going to stop hitting boys younger than yourself? 别孩子气,迈克尔,你什么时候才能不欺负比你小的孩子啊?

Grow up, you're not a baby any more! 不要老像个孩子,你已经老大不小了!

guess

1 by guess and by God/Godfrey/gosh/golly 凭猜测,凭直觉或估计

2 guess what 你看怪不怪

3 I guess 【美】我想，我认为

"Mummy, can I play with Snoopy?" "Sophie, you know dinner's nearly ready. But I guess it's all right." "妈妈,我能和史努比玩一会吗?""索菲,你看饭马上就好了,可是我想你去玩一会也行。"

4 (it's) anybody's/anyone's guess 谁也说不准

It's anybody's guess who will win the next race! 谁也说不准下轮比赛谁赢！

What will happen next is anyone's guess! 下一步会出现什么事谁也说不准。

5 keep sb. guessing 让某人捉摸不定

A good story is one that keeps others guessing till the last minute. 好的故事应该是让别人直到最后一刻才能猜透的。

6 one man's guess is as good as another's 猜测终究是猜测

The future is so uncertain that one man's guess is as good as another's. 未来的事情很难臆测,大家都无法确定。

7 your guess is as good as mine 我和你一样不知道

"When is the bus coming?" "Your guess is as good as mine! They seem to turn up whenever they want to!" "公共汽车什么时候来?""我也不知道,看来他们是什么时候想来就什么时候来。"

guest

be my guest 请便；【美俚】悉听尊便（常用于讽刺）

"May I have some more?" "Be my guest!" "我可以再来一点吗?""请便。"
You want to tell the cop he's wrong? Be my guest. 你想要告诉警察说他错了? 悉听尊便。

gum

by gum 【粗】老天,哎呀,糟糕,好家伙（表示惊讶、懊丧）

gun

1 give it/her the gun 【口】加大油门,加速

2 great guns 哎呀,好家伙,糟糕（表示惊愕、谴责、惋惜）

3 jump/beat the gun 比赛时运动员偷跑；提前行动,过早行动

We jumped the gun by saying that you could buy televisions more cheaply. This is a plan to do this, but it is not yet in operation. 我们说你可以买到便宜的电视机还为时过早，现在倒是有一个计划要这样做，但尚未实施。
Newspapers both at home and abroad began to jump the gun and talk about impeachment. 国内外报纸开始过早地谈论弹劾问题。

gut

1 gut it out【美】强硬到底，坚持到底，熬到头
Smelly boy! Gut it out! 臭小子，坚持到底！

2 have one's guts for garters 抽……的筋，教训……，惩罚……
If that boy has taken my bike again, I'll have his guts for garters! 那个男孩儿要再动我的自行车，我就抽他的筋，剥他的皮。

3 run/scream one's guts out 拼命奔跑

4 sweat/work/slog one's guts out 拼命工作
I'm not going to work my guts out for only $10 a day. 我不会为一天十美元去卖命的。
I slog my guts out and get paid only a hundred pounds a week. 我工作非常努力，但每星期只有100英镑的报酬。

H

habit

habit is second nature 习惯成自然

hail

1 drink hail（祝酒时）干杯
2 hail Columbia【美】挨揍；该死，混账（原系歌名，现用作 hell 的委婉语）
3 hail from【美】来自何处；出生于
The other six hail from China, Greece, France and Cyprus. 其他六位来自中国、希腊、法国及塞浦路斯。
4 hail to the winner 向胜利者致敬
5 out of hail 在远处，在听到/听不到招呼的地方
6 within hail/call 在附近，在听到呼喊的地方
Born almost within hail of it, he could remember it from 1860 on. 由于他的出生地点离这里只有一箭之遥，1860 年以来的事情他全部记得。

hair

1 be/get in one's hair 烦扰……，使……受烦扰；激怒……，惹恼……
The children kept getting in my hair. 孩子们不停地惹恼我。
2 be out of one's hair 不再烦扰……
You know what, just give me a second and I'll be out of your hair. 你猜怎么着，只耽误你一会儿工夫我就不再烦你了。
3 comb one's hair for 申斥……，斥责……
Your wife will comb your hair for you. 你妻子会痛骂你一顿的。
4 comb/stroke one's hair the wrong way 使……恼怒，触怒……，犯……之忌
The worker combed his boss's hair the wrong way. 那个工人惹恼了老板。
5 curl one's hair 使人毛骨悚然
The prices here will curl your hair. 这儿的东西贵得吓死人。
The movie about monsters from another planet curled his hair. 有关来自

另一星球的怪物的电影使他毛骨悚然。

6 get gray (hair) 担心

"If John doesn't join the team, I won't get gray hair over it," the coach said. 教练说:"如果约翰不加入我们队,我一点也不担心。"

Naughty children are why mothers get gray. 顽皮孩子的母亲衰老得快。

7 get/have sb. by the short hairs/get sb. where the hair is short 任意摆布某人,控制住某人

Someone nasty and ruthless has him by the short hairs. 有个心狠手辣的家伙在摆布他。

8 get sb. out of one's hair 摆脱某人的烦扰

They sent him to America, just to get him out of their hair. 他们送他去美国,只是图个眼不见为净。

9 one's hair stand on end 吓得毛骨悚然

When James heard the strange cry, his hair stood on end. 詹姆斯听到奇怪的喊声吓得毛骨悚然。

10 hang by a hair/thread 千钧一发,岌岌可危,摇摇欲坠

For three days Tom was so sick that his life hung by a hair. 汤姆病重三天来真是命若游丝。

As Joe got ready to kick a field goal, the result of the game hung by a hair. 当乔准备射门时,场上的胜负真是千钧一发。

11 harm a hair of one's head 损伤……一根毫毛

If you harm a hair of my daughter's head, I'll kill you. 要是你敢伤我女儿一根毫毛,我宰了你。

12 keep one's hair/shirt on 保持镇静,不发火

Keep your hair on, Rod! I only asked if I could borrow the car for this evening, not for you to give it to me for ever! 别发火,罗德,我只不过问一下今晚能否借用你的车,并不是要你把车送给我!

"What are you doing with my radio?" "Keep your hair on! I'm just putting a new battery in it for you!" "你摆弄我的收音机干吗?""别激动,我只不过给它装上了新电池。"

13 let one's hair down/let down one's hair 不拘礼节,无拘无束,坦率直言;自由自在,放松一下

My father is very busy, he can seldom let his hair down. 我父亲工作很

忙,难得放松一下。

Go on, let your hair down this evening. You deserve it after the busy week you've had at work. 来吧,今天晚上你要好好放松一下。这是你紧张工作一周后应得的。

14 let your hair dry【美俚】别摆架子,别神气

Let your hair dry! You will fail soon. 别那么神气!你很快就会失败的。

15 lose one's hair【俚】发脾气,发怒

16 make one's hair stand (up) on end/make one's hair curl 使……毛骨悚然,使……害怕

17 split hairs 吹毛求疵

John is always splitting hairs, he often starts an argument about something small and unimportant. 约翰喜欢吹毛求疵,总是在一些鸡毛蒜皮的小事上争论不休。

Don't split hairs about whose turn it is to wash the dishes and make the beds; let's work together and finish sooner. 何必斤斤计较轮到谁洗碗、铺床,咱们一起动手干吧,可以更快干完。

18 tear one's hair (out) 扯自己的头发(表示强烈的愤怒、焦虑、悲伤等情绪)

Ben tore his hair when he saw the wrecked car. 本看到被撞毁的车子,怒气冲天。

The teacher tore his hair at the boy's stupid answer. 老师对这个学生的愚蠢回答感到泄气。

half

1 a... and a half 非常出色的;特大的;不一般的;更多的

That's a book and a half. 那是一本非常精彩的书。

I've come here for a purpose and a half. 我到这里来有特殊的目的。

2 by half 极大地,大大地

Jessie is the better singer by half. 杰西是一位实力强得多的歌手。

It helped to reduce street violence by half. 那有助于大大减少街头暴力。

3 by halves 部分地,不完善地,不完全的,不太热心地

Hansen paid his bills by halves. 汉森付了部分账单。

James never does things by halves. 詹姆斯做事从不马虎。

4 **go halves (on/in sth.) (with sb.)** 与某人平分某物；与某人均摊费用
The two boys *went halves on a piece of cake*. 两个男孩平分一块蛋糕。
Jonson *went halves with his brother* when they bought their mother some flowers. 琼森和兄弟买了一些花，费用平摊。

5 **half a loaf is better than none/no bread** 有一点总比没有好，聊胜于无
Albert wanted two dollars for shoveling snow from the sidewalk but the lady would only give him a dollar. And he said that *half a loaf is better than none*. 艾伯特想要两元作为他清扫人行道上积雪的报酬，但那妇人只肯给一元。他只好说聊胜于无。

6 **half a mind/notion** 有意，正想
I have *half a mind* to stop studying and walk over to the brook. 我正想暂停学习，去河边散散步。
Jerry went home with *half a mind* to telephone Betty. 杰里回家就想着要给贝蒂打电话。

7 **half a moment/half a mo/half a tick/just a moment/just a minute/just a sec/just a second/just a tick** 等一下

8 **half an eye** 瞟一眼；一望便知
The substitute teacher could see with *half an eye* that she was going to have trouble with the class. 代课老师一望便知驾驭这个班可不容易。
While Mary was cooking, she kept *half an eye* on the baby to see that he didn't get into mischief. 玛丽一边做饭，一边不时地瞟一眼婴儿，确保他没有淘气。

9 **not half** 很小程度地；一点也不，毫不；非常；差距很大地
They were *not half* done with the work. 那工作他们才做了一点点。
Lamb hasn't *half* enough money. 兰姆的钱还差很多。

10 **not half as** 远非，差得远，绝不是
Malan didn't feel *half as* bad when he got there. 马伦到达那儿时感觉好多了。

11 **the half of it** 整个情况或麻烦的一部分；较重要的一部分
If I told you *the half of it*, you'd be shocked. 如果我把实情告诉你，你会震惊的。
You've not seen *the half of it* yet. 你还没有看到事情要紧的那部分呢。

12 **too... by half** 太，过于

The play is too long by half. 这戏太长了。

You did that too quickly by half. It's all wrong. 你做得太快了,全都错了。

hand

1 a big hand for 请鼓掌欢迎

A big hand for Toby Tootall, the greatest circus acrobat of all time! 请鼓掌欢迎我们最杰出的马戏团杂技演员托比·图托。

2 a hand's turn 举手之劳(常用于否定句)

The lazy girl doesn't do a hand's turn in the house. 那懒姑娘在家里什么事也不干。

3 an open hand 慷慨,大方

Mark used to have an open hand. 马克过去一向挥金如土。

4 at hand 在近处,在手边,供使用;即将来到,被考虑中

When Kennedy writes, he always keeps a dictionary at hand. 肯尼迪写作时总放本词典在手边。

Your question is not related to the matter at hand. 你的问题与眼下审议的事无关。

5 bear a hand 帮帮忙,出把力

Will you bear a hand? 请你帮帮忙好吗?

6 bite the hand that feeds one 恩将仇报,忘恩负义

Even a beast don't bite the hand that feeds one. 最残忍的人也不会恩将仇报。

7 dirty one's hands 弄脏……的手,玷污……的名声

Do you think I would hit you? I wouldn't dirty my hands on you. 你以为我会打你？我才不会打你而弄脏我自己的手呢。

Parker never dirtied his hands with political intrigue. 帕克的名声很好,因为他从未参与任何政治阴谋。

8 give a (helping) hand 给予帮助,助一臂之力

Lewis has always been willing to give a hand to anyone who asked. 任何人有求于刘易斯,他都乐于帮助。

9 hand and/in glove 亲密合作;勾结

The feudal and religious forces worked hand in glove to oppress and exploit the people. 封建势力和宗教势力狼狈为奸,压迫和剥削人民。

10 hand it to sb. 赞扬某人，承认某人的长处

You've got to hand it to him; he's quite a salesman. 你不能不称赞他，他是个蛮不错的推销员。

11 hands off 不许碰，不许干涉

Hands off that machine—it's dangerous, you know! 别碰那机器，危险！

Hands off! She's my girlfriend, if you don't mind! 住手！对不起，她是我女朋友。

12 hands up 举起手来（要对方缴械投降）；举手（表示同意）

"Hands up, all those who want to go swimming," the teacher said. "想去游泳的举手！"老师说。

Hands up if you know the answer. 知道答案的举手。

13 raise one's hand against 举手要打，威胁要攻击

Don't you ever raise your hand against your father again! 看你还敢不敢威胁要打你父亲！

14 shake hands 握手（表示欢迎、问候或达成协议、表示和解等）；握手言和，重归于好

When I was introduced to Mr. Page, we shook hands. 当我被介绍给佩奇时，我们握手问候。

They shook hands after their quarrel. 他们争吵过后又握手言和。

15 sit on one's hands （对演出等）不热烈鼓掌，反应冷淡；什么都不干

I asked him for help, but he sat on his hands. 我请他帮助，但他没有行动。

16 take sb./sth. in hand 担负起对某人的责任，照管，承接，处理某事

Somebody far more expert than Sammy has taken Madge in hand. 一位比萨米经验丰富得多的人已接手管教玛奇。

The matter will be taken in hand before long. 这事不久将着手处理。

17 with one hand tied behind one's back 轻而易举地，易如反掌地

It is difficult for you to carry the box on your own. But I can carry it with one hand tied behind my back. 对你来说，自己扛这个箱子很难，但我可以毫不费力地扛起它。

18 have one's hand/fingers in the till 监守自盗

The store owner thought his business was failing until he discovered that the treasurer had his hand in the till. 店主原以为是他的生意失败，后来才

发现是财务会计监守自盗。

handful

a handful 难控制的人或物；费劲的事，麻烦的事
That child is quite a handful. 那男孩子真难管。
I shall have a handful when those boys come home for the holidays. 等那些男孩子回家度假时，够我麻烦的了。

handle

1 fly off the handle 大发雷霆，勃然大怒；十分激动，失去自制
Rosa flew off the handle for nothing. 罗莎无缘无故地大发雷霆。
2 handle with (kid) gloves 温和对待，小心处理，小心翼翼
This kind of dispute, we have to handle with kid gloves. 对于这类争端，处理时我们必须谨慎。
3 handle without (kid) gloves/mittens 粗暴对待，严厉对待，毫不留情地对待
The police chief declares that it is time for the good and true men to handle the impostors without gloves. 警察局长宣称，现在是那些善良诚实的人严厉处理那些骗子的时候了。

handsome

handsome is as handsome does 优雅慷慨始为美
Everyone thinks that Bob is a very handsome boy, but he is very mean too. Handsome is as handsome does. 大家都认为鲍勃长相帅气，其实他很自私刻薄。一个人行为优雅、慷慨大方始为美。

hang

1 give/care a hang/rap/straw 参见 give 3
2 (a) hang of a【澳新】极其，非常（用于加强语气）
It's a hang of a wet day. 天气十分潮湿。
3 be hanged 见鬼，该死（表示恼怒、不耐烦）
Next time be hanged! It won't come in a thousand years. 绝不会有下一次了。再过一千年，我也不会来了。
4 get the hang of 掌握……的窍门，熟悉……的用法，懂得……的意义

Once you **get the hang of** writing poetry, there's almost nothing you can't do with it. 一旦你掌握了写诗的窍门,关于诗就几乎没有什么可以难倒你的了。

5 go hang 不再被关心,被忽略,被遗忘;自顾自,不打扰别人

Norris let an opportunity **go hang**. 诺里斯错过了一个机会。

Practise your English everyday. You shouldn't let it **go hang**. 你们要天天练习英语,不要把它荒废了。

6 hang around/about 闲荡

Philip stopped **hanging about** and did something useful. 菲利普不再东游西逛,而是做了一些有益的事。

Don't **hang about** with them. 不要和他们鬼混。

7 hang in (there) 不泄气,不胆怯;坚持下去

Be prepared for a rough time, and **hang in** there. 准备吃苦,坚持下去。

Hang in there, old buddy; the worst is yet to come. 老伙伴,坚持住,还会有更糟的情况出现。

8 hang in the balance 难分高下,未见分晓

Until Jim scored the winning touchdown, the outcome of the game **hung in the balance**. 在吉姆触地得分前,比赛一直难分高下。

Polly was very sick and her life **hung in the balance** for several days. 波莉病得厉害,几天来生死不明。

9 hang it (all) 可恼,该死;岂有此理,见鬼(表示愤怒、烦恼、吃惊、不耐烦)

Oh, **hang it**! I forgot to bring the book I wanted to show. 可恼,我忘了把要给你看的书带来了。

Hang it all! You've had three weeks to plant the seeds and you say you've not even started! 真见鬼,你已经种下种子三个星期了,却说还没有开始!

10 hang on 等一下(要对方别挂断电话);请讲点道理;哎呀(表示惊讶)

Hang on—I'll just got a pencil and jot down the details. 请等一下,我拿支铅笔,详细记下来。

Hang on—don't I know you? Weren't we at school together? 什么? 我不认识你? 我们不是中学的同学吗?

11 hang/hold on to your hat 留神,小心

"**Hold on to your hat**," said Jim as he stepped on the gas and the car shot forward. "小心!"吉姆边说边踩油门,车便飞一般地向前冲去。

12 hang out 鬼混，居住；闲逛

The teacher complained that Joe was hanging out in pool rooms instead of doing his homework. 老师指责乔终日在台球室鬼混，不做功课。

Two policemen stopped the stranger and asked him where he hung out. 两个警察拦住一个陌生人，问他家在何处。

13 hang out one's shingle 贴出开业通告，挂牌开业；开始营业

The doctor hung out his shingle at the beginning of this year. 这位医生今年年初挂牌开业了。

The doctor has to take the exam before he can hang out his shingle. 医生在挂牌营业前必须通过考试。

14 I'll be hanged（用于赌咒）如果我……就不得好死；我死也不

I'm hanged if I know. 我要是知道，就不得好死。

I'll be hanged if I'll apologise this time—he should say he's sorry first. 这次我绝不向他道歉，他应该先认错才是。

15 hang you/you be hanged 该死的家伙，去你的吧（表示愤怒、烦恼、不耐烦、不满等）

16 let it all hang out 放轻松些，不拘礼节

"We are just off to the party." "Enjoy yourselves—let it all hang out." "我们就要去参加舞会。""大家玩个痛快，轻松随便些。"

happen

1 as it happens 碰巧，偶然

As it happens I have my notebook with me. 碰巧，我带着笔记本。

2 it (so) happens that 碰巧，恰巧

It so happens that I saw him yesterday. 昨天去碰巧看见他了。

3 it's all happening 一切顺利，一切都能如愿以偿

It's all happening here today! 今天这儿一切顺利！

It's all happening in Birmingham at the moment it's got a new shopping centre, good concert halls, and an excellent library—what more could you want? 现在伯明翰可好啦！那儿有一个新的购物中心，一些优秀的音乐厅，一个出色的图书馆。你还有什么要求不能满足呢？

happy

(as) happy as Harry/as happy as the day is long 极为快乐，非常幸福

Give my husband an old motorbike to tinker with and he's as happy as the day is long. 给我丈夫一辆老式摩托车让他修理,他就非常高兴。

hard

1 be hard put (to it) to do sth. 为难,在窘境中,进退维谷
John was hard put to find a good excuse for his lateness in coming to school. 约翰很难找到上学迟到的借口。
They found themselves hard put to it to find the way home. 他们发现很难找到回家的路。

2 be hard up 穷,缺钱,短缺
I'm a bit hard up this month. Can you lend me some money? 我这个月手头有点紧,你能借点钱给我吗?

3 be hard up against it/have it hard 【美】处境艰难,面临种种困难
The widow was hard up against it, ever so hard. 这位寡妇吃了很多苦,生活真是苦极了。

hash

1 hash out 【美】充分讨论或辩论
The teacher asked Susan and Jane to sit down together and hash out their differences. 老师要苏珊和简坐下来,把她们的分歧好好讨论一下。
The students hashed out the matter and decided to drop it. 学生们把问题彻底讨论后决定放弃。

2 hash over 【美】充分讨论;回忆过去
I have something I want to hash over with you. 我有事要跟你好好谈谈。

3 hash up/make a hash of 搅乱,弄糟,弄砸
Bob really hashed up that exam and failed the course. 鲍勃真的把考试弄砸了,这门功课不及格。

4 settle one's hash/settle the hash of sb. 制服……,使……哑口无言
That remark settled her hash. 那句话说得她哑口无言。
It's very probable, sir, that you won't be wanted upstairs for several minutes, sir, because my master is at this moment particularly engaged in the settling the hash of your master. 先生,可能暂时用不着你上楼去,因为我的主人这时候正在收拾你的主人呢。

hat

1 by this hat/my hat to a halfpenny 我敢拿一切来担保，我敢打赌；千真万确，毫无疑问
My hat to a halfpenny! This story is true. 我敢担保，这个故事是真的。

2 hang one's hat on 【美】依靠，指望
The old man had nothing to hang his hat on. 那个老人没有什么可依靠的。

3 hang up one's hat 在某处住下来，停止惯常的活动
At the age of 60, Pope hung up his hat. 波普60岁时退休了。

4 hat in hand/(with) one's hat in one's hand 毕恭毕敬，卑躬屈膝
The student was standing hat in hand before his teacher. 那个学生恭恭敬敬地站在老师跟前。

5 hats off to 让我们向……表示敬意
Hats off to this company for making such a fine product. 让我们向这家制造出这样好的产品的公司致敬。

6 keep sth. under one's hat 保密
Mr. Jones knew who had won the contest, but he kept it under his hat until it was announced publicly. 琼斯先生知道谁赢了这场比赛，但他一直保密，直到公布时为止。
I hear that John and Mary are getting a divorce, but keep it under your hat. 我听说约翰和玛丽准备离婚，不过请保密。

7 my hat 啊（表惊讶）；胡说，我不信
Seventy, my hat! Surely you're only around fifty! 七十岁，天哪！实际上你只有五十岁呀！
My hat! It's cold today, isn't it? 天哪，今天真冷，不是吗？

8 old hat 不合时宜的，老式的，过时的
This camera looks pretty old hat. 这相机看上去过时了。
Mary thought her mother's ideas about dating were old hat. 玛丽认为她母亲对约会的看法太古板。

9 out of a hat 随便地，任意地；像耍魔术般变出一个……
Take one out of a hat. 随便拿一个。

10 pull out of a/one's hat 变出，编出；发明；想象
When the introduction to a dictionary tells you how many hours went into its making, these figures were not pulled out of a hat. 字典的前言中说编

篡工作历时多久,这数字可不是瞎编的。
Let's see you pull an excuse out of your hat. 看你能编出什么理由。
11 put that/this in/under your hat 【美】记住这一点吧;你好好琢磨琢磨吧
12 raise/take off one's hat to sb. 向某人致意,向某人表示钦佩
I take off my hat to him for his courage. 我钦佩他的勇气。
I take off my hat to you. I thought you were wrong from the very first, but I guess you know this game better than I do. 我真佩服你。起初我以为你错了。可现在我看你对这套把戏比我在行多啦。
13 shit in your hat 【美】去你的
14 talk through/out of one's hat/talk wet 【美】信口开河,胡说八道
Don't take any notice of what he says, he's just talking through his hat. 别听他的话,他在胡说八道。
John said that the earth is nearer the sun in summer, but the teacher said he was talking through his hat. 约翰说夏天地球比较接近太阳,但老师说他是瞎说。
15 throw/toss one's/a hat in/into the ring 参加竞选或竞赛、讨论等
A former senator from Massachusetts named Paul Tsongas was the first Democrat to throw his hat in the ring for this year's presidential election. 麻省一位名字叫保罗·聪格斯的前参议员是第一个决定参加今年总统竞选的民主党人。

hatch

down the hatch 【美】干杯(饮酒前朋友之间的互祝之词)
Well, down the hatch. 好吧,干杯。

haul

haul down one's flag 屈服,投降;认输
They can either haul down their flag or run away. 他们要么投降要么逃跑。

have

1 **have a ball** 玩得高兴,过得愉快
John had a ball at camp. 约翰在露营时玩得很痛快。
After their parents left, the children had a ball. 父母离开后孩子们玩得很

开心。

2　have a care 当心

Jane, have a care what you are doing with that valuable glass. 珍妮,当心那只珍贵的玻璃杯。

The judge told him to have a care what he said in court. 法官叫他注意法庭上的语言。

3　have a finger in the pie 参见 finger 2

4　have/throw a fit/fits 生气,发怒

When John decided to drop out of college, his parents had fits. 当约翰决定退学时,他父母很生气。

5　have a go at 跃跃欲试

Bob asked Dick to let him have a go at shooting at the target with Dick's rifle. 鲍勃请求迪克让他用迪克的枪射一回靶。

Rhodes had a go at archery, but did not do very well. 罗兹尝试射过箭,但成绩不太好。

6　have a heart 发善心,发慈悲,行善事

Have a heart, Bob, and lend me two dollars. 鲍勃,行行好,借给我两块钱。

Robbins didn't know if the teacher would have a heart and pass him. 罗宾斯不知道老师会不会发善心让他及格。

7　have a screw loose 行为古怪,疯疯癫癫,傻里傻气

Now I know he has a screw loose—he stole a police car this time. 现在我才知道他是有点疯——这次他竟然偷了辆警车。

Samuel was a smart man but had a screw loose and people thought him odd. 塞缪尔是个聪明人,但行动有点怪异,因此人们认为他太古怪。

8　have a time 遇到麻烦,过一段痛苦的时间;欢乐时光,愉快

Poor Susan had a time trying to get the children to go to bed. 可怜的苏珊为了哄孩子睡觉,要费好大的劲。

John had a time passing his math course. 为了通过数学考试,约翰熬了一阵子。

9　have all one's buttons/marbles 精神正常,头脑清醒(通常用于否定句或条件句)

Mike acts sometimes as if he didn't have all his buttons. 迈克有时表现得

像脑子有问题似的。

Kingsley would not go to town barefooted if he had all his marbles. 如果金斯利头脑清醒,他就不会赤脚进城。

10 have/keep an ear to the ground 注意舆论动向

The city manager kept an ear to the ground for a while before deciding to raise the city employees' pay. 市长在决定给城市职工加薪之前,一再细心地注意舆论动向。

Reporters keep an ear to the ground so as to know as soon as possible what will happen. 记者们一直注意舆论动向,以便尽快地掌握最新动态。

11 have an edge on 占优势;略胜一筹;微醉

I can't beat you at tennis, but I have an edge on you in ping-pong. 网球我无法赢你,但打乒乓球我胜你一筹。

Joe sure had an edge on when I saw him last night. 昨晚我看见乔时,他一定是喝了几杯,有点儿醉了。

12 have an eye for 能鉴别好坏,有眼光

Lily has an eye for color and style in clothes. 在鉴别服装的颜色和式样方面,莉莉很有眼光。

Martin has an eye for good English usage. 马丁能识别正确的英语用法。

13 have an/one's eye on 把目光投向;集中注意于;想要……;想以……为目标

I bought ice cream, but Jimmy had his eye on some candy. 我买冰激凌,但吉米却想要糖果。

John has his eye on a scholarship so he can go to college. 约翰想得到奖学金,这样他就能够上大学了。

14 have/keep/with an/one's eye out 留心,注意

Keep an eye out. We're close to Joe's house. 当心,我们已接近乔的房子了。

Mary has her eye out for bargains. 玛丽最留心商品大减价的信息。

15 have/with an eye to 留心,注意;打算,计划

Have an eye to spelling in these test papers. 留意试卷上的错别字。

John is going to college with an eye to becoming a lawyer. 约翰要上大学,打算当律师。

16 have been around 经验丰富,见过世面

Uncle Willie is an old sailor and has really been around. 威利叔叔是个老水手,见过世面。

It's not easy to fool Garcia, he's been around. 欺哄加西亚可不容易,他是见过世面的。

17 have had it/sb./sth. 吃够了苦头,受够了,忍无可忍;感到厌烦;行将就木;已失去机会或效用;没落;不再受欢迎

I've been working like a fool, but now I've had it. 我一直像个傻瓜似的干着,但现在我可受够了。

His bicycle looks as though it's had it. 他的自行车看上去已经坏得没法收拾了。

I've about had pop music. 我对流行音乐已没有多大兴趣了。

18 have it 说,找到或想出答案;处境(好或坏)

Shakespeare has it that all the world is a stage. 莎士比亚说整个世界是个大舞台。

Rumor has it that the school burned down. 谣言说学校已经被烧毁了。

19 have it all together 【美】把生活安排得有条不紊;使身心都得到平衡

Why is it that some people seem to have it all together while others are shy and afraid? 为什么一些人似乎能把生活安排得井井有条而另一些人却害羞、恐惧,生活一团糟?

20 have it bad (for) 对……怀有一片痴情

I love my girlfriend. I really have it bad for her. 我爱我的女友,我疯狂迷恋着她。

21 have it/that coming (to sb.) 应该,活该

John had that defeat coming to him. 约翰那次失败是活该。

Jack had it coming when he won the scholarship. 杰克获得奖学金是应该的。

22 have it good 过得舒心快乐

Alice really has it good. Everybody caters to her every need. 爱丽丝真是享受得很,大家都迁就他。

23 have it in for sb. 对某人有恶感,总想伤害某人

George has it in for Bob because Bob told the teacher that George cheated in the examination. 鲍勃告诉老师说乔治考试时作弊,乔治怀恨在心,想伺机报复。

I don't think Morgan *has it in for you*. 我认为摩根对你并无恶意。

24 have (got) it made 一定成功,不愁没出路
With her fine grade, Alice *has it made* and can enter any college in the country. 凭爱丽丝的优异成绩,她肯定能顺利地进入国内的任何大学。

The other seniors think Joe *has it made* because his father owns a big factory. 其他毕业生们认为乔不愁找工作,因为他父亲拥有一家大工厂。

25 have kittens 忐忑不安,忧心忡忡
Mrs. Jones was *having kittens* because it was very late and Susan wasn't home yet. 夜已深,苏珊尚未回家,琼斯太太因而忧心忡忡。

26 have no business 无权,没有理由
Jack *had no business* saying those nasty things about Dick. 杰克没有理由说迪克的坏话。

Mike's mother told him he *had no business* going swimming that day. 迈克的母亲说他那天实在不该去游泳。

27 have none of 不许
The teacher said she would *have none of* Tom's arguing. 老师说她不许汤姆争辩。

When the fullback refused to obey the captain, the captain said he would *have none of* that. 当后卫拒绝服从队长时,队长说他决不允许这种行为发生。

28 have nothing/anything on 不优于,未胜过;没有证据、把柄
Susan is a wonderful athlete, but it comes to dancing she *has nothing on* Mary. 苏珊是个优秀的运动员,但谈到跳舞她就不如玛丽了。

Even though he is older, John *has nothing on* Peter in school. 虽然约翰年纪大些,但他的功课并不比彼得强。

29 have on 有计划,有约会;戏弄,欺哄
Harry *has* a big weekend *on*. 哈里计划好好度过周末。

Don't take any notice of what he says, he's just *having you on*. 别理会他说的话,他在骗你。

30 have oneself (sth.) 给自己某物;使自己做某事;痛快地享受
I *had myself* a small brandy. 我自己喝了一点白兰地。

After working hard all day, John *had himself* a good night's sleep. 辛苦地工作了一天,约翰好好地睡了一夜。

31 have one's hand/fingers in the till 参见 hand 18

32 have one's ear 受到……重用；对……有影响

Watts is nowhere near as arrogant as you were when you *had Kennedy's ear*. 肯尼迪重用你的时候，你比沃茨可狂妄多了。

My friend *has the boss's ear* and could put in a good word about you. 我朋友在老板那里说得上话，能帮你美言几句。

33 have one's hide 严惩，惩罚

John's mother said she would *have his hide* if he was late to school again. 约翰的母亲说如果他再迟到将受到严惩。

34 have rocks in one's head 昏了头，做错误决定

When Mr. James quit his good job with the coal company to begin teaching in school, some people thought he *had rocks in his head*. 詹姆士先生辞去了煤矿公司的好工作去教书，有人认为他简直是昏了头。

35 have sth. on sb. 有某人的把柄

Mr. Jones didn't want to run for office, because he knew the opponents *had something on him*. 琼斯先生不想竞争公职，因为他知道自己有把柄落在对方手里。

36 have (got) sth. on the ball 很伶俐，很老练

You can trust John; he's *got a lot on the ball*. 你可以信赖约翰，他很老练。

37 have/get the best/better of 赢取，获益；赢得，打败

Bill traded an old bicycle tire for a horn; he *got the best of* that deal. 比尔用旧自行车轮胎换了个喇叭，他占了便宜。

Our team *had the best of* it today, but they may lose the game tomorrow. 我们队今天赢了，但明天可能会输。

38 have/get the goods on 参见 get 63

39 have/get the jump on 占优势，领先，胜过

Don't let the other boys *get the jump on* you at the beginning of the race. 比赛一开始就不能让别的男孩儿占优势。

Our team *got the jump on* their rivals in the first minutes of play, and held the lead to win. 我们队一开始就领先对方，直至赢得胜利。

40 have/get the worst of 失败，被击败；遭受极大痛苦

Joe *got the worst of* the argument with Molly. 乔在辩论中败给了茉莉。

If you start a fight with Jim, you may have the worst of it. 你要是和吉姆起争端,你可能要倒霉了。

41 have to be 【美】无疑,必定
You have to be joking! 你一定是在开玩笑吧!
This has to be the best movie of the year. 这部电影无疑是今年最好的。

42 have two strikes against/on 情况不利,困难重重
Children from the poorest of a city often have two strikes against them before they enter school. 贫困地区的孩子上学很不容易。
George has two strikes against him already. Everybody is against what he wants to do. 乔治处境很不好,大家都反对他想做的事。

43 I have and I haven't 我说不上来(回答别人询问时模棱两可的答复)
"Have you spoken to Mr. Smith about a pay rise?" "I have and I haven't—not directly yet, but I promise tomorrow." "你问过史密斯先生关于加薪的事了吗?""啊,说不上来,还没直接说,不过明天我一定说。"
"Have you got any work for me to mark?" "Well, I have and I haven't." "你有什么作业要我批改的吗?""啊,说不上来。"

44 I wouldn't have it if you give it to me 你就是送给我,我也不要
That car of yours is so old, I wouldn't have it if you give it to me! 那车子太旧了,你就是送给我,我也不要。

45 let's be having you 对不起,请离开这儿(公共场所的侍者、工地的领班、现场的警察等说的话)
Come along now, let's be having you, please! 啊,对不起,请各位离开!
Ladies and gentlemen, let's be having you; the museum closes in ten minutes. 女士们先生们,请原谅,博物馆还有十分钟就要关门了,请离开吧。

46 you shouldn't have 非常感谢(用于接受别人礼物时)
"Auntie, we've brought you some flowers, and all the family hope you'll get better soon." "Oh, you shouldn't have! Aren't they lovely!" "姨妈,我们给你买了些鲜花来,大家都希望您早日康复。""啊,太感谢啦,这花多美啊!"

head

1 above one's head/the head of sb. 太高深,难理解

Your lecture was a bit above my head. 你的演讲比较深奥，我不太理解。We shouldn't talk above the head of our students. 我们讲的内容不应超过学生的理解水平。

2 an old head on young shoulders 少年老成

Moulton has an old head on young shoulders. 莫尔顿少年老成。

3 bang/beat/bash one's head against a (brick) wall 徒劳无功，无谓挣扎

Trying to make him change his mind is just beating your head against a wall. 要想改变他的想法是徒劳无功的。

4 beat/bang/hammer/knock sth. into one's head 向……灌输，反复说教

Tom is lazy and stubborn and his lessons have to be beaten into his head. 汤姆懒惰固执，他的功课必须反复督促、硬性灌输才行。

I cannot beat it into his head that he should take off his hat in the house. 在室内摘下帽子一事，我不知对他说了多少遍，他就是记不住。

5 big head 目空一切，狂妄自大

When Jack was elected captain of the team, it gave him a big head. 杰克被选上队长以后就变得目空一切了。

It was his social position that was giving Parker the big head. 社会地位使帕克变得自高自大起来。

6 bite/snap one's head/nose off 大声怒吼，气势汹汹地回答……，声色俱厉地训斥……

I only asked you a question. There's no need to bite my head off. 我只问了你一个问题，你何必对我这么凶。

You don't have to bite my head off. 你没有必要这样对我大发脾气。

7 bury one's head in the sand 不肯正视事实

Never bury your head in the sand; you need to face what has already happened. 不要逃避现实；你必须正视已经发生的事情。

8 by the head 微醉

Robbins was a little by the head. 罗宾斯微有醉意。

9 carry/hold one's head high 趾高气扬

A mark of true nobility is, not to hold one's head high, but to bear oneself humbly in high station of life. 真正高贵的标志并不是趾高气扬，而是身居高位仍然谦虚谨慎。

10 come into one's head/enter one's head 想起

Sally gave the first name that *came into her head*. 萨莉把想到的第一个名字随口说出。

It hasn't even *entered my head*. 我连想都没想到。

11 come to a head 达到决定阶段,达到顶点,紧要关头

Things *came to a head* in mid-August. 八月中旬情况到了紧要关头。

The dispute *came to a head* yesterday. 昨天那场争论达到了白热化程度。

12 get (sth.) into/through (one's) head 充分理解,明白,相信;固执地认为

At last Rudolf *got it into his head* that some newspapermen have been out to smear him. 鲁道夫固执地认为有些新闻记者蓄意诽谤他。

13 get one's head down 躺下睡觉;重新坐下来工作

I'll have to *get my head down* for a bit before going out. 我要先睡一会儿再出去。

I'll have to *get my head down* in order to finish all this work. 为了完成这些工作,我还得坐下来好好干。

14 get/put sb./sth. out of one's head 不去想,尽量忘掉

I wish I would *get* the picture of that awful accident *out of my head*. 但愿我能把那次事故的可怕情景忘掉。

Susan tried in vain to *put* him *out of her head*. 苏珊竭力不去想他,可是不行。

15 give sb. his head/let sb. have his head 让人随意而为、随心所欲

Give him *his head*. 随他便吧。

16 go to one's head 使……入迷,使……沉醉;使……冲昏头脑

Sweet was very busy writing a book and it's *gone to his head*. 斯威特正忙着写一本书,已经写得入迷了。

You mustn't let this success *go to your head*. 你不能让这次胜利冲昏了你的头脑。

17 have a good/no head for 在……方面有天分/在……方面缺乏天分

Taylor *has a good head for* figures. 泰勒擅长演算。

Pound *has no head for* figures. 庞德不善演算。

18 have a (good) head on one's shoulder/have (got) one's head screwed on (the) right way 精明,有见识(尤指会做生意)

Soames did very well; he's *got his head screwed on the right way*. 索米斯干得很好,他很精明。

19 have/keep a level/cool/one's head 保持镇静

Pansy has a level head in emergencies. 潘西临危不乱。

Luckily the driver kept his head, or there might have been a serious accident. 幸亏司机保持镇静，否则可能发生严重车祸。

20 have a long head 有远见，有先见之明

Mr. Smith is a person who has a long head. 史密斯先生是一个有远见的人。

21 have a swollen/swelled head 自负，骄傲自大

Peter has had a swelled head since he went to Harvard. 彼得自从进入哈佛大学之后，他就忘乎所以骄傲自大起来。

22 have one's head in a tar barrel 【美】陷入困境；闹出笑话

Peter had his head in a tar barrel sure enough. 不出所料，彼得陷入了困境。

23 have one's head in the clouds 心不在焉，想入非非

If you think oil companies are going to help destroy their own industry by developing alternative energy sources, you have your head in the clouds. 如果你觉得石油公司会放弃他们的产业发展而致力于替代能源开发，那你就太富于幻想了。

24 head and ears 完全地，深深地

Nancy is head and ears in debt. 南希背了一身债。

25 head and shoulders above 远远地超过，出类拔萃

Morley towers head and shoulders above all his contemporaries. 摩利在同辈人中是出类拔萃的。

Martha is head and shoulders above the rest of the class in singing. 马莎的歌唱得比班上其他人都好。

26 heads or tails 正面还是反面（在游戏中用猜硬币的正反面决定次序、胜负）

"Let's toss for it—heads or tails?" "Heads!" "Heads it is!" "让我们抛硬币定输赢吧。正面还是反面？""正面。""不错，是正面。"

27 heads up 注意，当心

Heads up, boys! A train is coming. 注意，孩子们！火车来了。

Heads up now! You can do better than that. 这次注意点，你就能做得更好。

28　keep one's head/wits 保持冷静，处之泰然，不动声色

The boy managed to keep his head in a difficult situation. 那个男孩儿在困境中设法保持清醒的头脑。

29　keep one's head above water 凑合着过日子，勉强维持生活

A man who loses his job tries to keep his head above water until he finds a new job. 一个失业者在找到新工作之前只能凑合着过日子。

30　keep one's head above ground 活着，保住生命

31　knock... on the head 使……落空

The increase in the price of cars knocked their hopes for a new one on the head. 汽车涨价使他们购置新车的希望化为泡影。

32　knock one's heads together 用武力（断然手段）制止争吵，强迫争议双方接受和谈

You should knock their silly heads together. 你应设法让他们明白事理。

33　knock one's head off （为惩罚或报复威胁要）揍扁……，痛打……，让……吃苦头；轻易胜过……

If I see that kid in my orchard again I'll knock his head off. 我要是再看到那个小孩到我的果园里来，我就揍他。

34　laugh one's head off 大笑，狂笑

The joke was so funny that I almost laughed my head off. 这个笑话太滑稽了，让我大笑不止。

35　lay/put (one's) heads together 共同商量

They laid their heads together and formed a plan. 他们集思广益，制定了一个计划。

You didn't put your heads together as to what you would say to us? 你们要对我们说的话事先没有商量过吗？

36　lose one's head 昏头昏脑，惊慌失措

Don't lose your head in an emergency. 遇到紧急情况不要慌乱。

Mary saw the train coming, she lost her head altogether and stepped on the gas. 玛丽看到火车来时，惊慌失措反而猛踩油门加速。

37　make head or tail of 弄清楚，了解（常用于否定句）

I can't make head or tail of her letter. 我一点也看不明白她的信。

It is difficult to make head or tail of the whole business. 要摸清整个事情的底细很困难。

38 off with one's head 处死……

The women sat knitting in front of the guillotine. "Off with his head!" they shouted. 妇女们坐在断头台前织着毛衣,她们怒吼:"绞死他!"

39 open one's head 【美】说,开口

Lewis didn't open his head for the whole ten miles. 走了十英里路,刘易斯一句话也没说。

40 put a head on sb. 【美】痛揍某人,迫使某人不敢开口;击败某人

I'll try my best to put a head on the other contestants. 我要竭尽全力击败其他选手。

41 talk one's head off 对……唠叨不休;(自己)喋喋不休,说得天花乱坠

Penn will talk your head off if you give him a chance. 佩恩一有机会就会对你说个没完。

Be careful, she'll talk your head off. 小心,她会对你喋喋不休地说个不停。

42 throw/fling oneself at someone's head 极力讨好

Louise threw herself at his head, but he was interested in another girl. 路易丝极力讨好他,但他对别的女孩儿感兴趣。

43 work one's head off 苦干,拼命干活

Lucy worked her head off as an actress so that she could make more money for her family. 露西作为演员干活很拼命,这样她才能挣更多的钱养家。

headache

1 a headache/headaches 令人头痛的人或事

This is one of her little headaches in her life. 这是她生活中令她头痛的一件琐事。

That kid is a real headache. 那孩子真叫人头痛。

2 be no more use than/as good as a (sick) headache 毫无用处

This contract is as good as a sick headache. 这份合同丝毫不起作用。

health

your health/good health/to your health/your (very) good health 祝你健康(敬酒用语)

Your health, Pat—may you have prosperous time in Scotland! 帕特,祝你健康,祝你在苏格兰一帆风顺!

The whole gathering raised their glasses and the chairman spoke, "Your very good health, colonel Digby!"全体与会者举起酒杯,主席说:"迪格拜上校,祝你健康!"

hear

1 hear, hear 听啊,听啊;说得好,说得好(表示赞同的喝彩声)
"The government may decide in certain circumstances to reduce the amount of tax paid." "Hear, hear!" "政府可能决定在一定情况下削减缴纳的税款。""好哇,好哇!"
I think I'd better go and do washing-up!" "Hear, hear!" "我看还是我去洗餐具吧。""好哇,好哇!"

2 I've heard that one before 我不信;别找借口了
"Let's go to the disco on Friday!" "I've heard that one before—you always say that and then forget about it later!" "我们星期五去参加迪斯科舞会吧!""我才不信呢,你老是说要去,可是过后又忘了。"

3 that's a good hearing 这倒是个好消息

4 to hear some people tell it 听人说

5 will not hear of 不允许,拒绝考虑
I want to go to the show tonight, but I know my mother will not hear of it. 今晚我想看演出,但我知道母亲不会允许的。
Mary needs another day to finish her book report, but the teacher won't hear of any delay. 玛丽需要再多一天完成读书报告,但老师不允许她拖延。

heart

1 after one's (own) heart 合……心意
You are a man after my own heart. 你很合我心意。
Thanks for agreeing with me about the class party; you're a girl after my own heart. 感谢你在班会上和我意见一致,你是个令人愉悦的女孩儿。

2 at heart/in heart/in one's heart (of hearts) 内心里,实质上
Frank is not mean at heart. 弗兰克心地并不坏。
Helina knew in her heart of hearts that it was a lie. 赫莉娜心里明白那是谎话。

3 bless one's heart/heart and soul/life/me 哎呀,好家伙,我的天哪(表示惊愕、意外、喜欢、感谢等)

Bless her heart, hasn't she grown into a beautiful lady! 哎呀,她已长成一个漂亮的少女了!

Bless your heart, you shouldn't have spent so much money on me! 哎呀,你真不该为我破费这么多!

4 bring one's heart into one's mouth/make one's heart leap out of one's mouth 使……吓得要命

The sound brought my heart into my mouth. 这响声把我吓得要命。

5 cross one's heart (and hope to die) 在胸口划十字(发誓说真话或不泄密)

Cross my heart, I didn't hide your dictionary. 我发誓我没有藏你的词典。
Promise me you won't tell him what I have said. Cross your heart and hope to die! 你答应我绝不把我说的话告诉他,你发誓,说了不得好死。

6 dear heart 哎呀,糟糕,我的天哪(表示惊讶、懊丧)

Dear heart, it's half past two; I must be off! 哎呀,已经两点半了,我得走了!

7 eat one's heart out 忧伤、沮丧;因忧虑或渴望而憔悴

For months of her son's death, she simply ate her heart out. 在她儿子死后的几个月内她悲痛欲绝。

8 find (it) in one's heart to do sth. 甘心,忍心,情愿(一般用在否定句中)

I cannot find it in my heart to disappoint you. 我实在不忍心使你们失望。
John could not find it in his heart to tell her about her mother's death. 约翰不忍心把她母亲的死讯告诉她。

9 have a heart 参见 have 6

10 heart and hand 热心地,尽心尽力地

I am with you heart and hand. 我全心全意地支持你。

11 heart and soul 全心全意,竭诚地,完全地

Eden is heart and soul in his work. 艾登一心一意地工作。
I put my heart and soul into writing that speech, so don't tell me it wasn't worth it! 我全身心投入地写这篇演讲稿,所以请你别对我说那不值得。

12 heart goes out to 深表同情

Frank's heart went out to the poor children playing in the slum street. 弗兰克对在贫民区街上玩耍的穷孩子深表同情。
Our heart went out to the young mother whose child had died. 我们对丧

子的年轻母亲很同情。

13 hearts and flowers【美】伤感,多愁善感

Just don't come around here with hearts and flowers. 可别带着伤感之情来这儿。

14 my heart bleeds/aches for sb. 幽默地表示遗憾

"I've got to be up by seven tomorrow to get to work early." "My heart bleeds for you—I get up at six every day at the moment." "我明天早上得在七点钟起床去上班。""你真走运呀,我一直都是六点钟起床的。"

15 with all one's heart 全心全意地,真心实意地

Ferdinand welcomed the visitors with all his heart. 费迪南德竭诚欢迎来访者。

I will do it for you with all my heart. 我十分愿意为你效劳。

16 with half a heart 半心半意地,不大愿意地,勉勉强强地

The house maid always does her work with half a heart. 那个女佣干活总是半心半意。

heave

1 heave away 用力拉呀（水手在起锚时的呼喊）

Everybody, heave away! 大伙儿用力拉啊!

2 heave to 停下,停止

"Heave to!" the captain shouted to his crew. "抛锚!"船长对船员们喊道。

We fired a warning shot across the front of the pirate ship to make her heave to. 我们在海盗船前鸣枪示警,令其停航。

3 heave up 起锚;呕吐

They heaved up the anchor by means of a donkey engine. 他们用辅助发动机把锚拖了出来。

The boy ate some green apples, and not long after, he was sick and heaved up. 那男孩吃了几个青苹果,不久他就开始作呕,接着就吐了出来。

heaven

1 by heaven 哎呀,天哪（表示惊奇、不信、厌烦等）

By heaven! It's snowing at last. 哎呀,终于下雪了!

**2 for Heaven's/God's/Christ's/goodness'/mercy's/pity's sake 看在上帝的份上,行行好吧,请帮帮忙;天哪,哎呀（用于加强请求的语气或表示厌烦、

惊奇)

For goodness' sake, stop arguing! 看在老天爷份上,别再争论了!

Why for heaven's sake didn't you tell me you were feeling ill? 天哪,你为什么不告诉我你感觉不舒服?

3 good heavens/lord 参见 good 8

4 Heaven/God forbid 参见 god 5

5 Heaven/God/Goodness/Lord knows 参见 god 8

6 heaven and earth 天哪,好家伙,糟糕(表示惊愕、惋惜等);千方百计,竭尽全力;天地,宇宙万物,天上人间

The difference is not unlike between heaven and earth. 何啻天壤之别。

7 heaven on earth 地上天堂,极大快乐

Autumn is not always heaven on earth. 在人世间秋天并不总是天堂。

8 Heaven/God/Saints preserve us 参见 god 9

9 Heavens above 天哪(表示惊讶、怀疑、烦恼)

Heavens above! That's Jane Mitcham over there—I've not seen her for years! 天哪,那不是简·米切亚姆吗! 我已多年没见到她了。

Heavens above, child! Can't you be quiet for two minutes? 天哪,孩子,你能安静两分钟吗?

10 in heaven 究竟,到底(加强语气)

Where in heaven were you? 你当时究竟在哪里?

What in heaven happened? 到底发生了什么事?

11 in Heaven's/God's name 参见 god 15

12 in (the) seventh heaven 在七重天,如登天堂,在极乐世界

The child was in the seventh heaven with his new toys. 那孩子有了新玩具快乐极了。

13 move heaven and earth 参见 earth 3

14 thank heaven(s)/God/goodness/God be thanked 参见 god 17

15 under heaven 到底,究竟(加强语气)

Who under heaven would have done such a thing? 天底下谁会干出这种事?

heck (hell 的委婉语,用于加强语气或表示恼怒、诅咒、厌烦等)

1 heck no 决不

2 oh, heck 真见鬼

3 to heck with 见……鬼去吧

One day you say,"To heck with this." 有一天您会说"去他的"。

4 where (in) the heck/on earth have you been 你刚才到底上哪儿去了

heel

1 at heel/at/on/upon one's heels/the heels of sb./sth. 跟在后面,尾随,接踵而至

The boy got tired of having his little brother at his heels all day. 这男孩厌烦小弟弟整日跟在自己后面。

I came that morning on the heels of my letter. 那天早上我的信刚到,我也跟着到了。

2 cool/kick one's heels 参见 cool 2

hell

1 a hell of 糟糕的,坏透的,很艰难的,很麻烦的;极好的,影响极大的,极度的,异常的

The company is in a hell of a mess. 这家公司情况糟透了。

We had a hell of time on holiday last year. 我们去年度假时玩得很痛快。

2 a hell of a lot 许多,大量;非常,远远

A hell of a lot has happened. 发生了许多许多事情。

Rebecca likes her child a hell of a lot. 丽贝卡非常喜欢她的孩子。

3 a hell of a note 怪事,坏事,令人瞠目结舌的事

A lot of people don't like dogs, it's a hell of a note. 很多人不喜欢狗,真是怪事。

4 as hell 非常地,极端地,可怕地(强调激动)

I'm sorry/grateful as hell about all of this. 对这一切我非常抱歉/感谢。

5 be hell on 【美】对……来说很痛苦/很不愉快/很困难;对……十分严厉或苛刻;对……极端有害

I do know it's been hell on you. 我确实知道这一阵子够你受的。

It's going to be hell on wheels. 这对车轮十分有害。

6 come hell or high water 不论发生何事;无论如何

Grandfather said he would go to the fair, come hell or high water. 祖父说他无论如何也要去参观博览会。

I'm determined to finish the job come hell or high water. 不管有多大困难,我决心把那件工作做完。

7 go through hell (and high water) 赴汤蹈火,出生入死,经受重重困难

John is ready to go through hell and high water to help his friend. 约翰正准备为帮助他的朋友而赴汤蹈火。

The soldiers went through hell and high water to capture the fort. 士兵们经过浴血奋战才夺下了这个堡垒。

8 go to hell 越来越糟,恶化;见你的鬼,去你的吧

The whole town's gone to hell with that new mayor. 那个新市长上任以后情况越来越糟。

"Can I have a word with you for a moment?" "No, I'm tired of you annoying me all day—go to hell!" "我能和你谈一会儿吗?" "不行,我讨厌你整天缠着我。你给我滚开!"

9 go to hell in a hand basket/a bucket 急剧恶化

The company can only go to hell in a hand basket with this damned dead cat bounce. 该死的"死猫反弹"只能使该公司的处境迅速恶化。

10 have a/the hell of a time 度过一段非常艰苦的日子;经历一段可怕的生活;过得非常快乐,玩得非常痛快

They had a hell of a time in the desert. 他们在沙漠中度过了一段非常艰苦的日子。

You really ought to have been at the dance last night. It was very jolly and we had the hell of a time. 你真该去参加昨晚的舞会,实在太好了,我们玩得非常痛快。

11 hell and Tommy 彻底毁灭

12 hell for leather 飞快地,高速地

Malan was running hell for leather across the grass. 马伦飞快地跑过草地。

Norris rode hell for leather down the street. 诺里斯策马飞驰过街道。

13 hell's bells/teeth 见鬼

Hell's bells! How many more times do I have to tell you to shut up? 真见鬼!我还要对你说多少遍才能叫你闭上嘴呢?

14 hell to pay 大麻烦,重罚,痛骂

If he's late, there'll be hell to pay. 他如果迟到就要吃苦头了。

15 hope/wish to hell 渴望，从心眼里盼望

I *hope to hell* you would come earlier. 我很希望你早些来。

16 in hell 到底，究竟（表示恼怒、惊奇）

Where *in hell* have you been? 你究竟到哪里去了？

Who *in hell* are you? 你到底是谁？

17 like hell/the hell you will/can 非常厉害地；拼命地；哪能有这种事，绝不会

It's raining *like hell*. 雨下得大极了。

Grace always works *like hell* before exams. 格雷斯总是在考试前拼命用功。

18 play hell with 破坏，损坏，制造麻烦

If you drive badly, it *plays hell with* the tyres of your car. 如果你胡乱驾驶，你会损坏车轮。

Grey is a splendid speaker. He absolutely *played hell with* his opponents. 格雷是个出色的演说家，将对方驳得体无完肤。

19 raise hell 大吵大闹，引起骚动；制造麻烦

They *raised hell* with neighborhood children. 他们跟邻居的孩子大吵起来。

They *raised hell* about pollution. 他们为污染问题大兴问罪之师。

20 the hell of it is 【美】妙就妙在……；麻烦就在于……

The hell of the plan is that it works. 这计划好就好在行得通。

The hell of it is, how do you refute the charges. 问题在于你如何驳斥那些指责。

21 the hell you say 真出人意料

22 there will be hell to pay 那就不得了啦，那就麻烦啦，后果不堪设想

If and when prices crash, *there will be hell to pay*. 万一要是价格暴跌，后果不堪设想。

23 to hell and gone 极度，极远，永远

Henry says London is *to hell and gone* from here. 亨利说伦敦离这儿很远。

The line parted and the boat was carried *to hell and gone*. 绳子断了，小船漂向了远方。

24 to hell with 让……见鬼去吧

No need to worry; to hell with all this. 不必操心，让这一切都见鬼去吧！
To hell with this essay—I've spent hours on it already, but I don't seem to be getting anywhere! 让这篇文章见鬼去吧，我已经为它花了好几个小时，但似乎并没什么进展。

25 until hell freezes over 永远地

Hoover can argue until hell freezes over; nobody will believe him. 胡佛辩论不休，但没人会相信他。

26 what/how/where/who/why, etc. the hell/heck 到底，究竟（表示不在乎或无可奈何）

I know the fare is expensive, but what the hell. 我知道车费很贵，但这没关系。

How the hell are we going to get out of this mess? 我们究竟怎样才能摆脱这一困境呢？

Who the hell do you think you are coming in here without even knocking? 你以为你是谁呀？不敲门就闯进来。

27 when hell freezes over【美】绝不会有的事，决不

I'll believe when hell freezes over. 我决不相信会发生这种事。

help

1 cannot help but 不得不

I cannot help but admire his courage. 我不得不赞赏他的勇气。

When your country calls you to help, you cannot help but go. 一旦国家需要你，你必须尽力为国效劳。

2 God/heaven help sb. 参见 help 6

3 help yourself to 请随意用，不要客气

Help yourself to another piece of pie. 请再吃一块馅饼吧。

John helped himself to some candy without asking. 约翰没有询问就自己拿了一些糖果吃。

4 I can't help it 我实在没有办法，这不能怪我

I mean, whenever I see him or think of him, I can't help it, this smile comes across my face. 我的意思是说，无论何时我看见他或者想起他，我控制不了，我脸上就会露出微笑。

5 it can't be helped 这是无可奈何的事

This is a law of nature and *it can't be helped*. 这是自然规律，没有办法。

6 **not if I can help it/not if I know it** 我实在没有办法，这不能怪我

I won't pay the money on time, *not if I can help it*. 我不能按时付这笔钱，这不能怪我。

Not if I know it, you won't borrow my car! 不行，你不能借我的车，这不能怪我。

7 **so help me** 我保证，我发誓

I've told you the truth, *so help me*. 我发誓，我已告诉你事实了。

If you're not at the theatre tonight, *so help me*, I'll resign as your agent! 如果你今晚不去剧院，我发誓，再也不当你的经纪人了。

8 **so help me God** 参见 god 16

9 **there is no help for it** 这件事实在没有办法

There is no help for it but to delay our journey. 没办法，只好推迟我们的旅行。

here

1 **here goes** 看我的，我开始啦

"*Here goes*!" said Charley, as he jumped off the high diving board. 查利从高台上跳水时叫道："看我的！"

"*Here goes*!" said Mary as she started the test. 玛丽开始做测验时说："我开始啦！"

2 **here goes nothing** 没什么了不起；大不了失败吧

"*Here goes nothing*," said Bill at the beginning of the race. "就算滥竽充数吧，"比尔在比赛开始时说。

3 **here you are** 给你，（你要的东西）来了，你到了……；你看吧，请把……

Here you are, madam, what you ordered, roast chicken and peas. 来啦，夫人，这是您要的烤鸡和青豆。

You say you want to go to the States in July but, *here you are*, it's January already and you've still not got any money—you'd better start saving, my lad! 你说你打算七月份去美国，可是你看，现在已是一月份了，你还没有弄到一点钱。伙计，我看你最好还是先攒点钱吧。

4 **here's to/【美】here's how** 祝你健康，敬你一杯，为……干杯

Here's to the bride and groom! 为新娘新郎的幸福干杯！

Here's to a long and happy life! 祝长寿愉快!

5 look here/【美】see here 听我说(引人注意)

6 same here 彼此彼此,我也一样

"I'd like to see you again, sir." "Same here!" "很想再见到你,先生。""我也一样。"

Hey

1 Hey presto (感到突然或意外)嘿;(变戏法者用语)嘿,变

Do you see this smart top hat? Hey presto, here are two rabbits jumping out of it! 请看,这是一只平顶帽子。嘿,变! 现在从里面跳出两只野兔。The doorbell rang. I went to see who it was. Hey presto! It was my brother, Jason, who I'd not seen for years! 门铃响了,我去看谁来了。嘿,真想不到,竟是我弟弟杰森,我多年没见到他了。

2 Hey, that's nice 嘿,真妙

high

1 high, wide and handsome 【美】无忧无虑地,充满自信地;轻而易举地,成功地

Tom could talk high, wide and handsome when he set out to. 汤姆一旦打开话匣子,就会没完没了地说个不停。

2 how is that for high 【美】你说妙不妙,你说怪不怪

I didn't pass the exam, how is that for high? 我考试没有及格,你说怪不怪?

hint

hint, hint 喂,喂(委婉地表示应该做什么事)

"It's ten o'clock, hint, hint!" muttered Sue quietly. Sam understood. "Yes, I think it's time we went," he said. "现在是十点钟啦,喂,喂!"苏轻轻地咕哝了一句。山姆明白她的意思,说:"对,我想我们该走了。"
A cup of tea would be nice—hint, hint! 要有一杯茶就好了,噢,噢。

hip

hip, hip, hurrah 希普,希普,万岁(由带头欢呼者呼喊 hip, hip,众人跟着喊 hurrah,如此反复喊三遍)

Congratulations to the team for coming first in the competition! Hip, hip, hurrah! Hip, hip, hurrah! Hip, hip, hurrah! 祝贺赢得比赛冠军的队伍，希普，希普，万岁！希普，希普，万岁！希普，希普，万岁！

hit

1 hit between the eyes 留下深刻的印象；大为惊讶

Let us suppose that this man gets hit between the eyes. 我们假设，这个男的受宠若惊。

2 hit it off 相处融洽，志趣相投

From the first time they met, they hit it off. 他们一见如故。

Mary and Jane hit it off from the first. 玛丽和简一开始便十分合得来。

3 hit the books 参见 book 7

hold

1 hold cheap 不重视，瞧不起，低估

Those who look big are always held cheap by others. 自高自大的人往往被别人瞧不起。

2 hold hard 等一等，停住

Hold hard! There's no great hurry to start. 等一等，不要急着开始。

3 hold it/everything 参见 everything 3

4 hold on 等一下（打电话时叫对方别挂断）

"Is Mr. Jackson there, please?" "Hold on, I'll see if he's available." "请杰克逊先生接电话。""等一下，我去看看他在不在。"

Hold on a minute! Aren't you the man the police are looking for in connection with the robbery? 等一等，你不就是警察正在搜捕的那个与劫案有关的人吗？

5 hold one's horses 站住，等一等，忍一忍

"Hold your horses!" Mr. Jones said to David when David wanted to call the police. 戴维要喊警察，琼斯先生对他说："等一等！"

6 hold one's noise/peace/tongue/jaw/mouth 保持沉默，闭口不言，住嘴，别嚷

Hold your peace, sir, … and keep your own breath to cool your own porridge. 别多嘴，先生，……还是少管闲事吧。

If people would hold their tongues from unkind speech, fewer people would be hurt. 人们如果不说不友好的言论,受到伤害的人就会少一些。

7 hold out on 不答应;不向……屈服

The boss has been *holding out on* me. 老板一直不答应我的要求。

Holy

1 holy hell 臭骂,训斥;严惩

I caught *holy hell* when the thing broke. 这东西打碎后我挨了顿臭骂。

2 holy Mackerel/Moses/smoke/cow/cats 参见 cat 5

home

1 be at home in/on/with 精通或熟悉某一问题、行业

Jack is not much *at home in* the art of spelling. 杰克拼写还不够熟练。

This is a subject on which he is much more *at home* than you. 这个问题他要比你内行得多。

2 go home 滚回去(标语口号)

Prime Minister *go home*! 首相滚回去!

Foreign troops *go home*! 外国军队滚回去!

3 home, James 开车回家(招呼司机开车回家的幽默用语)

The children got into the back of the car and called out "*Home, James*!" to their father. 孩子们钻进汽车后座向父亲喊道:"开车回家!"

4 home was never like this 【美】真开心,太好了

5 make yourself at home 请随便些,像在自己家里一样,请不必客气

Do come in and *make yourself at home*! Would you like something to eat? 请进,别客气,像在自己家里一样。你想吃点什么吗?

Sit down and *make yourself at home*, while I put the kettle on for a cap of tea. 请坐,别客气。我去给你沏杯茶。

6 nothing to write home about 平淡无奇,平凡;无聊

We certainly don't know why she wants to marry him. He's as ugly as sin, and his brains are *nothing to write home about*. 我们当然不明白她为什么想嫁给那个男人,论相貌,奇丑无比,论头脑,也是稀松平常。

7 who's... when he's/she's, etc. at home ……是谁,我怎么没听说过这个人

"I'm off to see Tracy Rossiter." "Tracy Rossiter? *Who's she when she's at home*?" "我要去看特蕾西·罗西特。""特蕾西·罗西特,她到底是谁?"

honest

1 honest Injun 【美】绝对不假,天地良心(Injun 是 Indian 的误用)

I've never seen her before in my life, honest Injun! 说真的,我以前从未见过她。

2 honest to goodness/God 参见 God 14

honour

1 do the honours 尽地主之谊,招待客人

The wine is over there—will you do the honours? 酒在那儿,你去向客人们敬一杯好吗?

The president of the club will do the honours at the banquet. 社团的会长将主持宴会。

2 God's/Scout's honour 真的,千真万确

God's honour! I'm telling the truth! 真的,我说的是实话!

I am really going to finish my work tonight, Scout's honour! 真的! 今晚我一定完成我的工作。

3 honour bright/on my honour 真的,一定

On my honour, we will do all we can to help you. 真的,我们一定尽力帮助你。

"John earns ＄20,000 a year." "Honour bright?" "Honour bright!" "约翰一年赚两万美元。""真的吗?""真的!"

hook

1 hook, line, and sinker 完全,全部

Johnny was so easily fooled that he fell for Joe's story hook, line and sinker. 约翰尼总是轻信他人,所以他毫不怀疑乔编的故事。

Mary was such a romantic girl that she swallowed the story Alice told her about her date, hook, line, and sinker. 玛丽是一个充满幻想的女孩,她完全相信爱丽丝告诉她的关于她约会的故事。

2 on one's own hook 独自地,独立地

I must think of starting in business on my own hook with the new year. 我必须打算明年开始自己做生意。

Let me help you. It's no easy thing to go on your own hook here. 让我帮

帮你吧,在这儿孤军奋战可不容易呀。

3 sling/take one's hook/hook it 逃走,溜走

I'm tired of school, let's hook it for the day! 我讨厌上学,我们今天逃一天学吧!

4 throw the hooks into 【美】欺骗,使上钩

hookey/hooky

1 by hookey/the living hookey 【美】岂有此理;真的,绝对可靠

2 play hookey【美】/truant【英】逃学

Carl is failing in school because he has played hookey so many times during the year. 卡尔今年考试不及格,因为他经常逃学。

hoop

1 go through the hoop/hoops 经受考验,历尽沧桑;饱尝辛酸;久经磨炼

They went through the hoop in the countryside. 他们在农村经受过磨炼。

2 jump through a hoop/hoops【美】经受考验,做最大努力;对……俯首帖耳,对……百般讨好

Bob would jump through a hoop for Mary. 鲍勃对玛丽唯命是从。

hoot

1 not care/give/matter a hoot/two hoots 不在乎,根本不在意

I don't care a hoot for what you do or say. 你要做什么说什么我都不在乎。

You can stay or go just as you please—it doesn't matter a hoot to me. 去留听便,与我毫无关系。

2 not worth a hoot/leek 一钱不值

What the CEO of the company said is not worth a hoot. 公司首席执行官所说的话毫无价值。

hop

1 catch/take sb. on the hop 使某人措手不及;当场抓获某人

Our visitors arrived early, and caught us on the hop. 客人提早到达,令我们措手不及。

2 hop in 上车

I've never given anyone a lift, but you hop in! 我从来不让任何人搭车,可是你上车吧。

3 hop off/out 下车;离开;起飞;死亡

The little girl was not willing to hop off as I drove at the gate of her house. 我把车开到小姑娘家门口时,她还不肯下车。

The old man had hopped off when the ambulance reached the hospital. 当救护车开到医院时,那个老人已经死了。

4 hop it 走开

Hop it, Pete, we don't want you around! 走开,皮特,别在我们跟前捣乱!

5 hop to it【美】开始做事;赶紧

There's a lot to do today, so let's hop to it. 今天要做的事很多,我们开始吧。

We shall have to hop to it if we're to catch the train. 我们要赶上这班火车,就得抓紧时间。

6 on the hop 忙碌,忙乱,奔忙

Jackson was kept on the hop yesterday. 杰克逊昨天忙得团团转。

hope

1 hope against hope 在绝望中仍抱希望

Katharine continued to hope against hope that her son had survived the shipwreck. 凯瑟琳对儿子在船只失事中能幸免于难仍抱一线希望。

Jane hoped against hope that Joe would call her. 明知没有希望了,简仍然盼望乔会打电话给她。

2 I hope you feel proud of yourself 我希望你争气

I hope you feel proud of yourself, Sarah! Your silly behaviour in the restaurant really made your mother and me feel embarrassed! 我希望你争气,萨拉,你在餐馆里的愚蠢行为,真使我和你母亲十分难堪。

3 some hope(s)/not a hope/(a) fat chance 参见 chance 1

horn

1 blow/toot one's own horn 参见 blow 9

2 draw/haul/pull in one's horns 收敛傲气,软下来,缩回去,打退堂鼓;缩减开支

The fellow drew in his horns, and acknowledged he might have been mistaken. 那家伙软了下来,承认可能是他自己搞错了。

Lamb said he could beat any man there single-handed, but he pulled in his horns when Jack came forward. 兰姆说他可以独自打败那里的任何人,可是当杰克向他挑战时,他却退缩了。

3 horn/butt in 插嘴;闯入,侵入;干涉

Louise loves to horn in on her husband's official functions. 路易丝老爱干预她丈夫的公务社交。

Mary was explaining to Jane how to knit a sweater when Barbara butted in. 玛丽正在向简讲解怎样织毛衣,芭芭拉却在一旁插嘴。

4 lift/raise up the horn 得意忘形,趾高气扬;显示斗志,不示弱,不屈服

5 lock horns 【美】抵触,冲突,斗争,较量

Lucy locked horns with him over the subject of equal pay for women. 露西和他就妇女同工同酬的问题争得不可开交。

6 lower one's horn 卑躬屈膝,收敛气焰

Pride when it has lowered its horn as it skirted by ruin, now raises it again as it touches success. 一个人的骄气在遇到挫折时会消沉下来,而一遇到成功便会重新抬头。

7 show one's horns 凶相毕露

8 take the bull by the horns 参见 bull 2

horse

1 a horse of another/a different color 参见 color 3

2 a horse of the same color 完全是一回事

3 back the wrong horse/bet on the wrong horse 参见 bet 3

4 be on/get on/ride the high horse 目空一切,傲气凌人

Edith appeared to be on her high horse tonight. 伊迪丝今天晚上看上去真是目空一切。

5 buy a white horse 浪费钱财

It's a crime to buy a white horse like that. 那样浪费金钱是一种罪过。

6 come off the/one's high horse 放下架子

Nancy's father frequently asked her to come off her high horse and make friends with other girls. 南希的父亲屡次告诫她不要自视过高,要与其他女孩子交朋友。

7 hitch one's horses together【美】/put up one's horses together【英】意见一致；同心协力；情投意合

We can't keep harmony with each other all the time, contrarily, we have to hitch our horses together with. Meanwhile, it is a common phenomenon for us to stand our own opinions for same questions. 人与人之间的相处不可能一直都十分融洽，难免会有磕磕碰碰的时候。同时，对同样的问题持不同的意见，也是很平常的事。

8 hold one's horses 参见 hold 5

9 horse around 玩耍，哄闹，捣蛋

John horsed around with the dog a while when he came in from school. 约翰放学回家后逗了一会狗。

The pupils spoke in low tones and there was none of usual horsing around. 学生们轻声细语地说话，再不像往常那样哄闹。

10 horse sense 常识，判断力

Bill had never been to college, but he had plenty of horse sense. 比尔从未上过大学，但他却有丰富的常识。

Some people are well educated and read many books, but still do not have much horse sense. 有些人受过良好的教育，读过许多书，但一点生活的常识和判断力都没有。

11 wild horses shall/would not drag it from/out of me 休想从我这里探到口风

The newspaper reporters wanted to know why I had resigned from the cabinet but wild horses wouldn't drag it out of me. 新闻记者想知道我为什么辞去内阁职务，但是他们休想从我这里探到口风。

hot

1 give it to sb. hot/give it hot to sb./make it hot for sb. 痛打某人；狠狠责罚某人；与某人为难，使某人难堪

I gave it to him hot for that matter. 为那事我把他臭骂了一顿。

2 hot air 空话，大话

This was not just inaugural hot air. 这并不是就职时讲的空话大话。

His utterances are so much hot air. 他的发言大话连篇。

3 (all) hot and bothered 慌张；激动；忧虑，困惑；气冲冲地

Fritz got all hot and bothered when he failed in the test. 弗里茨考试失败以后焦虑不安。

Jerry was hot and bothered about his invention when he couldn't get it to work. 杰里为他的发明未能成功而忧虑。

4 hot and heavy/strong 猛烈地，激烈地

The partners had a hot and heavy argument before deciding to enlarge their store. 合伙人经过激烈的辩论之后才决定扩大营业规模。

5 hot dog 参见 dog 5

6 hot number 热门的，流行的；引人注目的

The boys and girls thought that song was a hot number. 青年男女都认为那首歌挺时髦。

The new car that Bob is driving is a real hot number. 鲍勃驾驶的那辆新车真棒。

7 hot one 出众的，非凡的

Joe's joke sure was a hot one. 乔的玩笑果然不凡。

Sue Beever is a hot one, isn't she? 苏·比弗是个出众的女孩，不是吗？

8 hot potato 难处理的问题

In the meantime, passing the buck like a hot potato does not work. 同时，将美元像个烫手山芋一样推出去是做不到的。

9 hot seat 电椅；不好办的差事，尴尬的局面

Tony Blair—his friend and erstwhile boss, who takes the hot seat soon—will have been watching anxiously. 作为他的朋友和过去的老板，托尼·布莱尔不久将如坐针毡，并将一直焦急地关注此事。

10 hot water 麻烦

11 not so/too hot 【美】普普通通的，没什么了不起的

Edward didn't flunk out, but his record isn't so hot. 爱德华没有退学，但成绩不太好。

Foster has not been feeling too hot recently. 近来福斯特感到身体不太好。

how

1 and how 【美】当然喽，那还用说（表示强调或讥讽）

Am I happy? And how! 问我幸福吗？当然幸福！

"So you have a good time in London?" "And how! It was all so dirty, the hotel was expensive, the trains were all late—we're never going back there!" "你们在伦敦玩得很痛快吗？""嗐，别提了！那里一片肮脏，旅馆又贵，火车总是晚点——我们这一辈子再也不想去那里了。"

2 and old how 粗枝大叶地，胡乱地

3 how are you/how are things/how are you keeping/how's yourself 你好吗，你身体怎么样，你好（问候用语）

4 how come 参见 come 15

5 how comes it/how is it 怎么啦，这是怎么搞的

How is it you always arrive late on Mondays? 为什么你星期一老是迟到？

6 how do you like them apples 【美】你们看棒不棒（炫耀）

I got her number, how do you like them apples? 我要到她的号码了！瞧我牛吧？

7 how is it for 在（特点方面）还满意吗

"Do you want to try on this coat?" "Yes, let's." "How is it for size?" "你想试试这件大衣吗？""对，让我试试。""尺码还合适吗？"

8 how now 这是怎么回事，这是什么意思

9 how so 怎么会这样，为什么

"I thought the concert was very disappointing." "How so?" "The lead singer didn't turn up, and the understudy couldn't reach the high notes properly." "我认为这个音乐会很令人失望。""怎么啦？""领唱没有来，替代者达不到高音部的要求。"

I said the party was a failure and she asked, "How so?" 我说舞会很不成功，她问道："为什么？"

10 how's that 你的意见怎么样，你怎么看；你说什么，再说一遍好吗；为什么

"I'm not sure I'll be able to come and visit you again." "How's that?" "我不能肯定还能不能来看你。""为什么？"

"I'm going to be an astronaut when I grow up." "How's that?" "I said I'm going to be an astronaut when I grow up." "我长大了要当个宇航员。""你说什么？""我说我长大了要当宇航员。"

11 how's that for 赞扬（某事物的特点）或引起注意

How's that for economy! It's the cheapest small car available! 价钱可真不错！这是最便宜的一辆小汽车了。

How is that for impudence! 多么放肆！

12 how's tricks 【美】你好吗；情况怎么样

How's tricks in the grocery trade this week? 这个星期的食品生意怎么样？

13 how then 这是怎么回事；这是什么意思；后来怎样；还有什么

14 how are they hanging 【美】(男子间的问候语)你好吗

How are they hanging here in the ghetto? 在贫民窟里感觉怎样？

hundred

1 a cool hundred 【口】巨款，百镑巨款

Why did the corporation lose *a cool hundred* machine tools? 那家公司为什么损失了整整100台机床？

2 like a hundred of bricks 势不可挡地，来势凶猛地；气势汹汹地

The boss come down upon the worker *like a hundred of bricks*. 老板严厉训斥了那个工人。

I

I

I'll be【美】哎呀,好家伙(表示吃惊、诧异)

ice

1 break the ice 给难办的事开个头;打破沉默;使气氛活跃
Fortunately, we had the baby with us when we went round there for tea, so that helped to break the ice. 幸好,我们去那儿喝茶时把小宝宝也带了去,这才打破了拘束,气氛变得自然些了。
They nodded to each other by way of breaking the ice of unacquaintance. 他们彼此点点头,以便打破不相识的尴尬僵局。

2 cut no/any/much ice 不起作用/起任何作用/起很大作用;没有影响/有任何影响/有很大影响
The argument cut no ice with me. 那个论据一点也说服不了我。
When Frank had found a movie he liked, what others said cut no ice with him. 只要弗兰克认为这是一部好电影,谁也无法改变他的看法。

3 on ice 必胜无疑的;保存着,暂时搁置
With their lead they had the game on ice. 有了领先的优势,他们肯定会赢得比赛。
You will have to put your vacation plans on ice until your debts are paid. 你在未偿清债务前,必须暂停度假计划。

4 put... on ice【美】把……忘掉;把……暂时搁置
We'll put the project on ice. 我们要把这项工程暂时搁置起来。

idea

1 big/grand/great idea 高见,好主意,妙招(含讽刺意味)
2 get/have ideas (into one's head) 抱有不切实际的或有害的想法
Don't get any ideas into your head about buttering her up because it won't work. 别打主意拍她马屁了,她不吃这一套。
3 it's/that's an idea 这可是个好主意

"Shall we go to America for the day?" "That's an idea! I'd never thought of that!" "我们就在这天去美国好吗?""好啊,我怎么没想到这点!"

4 one's idea of ……对……的看法

It's not my idea of the thing. 这不是我对这件事的看法。

Camping in the rain is not my idea of fun. 我觉得在雨中露营不是有趣的事。

5 that's the idea 对了,就是这个意思;我赞成,这行

"Listen, Mum, to me playing this piece by Mozart." "Yes, that's the idea! You are coming on very well now." "妈妈,听我演奏莫扎特的这支曲子吧。""好啊,你现在进步很快呀!"

6 what an idea/the very idea 这是什么话,多么荒唐,真是异想天开

What an idea, thinking mother was my sister! 多么荒唐,竟以为母亲是我的姐姐!

The very idea of Tom bringing that dirty dog into my clean house! 真不像话,汤姆竟把这么脏的狗带进了我干净的房子!

7 what's the (big) idea 这是什么馊主意;你要干什么

The Smith family painted their house red, white and blue. What's the big idea? 史密斯一家把房子刷成红、白、蓝三色,这是要干什么?

What's the big idea of gossiping about me behind my back? 背后散布我的流言蜚语,你想干什么?

if

1 if/well if 表示惊奇、沮丧或恼怒(与动词否定式连用)

Well if that isn't limit! 唉,实在是忍无可忍了。

If it isn't spotty Brian from London! What are you doing here in America? 那不是从伦敦来的该死的布莱恩吗?你到美国来干什么?

2 if anything 更像是,不如说是

The weather forcast is not for cooler weather; if anything, it is expected to be warmer. 气象预报没说天气会转凉,倒像是要变暖。

Joe isn't a bad boy. If anything, he's a pretty good one. 乔并不坏,说他是个好孩子更好些。

3 what if 如果……将如何呢;假设

What if you go instead of me? 你代替我去怎么样?

What if the President were shot? 要是总统真的被刺杀了后果会怎样呢?

ill

1 ill at ease 局促不安,不自在
The principal appeared ill at ease at the party. 在宴会上校长显得局促不安。

2 make sb. ill 使某人生气,使某人讨厌;使某人恶心
What my young sister said made me ill. 我妹妹说的话使我很生气。

imagine

(just) imagine (that/it) 亏你想得出来,难以想象(表示惊奇或反对)
Just imagine! After all these years of buying British, he's now bought a foreign car! 亏他想得出来,这些年都买英国车,可现在他竟买了一辆进口车!
"My dad's a driver on one of the new fast trains!" "Imagine that! I thought he was a ticket-collector!" "我爸爸是新型高速列车的司机!""哎呀,真了不起,我以为他是检票员呢!"

in

1 be in for it 骑虎难下,没有退路;势必受罚
Now that you are in for it, you must carry on. 你既然沾上了手,就得干下去。
The children knew they were in for it. 孩子们知道他们肯定要受处罚了。

2 be in at …… 发生时在场
They were in at the start of the economic boom. 他们赶上了经济繁荣时期。

3 be in on it 熟悉内情
The hotel manager says it's to fix a broken pipe, but he may be in on it too. 酒店经理说他们是去修理破裂的水管,但他也有可能混入其中。

4 have it in for 对……怀有仇恨,伺机报复……
Some politicians seem to have it in for the environment these days. 近来,一些政客们似乎总是和环境过不去。
Adams seems to have it in for me for some reason. 不知为什么,亚当斯对我似乎总是耿耿于怀。

5 in on 参与……；对……有所闻

The police are in on the case. 警察正在查办这个案件。

The monitor should be let in on secrets. 应该让班长知道这个秘密。

6 in with you 进去

7 in a bind/box 身处窘境，左右为难

OPEC's de facto leader and the world's largest exporter, Saudi Arabia, finds itself in a bind. 全球最大的石油出口国、欧佩克的实际领导者沙特阿拉伯发现自己正身处困境。

8 in a hole/spot 处境尴尬，陷入困境

I'm in a hole. Can you help me? 我遇到麻烦了，你能帮我忙吗？

9 in way over one's head 搞不清楚状况

Stanley, you're in way over your head. 史丹利，你根本没搞清状况。

Irish

get one's Irish/dander up 参见 dander

iron

1 iron out 解决困难、纠纷

All difficulties were finally ironed out and the contract signed. 一切困难终于解决了，合同签订了。

2 put all irons/every iron in the fire 使用种种手段，用尽一切办法

Peter had begun to canvass and was putting every iron in the fire. 彼得已开始游说活动，正采取各种手段来达到目的。

issue

the whole issue 全部

Not a soul got back, the whole issue was done in last night. 昨晚没一个人活着回来，全完了。

it

1 at it 忙个不停；正在工作，从事某项活动

John is at it night and day. 约翰日夜奔忙。

I caught William at it red-handed. 威廉正干得起劲，被我当场逮住了。

2 be it 在某一方面很了不起，是杰出的专家

Do you mean to tell me you don't know his name? Why, among biologists, he's it! 你真的不知道他的姓名吗？在生物学家当中，他是最出色的一个！

3　have it in 有能力，能做到

I knew Oscar had it in him. 我知道奥斯卡能做到。

4　in it 有好处的，得益的；参与的；足以形成对抗的（常用于否定句）

I can't see what there was in it for Mrs. Plum. 我看不出这对普卢姆夫人有什么好处。

They had a good time, but I was not in it. 他们玩得很痛快，可没我的份。

5　it couldn't happen to a nicer guy【美】活该（常指被开除或受罚）

6　it shouldn't happen to a dog【美】即使是狗也不该受这份罪

7　it's you 这东西配你是再合适不过了

8　think sb. is it【美】自以为了不起

They thought they were it. 他们自以为了不起。

J

Jack

1 before you can say Jack Robinson/knife 参见 before 3

2 I'm all right, Jack 老兄,我没事(表示只求自己没事的自私心理)

We're going to make sure that our union gets the highest pay settlement this year. Workers in other industries don't count; it's "I'm all right, Jack", that's important. 我们将确保我们的工会行业今年获得最高的工资,至于别的行业就不在其列了。这就是典型的"老兄,我没事儿"的心态,这一点很重要。

Ford adopted an "I'm all right, Jack" attitude in leaving his convoy. 福特离开护卫队时摆出一副"老子没事"的得意架势。

3 Jack at a pinch 紧急时有用的人或物;临时找来代替的人

4 Jack of all trades 万能先生,万事通,万金油,博而不精的人

The "Jack of all trades" question is something I've struggled with for a long time. "是否做博而不精的人"这个问题曾经困扰了我很长一段时间。

jacket

1 dress down/dust/trash/trim/warm one's jacket 殴打……,痛骂……

The father has dusted the boy's jacket for telling a lie. 那位父亲因孩子说谎而痛打了他一顿。

2 pull down your jacket 冷静点

Pull down your jacket, young man! 小伙子,镇定,别激动!

jam

1 (have) jam on it 好上加好,十分走运

You have a well-paid job and a company car, and now you're asking for travelling expenses. What do you want, jam on it? 你有一份收入丰厚的工作、一辆公司的汽车,现在你又要求差旅费。你想干什么,好上加好吗?

2 all jam 轻松的工作;令人愉快的事物;好运气

The job isn't all jam. 这工作并不轻松。

3 like/want jam on it 一心想好上加好；过分奢望，不知足
4 real jam 难得的享受；叫人高兴的事物；轻松的活儿

jaw

1 hold/stop your jaw 住口，别废话
2 jaws tight 生气；紧张
Why are you getting your jaws so tight? 你为什么生那么大的气？
3 one's jaw drops (a mile) ……惊讶得目瞪口呆
Tom's jaw dropped a mile when he won the prize. 汤姆获奖时惊讶得目瞪口呆。

jazz

jazz sth. up 使某事更有趣，使某事更令人兴奋
The party was very dull until Pete jazzed it up with his drums. 他们的舞会本来很沉闷，后来皮特表演击鼓，气氛才活跃起来。

jeeper

jeepers/jeepers creepers【美】天哪，哎呀（表示惊讶）
Jeepers creepers, Auron's coming down the drive—we'd better move! 哎呀，奥隆要来赶我们走。我们快搬家吧！

Jerusalem

Jerusalem 啊，天哪
Geoffrey looked at his watch and cried, "Jerusalem! It's nearly five o'clock." 杰弗里看了看表，嚷道："啊，都快五点了！"

Jesus

1 beat/knock the Jesus out of【美】把……揍得屁滚尿流
I'm going to knock the Jesus out of him for doing that to my girlfriend. 他那样对待我的女朋友，我要把他好好收拾一顿。
2 by Jesus/Jesus wept 天哪（用于起誓或表示不信、惊讶、不耐烦等）
By Jesus, did you see that! 天哪，果然被你看见了！
George is so spineless, Jesus wept! 老天爷，乔治真是个大草包！

jiffy

1 in a jiffy 瞬间，马上；一下子

I'll be ready in a jiffy. 我马上就好了。

2 wait half a jiffy 稍等一下

Please wait half a jiffy. 稍等片刻。

jig

1 in/on jig time【美口】马上，迅速地

I guarantee you'll have a job in jig time. 我保证你马上就能找到工作。

2 the jig is up/over 把戏已拆穿，一切全完了，已无成功希望

As soon as the jig is up, he flew off to Paris. 一看到把戏已被拆穿，成功无望，他就飞到巴黎去了。

The jig's up; the principal knows the boys have been smoking in the basement. 这下完了，校长已经知道男孩们在地下室里抽烟的事了。

jigger

1 jigger it 去他的，该死的

2 jiggered 该死的；天哪（damned 的委婉语）

It's Pete! Well, I'm jiggered! Who would have thought of meeting you here! 天哪，这不是皮特吗！谁想到会在这儿遇见你！

I'm jiggered if I'll let him get away without being punished! 我要是就这样便宜地饶了他，我就不是人！

3 jiggers【美】注意，当心，快跑

4 not worth a jigger/dime 一文不值，毫无价值

These shoes are not worth a jigger. 那些鞋一文不值。

jiminy

jiminy/by jiminy/jiminy crickets/jiminy Christmas 哎呀，天哪（表示惊讶、敬畏或用于起誓）

By jiminy—you're right that is Margaret over there! I wonder what she's doing here. 哎呀，不错，那是玛格丽特！我不知道她来这儿干什么。

jingo

by (the living) jingo 老天作证；注意，一定；天哪（用于起誓或表示强调、惊讶）

By jingo, the bus is on time! 啊，汽车准时来啦！

By jingo, Mary's passed her driving test! 天哪，玛丽通过驾照考试啦！

job

1 a bad job 坏事，白费力气的事；令人不满意的状况

George gave up the plan as a bad job. 乔治放弃了这个没有成功希望的计划。

2 a good job 好事，幸运事；令人满意的状况；干得出色的活

It's a good job we brought our raincoats. 幸好我们带了雨衣。

3 a job of work 重要的工作；干得出色的活

The report was really a solid job of work. 这份报告确实写得很充实。

4 do a job on 严重破坏，伤害；变丑

The baby did a job on Mary's book. 婴儿把玛丽的书弄坏了。

Jane cut her hair and really did a job on herself. 珍妮把头发剪得糟透了。

5 fall down on the job 工作不力；无法做到

The boss was disappointed when his workers fell down on the job. 老板看到工人不好好干活很失望。

6 jobs for the boys 给追随自己的人的肥缺

7 job's jobbed【俚】全完了

8 just the job 正是想要的东西

Thanks for that screw, it was just the job. 谢谢你给我那个螺丝，我正需要它。

So I could stay with you in Birmingham and then drive up to Edinburgh the next day? That's just the job! 那么我可以同你待在伯明翰，第二天驱车前往爱丁堡喽？那太好了！

9 lie down on the job 偷懒；闲逛；有意失职

Bill isn't trying to learn his lessons. He is lying down on the job. 比尔不努力学习功课，他是故意偷懒。

If you lie down on your job, you will lose it. 你干活故意吊儿郎当就会失业。

10 on the job 努力工作，不浪费时间

Joe is on the job all of the time that he was at work. 乔工作时总是全力以赴。

The school paper came out on time because the editors were on the job. 学校的报纸能准时印出是因为编辑们都很努力。

11 pull a job 抢劫

They pulled a bank job. 他们抢劫了银行。

Joe

Joe Doakes/Blow 一般人，普通人，老百姓

Let us say that Joe Doakes goes to the movies three times a year. 假定一般人平均每年看三次电影。

John

1 John Q Public/Citizen 【美】公众，民众，公民

It is John Q Public's duty to vote at each election. 投票选举是公民的义务。

2 John Doe 张三，李四；某人

The alarm went out for a John Doe who stole the diamonds from the store. 警铃响着，警察正在寻找一个偷了店里钻石的家伙。

joke

1 beyond a joke 并非戏言，使人极为难堪、恼火，超出开玩笑的限度

Your bad behaviour is beyond a joke. 你的不良行为超出玩笑的界限。

2 crack a joke 开个玩笑，讲句笑话

It's serious. This is no time to crack a joke. 这是很严肃的，不是开玩笑的时候。

3 it's/it was no joke 这是严肃的事

It's no joke walking alone a country lane in the dark. 夜间走乡间小道可不是一件小事。

It was no joke carrying all your suitcases from one side of the station to the other—what did you put in them? 把你的这些箱子从车站一头扛到另一头真不容易，你这里面到底放了些什么？

4 (all) joking apart/aside 言归正传，说正经的

Joking aside, although the conditions were not very comfortable, we had a wonderful time. 说真的,虽然条件不十分好,但我们玩得很高兴。
Joking apart, there must have been over a handred people in the room. 这不是夸张,屋里肯定有一百多人。
5 you must be/are/have got to be joking 你一定是在开玩笑
"Goldie's just won first prize in the beauty competition!" "You must be joking!" "戈尔黛在选美比赛中获得了第一名。""你一定是在开玩笑!"
"Have I told you we're emigrating?" "You're joking!" "我不是告诉你我们要移居国外了吗?""你骗人!"

Jove

by Jove/thunder 哎呀,天哪;我发誓,这是真的(表示惊讶、赞同或强调)
By Jove, I think you've guessed it. 啊,看来让你猜到了。
By Jove, I'll get you back for what you've done to me, if it's the last thing I do! 我发誓,我要用你对我的手段对付你,尽管这是我最不愿干的事!

joy

1 God give you joy/joy go with you 希望你幸福
2 (get) no joy 不成功,不走运
"Did you manage to find the book you were looking for?" "No joy!" "你找到你要找的那本书了吗?""没有!"
3 wish/give sb. joy (of) 向……致贺(多用于讽刺、反义)

judgement

judgement on you 报应
"I've just got absolutely soaked running for the bus!" "It's a judgement on you for breaking Mrs. Jones's window!" "为了追赶公共汽车我跑得浑身都湿透了!""活该! 这就是你打碎琼斯夫人窗户的报应!"
It's a judgement on you for getting up late. 这是你睡懒觉的报应。

jump

1 (at a) full jump/on the jump/upon the jump【美】迅速地,全速地
We heard it coming and coming on the jump, too. 我们听出他们已经快到了,而且来势极猛。

2 at one jump【美】一下子

They came to the conclusion at one jump. 他们一下子就作出了结论。

3 at the (first) jump/from the (very) first jump 一开始

4 all of a jump【美】心惊胆战

The new soldier felt all of a jump at the battlefield. 在战场上,那个新兵心惊胆战。

5 get/have the jump on 参见 get 62

6 jump/land on/all over 责骂,批评,埋怨

Tom's boss jumped all over Tom, because he made a careless mistake. 汤姆不小心犯了错,挨了老板的骂。

Jane landed on Robert for dressing carelessly for their date. 简埋怨罗伯特约会时穿着随便。

7 jump/leap out of one's skin 吓坏了,十分惊讶

The lightning struck so close to Bill that he almost jumped out of his skin. 闪电来得如此靠近比尔,他几乎吓坏了。

8 jump through a hoop/hoops 参见 hoop 2

9 jump to it 赶快行动,积极干起来

Get the table set and cut the bread up, jump to it! 去把桌子摆好,面包切开,快点!

If you don't jump to it you will miss the train. 要是你不赶快些,会误了火车的。

We'll have to jump to it to get our work finished by the time Pete comes round for us! 我们得马上动手干起来,一定要在皮特来找我们之前把事情办完。

10 take a running jump 滚开

"You've really got on my nerves this morning!" "Yes, and you've got on me!" "Why don't you take a running jump!" "今天早晨你可把我烦死了!""你也把我烦死了!""你干吗还不快点滚开!"

And then Nancy told Owen to go and take a running jump—you can imagine what sort of an effect that had! 于是后来南希就叫欧文赶快走,赶快离开她,其结果如何可想而知了。

Jupiter

by Jupiter 哎呀，天哪，好家伙

just

1 isn't/wasn't, etc. it/he/she, etc. just 是呀，可不是吗（有时用作反义）

"Wasn't that book interesting?" "Wasn't it just! Once I started it, I couldn't put it down!" "那本书不是很有趣吗？" "不错，我一读起来就放不下！"

"Isn't Perry helpful around the home?" "Helpful? Isn't he just—he sits there all the time, watching TV, and never even asks if he can help at all!" "佩里在家里不是个帮手吗？" "帮手？可不是吗！他只要一坐下来看电视，就什么都不管了，还说给你当帮手呢！"

2 just a moment 且慢，等一等；哎呀（表示惊讶）

Just a moment! What about the plans for the other side of the building? Has everyone forgotten them? 且慢，这大楼另一边的方案如何？难道大家忘了吗？

Just a moment! Aren't you the chap we met in the bank? Yes, look your beard's falling off! 哎呀，莫非你就是我们在银行里遇见的那个小伙子？就是你，你的假胡子正在往下掉呢！

3 just/quite so 不错

"I'll come and pick you up at six o'clock and then we can drive on to Ralph's tonight." "Just so!" "六点钟我开车来接你，今晚我们可以驱车去拉尔夫家。""那好哇！"

"I'm sure Harvey's the best tennis player we've ever had, isn't he?" "Quite so!" "我敢断定哈维是我们这儿最优秀的羽毛球选手，不是吗？" "一点不错！"

4 just what the doctor ordered 参见 doctor 2

keep

1 keep after 一再要求，不断提醒

Some pupils will do sloppy work unless the teacher keeps after them to write neatly. 有些学生作业写得潦草，除非老师一再提醒他们写得整齐些。

Mother kept after me for not getting enough sleep. 母亲老是提醒我，说我睡眠不足。

2 keep oneself to oneself 不与人来往，离群索居

They kept themselves to themselves ever since they had come here. 他们搬到这里之后从不与他人交往。

3 keep one's fingers crossed/cross one's fingers 使两指交叉以求好运

Mary crossed her fingers during the race so that Tom would win. 比赛中玛丽两指交叉希望汤姆获胜。

Keep your fingers crossed while I take the test. 我考试时请你交叉两指祝我好运。

4 keep one's nose clean 安分守己，不惹麻烦

The boss said Jim could have the job as long as he kept his nose clean and worked hard. 老板说吉姆只要不惹麻烦、勤奋工作就可以获得这份工作。

The policeman warned the boys to keep their nose clean unless they wanted to go to jail. 警察警告男孩们不要惹麻烦，除非他们想坐牢。

5 keep/have/hold one's nose to the grindstone 努力不懈，终日忙碌

His wife was wasteful and he had to keep his nose to the grindstone. 他妻子花钱很随便，他只好终日忙碌，努力挣钱。

6 keep one's shirt/hair on 参见 hair 12

7 keep shady【美】(不声不响) 避免被人注意，藏匿；光线不好

8 keep sb. guessing 参见 guess 5

9 keep smiling 别紧张，别担心，保持乐观，不泄气

Whatever troubles you may be going through, remember, "Keep smiling."

无论你遇到什么样的困难,你都要记住,"沉着冷静!"

10 keep sth. dark 保密

You can tell everything to her. She can keep it dark. 你可以把什么事情都告诉她,她能替你保密。

11 keep tab(s) on 记录;注视;检查

The government tries to keep tabs on all the animals in the park. 政府要将公园里的所有动物记录下来。

The house mother kept tabs on the girls to be sure they were clean and neat. 舍监经常检查女孩们是否干净整洁。

12 keep the ball rolling 保持活跃,使(谈话、活动等)继续下去,使(谈话、活动等)不中断,继续(做某事)

Let's keep the ball rolling on this project. 让我们保证这个项目的进度。

13 keep the wolf from the door 免于饥饿

John earned very little money and could hardly keep the wolf from the door. 约翰挣钱太少,不免经常挨饿。

14 keep to oneself 不与人交往

Peggy kept to herself in the ship and would speak to no one. 佩吉在船上一人独处,不愿与人交谈。

When Mary first moved to her neighbourhood she was very shy and kept to herself. 玛丽刚搬来时很害羞,不和邻里来往。

15 keep sth. under one's hat 参见 hat 6

16 you can keep 你留着自己用吧,我才不稀罕呢

You can keep your burnt pie—I'm going out for a take away! 那块烧焦的馅饼你自己留着吧,我要点外卖!

You can keep it. 你自己留着吧。

kettle

1 another/a different kettle of fish 截然不同的人或物

Your brother is a different kettle of fish from you. 你兄弟和你完全不同。

I thought he needed money, but it was another kettle of fish—his car had disappeared. 我以为他需要钱,其实是另外一回事,他的车子丢了。

2 (that's/it's) a fine/nice/pretty kettle of fish 难办的事,尴尬的局面,一团糟

That is a fine kettle of fish! I forgot my book. 这可糟了,我忘了把书带来!

Orlando had two flat tires and no spare on a country road at night, which was certainly *a pretty kettle of fish*. 在晚上乡间的路上奥兰多两个轮胎都漏气了,又没有备胎,真是糟透了!

kick

1 **a kick in one's gallop** 古怪念头;异想天开

2 **a kick in the pants/teeth** 责备;非难;拒绝;重大挫折

All she got for her trouble was *a kick in the teeth*. 她费尽周折换来的却是责备。

You deserve *a kick in the pants* making such a darned slob of yourself. 瞧你这副懒散的鬼样子,活该栽大跟头。

3 **a kick in the ass**【美】出乎意料的拒绝;坏消息;鞭策;使人振奋的事物

It may not be much, but it's better than *a kick in the ass*. 所得可能不多,但总比一无所获好些。

4 **for kicks/the hell of it** 为了取乐,寻求刺激

Paul drives fast just *for kicks*. 保罗高速驾车只是为了寻求刺激。

The boys stole the car and drove it round town just *for the hell of it*. 孩子们偷了车开着它在镇上到处跑,只是为了好玩。

5 **kick about/around** 轻蔑对待,粗暴对待,虐待,欺凌;被忽视,被冷落;漫谈;经常移动;常换职业

Business was so good that he felt he could *kick* the customers *around* a little. 生意如此兴隆,他认为稍微怠慢一下顾客也无妨。

Harry has *kicked around* all over the world as a merchant seaman. 哈里作为一个商船船员走遍了世界各地。

6 **kick back** 贿赂,回扣

Philip was arrested for making *kick back* payments. 菲利普因贿赂而被捕。

I will do it if you *kick back* a few hundred for my firm. 如果你给我公司几百元回扣,我就给你做。

7 **kick/chip in** 捐助;死亡;开启(暖气装置)

An unknown contributor *kicked in* with $50,000. 一位匿名捐款人捐了

五万元。

Pullman kicked in at the ripe old age of 90. 普尔曼死时 90 岁，寿尽天年。

8 kick it【美】戒掉恶习

Richards finally kicked it; he's in good shape. 理查兹终于戒除了坏习惯，他现在状态很好。

9 kick off 开始；引起；死亡；【美】出发

The concert kicked off with a folk song. 音乐会以一曲民歌开始。

The candidate kicked off his campaign with a speech on television. 候选人在电视上发表演说开始其竞选活动。

10 kick on 打开（开关等）；（机器等）开始启动

Suddenly the motor kicked on. 马达突然启动了。

11 kick oneself 责备自己，感到内疚，懊悔

I kicked myself for letting that opportunity slip by. 我为错过了那个机会而懊悔。

When John missed the train, he kicked himself for not having left earlier. 约翰没赶上火车，他后悔没早点出发。

12 kick over （引擎）启动；【美】捐款；抢劫；袭击；搜查

The engine kicked over and the plane started on its take-off. 引擎启动了，飞机开始起飞。

The police kicked over the spot. 警方搜查了现场。

13 kick the bucket 死亡

Old Mr. Jones kicked the bucket just two days before his ninety-fourth birthday. 老琼斯先生死时正是他 94 岁生日前两天。

14 kick up 出了毛病；升起；激起；引起

John had had too much to eat and his stomach started to kick up. 约翰吃得太多，他的胃出了问题。

After working well for a year the air conditioner suddenly started kicking up. 运转良好一年多的空调突然出了问题。

15 kick up a fuss/row/dust 参见 dust 3

16 kick up one's heels 欢度时光，热烈庆祝

When exams were over, the students went to town to kick up their heels. 考试一结束，学生们便进城去庆祝一番。

Mary was usually very quiet but at the farewell party she kicked up her heels and had a wonderful time. 玛丽一向沉静,但在惜别会上她尽情欢乐,玩得很痛快。

17 kick upstairs 明升暗降

The only way to get rid of old Smith is to kick up him upstairs. 赶走老史密斯的唯一办法就是将他明升暗降。

18 kicking ass【俚】快乐时光

We went downtown and had a kicking ass. 我们去了市中心,玩得很痛快。

19 more kicks than halfpence 苛待多于优遇,责怪多于表扬

You get more kicks than halfpence in this job. 你这种工作真是吃力不讨好。

kid

1 I kid you not【美】我可是说正经的;我骗你不是人

I kid you not, during my internship I discovered that the coeds liked being around me. 不瞒你们说,实习的时候我发现女同学喜欢和我在一起。

2 no kid 不骗你

True story, no kid. 这是真的,不骗你。

3 no kidding 是真的;【美】我不相信

I'll beat you in the long jump today—no kidding. 今天的跳远我要超过你,真的。

"The cemetery has a lake with ducks." "No kidding!" "墓地里有个养鸭子的小湖。""我才不信呢!"

4 handle/treat sb. with kid gloves 小心、谨慎、温和地对待某人

Sally is such a baby that she cries if the teacher does not handle her with kid gloves. 莎莉是个老师对她不和气便会哭泣的孩子。

Don't treat these criminals with kid gloves. 不要对那些犯罪分子心慈手软。

kill

1 be dressed/dolled up (fit) to kill 打扮得花枝招展

Tina was dressed up (fit) to kill for her date on Saturday night. 周六的晚上,蒂娜打扮得漂漂亮亮地去赴约。

2 kill oneself 自杀;使自己过分劳累

I had killed myself over my manuscript during the summer. 在夏季我把全

部精力都花费在那篇稿子上了。

3 kill the goose to get the eggs 杀鸡取卵，竭泽而渔，只顾眼前利益
To sell the firm is equal to kill the goose to get the eggs. 卖掉公司等于杀鸡取卵。

4 (it) won't kill you/him, etc. 这对你/他等没什么大不了的
A little hard work won't kill you. 稍微辛苦一下对你算不了什么。

kind

1 a kind/sort of 有几分，稍稍；一种
I had a kind of feeling you'd be offered the job. 我有一种预感，你会得到这个工作的。
Dodd always has a sort of mental blockage when it comes to buying other people presents. 只要一提到给别人买礼物，多德就会出现一种精神障碍。

2 answer/repay/return/pay back in kind 以其人之道还治其人之身
Don't get sarcastic with him; he can pay you back in kind. 不要跟他说挖苦话，他会照样回敬你的。

3 kind/sort of 有一点；相当；可以这么说
It's kind of late to begin now. 现在开始有点晚了。
I kind of love Raymond. 我有点喜欢雷蒙德。

4 some kind of【美】很好的，有效的
God, isn't Swift some kind of a singer? 天哪，斯威夫特是个很棒的歌手，不是吗？

5 the worst kind【美】极其，非常
Chaucer loves Sal the worst kind. 乔叟非常爱莎尔。

kiss

1 kiss and tell 泄密，辜负信任
I'm not a man to kiss and tell. 我不是一个背信弃义的人。

2 kiss... goodbye 放弃，失去；丧失获得……的希望
If you don't work hard, you can kiss your bonus goodbye. 如果你不努力工作，你就别想得到奖金。
If the war escalates, then you can kiss all thoughts of negotiations goodbye. 如果战争升级，你那些关于谈判的想法都得泡汤。

3 (kiss) my foot 见鬼去吧（用于拒绝请求等场合）

You think Yorkshire is the best cricket side? My foot! 你以为约克郡队是最好的队吗？算了吧！

4 kiss off 走开；死去

Kiss off, I told you, Mary's not here. 走吧，我跟你说过，玛丽不在这里。

kite

go fly a kite 参见 go 14

knife

1 before you can say Jack Robinson/knife 刹那参见 Jack 1

2 twist/turn the knife (in the wound) 揭人伤疤，落井下石

Just to turn the knife a little, he told me he'd seen my old girlfriend with her new man. 他告诉我他看到我前女友另结新欢，这不是揭人伤疤吗？

knock

1 knock about/around 漫游；虐待

Marion has knocked about all over the world. 马里恩曾在世界各地漫游。
My poor child, who they've knocked you about. 可怜的孩子，他们这样虐待你。

2 knock back 一下子吃下，喝掉；使花费；使吃惊

Macaulay knocked back four pints of ale. 麦考利一口气喝下四品脱啤酒。
The news knocked Philip back. 那消息使菲利普吃惊。

3 knock down 降价，杀价；要求

Tommy asked 500 dollars for his car but I knocked him/his price down to 450 dollars. 汤米的汽车要价 500 美元，但我给他还到 450 美元。
Virginia knocked me down for a song. 弗吉尼娅要求我唱首歌。

4 knock/throw for a loop 使大吃一惊

When I heard they were moving, I was really knocked for a loop. 听到他们正在搬家，我大吃一惊。
The news of their marriage threw me for a loop. 他们结婚的消息使我大吃一惊。

5 knock it off【美】住手，住嘴，别闹了（用于制止喧哗、骚乱、斗殴、争论、哄笑等）

Knock it off, you two. Can't you see I'm trying to work? 别闹了，你没看

见我正在工作吗？
Come on, Joe, knock it off, you're not making any sense at all! 好了，住口吧，乔，真不知道你在说些什么！

6 knock off（从账单中）减去，除去；降价；中断工作，下班；完成，写完，仓促做完；破坏；击败；消除；盗窃；杀害
They knocked $10 off the price. 他们把价格降低了 10 美元。
I've a lot of work to knock off before I can take my holiday. 我有很多工作要赶完才能去度假。

7 knock out 仓促写成；草草拟出（计划）；随便地演奏
Raymond knocked out a tune on the piano. 雷蒙德在钢琴上即兴弹了支曲子。
Samuel knocked out a plan in half an hour. 塞缪尔在半小时内就拟出了一份计划。

8 knock over 偷盗；抢劫
Where did you get all these watches? Did you knocked them over? 你从哪儿弄来的这些手表？是偷来的吗？

9 knock sb./sth. sideways 使目瞪口呆；对……起作用
The rise of the price of oil has knocked the cost of living sideways. 石油价格上涨已经影响了生活费用。

10 knock the (living) daylights out of 使惶惑，使茫然；狠揍某人
The news almost knocked the living daylights out of me. 这消息使我几乎昏昏沉沉，不知所措。

11 knock up 使筋疲力尽；挣得；赶制；仓促建造
The long journey knocked her up. 长途旅行把她累坏了。
After yesterday's exertion I feel quite knocked up. 昨天我费尽了力气，现在感觉疲乏极了。

12 you could have knocked me/him/her, etc. down with a feather 我/他/她等极为惊讶
Say, you could have knocked me down with a feather. 咳，你简直把我惊呆了。

knot

1 at a/the rate of knots 极快地，飞快地

Peter went out of the house at a rate of knots. 彼得大步流星走出屋去。

2 get knotted 别烦我，滚开，见鬼去吧

Get knotted, you ruddy troublemaker! 去你的，你这讨厌的捣蛋鬼！

"Can I borrow your pen?" "Get knotted! You never gave me back the last one you took!" "我能用你的笔吗？""去你的，你上次借我的还没有还给我呢！"

I told her to get knotted. 我叫她滚开。

3 tie the knot 结婚；主持婚礼

Diane and Bill tied the knot/Bill tied the knot to Diane yesterday. 黛安和比尔昨天结婚了。

The minister tied the knot for Diane and Bill yesterday. 牧师昨天为黛安和比尔主持了婚礼。

4 cut the Gordian knot 快刀斩乱麻，办事果断

The Senate would like to take this opportunity to change their position to "cut the Gordian knot". 参议院希望借这个时机促使他们转变立场，达到"快刀斩乱麻"的效果。

know

1 all one knows 全部能力、才智；尽全力，尽一切可能

They tried all they knew to be prepared. 他们竭力做好准备。

It cost Faulkner all he knew to restrain his anger. 福克纳尽力抑制自己的愤怒。

2 and I don't know who/what ……的许多其他的人/物也……

There was the mayor, the school governors, the chaplain, and I don't know who at the dinner. 市长、学校领导、牧师，还有许多其他人也参加了宴会。

In the room books, packs of cards, empty boxes, and I don't know what, had just been thrown about. 书、成捆的卡片、空盒子还有许多其他东西被扔得满屋都是。

3 as you know 如你所知，尽管你已经知道（用于进一步介绍情况）

As you know, Pete's got a place at university. Well, he starts next month. 你已经知道皮特在大学里找到了一份工作，而且他下个月就去上班。

4 before one knows where one is 立刻，刹那

5 don't I know it 我知道了，我何尝不知道（表示不情愿的认可）

I've got to wash all those dishes, don't I know it. 我知道了，我得洗所有这些盘子。

I got up at 5 o'clock this morning to finish my work, and don't I know it. 今天早晨我五点钟起床去完成我的工作，我怎么会不知道。

6 don't you know 你也知道（用于加强语气）

It's such a nuisance, don't you know, travelling by train. 你也知道，坐火车旅行是一件讨厌的事。

It's such a bore, don't you know. 你也知道，那是多么乏味的事。

7 Heaven/God/Goodness/Lord knows 参见 god 8

8 I don't know 哎呀（表示恼怒或惊讶）；我不能肯定

I don't know! You children are really getting on my nerves this morning! 哎呀，你们这些孩子今天早晨把我头都闹昏啦！

Well, I don't know! Imagine her entering a beauty competition with a figure like that! 哎呀，想象一下她那样的身材居然去参加选美比赛！

9 I don't know about that 我看不是这么回事

"Robert's getting on very well at school these days, isn't he?" "I don't know about that—though he's certainly not bottom of the class any more." "罗伯特这一段时间在学校里学得很好，是吗？""我看不是那么回事，当然喽，他现在已经不是班上的最后一名了。"

10 I don't know, I'm sure 真弄不明白，到底发生了什么事（语气带有焦急、烦躁）

What's the country coming to? I don't know, I'm sure! 我真不明白，这个国家会弄到什么地步！

11 I don't know that 我看不见得，很难说

"Tom's quite a good friend, isn't he?" "I don't know that—he's never helped me much." "汤姆是个好朋友，不是吗？""我看不见得，他从未给我帮过什么忙。"

I don't know that I like this arrangement. 很难说我喜欢这样的安排。

12 I knew it 我早就知道事情会是这样

I knew it! As soon as I left the room, you stopped working! 我早就知道，我一离开房间，你就开始偷懒！

13 I know just how it is 我知道这是怎么回事；我知道这有多难(表示关切、同情)

14 I know what/I tell you what/I'll tell you what 我有个主意

I know what, let's go and see Pat tonight. 我倒有个主意,今晚我们去看帕特吧。

I tell you what, we'll have a cheap holiday and stay at home this year—that'll save us some money. 我有个主意,今年我们在家里过一个廉价的假期,这会省些钱。

15 I/you, etc. wouldn't know 我/你等没有这方面的知识；我说不上来；(有时表示讥讽)

"Is this the way to the station?" "I'm sorry, I wouldn't know—I'm a stranger here myself." "这是到车站去的路吗？""对不起,我说不上来,我也是个外地人。"

Of course you wouldn't know what it was like spending all day at home doing the housework, would you? 当然喽,我看你也说不清成天待在家里做家务是个什么滋味,不是吗？

16 I'd have you know 我老实告诉你；你倒是好好看看(用于加强语气或反驳对方的话)

"The car doesn't look too clean, does it?" "I'd have you know I've just spent an hour washing it!" "这车看上去不太干净,是吧？""我老实告诉你,我刚花了一个小时清洗它的。"

17 I want to know 【美】哎呀,你看,真的,会有这种事

18 in the know 知情的,消息灵通的

We're not in the know on the disarmament question. 我们不了解裁军方面的内情。

Caroline enjoyed the feeling of being in the artistic know. 卡罗琳因觉得自己熟谙艺术而洋洋自得。

19 know beans/know black from white/know chalk from cheese/know how many beans make five/know one's way about/know what's what 有判断力,机敏,精明干练

I had so much claret—I did not much know what was what. 我喝了那么多的红葡萄酒,我头脑是有点糊涂了。

Believe me, Tommy knows what is what. 相信我,汤米这个人很精明。

20 know better 有头脑,有见地;更加谨慎,学乖了,有主张,不会上当

Give Virginia a piece of your mind and then she'll know better. 你把弗吉尼亚训一顿,以后她就会更加小心。

Fool may believe you, but Valentine knows better. 傻子或许会相信你,可是瓦伦丁不会相信你。

21 know enough to come in out of the rain 有见地,知道自我照顾

Sally may look stupid, but she knows enough to come in out of the rain. 莎莉可能看起来很笨,但她却很有见地。

22 know if/whether one is coming or going 思路清晰;应付自如(常用于否定句)

My cousin is so much in love that she scarcely knows whether she's coming or going. 我的表姐深陷情网,整日心不在焉。

23 know sb. is alive 注意某人(与否定句连用),没有忽视某人

Sally was a good looking girl, but she didn't know I was alive. 莎莉是个漂亮的女孩儿,但她不曾注意过我。

24 know one's goods/stuff【美】精通本行业务,有专门知识,内行

Tom is a person who knows his stuff. 汤姆是个内行。

25 know one's way around/about/know one's onions/stuff 精于世事;老于世故;能随机应变;有阅历;熟悉周围情况

The sailor had been in the wildest ports in the world. He knew his way around. 这个水手到过世界上最荒凉的港口,经验丰富。

26 know sth./sb. as a person knows his ten fingers/as well as a beggar knows his bag/like a book from A to Z/like the palm of one's hand 了如指掌,一清二楚

Jason knows the truth as well as a beggar knows his bag. 杰森对这事的内情知道得一清二楚。

27 know the time of the day 机灵,能随机应变,消息灵通

Williams doesn't know the time of the day. 威廉姆斯不够机灵。

28 know what one is about 做事精明,有把握

29 know where one stands/is 知道别人如何看待自己

Dennis never quite knew where he stood with Emily. 丹尼斯从来不清楚艾米丽对自己是怎么个看法。

30 know which side one's bread is buttered on 善于趋利,知道讨好谁以

获利

Dick was always polite to the boss; he knew which side his bread was buttered on. 迪克对上司总是彬彬有礼，他知道靠山吃山的道理。

31 knowing/if I know sb./sth./you know what sb./sth. is/are 因为我很熟悉某人/某物的性格,所以我确信……

If I know the weather, it'll rain on sports day—it does every year. 我了解气候的规律,开运动会一定会下雨。

You know what Perry is, he always has some excuse for missing a French test. 我很了解佩里,可以肯定他总是为逃避法语考试找借口。

32 not if I know it/not that I know of 如果我知道(就不这样做了);据我所知,不是这样;我不知道,我不清楚

After that, do you think I could marry you? Not if I know it. 事已至此,你想我还能和你结婚吗？我认为这是不可能的。

I was told that he failed in the test. Not that I know of. 听说他考试没通过,据我所知并非如此。

33 not that you know of 你办不到,休要妄想

34 that's all you know (about it) 你(对此)全然无知

"Pete's started to go out with my sister!" "That's all you know about it! It's been going on for weeks!" "皮特同我妹妹出去了。""你还蒙在鼓里呢,这已经好几个星期了。"

35 there's no knowing/telling 谁也说不上来

There's no knowing what we could do to help, if we had more money. 如果我们有了更多的钱我们能做什么事更好,这谁也说不上来。

You'd better take your boots with you. There's no telling how deep the snow will be if it keeps falling like this. 你最好把你的靴子带上,很难说,如果这场雪像这样一直下下去的话地上的雪会积多深。

36 what do you know (about that) 【美】你看怪不怪,真想不到(惊讶)

What do you know about that? The tire blew out again! 真想不到,车胎又爆了！

Now, what do you know about this? Such colours! 你看怪不怪,这样的颜色！

37 who knows 谁知道呢

38 wouldn't you (just) know 真想不到,请想象一下

39 you don't know when you're well-off/alive/born 你是身在福中不知福

You don't know when you're well-off! You've got a good job, a house, a colour TV; just think of what the rest of the world has got compared with you! 你真是身在福中不知福!你有一份好工作、一套房子、一台彩电,想想看,世界上其他的人和你比起来,他们又有些什么呢?

Why are you moaning? You've passed your exams, got into college, and you're doing pretty well—you don't know you're alive! 你为什么牢骚满腹?你通过考试进了大学,现在还学得相当不错。你真是身在福中不知福。

40 you know 你知道,你要知道(交谈时提醒对方)

You'll have to try harder, you know, if you want to succeed. 你要知道,要想获得成功,你就得更加努力。

41 you know something/what 要不要我把真相告诉你,听我说

You know something, Mary? Mr. Harris is the richest man I knew, except my father. 我来告诉你吧,玛丽,哈里斯先生是我知道的除了我父亲以外最富有的人。

You know what? I've never told you this before, but this is my second marriage. 告诉你,这是我的第二次婚姻,这点我之前从未对你说过。

42 you know what you can do with 真不像话(表示轻蔑的粗鲁态度)

I'm fed up with your Aunt Agatha! You know what you can do with her! 我对你的阿加莎婶婶厌烦透了,她真不像话!

Your pen never works! You know what you can do with it. 你的笔从来都不能用,干脆扔了算了。

43 you never know/never can tell 很难说,很难预料

"Do you think you'll be able to come and stay with us in Malaysia sometime?" "You never know! My firm might give me a job there!" "你说你将来有可能来马来西亚和我们待在一起吗?""很难说,我们公司可能在那儿给我提供一份工作!"

You'd better take an umbrella; you never can tell if it's going to rain. 你最好带上雨伞,很难说会不会下雨。

44 not know sb. from Adam 素昧平生

Why should Eric lend me money? He doesn't know me from Adam. 埃里克为什么借钱给我? 他根本不认识我。

known

1 make it known that 公布，发表，宣称

Faulkner made it known to his friends that he did not want to enter politics. 福克纳向朋友们声明，他不想进入政界。

2 make oneself known to 向……作自我介绍

There's your tutor; you'd better make yourself known to him. 你的导师来了，你最好向他作自我介绍。

lady

1 lady/ladies first 女士优先
2 your good lady 尊夫人，您的妻子

lake

go (and) jump in the/a lake【美】走开，滚开，别惹人嫌
How dare you speak to me like that! Go and jump in a lake! 你怎敢这样对我讲话！滚开！
George was tired of Tom's advice and told him to go jump in the lake. 乔治厌烦汤姆的劝告，叫他走开。

land

1 land【美】上帝，主啊，天啊（Lord 的委婉说法）
We've only got another week, for land's sake. 天啊，我们现在只剩下一个星期了。
My land! If Clare sees me here, he'll kill me. 天啊，如果克莱尔看见我在这儿，他准会把我宰了。
2 land/jump on/all over 参见 jump 6
3 land on one's/both feet 参见 foot 9
4 happy landing 干杯；(飞机起飞前向乘机者告别用语)祝您一路平安
Have a happy landing! 祝您一路平安！

lap

1 drop/dump/throw sth. in/into/on one's lap 将某事交给……处理、负责；将某事推给……
Don't drop all your personal problems in my lap. 不要把你所有的个人问题都交给我处理。
I'll throw this into John's lap, I don't want to be mixed up in it. 我将把此事交给约翰去办。我不愿牵扯在里面。

2 in the lap of fortune/Providence 走好运

Elizabeth was born in the lap of fortune. 伊丽莎白生来就有福分。

3 in the lap of luxury 在优裕的环境中

Edward was brought up in the lap of luxury. 爱德华从小就养尊处优。

Mike grew up in the lap of luxury. 迈克在优裕的环境中长大。

4 in the lap/on the knees of the gods 听天由命

The outcome of this war is in the lap of the gods. 这场战争的结果如何只好听天由命了。

Frank had worked hard as a candidate, and as election day came he felt that the result was in the lap of the gods. 作为一名候选人弗兰克下了很大功夫,但在选举那天,他觉得结果只能听天由命。

5 lap up 轻信;爱听,爱看,热切地享受(知识等)

Fox laps up old horror films. 福克斯爱看那些老旧的恐怖电影。

Funk flatters Gilbert all the time and he just laps it up. 芬克一再向吉尔伯特献媚,吉尔伯特也乐于享受。

large

1 at large 自由自在,不受限制;一般而言;整体

The murderer is still at large. 杀人凶手仍逍遥法外。

2 be large for【美】对……狂热之至,热衷于……

3 by and large 大部分地;一般地,通常地

Taking it by and large, the conditions of employment are good. 从大体上来说,就业环境是好的。

4 in large 大规模地

We bought in large stocks of tinned goods for the tour. 我们为旅行买进大量罐头食品。

lark

1 as cheerful/gay/merry as a lark 非常快乐

The old man became as cheerful as a lark when he heard that his grandchildren were coming for a visit. 老爷爷听说他的孙子孙女们要来看望他,简直高兴极了。

2 for a lark 当作玩笑

They stole the car for a lark, but now they're in trouble. 他们偷车只是觉

得好玩,可是现在麻烦了。

3 rise/be up with the lark 早起

To catch a glimpse of sunrise on the lake, we shall have to be up with the lark. 为了看湖面上的日出,我们得早早起床。

4 what a lark 真有趣

The murderer thinks he is clever, what a lark! 凶手还自以为聪明,真有意思!

last

1 every last man/every man Jack【美】人人,个个

And for the briefest of moments, every last man at Shawshank felt free. 就在那一刹那,每一位在肖申克监狱的人都感到了自由。

2 every single/last【美】每一个

And this is true for every single component. 这对每一个组件都是成立的。

3 first and last 主要地,总的来说,整体看来;彻头彻尾,始终,完全

It was the first and last time we ever went out to a dinner like that. 这是我们俩第一次,也是最后一次去这样的一个地方吃饭。

4 have/get the last laugh/the laugh on one's side 让讥笑者尴尬,获得最后的胜利

The boys thought they had tricked the girls by locking them in the kitchen. But the girls had the last laugh when the boys got hungry and realized they couldn't get into the kitchen for food. 男孩儿们把那些女孩儿锁进了厨房就自以为计谋得逞了,但是女孩儿们笑到了最后:男孩儿饿了想吃东西的时候才想起他们进不去厨房了。

5 haven't heard the last of ……还没有了结

We haven't heard the last of George. 乔治的事还没有了结呢。

You haven't heard the last of this, I can tell you. 告诉你,你这事还没有了结呢。

6 last but not least 最后的但并非最不重要的

Last but not least, I must thank our host for his hospitality. 最后的但并非最不重要的,我得感谢主人的热情款待。

Billy will bring sandwiches, Alice will bring cake, Susan will bring cookies, John will bring potato chips, and last but not least, Sally will bring the lemonade. 比利带三明治,爱丽丝带蛋糕,苏珊带曲奇饼干,约翰带马铃薯片,莎莉最后但同样重要,她带的是柠檬汁。

7 (to the) last ditch 战到最后,坚守到底

They will fight the enemy to the last ditch. 他们要与敌人战斗到底。

8 last word 最新式的东西;最后的决定权;最后一句话

These studies are not the last word. 这些研究并不是最后的定论。

9 last words 临终遗言

His last words is still ringing in my ears. 他最后的遗言依然在我的耳边响起。

10 stick to one's last 不管闲事,只做自己会做的事

Don't play around with jobs that are really outside your field; stick to your last. 别管那些对你来说是外行的事,只干你会干的事吧。

latch

1 latch on/onto 抓住,缠住;拥有,得到;理解

My host latched onto me at the door saying I must not go yet. 在门口主人拖住我,叫我再待一会儿。

The new radio direction-finding device could latch onto a transmission with remarkable speed. 新的无线电测向设备能以惊人的速度捕捉传送中的信号。

2 the latch string is out/have one's latch string out 热烈欢迎

Mary has her latch string out for everyone who comes. 玛丽热烈欢迎每一位来客。

late

1 late in the day 最后,最后阶段

It was the pensioner's vote late in the day that influenced the election of Mr. Sweet. 最后是领取养老金者的选票影响了斯威特先生的当选。

It's a little late in the day to talk about policy changes. 现在谈改变政策已经有些晚了。

2 of late 近来

There have been too many school dropouts of late. 最近有太多学生中途退学。

I haven't seen him of late. 近来我没有见到过他。

3 of late years 近年来

Swedish industry has *of late years* grown with leaps and bounds. 瑞典的工业近年来增长迅速。

4 will/would be late for one's own funeral 老是迟到

You have missed your train three times this week—you'd *be late for your own funeral*. 这个星期你有三次没赶上火车了,你老是迟到。

lather

1 a good lather is half a shave 良好的开端是成功的一半

2 in a lather 非常激动,紧张

I couldn't get across to Joe, he was all *in a lather*. 我无法和乔交谈,他现在太激动了。

laugh

1 a laugh and a half 引人发笑的事,笑料,笑柄

2 be laughing 走运

If the electricity bill is as low as the gas bill, *we're laughing*. 要是电费和煤气费一样低廉,我们可走运了。

3 be laughing all the way to the bank (尤指战胜困难而)发大财

Now I'm the one who's *laughing all the way to the bank*. 现在我就是那个发财得意的人。

4 don't make me laugh 别让我笑掉大牙,别开玩笑了,别胡说八道

Tom's innocent? *Don't make me laugh*. 汤姆会是无辜的? 别开玩笑了。
"Did I tell you I'm going to buy a brand new sports car?" "*Don't make me laugh*! You've not got enough money for your bus fare into town!" "我不是对你说过我要买一部名牌的新跑车吗?""别胡扯啦,你连进城买车票的钱都不够,还说买车!"

5 have/get the last laugh (尤指看上去必败时)获得最后胜利

They laughed at us, but look, who's *got the last laugh*? 他们曾讥笑我们,看吧,究竟是谁笑到了最后。
Henry has outlived all the others to *have the last laugh*. 亨利因为比所有的人都活得长而扬扬得意。

6 have/get the laugh of sb. (在辩论等场合击败对方而)使某人出丑

They racked their poor brains to *get the laugh of us*. 他们搜肠刮肚、绞尽

脑汁,对我们反唇相讥。

7 have the laugh on one's side 转败为胜,扭转形势
You *have the laugh on my side* this time. 这次你可以讥笑我了。

8 have/get the laugh on/over sb. 反唇相讥,占某人上风
Henry *had the laugh on all of us* when his blind date turned out to be the prettiest girl at the party. 当亨利初次约会的对象结果是晚会上最美的姑娘时,轮到亨利来取笑我们大家了。

9 he who laughs best laughs last/he who laughs last laughs longest/loudest 谁笑在最后,谁笑得最好

10 kill oneself laughing/with laughter 【口】笑痛肚皮,笑死人
The children were *killing themselves with laughter* over the joke. 孩子们听了那笑话后笑得要死。

11 Laugh! I thought I'd die! 可把我笑死啦!

12 laugh on/out of the wrong/other side of one's mouth/face 觉得难过或不安,哭泣;转喜为忧
They were made to *laugh on the wrong side of their mouths* by an unforeseen occurrence. 一件不测的事件使他们变喜为悲。
I have got some news here that will make you *laugh out of the other side of your face*! 我这儿有些会使你转喜为忧的消息。
This will make them *laugh on the other side of their faces*. 这会使他们转喜为悲的。

13 laugh up/in one's sleeve/laugh in one's beard 偷偷地笑
We were *laughing in our sleeves* at the teacher when he was up at the blackboard explaining the math problem. He had a rip in the back of his pants. 当老师在黑板前讲解数学题的时候,我们都偷偷地笑,因为他裤子后面有个裂缝。

14 you're/you'll be laughing 你要走运啦
If you get that amount of money for your new job in Saudi Arabia, *you're laughing*! 如果你因在沙特阿拉伯的新工作而获得那么一大笔钱,你就走运啰!

15 laugh against one's will 违心地笑

16 laugh like a drain 放声大笑,开怀大笑;难听的笑声
Mom, I don't like Uncle Zhong, he *laughs like a drain*. 妈妈,我不喜欢钟

叔叔,他笑得太难听了。
The professor sat in front of the television, watching the rather rude jokes and laughing like a drain. 教授坐在电视机前,看着那些粗俗的恶作剧放声大笑起来。

law

1 lay down the law 说话武断;发号施令;迫使接受;呵斥
The teacher lays down the law about homework every afternoon. 老师每天下午严格规定学生的家庭作业。
The teacher laid down the law to two boys who skipped classes. 老师严厉斥责两名逃课的学生。

2 necessity/need has/knows no law 事急无法律
Necessity knows no law. 【谚】情出无奈,罪可赦免。

lay

1 lay for 埋伏等待
The bandits laid for the policemen along the road. 匪徒埋伏在路旁等候警察。

2 lay into 狠打,打斗,攻击;责骂;大吃
The two fighters laid into each other as soon as the bell rang. 铃声一响,两个拳击手就使劲对打起来。
John loves Italian food and he really laid into the spaghetti. 约翰爱吃意大利食物,他真吃了不少通心粉。

3 lay/pile/put/spread it on (thick) 奉承,献媚;言过其实
To call Thomson a genius is laying it on a bit too thick. 称汤姆森为天才有点言过其实。
Gabriel laid it on thick to his rich aunt. 加布里埃尔拼命讨好他那有钱的姑妈。

4 lay off【美】临时解雇;停下休息;暂时停止打扰、取笑、批评、干涉等
They laid us off (work) for three months. 他们临时停工三个月。
You'll have to lay off smoking or it will kill you. 你必须戒烟,否则它会毁了你。

5 lay on 痛殴,猛攻;安排文艺节目
As he laid on blows to the boy's back, a man came up and took the whip

out of his hand. 他鞭打男孩背部时，一个男人走过来夺走了他手中的鞭子。

Stage shows were laid on to entertain the foreign guests. 安排了几场演出招待那些外宾。

6 lay/put sb./sth. on the line 付款；冒险；坦白地说

The sponsors had to lay nearly a million dollars on the line to keep the show on. 赞助商几乎要付一百万美元才能使节目上演。

I'm going to lay it on the line for you, Paul. You must work harder if you want to pass. 保罗，老实告诉你，如果你想通过考试，必须更加努力。

7 lay (it) on with a trowel 露骨地吹捧，言过其实，竭力恭维，过分夸奖，厚厚地涂抹

Newman laid on the horror with a trowel and made everybody feel sick. 纽曼过分地渲染恐怖场面使大家觉得恶心。

8 lay/put one's cards on the table/lay down one's cards 坦诚表示

In talking about buying the property, Peterson laid his cards on the table about his plans for it. 彼得森在谈到置产时坦诚地表明了他的计划。

9 lay oneself out 尽力，特别卖力

Harry wanted to win a medal for his school, so he really laid himself out in the race. 哈里想要为学校赢得奖牌，他在比赛时真是竭尽全力。

10 lay over 【美】作短暂停留；使延期；胜过，优于

We had to lay over here for two hours waiting for a plane to New York. 我们得在这里停留两个小时，等待去纽约的飞机。

The vote will have to be laid over until next week. 投票将推迟到下周举行。

11 lay out 捐款；投资；花一大笔钱；击倒，打昏

Owen had to lay out all he had on the airline tickets. 欧文得倾其所有去买飞机票。

A stiff right to the jaw laid the boxer out in the second round. 在第二个回合这个拳击手下颚挨了一记右手重拳，被打昏了。

12 lay to rest/sleep 埋葬；消除（疑虑等）；结束；忘却

They laid Richard to rest. 他们把理查德安葬了。

The rumor was laid to rest. 谣言平息了。

lead

1 lead astray 把……引入歧途
They've led Newman astray. 他们把纽曼带坏了。

2 lead by the nose 摆布，牵着别人鼻子走
Many people are easily influenced and a smart politician can lead them by the nose. 很多人容易受人影响，高明的政客可以牵着他们的鼻子走。
Don't let anyone lead you by the nose, use your own judgment and do the right thing. 不要任人摆布，要自己判断行事。

3 lead captive 押走
The policemen led them captive to a distant land. 警察把他们押送到远方去了。

4 lead nowhere 毫无结果
This idea led nowhere. 这一想法毫无结果。

5 lead off 领头，开头
Who is to lead off the debate? 辩论由谁开始？
Rebecca led off the show with a song. 丽贝卡以一首歌开始了这场演出。

6 lead on 怂恿……在歧途上走得更远；把人带坏；引诱；骗人，使人误信
Sally led Roy on to think that she would eventually marry him. 萨莉使罗伊误以为她最终会嫁给他。
Terry's leading Sophia on to bad ways. 特里正把索菲娅往邪路上引。

7 lead with one's chin 言行轻率；鲁莽从事
Let him lead with his chin. We'll work undercover. 让他毛手毛脚地去干吧，我们要悄悄地干。

8 lead a cat-and-dog life 争吵不休

9 lead a double life 婚外恋，婚外情
People around here all feel that he's leading a double life. 我们这片儿的人都感觉到他有婚外恋。

10 lose the lead （在赛跑或做生意时）落后
If the Roxs lose the lead, I will switch to FSN for good. 如果火箭队丢掉了领先优势，我就转到福克斯体育网。

11 take over the lead 领先
But right now, they've got a chance to take over the lead in the West. That's enough motivation for them. 但是现在，他们有机会领跑西部。这

对于他们是个足够大的动力。

12 pump lead into sb. 【美】向某人扫射，连续向某人开枪

The killer pumped lead into the audience. 枪手连续向观众开枪。

13 swing the lead (以装病等)逃避工作；(以说谎)回避真相

The doctor thought the young man was swinging the lead and sent him back to work at once. 医生认为年轻人是在装病，就立刻打发他回去工作。

Don't believe his tale; he's just swinging the lead. 别信他那套，他只是瞎吹。

leaf

1 borrow/take a leaf from/out of one's book/notebook 以……为榜样

You ought to take a leaf out of your brother's book. He was never late. 你应当学习你的弟弟，他从来不迟到。

2 turn over a new leaf 洗心革面，重新开始，改弦更张，开始新的一页

I have been very lazy, but I'm going to turn over a new leaf and work hard. 我过去一向很懒，但我将改过自新，努力工作。

The conservative editorial board was turning over a new more open-minded leaf. 立场保守的编委会正变得较为开明。

league

1 in one's league 与……同类型

Susan was bored because Tony obviously wasn't in her league. 苏珊感到厌烦，显然托尼和她并不是同一类型的人。

2 out of one's league 与……不同类型

Vincent was so sophisticated, just someone way out of her league. 文森特是那么老于世故，和她完全是两路人。

leap

1 a leap in the dark 冒险举动，瞎闯

His move to America was a leap in the dark. 他迁居美国是件冒险的事。

2 by/in leaps and bounds 非常迅速地

The population of Africa is growing by leaps and bounds. 非洲人口正在极其迅速地增长。

The school enrollment was going up by leaps and bounds. 入学人数迅速增加。

leave

1　by/with your leave 请允许我；对不起（常用在冒昧行事或说不受欢迎的话时）

By your leave, I'll shut this window, I'm feeling the draught. 请原谅，我觉得有过堂风，想把窗户关上。

2　get left 被遗弃；受挫折；竞赛中被击败；失望

I got left when all the others ran ahead, as I could not run so fast. 其他人都跑到前面去了，我落在了后面，因为我跑不快。

When the examination results came out, Jack had got left as usual. 考试成绩出来了，杰克照例是不及格。

3　leave sb. be 不打扰

"The baby's crying!" "Leave him be; he'll soon stop." "小宝宝哭了！""别管他，一会儿就不哭了。"

4　leave sb. flat 悄然离开，遗弃某人；驳得某人哑口无言

Sam found that being a member of the trail-clearing group was a lot of hard work, so he left them flat. 山姆发现道路清洁小组的工作很苦，就悄然离开了。

My car was ran out of gas and left me flat, ten miles from town. 我的车子在离城10英里时没汽油了，可把我害苦了。

5　leave go/hold/loose of 放开，放手

Leave go of my hair! 放开我的头发！

6　leave holding the bag/sack 使……的需要落空

In the rush for seats, Joe was left holding the bag. 大家争抢座位，乔没抢着。

7　leave it at that 行啦，好啦，到此为止吧，别太过分啦

We'll leave it at that. You will pay half the expenses. 这事就这样吧，你得付一半费用。

I think I've given you a strong enough warning; we'll leave it at that for the moment. 我想我已经给了你足够的警告，这事就到此为止吧。

8　leave off 停止

The rain hasn't left off. 雨还没停。

Leave off interrupting me whenever I'm talking! 我讲话时别打断我!

9 leave/let well (enough) alone【美】不要画蛇添足,不要弄巧成拙

John wanted to make his kite go higher, but his father told him to let well enough alone because it was too windy. 约翰想让他的风筝飞得更高,但他的父亲叫他适可而止,因为当时风太大了。

Waters polished up his car until his friends warned him to leave well enough alone. 沃特斯把车子擦个不停,直到朋友们告诫他不要擦过了头,他才住手。

10 neither with your leave, nor by your leave 无论你喜欢不喜欢,不管你赞成不赞成

11 take it or leave it 要不要随你便

Paddy said, real sore, "Personally, I can take it or leave it alone." 帕迪气恼地说,"就个人而言,我要么接受,要么就不管这件事。"

12 without a with your leave/by your leave 不征得同意擅自行动

The girl stormed in, grabbed her books and stormed out again without so much as a by your leave. 那个姑娘冲了进来,抓起她的书,一言不发又冲了出去。

leg

1 get a leg in 取得……的信任

If I could get a leg in, I could persuade him. 如果我能得到他的信任,我就能够说服他。

2 hang a leg 犹豫不决

You have your hands on thousands, you fools, and you hang a leg! 你们这些傻瓜,只要一伸手就可拿到成千上万的钱,你们还犹豫不决!

3 have sb. by the leg【美】使……处于不利地位

4 have not/not have a leg to stand on (论点、要求等)站不住脚;完全缺乏根据

This theory has not a leg to stand on. 这种理论是站不住脚的。

Without evidence, the prosecutor doesn't have a leg to stand on. 由于缺乏证据,原告的起诉站不住脚。

5 have the legs of/on 比……跑得快

6 pull/draw one's foot/leg 参见 foot 15

7 put one's best leg forward/foremost 以最快的速度走或跑

You must put your best leg foremost, we are rather late. 你必须拼命地赶,我们已经相当晚了。

8 shake/show a leg 赶快

Shake a leg there! We've got to get this work done soon, you know! 快点! 我们得马上结束这个工作,明白吗!

Shake a leg there! We'll never finish if you don't hurry up! 快点吧! 你再不抓紧,我们就完成不了工作啦。

9 talk a donkey's/dog's hind leg off/talk the hind/back leg off a donkey/dog/horse/mule 说话滔滔不绝

Susanna would talk a donkey's hind leg off if you gave her the chance. 只要你给苏珊娜机会,她就会说起来没完没了。

10 try it on the other leg 用最后的办法去试,采取最后的手段

Let's try it on the other leg as this method doesn't seem to work. 既然这个法子看来不管用,咱们试试最后一个办法吧。

length

1 go (to) all lengths/go to any length(s)/go (to) the length of/go to great lengths 什么都干得出来;为达目的不遗余力;无所顾忌

Sarah will go to any lengths to get promotion. 为了要得到提升,萨拉什么事都干得出来。

Bill will go to any length to keep Dick from getting a date with Mary. 比尔会竭尽全力阻止迪克和玛丽的约会。

2 know/find/get/have/take the length of one's foot 深知……;了解……的特性等

I know the length of his foot, but he does not know mine. 我完全了解他的情况,可是他对我却一无所知。

less

1 less of/no more/none of your cheek/less of sth. 不要,别(用于祈使句)

Less of your impudence! 放规矩些!

Less of your cheek, young man! 不得无礼,年轻人!

2 less than no time 很快,迅速

We can be ready to go in less than no time. 我们很快就能准备好出发。
It took mother less than no time to get dinner ready. 母亲很快就准备好了晚餐。

3 much/still less 更不用说，更何况

Ruskin wouldn't take a drink, much less stay for dinner. 罗斯金连饮料都不肯喝，更别说留下吃饭了。

French is not the private property of Frenchmen, and still less is English the private property of Englishmen. 法语不是法国人的私有财产，英语就谈不上是英国人的私有财产了。

4 no less 竟，居然(表示惊奇或钦佩，常含讽刺意味)

Good heavens! It's the president himself, no less! 天哪,那竟是总统本人！
Marshall gave me ＄50, no less. 马歇尔居然给了我50美元。

let

1 let alone 更不用说

I can't add two and two, let alone do fractions. 我连2加2等于多少都不知道，更不用说做分数了。

There are seven people in the car, let alone a pile of luggage. 汽车里已经有七个人，更不用说还有一大堆行李。

2 let George do it【美】期望他人代劳

Many people expect to let George do it when they are on a committee. 委员会里的很多人都希望事情都让别人去做，而自己坐享其成。

3 let it all hang out 毫不掩饰，供出实情

Sue can't deceive anyone; she just lets it all hang out. 苏不会骗人，她有什么说什么。

4 let it go at that 不再多说；不再操心

Lynd said he hadn't understood the rules, and we let it go at that. 林德说他不懂这些规则，我们也就不再追究了。

5 let it lay 别提了；别理它(常用于祈使句)

Don't get involved with Max again—just let it lay. 别再和麦克斯纠缠了——别理他就是了。

6 let it rip 别担心，别理会后果；用心好好干(祈使语气)

Why get involved? Forget about it and let it rip. 何必操那些心，随它

去吧!

Come on, man, give it all you've got and let it rip! 大伙加油,拼命大干一场!

7　let me/us see 试试看;让我想想看

I can't come today. Let me see. How about tomorrow? 我今天不能来,让我想想看,明天怎么样?

8　let/blow off steam 静极思动;发泄精力或情绪

After the long ride on the bus, the children let off steam with race to the lake. 坐了很长时间的公共汽车之后,孩子们一下车就尽情地飞跑到湖边。

When the rain stopped, the boys let off steam with a ball game. 雨停了以后,孩子们就尽情地打起球来。

9　let sb. off the hook 错过机会

We almost scored a touchdown in the first play against Tech but we let them off the hook by fumbling the ball. 对工学院的第一个回合我们几乎触地得分,却因漏球错过了机会。

The boxer let his opponent off the hook many times. 拳击手错过好几次打倒对手的机会。

10　let on 泄露秘密;流露真情

Marion never let on that he was married. 马里恩从不让人知道他已结婚。

Never let on to anybody. 千万别对任何人说。

11　let one's hair down/let down one's hair 随意,自由自在,轻松

The teachers can seldom let their hair down. 老师们难得轻松一下。

After the dance the college girls let their hair down and compared dates. 舞会以后女大学生们随意评论她们的舞伴。

12　let one's left hand know what one's right hand is doing 使人认清应该做什么

Tom told Fred and Bill to meet him in town, but he forgot to tell them where. Next time he'll let his left hand know what his right hand is doing. 汤姆告诉弗雷德和比尔在镇上和他见面,但忘了说明地点,下次他应该会说清楚。

13　let out 任其奔驰;不为难……;解雇,解散,放出

The rider let out his horse to try to beat the horse ahead of him. 骑手放马

飞奔,想追上领先的那匹马。

Last time I let you out of it when you were late. I'll have to punish you this time. 上次你迟到了,我没为难你,这次我必须惩罚你。

14 let ride 同意照旧;暂时接纳

The class was rather noisy but the teacher let it ride because it was near Christmas. 班上非常吵闹,因为圣诞节快到了,老师也就暂时不管它了。

Ruth's paper was not very good, but the teacher let it ride because he knew Ruth had tried. 露丝的试卷写得不好,老师姑且认可,因为她已尽力了。

15 let sb. have it【美】打击某人;向某人射击;刀刺某人;谴责、攻击、批评某人;讲述有关的

The gunman threatened to let the teller have it if he didn't obey. 武装匪徒威胁出纳员,要是不听话,就开枪打死他。

Mary kept talking in class until the teacher became angry and let her have it. 玛丽上课时老是讲话,老师生气地把她批评了一顿。

16 let slide 听其自然

You should not let your studies slide. 你不该在学习上放任自流。

17 let slip 放开,放手;放过;错过

When the game was started, the hunter let the dogs slip. 当猎物惊起时,猎人放狗追赶。

Nicholas was invited to America several years ago, but he let the chance slip. 几年前尼古拉斯被邀请去美国,但他放弃了这个机会。

18 let up 暂停,停止;放松;减弱

The rain will soon let up. 雨很快就会停的。

His mind never let up for an instant. 他的思想一刻也没放松过。

19 let up on 较宽容地对待

Let up on her. She is sick. 别对她太严厉了,她在生病。

20 let's don't/don't let's 不要做

"Let's go out and play," said Fred. "Let's don't until the rain stops," said Mary. 弗雷德说:"我们出去玩吧。"玛丽说:"雨没停,不要出去。"

Don't let's go now. Let's go tomorrow instead. 现在别去,我们明天去吧。

21 let's us/let's you and I/me/us【美】让我们

Let's us go too. 让我们也去吧。

level

on the level 【美】公平，正直；实实在在；老实说

Bud acted *on the level*. 巴德处事公正。

Our teacher respects the students who are *on the level* with her. 我们的老师尊重对她诚实的学生。

liberty

what a liberty 真失礼，真放肆，真不像话

What a liberty! He's taken my car without even asking my permission! 真不像话！他竟然不经我允许开走了我的车！

Who does she think she is? She just walked past me without even saying a word! *What a liberty*! 她以为她是什么人？刚才她从我身边走过连个招呼都不打，真不像话！

lick

1 lick (all) creation/lick everything 出乎意料；胜过一切，出众，闻所未闻

2 a lick and a promise 潦草从事，马马虎虎，随随便便

You didn't wash your hands. You just gave them *a lick and a promise*. 你没把手洗干净，只是马马虎虎地洗了一下。

The boys didn't cut the grass properly. All it got was *a lick and a promise*. 孩子们没把草剪好，只是随便剪了一下。

3 lick one's boots/feet/shoes 参见 boot 8

4 lick one's chops 想到得意的事而沾沾自喜

John is *licking his chops* about the steak dinner tonight. 约翰想着今晚的牛排晚餐喜不自胜。

Our team *is licking its chops* because we beat the champions last night. 昨晚我队获得冠军，全体队员喜气洋洋。

5 lick/whale the daylights/living daylights out of 痛打，把……打得鼻青脸肿，把……打得失去知觉

The big kid told Charlie that he would *lick the daylights out of* him if Charlie came in his yard again. 那个大男孩告诉查理如果他再闯入院子，一定要狠狠揍他一顿。

6 put in best/solid/big licks 【美】尽最大努力，不断努力，苦干

lid

1 blow one's lid【美】发脾气,勃然大怒,大发雷霆

2 blow/take/lift the lid off 揭盖子,揭露

The police blew the lid off the gambling operations. 警察揭露了赌场内幕。

The clever journalists blew the lid off the Watergate scandal. 聪明的新闻工作者揭露了水门丑闻的真相。

3 clamp/put a lid on 限制,抑制,制止;取缔

Put a lid on rumors by using plain, simple language. 运用平实、简单的语言就能遏止流言。

4 flip one's lid/wig 发脾气;狂怒;发疯

Don't go flipping your lid. 别发火!

When that pushy salesman came back, mother really flipped her lid. 那难缠的推销员又来了,母亲真的生气了。

5 keep the lid on 保守秘密

Harriman is unable to keep the lid on his role in the murder. 哈里曼无法隐瞒自己在谋杀案中充当的角色。

John kept the lid on his plans until he was ready to run for class president. 约翰没有泄露他竞选班长的计划,直到他一切准备就绪。

6 put/place the lid on 阻止或破坏(计划、行动等)

These latest regulations have put the lid on our plans. 最近这些规定使我们的计划泡汤了。

The chief of police placed the lid on gambling in the town. 警长扫除了镇上的赌博之风。

7 with the lid off 真相大白,原形毕露

lie

1 as far as in my lies 尽我所能

As far as in my lies, I will try to bring this business back to prosperity. 我要全力以赴使这家商行重新繁荣昌盛起来。

2 I tell a lie 啊,我错了

I saw him yesterday—no, I tell a lie—it was the day before. 我昨天看见他,啊,不对,我是前天看见他的。

3 it lies with you 随你的便

It lies with you to accept or reject the proposals. 接受还是拒绝这些建议由你来决定。

4 lie doggo 静待时机，隐蔽躲藏

The escaped prisoners lay doggo in a haystack until the searchers had gone away. 越狱的囚犯们一直躲在干草堆里，直到搜寻者离去。

5 lie down on the job 参见 job 9

6 lie/lay low 藏身，躲避；保持低调，韬光养晦

After holding up the bank, the robbers lay low for a while. 抢了银行以后，劫匪们暂时藏了起来。

life

1 for dear/one's life 拼命地

Hobbes was running for dear life toward town. 霍布斯拼命地向城里跑去。

When the horse began to run, Jean held on to the reins for dear life. 当马开始跑的时候，琼死命地抓紧了缰绳。

2 for one's life/for the life of sb. 死也……，无论如何也……；拼命地，急忙地

Walter, for his life, would have hardly called her by her name. 华尔特死也不肯用她的名字称呼她。

Run, run for your life! 快跑，赶快逃命！

I can't for the life of me remember her name. 我无论如何也想不起来她的名字。

I can't understand it for the life of me. 我无论如何也弄不懂。

3 get the fright of one's life【口】从来没有这样惊吓过

4 have the time of one's life【口】从来没有这样快活过，过着最快活的生活

5 how's life【口】你近来生活好吗？近来怎么样？

6 lay down one's life 牺牲生命

Man can have no greater love than to lay down his life for his friends. 牺牲自己的生命去救朋友，没有比这更伟大的爱了。

7 on your life/nelly 一定，务必，在任何情况下；绝对（用于否定句）

Obey them on your life. 一定要服从他们。

"Do you really expect me to believe that excuse?" "Not on your nelly!" "你以为我会相信那个借口吗？""绝对不会！"

8 put some life into it 鼓起劲来干

9 risk life and limb 冒生命危险

Viewers will remember the dashing hero, Dirk, risking life and limb to rescue Daphne from the dragons. 观众不会忘记英勇的男主角德克冒着生命危险把达芙妮从恶龙爪下救出的情形。

10 that's life 事情就是这样；情况就是如此

It's a pity, Colin and Rowena got divorced, but then that's life! 真可惜，科林和罗伊娜离婚了。事情就这样发生了。

11 this is the life 这才叫生活呢

A sandy beach, plenty of hot sun, lots of nice people! This is the life! 海滨沙滩上，温暖的阳光，快乐的人群尽情享受大自然的恩赐，这才叫生活呢！

12 to save one's life 死也……；怎么也……

Lincoln could not help laughing to save his life. 林肯怎么也忍不住笑。

Judith couldn't play football to save his life. 朱迪思怎么也学不会踢足球。

13 upon my life 我敢以生命担保，我敢说

Upon my life, you are enough to vex a saint! 我敢说，再有涵养的人也会被你惹恼。

You are, upon my life, a strange instance of the little frailties that beset a mighty mind. 说句良心话，你这人真是个奇怪的典型：一方面有坚强的精神，一方面又摆脱不掉许多小缺点。

14 what a life 人生太苦了

What a life, I get up at half past five every day, work solidly for eight hours, come home, have my meal and go to bed. It's all so monotonous! 这算什么日子啊！我每天早晨五点半起床，紧张地工作八个小时后回家，吃了饭就上床睡觉。整个生活就是这么枯燥单调。

15 you bet your life/boots 的确，不错，肯定

Do I like to ski? You bet your life I do. 我喜欢滑雪吗？我的确很喜欢。

light

1 be/go out like a light 【美】很快入睡,酣睡;失去知觉

As soon as the lights were turned off, Peter was out like a light. 灯一熄,彼得就睡着了。

Tom was hit by a stone and went out like a light. 汤姆被石块击中,立刻昏了过去。

2 see the light 明白,领悟;同意

I did not approve of his plan, but he explained and then I saw the light. 我不赞成他的计划,但他解释了以后,我就同意了。

3 see the light of day 出生,问世;发表

They visited the old house where their grandfather first saw the light of day. 他们参观了祖父出生的老房子。

The report saw the light of day last month. 那篇报道在上个月发表了。

like

1 I don't half like it 我一点也不喜欢

2 I like that 哪能这样,哪有这样的道理;亏你说得出口

"Everyone knows that restaurant's kitchens are dirty." "I like that! It was you who advised me to go there!" "人人都知道那家餐馆的厨房很脏。""亏你说得出口!是你建议我到那儿去的!"

"I said this department store wouldn't have what we were looking for!" "Well, I like that! It was you who suggested that we come here!" "我说过这家百货商店没有我们要买的东西。""好哇,亏你说得出口!正是你建议我们到这儿来的!"

3 I'd like to 我喜欢,我想要

I'd like to know what he means by that. 我想知道他那样讲是什么意思。If he thinks he's so smart, I'd like to see him come round and mend this bike; I can't. 如果他认为他那么能干的话,我倒想看看他能不能来修好这辆自行车。我可修不好。

4 if you don't like it, you may lump it 不高兴也得忍耐

5 if you like 如果你愿意的话(用于提议);如果你一定要这样看的话(用于加强语气表示勉强同意)

"I'd thought of asking Julie to give me some driving practice. What do you think she'd say?" "I'll ask her, if you like." "我想请朱莉教我练习开车,你看她会同意吗?""如果你愿意的话,我会去问问她。"

I may be mean with money, if you like, but my wife certainly isn't. 也许我对钱看得很重,如果你这么认为的话,可是我的妻子肯定不是这样的。

6 (as) like as not/like enough/very like 大概,很可能,十之八九

Like as not, the guards outside the keep would stop them. 监狱外的那些守卫十有八九会拦下他们的。

7 like hell 用劲地,死命地;见鬼,不信

As soon as they saw the cops, they ran like hell. 他们一看见警察就拼命地逃跑。

Like hell you're going to bring me my dough! 见鬼,我不信你会带钱给我!

8 like mad/crazy 疯狂地,拼命地,尽快地

We had to drive like mad to get there on time. 我们必须尽快开车,才能准时到达。

9 like water off a duck's back 不起作用,无效

Advice and correction roll off him like water off a duck's back. 劝导和处罚对他丝毫不起作用。

Many people showed Hughes they didn't like what he was doing, but their disapproval passed off him like water off a duck's back. 很多人向休斯表示他们不喜欢他的行为,但这对他没有丝毫影响。

10 that's more like it 那样就好得多了

"I got sixty per cent in my history test this week." "That's more like it! That's a lot more than you've had recently." "这周的历史考试我得了60分。""这才像话嘛,这说明你近来大有进步。"

likely

1 a likely story/tale 说得倒像是真的,我才不信呢

2 as likely as not/most likely/very likely 大概,很可能

3 not likely 绝不可能,才不呢

"Would you be willing for your name to be put forward as chairman of the committee?" Pete asked. "What me? Not likely!" Bob exclaimed and walked out of the room. 皮特问道,"你愿意你的名字作为委员会的主席排在前面吗?""什么? 我的名字! 绝不可能!"鲍勃叫喊着走出了房间。

limit

1 off limits 【美】止步；禁止入内
Off limits to all unauthorized personnel. 闲人免进。
No knowledge is off limits, and nothing is impossible. 知识没有止境，万事皆有可能。

2 that's the limit 这算到了头了，不能再容忍了

3 the frozen limit 讨厌到极点，恶劣到极点，忍受极限

4 to the limit 【美】到极点，极端地

line

1 all/right along/down the line 到处，在全线；全部
The attack was successful all along the line. 进攻获得全线成功。
The politician supported the government's actions all down the line. 这位政治家全心全意地支持政府的各项措施。

2 blow one's lines 【美】忘记台词，背错台词
The noise backstage scared Peter and he blew his lines. 后台的噪音使得彼得惊慌起来，他忘了台词。

3 down the line 在前面街上，沿街一直往前；全部地，彻底地
The post office is down the line a few blocks. 往前一直走过几条街就是邮局。
Frank always follows the teacher's directions right down the line. 弗兰克一向完全听从老师的指导。

4 drop a line 简略写几句寄来
Judy's friend asked her to drop a line while she was away on vacation. 朱迪的朋友请她在度假时写信。

5 get a line on sb./sth. 【美】得到情报、消息，打听明白
See if you can get a line on the new man. 看你能否打听到新人的情况。

6 give sb. a line on sb./sth. 【美】把有关某人/某事的消息告诉某人
Can you give me a line on the new boss? 你能跟我讲讲新老板的情况吗？

7 line one's pockets/purse 贪污
The policeman lined his pockets by taking bribes. 这个警察贪赃枉法，收了不少贿赂。

8 line up 妥善安排，组织；邀请

Henry's friends lined up so many votes for him that he won the election. 亨利的朋友为他拉到许多选票,他因而当选。

They've lined up some excellent entertainers for our show. 他们邀请了几位出色的艺人参加我们的演出。

9 offline 不在工作或运行;离线,下线;脱机;线下

You can do all of this processing offline without any impact to the processing on the database server. 可以在脱机情况下完成该处理的所有工作,不会对数据库服务器上的处理产生任何影响。

10 on line 正在工作或运行;线上,在线

Evans has been back on line after his illness. 埃文斯生病后已经回来工作了。

11 on the line 【美】马上,立刻;处境危险;模棱两可

Remember, your hotel's reputation is always on the line. 谨记一点,你的酒店声誉永远是第一位的。

12 out of line 行为出格,举止不当

They were severely punished for stepping out of line. 他们因行为出格而受到严厉惩罚。

Eden was out of line for criticizing his wife publicly. 艾登当众指责妻子,真是不近人情。

13 shoot a line 吹牛

Dick's only shooting a line. Don't believe him. 别信迪克的,他只不过是吹牛罢了。

lip

1 bite one's lip(s)/tongue 咬住嘴唇(抑制喜怒等感情的流露),克制自己,保持沉默

It was scary. A dozen times I wanted to yell "Not so fast! Not so fast!" or "Look out for that car!" But I managed to bite my lip and we got through it without an accident. 那真吓人。有好多次我都想大叫:"别开那么快!别开那么快!"或者"当心那辆车!"但是我竭力忍住了没开口。我们总算平安无事地到达了目的地。

It is wise to bite one's tongue on a controversial issue. 对有争议性的话题,还是少说话为妙。

2 button/zip one's lip/keep one's lip buttoned 使闭嘴，使安静

The man was getting loud and insulting and the cop told him to button his lip. 这人大声地叫嚷、辱骂，警察叫他住口。

John wanted to talk, but Dan told him to keep his lip buttoned. 约翰想说出来，但丹叫他别作声。

3 carry/keep a stiff upper lip 不灰心，不气馁

I want you to carry a stiff upper lip whatever happens. 我希望你们无论如何不要灰心丧气。

Cooper was very much worried about his sick daughter, but he kept a stiff upper lip. 库珀为生病的女儿担忧，但他并不气馁。

4 curl one's lip 撇嘴（表示轻蔑）

5 escape one's lip/slip of the lip 脱口而出，说走了嘴

The manager didn't mean to hurt you. He only made a slip of the lip. 经理只是说走嘴了，他根本没有想伤害你的意思。

6 lick one's lips 舔嘴唇（表示满意、赞赏、渴望等）

7 none of your lip 不得无礼，不要放肆

Do as I tell you and it's none of your lip! 照我的吩咐做，不许顶嘴。

8 read my lips/can you read lips 看我嘴唇动作就行了，注意听；仔细听清楚；不说也知道

You want me to kiss his ass? Read my lips: No Way! 你要我拍他马屁？仔细听好：门儿都没有！

9 seal one's lips 封……的嘴，不准……讲，阻止……说出某事

"OK—it's a secret, remember—don't tell anyone!" "Right, my lips are sealed." "好吧，这是个秘密，记住，对谁也不能说。""对，我一定保守秘密。"

10 shoot out one's lips/make (up) a lip 噘嘴，撇嘴（表示轻蔑）

11 smack one's lips 咂嘴（表示满意、赞赏或渴望等）；不胜向往未来的欢乐

Sally and I will fly to Hawaii for two weeks. I smack my lips every time I think about us lying on a white sand beach with the waves rolling in and palm trees rustling around us, or luau feasts and hula dancers and that beautiful scenery. 萨莉和我要去夏威夷度假两星期。现在我想象我俩躺在白沙海滩上，层层细浪席卷而来，四周棕榈树沙沙作响。我还想到夏威夷的欢乐宴会和草裙舞娘，更想到了美不胜收的风景，这一切都无限

美好。

12　white at the lips 气得/吓得嘴唇发白

little

1　a little bird told me 我自然知道，有人告诉我

2　little or no/little if any 极少，几乎没有

Then, emergency workers were sent in with little or no protection to deal with the fallout. 那时，被派到那里的应急工作人员几乎没有任何防护地处理辐射。

3　little or nothing/anything 没有什么东西，简直没有

The truth is that fun and happiness have little or nothing in common. 事实是乐趣和幸福几乎没有共同点。

4　make little of 轻视；怠慢；不太理解

Jenny thought Tom was looking for another way to make little of her. 珍妮认为汤姆在找别的法子来冷落她。

I could make little of his instructions. 我对他的指示不太理解。

5　not a little 许多

I am so sorry to give you not a little trouble. 真抱歉给你添了这么多麻烦。

6　quite a little 相当多

My pedagogue is quite a little gentleman! 我的启蒙先生可以说是一个相当有教养的人！

7　think/make little of sth. /set little by sth. 不重视，不在乎某事

The critic thought little of the new novel. 评论家认为这部新小说没什么价值。

Bob thought little of walking three miles to school. 鲍勃认为步行三英里去上学算不了什么。

live

1　as I live and breathe 参见 breathe 1

2　live high off the hog/eat high on the hog 生活很富裕

The Jones family lived high off the hog after they struck oil. 琼斯一家人在发现油矿后生活得很富裕。

Mr. Harris wasn't really rich, but his family always ate high on the hog.

哈里斯先生并不真正富有,但他们一家生活得一直很富裕。

3 live it up 追求欢乐;爱好球赛或夜生活

Joe had had a hard winter in lonesome places; now he was in town living it up. 乔曾在偏僻之地度过严冬,现在他在城里尽情享乐。

4 where one lives【美】要害

Her words go right in where he lives. 她的话正击中他的要害。

Hit him where he lives! 把他往死里打!

5 you've not/never lived 你还没有真正体会到生活的全部含义

You've never flown in an aeroplane before? You've never lived! 你从未开过飞机吗?那没有什么值得夸耀的!

You've not lived until you've seen the Niagarra Falls—they're magnificent! 你看过尼亚加拉大瀑布才算真正开了眼界——那真叫了不起!

lo

lo and behold 你瞧,真怪

I'd just come in, when, lo and behold, your old friend Mandy came to the door! 你瞧,真怪,我刚到家,你的老朋友曼迪就来到了门口。

load

1 get a load of this 参见 get 3

2 have/get a load on【美】喝醉

You've got a load on and no mistake. 你已经喝醉了,毫无疑问。

loaf

use your loaf/brain 动动脑筋

Use your loaf! Can't you be more tactful? 动动脑筋,你能不能更谨慎些?

lock

1 lock up【美】胜券在握,有成功把握

"How did your math test go?" "I locked it up, I think." "你的数学测验成绩如何?" "我想一定很好。"

It became apparent that he had the presidential nomination locked up. 显然他被提名为总统候选人已成定局。

2 lock, stock and barrel 全部，完全地

Before they were repatriated, they sold all their possessions, lock, stock and barrel. 他们在被遣返前把所有财产都卖完了。

long

1 by a long chalk/long chalks/a long way/a long shot 参见 chalk 2

2 not by a long chalk/shot 参见 chalk 3

3 now we shan't be long 好啦，差不多啦（一般用作讽刺）；一切顺利（暗示事情终结）

4 so long 再见

So long, Tom! See you next week! 再见，汤姆，下星期见！

I'm going now, but I'll be back tomorrow. So long! 我要走啦，但我明天会再来，再见！

look

1 be looking for a fight/trouble 想找事；想挑衅；想露一手；气势汹汹

"Are you looking for a fight?" "No!" "Then shut up!" "你想找事吗？""不！""那就闭嘴！"

Three youths were going round the streets late at night—you could tell from their faces that they were looking for trouble. 三个年轻人深夜在街上闲逛，从他们脸上可以看出他们是想惹事。

2 look after yourself 小心（再见时说）

"Look after yourself, Julia!" "Yes, I will, thank you." "小心，朱莉娅。""知道了，谢谢你。"

3 look/see here 哎，喂，注意（唤起注意、表示不悦、规劝等）

Look here, young man, I've had about enough of all this noise. Now turn that radio down or I'll report you. 听着，年轻人，这噪音真把我烦死了。请把收音机开小点，不然我可要去告你们了。

Now see here, I won't have you speaking to my daughter like that! Apologise at once! 听着，我不允许你这样对我女儿说话！立刻向她道歉！

4 look like a million dollars 参见 dollars 3

5 look lively/smart 快些

Look lively, teacher's coming! 快点，老师来了！

You'll just catch the bus if you look smart. 你动作快点就能赶上公共

汽车。

6 look what you've done 看你干的好事（口气温和地责备）

Look what you've done! You've woken the baby after we've spent an hour trying to get him to go to sleep. 看你干的好事！我们花了一个小时才把婴儿哄睡，你又把他弄醒了。

7 look you 注意，听我说

Look you, take my advice, or you'll regret what you're about to do. 听我说，接受我的意见。否则你会对你要做的事后悔的。

loose

stay loose 【美】保持镇静，不着急

Stay loose, the fire has been brought under control. 别紧张，火势已经被控制住了。

loosen

loosen up 【美】无拘束、无顾忌地说话；慷慨解囊，花钱大方；自然，随便，不拘束

You're tight-mouthed. Loosen up! 你嘴太紧了。讲出来吧！
After the death of his stingy wife, Bill loosened up a great deal. 比尔在吝啬的妻子死了以后花钱大方多了。

lose

1 lose one's shirt 【美】丢得精光，一无所有

Uncle Joe spent his life saying to buy a store, but it failed, and he lost his shirt. 乔叔叔一生都在说要买一家铺子，但这个愿望没有实现，他现在一无所有。

2 lose one's tongue 困窘慌乱，张口结舌

The man would always lose his tongue when he was introduced to new people. 这人在被介绍给生人时总是窘迫得说不出话来。

3 lose out 输掉，失败

Our team lost out in the finals. 我们队在决赛中输掉了。

4 lose out on 错过，没赶上，没得到

Kelsen lost out on the special sale because he did not read the advertisement announcing it. 凯尔森错过了那次大促销，因为他没有看到

广告。

lost

get lost 参见 get 31

lot

1 a fat lot 极多,极大(反语,实指极少、几乎没有)

A fat lot of good you are! 你可真是个大好人!

Leonard gave us a pat on the back. That's a fat lot of encouragement. His time and money are more important to us than his words! 伦纳德拍了拍我们的背,那真是给了我们极大的鼓励! 他的时间和金钱对我们来说比他的言语更重要!

2 a lot of doing 费劲;难以

His story takes a lot of believing. 他的说法很难令人相信。

That won't take a lot of doing. 那件事并不难办。

3 that's your lot/you have had your lot 你命该如此

Well, that's your lot. I've checked all the lists for you and the amount is correct. 好啦,你命该如此,我为你检查了所有的账目,总数没错。

louse

louse up 混乱了,弄糟了;弄错了

When Mansfield got there, he found that the hotel reservation had gotten loused up. 曼斯菲尔德到那里后发现预订房间的事搞错了。

The rain loused up the picnic. 这场雨把这次野炊破坏了。

love

1 for the love of God/Heaven/Christ/Mike/mercy 看在上帝的份上;求求你;哎呀(表示惊讶、烦恼)

For the love of Christ, don't go until I finish what I have to say. 看在上帝的份上,让我把话说完你再走。

For the love of Mike (St Michael), stop complaining, and get on and do some work! 求求你们,别抱怨啦,开始干活吧!

2 I love you, too 得了吧,真见鬼(表示不愉快、不耐烦)

"I'll have my meal now and you can wait for yours!" "I love you, too!"

"我先吃饭啦,你等你那份吧!""得了吧,你吃你的!"
"You're absolutely hopeless, aren't you!""I love you, too!""你这人真没治!""见鬼去吧!"

3 I must love you and leave you 我得走啦

"Time's getting on—I must love you and leave you!""OK, see you next week.""时间到了,我得走啦!""好吧,再见!"

4 Lord love you/your heart 哎呀,真是

Quiet! Lord love you! Never heard a noisier little urchin! 安静!哎呀,真没遇到过比你更会吵闹的淘气鬼!

5 not for love or/nor money/【美】not for the love of Mike 无论怎样也不

Fast wouldn't tell me for love or money. 法斯特无论怎样也不肯告诉我事情真相。

Edith can't find a flat for love nor money. 伊迪丝无论怎样也找不到一套住房。

luck

1 as ill/bad luck would have it 不幸得很,倒霉的是

As bad luck would have it, captain Anthony has no mother living. 不幸得很,安东尼船长的母亲不在世上了。

2 as luck would have it 碰巧,真幸运;不巧,真倒霉

As luck would have it, no one was in the building when the explosion occurred. 真幸运,发生爆炸时大楼里没有人。

Edward was a young keeper, as luck would have it, and new to the business. 不幸的是,爱德华是个年轻的管理员,对业务还很生疏。

3 bad luck/hard luck/tough luck/hard lines 真倒霉

Bad luck! How awful that you didn't pass the exam! 真倒霉!你考试没有及格,真可怕!

"I've just heard they are not picking me for the football team.""Hard luck!""我刚听说他们没有选我进足球队。""真倒霉!"

4 by (good) luck/by the skin of one's teeth 凑巧,幸亏,侥幸地,九死一生,一线生机,幸免于难

I have escaped death by good luck. 我侥幸躲过了一劫。

5 by ill luck 不巧,不幸

By ill luck it was a rainy evening. 不凑巧，那晚偏偏在下雨。

6　by the luck of Eden hall 全仗好运

7　crowd/press/push one's luck 得寸进尺，贪心不足；进一步碰碰运气

You'll really be *pushing your luck* if you miss class again. 如果你再次旷课，你就是得寸进尺。

8　down on one's luck 不幸的；穷困潦倒的，不走运的

The Nobel laureate would not hesitate to give money to anyone *down on his or her luck*. 那个诺贝尔奖得主对任何不幸的人都很慷慨。

9　good luck 祝你好运

"*Good luck*, Andy!" my friends all shouted as the train pulled out. "祝你一路顺风，安迪！"火车开动时我的朋友们一齐喊道。

Good luck to you at college! 祝你在大学里一帆风顺！

10　in luck/in luck's way 走运

They are *in* great *luck* this year. 他们今年鸿运当头、吉星高照哇。

11　just one's luck 真倒霉

It was *just my luck*! 唉，我可倒霉了！

Just my luck! The day I want to travel by train was the day of the national rail strike. 真倒霉，那天我正要乘火车旅行却碰上全国铁路大罢工！

12　luck out 意外的财气，运气好

I was sure I was going to miss the train as I was three minutes late; but I *lucked out*, the train was five minutes late. 因为已经迟到了三分钟，我想一定赶不上火车了，但我运气好，火车晚点五分钟。

13　out of luck 运气不好，不凑巧，倒霉

Those who arrive by air, however, are *out of luck*. 但那些乘飞机来的顾客就没这么幸运了。

14　try one's luck 碰碰运气，撞大运

And also there's one jade bazaar near the Yurungkash River (the Jade Drageon Kashgar River). Varieties of colorful jades and stones are sold there. Many people go there to *try their luck*. 玉龙喀什河边还有一个玉石集市，琳琅满目的玉石在那里出售，许多人都愿意去那里碰碰运气。

15　with (any) luck 如果一切顺利的话

The two volumes will, *with luck*, appear in English before long. 如果一切顺利的话，那两册书不久将出英文版。

With any luck we should be there by two o'clock. 一切顺利的话,我们在两点钟前可到达那儿。

16 worse luck 不幸,倒霉

We won't be able to get away this weekend, worse luck! 我们本周末走不成了,真倒霉!

"Do you know Robert Hampshire?" "Yes, I have met him before, worse luck!" "你认识罗伯特·汉普谢尔吗?""认识,我以前见过他,真倒霉!"

17 you never know your luck 一个人说不准什么时候会走运

"Let's have another go on the space invader! I may beat you this time!" "You never know your luck!" "让我们再来一次'空中袭击',也许这次我能打败你。""那可说不准。"

mad

1 (as) mad as a hatter/March hare 发狂,疯狂,疯疯癫癫

Anyone who thinks the moon is made of green cheese is mad as a hatter. 以为月亮是绿色干酪做的人一定是疯了。

Hamilton was mad as a March hare about electricity. 汉密尔顿迷恋电器迷得发狂了。

2 (as) mad as a hornet/hops/a wet hen【美】气得发疯,狂怒

Gray was as mad as a hornet when he heard how the election went. 格雷听到了选举进行的情况气得发疯。

When my father sees the dent in his fender, he'll be mad as a hornet. 当父亲看到车子挡板上的凹陷时一定会气疯。

3 like mad 疯狂地,拼命地,猛烈地,极快地

I was very frightened and clinging on like mad. 我吓坏了,拼命地紧抓不放。

We were arguing like mad as to what it was. 对于那是什么我们争论得非常激烈。

4 stark raving/staring mad 完全疯了,傻透了

Fred must be stark staring mad if he thinks they're going to pay him for work he hasn't done. 如果弗雷德认为他没干活他们也会付他钱,那他一定是疯了。

made

1 have (got) it made 参见 have 24

2 what sb. be made of 真才实学,真本领

The race next week will be a chance for her to show what she's made of. 下周的比赛就是她大显身手的时候了。

All right, let's see what you're made of! 好吧,让我们来领教一下你的真本事吧!

make

1 make a dent in 略少一些，略为减少
Mary studied all afternoon and only made a dent in her homework. 玛丽整个下午都在学习，但作业只做了一点点。

2 make a face 做鬼脸
The boy made the baby laugh by making a face at him. 那个男孩扮鬼脸把婴儿逗笑了。

3 make a fool of 愚弄，欺骗，使出丑
If you pretend to know what you don't know, you'll only make a fool of yourself. 不懂装懂只会愚弄自己。

4 make a go of 获得成功，取得好成绩
Evans was sure he could make a go of the filling station. 埃文斯确信他能使加油站获得成功。

5 make a hash/hay/mess/muddle of 弄错，弄糟
Edith made a mess of her life. 伊迪丝把自己的生活弄得一团糟。

6 make a hit 大出风头，大受欢迎；进展顺利
Mary's new red dress made a hit at the party. 玛丽的红色新衣在舞会上大出风头。

7 make a night of it 通宵活动
The boys and girls at the dance made a night of it. 男孩和女孩们通宵都在跳舞。

8 make a pass at 感情进一步发展；越轨（指性方面）
We've been dating for four weeks but Joe has never even made a pass at me. 我们已经约会四周了，但乔对我从未有越轨举动。

9 make a play for 讨好，勾引；卖弄
Bob made a play for the pretty new girl. 鲍勃对这个新来的漂亮女孩尽力讨好。

10 make away with 带走；偷走；杀死；吃光；浪费
His father tried to make away with himself by drinking poison. 他的父亲企图服毒自杀。
As to the pure coffee, which was something that grandpa and grandma would rather make away with than accepting it. 纯咖啡是爷爷奶奶宁可让其浪费也不能接受的。

11 make fun of/poke fun at 参见 fun 4

12 make head or tail of 了解,懂得

Can you *make head or tail of* the letter? 你能看懂这封信吗?

13 make it 达到目标,成功,做到;发迹;及时抵达,赶上;(病痛等)好转,得救

The charts showed we had *made it* and big. 图表显示我们成功了,大大地成功了。

The doctor knew that the patient was unlikely to *make it*. 医生知道那个病人没有什么希望了。

14 make it hot for sb. 使某人日子不好过,刁难某人

I don't want to *make it hot for you*. But I won't tell you the true story of that till you return the letter to me. 我不想刁难你,但如果你不还给我那封信,我就不会告诉你那件事的实情。

15 make it snappy 赶快,快走

"*Make it snappy*," mother said, "or we'll be late for the movie." 母亲说:"快点,否则我们赶不上电影了。"

16 make like【美】假装;扮演;充任

Well, it could *make like* the Dutch and convert it into a temple of books. 嗯,可以模仿荷兰人,把它改建成一座图书的殿堂。

17 make no bones/mistake 毫不犹豫;不反对;公开承认

Bill *makes no bones* about telling a lie to escape punishment. 比尔直言不讳地承认,为了逃避惩罚,他说了谎。

I shall be coming back, *make no mistake* about it! 我要回来的,毫无疑问!

18 make no never mind 没有影响,不起作用

Make no never mind what he thinks, I'm going. 不管他怎么想,我去定了。

19 make one's/the blood boil 参见 blood 4

20 make oneself scarce 吓跑;溜走;不出来

The boys *made themselves scarce* when they saw the principal coming to stop their noise. 孩子们看到校长走来制止他们吵闹全都溜走了。

21 make out 过日子;进展;尽力做到,尽力应付

How are things *making out*? 情况进展如何?

Crane *made out* very well as a salesman. 克兰当推销员干得不错。

22 make the feathers/dust/fur fly 参见 fur 1

23 make the grade 成功

It takes hard study to make the grade in school. 在学校里必须用功学习，才会有好成绩。

24 make the scene 出席，到场；露面；参加

I hope everybody can make the scene. 我希望大家都前去参加这次活动。

25 make time 准时到达，腾出时间；抽空；争取时间

Make time to spend with them. 花些时间和他们待在一起。

26 make tracks 快走，快点

Man, it's time we made tracks! 唉，我们得赶快出发了！

27 make up to 讨好，奉承，巴结；报答，酬谢

I don't like being made up to. 我不喜欢人家巴结我。

How can we make it up to them for all the worry we've caused them? 他们为我们担惊受怕，我们怎么才能报答他们呢？

28 make waves 兴风作浪，制造骚乱

Joe is the wrong man for the job; he is always trying to make waves. 乔不适合这项工作，他总爱惹是生非。

29 on the make 形成中，增长中；唯利是图，损人利己，追求名利

He's always on the make; I have never known him do a disinterested action. 他这个人一贯唯利是图，我从来不知道他做过什么无私的事。

30 that makes two of us 我也是这样

"I'm going to Birmingham University in October!" "That makes two of us—I'm as well." "十月份我要到伯明翰大学去。""我也是。"

31 make a monkey out of 愚弄，戏弄

Some people make a monkey out of themselves by acting foolish or silly. 有些人做了一些荒唐可笑的事情，把自己给嘲弄了。

man

1 be a man 拿出勇气来，拿出大丈夫气概

Be a man! You can beat him easily! 拿出勇气来，你能轻易战胜他！

Go on, be a man, accept the bet! 干吧，拿出勇气来，同他打赌！

2 go, man, go 参见 go 22

3 I'm/he's, etc. your man 我/他等是适合做这事的人；我来应征

I'm your man! I'll accept that offer and start immediately! 我来应征,我接受那个条件并马上开始!

If you want any plumbing work done, then he's your man. 如果你要找安装管道的人,那么他是合适的人选。

4 man alive 参见 alive 2

5 man to man 坦率地,真诚地;面对面地,私下地

As man to man, I think you should admit your mistakes. 坦率地讲,我认为你应该承认自己的错误。

That evening she wanted to speak to her father man to man. 那天晚上她想和父亲单独谈谈。

6 may the best man win 愿最佳者获胜

"I'd like to wish you every success!" "Thank you, and may the best man win!" "我衷心祝愿你成功!" "谢谢,自然是最佳者获胜啦!"

7 my good man 伙计(不礼貌的称呼)

Look here, my good man! How dare you speak to me like that! 听着,伙计,你怎么敢这样对我讲话!

8 oh man 哎呀(表激动、惊讶、愉快等)

Oh man, was I pleased to see her! 哎呀,我见到她真高兴!

Oh man, you really get on my nerves, you know! 天哪,你可真使我心烦!

9 see a man about a dog/horse/wallaby 要去一下洗手间;有点急事先行告辞(通常用来作为离开或缺席的借口)

Excuse me, I gotta see a man about a dog. 对不起,我要方便一下。

10 separate the man from the boys 从一群人中找出真正有魄力、有才干的人

The mile run separates the man from the boys. 从一公里赛跑可以看出谁是真正的英雄好汉。

11 so's your old man 【美】去你的吧,胡说

So's your old man! When had I said that? 你简直是胡扯! 我什么时候说过那样的话?

marine

tell it/that to the marines/horse/Sweeney 【美】鬼才会相信

"I've just been to tea at Buckingham Palace." "Tell that to the marines."

"我刚才在白金汉宫参加茶会来着。""鬼才会相信。"
John said, "My father knows the President of the United States." Dick answered, "Tell it to the marines." 约翰说:"我父亲认识美国总统。"迪克回答说:"鬼才相信。"

mark

1 God/Heaven bless/save the mark 天哪(表示惊愕、轻蔑、抱歉、讽刺等);上帝保佑我,真要命,对不起

God save the mark! 上帝宽恕我这样说! 罪过罪过!

2 off the mark 不正确,不可信

Whoever told you that was right off the mark. 不管谁告诉你,都不可信。

matter

1 for that matter/for the matter of that 就此而言,而且

I don't know, and for that matter, I don't care. 我不知道,而且,我也并不在意。

The old lady had a good many goddaughters—and godsons, for that matter. 那个老太太有许多教女,还有许多教子。

2 no matter 没关系

"I've just broken one of your mugs!" "No matter! They were only cheap ones!" "我刚才打破了你的两个杯子!""没关系,那都是些不值钱的东西!"

3 no matter how/who/what, etc. 不管怎样/是谁/什么等

4 what matter 这有什么关系,这无须担心

What matter if we meet some difficulties? 即使我们遇到一些困难,又有什么了不起?

What matter if there's a strike, we'll muddle through somehow. 即使发生了罢工,又有何妨。我们总能对付过去。

mean

1 and I don't mean maybe 我说话算话

I want this work done for ten this evening, and I don't mean maybe! 我要求这项工作在今天晚上十点钟完成。我是认真的!

2 mean business 参见 business 15

3 what do you mean by 你做……的目的何在；你怎么竟敢

What do you mean by getting me up in the middle of the night? 你半夜把我弄起来到底要干什么？

What do you mean by that? Please explain, as I'd like to know! 你这是什么意思？请解释一下，我想知道究竟。

means

1 by all means 务必，一定；当然没问题，自然可以

"Can we come aboard?" "By all means! You are most welcome!" "我们可以登机了吗？""当然可以，非常欢迎！"

By all means use my name when you apply for the job. 你申请工作时一定要用我的名字。

2 by any means 无论如何，不惜一切代价

It's not an easy beat to cover by any means, and the media may be falling down on the job. 无论如何，这都不是一件容易报道的事，媒体可能一直在拖延时间。

3 by no means 决不，决没有；一点也不

That's by no means the last you've heard of this. 那决不是你最后一次听说这件事。

Evans is by no means considered to be a great explorer. 人们决不会认为埃文斯是个伟大的探险家。

mention

1 don't mention it 别客气，没什么；别介意，没关系

"Thanks so much for lending me your typewriter!" "Don't mention it!" "非常感谢你借给我打字机用。""别客气。"

"I apologize for what I've said." "Don't mention it!" "我为我说的话向你道歉。""没关系，不必介意。"

2 I hate to mention it, but... 对不起，我想问一下（不愿提及对方忽略、忘记的事）；如果你不介意的话

I hate to mention it, but what about the money you owe me? 对不起，我想问一下，你欠我的钱怎么办？

3 not to mention/not to speak of/to say nothing of/without mentioning 除此之外，更不用说

It was a awful hotel, with poor meals, hopeless service, not to mention the noise outside. 这是个很糟的旅馆,饮食太差,服务质量低劣,除此之外,外面还有噪音。
Dave is handsome and smart, not to mention being a good athlete. 戴夫英俊又聪明,还是个优秀的运动员。

mercy

1 mercy me 哎呀(表示惊愕、惊恐、烦恼等)
2 what a mercy 多幸运
What a mercy (that) you could go to college! 你能上大学多么幸运!

merry

1 (as) merry as a cricket/grig/lark/marriage-bell/the maids 非常快乐,兴高采烈
I have not had all the luck I expected, but I'm as merry as a cricket. 我没有碰到我期望的好运气,但我还是很快乐。
2 make merry 尽情欢乐,寻欢作乐
I don't think that you are able to eat and drink and make merry while Africans are being oppressed. 我认为在非洲人受到压迫的时候,你不可能继续大吃大喝尽情享乐。
3 make merry over/about/of 嘲笑,取笑,嘲弄,挖苦
John used to make merry over the cleverness of women, but I have not heard him do it of late. 约翰过去常常对女人的聪明机智加以嘲讽,近来我很少听到他这样做了。

middle

knock/send sb. into the middle of next week 痛打某人;使某人大吃一惊;把某人打昏;杀死某人;把某人撵走;严惩某人
His father often knocked him into the middle of next week. 他父亲以前常常揍他揍得很惨。

might

1 might (just) as well 倒不如,大可,不妨
There is nothing worth watching on the television, so we might as well go

to bed. 没有什么值得看的电视节目，我们还是睡觉吧。

2 might well 很可能

The president might well come. 总统很可能来。

3 with/by all one's might and main 竭尽全力地

Geoffrey pushed and pulled with all his might and main but the door remained firmly closed. 杰弗里拼命地又推又拉，但门仍然紧闭着。

mill

through the mill 通过严格的训练或考查；经受磨炼；饱尝辛酸

Hamilton is an excellent soldier, having gone through the mill at military school. 汉密尔顿是个杰出的军人，在军校受过严格的训练。

The new car was put through the mill. 这辆新车经过了严格的检测。

million

1 a million and one 许许多多

I've got a million and one things to do today. 今天我有许许多多的事要做。

2 feel like a million (dollars) 参见 dollar 1

3 look like a million dollars 参见 dollar 3

mind

1 a bit/piece of one's mind 严厉的责备，坦率的批评，直言不讳

Today I'll give my business manager a piece of my mind. I'm tired of him coming in an hour late every day. I'll tell him to be here on time or look for a job some place else. 今天我得好好地把业务经理说一顿。他每天迟到一小时，真叫我讨厌。我要叫他准时来上班，否则就另谋高就。

2 be in two/many minds 三心二意，犹豫不决

The committee itself appeared to be in two minds over this. 看来委员会本身对这事就拿不定主意。

3 bend one's mind to 专心致志于

I can't really bend my mind to this new work. 我真的不能全身心地投入这项新工作。

4 do/would you mind doing sth./if …… 可以吗，好吗，你不反对吧，请你……

"Do you mind if I smoke?" "No, that's quite all right." "我抽烟你不介意吧?""没关系,请吧。"

"Would you mind opening the window, please?" "Yes, it is a bit hot in here, isn't it?" "请打开窗户,好吗?""好的,这儿是有点热。"

5 do you mind 住手,住口,站住,得了,请不要这样,你太冒失了

Do you mind! That's my parking space you've taken! 站住! 你占了我的停车位!

6 don't mind if I do 好的,我会这样做的,谢谢

"Have another cake." "Thank you. I don't mind if I do." "请再来一块蛋糕。""好的,谢谢,我自己来。"

7 don't mind me/him, etc. 别管我/他等,别为我/他等担心;你这样做像话吗;别对我这样冒失

Just carry on working! Don't mind her! 继续干吧,别管她!

Don't mind me—I can manage quite well while you're away! 别为我担心,你走了我能应付一切的。

8 great minds think alike 英雄所见略同

"Let's go to Brighton this afternoon." "Great minds think alike—I just about to suggest that myself!" "我们今天下午到布赖顿去吧。""真是英雄所见略同,我本来想这样建议的。"

9 have a mind of one's own 有自己的看法,能独立思考

Hobson has a mind of his own and will not be persuaded by what others think. 霍布森有自己的见解,不会被别人的想法左右。

10 I wouldn't mind 我想要……(提出客气的请求)

"I wouldn't mind a nice cup of tea." "All right. I'll go and make one for you." "Thank you!" "我想要一杯清茶。""好的,我去给您沏一杯来。""谢谢!"

11 if you don't/won't mind 如果你同意的话(提出要求或命令)

Please wait over there, if you don't mind. 请到那边去等一下。

If you won't mind, I'll see you in a few minutes. 可以的话,我会在几分钟后来看你。

12 it's all in the mind 这不过是你的想象而已

"I think Jane's in love with me!" "It's all in the mind." "我认为简爱上我了。""这不过是你的想象而已。"

"I feel awful with this stomachache." "It's all in the mind; you're perfectly all right really." "这次胃疼使我感到很不舒服。""这不过是你的心理作用罢了,其实你状态很好。"

13 know one's own mind 有自己明确的想法或愿望;有决断

You ought to have known your own mind on a point of such vital importance. 在如此至关重要的问题上你应该有自己明确的意见。

14 mind how you go 您慢走

Mind how you go! See you next week! 您慢走,下星期再见!

15 mind (out) 当心

Mind out! Don't go too near the edge! 当心,不要走得太靠边了!

Mind! The plate's hot! 当心,碟子烫手!

16 mind (you)/mark you 听我说(用于限定、反对或强调刚才说过的某事);请听清楚;请注意;说真的

I wouldn't help everyone, mind. 说真的,我不会帮助大家。

John's a very nice fellow, mind you, but I wouldn't want to marry him. 说真的,约翰是个好人,但我不想嫁给他。

17 mind you do it/that 务必要做

18 never mind 别担心,没关系;不用了,别费事;别管他;更不用说,更谈不上

Do what the doctor says; never mind the advice of your friends. 照医生的话去做,别管朋友们怎么说。

Never mind about yesterday; it's today I'm interested in! 别管昨天的事,我关心的是今天!

19 never you mind 这与你无关,用不着告诉你

"Where did you two go last night?" "Never you mind!" "你们俩昨晚到哪儿去了?""这你管不着!"

20 out of one's mind 精神错乱,发狂(尤指因生病或忧虑)

Faulkner was out of his mind with grief. 福克纳伤心得精神错乱。

21 pay no mind/not pay any mind 【美】不在意,不在乎,不理睬

I used to laugh at him, but he didn't pay any mind. 我常常嘲笑他,但他从不在意。

22 the mind boggles 对……感到奇怪;感到不知所措;令人难以想象

The mind boggles at how she managed to bring up seven children by herself. 令人费解的是,她是怎样独自一人把七个孩子带大的。

Three bathrooms and seven bedrooms in the house! The mind boggles! 那套房子里有三间浴室和七间卧室,真不可思议!

mirror

it's all done by/with mirrors 这就和变戏法一样

"You see that new machine I've made for brewing tea?" "Yes, how does it work?" "Ah, it's all done by mirrors, you know!" "你看见我煮茶用的新器具了吗?""看到了,那是怎么用的呀?""啊,那就跟变戏法一样!"

mischief

1 do sb. a mischief 使某人受到损害

It will be as well to stop that young screamer though, in case I should be tempered to do him a mischief. 最好让那个在尖叫的孩子住嘴,不然我可要对他不客气了。

2 go to the mischief/dogs 堕落

Then I will follow you, comrade, and be drunken and go to the mischief. 那么我就要跟随你,伙伴,喝得烂醉走向堕落灭亡。

3 make mischief 搬弄是非,制造混乱

4 play the mischief with 损害(健康);弄坏(机器);搞糟(计划)

An accident played the mischief with his plans. 一桩意外的事故打乱了他的计划。

The wind played the mischief with my papers. 风把我的文件吹得乱七八糟。

5 raise (the) mischief 大吵大闹,闹事,闹乱子

If you find they raise the mischief again, please call the police. 如果你发现他们再闹事,那就打电话报警。

miss

1 give a miss 避开,不予理会

We visited the place last time, so we give it a miss this time. 上次我们去过那个地方,这次就不去了。

2 miss the boat/bus 参见 boat 3

Missouri

be/come from Missouri 【美】多疑的,不相信的
I'm from Missouri; you've got to show me. 我是不会轻易相信的,你得拿出证据来。

mistake

1 and no mistake 确确实实,一点没错
Grant's the one I saw and no mistake. 格兰特就是我见到的那个人,没错。

2 make no mistake about it/that 千万不要听错了;绝对如此
If you don't mend your ways, you'll be punished, make no mistake about it. 如果你不改过自新,你将受到惩罚,这点毫无疑问。
Make no mistake about it we are going to win. 毫无疑问我们将获得胜利。

3 there's no mistake about it 绝对没错,毫无疑问
There's no mistake about it that this is quite simply the best car on the market, sir. 毫无疑问,先生,这的确是市场上最好的小汽车。

4 there's no mistaking sb./sth. (某人或某事)绝不会被认错或误会
There was no mistaking Isabel. 伊莎贝尔不可能被认错。
There is no mistaking his meaning. 他的意思不可能被误解。

moment

1 have one's moments 曾经走红、得意;显赫一时
The book has had its moments. 这本书也曾畅销过。
I may not be of much importance now, but I've had my moments. 也许我现在没有那么重要了,但我也曾显赫一时呢。

2 live for/in the moment 得过且过
Kelsen lay on the bed most of the time, living for the moment. 凯尔森大部分时间躺在床上,过一天是一天。

3 never a dull moment 从不感到乏味,总是丰富多彩
"As a teacher, it's all go from the moment I come into school to when I leave." "Yes, never a dull moment." "作为一名教师,我从一进校门到离开学校回家,一直忙个不停。""是呀,那生活真是丰富多彩呀!"

4 not/never for a moment 决不,从来没有
I don't think for a moment that he believed my reason. 我从来没有认为他

会相信我的借口。

5 not have a moment to call one's own 忙得不可开交，抽不出一点时间
You'll not have a moment to call your own this week. 本周你甭想有自己支配的时间了。

money

for one's money 据……看来；以……的意见
For my money, Marian was responsible for the trouble we'd had. 据我看来，玛丽安应对我们遇到的麻烦负责。

monkey

1 get/put one's monkey up 生气，使……生气
Catharine gets her monkey up if you tell her that she's wrong. 如果你说凯瑟琳错了，她会火冒三丈。
What the wife said put the husband's monkey up. 妻子说的话使丈夫很生气。

2 I'll be/I am a monkey's uncle 天哪，哎呀（表示惊奇）
Well, I'll be a monkey's uncle. I never thought Bill would remarry. 天哪！我从来都没想过比尔会再婚。

3 make a monkey out of 参见 make 31

moon

1 be/jump over the moon 非常快乐
Leighton's a grandfather for the first time. And he's over the moon about it. 莱顿第一次当了爷爷，高兴极了。
Rosalind's over the moon about her new job. 罗莎琳德为她的新工作高兴万分。

2 to the moon and back 永远；很多
I love you to the moon and back, I swear. 我发誓永远爱你。

more

1 and what is more 更重要的是，更有甚者，而且
You've come late for school, and what's more, you've lost your books. 你上学迟到而且丢了书。

The price is too high, and what's more, the style is too old-fashioned. 这价钱太高,况且式样太陈旧。

2 more than 非常,极其;超出

They were more than willing to help. 他们非常愿意帮忙。

Some of the stories were really more than could be believed. 有些故事实在不能相信。

3 more... than 与其……倒不如……

The child was more frightened than hurt. 这孩子伤倒没什么要紧,只是受惊不小。

mother

the mother and father of 最好的

We had the mother and father of all arguments last night. 昨天晚上我们进行了一场最精彩的辩论。

motion

go through the motions 装样子,做姿态;不花力气,敷衍

When her mother told her to clean her room she just went through the motions. 她母亲叫她打扫房间,她只敷衍了一下。

It would be better if we at least go through the motions of an investigation. 即使装样子,走过场,我们也最好调查一下。

mouth

1 be all mouth and trousers 只说不做

Their trouble was that they were all mouth and trousers. 他们的毛病是光说不做。

2 blow/shoot off one's mouth/blow/shoot one's mouth off/run off at the mouth 夸夸其谈,胡吹;滔滔不绝地谈论

I've never heard him shooting off his mouth on subjects about which he knew nothing. 我从未听到过他侈谈自己一窍不通的领域。

Sure, I'll say nothing, and I'm sorry, I shot my mouth off. 对不起,我说漏了嘴,我保证今后守口如瓶。

3 down in/at the mouth/down in the dumps 垂头丧气

The boys were certainly down in the dumps when they heard that their team had lost. 听说自己的队输了,孩子们垂头丧气。

4　foam at the mouth 非常恼火

Henry had the third flat tire, and he was really foaming at the mouth. 当车第三次爆胎时,亨利真是气极了。

5　give it mouth 滔滔不绝地讲;慷慨陈词

6　have a big mouth 大声说话;喋喋不休;随便乱说

If I told you, he would say I have a big mouth. 如果我告诉你,他就会说我说话冒失。

You might have a big mouth, so I can't tell you. 你也许无法保守秘密,所以我不会告诉你。

7　mouth on sb.【美】告发某人

The criminal threatened to mouth on him. 那个犯罪分子威胁说要告发他。

8　put one's foot in/into it/in one's mouth　参见 foot 19

9　shut one's mouth/keep one's mouth shut/button up one's mouth 闭口,停止讲话

Shut your mouth! 住口!

I decided I'd better shut my mouth in case I said the wrong thing. 我决定还是不开口的好,免得说错话。

10　shut/stop one's mouth 使闭嘴;堵住……的嘴;杀人灭口

Tell him we'll shut his mouth (for him) if he talks to the police. 告诉他要是他向警方告密的话,我们就要他的命。

11　straight from the horse's mouth 直接从权威方面得来的消息

Believe it or not! I got the information straight from the horse's mouth! 信不信由你,我的消息非常可靠!

12　watch one's mouth 说话小心,不说下流、粗暴挑衅的话

Just watch your mouth! 你说话注意点!

13　well, shut my mouth【美】哎呀,真想不到

move

1　get a move/wiggle on　参见 get 4

2　have all the moves【美】(尤指对运动或游戏)技术精湛,(对运动等)精通熟练

3 make a move 离去，离席；采取行动或措施
Come on, it's time we were making a move. 快点，我们该走了。
Don't make a move without phoning me. 在采取行动前必须打电话给我。

4 make one's move【美】采取行动，有所动作
The cops are just waiting for the guy to make his move. 警察正等着那家伙采取行动。

5 move in 接任，接手；强行插手；进行操纵；【美】夺走
Lewis was appointed Defense Minister when the new Administration moved in. 新政府上台时刘易斯被任命为国防部长。
Professional drug pushers moved in and organized the trade. 职业毒贩进行操纵，把这种买卖包揽下来。

6 on the move 在行进，在奔波，在迁移；动个不停
It was vacation time, and the highways were full of families on the move. 那是度假时节，公路上驾车出游的家庭络绎不绝。
The boy's limbs were always on the move. 这男孩的手脚一直动个不停。

much

1 as much as to say 等于在说，好像是说
The dog wagged its tail, as much as to say "Thank you!" 狗摇摇尾巴，好像是说"谢谢你!"

2 it's a bit much 你的期望值太高了
It's a bit much that you want this shirt now, when you know I've not done the ironing. 你现在就要这件衬衫，未免太性急了，你看我还没有熨好呢。
You come in late and want your dinner immediately—it really is a bit much, you know! 你回来得晚，马上就要吃饭，你的要求也太高了。

3 not much 不十分好，不怎么样；哪里的话；当然不；未必，不大可能
Kitty's not much to look at. 基蒂长得不怎么好看。
I'm not much for politics. 我对政治不怎么感兴趣。

4 not much of a 不是什么了不起的；算不上好的
If you're not much of a Hayden Christensen fan, I think you'll be surprised by how well he does in this flick. 如果你不是很喜欢海登·克里斯滕森，那么你一定会为他在这部电影中的精彩表演而感到惊讶。

5 not up to much 不十分符合标准；不怎么令人满意

"How is your mother today?" "Not up to much." 今天你母亲身体怎样？""不太好。"
I don't think the party was up to much. 我觉得那次聚会不怎么令人满意。

6 so much for 关于……就谈这么多；……到此为止；原来不过如此
Now it started raining so much for my idea of taking a walk. 下雨了，我想散步的打算只好作罢。
So much for your bright idea. 你那高明的主意原来不过如此。

7 too much 太过分，太糟糕，太不像话；【美】太棒了，妙极了
This is too much. 这太过分了。
The stench was too much for me. 那臭气我实在受不了。

muck

1 (as) common as muck 举止粗俗，没有教养
When Jane started talking, you'll realize that she's as common as muck. 简一开口讲话，你就知道她缺乏教养。

2 drag through the muck 玷污，诋毁
Your behaviour is causing our reputation to be dragged through the muck. 你的行为在玷污我们的名声。

3 make a muck of 弄脏；弄糟，打乱安排
Don't make a muck of the dictionary. It is newly bought. 别把字典弄脏了，这是新买的。

mud

1 drag in/into/through the mud 玷污，诋毁
His name was dragged in the mud. 他的名声被毁了。

2 (here's) mud in your eye 干杯，祝你健康（第一次世界大战时士兵在战地祝酒用语）
"Yeah, mud in your eye!" I said and swallowed it quickly. "好，干杯！"我说完一饮而尽。

3 (it's) as clear as mud【讽】一点也不清楚，使人莫名其妙
"Is my explanation clear?" "Yes, as clear as mud, thanks!" "我解释得清楚吗？""是呀，清楚得叫人莫名其妙，谢谢！"

4 name is mud 名声扫地；倒霉
Her name has been mud around here. 她在我们这儿已经名声扫地。

If you tell mother I spilled ink on the rug, my name will be mud. 要是你告诉妈妈我把墨水洒在地毯上,我就要倒霉了。

mum

1 mum's the word 别多嘴,嘘,绝对保密

"I don't want her to know about the present till Christmas day!" "OK, Mum's the word!" "我不想让她在圣诞节前知道给她什么礼物。""好吧,我们保密!"

We are planning a surprise party for John and mum is the word. 我们在为约翰筹办一个惊喜派对,别走漏风声。

2 keep mum about 这事不要说出去,保密

Eric tells Encai to keep mum about this matter, and instructs her to deliver the documents to his lawyer. 埃里克不但要恩才对这件事情保密,同时还吩咐她将文件交给他的律师。

music

face the music 参见 face 1

my

1 my, my 哎哟(表示惊讶、高兴)

My, my! How nice to see you again after all these years! 哎哟,多年没见到你,真高兴呀!

My, my! Who's grown so much, then? You're a big boy now, aren't you? 哎哟,瞧你长这么高了,完全成了个大孩子了!

2 oh my 哎呀(表示惊讶、怀疑、烦恼)

Oh my! It's just been all of five years since we last saw you! 哎呀,自从上次我们见到你以来,已经过去整整五年了呀!

3 my aunt/eye/eyes/hat/stars/word/world/lord/goodness/stars and garters 哎呀,天哪,好家伙,你看,真要命(表示惊讶、赞叹、懊丧)

4 my foot 胡说,没这回事

N

nail

1 **(as) right as nails** 十分准确，毫厘不爽；完全健康
In a fortnight I shall be **as right as nails**. 两周后我就会完全恢复健康。

2 **(as) tough as nails** 身体结实；冷酷无情；性格坚强
Some people consider Rembrandt a sentimentalist, but he can be **as tough as nails**, as he is in this picture. 一些人认为伦勃朗是个感伤主义者，其实他也像他的这幅画一样坚强。

3 **bite one's nails** 急躁不安，束手无策
The companies are **biting their nails** at the prospect of a national strike. 面对全国罢工的前景，各家公司都坐立不安。

4 **hit the (right) nail on the head** 正中要害；猜中；说得好；做得好
Your criticism really **hit the nail on the head**. 你的批评确实一针见血。
In so saying, you **hit the right nail on the head**. 你这样说确实击中了要害。

5 **nail a lie/lies** 揭发弊端；拆穿谎言

6 **nail one's ass** 教训……一顿；给……一点颜色看看
Because if he doesn't, I'm really going to **nail his ass**. 要是他不听，我就会给他好看。

7 **nail sb. down to the truth** 使某人挑明真相，说出真相
The cop really wants to **nail her down to the truth**. 那个警察真想逼她说出真相。

name

1 **call sb. names** 谩骂……（比较：call one's name 点名）
They **called each other** all sorts of **names**. 他们恶语相加，互相谩骂。
Bill got so mad and started **calling Frank names**. 比尔愤怒万分，破口大骂弗兰克。

2 **give it a name** 你要什么尽管讲（尤用于请人喝酒时）

3 **in God's/Heaven's name** 天哪，究竟，真没想到

How in Heaven's name could they raise a sum like that? 天哪，他们怎么会筹集到这么一笔钱呢？

4 ... be my middle name 我以……著称（常用于幽默场合）

"I gave a good speech tonight!" "Modest, aren't you?" "Yes, modesty is my middle name!" "今晚我作了一个很好的演说！""你不是谦虚吧？""不错，我正是以谦虚著称呢！"

5 or my name's not 我确信

I'll do that for you immediately, sir, or my name's not Peter Perkins! 我马上给你办这事，先生。否则我就不是彼得·帕金斯。

6 take one's name in vain 滥用……的名义；亵渎……的名声；【谑】（轻慢地）提到……的名字

Yes, when we came to discussing the photographs, I heard them taking your name in vain. 是的，当我们讨论这些照片时我听到他们极不严肃地提到你的名字。

"Hello, Ken!" Pete called out. Ken turned round to see who it was and said, "I thought I heard my name being taken in vain!" "你好，肯！"皮特叫道。肯回过头来看是谁在喊他，说道："我以为有人乱喊我的名字呢！"

7 the name of the game 参见 game 8

8 you name it 无所不包，无奇不有，只要你想得到的

Williams stepped back with a look I will never forget, hatred, disgust, you name it. 威廉姆斯步步后退，脸上的表情我一辈子也忘不了——憎恨、厌恶，反正什么样的表情都有。

You name it, and we've got it. 凡是你想得到的，我们都有。

9 what name shall I say 请问您的名字（常用于电话接线台）

I'll put you through to Mr. Longfield. What name shall I say? 我给您接通朗费尔德先生家的电话，请问您的名字？

nature

1 like all nature【美】无可比拟地，拼命地，猛烈地；非常，极其

The troop started to attack the enemy like all nature. 部队开始猛烈地进攻敌人。

2 nature calls/answer/obey the call of nature/nature's call 上厕所

Sorry, nature calls, I must leave you for a moment. 对不起，我要去一趟

洗手间,请你等一下。

naughty

naughty, naughty 真讨厌,烦死人,好啦好啦

Naughty, naughty, Eric—why did you have to empty all your toys out of the box? 真淘气,艾瑞克!你为什么把玩具都从盒子里倒出来?

Naughty, naughty! We know what you two are up to! 得啦,得啦,我们知道你们俩在搞什么名堂!

near

1 (as) near as dammit/damnit 完全差不多,确实

They near as dammit showed interest in the matter. 他们确实对此事表示有兴趣。

2 as near as makes no difference/matter/near enough 几乎丝毫不差,确实

They are the same height, or as near as makes no difference. 他们俩一样高,简直分不出高低。

3 damn near 差不多,几乎

By the end I damn near had myself convinced that I was wrong. 到最后,我几乎相信是我错了。

4 not near 远远不,根本不

The kind of work is not near as complicated as searching for a cure of cancer. 这种工作远远没有探求治疗癌症的药物那样复杂。

neck

1 break one's neck (做事)拼命

We've (nearly) broken our necks looking for you. 我们找你找得好苦啊。

2 breathe down one's neck 紧跟在……后面;监视……

The manager was always breathing down her neck, telling her to do this or that. 经理老跟在她的后面,叫她做这做那。

3 catch/get/take it in the neck 受到当头一棒;受到严厉谴责或惩罚

If you don't do better than that, you'll get it in the neck from the manager. 你要是不好好干,就要受到经理的惩罚。

They'll get it in the neck in real earnest one of these days. 总有一天他们会受到严厉的惩罚。

4 have the/a neck to do/doing sth. 厚着脸皮做某事

Frederick had had the infernal neck to say that I was going to marry him. 弗雷德里克竟死不要脸地说我要嫁给他。

You've got a neck asking/to ask that! 你这个厚脸皮,亏你还好意思问!

5 neck or nothing 孤注一掷,不顾死活

I'll have a try. It's neck or nothing. 我来试试看,成败在此一举。

6 neck up a storm 【美】拼命地搂着亲嘴

7 off one's neck 从身边打发开,不再烦……

Can't you keep the kid off my neck? 难道你不能把孩子从我这里引开吗? One more question and I'm done. After that I'll be off your neck. 再问一个问题,我就结束。以后不再纠缠你了。

8 on/round one's neck 缠住……,麻烦……

My kid has been on my neck for weeks about going to the zoo. 我的孩子缠了我好几个星期,要去动物园玩。

9 save one's neck 使……免受绞刑,保全……

If you would save your neck, write me swiftly an obligation for twenty pounds. 如果你想保住脑袋的话,马上给我写一张二十英镑的借据。

10 talk/speak through (the back of) one's neck 信口开河

Green didn't know a thing about it and was certainly talking through the back of his neck. 格林对此事一无所知,自然是信口开河乱说一气。

11 stick one's neck/chin out 参见 chin 3

12 up to one's neck/ears 参见 ear 16

need

1 as/when/if the need arises 需要时,必要时

What's more, if you think about how to survive now, you'll be well prepared to change direction if the need arises. 更为重要的是,如果你现在考虑如何生存的问题,那么一旦有需要的时候你就会对改变方向做好万全的准备。

2 at need 困难时,必要时

At need one sees who his friend is. 患难见知交。

3 have need to do 需要,务必,应该

You had need to remember his name. 你务必记住他的名字。

Jimmy has need to be reminded about it. 这事有必要提醒吉米。

4 have need of 需要，要有

Jackson has no need of your charity. 杰克逊用不着你来发慈悲。

5 if need(s) be/require 需要的话，必要的话

If need(s) be, Hal would go and consult a doctor. 如果需要，哈尔会去找医生看病。

6 that's all I needed/need 这是我最不愿干的事；这是我最不愿遇到的事

What a day it's been—Rod had an accident on the way to school, the car's broken down, and now you say you're leaving me! That's all I needed! 今天我多倒霉啊！罗德上学出了车祸，车子撞坏了，现在你又要离开我。我真不幸啊！

7 who needs it 这种货色有谁要，这种东西有何用

needle

1 give sb. the needle 激励某人；挑逗某人；惹某人发作

It would give him the needle to make him do the work. 叫他干这件事可以激励他一下。

2 stick needles in sb. 促使某人；刺激某人

3 on pins and needles 如坐针毡

Jane's mother was on pins and needles because Jane was very late getting home from school. 简的母亲因为她放学后迟迟未回家而坐立不安。

nerve

1 have a/the nerve to do/doing sth. 厚脸皮

Nelson had a nerve dragging her out just for this. 尼尔森拖她出去就是为了这事，真不像话。

Rebecca had the nerve to ask for more. 丽贝卡脸皮真厚，一个不够还要更多。

2 lose one's nerve 心慌，胆怯，失去勇气

The men inside the building lost their nerve and opened fire on the crowd. 大楼内的人惊慌失措，向人群开了枪。

3 strike/touch a nerve 触及要害

Rosa's expression told me that I'd touched a sensitive/raw nerve. 罗莎的表情说明我触及了要害。

4　what a nerve/got a nerve/some nerve/the nerve of it 恬不知耻

What a nerve! Sally's the richest person I know and now she asks me if she can borrow some money! 真不要脸！萨莉是我认识的最有钱的人了。可她现在还好意思开口向我借钱！

Sharp's got a nerve, hasn't he, coming in here, taking my car keys off the desk without even asking! 夏普脸皮真厚，不是吗？进来以后从桌上拿走我的车钥匙，连招呼都不打一个！

never

1　do a never 开小差，磨洋工

2　never ever 永不，永无，从不，从未

Stevenson was ordered never ever to do that again. 上级叮嘱史蒂文森再也不要做那样的事了。

Temple never won anything, ever. 坦普尔从未赢过任何东西。

3　never is a long time/word/day 莫轻言"决不"，莫把话说绝

4　never so much as 甚至不，甚至没有

Valentine never so much as said "thanks". 瓦伦丁甚至连"谢"字都没说一个。

5　well, I never (did) 我真没想到/听到/见到（表示惊异）

Well, I never! It's Mr. Oliver. I'm pleased to meet you. 真没想到，是奥利弗先生，很高兴见到你。

new

what's new 【美】你可好，怎么样，还好吗（用作打招呼）

news

1　be news to sb. / come as news to sb. 对某人来说是新闻

Did you say that the meeting is cancelled? Well, that's news to me. 你刚才说会不开了吗？哟，我还不知道呢。

2　good news goes on crutches, ill news comes apace/flies fast/travels quickly 好事不出门，坏事传千里

3　no news is good news 没有消息就是好消息

No news is good news as far as I'm concerned. 对我而言，没有消息就是最好的消息。

next

1 be next to/on 【美】熟悉,了解
Sure, Tyler's next to the game. 当然,泰勒对这游戏很在行。

2 get next to/on 【美】开始熟悉,开始了解
If Tom can't get next to what we're about, we'll just have to school him. 要是汤姆不明白我们要干的事,我们只好让他开开窍。

3 next to 几乎
We had next to nothing to say to one another. 我们之间几乎没有什么话好说。
I know next to nothing about Ulysses. 我对尤利塞斯几乎一无所知。

4 what next 有比这更稀奇(更岂有此理)的事吗;下一步怎么办
What next to me? 下一步我怎么办?
A new car! A new house! What next? 又是要新车,又是要新房子,下面不知还要什么新玩意呢!

nice

1 make nice 【美】爱抚;表示亲昵
Public officials have to make nice to politicians they cannot stand. 公务员们不得不对那些使他们不能忍受的政客们表示亲热。

2 nice and 很,挺;倒好(表示轻微的不满)
Tom likes his tea nice and hot. 汤姆喜欢喝滚烫的茶。
You're nice and late getting to work today. 你倒好,今天上班迟到了。

3 not very nice 使人不愉快的,讨厌的

nickel

don't take any wooden nickels 【美】好好保重,别上当,别受人骗(告别时的嘱咐)

night

1 call it a night 今晚到此为止
I'm tired; let's call it a night and go to bed. 我累了,今晚就到这吧。

2 make a night of it 痛快地玩一个晚上
You can call a few friends to make a night of it. 你可以叫上几个朋友玩一晚上。

nip

nip and tuck【美】比赛中不相上下，难分高低，概率相等

It was nip and tuck who was going to win the game. 这场比赛的胜负很难预测。

The game was nip and tuck until the last minute. 比赛结束前双方势均力敌。

nix

nix on 当心，住手

Nix on it! 给我住手！

no

1 no end to/of 参见 end 3

2 no deal/dice/go/sale/soap 参见 dice 2

3 no end 很，非常；不断，继续

Jim was no end upset because he couldn't go swimming. 吉姆很烦恼，因为他不能去游泳。

The baby cried no end. 这个婴儿哭个不停。

4 no great shakes 平凡的，不重要的

Joe is no great shakes. 乔是个平凡的人。

5 oh no 当然不是；自然没有；哎呀不好

"Harry's had to go back into hospital, I'm afraid." "Oh no, how awful—I'm sorry." "我看哈里只好再进医院了。""哎呀，真可怕！我非常难过。"

Oh no, that's the third time the line's engaged; how can I get in touch with him? 哎呀，这是电话第三次占线了，我怎么才能和他联系上呢？

nod

1 a nod is as good as a wink/blind man/horse/bat/beggar 心中有数，心照不宣

Malory gave me one look and I nipped out. A nod's as good as a wink, you know. 马洛里朝我看了一眼，我就一溜烟跑了出去。这叫心领神会嘛！

2 get the nod【美】得到同意；被挑中

The manager is going to pick the new sales manager. I hope I could get the nod. 经理要挑选新的销售部经理，但愿我会被选中。

3 give the nod 【美】同意；挑中
All other things being equal, I'd give the nod to an ugly candidate. 其他条件相同的情况下，我会给难看的应聘者投一票。

4 on the nod 以点头表示同意或默许（未经正式表决或讨论）；用赊购的办法；处于昏迷状态（服用药剂后）
The chairman's proposals are usually passed on the nod at the shareholders' meeting. 在股东大会上，主席的提议通常在无人反对的情况下通过。

noise

1 make a/some noise about 为……而埋怨，为……而吵闹
The bus was late again today. Let's make a noise to the company about it. 公共汽车今天又晚点了，我们向公司投诉去。

2 make a noise in the world 轰动一时，扬名
This scandal will make a noise in the world. 这桩丑闻将轰动全世界。

3 make (all) the right noises 随声附和，故作踊跃
Nancy said I would have to come and visit her. I made the right noises, then changed the subject. 南希说我得来看望她，我就随声附和。接着便换了话题。

4 make noises 模仿各种声音；口头上表示，嘴上说说
The government makes noises about better relations with it's neighbouring countries. 政府再三讲要处理好同邻国的关系。
Do they mean it, or are they making mere noises? 他们是真心想干，还是仅仅说说而已？

none

1 have none of 不参与；同……不沾边；不准，不接受
Father said that he would have none of my arguing. 父亲说他不准我争辩。
When the firm refused to negotiate, the workers would have none of that. 公司拒绝谈判，工人们坚决不答应。

2 none of 不要，别
None of your stupid remarks, young man! 别说蠢话，年轻人！
None of your impudence! 别那么厚颜无耻！

nose

1 bite/snap one's nose/head off 参见 head 6

2 bloody one's nose 伤害……的自尊心；挫伤……，打得某人鼻孔流血

3 bring/hold/keep/put one's nose to the grindstone 参见 keep 5

4 count/tell noses 清查人数；数投票数
Let's tell noses and call it a day. 咱们清点一下人数收工吧。
Each time the troop assembled the leader counted noses. 部队每次集合时队长都清点人数。

5 cut off one's nose to spite one's face 拿自己出气；因一时恼怒反害自己
By refusing to work they are cutting off their noses to spite their faces because the company will close down. 他们拒绝工作，这是跟自己过不去，因为公司会倒闭。
If you refuse her help because you're angry with her, you're cutting off your nose to spite your face. 如果你是因为跟她赌气而拒绝她的帮助,那你是自讨苦吃。

6 get it up one's nose 发怒,恼怒；入迷,迷恋

7 get one's nose down 专心致志于
They are getting their noses really down to business. 他们当真专心致志地干起来了。

8 get/have one's nose (stuck) in/into a book 埋头看书
Petty always has her nose (stuck) in a book when she is not doing the housework. 佩蒂不做家务的时候就一头钻进书里。

9 get up one's nose 惹怒……
The homeless alcoholics get up the public's nose too much. 这帮流浪的醉汉使公众大为恼火。

10 go into a tailspin/nose dive 走下坡路；崩溃；放弃尝试；焦虑,沮丧,意志消沉
That would lessen Japan's dependence on exports for growth, a dependence that caused the economy to go into a nose dive when world trade halted late last year. 这将降低日本经济增长对出口的依赖,在全球贸易去年晚些时候停滞不前之际,这种依赖导致日本经济急剧下滑。

11 hold/stick one's nose in the air 鼻孔朝天,目中无人
Ralph's been holding his nose in the air since he won the prize. 拉尔夫自

从得奖以后就目中无人了。

12 hold one's nose to it 支持下去，支撑下去

13 keep one's nose clean 参见 keep 4

14 keep one's nose out of 不探问，不干预

Keep your nose out of our business. 我们的事不要你管。

15 lead by the nose 参见 lead 2

16 look down one's nose at 不把……放在眼里

I gave the dog some lovely steak, but it just looked down its nose at it. 我给了那只狗一些挺好的牛排，可它却看不上。

17 measure noses 遇见

They measured noses at the crossroad. 他们在十字路口相遇。

18 nose about/around 搜索，寻找；探问

The detective was nosing around in the crowd for pickpockets. 侦探在人群里查看有无扒手。

The writer is nosing around for a new book. 这个作家正在找一本新书。

19 nose into 探问；干预

Rosa is always nosing into other people's affairs. 罗莎老是管别人的事。

20 nose out 嗅出，搜出，找到；【美】略胜一筹

The journalist has nosed out the story. 记者已经摸清了事情的来龙去脉。

21 pay through the nose 付费太高；花太大代价

There was a shortage of food; so you had to pay through the nose for what you could find. 食品短缺，所以能买到的话就得花大价钱。

22 poke/stick/thrust/push/have one's nose into/in 探问；干预

Don't ask questions and poke your nose into other people's business. 不要问长问短，干预别人的事。

23 put one's nose out of joint 挤掉……，取代……；夺走……的恋人；使……心烦意乱；扰乱……的计划

Sophia keeps an eye on her boyfriend for fear someone else should put her nose out of joint. 索菲娅密切注意男朋友的行动，生怕别人把他夺走。

It puts his nose out of joint to see others being successful. 看见别人成功，他就心烦意乱。

24 rub/push one's nose in it/the dirt/the mess 揭……疮疤，使……不愉快

I know I'm wrong, but there's no need to rub my nose in it. 我知道我不

对，可是也没有必要揪住这事不放呀。

25 skin off one's nose 使人感兴趣、使人关心或使人感到麻烦的事；不相干（常用于否定句）

Go to Jake's party if you wish. It's no skin off my nose. 如果你想参加杰克的聚会，你就去吧。这与我无关。

You could at least say hello to our visitor. It's no skin off your nose. 你至少可以跟我们的客人打个招呼，这不会给你添麻烦。

26 turn up one's/the nose at 不把……放在眼里，蔑视

You shouldn't turn up your nose at good food—some people would be glad to have a meal like that. 你不要把这好端端的食物不放在眼里，有人能吃上这顿饭会庆幸不止呢。

27 under one's (very) nose/the nose of 就在……的眼前，当……的面

The thief walked out of the museum with the painting, right under the nose of the guards. 那个小偷带着名画，就在守卫人员的眼皮底下走出了博物馆。

nosey

nosey got shot 别自找苦吃

"What were you saying about me to Jane?" "Mind your own business! Nosey got shot!" "你们对简说了我哪些闲话？""少管闲事！否则你会自找苦吃！"

not

1 not for Joe 我才不呢，决不干；无论如何不行，当然不行

2 not for worlds/the world 决不，断无

I wouldn't hurt his feelings for the world. 我决不会伤他的心。

3 not that 并非，并不是说；并不特别地；不那么大

If Peter said so—not that he ever did—he lied. 如果彼得这样说——并不是说他真的这样说过——他是在撒谎。

We were allowed at last to rest, not that much of the night remained. 我们终于被允许休息，虽然离天亮不远了。

note

1 compare notes 对笔记；交换意见

I think there are a few things we might compare notes on. 我认为有几件事情我们可以交换意见。

2 sound/strike a false note/strike the wrong note 说错话；办错事；走调；说话听起来虚伪

3 strike a... note/a note of 带有……口吻；形成某种特征；表达某种意思
The report struck an occasional frivolous note. 这份报告偶尔带有轻佻的口吻。
Let me strike a note of hope the exam will not be as difficult as we expect. 我来说句鼓励的话，这次考试并不像我们预料的那么难。

4 strike the right note 说话听起来真实；做事对头；说话、办事妥当
Nixon with his mastery of intangibles knew how to strike the right note. 尼克松由于擅长掌握不可捉摸的事物，完全明白怎样讲才恰到好处。

nothing

1 have nothing on 【美】比不上，不及；缺乏指控的证据
Jack had lived in many a countries, but he said that living abroad had nothing on living in London. 杰克在许多国家住过，他说住在国外不如住在伦敦。
The police had nothing on that suspect. 警方未掌握那个嫌疑犯的犯罪证据。

2 here goes nothing 真是白费心思，不会有什么希望（尤指做某种依靠技术、勇气、运气的事前）
"Here goes nothing," said Bill at the beginning of the race. "这没有什么希望，"比尔在比赛前说。

3 in nothing flat 马上，很快
My mother can whip up a salad in nothing flat. 我妈妈可以眨眼间就飞快地做好一份沙拉。

4 it was/it's nothing 不值一谢，不必客气，不算什么（常以谦卑、惶恐的口气）
"Thank you for all the help you've given us over the last few days—you've been tremendous!" "It was nothing—all I've done is cook a few meals and tide up a bit." "谢谢你这些天来给予我们的帮助。你的服务是一流的。" "不必客气，我只不过给您做了几顿饭、打扫了一下房间而已。"

5 no nothing 什么都没有（用于否定句列举之末）

There was no bread, no butter, no cheese, no nothing. 面包没有，黄油没有，奶酪也没有，什么都没有。

6 nothing doing 绝对不；当然不；没有结果；没有办法；事情行不通；没有什么重要的事情或活动

Jane looked for her handbag all afternoon, but nothing doing. 简找手提包找了一个下午，可连影子都没见到。

There's nothing doing in this town. 这个镇里的生活平淡无奇。

7 nothing like 完全不像；没有什么能比得上的；没有；不到

James is nothing like his father. 詹姆斯一点也不像他的父亲。

There's nothing like leather for shoes. 用皮革做鞋再好不过了。

8 nothing much 没有什么，很少

There's nothing much to be done about this. 对这事已经无能为力了。

9 nothing near so 远不及，差得远

This building is not inferior to that one but nothing near so large. 这座建筑并不比那一座差，只是远不及那座大。

10 nothing of the kind 哪儿的话，没有那回事

"I'm sorry to cause you trouble." "It's nothing of the kind." "真对不起，给你添麻烦了。""哪里，哪里。"

11 nothing to it 不费事，不要紧；没有道理；没有真情

Nothing to it, I'll fix it in a jiffy. 没关系，我马上就修好。

This is how you ride a bike… You see, there's nothing to it. Now you try. 自行车就是这样骑的……你看，很容易，你来试试。

12 nothing to write home about 参见 home 6

13 nothing very much 没有什么特别的；将就过得去；平平常常

14 thank you for nothing【讽】不劳费心，敬谢不敏

"I can't get that coat cleaned for you by tonight, I'm afraid." "Well, thank you for nothing!" "恐怕我今晚前不能把您的外衣洗干净了。""那就不劳费心了。"

15 there's nothing for it 实在没有办法，只好

There's nothing for it—we'll just have to sell the car to pay off our debts, that's all. 实在没有办法，我们只好卖掉汽车还债，就是这样。

16 there's nothing in it 全是假话；与事实不符；不重要；不相干；没道理；机

会均等(竞争者之间)
"Have you heard about Rob and Sheila?" "Yes, but there's nothing in it, I'm sure!" "你听说关于罗布和希拉的事了吗?""是的,听说了,可那全是捕风捉影的事。"
There's nothing in it as they're coming up to the last hedge! 他们在临近最后一个跨栏时仍然不分高下。

17 think nothing of it 别放在心上,没什么
"Thank you for lending me your bike last night." "Think nothing of it!" "谢谢你昨晚把自行车借给我用。""没什么。"
"Thank you very much for all your help!" "Think nothing of it! It's my pleasure." "非常感谢你的帮助。""不用客气,愿为您效劳。"

18 to say nothing of 更不用说,何况
Mark takes singing and dancing lessons, to say nothing of swimming and tennis lessons. 马克上音乐课和舞蹈课,更不用说游泳课和网球课了。
Three people were badly hurt, to say nothing of damage to the building. 三人重伤,更不用说大楼受到损坏。

notice

sit up and take notice 对……刮目相看
George's sudden success made the town sit up and take notice. 乔治的突然成功使全镇的人都对他刮目相看。
His new book made the whole literary world sit up and take notice. 他的新书使整个文学界都对他刮目相看。

now

1 now for 现在着手干
I think we've finished with that point. Now for the next item on the agenda. 我看我们已经完成了这一项,现在来进行下一个议程。
The matter is settled. Now for the next question. 这件事解决了,现在来讨论下一个问题。

2 now, now/now then 好了,好了(表示告诫或引起注意)
Now, now, child. Stop crying! 得了,得了,孩子,别哭了!
There we were, we'd climbed halfway up. Now then, it started to snow—so what do you think we did? 当时我们爬山刚爬到一半,你看,就下起雪

来了。你猜我们当时干什么来着？

3 now or never/now for it 机不可失，莫失良机

They knew that it was now or never. 他们知道机不可失，时不再来。

If we don't buy that car now, we never will—it's now or never! 如果我们不马上买那辆车，就再也买不到了。机不可失！

4 there now 瞧，看（表示告诫或引起注意）

There now, I've at last got the engine started. 瞧，我终于把发动机启动了。

nowhere

nowhere near 远远不，完全不，远没有，远不及

Your work is nowhere near good enough. 你的工作连尚好都谈不上。

The nation's political crisis is nowhere near a solution. 这个国家的政治危机眼下根本无法解决。

number

1 any number of 好多，许多

I must have seen her any number of times. 我肯定见过她好多次了。

I know any number of men who can do this job. 我认识的人当中能做这件工作的非常多。

2 get/have one's number 对……心中有数，看清……的本质和动机

McDonald's rather transparent. I have his number. 麦克唐纳非常坦率，我十分了解他。

I used to think Norris was a friend of mine, but now I've got his number. 我以前一直认为诺里斯是我的朋友，可现在我可把他看透了。

3 make one's number 接洽，报到

On arrival, O'Connor made his number at the local office. 奥康纳一到就同当地的办事处接上了头。

4 number one 自己，自身

I can certainly assure you I'm looking after number one all right. 我向你保证，我一定会照顾好自己。

Philip was well known for his habit of always looking out for number one. 菲利普那只顾自己的脾气是众所周知的。

5 one's number has gone/is up 气数已尽，死期已到

When the police arrive, the thieves knew *their number was up*. 警察一到，盗贼就知道自己的死期已经来临。

6 one's (lucky) number comes up 走运了

Karl wants to buy a sports car when *his number comes up*. 当卡尔发财时，他想买一部跑车。

If *my lucky number comes up*, we'll have a holiday in Venice. 如果我走运的话，我们就去威尼斯度假。

nut

1 a hard/tough nut (to crack) 难题，难事；难缠的人

The question of world hunger is *a hard nut* to crack. 世界范围的饥荒是个难以解决的问题。

Don't annoy him, he's a real *tough nut*. 别招惹他，他这个人实在难缠。

2 be (dead) nuts on 精通，对……了如指掌；是……的能手；对……非常喜爱，迷上

The boy could read, write and *was nuts on* figures. 那孩子会读会写，还善于计算。

Michael's such *dead nuts on* her that he's getting dull. 迈克尔爱她爱得发狂，以致变得呆头呆脑的。

3 be nuts to 给……以极大满足、愉快等，对……来说是极大的满足

4 do one's/the nut(s) 心烦意乱，发狂，大发雷霆

Quiller will *do his nut* when he sees the damage you've done to his new car. 奎勒要是看见你把他的新车弄坏了会大发雷霆的。

5 for nuts 根本，一点也（用于否定句）

Theresa can't cook *for nuts*. 特里萨根本不会做饭。

6 nuts and bolts 具体细节，基本要素，基本要点

So what are the *nuts and bolts* of a healthy fight? 所以保持健康争吵方式的具体细节是怎样的呢？

7 off one's nut 发呆，发狂

You must be *off your nut*! 你一定是昏了头了！

Toby's simply gone *off his nut*. 托比简直是疯了。

o

o for 唉，要有……该多好啊

O for a horsecar to take me home! 唉，要有辆马车送我回家多好啊！

oar

1 get one's oar in 插手

All are trying to get their oar in. 大家都想插一手。

2 have an oar in every man's/another's boat 多管闲事

Kent must be kept out of this affair. He'll interfere and tries to have an oar in every man's boat. 这事可不能让肯特参与。他一定会横加干涉，多管闲事。

3 pull a respectable oar 表现出色

There he won First Class Honours in Arabic and pulled a respectable oar. 在那儿他获得了阿拉伯语一等荣誉学位，表现出色。

4 pull a strong oar 发挥强有力的影响

A man's wife always pulls pretty a strong oar. 一个男人的妻子总是起着强有力的影响。

5 put one's oar in/into 干涉，干预

No one asked you to put your oar in. 没人叫你多管闲事。

oat

1 feel one's oats 【美】兴高采烈；自命不凡

When they first got to camp, the boys were feeling their oats. 孩子们第一次参加野营，个个兴高采烈。

The new gardener was feeling his oats and started to boss the other men. 这名新园丁自命不凡，开始指挥他人。

2 know one's oats 消息灵通；精通业务；懂行

Thomson really knows his oats where skiing is concerned. 就滑雪而言，汤姆森确实是内行。

3 off one's oats 胃口不好

oddly

oddly enough 说来也奇怪

<u>Oddly enough</u>, nothing valuable was stolen. 说来也奇怪，值钱的东西一件也没被偷。

odds

1 **give/lay odds** 预测，猜测

I'll <u>lay odds</u> that Vincent won't come tomorrow. 我估计文森特明天不会来。

2 **make no/little odds** 没有/仅有一点点差别

It <u>makes little odds</u> which party we vote for—nothing ever seems to change much! 我们无论投哪一党的票都差不多，看来情况不会有多大变化。

It <u>makes no odds</u> which road we take, we'll come to the same place in the end. 无论我们走哪条路都无所谓，反正最终我们会到达同一地点。

3 **make odds even** 消除差别，拉平，使平等

Death <u>makes</u> the <u>odds</u> all <u>even</u>. 生命终结时，一切归于原点。

4 **shout the odds** 说大话，夸口

No one in our class <u>shouts the odds</u> quite so much as he does. 我们班谁也不像他那样会吹牛。

5 **what's the odds** 那有什么关系，那有什么要紧

<u>What's the odds</u>? Whatever we do, we're bound to lose money! 那有什么关系？无论干什么，我们都得花钱！

off

1 **how... off for** 有多少

<u>How</u> are you <u>off for</u> money at the moment? 眼下你有多少钱？

2 **it's/that's a bit off** 真奇怪；真是的

<u>It's a bit off</u> not letting us know you'd be coming on a late coach—we've been waiting around for two hours! 真是的，为什么不告诉我们说你们乘的是晚班车来的，害得我们在这儿等了两个小时。

3 **off again, on again/on again, off again** 不固定，时有时无，断断续续；反

反复复

John and Susan had an off again, on again romance. 约翰和苏珊的罗曼史断断续续。

I don't like this off again, on again business. Are we going to have the party or not? 我不喜欢反复无常,派对到底开不开?

4 off and 忽然,意外地

5 off and on/on and off 断断续续;偶尔,有时

Rather, this is something that I have been thinking about, off and on, for some time. 相反,这是我断断续续地思考了一段时间的问题。

6 off base 与事实不符的,大错特错的;出其不意地,乘人不备地

The report was well written, but it was slightly off base. 这篇报告的文笔不错,但是立意错了。

7 be off (one's) feed 参见 feed

8 get off one's back 参见 back 1

9 get sth. off one's chest 参见 chest 1

10 come off the/one's high horse 参见 horse 6

11 off one's rocker/trolley 愚笨;疯狂;神经失常,缺乏理智

Tom is off his rocker if he thinks he can run faster than Bob can. 如果汤姆认为他跑得比鲍勃快,那就大错特错了。

Mathilda went off her rocker and had to be put away in a mental home. 马蒂尔达精神失常了,不得不送进精神病院。

12 off-the-cuff/off the cuff 即席的,未经准备的;临时地;非正式地

The prime minister keeps making off-the-cuff remarks that get him into trouble. 首相总是没有准备就即席发表讲话,使他麻烦不断。

Considering that the speech was off the cuff, it was rather good. 由于这发言是即席演讲,所以它还算是不错的。

13 off the top of one's head 不假思索地,很快地

Vin answered the teacher's question off the top of his head. 温不假思索就回答了老师的问题。

14 off with 走开,去掉,脱掉

Off with your coats—they're soaking wet! 脱掉你的外衣,它们全湿透了!

Off with you! What are you doing here anyway? 你给我滚开! 你到底在这儿干什么?

offence

no offence (meant) 没有触犯你的意思；并无恶意，请勿见怪
Your necktie is wry, no offence. 您的领带戴歪了，请勿怪我提醒。

oil

1 pour oil on the flame(s) 火上浇油，使争吵更激烈
Yes, Tina was fired by her boss. Don't bother her, or you'll pour oil on the flame. 是的，蒂娜被老板开除了。不要烦她，否则你会火上浇油的。

2 pour oil on troubled waters 平息风波，劝和，息事宁人
In a speech to the Conservatives Edmund tried to pour oil on troubled waters. 在对保守党人作的一次演讲中埃德蒙试图调停争端。

old

1 any old how 随便地，马马虎虎地
We can paint the back of this cupboard any old how, as no one will ever see it. 我们可以把食品柜的背面随便油漆一下，因为没人看背面。

2 old 老……；极其（加在名词或形容词之前，表示亲密、戏谑、厌恶或加强语气）
Old Joe! 老乔！
You old silly! 你这个老傻瓜！
Old Hitler. 希特勒那混蛋。
Have a good old time. 过得极其愉快。

3 old bloke/buffer/card/codger【蔑】不中用的老家伙；老古板
4 old boat/crate/relic/tub/wreck【美】破旧汽车，老爷车
5 old bean/boy/chap/cook/egg/fruit/fellow/man/ship/thing/top 参见 bean 4
6 old Harry/Nick/Scratch/gooseberry【谑】恶魔，魔王
7 old hat 老式的，过时的
They are more old hat than progressive. 他们固步自封，不求进步。
8 old stager/【美】coon 经验丰富的人，老手，识途老马
9 one's old Dutch/woman 老婆
10 the old one 老头儿，父亲

on

1 be on about 反复地讲，唠叨个没完
You mean the thing Carol is always on about. 你指的是卡罗尔常常谈到的那件事。

2 be on at 唠叨，不停地催促或责怪
Ann has been on at me for 30 minutes to take her down to the shops. 安要我带她去逛商场，她已唠叨了三十分钟了。

3 be on it【美】熟练，准备就绪；决定动手做某事
Whenever I'm at home, if my computer is on, I feel obligated to be on it and working. 不管我什么时候在家，只要电脑开着，我就觉得自己有必要用它来工作。

4 be on to 了解……的情况；查明；跟……联系；找……的岔子
I have a reasonable level of success, so I must be on to something. 我就是这么做的，而且成功率还不低，因此我肯定有些发言权。
The teacher is on to me. 那个老师很了解我。

5 have/get something/nothing on sb. 掌握/没有掌握某人的情况
They're through with me now. They have nothing on me. 他们现在对我无可奈何，他们抓不到我的把柄。

6 it's (just) not on 真不像话
It's just not on, son, coming home so late without even ringing—your mother was worried stiff about you. 孩子，你真不像话。这么晚才回来，也不打个电话，你母亲为你担心死了。

7 on with 穿上，戴上；开始；继续
I'll help you on with your coat. 我来帮你穿上衣服。
On with the show! 开始/继续表演！

8 you're on 行啦，我接受这条件（开价、打赌等）
"I bet I can get to the windmill before you!" "Right, you're on!" "我打赌我能比你先跑到风车磨房。" "行啊，赌就赌。"
"OK, so let's say $1,000 for the car then." "All right, you're on." "好吧，我们讲定一千美元买那辆车。" "行，一言为定。"

once

1 at once... and... 既……又……

This book is at once interesting and instructive. 这本书既有趣又有教益。

2 once too offen 多次幸运，一次遭殃
Smith exceeded the speed limit once too offen and was fined. 史密斯多次超速开车未被发现，这次被罚了款。

3 once in a blue moon 难得的机会，千载难逢；极为罕见
You should be grateful for the extra job offer. Things like that come along only once in a blue moon. 你应该对额外的工作机会抱有感激之心；这样的事可是极其难得的。

one

1 a dead one 【美】吝啬鬼；笨蛋，无用的人

2 a right one 笨蛋
You are a right one, losing the tickets again! 你这个笨蛋又把门票弄丢了！

3 be all one (to) 对……反正一样
It's all one to me where we go—round the shops, to the museum again; I'm getting rather bored with all this sightseeing anyway. 到哪里去我都无所谓，逛商店也好，参观博物馆也好。我已经渐渐对所有这些游览活动不感兴趣了。

4 hang one on 【美】狂饮，喝醉；狠狠地朝……打一下
Fred was hacked and went out to hang one on. 弗雷德很生气，于是到外面去喝了个一醉方休。

5 have one over the eight 喝醉；微醉
David has had one over the eight and shouldn't be allowed to drive his car. 戴维已有三分醉意，不应该让他开汽车。

6 for one 举例来说
I for one think Tom's nice. 拿我来说，我就觉得汤姆挺好。
I, for one, don't think it's a good idea. 拿我来说，我就觉得这个主意不够好。

7 one for the book(s) 【美】值得大书特书的，值得记载的
That storm was really one for the book. 那场风暴实在是空前的，值得大书特书。

8 one to do sth. /one for doing sth. 是喜欢或愿意做某事的那种人
Bacon's not usually one to talk about people behind their backs, but I did

hear him being rather nasty about Peter, you know. 培根平常不是个背后议论别人的人,但你知道,我的确听见他说彼得的坏话。

I'm not really one for eating lots of cakes, but since you insist, I think I will have another one. 我的确不喜欢吃太多的蛋糕,既然你这么热情,我就再吃一块。

9 one up on 比……略胜一筹

John graduated from high school; he is one up on Bob, who dropped out. 约翰中学毕业了,他比中途辍学的鲍勃略胜一筹。

ooh

ooh 唷(表示惊讶、赞美、喜悦、恐惧等)

Ooh, this cream cake's delicious. 唷,这奶油蛋糕好吃极了。

oops

oops 哎呦(表示惊讶、沮丧、道歉等)

Oops, the rain began falling again! 哎呦,又下雨了!

open

1 be open to 乐意接受;愿意考虑;容易受到;对……开放;是……的自由

We are open to suggestions. 我们乐意接受建议。

It was open to Mr. Smith to sign the agreement. 签不签此项协议是史密斯先生的自由。

2 open out 畅谈,倾心交谈

Bessie found it difficult to open out to people. 贝西感到很难同人们无拘无束地交谈。

The two friends opened out to each other. 两个朋友倾心交谈。

3 open up 自由自在地谈,无拘无束地谈

Louise was disappointed that the manager hadn't opened up about Gretchen. 经理未能直陈格雷琴的情况,为此路易丝很失望。

You must open up and tell us all about what happened. 你一定得把发生的事情毫无保留地全部告诉我们。

4 throw open 开放

The universities were thrown open to all. 各个大学向所有人开放。

order

1 in apple-pie order 并然有序，有条不紊

The room was in apple-pie order. 房间里整整齐齐。

Blume wanted the account put in apple-pie order. 布卢姆要求把账目记得清清楚楚。

2 in short order 【美】立即，毫不耽搁地

Half was through the garden party my sister became ill and we had to leave in short order. 花园招待会进行到一半，我姐姐病了，我们只好马上离开。

3 just what the doctor ordered 参见 doctor 2

4 large order 过分的要求；难办的事；大批订货

The company received a large order for computers. 这家公司接到一份要求大量供应电脑的订单。

5 tall order 困难的任务；过分或不合理的要求

I know it sounds like a tall order, but remember, this is your quality of life we are talking about. 我知道，要做到这些似乎困难重重，但是请记住，这关系到我们现在讨论的话题——你的生活质量。

out

1 be out for 一心谋求，力图获得

I am not out for power. 我并不追求权势。

2 on the outs (with) 与……不和

Catharine is on the outs with a childhood buddy. 凯瑟琳和一个童年时的好友闹翻了。

Are you two on the outs? 你们俩是不是吵架了？

3 out and out 完全地；不折不扣地

Clarissa knows English out and out. 克拉丽莎精通英语。

4 out cold 失去知觉，昏迷

The stone hit Jack in the head and knocked him out cold for several minutes. 石头击中杰克的头，他昏迷了好几分钟。

They tried to lift Mary when she fell down, but she was out cold. 他们想把倒下的玛丽扶起来，但她已失去知觉。

5 out from under 脱离困境，脱离危难

The bankrupt tried to get out from under but he couldn't make it. 那个破产者试图摆脱困境,但他失败了。

John had so many debts, he couldn't get out from under. 约翰债务缠身,简直无法了结。

6 out in left field 错得太远;行为怪异;疯癫

Johnny tried to answer the teacher's question, but he was way out in left field. 约翰尼试图回答老师的问题,但却错得离谱。

The girl was always queer, but after her father died, she was really out in left field and had to go to a hospital. 这女孩平时行为怪异,但她父亲死后,她真的疯了,只得住进医院。

7 out in the cold 孤单,被冷落,被排除在外

All the other children were chosen for parts in the play, but Johnny was left out in the cold. 所有的小朋友都被选上参加演出,只有约翰尼除外。

8 be/go out like a light　参见 light 1

9 out of circulation 不交际,不活动

John has a job after school and is out of circulation. 约翰下课以后外出打工,他不能和朋友一起玩了。

10 out of it 在局外的,未被邀请加入的,感受冷落的;神志不清的;糊涂的;不合潮流的;被淘汰的

Mary felt out of it as she watched the others set out on picnic. 看到别人出发去野餐,玛丽因自己未被邀请参加而感到难过。

If our team loses two more games, we'll be out of it. 如果我们队再输两场,我们将被淘汰。

11 out of one's hair 摆脱困扰、纠缠

Harry got the boys out of his hair so he could study. 哈里摆脱孩子们的纠缠,开始学习。

12 out of one's head/mind/senses/off one's head 发狂,行为疯狂

The patient was feverish and out of his head and had to be watched. 病人高烧后发狂,必须实行监护。

13 come out of one's shell 不羞怯;大方交谈

John wouldn't come out of his shell at the party. 约翰在舞会上显得十分羞怯。

14 out of the blue/a/the clear (blue) sky 出其不意,晴天霹雳

It came quite literally and metaphorically out of the clear blue sky. Nobody saw this coming. 它真的就像是晴空中的一道霹雳，来得毫无征兆。

15 out of the hole 打破零分；（比赛中）扳成平局；债务状况良好，免于负债

It's one thing to have the worst record in the Eastern Conference, but quite another to have no plan to start digging out of the hole. 我们是东部战绩最差的球队，但我们确实需要一个计划确定如何打破僵局摆脱困境了。

16 out of this world 棒极了

The dress in the store window was out of this world! 商店橱窗里的那件衣服棒极了！

17 out of whack 有故障，待修；不一致，不相符

The lawn mower got out of whack. 割草机坏了。

The things Mr. Black does are out of whack with what he says. 布莱克先生言行不一。

18 out with 说出；拿出；赶出；与……不和

Gilbert outs with his money. 吉尔伯特把钱拿了出来。

If you are out with Ferdinand, then I shall not visit him. 如果你和费迪南德有矛盾的话，我就不去看他了。

19 out with it 全说出来

You're worrying about something, aren't you? Come on, out with it! 你在为什么事发愁，是吗？得了，说出来吧！

Don't just stand there! Out with it! Who won? 别光站在那儿呀，说出来，是谁赢了？

20 out you go 出去

over

1 over a/the barrel 受制于人，一筹莫展，不知所措

The criminal had no other alternative but confess; we had him over a barrel. 那个犯罪分子没有办法，只好坦白，我们迫使他乖乖地听话。

2 over and out 通话完毕（无线电通信用语）

Alice two, will go to scene of accident. Over and out. 爱丽丝等二人将去出事现场，通话完毕。

3 over the hill 今不如昔；老迈不中用；在衰退中；擅离职守，开小差

The fact is I'm a little **over the hill** to be playing contact sports. 事实上，我现在再参加这种会磕磕碰碰的体育活动年龄确实有点大了。

4 over the hump 渡过危机；冲过难关
With half the race done, he was **over the hump**. 比赛过了一半，他已经渡过最困难的阶段。

5 over with 结束，了结
It should have been all **over with** and forgotten by the first of last February. 它早该在去年二月的第一天就结束了，然后被人忘得干干净净。

owe

owe it to oneself to do sth. 认为自己应该、有必要做某事
We **owe it to ourselves to explain how it all happened**. 我们认为有必要解释一下事情发生的经过。

own

1 on one's own (account/hook) 为自己的缘故；自动的；自己负责的
The COO of the firm did it **on his own account**, not for anyone else. 公司首席运营官做这件事是为自己的利益，而不是为别人。
No matter what is, they are all need to create **on one's own account**, isn't it? 无论哪种，都要靠自己的能力去创造，不是吗？

2 own up 承认错误，引咎自责
John **owned up** when Mr. Jones asked who broke the window. 琼斯先生问是谁打破了窗子，约翰承认是他干的。
You had better **own up** to your faults. 你最好坦白认错。

P

pace

1 go the pace 高速行进；挥霍放荡

The blacksheep is going the pace and his property will soon run out. 那个败家子生活奢侈，财富很快就会败光。

2 go through/show one's paces 显身手，显本领

The young actor must be given the chance to show his paces. 必须给那个年轻演员一个大显身手的机会。

3 put/try sb./sth. through his/its paces 测试某人的本领，测试某物的性能

Kennan put his new car through its paces. 凯南测试新车的各项性能。

Many different problems put the new mayor through his paces in the first mouths of his term. 新市长上任的头几个月遭遇到的各种问题考验了他的能力。

pack

1 pack in 大批地吸引观众；停止工作；停止起作用；辞职；放弃；对……不感兴趣；同男友终止关系

Star Wars was really packing them in. 《星球大战》的确吸引了大批观众。

The girl had only worked for a week when she packed in. 这姑娘只干了一个星期就不干了。

2 pack it in/up 结束，停止，放弃，离开

I ought to begin to think of packing it in as an actor. 我应当开始考虑结束演员生涯了。

Pack it up, will you! You're so noisy. I can't hear myself think! 好啦，好啦，别闹啦。你们吵闹得我无法想问题。

3 pack oneself off 卷铺盖，离开

I wish you would pack yourself off at once. 我巴不得你马上给我滚开。

4 pack up （发动机等）停止转动，出了故障；使停止；死去

My watch has just packed up. 我的表刚停。

One of the aircraft's engines packed up. 飞机的一个引擎出了毛病。

paddle

paddle one's own canoe 独自为生，自立谋生
After his father died, John had to paddle his own canoe. 约翰的父亲死后，他只得自立谋生。

pair

1　I have only one pair of hands 我只有一双手（表示埋怨）
"Rob, could you do the washing-up and then make a start on the housework, please?" "Wait a minute, I've only one pair of hands, you know." "罗布，你先把餐具洗一洗，然后再开始做家务，好吗？""等等，你看我只有一双手呀。"

2　pair off 结婚
I suppose Mr. Lin will pair off with Miss Wu in the end. 我料想到头来林先生还是会和吴女士结婚的。

palm

1　bear/take/carry (off) the palm 得胜，获奖，博得无上荣誉，夺魁
Malory carried off the palm by sheer perseverance. 马洛里靠坚忍不拔的精神取得了胜利。
Of all the cities of Europe I think that Paris bears the palm. 我认为巴黎是欧洲所有城市中最好的。

2　grease the palm of sb. / grease one's palm 向某人行贿
The couple had to grease the palm of the waiter to get a table in the crowded restaurant. 那对夫妇只得贿赂服务员以便在拥挤的餐馆里得到一张桌子。

3　have an itching palm/itching palms 贪财
That old woman has an itching palm. 那个老太婆贪财。

4　yield the palm to 认输；承认不如……
After listening to everyone's opinions, he yielded the palm to my good judgement. 听了大家的意见之后，他承认还是我的判断力好。

5　palm off 使人得出错误印象；用欺骗手段销售
The fruit seller palmed off some bad oranges onto the old lady. 水果贩子

把一些坏橘子卖给了那个老太太。
North palmed him off with the excuse that she had no money. 诺思谎称没钱把他打发走了。

pan

1 on the pan【美】受严厉批评
A professor who wasn't there was on the pan. 一个不在场的教授受到了严厉的批评。

2 pan off/out 结果是,证明是；成功
His plan to remodel our house panned out poorly. 他改建我们房子的计划效果不佳。
His new job is panning out well for him. 他的新工作很适合他。

panic

press/push/hit the panic button【美】(紧要关头)惊慌失措
Keep cool, don't hit the panic button! 要冷静,不要惊慌失措!

pants

1 ants in one's pants 坐立不安,神不守舍
You have ants in your pants today. Is something wrong? 你今天坐立不安,有什么不对劲的事吗？

2 beat the pants off 把……打得屁滚尿流,大获全胜
By 1941, zippers beat the pants off buttons in the Battle of the Fly. 1941年,在与纽扣的战争中,拉链大获全胜。

3 bore the pants off 使……厌烦透顶
The professor bore the pants off us during every class of the semester. We were so ready to be done with him. 这个教授整个学期的每节课都无聊透顶。我们只想早日结束他的课。

4 catch one with one's pants down 突陷窘境,十分尴尬
They thought they could succeed in the robbery, but they got caught with their pants down. 他们原以为可以抢劫成功,谁知被逮个正着。
Abbot entered the room for ladies by mistake and was caught with his pants down. 阿博特误入女厕,万分尴尬。

5 frighten/scare the pants off 吓得魂不附体

The new roller coaster ride at the amusement park *frightened the pants off me*. 乘坐游乐场里那辆新的过山车吓得我魂飞魄散。

6　get the lead out of one's pants 忙碌，加紧工作

The captain told the sailors to *get the lead out of their pants*. 船长要水手们加紧工作。

7　wear the pants【美】掌权，当家

Mr. Jones *wears the pants* in that house. 那家子由琼斯先生当家。

My mom *wears the pants* at home, my dad is my mom's puppet. 在我家里是妈妈当家，爸爸听妈妈的。

paper

peddle one's papers【美】别管闲事，走开

I told him to go *peddle his papers*. 我叫他走开，别管闲事。

par

par for the course 意料中的事，不足为奇

Only ten students passed the examination this time, but it's *par for the course*. 这次考试只有十个学生及格，不过这种情况是正常的。

pardon

1　I beg your pardon 请原谅，对不起，请再说一遍

2　(if you'll) pardon the expression 请原谅我使用这个词语

I think they're full of—*pardon the expression*—bull. 我认为他们是，废话连篇，请原谅我这么说。

3　pardon me for existing/living/breathing【反讥】请原谅我活着让你受气了

part

1　look the part 看样子像那种人

If John wasn't actually a thief, he certainly *looked the part*. 如果约翰真的不是小偷，但模样却够像的。

2　take... in bad/evil part 对……见怪，不乐意地接受

I will not *take* anything you say *in bad part*. 你怎么讲我都不会见怪。

3　take... in good part 对……不见怪，欣然接受

I hope you will take the advice in good part. 我希望你能愉快地接受这个劝告。

pass

1 let it pass 暂且不谈；暂且不去管它

Kelsen shouldn't have said that, but let it pass. 凯尔森不该那么说，不过暂且不去管它。

2 pass muster 通过考试，及格；合格

After a practice period, Sam found that he was able to pass muster as a lathe operator. 经过一段时间实习，山姆已经成为了一名合格的车床操作工。

His work was done carefully, so it always passed muster. 他的工作做得很细心，所以一直是合格的。

3 pass out 失去知觉；大醉；死去

Mary went back to work while she was still sick, and finally she just passed out. 玛丽抱病上班，后来终于昏倒了。

After three drinks, Lowell passed out. 酒过三巡，罗威尔醉得不省人事。

4 pass the buck 推卸责任，委过于人

If you break a window, do not pass the buck, admit that you did it. 如果是你打碎了窗子，别推卸责任，要坦白承认。

passenger

wake up the wrong passenger 【美】怪错了人，骂错了人，惹错了人

Sometimes it's not your fault, but the boss wake up the wrong passenger, how do you handle it? 有时，不是你的错误，但你老板错怪了你，如何处理？

past

1 not put it past sb. (to do sth.) 认为某人很有可能做某事

Margery may have killed Rebecca, I wouldn't put it past him. 马杰里可能杀了丽贝卡，我认为他很有可能干这种事。

I wouldn't put it past them to try a last throw. 我认为他们很可能孤注一掷。

2 past it 不能工作（因为年老）

You should start saving money for the time when you get past it. 你应该开始攒钱，以备年老不能工作时用。

pat

1 have/know (sth.) down/off pat 完全掌握，彻底了解

If you want to have English down pat, you must study even harder. 如果你想完全掌握英语，你必须更加刻苦地学习。

2 pat/give sb. a pat on the back 鼓励某人，赞许某人

The coach patted the player on the back and said a few encouraging words. 教练拍拍选手的背，说了几句鼓励的话。

I gave her a pat on the back and told her she had done fine work. 我拍拍她的背鼓励她，并说她做得很好。

patch

1 don't put a patch upon it 别再表白啦，欲盖弥彰

2 go through/be in/hit/strike a bad patch 倒霉，不走运

Arsene Wenger once said that every player should go through a bad patch in their careers so they can learn how to handle disappointment. 阿尔赛纳·温格说过，每个球员都要经历挫折，才能学会如何面对沮丧。

3 not a patch on 比不上，远不如

As a scholar, Laurie is not a patch on his predecessor in the past. 作为一个学者，劳里远不如他的前任。

path

beat a path to 纷纷前去，争先恐后地去

Edith was now so famous that the newspaper reporters were beating a path to her door. 伊迪丝现在大名鼎鼎，报社记者纷纷上门采访她。

pay

1 pay as you go 【美】付现款，不赊欠

It is best to pay as you go; then you will not have to worry about paying debts late. 最好能付现款，这样就不必担心日后负债。

2 hit/strike pay dirt 【美】发现财源，获得发财的机会；发现有益的线索

After days of questioning, the police struck pay dirt. 经过几天的审讯，警

察获得了有益的线索。

The author believes if he writes a good book he will finally hit pay dirt. 这位作者相信,如果他写一本好书,他终会找到财源。

3 pay off 报复;惩罚;向……行贿;赚回;获利;换回,得到回报

You will be paid off for your negligence. 你将因你的失职受到处分。

At first Mr. Harrison lost money on his investments, but finally one paid off. 哈里逊先生原先多项投资都赔了钱,但最后有一项赚了。

4 pay through the nose 付出惊人巨款;付出很大代价

Remember one thing, you'll pay for this and pay through the nose. 记住:你要付出代价,而且是很大的代价。

There was a shortage of cars; if you found one for sale, you had pay through the nose. 汽车缺货,如果你想买待售的车,就得付高价。

5 something is to pay【美】情况不妙,事情有点不对头

6 what is to pay【美】怎么啦,出了什么事

peace

hold/keep one's peace 保持沉默,住嘴

I kept my bitter peace. 我憋着气一声不吭。

Hold your peace while I'm talking. 我讲话时你别开口。

pecker

1 keep one's chin/pecker up 参见 chin 2

2 put up one's pecker 惹恼……,得罪……

What the fellow said put up the young man's pecker. 那个家伙说的话惹恼了那个年轻人。

peg

1 a square peg in a round hole/a round peg in a square hole 方枘圆凿,格格不入,德不配位

Jane was the odd one out, just as she had been at school and university: a square peg in a round hole. 简比较怪僻,像在中学和大学里一样,不适应周围的环境。

2 bring/take sb. down a peg (or two) 杀杀某人的威风;打掉某人的傲气

Emma ought to be taken down a peg or two. 应该杀杀埃玛的威风。

The team was feeling proud of its record, but last week *the boys were taken down a peg* by a bad defeat. 这支球队为它的战绩自高自大,目空一切。但上周他们的惨败挫了他们的锐气。

3 come down a peg (or two) 气势稍减;受屈辱;丢面子;降低身份

The US *has come down a peg or two* in dealing with all other countries in the world, not just China. 在与世界上其他国家打交道时,美国已放低身段,并非只是对中国如此。

4 peg out 筋疲力尽;失败;完蛋;死去

I've got to find something, or *peg out*. 我得去找点什么,不然就没命了。

penny

1 a penny for your thoughts 你在呆想什么呢

A penny for your thoughts, Martin? You've not said a word all evening! 你在呆想什么呢,马丁? 整个晚上你没说一句话。

2 a pretty penny 一大笔钱

That will cost you *a pretty penny*! 那得花去你不少钱呢。

3 not a penny the worse 一点不比以前坏;一点也没吃亏;毫不逊色

4 not have a penny to bless oneself with/one's name/two pennies to rub together 不名一文,穷得叮当响

How can they afford a holiday? They haven't got *two pennies to rub together*. 他们怎么有钱去度假呢? 他们穷得叮当响。

5 pinch pennies/a penny 精打细算,点滴积攒

When Tom and Mary were saving money to buy a house, they had to *pinch pennies*. 汤姆和玛丽为了存钱买房,不得不精打细算。

6 the penny dropped 最后明白了;这才达到效果

I stared at him for a long time and *the penny dropped*. 我盯着他看了很久,后来终于明白了。

We tried to suggest that she might give us a lift home, but she didn't seem to understand. Then suddenly *the penny dropped* and she said, "Can I take you home now?" 我们竭力向她暗示,请她顺便带我们回去,但她好像没有明白我们的意思。然后突然她恍然大悟,问道:"我可以送你们回家吗?"

7 two/ten a penny 非常便宜的,不值钱的;很平常的

University degrees are two a penny these days. 大学文凭现在不值钱了。
We have 50 men like that—drivers are two a penny. 像这样的人我们有50个，驾驶员一抓一大把。

pennyworth

1 get/have one's pennyworth of 【口】钱花得合算；挨了一顿打

2 not a pennyworth 一钱不值；丝毫不

The diamond is not a pennyworth, because it's fake. 那颗钻石一钱不值，因为它是赝品。

perch

1 come off your perch 别那么自命不凡，放下你的臭架子

Come off your perch! We've seen you through. 别装模作样了！我们已看透了你。

2 hop/tip over the perch 死掉；败落

3 knock sb. off his perch/throw/turn sb. over the perch 击败某人；杀死某人；杀某人的威风

peril

at one's peril 自担风险，自己负责（告诫……别做某事）

You do it at your peril. 你要做这事就得自担风险。

You become neglectful at your peril. 你若粗心大意，就要自己负责。

perish

perish the thought 想也别想；但愿不是

If John fails the college entrance exam—perish the thought—he will go back to high school for one more year. 如果约翰考不上大学，他得回高中再读一年，唉，但愿不会。

Perish the thought that Mary should have cancer. 但愿玛丽不是得了癌症。

person

1 I'd be the first (person) to 我很愿意

I'd be the first person to say we must decide on our priorities immediately. 老实说，我认为我们必须立即决定那些优先考虑的问题。

2 I'd be the last (person) to 我不愿意

I'd be the last person to criticize someone else for their failures. 我不愿意批评别人的失败。

3 in (one's own) person 亲自

You can vote either in person or by proxy. 你可以亲自投票或请人代理。

4 in the person of 以……身份或资格,代表

He spoke in the person of Xinhua News Agency. 他代表新华社讲话。

phooey

phooey 啐,呸(表示轻蔑、厌恶、不信、失望等)

Phooey on love! 我才不信什么爱情呢!

phrase

coin a phrase 参见 coin 2

pick

1 can really pick'em【美】很会挑选东西(常用作反语)

Is this turkey your idea of a good show? You can really pick'em. 挑选这种准演砸的东西充当好节目吗? 你可真是别具慧眼。

2 have a bone to pick with 有理由找……的麻烦,与……争论;对……有怨言

I have a bone to pick with you, Wallace. I heard how you criticized me at the meeting last night. 华莱士,我要和你理论一下。我听说了昨晚开会时你怎么批评我的。

3 pick a hole/holes in 找毛病,挑刺;批评,埋怨

Mary is always picking holes in what the other girls do. 玛丽总是挑别的女孩的毛病。

4 pick and choose 挑挑拣拣,挑三拣四

In work, one mustn't pick and choose or change one's mind the moment one sees something different. 对工作不应见异思迁,挑挑拣拣。

5 pick apart (to pieces) 苛责,找错

After the dance, the girls picked Susan apart. 舞会后女孩们严厉批评苏珊。

6 pick on/at 找……的岔子,对……指责;捉弄,惹恼

Why pick on me? 为什么偏要和我过不去？
They picked on smaller boys. 他们欺负比自己小的孩子。

7 pick up 为大家付账；逮捕；转佳，复原；改进
After lunch in the restaurant, Uncle Bob picked up the check. 在餐馆吃完午餐后鲍勃叔叔为大家付了账。
Police picked the man up for burglary. 警察逮捕了那个窃贼。

8 pick up on【美】理解；赏识；了解到，注意到；获得
Other people can pick up on this just by watching our faces. 其他人能仅仅靠观察我们的面部表情就注意到这些。

pickle

1 in a fine/pretty pickle 十分混乱，乱七八糟；处境尴尬
The papers lay in a fine pickle. 文件乱七八糟地堆放着。

2 in pickle 准备好待用，备用
She went away in an opposite direction turning her head and saying to the unconscious Jim, "There is a fine rod in pickle for you, my gentleman, if you carry out that pretty scheme."
她朝相反的方向走去，转过头来向失去知觉的吉姆说道："还有严厉的惩罚在等着你呢，我的先生，如果你按照你的鬼计划行事的话。"

picnic

no picnic 不是轻松的事
Geoffrey might have warned that nation building is no picnic, either. 杰弗里警告说，国家的建立从来都不是一件轻松的事。

picture

1 come into/enter the picture 被牵连进去
I don't think you come into the picture at all. 我认为这与你根本无关。

2 in the picture 熟知一切，知道内情
Katharine always wants to be in the picture. 凯瑟琳什么事情都要了解。

3 out of the picture 不了解情况，不知内情
I've been away for a few weeks so I'm rather out of the picture. 我离开这里几个星期了，所以我不太了解情况。

pie

1 cut a pie【美】卷入某事，多管闲事，妄加干预

2 have a/one's finger in the/every pie 参与

Tommy likes to have a finger in every pie. 汤米爱多管闲事。

piece

1 a piece of cake 容易的事情，轻松、愉快的事情

2 give sb. a piece of one's mind 参见 give 6

3 go (all) to pieces（在身体、精神、道德方面）崩溃，垮掉；停止活动；报废，损坏

Lena went to pieces when her husband died. 丈夫死时莉娜悲痛欲绝，心力交瘁。

After 100,000 miles the car went to pieces. 跑了十万英里以后，这车子就报废了。

4 pick/pull to pieces 严厉批评，把……批得体无完肤

Lucius pulled their argument to pieces. 卢修斯把他们的论点批得体无完肤。

5 pick up the pieces 收拾残局，恢复正常

They can pick up the pieces, reshuffle the deck and create together the relationship of both of their dreams—at any age. 他们可以收拾残局，修复感情，然后一起创建他们梦想中的美好关系——无论什么年纪。

6 speak/say/state one's pieces【美】说自己要说的话

If you don't let him speak his pieces he'll think that you've made him work for nothing. 要是你不让他诉诉苦，他就会认为你让他白干了。

pig

1 in a pig's ass/ear/eye【美】决不，当然不，不可能

In a pig's eye, I will! 我才不会呢！

2 in less than a pig's whisper/whistle 马上，立刻，一眨眼工夫

The thief ran away in less than a pig's whisper. 那个小偷一眨眼工夫就不见了。

3 live like pigs in clover 生活优裕，养尊处优

We live like pigs in clover. 我们生活得非常优裕。

4 make a pig's ear (out) of 把……弄糟,弄得一团糟

Tim *made a pig's ear of* repairing my car. The car was almost broken. 蒂姆把我的车修得一塌糊涂,几乎全毁了。

5 on the pig's back 走运,幸福之极,扬扬得意

John is *on the pig's back* when he passed the exam. 约翰因为考试过关而扬扬自得。

6 pigs might fly (if they had wings)【讽】无稽之谈,无奇不有

We might win! *Pigs might fly.* 我们会赢,那才怪呢!

"I might get a job one day soon!" "*Pigs might fly!*" "我可能在一天内找到工作。""真是异想天开!"

7 please the pigs【谑】如果上天保佑的话,如果走运的话

Please the pigs, I will win the game. 若走运,我会赢得这场比赛。

8 teach a pig to play on a flute 做荒诞或不可能做到的事

Teach him to learn French is like to *teach a pig to play on a flute*. 教他学法语绝不可能成功。

9 when pigs fly 决不可能,决不,永不,除非猪会飞

Sure our boss willpay for the drinks? *When pigs fly*! 我们老板当然会付这些酒钱——只要猪能上天!

10 make a silk purse out of a pig's/sow's ear 猪耳朵做出丝绸钱包,朽木不可雕

You can't *make a silk purse out of a pig's ear*. 朽木不可雕也。

11 make a pig of yourself【口】吃得过多;狼吞虎咽

Don't *make a pig of yourself* at dinner party! 别在正式宴会上狼吞虎咽,那样很不礼貌!

pile

1 a pile of shit【美】胡说八道,废话,谎言;破烂货,废物

You are without rights, dishonorable and defenseless. You're *a pile of shit* and that is how you're going to be treated. 你没有权力,没有自尊,没有反抗能力。你就是一个废物,这就是你应得的待遇!

2 make a/one's pile 赚钱,发财

McCarthy *made his pile* by selling tea. 麦卡锡贩卖茶叶发了财。

pin

1 can/could/be able to hear a pin drop/fall 静得连针掉在地上都听得见
When he started to tell us about how his son died, there was a sudden hush—you could have heard a pin drop. 当他开始向我们讲述他儿子死时的情景时,大家突然静了下来,静得连针掉在地上都听得见。

2 for two pins 恨不得,巴不得
Monroe laughed at me. For two pins I could have hit him in the face. 门罗笑话我,我真恨不得打他一记耳光。

3 knock sb. off his pins 使某人大为震动;使某人大吃一惊;把某人打倒在地

4 not care/give a pin/fig for 对……毫不在乎
I do not care a pin for his opinion. 我毫不在乎他的意见。

5 not worth a pin 一钱不值
That ring is not worth a pin. 那个戒指不值钱。

6 on pins and needles 如坐针毡,焦躁不安
The colonel, on pins and needles, did what he could to speed up the departure of the countryside guests. 如坐针毡的上校尽快打发走了乡下的来宾。

7 on the pin 注意,留神

8 quick on one's pins 腿快,行动迅速

9 stick pins into 戳进……;激励……;激怒……
Don't stick pins into the chair! 不要把大头针戳进椅子里!

10 slow/weak on one's pin 腿有毛病,走得慢

11 pin down 确认,辨明,选定
I can't quite pin my feeling down. 我很难弄清楚自己的感觉。

pinch

1 at/in a pinch/if/when it comes to the pinch 在必要时,在紧要关头
In a pinch it can be used as a weapon. 必要时可以把它当作武器。

2 with a pinch of salt 半信半疑
His remarks should be taken with a pinch of salt needed in that atmosphere. 对他的话要半信半疑,这在那种环境下是必要的。
We took uncle George's stories with a pinch of salt. 我们对乔治叔叔的故

事半信半疑。

pink

in the pink 身体棒极了

"How are you?" "Oh, I'm in the pink." "你好吗?""哦,很好。"

pip

1 give sb. the pip 使某人恼怒,使某人精神抑郁

His disgusting jokes gave everybody the pip. 他那些令人作呕的笑话弄得大家都不痛快。

The general's wishy-washy talk gave her the pip. 将军那不痛不痒的话使她很恼火。

2 have/get the pip 沮丧,情绪不佳;不适,有病

I've had the pip since I came back from New York. 我从纽约回来后心里一直不痛快。

pipe

1 dance after/to one's pipe 听从……的指挥

I don't think Mary will dance after Bill's pipe. 我认为玛丽是不会任比尔摆布的。

2 fill one's pipe 致富,发财

3 hit the pipe 【美】抽大烟,吸鸦片;吸毒

The old man told about the days when they went down to Chinatown to hit the pipe. 那个老人讲述了那时候他们到唐人街去吸鸦片烟的事情。

4 pipe down (使)安静下来;(使)停止说话;不再十分坚持,不再十分自信

Pipe down, you boys at the back there. 后面的孩子,安静下来。

Won't you two please pipe down? 请你们俩安静点好吗?

5 pipe up 讲话,说出

Everyone was afraid to talk to the police, but a small child piped up. 人人都怕跟警察谈话,但一个小孩子却敢于开口讲话。

6 put that in your pipe and smoke it 这事你好好考虑一下(要求对方接受他不愿意的事情);了解,承认是事实

I am not going to do it, and you can put that in your pipe and smoke it. 我不打算做这事,你考虑考虑,别再勉强我。

You can't spend any more money, as we simply haven't got any more! So you can put that in your pipe and smoke it. 你再也不能多花钱了,因为我们实在是没有多少钱了!这事你好好考虑一下。

piss

1 on the piss 暴饮,喝酒过多

I was on the piss last night. 我昨晚酒喝多了。

2 piss about/around 游手好闲;胡闹

Stop pissing about. I've got work to do. 别胡闹了,我还有活要干。

3 piss and wind 夸夸其谈,空话

The crooked politician's speech was full of piss and wind. 那个奸诈政客的演讲都是空话。

4 piss and vinegar 精力,活力;顽皮,淘气

We were filled with piss and vinegar like many teenage boys. 我们精力充沛,像十几岁的青少年。

5 piss in the wind 浪费时间和人力做某事却没效果

Telling the president that invading other countries is unpopular with many voters is like pissing in the wind. 告诉总统侵略其他国家会遭到许多投票者的反对,但这种警告不会有什么作用。

6 piss away 浪费,滥用,挥霍

The old man has got enough to piss away from now until the day he dies. 老人有足够的钱供他挥霍一辈子。

7 piss down 下大雨

It's been pissing down for three days. 这场大雨已经下三天了!

8 piss off 立即走开,滚开;使……讨厌

The old fisherman told me to piss off, or he'd clobber me. 那个老渔夫叫我滚开,不然就要揍我了。

9 piss on ice 【美】生活优裕,生活奢侈,大为走运,大为成功

The old couple has been pissing on ice for the recent years. 最近几年那对老夫妇生活一直很奢侈。

10 take the piss out of 【英】取笑,嘲弄

We mercilessly take the piss out of people we like or dislike basically. 不论对喜欢还是不喜欢的人,我们都无情地嘲笑。

pitch

1 in there pitching【美口】尽力地；非常成功地
No matter what happened, John stayed in there pitching. 不管发生什么事，约翰总是一个劲地干。
I'm on the go night and day, and I'm in there pitching. 我日夜拼命干，时刻都不松懈。

2 make a pitch for【美】为……宣传，替……说好话
Nelson made a strong pitch for his tax reform bill. 纳尔逊竭力为自己的税改法案作宣传。
Both presidential candidates have promised to make a pitch for better roads and schools. 两位总统候选人都许诺一定会改善交通和教育。

3 make one's pitch【美】定居，落户

4 pitch in 把……投入；动手干，使劲干；协力；作出贡献
Everywhere people pitched in to help. 到处都有人出力相助。
We all pitched in a quarter to buy Nancy a present. 我们每人拿出25美分，给南希买了一份礼物。

5 pitch into 把……投入；开始干，动手干；开始大吃；迫使处于；迫使接受；猛烈攻击
I didn't ask for the championship, I was pitched into it. 我不想当冠军，我这是被赶鸭子上架。
I pitched into the work on my desk. 我开始埋头干我桌上的工作。

6 pitch woo【美】抱吻
Mary and John pitched woo in the movies. 玛丽和约翰在电影院里接吻。

7 queer one's pitch/queer the pitch for sb. 破坏、阻扰某人的计划或安排
By acting in that way you have queered my pitch. 你那样做坏了我的事。

pity

1 for pity's sake 天哪，发发慈悲吧（表示惊讶、恼怒、不快、请求等）
For pity's sake, be quiet! 行行好，安静一点吧！

2 it is a thousand pities 万分可惜
It is a thousand pities that such accidents should have happened. 竟然会发生这种事故，太遗憾了。

3 more's the pity 不幸的是，真可惜；真糟糕

Oliver's got a bad reputation, and it's true, more's the pity. 奥利弗名声不好,更糟的是恶名与恶行相符。

There's a rumour going round that they're getting divorced, and it's true, more's the pity. 据说他们要离婚,居然是真的,真可惜。

place

1 a place in the sun 有利的环境;显赫的地位

The new generation of writers has achieved a place in the sun. 新一代的作家已经功成名就。

2 fall into place 情况变得清楚

Pressures are relieved. Things begin to fall into place. 压力解除了,情况开始明朗起来。

3 go places 旅行;取得成功

This child will really go places one day. 这孩子将来能成气候。

We have very reason to expect him to go places in business. 我们有充分的理由认为他在经商方面会有成就。

4 in the first place 首先

And, in the first place, was that silver ours? 首先,那些银器难道真是我们的吗?

5 know/keep one's place 自觉安分,知趣,识相

One of the reasons that adults don't like young people is that they don't know their place. 成年人之所以不喜欢年轻人,其原因之一就是年轻人不知天高地厚。

6 put/keep sb. in his place 使某人安分,杀某人的威风

The teacher put the boy in his place with just a glance. 老师只投去一瞥就使那男孩规矩了。

plague

(a) plague on/take you/him, etc. 愿上天降祸于你/他等;该死,遭瘟

Plague take the fellow! 那家伙真该死!

A plague on you! Why do you always turn up so late? 该死的,为什么你总是来这么晚?

plate

1 have/give/hand sb. sth. on a plate 乐意地、爽快地给予，奉送，白送

You can't expect people to give you all the answers on a plate. 你不要指望人家会把全部答案顺顺当当地告诉你。

The team was given the first prize on a plate. 该队轻而易举地获得了第一名。

2 have/get a lot/too much on one's plate（要做的工作或事）很多

Pitman's got a lot on his plate these days. 这几天皮特曼有很多工作要做。

play

1 have sth. to play with 有某物（钱、时间等）可供支配

How much money have we got to play with? 我们有多少钱可以花？

2 make a play for 【美】挖空心思地吸引、勾引（异性）；想方设法得到

If I was Peter, I definitely would not make a play for Jane. 如果我是彼得，我肯定不会勾引简的。

3 play double 耍两面派，两面讨好；双打

Will you play single or double in the tennis game? 网球比赛你单打还是双打？

Our coworker always plays double. 我们的合作者老是耍两面派。

4 play fair/cricket/the game 参见 game 4

5 play fast and loose 反复无常，耍滑头；为所欲为；不可靠

Spencer played fast and loose with the company's good name. 斯宾塞肆无忌惮地破坏公司的信誉。

6 play havoc/hell/hell and Tommy/hob/Old Harry/the bear/the deuce/the very deuce/the devil/the devil and all/the very devil/the dichens/the very dichens/the mischief/old gooseberry with 蹂躏，糟蹋，破坏；造成巨大混乱

An unhappy marriage can play such havoc with other lives besides one's own. 不幸的婚姻，不但会破坏自己的一生，还会破坏别人的一生。

Mother's illness played hob with our party. 我们因为母亲生病而取消了聚会。

7 play high/for high stakes 豪赌，出大牌

Elizabeth often plays high. 伊丽莎白赌注常下得很大。

Disney is playing for high stakes. 迪斯尼这样做是冒了很大的风险的。

8　play it low down on/upon sb. 用卑鄙手段对某人；利用某人弱点进行欺骗

The cheat always plays it low down upon the innocent. 那个骗子经常用卑鄙手段欺骗那些无辜的人。

9　play one's cards right/well 善于运用本领或机会获得成功，把握良机，相机行事

Within seven to ten years, if we play our cards right, China will be one of the biggest markets inbound to America. 如果我们的策略得当，在7至10年，中国就将成为美国最大的旅游客源市场之一。

10　play out 用完，耗尽；精疲力竭；失去作用；过时

It had been a hard day and by night he was played out. 劳累了一天，到晚上他已是疲惫不堪了。

11　play possum (over/with) 【美口】装睡；装死；装病；装傻，装糊涂

Two naughty brothers, Jimmy and Tony played possum when their mum came upstairs to see whether they had gone to bed or not. When their mum walked away, they started to play again in the room. 当妈妈上楼来看吉米和托尼是否在睡觉时，调皮的兄弟俩装睡，等妈妈一走开，他们马上又开始玩起来。

12　play (it) safe 稳扎稳打，谨慎行事，明哲保身

The country's scientists hesitate to draw inferences when there is uncertainty, she says, instead preferring to play it safe and be cautious in their words and assessments. 她说，当存在不确定性时，这个国家的科学家在做出推论方面犹豫不决，相反却更愿意保持四平八稳，在措辞和评估上保持谨慎。

13　play sb. for 【美】把某人当……利用；为……而利用某人

We are being played for suckers. 我们在被人当傻瓜利用。
You are only playing me for what you can get out of me. 你只是在利用我，想从我身上捞点什么。

14　play the field 拈花惹草；不专一，三心二意

You'll never get Bill to give up other women. He likes to play the field. 你不可能让比尔放弃别的女人，他喜欢广交女朋友。

15　play truant/hookey 参见 hookey 2

16　play up to 献媚，取悦；利用某事达到目的

Thomas played up to the boss. 托马斯向老板献殷勤。

17 child's play 简单的东西；容易的事情

Many of my contacts and friends within Facebook are senior managers, directors, VPs, and CEOs, this is not child's play. 我在脸书上的许多联系人和好友都是高级经理、董事、副总和首席执行官，这可不是小孩子的游戏。

18 what are you/is he, etc. at 你/他等在搞甚么名堂

please

1 if you please （表示客气礼貌）烦请，如果你愿意的话，如果可以的话；（表示强调或要求注意）请听我说，对不起；（表示惊奇、气愤或难以置信）真怪，竟然

Step this way, ladies and gentlemen, if you please. 女士们，先生们，请走这边。

Tyler crashed my car, and now, if you please, he expects me to pay for the repair bill! 是泰勒撞坏我的车，现在倒好，他要我付修理费，真是岂有此理！

2 please oneself 愿意怎样就怎样

Please yourself when you start—eight or nine o'clock, as long as you do your eight hour's work, I don't mind. 你什么时候上班都可以，八点或九点，只要上够八个小时，我就没意见。

pleasure

1 at one's pleasure/during one's pleasure 随……之便

2 it's my/a pleasure 别客气

"Thank you for the dinner." "It was my pleasure. (Pleasure was all mine.)" "谢谢你请我吃晚饭。""别客气。"

3 may I have the pleasure of 我可以有幸……

May I have the pleasure of the next dance? 我可以有幸邀请你跳下一支舞吗？

4 what's your pleasure 【口】你想要什么

5 with pleasure 当然可以，很乐意

"Could you post these letters on your way home, please?" "With pleasure!" answered John, eager to please as ever. "请你在回家的路上把

这些信寄出好吗？""当然可以，"约翰像往常一样受宠若惊地回答道。

pocket

1 be in pocket 有钱，赚钱

Garcia is never in pocket. 加西亚从未有过钱。

2 be low in (one's) pocket 一个钱也没有，手头拮据

3 be out of pocket 没钱，赔钱

Hardy was out of pocket by the transaction. 哈代这回买卖赔了钱。

4 have sb. in one's pocket 可以左右某人，可以操纵某人

Halifax has had half the Cabinet in his pocket. 哈利法克斯控制着内阁中一半的成员。

5 in one's (hip) pocket 在……掌握之中，受制于……；与……形影不离

point

1 at/on the point of 正当……之际，就在……之时

The roof seems on the point of falling in. 这屋顶眼看就要塌下来了。

A visitor came when Isaac was at the point of leaving. 艾萨克正要离开时一位客人来访。

2 I take your point/point taken 你说得是

I take your point about needing new recordings. 你说得对，是需要添置些新的录音材料了。

3 in point of fact/law 事实上；法律上

In point of fact the only progress we made in that academy was towards freedom. 实际上，我们在这所学校里唯一的进步就是走向自由。

The judge remarked that omitting to tell the truth was next door to lying in point of law. 法官说，从法律上讲，不说实话无异于欺骗。

4 not to put too fine a point on it 直言不讳，实话实说

Not to put too fine a point on it, your work has been unsatisfactory recently! 实话实说，你近来的工作不能令人满意。

We're most unhappy about the lack of clear religious teaching in our schools, not to put too fine a point on it. 坦白地说，最令人感到不快的是，我们的学校缺乏明确的宗教教育。

5 that's not the point 你说的与我们正在讨论的无关

6 that's the (whole) point 这正是问题的实质

7 the point is 问题是,问题在于
8 you've (got) a point there 你说得对,你说的有道理
9 you've made your point 你说的我听懂了,你已说明白你的观点了
10 what's your point 你怎么认为

poison

what's your poison/name/pick/choose your poison【谑】你想喝什么酒
Name your poison, please. /What's your poison? 你们要喝什么酒?

poker

by the holy poker【谑】一定,老天在上(发誓用语)
I never saw anything to beat that by the holy poker, I never did. 我从来没见过有什么比得过那个东西,老天作证,从来没有。

pole

1 be poles apart/asunder 大相径庭,完全相反
They are poles apart in their attitude to education. 他们对教育的态度大相径庭。
The two brothers are poles apart in personality. 这兄弟俩的性格完全不同。

2 up the pole 在困境中;头脑有点失常;喝醉
Fielding's action has put us up the pole. 菲尔丁的行为弄得我们十分尴尬。
Eden's up the pole if he thinks I am going to do that work without being paid. 要是艾登以为我干那种工作不要报酬,那他的头脑就不正常了。

polish

1 polish off 飞快地完成;打败,制服;飞快地吃、喝完;【美】除掉,杀死;使失去知觉
I can polish off the work in five minutes. 我能在五分钟内把活干完。
You have to polish off three experienced players before you can win the prize. 你得战胜三个有经验的选手,才能获奖。

2 polish the apple 讨好,献媚
Mary polished the apple at work because she wanted a day off. 玛丽上班

时尽力讨好上司，因为她想休一天假。

Susan is the teacher's pet because she always polished the apple. 苏珊是老师的宠儿，因为她总是讨好老师。

3 polish up 使完善，改进

I must polish up my French before I go to Paris. 在去巴黎前，我得提高我的法语水平。

Jackson's polishing up on his German. 杰克逊在进修德语。

pop

1 pop off 睡着；突然死去；【美】杀死；乱发牢骚

All I need to do is lie down, and I can pop right off. 我只想躺下，而且马上就可以睡着。

The gangsters pop each other off. 歹徒们互相残杀。

2 pop on 一下子穿上（衣服）；啪地打开（电器等），瞬间出现

The actress popped her coat on. 那个女演员飞快地穿上外套。

Pop on a movie and do some stretching or yoga moves. 打开一部电影，做些伸展运动，或做做瑜伽。

3 pop out 突然死去；匆忙出去，突然走出，跳出来

A gust of wind made the candle pop out. 一阵风突然把蜡烛吹灭了。

I had just popped out for a breath of fresh air, and missed your telephone call. 我刚刚走出去呼吸了一下新鲜空气，没有接到你的电话。

4 pop the question【口】（男方向女方突然）求婚

You've decided to pop the question? That's wonderful! I think you should buy her roses and take her out for a nice dinner. 你决定向她求婚了！太好了，我觉得你得给她买玫瑰，再请她吃顿烛光晚餐。

pope

is the Pope Polish/Italian/Catholic【美】这还用问吗，这不是明摆着的吗

"Did he bet that day?" "Is the Pope Catholic?" "他那天赌博了吗？" "当然，这还用说吗？"

possess

what/whatever possessed you 你怎么这么鬼迷心窍

Whatever possessed you to act so foolishly? 究竟是什么使你干出这样的

蠢事?

What possessed you to behave in such a stupid way? 什么使你表现得如此愚蠢?

possum

play possum (over/with) 参见 play 11

post

pip at/on the post 在最后一刻击败

We didn't win the contract: we were pipped at the post by a firm whose price was lower. 我们未得到那份合同的生意,最后是一家出价更低的公司击败了我们。

pot

1 go to pot 堕落,衰落;完蛋,毁灭

If you don't attend to your garden, it will go to pot. 如果你不好好照看花园,它就会荒芜。

Mrs. Jones' health has gone to pot. 琼斯太太的身体一天不如一天。

2 keep the pot boiling 谋生,糊口;保持热度,继续干,兴致不减

The worker didn't earn much money—just enough to keep the pot boiling. 那工人挣钱不多,仅够糊口而已。

The government lent the company some money to keep the pot boiling. 政府贷给这家公司一笔款子,使其能够维持下去。

3 not have a pot to piss in 【美俚】一贫如洗,家徒四壁

My family didn't have a pot to piss in, but we were proud as devils. 那时我们家一贫如洗,但是我们自尊心很强。

4 shit or get off the pot 【美】不能举棋不定,应当机立断,别占着茅坑不拉屎

The union leader warned that the city had until Feb. 1 to shit or get off the pot. 工会领袖警告说,市政当局在2月1日之前必须做出决定。

5 take a pot at 朝……随意开一枪

The boy took a pot at the neighbour's cat with his air rifle. 那个男孩儿用气枪向邻居的猫打了一枪。

pot-luck

have/take pot-luck 吃顿便饭
Come and have pot-luck with us. 来同我们吃顿便饭吧。

potato

1 hot potato 烫手山芋，棘手的问题
Many school boards found segregation a hot potato in the early 1960s. 二十世纪六十年代初期许多学校当局觉得种族隔离是个棘手的问题。

2 the (clean) potato 正确的事物，正派的人
It's not quite the clean potato. 这事不大对头。
Julia had long known subconsciously that Kelvin was not the clean potato. 朱莉娅很久以来就隐隐约约地感到凯尔文不是个正派的人。

pound

1 a pound to a penny【口】十有八九，极为可能
I said it was a pound to a penny they'd get married within a year—they did! 我说过他们很可能在一年内结婚，果然不错。

2 get one's pound's worth 花钱划得来

3 pound the pavement【美俚】徘徊在街头寻找工作或行乞
John pounded the pavement looking for a job. 约翰来回奔走寻找工作。
Mary and Bill pounded the pavement to find an apartment. 玛丽和比尔到处奔波找公寓。

pour

pour it on【美】大肆吹捧；卖力干；比赛中连连得分；赶紧，快走
Isabel was good, but was there any need to pour it on like that? 伊莎贝尔固然很好，但是有必要那么大肆吹捧她吗？
Better pour it on if you're to catch your plane! 如果你想赶上那班飞机，最好快走！

powder

1 keep one's powder dry 做好行动准备，有备无患
Remember the old rule, keep your powder dry. 记住这条老规矩：有备无患。

Then we'll have to sue him in court so let's keep our powder dry. 那时候我们就得上法庭告他了,所以我们得做好一切准备。

2 not worth (the) powder and shot 不值得花费力气去做
Going all the way to town to look for him is just not worth the powder and shot. 大老远进城去找他未免太不值得了。

3 put more powder into it 加油,再加一把劲
Put more powder into it, Lancy! 加油,兰西!

4 take a (runout) powder 【美】匆忙离去,逃走,消失
All the gang had taken a powder when cops arrived. 警察赶到时,那一帮人早就逃之夭夭了。

power

1 all/more power to one's elbow 祝你成功,祝你一帆风顺
More power to your elbow! Keep on revising and you'll soon know it all! 坚持复习,你很快就能学会,祝你成功!
You are in for the job? I wish more power to your elbow. 你得到了那份工作? 我祝你一帆风顺。

2 be beyond/out of one's powers 不能胜任,力所不及
Not that I don't want to help you, but that it's beyond my powers to do so. 并不是我不想帮忙,而是我能力有限。

3 by (all) the powers/by merciful powers 我的天哪,上帝呀

4 do all in one's power 全力以赴,竭力
Lawrence will do all in his power to help you. 劳伦斯将竭尽全力帮助你。

5 have sb. in one's power 控制住某人
I have Geoffrey in my power at last. 我终于把杰弗里控制住了。

6 to the nth power 到极度,到极点
They are fools to the nth power. 他们真是愚蠢到了极点。

practice

make a practice 有……习惯,经常
MacArthur makes a practice of going to bed early. 麦克阿瑟习惯早睡。
Make a practice of being on time for work. 要养成准时上班的习惯。

practise

practise what you preach 身体力行，以身作则，言传身教

Where can someone find the time to practise what you preach? 人们在哪儿能够找到时间来实践你所宣扬的那一套呢？

praise

1 praise be (to God) 谢天谢地，感谢上帝

At last I've found you, praise be! 谢天谢地我总算找到你了！

2 that's praise indeed 那真是过奖了（有时表示讽刺）

"Lucy's the best student I've ever had!" "That's praise indeed!" "露西是我教过的最好的学生。""您过奖了。"

preserve

Heaven/Saints/God preserve us 参见 god 9

press

1 be hard pressed 处境窘迫

I'm hard pressed for time today. 我今天时间非常紧。

Norris was hard pressed with toil and worry. 诺里斯心力交瘁。

2 press ahead/on/forward 奋进，猛进

We hope both sides continue to press ahead in this direction. 我们希望各方继续做出努力朝着这一方向迈进。

price

what price 有没有希望，有没有可能，你以为怎么样；【讽】那算什么东西，有什么用处

What price fine weather for Sunday? 星期天天气会不会好？

What price that for a home-made motorbike? 你觉得国产摩托车怎么样？

proud

1 do oneself proud 养尊处优，生活阔绰

The girl always does herself proud, so she is not qualified to the work. 那个姑娘一向养尊处优，她不可能胜任这项工作。

2 do sb. proud/do credit 给某人面子，给某人荣誉，替某人争光；待客热

情；名副其实

His honesty did him proud. 他的正直为他争光。

They did us all proud at the hotel. 他们在酒店盛情款待我们。

pull

1 pull a fast one (on sb.) 捉弄某人，欺骗某人

Jackson tried to pull a fast one on us, but we caught on before he got away with it. 杰克逊想欺骗我们，但在他阴谋得逞前就被我们逮到了。

2 pull a good oar/pull one's weight 划得一手好船，划船划得好

The young man pulls a good oar. 那个小伙子很会划船。

3 pull caps/wigs 互相厮打；争吵

4 pull devil, pull baker/pull dog, pull cat 加油啊，干啊

Now you boys, get to it—pull devil, pull baker! 你们这群男孩们，现在开始，——加油，加油！

5 pull down 赚取；获得（工资、报酬、资金等）

Nicol pulled down five hundred dollars a month. 尼科尔每月赚500美元。

Owen pulled down an A in algebra by studying hard. 欧文努力学习，代数成绩得了优等。

6 pull for 对……极为同情，热情支持，给予帮助

We were pulling for their football team. 我们正在给他们的足球队打气。

7 pull in 获得（利益、报酬）；抓（嫌疑犯）

Connie pulled in about forty thousand dollars a year. 康尼每年挣四万美元左右。

8 pull/draw in one's horns 收敛傲气，服软；退缩不前；缩减开支

When he saw that I had the support of the majority, he pulled in his horns and admitted he might have made a mistake. 他见我获得多数人支持，就软了下来，承认自己可能错了。

After the business failed, he had to pull in his horns pretty sharply. 买卖失败后，他不得不大幅削减生活开支。

9 pull off 成功，做成；干坏事；捣鬼

That horse will pull off the race. 那匹马会跑赢比赛。

Nobody knows what he is trying to pull off here. 没人知道他想在这儿捣什么鬼。

10 pull oneself together 控制自己,镇静下来;重新振作起来

Stop acting like a baby! Pull yourself together! 别耍孩子气了,振作起来!

Clarissa had her ups and downs, but she had always managed to pull herself together. 克拉丽莎饱经沧桑沉浮,但她总能设法重新振作起来。

11 pull one's leg 骗人;取笑,戏弄

Western cowboys loved to pull a stranger's leg. 西部牛仔喜欢戏弄陌生人。

12 pull one's/any punches 未出全力打;掩饰不好的事

Jimmy pulled his punches and let Paul win the boxing match. 吉米未出全力而让保罗赢了这场拳赛。

The mayor spoke bluntly; he didn't pull any punches. 市长说话直率,未掩饰任何问题。

13 pull out of a/one's hat 变出;发明;想象

Those figures were not pulled out of a hat. 这些数字不是瞎编的。

Let's see you pull an excuse out of your hat. 看你能编出什么理由来。

14 pull rank 仗势欺人,摆架子;滥用职权,利用职权压制

When my assistant became obstinate I had to pull rank and insist that she obey. 当我的助手变得倔强不听话时,我只得利用职权,坚持要她服从。

Don't try to pull rank on me. We're all equals here. 别对我摆架子,这里人人平等。

15 pull round 使苏醒,使恢复健康

The doctor tried his best to pull the patient round. 医生尽力把那个病人的病治好。

16 pull strings/wires 幕后操纵,为……牵线

If you want to see the Governer, Mr. Root can pull strings for you. 如果你想见市长,鲁特先生可以为你从中牵线。

17 pull the other one (, it's got bells on) 我才不相信呢,你别开玩笑啦(幽默地表示嘲笑和轻蔑)

"I hear Mark's putting his car in for the London to Brighton race!" "Pull the other one! I don't believe it would get as far as the end of his drive!" "我听说马克要参加从伦敦到布赖顿的汽车拉力赛!""别开玩笑啦,我不相信他的车能开到终点!"

18 pull the plug on 揭发秘密行为;突然中断,停止

Given the chance, some officials would pull the plug on the Fed's second round of quantitative easing right now. 考虑到这种可能性,有些官员希望立即停止美联储的第二轮量化宽松计划。

19 pull the rug (out) from under 临场拆台,破坏计划,釜底抽薪
China may grumble about the dollar's dominance in the global trading system, but it has no desire to pull the rug out from under America's economy. 中国可能因美元在全球贸易体系中的支配地位而心怀不满,但中国并不想拆美国经济的台。

20 pull the wool over one's eyes 蒙骗……
It's no good trying to pull the wool over Harold's eyes, he's far too perceptive. 无法蒙骗哈罗德,他洞察力太强了。
Kennedy thinks by all this fast talking and flattery he can pull the wool over her eyes, but she isn't deceived. 肯尼迪以为像这样花言巧语加上奉承就可以蒙蔽她,但她没有上当。

21 pull up 制止;责备,责骂;纠正;在比赛中赶上
Caroline was pulled up for her error. 卡罗琳因过失而受到责备。
His mark in the geography paper pulled him up several places. 他的地理考分使他的名次提前了好几位。
The other boat pulled up with us. 另一条船追上了我们。

22 pull up stakes 搬家
The Jones family pulled up stakes three time in two years. 琼斯一家人两年内搬了三次家。

pumpkin

some pumpkins【美口】重要的人或物(用作单数)
I won't deny that her father is some pumpkins. 我不否认她父亲是个大亨。

punch

1 beat to the punch/draw 捷足先登
John was going to apply for the job, but Ted beat him to the punch. 约翰正要申请那份工作,但泰德却捷足先登了。

2 pack a punch/wallop 重击,出猛力
They both pack quite a punch. 他们两人出手都很猛。

pup

sell sb. a pup 欺骗某人；出售伪劣商品，商业欺诈行为
You've been sold a pup—that house is nearly falling down! 你上当了——那所房子快要塌了！

purse

1 control/hold the purse strings 掌握金钱，掌握开支
But it's important to remember you have little control over individuals who hold the purse strings and make decisions based on gut instinct. 但是你一定要记住你无法控制这些个人，钱掌握在他们手里，并且他们根据直觉做出决定。

2 loosen the purse strings 用钱大手大脚；慷慨解囊
My friends loosen the purse strings to help people suffered from Tsunami. 我的朋友慷慨解囊，帮助遭受了海啸的人们。

3 tighten the purse strings 节省用钱，紧缩开支
Always concerned about staying in touch with her subjects, Queen Elizabeth II has invited Britain's royal family to follow her example and tighten the purse strings during the financial downturn. 一直关心民生的英国女王伊丽莎白二世号召皇室家族成员们与其一同节省开支，避免浪费，以渡过金融危机。

push

1 at a push 在紧急时，在不得已时，在困难时
We can sleep seven or eight people in the house at a push. 不得已时，我们这间房子可以睡七八个人。
I'll be able to get the work done by five for you at a push. 必要时，我可以在五点钟前为你把这事办好。

2 push along 离开
I'm afraid I really ought to be pushing along now. 恐怕现在我真该走了。

3 push around 任意摆布，驱使，欺骗，烦扰
You can't push me around like you do to your poor wife. 你不能像对待你那可怜的妻子那样对待我。
Tom has been pushing himself around recently more than was necessary.

汤姆近来一直无端地烦扰自己。

4 push off 离开

It's time for us to push off now. 现在我们该走了。

Push off, will you—can't you leave us alone? 走开,你不能让我们安静一会儿吗?

5 push/hit the panic button 非常恐惧,紧张

Don't push the panic button! Keep cool! 别害怕! 冷静!

put

1 be (hard) put to it 为难,处境尴尬,没有办法

The boy was put to it to answer the teacher's question. 那男孩不知道怎样回答老师的问题。

I was hard put to it to please both parties. 我没有办法两面讨好。

2 not know where to put oneself 局促不安,十分尴尬

3 not (to) put it past 认为那是……的本分,认为……能做……

Burke wouldn't put it past them to make some grandstand play in the name of world peace. 伯克相信他们会借世界和平的名义做一些哗众取宠的表演。

4 not to put too fine a point/an edge on/upon it 直截了当地说出来,毫不客气地说出来

I don't much like modern music in fact, not to put too fine a point on it, I hate it. 我不很喜欢现代音乐——说句老实话,我其实很讨厌现代音乐。

Marcus is not to put too fine a point on it, a thorough scoundrel. 说得不客气一点,马库斯是个彻头彻尾的无赖。

5 put away 放好;大吃大喝;储存;关进监狱;杀掉(以解除痛苦);抛弃,放弃

You'd be surprised at the amount that the boy can put away in a single day. 这男孩一天能吃掉那么多东西,会使你惊讶不已。

The dog had to be put away. 为解除其痛苦,只好杀掉这只狗。

6 put down 批评,不赞成;镇压;写下;贬低;放下

Anna was put down for the way she dressed. 安娜的穿着方式受到指责。

7 put in 经过(一段时间)

There's still half an hour to put in before the meeting. 还要半个小时才开

会呢。

Alick put in many years as a printer. 阿利克做了多年的印刷工人。

8 put sb. in mind of 提醒,提议,使某人记起

Frances puts me in mind of my sister. 弗朗西丝使我想起我妹妹。

That puts me in mind of a story. 那使我想起一个故事。

9 put sb. in one's place 指责某人;挫某人的锐气;使某人规规矩矩

I'm pleased you told him off—it's about time somebody put that young man in his place. 我很高兴你把他数落了一番,到了该提醒那位年轻人注意一下自己地位的时候了。

If Oliver dares to be impudent with me again, I'll put him in his place. 要是奥利弗再敢对我无礼,我就要对他不客气了。

10 put it across 欺骗……;跟……算账;向……报复

Hornby put it across me by telling me that he was coming soon. 霍恩比骗我,说很快就会回来。

11 put it on 装腔作势;夸张;要高价

Mary wasn't angry really; she was only putting it on. 玛丽不是真的生气,她只不过是故作姿态而已。

12 put it/sth. over on【美】欺骗,愚弄

Gunter's not the sort of man you can put something over on. 冈特可不是你能愚弄的那种人。

13 put/stick it there【美】(表示同意、和解)跟我握手吧,一言为定

OK, so $500 it is, put it there. 好吧,就算五百元,一言为定。

"I think that's settled all over differences, hasn't it?" "Put it there, then, John!" "我看我们的全部分歧都算消除了,对吧?""对,咱们一言为定!"

14 put off 扰乱,使不快,使反感

I was rather put off by the shamelessness of his proposal. 他那无耻的建议使我反感。

Don't be put off by her sharp tongue. 别因为她说话尖刻而生气。

15 put on【美】欺骗

You're putting me on. 你在骗我。

16 put one across 欺骗,瞒过,使信以为真

They put one across their teacher. 他们瞒过了老师。

17 put one's back to it 努力,下功夫

You can finish the job by noon if you put your back to it. 你若肯努力,中午就可以把工作做完。

18 put one's best foot forward 参见 foot 16

19 put one's foot down 参见 foot 18

20 put one's foot in it/one's mouth 参见 foot 19

21 put one's money on a scratched horse 必输的赌博
You bet on the New York Mets to win the World Series? Why put your money on a scratched horse? 你赌纽约大都会队赢世界职业棒球大赛吗?为什么把赌注押在这必输的球队上?

22 put one's nose out of joint 参见 nose 23

23 put one's shoulder to the wheel 努力工作,全力以赴;助一臂之力
The only way we'll complete the job on time is for everyone to put our shoulder to the wheel. 按时完成这项工作的唯一办法是大家必须全力以赴。

24 put out 麻烦,打扰,引起不便;使出力量;尽一番努力
Don't put yourself out for my sake! 不要为我忙啦!
I hope I'm not putting you out. 但愿我没有打扰你。

25 put over 使成功,使被接受;赏识;理解;欺骗;愚弄
Jenny has put herself over the audience. 珍妮大受观众欢迎。
Jordan put over a complex and difficult business deal. 乔丹办成了一笔复杂而又困难的交易。

26 put the bite on 向……敲竹杠;借钱
A co-worker of his found out about his prison record and began to put the bite on him. 他的一个同事知道了他坐过牢,就向他敲竹杠。
Mike just put the bite on me. 迈克刚向我借了钱。

27 put them up 举起手来;举起你的拳头或武器(挑战用语)

28 put through it 对……的勇气或能力做严格的检查
Pearson had been put through it and had answered volumes of head breaking questions. 皮尔逊受到严厉的审讯,回答了许多令人头痛的问题。

29 put sth. through its paces 参见 pace 3

30 put/get/set to rights 办理妥当;清理
It took Mrs. Smith an hour to put the room to rights after the party. 史密

斯太太在舞会后花了一个小时才将房间整理好。

31 put up or shut up 要么来打赌,要么少饶舌;要么看行动,要么少废话

They called for the minister to either put up or shut up. 他们要求部长要么证明自己有理要么闭嘴。

32 put sb. up to 指挥他人;唆使某人做……

Older boys put us up to painting the statue red on Halloween. 大些的男孩鼓动我们在万圣节前夕将雕像漆成红色。

My older brother put me up to making a prank telephone call. 那个恶作剧电话是我哥让我打的。

33 put sb. wise 使某人明了,点醒某人

The new boy didn't know that Jim was playing a trick on him, so I put him wise. 新来的男孩不知道吉姆在捉弄他,所以我提醒他别上当。

It's kind of you to put me wise. I knew there was something wrong but I couldn't just put my finger on it. 承蒙你费心提醒了我。我明知事情有点不对头,但摸不清是怎么回事。

34 put up with 忍受,容忍

I can't put up with this noise. 我受不了这种喧闹声。

35 to put it mildly/to say the least 往轻处说,不夸张地说,实话说

These books are very, very expensive, to put it mildly. 老实说,这些书的确非常非常贵。

quite

1 quite a 异常的，出众的

It was quite a sight. 那是一个很特别的景象。

You have quite a memory. 你的记性真好。

2 quite so 正是这样，可不是吗

3 when you're quite finished 好嘛，你们已经干完了

When you're quite finished, children, thank you, we'll now start again!
好，孩子们，你们干完了，谢谢。现在我们重新开始！

R

rabbit

1 it's rabbits out of the wood 真是太妙了；真是上天的赏赐
2 produce the rabbit out of the hat （说话时）能随机应变

rack

1 rack back 训斥
2 rack off 走开；讲述
The professor racked off a miserable story. 教授讲了一个很凄惨的故事。
3 rack one's brain(s)/head/wits 参见 brain 1

racket

1 what's the racket 什么事，怎么啦
2 what's your racket 你从事什么行当

rag

1 chew the rag 聊天，争论，唠叨
Tom was chewing the rag at me the whole afternoon. 汤姆整个下午不停地数落我。
2 feel like a wet rag 感到疲倦，浑身没劲
I feel like a wet rag. 我感觉浑身没劲。
3 lose one's rag/get one's rag out 勃然大怒
Don't get your rag out! I only asked a question. 别发火，我只不过是提个问题而已。
4 take the rag off 【美】超过一切；独占鳌头，获得优良成绩
The safety first takes the rag off major events. 安全第一成为压倒一切的头等大事。

rage

1 all the rage 风靡一时的事物，流行式样，非常走红
Short dresses and long boots were all the rage last year. 去年短裙、长靴风

靡一时。
The man is *all the rage* there. 这人在那儿非常走红。
2 fly/fall into a rage 勃然大怒,大发雷霆
The fellow *flew into a rage* and tore at my hair. 那个家伙勃然大怒,要扯我的头发。

rain

1 as right as rain 非常健康
His teeth went and his hair got thin, but six months back in the hometown he was *as right as rain*. 他牙掉发稀,但是回到故乡半年之后,他竟然身强体健了。

2 (come) rain or shine 不论晴雨,无论如何
Sooner or later, *rain or shine*, Jim would do so. 无论如何,吉姆都会这么干的。
I'll see you again on Tuesday, *come rain or shine*. 我在星期二再来看你,风雨无阻。

3 rain on 诉苦;带来霉运
Don't *rain on* me. 不要向我诉苦。

raise

1 make a raise 弄到钱,筹集到一笔钱;借钱

2 raise Cain/hell/hell's delight/the devil/the mischief/【美】raise a big smoke 闹事,闹乱子;大叫大嚷,破口大骂
The children *raised Cain* in the living room. 孩子们在客厅里大闹天宫。
Some teenage boys *raised the devil* in town on Halloween. 一些青少年在万圣节前夕在街上胡闹。

3 raise money/the wind 筹款
Peter came to me this morning to *raise the wind*. 彼得今天早上来找我筹款。

rake

1 rake it in 捞进一大笔钱;赚钱
Peter has been *raking it in* since he started his new job. 彼得自从开始新工作以来,已经赚了很多钱。

2 rake over 旧事重提，反复提及

The questions were raked over in a thick report. 厚厚的报告中一再提到这些问题。

They like raking over old scandals. 他们喜欢翻出陈年丑闻谈个没完。

3 rake up 翻出往事，揭疮疤

Do not rake up old grievances. 不要再翻旧账。

ram

ram it 住手；去你的

rap

1 a bum rap 冤案

Gallup was sent to prison on a bum rap. 盖洛普遭冤案入狱。

2 be not worth a rap 一文不值

The chairman's opinion isn't worth a rap; the council votes as it pleases. 主席的意见一文不值，市政会总是按自己的意愿投票。

3 beat the rap【美】逃脱罪责，摆脱困境

The accused insisted that he would certainly beat the rap. 被告坚持认为他定会被宣判无罪。

4 rap it over 好好聊聊，把事情彻底谈清

You'd better rap it over right now. 你最好现在就把事情彻底说清楚。

5 stop your rap 别东拉西扯，别瞎扯

6 take the rap 承担罪责

Harold will never crack. He'll take the whole rap. 哈罗德决不会垮掉，他会承担全部罪责。

rat

1 do a rat 做卑鄙的事；变节

2 see rats 酩酊大醉，饮酒过量

3 have rats in the attic/garret 行为乖张，想法荒诞，精神失常；感觉不舒服，心情不好

4 rat race 横冲直撞；搞得一团糟

The dance last night was a rat race. It was too noisy and crowded. 昨晚的舞会搞得一团糟，人多又嘈杂。

School can be a rat race if you don't keep up your studies. 如果你不好好学习,你的功课将会一团糟。

5 rat out (on) 离去;遗弃

Joe ratted out on Susan when she was 7 months pregnant. 乔在苏珊怀孕七个月时遗弃了她。

6 smell a rat 感到可疑,感到事情不妙

Every time Tom visits me one of my ash trays disappears. I am beginning to smell a rat. 每当汤姆来看我时,我的烟灰缸就丢失一个,我开始怀疑起来。

7 like a rat in the hole 瓮中之鳖

The enemy was like a rat in the hole. 敌人已是瓮中之鳖,无处逃窜。

8 be in the rats【俚】发疯

Listen to what he said, don't you think that he is in the rats? 听听他说的话,你难道不认为他发疯了吗?

9 as wet as a drowned rat 浑身湿透;犹如落汤鸡

Walking in the rain for an hour, Mr. Smith was as wet as a drowned rat. 史密斯先生在雨中走了一小时,全身湿透了。

10 as poor as a rat/church mouse 一贫如洗;穷到极点

My aunt is as poor as a church mouse. 我姨妈穷得一贫如洗。

rate

1 at a rate of knots 极快地,迅速地

The rich man lent the servant his horse, and he duly set off for Samara at a great rate of knots. 富人把他的马借给了仆人,于是仆人就以极快的速度按时出发去萨马拉了。

2 at any rate 无论如何,至少,不管怎么说,反正

What a terrible thing to have to go through! At any rate you are all right now; that's the most important thing. 经历了多么可怕的事情啊,不过现在你一切安然无恙,这才是最重要的。

3 at that/this rate 那种/这种情形;既然那样/如此

At that rate we shan't see him today. 那样的话我们今天就不能碰见他了。We can't go on spending money at that rate. 我们可不能再照那样子花钱了。

rather

1 had/would rather/had sooner 宁可，宁愿，最好是

I would rather live in the city than on a farm. 我宁可住在城里，不愿住在农场。

I would much rather he had knocked me down. 我倒宁愿他把我打倒。

2 the rather that 何况，况且；正因为……，所以更加

I'm glad of it, the rather that you will benefit by it. 正因为这事对你有好处，所以我就更高兴了。

rattle

rattle off 一气呵成（说出或写出）

When Roger was seven he could rattle off the names of all the states in alphabetical order. 罗杰七岁时就能一口气将各州州名按字母顺序背出来。

raw

touch/catch/get/rub/sting sb. on the raw 触及某人痛处

My sarcasm seemed to have touched him on the raw. 看来我的讽刺触到了他的痛处。

read

1 read sb. like a book 了解某人，对某人了如指掌

John's girlfriend could read him like a book. 约翰的女友对他的情况了如指掌。

2 read one's mind/thoughts 看出……的心思

That's exactly what I was going to say. You read my mind well. 那正是我要说的，你看穿了我的心思。

3 read the riot act 强烈警告或谴责

Three boys were late to school and the teacher read the riot act to them. 三个男生迟到，老师给他们严重警告。

ready

ready, steady, go 各就各位，预备，跑

really

1 not really 事实上不是；不会；没有

"Are you happy to be here?" "Well, no, not really!" "你在这儿愉快吗？" "啊，不，怎么会呢！"

"Can you sew?" "No, I can't. Not really." "你会针线活吗？" "不会，真的不会。"

2 oh really 真是的（表示惊讶、怀疑、有兴趣等）

"I've been promoted!" "Oh really. That's good!" "我晋升了。" "啊，真是的，那太好了！"

Oh really! It's too bad for him. 啊，真是的，那真够他受的。

3 really and truly 果真，的确，千真万确

Did you really and truly say so? 你真的这样说的吗？

reason

1 in (all) reason 合情理的，有道理的

It is not in reason to ask him to do that. 要求他做那种事是不合情理的。

2 ours (is) not to reason why/ours but to do or die 我们无权问为什么，而只能照办

"Why on earth are they getting rid of this new metric size and going back to the old ones?" "Ours is not to reason why!" "他们到底为什么要废除新的公制尺寸，恢复旧制？" "我们无权过问，照办就是。"

3 stand to reason 合情理，是当然的，自不待言

It stands to reason that he won't go if we don't pay him. 我们不付钱给他，他当然不会去。

It stands to reason that if the government lowers taxes, then its income will be loss. 如果政府降低税收，其收入肯定会减少。

4 will/want to know the reason why 要追究原因；要大发脾气

The work had better be finished before tomorrow, or I'll know the reason why. 这活儿还是明天之前干完为好，否则，我是要追究的。

If I'm not home before 10 o'clock, my mother will want to know the reason why. 如果我不在十点钟以前回家，母亲就要大发脾气。

red

1 in the red【美】亏空，有赤字

A large number of radio stations operated in the red. 许多无线电台都亏损运营。

2 not care/give a red cent 毫不在乎，毫不计较

I don't care a red cent what you said. 你说什么我都毫不在乎。

3 not worth a red cent 一文不值

His advice wasn't worth a red cent. 他的意见毫无价值。

4 paint the town red 酗酒狂欢，大肆铺张，胡闹

When I meet my old friends, we are going to paint the town red. 每逢老朋友见面，我们总是狂欢痛饮。

5 see red 火冒三丈

When Lawrence started criticizing my work, I really saw red. 劳伦斯竟批评起我的工作，我不由得火冒三丈。

Whenever anyone teased John about his weight, he saw red. 每当有人拿约翰的体重取笑时，他必大怒。

6 was one's face red when 当……时……尴尬/惊讶极了

Was my face red when I discovered I hadn't brought out money with me and couldn't pay for bus ride. 当我发现身边没带钱而付不出车费时，真是尴尬极了。

remedy

what remedy【口】有什么补救办法

remember

something to remember me by 给……东西留念；【委婉】让……记住……的厉害

"Here's something to remember me by!" "Oh, a book on the English countryside! How lovely!" "给你件东西作纪念吧！""啊，一本关于英国乡村的书！太好了！"

If it's Malory again I'll give him something to remember me by. 如果又是马洛里的话，我要揍他一顿，让他知道我的厉害。

remote

not have the remotest (idea) 毫不明白

"Is he Italian or Greek?" "I haven't the remotest." "他是意大利人,还是希腊人?" "我完全不知道。"

respect

with (all due) respect 尽管对您尊敬之至(表示异议、提请注意时的谦语)

But Mr. Chairman, with all due respect, I feel that wouldn't work. 但是主席先生,请恕我直言,那个办法行不通。

With all due respect to the last speaker, I must point out that the lessons we can learn from history are rather different from those that he gave us. 尽管我们十分尊敬最后一位演讲人,可是我必须指出的是,他讲的一切和我们在历史课中所学的大相径庭。

rest

1 give it a rest 停下来,别说话

Give it a rest, Ron, we all know you can play the piano, but we'd like some peace and quiet, too! 别说了,罗恩,我们大家都知道你会弹钢琴,可是我们现在更需要安静。

2 (you can) rest assured 请相信,请放心

Rest assured, we are doing all we can to find your son. 请放心,我们会全力以赴去寻找你的儿子。

return

1 let us return to the muttons 【谚】言归正传吧

2 many happy returns of the day/your birthday (生日祝福语)福寿无疆,长命百岁,生日快乐

rib

1 dig/poke/nudge sb. in the ribs 为引起对方注意用手指或肘触碰某人的胸肋

His girlfriend at his side dug him in the ribs every time anyone told a joke. 每当有人说笑话时,他身旁的女友就用肘碰碰他的胸口,要他注意。

2 get into one's ribs 向……借钱

3 stick to the/one's ribs 饱餐一顿,填饱肚子
Farmers eat food that sticks to the ribs. 农民常吃些耐饥的食物。
Say, Joe, let's try that new Italian restaurant on First Street. People say the food is tasty and the prices are low. I am really hungry tonight so I want to eat something that sticks to my ribs. 嗨,乔,我们到第一街那个新开的意大利饭馆去试一试吧。人们说那儿的菜味道很好,价钱也便宜。今天晚上我真是饿极了。我得好好地饱餐一顿。

4 tickle the/one's ribs【口】逗人发笑
They conspire to tickle your ribs and give you the occasional choke. 他们会凑在一起设法逗你笑,叫你笑得喘不过气来。

rich

1 strike it rich 暴富;平步青云
The local lord struck it rich in real estate. 那个土豪做房地产生意发了财。

2 that's rich 真荒唐,真可笑
An Englishman teaching a Scotsman how to make kilts—that's rich! 英格兰人教苏格兰人制作苏格兰短裙,真可笑!

ride

1 hitch a ride【美】搭便车
It's dangerous to hitch a ride in the United States. 在美国搭便车是非常危险的。

2 ride herd on【美】密切注意,监督;仔细照顾
Mary rode herd on the small children walking home from school. 玛丽仔细照顾放学回家的孩子们。

3 ride high 大获成功,趾高气扬
Lena is riding high at the moment. 眼下正是莉娜春风得意之时。

4 ride off on 用……回避、掩盖要点
Don't ride off on a side issue. 不要用枝节问题掩盖重点。

5 take sb. for a ride 诈骗或欺骗某人,使某人上当
Keats had no experience in such transactions, and they took him for a ride. 基茨对这种买卖毫无经验,所以就上了他们的当。

riddance

(a) good riddance 庆幸摆脱；谢天谢地总算摆脱了

Their departure was a good riddance. 他们走了，值得庆幸。

Thank heavens we've finally sold that car—good riddance to it! 感谢上帝，我们终于把那辆车卖了，甩了一个包袱。

right

1 about right 恰当的，正确的；厉害的，重重的

Locke does his work about right. 洛克的工作做得好。

Marion was thrashed about right. 马里恩挨了一顿好打。

2 dead to rights【美】肯定无疑，无可抵赖；当场抓住的，无法逃脱罪责的

The thief was caught dead to rights. 那小偷当场被抓。

3 put (it) to rights 整理，整顿；收拾，纠正

Our room looked a mess when the maid arrived, but she soon put it to rights. 清洁女工来时，我们的屋里乱七八糟，但她很快就把房间收拾整齐了。

4 right along【美】进行顺利；不停止，不延缓

They fixed the engine and the train ran right along. 他们修好了引擎，火车开得很顺利。

Don't wait for me. Go right along. 你走你的，不要等我。

5 right and left 到处

Mike quoted right and left. 迈克从各方面引证。

6 right away/right off the bat 立刻

Frances was standing across the room but I recognized her right away. 弗朗西丝站在对面的房间里，但我立刻就认出了她。

7 right, left and centre 到处，周围

Colin was slightly drunk and hurling insults right, left and centre. 科林有点醉了，对周围的人破口大骂。

8 right on【美】完全正确，对啦，好啦

"You played real bad," said Dad. "You're right on there, father," she replied. 父亲说："你打得糟透了。"她回答说："你说得不错，爸爸。"

9 (how) right you are 你说得对，好吧，行，知道了

"Two coffees, please." "Right you are!" "两份咖啡。""好的。"

"You can come on Tuesday, if you want." "Right you are, then—see you next week." "如果可以的话,你在下星期二来。""好吧,那我们下星期再见。"

10 that's right 对啊,不错,完全正确

"You're filming a new series of the programme, I gather." "That's right, we've just started the third episode." "我想你们正在就这个节目拍一部系列片。""不错,我们刚开始拍第三集。"

11 too right/true 对啦,一点不错

"I'm a bit of a fool, aren't I? Coming out here and forgetting my map!" "Too right you are!" "我真笨,不是吗? 你看,出门来这里,却忘了带地图!""完全正确!"

ring

1 hold/keep the ring 不介入,袖手旁观

You should hold the ring while they are arguing about the matter. 他们争论那件事时,你最好不要介入。

2 make/run rings round/around 比……快得多;大大胜过

Morgan can run rings around us in everything. 无论做什么事摩根都比我们强得多。

3 ring down 鸣铃闭幕

The curtain has been rung down; the theatrical company are leaving here tomorrow. 帷幕随着演出结束的铃声落了下来,剧团明天就要离开这里。

4 ring in 把……纳入,偷偷带进;冒名顶替;暗中调换;打卡上班;鸣钟迎来

Nancy can't be kept out of the case entirely, after all, we'll have to ring her in. 不能把南希完全晾在这件案子之外,我们非把她牵扯进来不可。
Bob offered to ring Jim in on the party by pretending he was a cousin from out of town. 鲍勃说他可以带吉姆参加聚会,冒充他外地来的表弟。

5 ring off 住嘴;挂断电话

I'll have to ring off now, someone is knocking at the door. 我现在必须挂断电话,因为有人在敲门。

6 ring out 打卡下班;鸣钟送别

They are ringing out the old year and ringing in the new year. 他们敲起钟

声送走旧岁迎来新年。
They **ring out** at 5 p.m. every day. 他们每天下午5点打卡下班。

7 ring up 鸣铃开幕;打电话
The curtain **was rung up** on a new epoch in world history. 世界历史上一个新纪元的序幕揭开了。

rip

1 let her/it rip 让船、车等开足马力全速前进
Let her rip, Joe, we're out in the country now! 加足马力开起来,乔,现在我们已经来到郊区了。

2 let rip 自由自在,无拘无束,纵情欢乐,让感情奔放
Let your ambitions **rip**. This is no time to sit and dream. 让你的雄心壮志腾飞吧,现在可不是坐着空想的时候。

3 rip off 偷窃,抢劫;剥削;敲诈;强奸;剽窃
They went so far as to **rip off** banks in broad daylight. 他们居然在光天化日之下抢劫银行。
That store is known for **ripping off** the customers. 那家百货店以敲诈顾客而闻名。

river

1 sell down the river (在紧要关头)抛弃,不支持,出卖
Occam denounced the plan as **having sold** the whole peaceful prospect **down the river**. 奥卡姆痛斥该计划把整个和平的希望都抛弃了。

2 up the river 入狱,在狱中
Perkin was sent **up the river** for armed robbery. 珀金因持枪抢劫而入狱。

road

1 burn up the road 驾车急驶
Those who **burn up the road** often cause accidents. 那些开快车的人常常会出车祸。

2 down the road 在这条街上不远的地方;【美】将来,今后
There're shops just **down the road**. 就在这条街不远的地方有几家商店。

3 (one) for the road 以示送行
We gave him a final glass **for the road**. 我们斟上最后一杯酒为他送行。

4 go over the road 入狱服刑

The young man went over the road for stealing. 那个年轻人因盗窃而入狱。

5 hit the road 【美】启程，动身；开始流浪

Next day, we finally hit the road. 次日我们终于上路了。

6 take sb. over a rough road 【美】使某人处于困难、尴尬、狼狈的境地；申斥、痛骂某人

7 would not cross the road to do sth. 对做某事完全不感兴趣

rock

1 between the rock and the hard place 【美】左右为难，进退维谷

Couples are currently between the rock and the hard place; the economy is tightening while the cost of having babies is steadily going up. 如今夫妻们所处的境地很为难，经济在收紧，而抚养婴儿的花费在稳步上升。

2 have/get rocks in one's/the head 【美】愚蠢，神经不正常

You got rocks in your head for sending us on this cockeyed flight. 派我们做这次荒唐的飞行，你的神经一定不正常。

3 on the rocks 触礁；濒于破裂；毁灭，完蛋

His marriage is on the rocks. 他的婚姻濒于破裂。

4 rock along 【美】照老规矩办事

Everything is rocking along just like when Lena was here. 一切事情的安排都和莉娜在这里时一模一样。

5 rock the boat 惹是生非，捣乱，破坏良好的现状

What it needs is cheap labor and factories, and no one to rock the boat. 它所需要的是廉价劳动力和工厂，并且没有人来捣乱。

rocker

off one's rocker 参见 off 11

rocket

off one's rocket 发疯，神经失常（军队对 off one's rocker 的误用）

roll

1 get/set/start the ball rolling 开始活动，开始行动

George started the ball rolling at the party by telling a new joke. 乔治在宴会上首先说了一个新的笑话。

2 go and have a roll 走开,滚开(用于祈使句)

3 keep the ball rolling 保持活跃,不使衰退

John kept the ball rolling at the party by dancing with a lamp shade on his head. 约翰在舞会上头戴灯罩跳舞以提高大家的兴致。

4 roll around 定期或按时地回转

When winter rolls around, out come the skis and skates. 当冬天来临时,滑冰鞋和雪橇又都出来了。

5 roll in 滚滚而来;尽情享受;【美】就寝

Offers of help are now rolling in. 四面八方都伸出了援助之手。

6 roll on 但愿某一时刻尽快来临(用于祈使句)

Roll on spring! The winter's so long! 春天快来吧!冬天太长了!

Roll on the year that I retire! 我退休的年头快来吧!

7 roll up 乘车到达;(尤指在迟到、醉酒等情况下)到场;请进来(尤指看表演);积累,渐次增加

Roll up, roll up, ladies and gentlemen. 女士们,先生们,请进来观看。

The national debts of that country are rolling up. 这个国家的国债正在不断增加。

8 roll up one's sleeves 准备苦干

After the examination, John saw how little he knew about science. He rolled up his sleeves and went to work. 考试后,约翰看到自己对科学知之太少,于是他开始埋头苦干、刻苦学习。

roof

1 go through/hit the roof 暴跳如雷,大发雷霆;物价等上升到或超过最高限度

If William finds out what you did with the company's money he'll hit the roof. 假如威廉发现你这样处理公司的经费,他将大发雷霆。

Unemployment rates have gone through the roof. 失业率已超过最高峰。

2 raise the roof 欢呼庆祝,喧闹;大声抱怨,责骂,发怒

They raised the roof at the party with their noisy singing. 他们在聚会上大唱大嚷,闹翻了天。

Father will raise the roof when he hears what you've done. 父亲知道了你干的事一定会大发雷霆。

root

1 at (the) root 实际上，实质上

And of course there is no moral equivalence. But there is a psychological parallel, and at root it is not an unattractive spirit. 虽然这并不是道德的天平，但是从心理学上解释，这类行为的本质并不一定就是丑恶。

2 root, hog or die/root-hog-or-die 【美】不辛勤工作，便会挨饿；要么成功，要么失败；要么接受，要么拒绝

A red-faced rookie from the University of Michigan screamed, "Root, hog or die!" 密歇根大学队一名新队员急得满脸通红地喊道："要硬拼，不拼就完了！"

3 strike at the root(s) 摧毁……的基础；拒绝，根除

Give me the strength to strike at the root of penury in my heart. 请赐予我力量，使我能根除内心贫瘠的根源。

4 strike/take root 固定下来，成为风气；深入人心

His ideas have been taken root in the minds of his followers. 他的主张已经在他的追随者的心中扎了根。

rope

1 be on the high ropes 兴高采烈，趾高气扬；傲慢，自高自大

The prizewinner was quite on the high ropes. 那位中奖者非常得意。

2 fight with a rope round one's neck 拼死地抵抗，破釜沉舟，拼死决战

3 give sb. plenty of rope 给某人更多的活动余地，不干涉某人

4 give sb. rope enough to hang himself 任某人为所欲为而自食其果

5 know the ropes 内行，晓得诀窍；熟悉风俗习惯；熟悉内幕

Rebecca thought she knew the ropes about teaching. 丽贝卡认为她对教学很在行。

I've been to Japan before so I know the ropes. 我去过日本，所以我熟悉那里的风俗习惯。

6 learn the ropes/【美】get on to the ropes 熟悉内幕，搞清情况

Now you have to get in the swing of things and learn the ropes. 现在，你必须适应新环境，熟悉新工作。

7 rope in/into 欺骗，愚弄，使人中计，拉……加入，说服……去做

The company ropes in high school students to sell magazine subscriptions by telling them big stories of how much money they can earn. 这个公司用能赚大钱的谎话诱骗高中生推销订阅杂志。

Jerry let the big boys rope him into stealing some apples. 杰里被大男孩骗去偷苹果。

8 throw a rope to 在危难中帮助

9 work the ropes 操纵，暗中指使

rose

1 be not all roses （工作、事情等）并非完美

Life isn't all roses. 人生并不是一切都称心如意。

2 come out smelling of roses 出污泥而不染，保持清白

3 come up roses 结果良好

Everything came up roses. 结果一切都好。

4 gather (life's) roses 寻欢作乐

Her aim was to gather roses whilst she might. 她的生活宗旨是及时行乐。

5 under the rose 秘密地，私下地

William told me the whole truth under the rose. 威廉悄悄地把全部真相都告诉了我。

Do what you like under the rose, but don't give a sign of what you're about. 暗中怎么干都行，只是不要露出一点痕迹。

round

1 round on/upon 攻击；告密，出卖

Just because you've lost your temper, you needn't round on me. 你用不着因为自己发脾气就对我乱骂一通。

2 round up 集合，赶在一起，包围

rout

rout out 逐出；找来，拉来，拽起来

You should be routed out. 你得被赶走。

I routed him out of bed at dawn. 我在拂晓时拉他起床。

row

1 a hard/long/rough/stiff/the devil's own row to hoe 【美】困难、麻烦的事，艰巨的任务

It's possible, but he has a rough row to hoe. 这事虽有可能，但也够他干的了。

You are certainly given yourself the devil's own row to hoe. 你真是给自己找麻烦事做。

2 a new row to hoe 【美】新任务，新工作，新企图

Robin has a new row to hoe, a long and a rough one. 罗宾有个新工作要干，是个既费时间又费劲的工作。

3 hoe a big row 【美】干大事，执行重要任务，出色地完成任务

4 hoe another row 【美】从事新的事业；着手新的工作

5 hoe one's (own) row 【美】自力更生，自扫门前雪，独善其身，靠自己谋生，独立谋生

David's father died when he was little, and he has always had to hoe his own row. 戴维小时候就死了父亲，他只好自力更生。

6 hold your row 别吵，住口

Clay cried, "Hold your row, will you?" 克莱叫道："别吵了，好不好？"

7 make/kick up/raise a row/dust 参见 dust 3

8 what's the row 为什么吵闹，怎么回事儿

rub

1 rub along/on/through 勉强相处；相处融洽；勉强度日

In the past they managed to rub along together. 过去他们能友好相处。

In spite of financial difficulties, Orlando is rubbing along. 奥兰多经济虽然困难，但日子还过得去。

2 rub down 搜身；申斥，痛骂

The policeman rubbed down the suspicious stranger, who turned out to be a spy. 警察搜查了那个可疑的陌生人，原来是个间谍。

3 rub in/into 反复讲某种教训或不愉快的事；强调

The lesson needs to be well rubbed in. 这个教训有必要好好地讲。

Parents often try to rub into their children how much they owe to them. 父母常常试图向子女强调他们欠父母多少。

4 rub off 显得暗淡,减色

With the passing of time some of the glitter of the achievement has rubbed off. 随着时间的推移,这项成就渐失光彩。

5 rub off on/onto 因接触或相处而对……产生影响

Bad habits were rubbing off on them. 坏习惯正在传染给他们。

Jimmy is very lucky; I wish some of his luck would rub off on me. 吉米运气好,我希望也能沾他点光。

6 rub on 勉强对付过去,勉强度过;涂上,抹上

Every morning Nora rubs cold cream on her face. 诺拉每天早晨往脸上搽冷霜。

7 rub out 不念旧恶,忘掉宿怨;【美】杀死

The gangsters rubbed out four policemen before they were caught. 匪徒们在被捕前杀了四名警员。

8 rub the wrong way 使人不悦,引起反感,烦扰

John's bragging rubbed the other boys the wrong way. 约翰的高调炫耀让别的男孩反感。

9 rub up 温习,提高,唤起记忆

I'll have to rub up my French before I go to Paris. 我去巴黎前得把法语复习一下。

10 there's/here lies the rub 这就是困难所在,问题就在这里

We'd like to travel, but here lies the rub that we had no money. 我们喜欢旅游,问题是没有钱。

run

1 a run for one's money 剧烈的竞争;出了钱或力而得到的满足

One optimist argues logistics companies that kept NATO in supplies could give Pakistan's truckers a run for their money. 乐观者说,往来于北约与当地的物流公司给巴基斯坦的货运司机们带来了收入。

2 go and have a run 走开,滚,去你的

If you don't like the job, go and have a run. 如果你不喜欢这个工作,那就滚。

3 on the/a dead run 忙个不停

Mum is on the dead run from the time she wakes up at 7:30 a. m. until

1:30 a.m. next morning. 母亲从早上7点半醒来就一直忙到第二天凌晨1点半。

4 on the run 奔忙着，奔跑着，在逃

The speaker says the extremist cleric is on the run and keeps changing his locations. 发言人说，这名极端主义教士在逃，并不断改变地点。

5 run/chase around 交际，交友，交往

They've been running around together for some time. 他们交往已经有些时候了。

6 run down 批评，贬低，诽谤

Suzy ran down the club because the girls wouldn't let her join. 因为女孩们不接受她为会员，苏西就大肆诋毁这个团体。

7 (make a) run for it 快跑，躲避，奔跑逃命

As soon as they heard the siren, they ran for it. 他们一听到警报声就奔跑躲避。

8 run in 拘留；小坐一会儿

Partridge was run in for speeding. 帕特里奇因开车超速被拘留。
The neighbour boy ran in for a minute to see Bob's model rocket. 邻居小孩来小坐一会儿，看鲍勃的模型火箭。

9 run into the ground 过分的行动或要求

It's all right to borrow my hammer once in a while, but don't run it into the ground. 偶尔借用一下我的锤子倒没什么关系，可是别太过分喽。

10 run it close/fine （时间、金钱等）刚够用

On consulting his watch, he found he had run things rather fine. 他看了看手表，发现时间刚好来得及。

11 run out 【美】赶走

If Norris refuses to leave, they will run him out. 如果诺里斯不离开，他们将把他赶走。

12 run out on 突然离开，逃离；不支持；抛弃，遗弃；背弃诺言

John ran out on his poor wife. 约翰遗弃了他可怜的妻子。
Quiller ran out on the landlady without paying his rent. 奎勒没付给女房东房租就溜了。

13 run round 伺候

Don't expect me run you round for the rest of your life! 别指望我伺候你一辈子！

S

sail

sail in/into 毅然去做，精神抖擞地干起来；痛骂，猛击

Samuel saw his work and sailed in. 塞缪尔看到他应干的活，就精神抖擞地干了起来。

Taylor sailed in with one question after another. 泰勒开始进攻，提出一个又一个问题。

I couldn't understand why Ellen sailed into her sister so hard. 我真不明白，埃伦为什么这么严厉地责骂她的妹妹。

sake

1 for God's/Heaven's/land's sake 参见 heaven 2

2 sakes alive 参见 alive 4

salt

1 salt away/down 储存

Tony salted away part of his wages each month. 托尼每月把工资的一部分存起来。

2 salt of the earth 社会中坚，最优秀的人，最高尚的人

The newspaper described the young group who helped in the local old people's home as the salt of the earth. 报纸称帮助当地老人之家的年轻人群体是社会的中坚力量。

3 worth one's salt 称职的，胜任的，受尊敬的

Any engineer worth his salt should know how that machine works. 任何一个称职的技师都应该知道那台机器是怎么运行的。

sam

upon my sam 势必，一定，我敢发誓，实实在在，千真万确

same

1 all the same 完全一样，毫无区别，无所谓；仍然

If it all the same to you, I think I'll go now! 如果你无所谓的话，我想我现在就走！

I know he's rich, but all the same, it doesn't mean he's got an endless supply of money, you know! 我知道他很有钱，但他的钱并不是取之不尽的呀！

2 same here 参见 here 6

3 (the) same again, (please) （请）同样的再来一份

4 (the) same but/only different 几乎一样，略微不同

5 (the) same to you 我也同样祝愿你，你也一样（后跟 with brass knobs on 以加强语气）

"Happy Christmas!" "The same to you!" "祝你圣诞节快乐！" "祝你一样！"

"I wish you'd go and jump in a lake!" "The same to you!" "我愿你出去就掉进湖里！" "你也一样！"

sand

1 go/run into the sand(s) 陷入困境

There is a sense that the Asian upswing may have run into the sand slightly but it was coming from a very strong base so it was anticipated we would see some slowdown. 有迹象显示亚洲的复苏可能已经略微陷入困境，但是复苏源于一个十分坚强的基础，所以可以预见的是我们将会看见亚洲经济有些放缓。

2 have sand in one's craw【美】有勇气，有胆量，有毅力

If you have sand in your craw and determination, you'll succeed. 如果你有毅力和决心，你就一定会成功。

3 number/plough/sow the sand(s) 白费力气，徒劳无功

Pound was really just ploughing the sand. 庞德不过是在白费力气。

4 put/throw sand in the wheels/machine 妨碍，阻扰，捣乱

The terrorist attack put sand in the wheels of the ongoing peace talk. 恐怖袭击阻挠了正在进行的和平谈判的进程。

5 raise sand【美】引起骚乱，大吵大闹

6 the sands (of time) are running out 时间不多了，期限快到了

sauce

1 none of your sauce, child/not sauce 孩子，不要没规矩

Good boys don't sauce their mothers! 好孩子不会对母亲没规矩!
2 serve sb. with the same sauce 以其人之道还治其人之身

save

1 (God) save me from my friends 这样的好意我可受不了
2 save one's breath 省点力气,别费口舌
Save your breath, the boss will never give you the day off. 省点力气吧,老板绝不会准你假的。
3 save one's neck/skin 参见 neck 9
4 save the day 转危为安,反败为胜
The forest fire was nearly out of control when suddenly it rained heavily and saved the day. 一场森林大火几乎控制不住,但突然下起了大雨,我们这才转危为安。
5 save us 天哪(惊讶)
6 saving your presence 恕我直言,恕我冒昧
Saving your presence, I don't think the suggestion is very sensible. 恕我直言,我认为这个建议不太合情理。
7 you may save your pains/trouble 不必白费劲了

say

1 and so say all of us 我们也是这么说的,我们也是这个意思
"I'm sure we'll want to express our deepest gratitude to our guest speaker tonight!" "Yes, and so say all of us!" "我确信我们大家都愿意向今晚给我们讲话的客人致以最诚挚的谢意!""对呀,我们都是这个意思!"
2 as you say 是,遵命,照办(常用于说话人并不愿意)
"That's absolute nonsense!" "As you say so, sir!" "那全是胡说!""是,先生!"
"We must leave at once. Come on, pack your bags!" "As you say!" "我们必须马上离开这里,来吧,打好背包!""遵命!"
3 (do) you mean to say 你真的要……吗(表示惊讶、怀疑)
You mean to say you're leaving us? 你真的要离开我们吗?
Do you mean to say I've come all this way for nothing? 你真的以为我这趟来一无所获吗?
4 don't say 你是说……(表示烦躁、惊讶、反诘)

Don't say I've gone and locked my key in the car! 你是说是我走时把钥匙锁在车里了!

5　have nothing to say for oneself 没话可说;哑口无言

6　how say you 你还有什么要说的(用于法庭书记员宣读起诉书后,开始审判时法官问被告);诸位高见(法官请陪审团裁决时问)

How say you? Are you guilty or not guilty? 你还有什么说的,你认罪吗?

7　I can't say 我并不这样认为(委婉地表示否定)

To tell you the truth, *I can't say* I like your choice of wallpaper! 说实话,我并不十分喜欢你选的墙纸。

8　I couldn't say 我不知道,我说不上来

"How many people came to the party?" "*I couldn't say*—perhaps twenty, perhaps forty, it's difficult to tell." "有多少人参加了舞会?" "我说不上来,可能二十,也可能四十,很难说得准。"

9　I dare say 　参见 dare 2

10　I'll say 当然

I'll say this is a good movie! 这自然是部好影片。

11　I'll say this much 我要说的是(用以正面评价人或物)

I'll say this much for him—he's always honest, even if he is poor dressed. 我要说的是,他始终是个诚实的人,尽管他穿着朴素。

12　I'm not just saying this 我说话算话,我说的是实话

We've appreciated your help enormously, and *I'm not just saying this*. 我们非常感谢您的大力帮助,我说的是实话。

13　I'm not saying 我不愿作答,我不发表意见(表示拒绝回答)

14　I mean to say/I mean 哎呀(表示惊讶、怀疑或厌恶);我的意思是(表示澄清或进一步说明)

Well, *I mean to say*! Who does she think she is? Coming in here and telling us how to run the kitchen! 哎呀,我真不明白,她以她是谁? 居然跑到这儿来指手画脚教我们下厨房烹饪!

15　I must say 依我看,我认为(用以加强带有批评性的意见或评论的口气)

It's not the most exciting novel I've ever read, *I must say*, but it wasn't too bad. 依我看,这不是我读过的最令人激动的小说,但它也不算太坏。

16　I say 我说,听着(用以引起话头或注意);哎呀,你看,好家伙(表示轻微的惊讶、恼怒、遗憾等)

17 I should say 我猜想,我认为,大概,也许

18 I wouldn't say 我不得不承认(但仍有保留)

I wouldn't say we're not happily married—it's just that do seem to have more than our fair share of quarrels. 我不得不承认我们的婚姻也算得上幸福,但是在我们之间确实还存在着除了经常争吵以外的其他事情。

19 I wouldn't say no 好的,是(礼貌地回答)

"Would you like another piece of cake?" "I wouldn't say no!" "再来一块蛋糕好吗?" "好的。"

20 I wouldn't say that/I'm not saying that 我看不行(客气地表示不同意)

"So you think £100 will be enough?" "I wouldn't say that—I was thinking of nearer £500." "你看 100 英镑够吗?" "我看不行,我想在 500 英镑左右。"

21 if I may/might say so 照我看来(表示客气、委婉的语气)

If I may say so, that jacket doesn't quite fit you. 依我看,那件上衣不合你的身。

22 (let's) say 让我们说定

We'll meet, say, at six o'clock. 我们就定在六点钟见面吧。

What if I were to offer you, let's say, £1,000 for the whole lot? 我给你 1 000 英镑买下全部怎么样?

23 never say die 别灰心,别气馁

Margaret spoke to me gently, "Never say die! It won't last forever!" 玛格丽特轻声对我说:"别灰心,这种局面不会长久的。"

24 say away 有话就直说吧

25 say what you like 不管怎么说

Say what you like, it won't make me change my mind! 不管怎么说,这不会使我改变主意!

26 say when 可以了吗,好了吗(告诉对方可以开始或停止某个动作)

"Say when!" "Right, that's enough, thanks." "好了吗?" "好了,够了,谢谢。"

"Say when!" "When!" "好了吗?" "好了!"

As soon as you're ready, say when, and I'll switch on. 你准备好了就说一声,我就打开开关。

27 says you/says who 【美】你胡扯,去你的(表示不信、不接受或用于取

笑、反驳)

"Our team will win today!" "Says you! We'll beat yours easily!" "我们的球队今天会赢!""去你的,我们队毫不费力就能打败你们队!"

"I'm taking Jo to the party." "Says who? She's my girlfriend, not yours!" "我要带乔参加舞会。""去你的,她是我的女朋友,不是你的!"

28 so you say 是你这么说的吗(意指事实并非如此)

So you say the outside door was closed when you got here? 也就是说,当你到这儿的时候,外面的门是锁着的。

29 that's what you say 这只不过是你的看法罢了(意指还有人不同意)

That's what you say, but I'm sure your sister wouldn't agree with you! 那只是你的想法吧,但是我可以肯定你姐姐就不会同意!

30 they say 据说,听说,有人说

They say "Nothing succeeds like success." And I am certainly proving it in my business! 俗话说,"一事顺,百事顺。"我一定要在我的事业上证明这句话。

31 though I say it/so myself 不是我自己夸口

I think I've made a good job of decorating this room, though I say so myself. 不是我自己夸口,这房子经过我装饰以后大不一样了。

32 what would/do you say to 你同意吗,你看好不好

What would you say to a cup of tea? 来一杯茶怎么样?

What do you say to a walk? 出去散散步好不好?

33 when all is said and done 结果,到底,归根结蒂

When all is said and done, a person's most important possession is his health. 说到底,一个人最重要的财富还是健康。

34 you can say that (again)/you said it 我同意,你说对了

"I don't think he looks after his wife." "You can say that again he goes out drinking with his friends every night." "我看他根本不照顾他的妻子。""你说对了,他每天晚上出去和朋友喝酒。"

35 you could say that 可以这么说,但……

"He's plump, isn't he?" "You could say that, but he's not too fat, really." "他长得很壮实,是吗?""不错,但他并不太胖,真的!"

36 you don't say 未必吧,不会吧,没有的事吧,真的吗

"We're thinking of emigrating to Australia next year." "You don't say? I

thought you were very happy here." "我们打算明年移居澳大利亚。" "真的吗？我看你们在这儿不也是蛮好的嘛。"
37 you may well say so 你说得完全正确
38 you said it 对了，正是如此，我同意
"That sure was a good show." "You said it!" "那的确是一场精彩的演出。" "你说对了！"

saying

1 as the saying is/goes 正如俗话所说，常言道
Where you are dropped, as the saying is, is who you are, at least in a certain limited sense. 正如古语所言，你出生的地方决定了你是谁，至少在某种有限的意义上是这样的。

2 there's no saying 很难说，说不准
There's no saying how the experiment will develop. 说不准实验将如何进展。

scare

1 (as) scared as a rabbit 吓得要命，惊慌失措，如惊弓之鸟

2 scare out of one's wits/scare stiff/scare the daylights out of 吓坏了
The owl's hooting scared him out of his wits. 猫头鹰的叫声把他吓坏了。

3 scare/scrape up 努力收集，匆匆凑合
The boy scared up enough money to go to college. 这孩子筹措了上大学的钱。

score

1 clear/pay/quit a score/scores/pay off/settle/wipe off one's score 清账，还清债务
You'll clear a score after you get paid. 你领到钱后就可偿清债务了。

2 go/set off at score/go off at full score/start at score 情不自禁地说（做）；全速飞跑；精神抖擞地出发

3 (make a) score off sb. 驳倒某人
Ralph couldn't make a score off his opponent. 拉尔夫在与对手的辩论中无法占上风。

4 make a score off one's bat 独自干

5 **pay/wipe off old scores** 清算老账，报复

Now is the time for you to pay off old scores. 现在是你报仇雪恨的时候了。

Scott

Great Scott/guns 老天爷（表示惊讶）

Great Scott! Who stole my watch? 老天爷，是谁偷了我的表？

Great guns! The lion is out of his cage. 哎呀，狮子跑出笼子了！

scratch

1 **a/the scratch of a/the pen** 大笔一挥的签名；简单手令

The business could be settled by the scratch of a pen. 那件事大笔一挥签一下字就可以办成。

2 **from scratch** 从头开始，白手起家

They started their business from scratch. 他们白手起家办企业。

3 **no great scratch/shakes** 【美】没什么了不起，不重要，很平常

That restaurant is no great scratch. 那家餐厅很平常。

4 **scratch up**（艰难地）凑集，拼凑；挖出

I'll manage to scratch up some money somehow. 我要设法凑一点钱。

5 **up to scratch/par/snuff** 准备好；达到标准；处于良好状态

His health is not up to scratch. 他的健康状况不佳。

Also, I found that in a lot of fields my English vocabulary wasn't up to par. 我也发现在很多领域我的英文词汇没有达到一定的水平。

6 **without a scratch** 安然无恙，一点儿也没受伤

They might be, for example, in an accident, and come close to being killed, but walk away without a scratch. 比如说他们在事故中幸存，差点送命，但结果毫发无伤。

screw

1 **a screw loose** 故障，毛病

There's a screw loose in your affairs. 你的事情不是很顺利。

2 **have a screw loose/missing** 神经不正常，有点疯疯癫癫，古怪，低能

Tom was a smart man but had a screw loose. 汤姆长得很帅，可行为有点古怪。

3 put the screw(s) on/to sb. / apply the screw to sb. / turn the screws on sb. 对某人施加压力，强迫某人

If Needham won't give us the money, we'll have to put the screws on him. 如果尼达姆不给我们钱，我们就得对他施加压力。

4 screw around 游手好闲，溜达

You guys are no longer welcome here; all you do is screw around all day. 你们不再受欢迎，你们整天只是鬼混。

5 screw up 弄糟，毁坏，毁灭；使紧张，使神经失常；鼓起勇气，壮壮胆子

Isabel had screwed up and had to do it all over again. 伊莎贝尔把事情弄糟了，只好重新返工。

Halifax is really screwed up about his exams. 哈利法克斯对考试真是紧张得要命。

Hicks screwed up his courage to ask her to marry him. 希克斯鼓起勇气向她求婚。

sea

1 be (all) at sea 困惑，摸不着头脑

I'm all at sea when people talk about abstract painting. 当人们谈论抽象派绘画时，我不知所云。

2 go (and) jump in the sea 投海去死吧（表示恼怒、厌烦）

seam

1 burst at the seams 胀破；过于拥挤

The city is already bursting at the seams. 这座城市已经拥挤不堪。

John ate too much and was bursting at the seams. 约翰吃得太多，肚子快胀破了。

2 come/fall/break apart at the seams 破裂，崩溃，失败

Their friendship is falling apart at the seams. 他们的友谊正在破裂。

search

search me【美】我不知道，我怎么知道

"Where's Barry got to?" "Search me! I've no idea!" "巴里到哪儿了？" "我不知道，我一点也不知道！"

second

1　not for a second 毫不，一点也不

"Didn't you ever suspect he was guilty?" "No, not for a second." "你怀疑过他有罪吗?""没有，从来没有。"

2　second after 日复一日地

3　second to none 首屈一指，不比任何人差

As a football player, John is second to none. 约翰作为一名足球运动员是首屈一指的。

see

1　as far as I can see 就我看来，据我了解

As far as I can see, the only honourable course of action open to you is to resign immediately. 在我看来，对你来说唯一较体面的行动是立即主动辞职。

2　as I see it 我认为

As I see it, you can either invest the money or spend it! 我认为，这笔钱你可以用来投资，也可以花掉。

3　do you see (what I mean)/don't you see 你明白我的意思吗，你看见了吧

If you extend the shelves this way, then that'll give us a lot more room—do you see what I mean? 如果我们把书橱这样摆开，我们的房间就会有更大的空间。你明白我的意思吗？

4　I'll/we'll be seeing you 再见（用于朋友间）

5　I see what you mean 我明白你的意思了；正像你所说的

6　let me see 让我看看/想想

7　see about 考虑

We can't decide now, but we'll see about that. 我们现在还不能决定，但我们会考虑的。

8　see daylight 看见结局，成功在望；领会，搞懂

John explained it again, and at last I began to see daylight. 约翰又解释了一遍，我总算明白了。

9　see here 喂，听我说（引起注意或表示警告、不赞同等）

See here, boys, you mustn't ever do that again. 孩子们，听着，你们再也

不能干那种事了。

10 see nothing/much/a lot/little/more/less of 从来没有/经常/常常/很少/较多/较少见过……

The shoot took place four months before Marilyn tragically died, and yet we see nothing of a woman on the verge of a breakdown. 这张照片拍摄于梦露死前四个月,从照片中我们看不出一点崩溃的迹象。

11 see off 赶出,赶走;为……送行

They were seen off. 他们被赶走了。

Please don't trouble to see me off at the station. 请不用麻烦到车站送我了。

12 see red 参见 red 5

13 see sb. dead/damned/blowed/hanged/in hell/further (first) 绝不,死也不

I'll see you dead before I accept your terms. 见鬼去吧,我才不会接受你的条件呢。

14 see stars 眼冒金星,头昏眼花

My mother's head hit the desk. It made her see stars. 我妈妈的头撞在了桌子上,这使她眼冒金星,头昏眼花。

15 see the color of one's money 确认……有钱

Before I show you the diamond, let me see the color of your money. 在拿出钻石之前,请让我看看你是否确实有钱。

16 see the light 了解;同意

I didn't approve of his action, but he explained his reason and then I saw the light. 我并不赞同他的行为,但经他解释以后,我才了解。

17 see things 想象,以为不是真的

I had not seen him for twenty years and when we met on the street I thought I was seeing things. 我已经二十年没见到他了,当我们在街上遇见时,我还以为不是真的。

18 see to it that 注意,务必做到,保证

We'll see to it that she gets home early. 我们一定要让她早早回家。

19 so I see 这下我明白了;叫你说对了;那还用说

"I'm afraid I've brought in all this mud onto your carpet!" "So I see!" "我把泥土都带到你的地毯上来了!""那还用说吗!"

20 we'll see about it/that 你等着瞧吧（意欲制止某事）

You say the kids are playing behind the sheds again—we'll soon see about that. 你说那些孩子又在棚子后面玩，你等着瞧吧！

21 you see 你看，你知道，听我说，要知道（用作插入语）

22 you see if 你等着瞧吧

Hansom will quietly forget about all that money he owes you, you see if he won't. 汉萨会不声不响地把借你钱的事忘掉，你等着瞧吧。

sell

1 sell out 出卖，背叛；向……屈服，投降，被收买；牺牲

Daniel's going to sell out on us. 丹尼尔将出卖我们。

We would rather die than sell out our comrades. 我们宁死也不出卖自己的同志。

2 sell short 低估，轻视

Don't sell yourself short. 别低估你自己。

send

1 send down 判徒刑，使坐牢

Connor was sent down for ten years for robbing a bank. 康纳因抢劫银行而被判十年徒刑。

2 send sb. to hell (across lots)/the devil (across lots) 叫某人见鬼去吧

3 send up【美】判徒刑

Chapman was sent up for life. 查普曼被判处终身监禁。

sense

1 make sense 言之成理，合情合理

The plan made sense. 这项计划是合情合理的。

It makes sense to take care of your health. 注意身体健康是明智的。

What Browning says doesn't make sense. 布朗宁说的话毫无意义。

2 make sense of 理解，明白

Can you make sense of what he says? 你能明白他说的意思吗?

3 talk sense 说话有理

Beck was talking sense for once. 这一回贝克总算说出了一番有道理的话。

Don't interrupt him; he's talking sense. 别打断他，他说的有道理。

separate

separate the men from the boys 疾风知劲草，路遥知马力

When the ship hit an iceberg and sank, it separated the men from the boys. 当船撞上冰山而沉没时，便会知道谁是真正的男子汉了。

The mile run separates the men from the boys. 一英里赛跑可以测出人的体能和耐力。

serve

(it/that) serves sb. right 真活该，罪有应得

I've just heard Rod failed his exams—I think it serves him right as he didn't do any work for them. 我刚听说罗德考试不及格，这是他自作自受，因为他根本没做任何准备。

service

1 at one's service 听……吩咐，为……效劳，任凭……使唤

If you need any help I'm at your service. 如果你需要什么帮助的话，我当为你效劳。

The car is at your service. 这辆车供你使用。

2 it's all part of the service/it's what we're here for 这是我份内的事，这是应该的

"I want to thank you very much for seeing that I have all my shopping!" "It's all part of the service, madam!" "非常感谢你把我买的东西都送来了！""这是我份内的事，夫人！"

3 pay/give lip service to 口头承认/赞成/答应

Malory only pays lip service to that principle. 马洛里对那项原则只是口头上承认，并不真正执行。

set

1 all set 做好充分准备

I'm all set to go into chicken farming. 我已做好从事养鸡业的充分准备。

2 set about 袭击，攻击，抨击；开始做

They set about each other at once. 他们立刻互相扭打起来。

3 set back 使花费

The legal costs of the case set Luke back £10,000. 这场官司花了卢克一万英镑。

4 set/knock back on one's heels 突然惊扰别人, 扯人后腿

The question that set the press back on its heels was the last one. 让新闻界着实大吃一惊的是最后那个问题。

5 set down 谴责, 申斥, 训斥

I was obliged to set him down. 我不得不训斥他一顿。

6 set one's cap at/for/on sb. 参见 cap 3

7 set store by 爱好, 欣赏, 想要

George sets great store by that old tennis racket. 乔治极其喜爱那只旧网球拍。

8 set the world on fire 表现杰出, 大放异彩

Mary could set the world on fire with her piano playing. 玛丽能成为杰出的钢琴演奏家。

9 set to 开始起劲地干；开始大吃大喝；开始打起来、吵起来

We all set to and got the place cleaned up in no time. 我们一齐大干起来, 一会儿就把那地方打扫干净了。

When they reached home, they were hungry and at once set to. 他们回到家时都饿了, 马上狼吞虎咽地吃了起来。

10 set up 端上酒或饮料；他人付酒饭钱, 请客；冤枉, 诬陷

I'll set up next round. 下一回酒钱我付。

I'm not to blame; I've been set up. 我没有过错, 是遭人诬陷。

shade

1 put/throw/cast in/into the shade 使黯然失色, 使相形见绌

His sudden success put us all in the shade. 他的突然成功使我们大家相形见绌。

2 shades of 使联想起……

Shades of school! We were all treated at the conference as if we were children. 我联想到了学生时代, 在会上我们都被当成小孩子一样对待。

shadow

1 be afraid/frightened of one's (own) shadow 极为胆小

Adela won't stay alone in her house at night; she is afraid of her own shadow. 阿德拉晚上不肯单独留在家里，她连自己的影子都怕。

2 be worn to a shadow 极其虚弱，疲乏无力

Albert was playing football with the children all afternoon. He was worn to a shadow when he came in. 艾伯特整个下午都和孩子们踢足球，回来时已筋疲力尽。

3 catch/shoot at shadows/chase shadows/run after a shadow 捕风捉影，徒劳

You can't spend all your life chasing shadows. 你不能一辈子追求虚无缥缈的东西。

4 may your shadow never grow less 祝你永远健康，祝你长命百岁，愿你万事如意

shake

1 be on the shake 【美】参与敲诈、勒索等犯罪活动

2 give sb./sth. the shake 避开，摆脱某人/某事

3 in a shake/in two shakes/in half a shake/in two shakes of a lamb's tail/in a brace/couple of shakes 很快，马上

I'll be back in two shakes. 我马上就回来。

4 no great shakes 参见 great 4

5 put sb. on the shake/put the shake on sb. 【美】向某人勒索钱财

6 shake down 【美】勒索，敲诈

The gangsters shook the store owner down every month. 这帮歹徒每月向店主敲诈钱财。

7 shake it up 赶紧，加紧

Shake it up, we don't have much time. 快点，我们没多少时间了。

8 shake in one's shoes/boots 参见 boot 16

9 shake off 逃离，摆脱跟踪；除掉

A convict escaped from the prison and shook off the officers trying to follow him. 囚犯逃出监狱并摆脱了追捕他的警员。

Tom could not shake off his cold. 汤姆的感冒总是不好。

10 shake on it 握手（问候、和解时）

Arnold held out a hand to me,"Shall we shake on it?" 阿诺德向我伸出手

说:"让我们握手好吗?"

11 shake up 重新分配,改组;激励,使振作;困扰,打扰,使不安
The new chairman will shake up the company. 新任主席将重组公司。
The collision shook up both drivers. 两车相撞使双方司机受惊不小。

shame

1 cry shame on 指责……,痛斥……
The pavement was detestable; all foreigners cried shame on it. 路面糟透了,所有外国人都同声指责。

2 (fie) for shame/shame on you 真丢脸,真可耻,不像话
Shame on you, Peter, for behaving like that—I'd thought you'd know better! 彼得,你真可耻,竟然做那样的事! 我原以为你知道该怎么做!
Can you forget old friends? Fie for shame! 你把老朋友都忘了吗? 真不像话!

3 what a shame 多丢脸,多遗憾,多倒霉,太不像话
"Mary's cat has died.""What a shame!" "玛丽的猫死了。""多倒霉!"
What a shame that he didn't win! 他输了,多不走运!

shape

1 in (good/top) shape 处于良好状态;处于最佳状态
My health was in top shape again. 我的健康又达到了最佳状态。

2 lick/put/knock/whip/pound/hammer sth. into shape 把某物敲打成形;把某物整理好;使某物更完美
It cost me a lot of money to knock this old house into shape. 修整这座旧房子花了我不少钱。
I have a rough draft of the article finished, but I still have to lick it into shape. 这篇文章的草稿我已完成,但还得加以修改。

3 out of shape/in bad/poor shape 处于不良状态
I get tired easily; I must be out of shape. 我很容易感到疲劳,我的健康一定出了什么问题。

4 shape in with【美】与……鬼混,与……交往
Tell him not to go on shaping in with such company. 叫他别再跟那种人混在一起了。

5 shape up 使成形;发展顺利;准备就绪;循规蹈矩,变得守规矩

If the new boy doesn't begin to shape up soon, he'll have to leave school. 如果新来的男孩不好好用功,他只有离开学校。
Plans for our picnic are shaping up very well. 我们的野餐计划进展顺利。

share

go shares 分享;分担;合伙经营
Let's go shares, halves! 让我们一起分担,一人一半。

sharp

1 be sharp about it/sharp's the word 快点,赶快
2 look sharp 留神,注意;赶快
Now look sharp, or we'll be late. 好啦,抓紧些,否则我们要迟到了。
It pays to look sharp in traffic. 注意交通安全大有益处。
3 sharp as a needle 很有鉴别力,异常精明
William had a mind as sharp as a needle. 威廉是一个头脑精明的人。
4 sharp as a razor 异常锋利;非常精明的,非常机灵的
The fellow is as sharp as a razor. Be careful in your dealings with him. 这家伙厉害得很,你和他打交道时要特别小心。
5 sharp as a tack 干净利落;整整齐齐;很聪明
Tom is sharp as a tack; he got 100 on every test. 汤姆很聪明,每次测验都是 100 分。
6 sharp up【美】打扮得漂漂亮亮
We decided to sharp up for the dinner party. 我们决定要打扮一番去赴宴。

shell

1 come out of one's shell 参见 out 13
2 go/retire into/in one's shell 变得沉默寡言,不愿与人接触
After her mother scolded her, Mary went into her shell. 玛丽受母亲责备以后变得沉默寡言。
3 shell out 送给;交款,付款
Dick had to shell out a lot of money for his new car. 迪克为他的新车要付一大笔钱。
The note is due; shell out right off. 票据到期了,那就付款吧。

shine

1 shine up to【美】百般讨好

Men shine up to Mary like moths to the light. 男人们如同飞蛾扑火般地向玛丽献殷勤。

2 take a shine to【美】喜欢，喜爱

They took a shine to each other. 他们彼此爱恋。

3 take the shine out of 使失去光泽；使失去欢乐；使相形见绌

Liza's dress took the shine out of all the female guests. 丽莎的衣着使所有女宾的服装黯然失色。

ship

1 give up the ship　参见 bet 2

2 ship out 离职，辞职；解雇

Shape up or ship out! 放规矩点，要不就滚蛋！

3 when/if one's ship comes home/in 当发财的时候

When my ship comes in, I shall take a trip to Norway. 什么时候发了财，我就去挪威旅行。

shirt

1 bet/put/get one's shirt on 把所有的钱都押在……上，孤注一掷；确信

The horse lost, and Jim had put his shirt on it! 这匹马输了，而吉姆把钱全押在了这匹马身上！

2 have/get one's shirt off/out 发怒

3 give sb. a wet shirt 把某人累得汗流浃背

4 give the shirt off one's back　参见 give 35

5 keep one's shirt/hair on　参见 hair 2

6 lose one's shirt【美】失去一切，丧失全部财产；发怒，失去自制力

Mr. Matthews lost his shirt betting on the horses. 马修斯先生赌马，输得精光。

shit

1 eat shit 卑躬屈膝，蒙受屈辱

2 get one's shit/head together【美】镇静下来，稳定情绪，克制

3 in the/one's shit 处于困境

Kelvin's waist deep in his shit. 凯尔文现在处境异常狼狈。

4 not give/care a shit 毫不在意

I don't give a shit what other people say. 别人说什么我都不在乎。

5 not worth a shit/leek 毫无用处，分文不值

What he said is not worth a shit. 他所说的话毫无价值。

6 shit on 轻蔑对待

It throws shit on all pretensions and fictions. 它蔑视一切伪装和虚构的东西。

We all have shipmates we remember. Some of them were shit on and pissed on by the Pentagon. 我们都有袍泽丧命战场，有些甚至是被五角大楼的人所遗弃。

7 tough shit 要死，糟透了

8 when the shit flies/hits the fan 危机来临时，大祸临头时

When the shit hits the fan, I'll get covered with it. 一有麻烦，我就惨了。

When the shit hits the fan, I don't want to be here. 事情一旦败露，我就不想待在这儿了。

shoe

1 another pair of shoes 另外一回事，另当别论

"That, sir," answered Mr. Smith, "is quite another pair of shoes." 史密斯先生回答说："先生，那完全是另一回事了。"

2 be/stand in one's/the shoes of 取得……的地位；处在……的情况下

No man could tell what he would do if he were in the shoes of another man. 没有人能说出他取得别人的地位时他会怎么办。

3 blast my old shoes【美】见鬼，该死；如果不是，就叫我不得好死

I saw Jack in the bookshop. Blast my old shoes if I didn't. 我在书店看见了杰克，千真万确。

4 comfortable as an old shoe 参见 comfortable 1

5 common as an old shoe 参见 common 1

6 fill/step into one's shoes 代替……的地位

John could fill into Heyward's shoes well. 约翰能很好地接替海伍德的工作。

7 if the shoe fits, wear it【美】如果批评得对，就接受吧

Remember, if the shoe fits, wear it. 记住,如果别人批评得对,你就应该接受。

8 lick one's shoes/boots 参见 boot 8

9 put the shoe on the right foot/put the saddle on the right horse 赏罚分明,是非分明

It is quite natural that they should put the saddle on the right horse. 他们应该赏罚分明,这是理所当然的。

10 shake in one's shoes/boots 参见 boot 16

11 the shoe is on the other foot【美】情况大变,位置颠倒

Now that we are rich and they are poor, the shoe is on the other foot. 现在我们富了,他们穷了,位置颠倒过来了。

12 too big for one's shoes/boots【口】自高自大,目中无人

Raphael thought too much of himself and was getting too big for his shoes, though he kept his thoughts to himself. 拉菲尔少年得志,目中无人,不过没有表露出来。

13 what a pretty pair of shoes 好糟糕的局面

14 where the shoe pinches 问题的症结所在

shoot

1 I'll be shot if... 假如……的话,我就不得好死(表示否定的强调语气)

2 shoot at 试图(达到或完成);以……为目标,为……而努力

When it is achieved, there will be other goals for us to shoot at. 这事做成后,还有别的目标要我们去争取。

3 shoot down 击毙,打死;坚决拒绝;不批准;驳倒

Shoot down all who want to escape! 谁想逃跑就打死谁!

Any one of the above responses will let the person know you can easily shoot down anything they could possibly ask. 以上任何一个答案都将让那人知道,你能轻易地驳倒任何他们可能提出的问题。

4 shoot for【美】争取得到或完成;为……而努力

We're shooting this year for a 50% increase in sales. 我们正力争今年销售额增长 50%。

5 shoot off one's mouth/face 参见 face 5

6 shoot one's wad 花尽;道出心事,和盘托出

We've shot our wad for the summer and can't buy any new garden furniture. 我们夏天把钱花光了，无力再买新的花园家具。

Joe feels a lot better now that he's shot his wad at the meeting. 乔在会上说出了心里的话，感觉轻松多了。

7 shoot straight/square 言行正直，坦诚相待

You can trust that salesman; he shoots straight with his customers. 你可以相信那个售货员，他对顾客童叟无欺。

8 shoot/bat/fan the breeze/bull 参见 breeze 1

9 shoot the works 不遗余力取得或给予一切；孤注一掷；冒险

The Greens shot the works on their daughter's wedding reception. 格林夫妇倾尽全力操办他们女儿的婚礼。

The motor of Tom's boat was dangerously hot, but he decided to shoot the works and try to win the race. 船的马达已热得十分危险，但汤姆仍决定冒险干下去，以争取比赛胜利。

10 shoot up 开枪打伤，开枪乱射；制造恐怖

The cowboys got drunk and shot up the bar room. 牛仔喝醉了，在酒吧里开枪乱射。

The soldier was shot up very badly. 这名军人的枪伤很严重。

11 the whole bang shoot 全部，一切

I want all your furniture and books—the whole bang shoot—out of there by ten o'clock tomorrow. 我要你把你的家具、书等，总之一切的一切在明天十点钟以前全部搬出去。

shop

1 all over the shop 到处，四处；一片凌乱

My books are all over the shop. 我的书散得到处都是。

I searched for the dictionary all over the shop. 我到处寻找那本词典。

2 come/go to the wrong/right shop 在请求帮助、征求意见时找错/对了对象

They have come to the right shop for morals. 谈到培养德性，他们找对了地方。

What does he want? Money? Meat? Drink? He's come to the wrong shop for that, if he does. 他要的是什么呢？金钱吗？肉吗？酒吗？如果是这

样,那他就找错地方了。

3 talk shop 大谈行话,三句话不离本行
Two chemists were talking shop, and I hardly understood a word they said. 两位化学家大谈行话,我却一窍不通。

short

1 be short and sweet【谑】简短扼要,直截了当

2 get/have sb. by the short and curlies 控制住……
They've got us by the short and curlies. We have no choice but to agree. 他们完全控制了我们,我们无计可施只好同意。

shot

1 a bad shot 失算,搞错,猜错
My cousin? A bad shot, George, she's my sister. 我表妹? 你猜错了,乔治。她是我妹妹。

2 a good shot 神枪手;没失算,命中,猜中;差不多
Cowboy 3 is a good shot and can hit his target every time. 牛仔3号是一个射击好手,他每次都能击中目标。

3 a long shot 大胆的猜测或暗示,大胆的企图,可能性很小的事;一个长镜头
I admit Ellen's talented in many ways, but being a professional singer is really a long shot. 我承认埃伦在许多方面都很有才能,不过要当一个专业歌手实在是不太可能。

4 a shot in the dark 无根据的瞎猜,失策,鲁莽的行动
Because of pressure of time, the company's advertisements for their new ballpoint pen were just a shot in the dark. 由于时间紧迫,这家公司为他们的新圆珠笔做的广告真是失策。

5 be/get shot of 摆脱,完成,结束,解决,处理
I'm glad to be shot of the job. 我很高兴,摆脱/完成了那项工作。
There's a small problem I'd like to get shot of before I leave the office. 在离开办公室以前我还有个小问题要解决。

6 by a long shot/chalk 参见 chalk 2

7 call the shots/every shot 控制事态发展,操纵;发号施令;做决定
Before the union developed strength, the employers called all the shots. 在

工会羽毛未丰之时,一切还是雇主说了算。

Doyle has been calling every shot around here for almost two years. 多伊尔在这儿管事将近两年了。

8 have/take a shot at/for 尝试

I am doubtful whether I can solve the puzzle, but I'll have a shot at it. 我说不准能否解决这个难题,但我会试试看。

Why don't you take a shot at writing it yourself? 你为什么不试试自己来写?

9 like/in a shot 飞快地,立刻,突然;毫不犹豫地,乐意地

As soon as John heard the news, he was off like a shot. 听到这个消息,约翰马上就赶去了。

George would marry you like a shot. 乔治将乐意和你结婚。

10 not a shot in one's/the locker 身无分文,一文不名;毫无办法,一筹莫展

11 shot in the arm 激励,鼓舞

We were ready to quit, but the coach's talk was a shot in the arm. 我们已准备退出,但教练的话鼓舞了我们。

12 stand shot 负担全部费用,付账

Are you to stand shot to all this good liquor? 这些好酒都由你一人付账吗?

shoulder

1 lay/put/set one's shoulder to the wheel 参见 put 23

2 rub shoulders with 与(知名人士等)有交往;与……厮混在一起

It was a rare opportunity to rub shoulders with cabinet ministers. 跟内阁部长们来往是个难得的机会。

3 shoulder to shoulder 肩并肩地,齐心协力地

Mrs. Clinton spoke of standing "shoulder to shoulder" with her Democratic former rival; he gushed about "how good she is, how tough she is, how passionate she is". 希拉里称她将和她以前的对手奥巴马肩并肩地站在一起;而奥巴马则对希拉里的优秀、坚韧和热情赞不绝口。

4 square one's shoulders 挺直身子,勇敢面对

Young men must square their shoulders and face the world. 年轻人必须勇敢地直面人生。

5 straight from the shoulder 狠狠地；全力以赴地；坦率地，直截了当地
His remarks were straight from the shoulder. 他的批评一针见血。
In the end I had to speak straight from the shoulder. 最后我不得不直截了当地说了。

6 up to the/one's shoulders/ears/chin/elbows/eyes/knees/neck in 参见 chin 5

7 with a chip on one's shoulder 脾气坏，生性好斗
Rudolph is a man with a chip on his shoulder. 鲁道夫是个好寻仇吵架的人。

8 with one's shoulder to collar 紧张地，拼命地，勤劳地

shout

1 now you are shouting 你讲得好，你抓住了要害

2 shout from the housetops/rooftops 大肆宣扬
I've been wanting to shout it from the housetops that I have the best daughter in the world and this is my big chance. 我一直有个想法，就是能站在屋顶，告诉全世界的人们，我有一个世界上最棒的女儿，她是我的全部。

shove

1 shove around 摆布，虐待；盛气凌人
Kennedy would not be shoved around. 肯尼迪不会让人随便摆布。

2 shove off 离开
Shove off! I'm busy. 走开，我忙得很！
Lloyd put on his hat and shoved off for home. 劳埃德戴上帽子回家去了。

show

1 all over the show 【口】到处，遍地

2 bad/poor show (表示灰心或不满)真差劲
Bad show, Milton! A pity Joe was faster than you in the end! 真可惜，米尔顿！乔最后比你快！

3 give away the show/give the show away 泄露秘密
I wish he wouldn't give the show away. 但愿他不会泄露内幕。

4 good show 干得好，真棒

"I hear Jack's coming back from India!" "Oh, good show! I've not seen him for years." "听说杰克要从印度回来了。""啊,真棒!我有好多年没见到他了!"

Jolly good show you turned up—I was just giving up all hope of ever seeing you again! 你来得真是太好了! 我还在想恐怕再也见不到你了!

5 show sb. the ropes 指导,训练,传授秘诀

Zeke is going to break you in, show you the ropes. 泽克将会指导你、训练你。

6 get/put the show on the road 着手工作,付诸实践

We needed to put the show on the road. 我们需要开始干起来。

7 run away with the show 【美】取得特别突出的成就,特别引人注目;压倒所有的人

In the minor role of the hero's uncle, Sapir succeeded in running away with the show. 尽管萨皮尔扮演主角的叔叔这个次要角色,但在整出戏中他演得最出色。

8 run/boss the show 掌管一切;操纵局势

The press is running the whole show. 媒体在操纵局势。

9 show up 来到,出席,露面;(在智力、表现等方面)超过;使蒙羞,使难堪

Did everyone you invited show up? 你邀请的人都到了吗?

10 stand a show 有渺茫的机会;有可能,有希望

I think you stand a good show of seeing your opponent at the party. 我想你很有可能在聚会上见到你的对手。

11 steal the show 爱出风头,喧宾夺主;哗众取宠

This footballer is a sportsman who likes to steal the show. 这个足球运动员是个爱出风头的运动员。

Lisa loves to steal the show at parties. 丽莎喜欢在各种聚会上出风头。

12 show the white feather 胆怯,示弱,畏缩不前

Pull yourself together, do you want to show the white feather in front of these people? 振作起来,难道你要在这些人面前示弱吗?

shut

shut up/shut your face/mouth/trap/heads 闭嘴

Can you shut him up? 你叫他别说了,行吗?

Shut your heads, and let Tom go on! 别多嘴,让汤姆说下去!

shy

1 have/take a shy at sb. 嘲笑/挖苦/糟蹋某人;赏识某人

2 have/take a shy at sth. 试图击中某物;打算获得

Mathilda wants to have a shy at a new job. 马蒂尔达想尝试一项新的工作。

I've never played snooker before but I'll have a shy at it. 我从来没有玩过斯诺克台球,但我想试试。

sick

1 look sick 给人印象不深,显得差劲,相形见绌

Newman's such a good swimmer, he makes me look sick. 纽曼是一个非常优秀的游泳运动员,与他相比我大为逊色。

2 take/get sick/ill 【美】生病

Take this medicine with you in case you get sick. 如果你病了,吃这种药。

side

1 get up on the wrong side of the bed 醒来时心情不好

The man went to bed very late and got up on the wrong side of the bed. 这人很晚才睡,醒来时心情不好。

2 let the side down 使同事的努力遭受失败,使同事难堪或丢脸,使朋友失望

Petty will always do her part—she never let the side down. 佩蒂总是尽自己的一份力量,从来没让我们失望过。

3 look on/at the bright/black/dark/gloomy side of things 看局势光明/阴暗的一面,看事物有利/不利的一面,抱乐观/悲观态度

It is productive to always look on the bright side of things. 始终以乐观的态度看待事物是很有帮助的。

4 on one's bad side 不为……喜欢

Mary's boyfriend got on father's bad side by keeping Mary out too late after dance. 玛丽的男友因在舞会后带玛丽在外玩得太晚而不讨她父亲的喜欢。

5 on one's good side 为……喜欢

You'll have to get on his good side. 你一定得讨他的喜欢。

6 on the side 【美】作为兼职;【英】作为副业;私下,秘密地

His job at the hospital did not pay much, so he found another on the side. 他在医院的工资不高,所以又找了个兼职工作。

I'm telling you this on the side. 我私下里告诉你这件事。

sight

1 a sight for sore eyes/the gods 乐于看到的人或物,极受欢迎的人或物

You're a sight for sore eyes. 你是个极受欢迎的人。

2 be/look a perfect sight 不成样子,不成体统,极为难看,看起来可怕

In this hat Peg looks a perfect sight. 佩格戴上这顶帽子真难看。

3 not by a long sight 远非,决不,一点也不

We haven't given up hope, not by a long sight. 我们没有放弃希望,决不。

4 out of my sight 走开,滚开

Out of my sight! I never want to see you again! 走开!我再也不想看到你!

sin

1 as sin 非常,极端地

That new building is as ugly as sin! 那座新大厦难看死了。

Pitman would be as miserable as sin without company of his own age. 没有同龄人相伴,皮特曼会很可怜的。

2 for my sins 【谑】作为对我的报应/惩罚;自作自受

Quiller's left all the holiday arrangements to me, for my sins! 奎勒把一切假期活动安排都交给我来办,该我倒霉!

3 like sin 猛烈地,狂热地

It was raining like sin. 大雨倾盆。

sink

1 sink/soak in 完全了解

Everybody laughed at the joke but Joe; it took a moment for him to sink in before he laughed too. 除了乔,大家都被这个笑话逗笑了,过了一会乔才完全明白过来,也跟着笑了。

2 sink/get one's teeth into 参见 get 52

3 sink or swim 靠自己奋斗；不管成败如何

Faulkner was left by his family to sink or swim by himself. 福克纳家里人让他去独自谋生。

Sink or swim, I'll try. 不管成败与否，我都要试一试。

sit

1 sit down on 反对

The whole committee sat down on the suggestion as being unsuitable. 委员会全体反对这个建议，认为它不适当。

2 sit down under 忍受，默默接受，逆来顺受

Robbins should not sit down under these accusations. 罗宾斯不应该默默地忍受这类指责。

3 sit on/upon 拖延，压下；管教，压制；申斥；挖苦

They decided to sit on the bad news as long as possible. 他们决定尽量拖延时间不把这个凶信说出去。

Minnie sat on him for coming half an hour late. 明妮责备他来迟了半小时。

That impudent fellow wants sitting on. 应该给那个无礼的家伙一顿教训才是。

4 sit on a volcano 身陷险境

Bob was in that part of South America before the revolution began. He knew he was sitting on a volcano. 革命开始前，鲍勃就在南美洲的那个地方，他知道自己身陷险境。

5 sit on one's hands 游手好闲，拒绝工作

We asked Bill for help with our project, but he sat on his hands. 我们要比尔帮助我们的计划，可他拒绝帮忙。

6 sit tight 坐着不动；坚持主张，决不让步

We insisted but he sat tight. 我们一再坚持，但他毫不动摇。

Sit tight; I'll be ready to go in a few minutes. 等等，我一会就好。

7 sit up 警觉，关注；诧异

Gabriel really sat up when I told him the gossip about Tom. 我把有关汤姆的闲话告诉加布里埃尔时，他确实大吃一惊。

8 sit up and take notice 参见 notice

9 sit with 对……合适；被……接受；受……赞同

How did his plan sit with his supporters? 他的计划得到了他的支持者的拥护吗？

All this toughness does not sit well with everyone. 所有这种强硬的做法并非人人都能接受。

six

1 at sixes/dozens and sevens 参见 dozen 1

2 hit/knock for six 彻底打败；一击得最高分

The general urged the troops to knock the enemy for six out of Africa. 将军督促他的军队将敌人彻底赶出非洲。

3 six of one and half a dozen (of the other)/six and two threes 参见 dozen 3

4 six of the best 一顿痛打

Grant deserves six of the best for being so rude. 格兰特如此无礼，应该揍他一顿。

size

1 cut down to size 使知分寸，使有自知之明

Harvey has become too high-and-mighty. It's time someone cut him down to size. 哈维近来变得骄傲自大，该让他有点自知之明了。

2 size up 评估，品评，判断；认为，看作

A game of cards offers the best possible chance of sizing a man up. 打牌是鉴定一个人的最好机会。

Some people have the ability to size up a situation at a glance. 有些人对某一形势一眼就能估计得很清楚。

3 that's about the size of it 就是那么回事，情况大概如此

That's about the size of it—the roof will have to be repaired within a month or two, I'm afraid. 我看屋顶在一两个月内必须修缮了，情况就是这样。

skid

1 on the skids 待发出的；注定要失败的；在衰落，走下坡路

Is modern science on the skids? 现代科学在衰落吗？

2 put on the skid 说话小心，做事谨慎

3 put the skids under/on 催促；使走向失败/毁灭/堕落

We had better put the skids under the driver or we'll be late. 我们最好催司机快开车，不然要迟到了。

Isaac was doing fine until he met this girl. She really put the skids under him. 艾萨克在认识这个姑娘以前一直干得不错，是她使他开始堕落的。

skin

1 be in a bad skin 心情不好

Job was in a bad skin over his recent setback. 乔布因最近的挫折而心情不好。

2 be in one's skin 处在……的地位，站在……的立场

I wouldn't want to be in your skin for the world. 我决不愿处在你的地位。

3 by the skin of one's teeth 参见 luck 4

4 get under one's skin 使……生气；引起……极大关注；给……留下深刻印象

I must have said something. I've got under his skin. 我一定说错了什么。我使他很不高兴。

Her tearful face and pathetic appeal really got under his skin. 她泪流满面、神情哀伤的恳求确实深深打动了他。

5 give/get skin【美】握手问好

Give me some skin. 跟我握握手。

6 jump/leap out of one's skin 参见 jump 7

7 save/protect one's (own) skin 保全自己，使自己免受伤害/杀害

Daniel would give a friend away to save his own skin. 丹尼尔会出卖朋友来保全自己。

When they heard the police cars, they all set about saving their own skin. 他们听到警车开来，都忙不迭地各自逃命。

8 skin alive 参见 alive 5

9 the skin off your nose 干杯

Here's the skin off your nose! 干杯！

10 that's/it's no skin off one's nose/back 跟……毫不相干

You can sell the car or keep it. That's no skin off my back. 你卖不卖那辆车跟我毫不相干。

skip

1 skip/jump bail 交保后逃逸，弃保潜逃
The robbers jumped bail and fled to South America. 这批盗贼被保释后就潜逃到南美洲去了。

2 skip it 没关系，不要紧，别提了
Skip it! Can you two talk about anything but politics? 别提这个了，你们俩除了政治就不能谈点别的？

sky

1 out of a clear/blue sky 如晴天霹雳，出乎意外，突如其来
His visit came out of a clear sky. 他的来访实属意外。

2 the sky is the limit 没有任何限制，一切都是可能的
When these local hoteliers charge visiting foreigners, the sky is the limit. 这些当地的旅馆老板向来访的外国游客收费时真是漫天要价。

slap

1 a slap in the face 一记耳光；打击，侮辱
Their refusal was like a slap in the face to us. 他们的拒绝对我们不啻一记耳光。

2 a slap on the back 赞扬，鼓励
We got a slap on the back for staying late at work. 我们因工作加班到很晚而受到了表扬。

3 a slap on the wrist 轻微的处罚，轻描淡写的责备
Those who "have" get away with a slap on the wrist. Those who "haven't" don't. 有钱的受点轻罚就被放过去，而没钱的则不行。

4 slap down 粗暴地制止，断然拒绝，禁止，压制
The boss slapped down their idea of taking a nap on the job every afternoon. 老板断然拒绝了他们提出的每天午后上班时小睡片刻的要求。

sleep

1 sleep around 性关系随便
Sue is a nice girl but she sleeps around an awful lot with all sorts of guys. 苏是个可爱的女孩，但她乱搞男女关系。

2 sleep on 留到以后解决

I'll sleep on the matter, and write to you tomorrow. 这件事我再考虑一下，明天给你书面回复。

③ sleep like a log/top 酣睡，熟睡

Last night I slept like a log so now I feel refreshed. 昨天晚上我睡得很熟，所以现在觉得精神抖擞。

sleeve

① keep/have a card up one's sleeve 参见 card 1

② have/keep... up/in one's sleeve 伺机行事

Jimmy knew that his father had some trick up his sleeve because he was smiling to himself during the checker game. 吉米知道他父亲腹中定有妙计，因为他父亲在棋赛中一直对他微笑。

slip

① give... the slip 避开……，甩掉……

Make sure to give any tails the slip. 注意一定要把盯梢的人甩掉。

② slip a cog/gear 犯错误，出毛病

I must have been slipping a cog when I said that I would run for mayor. 我说我要竞选市长，那我一定是说错了。

③ slip one over on 欺骗，哄骗

The fox slipped one over on the hounds and got away. 狐狸对猎狗耍了个花招逃脱了。

④ slip up 失败；疏忽；跌倒；出错，犯错

It must have slipped up badly. 一定是出了大错。

smart

① look smart 赶快

Look smart, don't dawdle about like that. 快一点，别这么拖拖拉拉！

② play it smart 【美】干得好，做得对

You ought to play it smart and stop smoking. 你应该好好把烟戒掉。

smile

I should smile 【美】好得很，我很高兴；我才不干呢；我才不在乎呢

I should smile when I send you, who will soon obtain happiness, away. 我

应该微笑着送走即将得到幸福的你。

smoke

watch one's dust/smoke 参见 dust 6

snap

1 not care/give a snap 毫不在乎

They don't give a snap about what others think. 他们毫不在乎别人怎么想。

2 snap back【美】迅速跳回；迅速恢复；反驳

I snapped back to her and gave her a kiss. 我猛地回过头吻了她一下。

The production snapped back to normal. 产量迅速恢复了正常。

3 snap into it【美】加紧干，认真干

Oh, snap into it, or we can't sleep all night. 嗨，加紧干呀，否则我们通宵不能睡觉。

4 snap it up/snap to it【美】快干

It's a rush job. Snap to it! 这是件急活儿，快干吧！

5 snap one's fingers at 蔑视，轻视，不予重视，对……无礼

Helina snapped her fingers at the local gossip. 赫莉娜对当地的流言蜚语置之不理。

No petty official was going to stop Philip from getting into the enclosure. He would just snap his fingers at them. 没有哪位职位不高的官员敢阻止菲利普进入围栏，即使有人阻止，他也会不屑一顾。

6 snap out of 迅速恢复过来；迅速改变

The loud noise snapped him out of his daydream. 巨大的喧闹声把他从白日梦中惊醒过来。

The coach told the lazy player to snap out of it. 教练叫那个懒惰的队员改变懒惰的习惯。

7 snap/bite one's head/nose off 参见 head 6

8 snap up 迅速地拿来、买来或接受；咬住；攫取

The bargains were quickly snapped up by the crowd of women shoppers. 这批便宜货立刻被那群女顾客抢购一空。

snook

cock/cut/make a/one's snook at sb. 对某人做侮辱性的轻蔑手势
Poor and bored, they think it's a bit of a laugh to cock a snook at the cops, and at the "rich people" who own businesses. 他们又穷又无聊,觉得对警察和那些经营自己生意的"富人"做出侮辱性的轻蔑手势可以聊以博自己一笑。

snow

snow under with 忙得不可开交
I've been so snowed under with work, so I just didn't have the time. 我近来忙得不可开交,所以抽不出时间来。
I was snowed under with my work. 我被工作压得喘不过气来。

so

1 be it (so)/so be it 就那样吧
If you don't wish my friendship, so be it. 要是你不愿和我交朋友,那就算了。
If that's what you want, so be it, though it's not what we'd have chosen for you! 如果那就是你想要的,你拿去好了,虽然那并不是我们为你挑选的。

2 is that so 是真的吗
"Brian's coming to see us tonight, you know." "Is that so? I thought it was tomorrow!" "布莱恩今晚要来看我们。""真的吗?我还以为是明天呢!"

3 it is so 正是这样(反驳否定问句)
"It's not raining, is it?" "It is so!" "现在没有下雨吧?""正下着呢!"

4 like so 像这样,照这样
And due to an explosion, an iron rod passed through his head like so. 因为一次爆炸,一个铁棒像这样穿过了他的头颅。

5 so help me 我保证,我发誓
I've told you the truth, so help me. 我发誓,我说的是实话。
So help me, there was nothing else I could do. 我发誓,我再也没有别的办法了。

sock

1 pull one's socks up 加紧努力，努力改正
We should pull our socks up and see whether by more sufficient approaches we can improve our work. 我们要加紧努力，看是否能用更为有效的方法改进工作。

2 put a sock in it【谑】不出声，别动
Put a sock in it! Why don't you shut up? It's two o'clock in the morning, and I've got to be up at six! 别说了，你们俩为什么还不住口！现在是凌晨两点了，而我六点钟就得起床。

3 sock away【美】储蓄
His main occupation is to sock away a fortune for himself. 他主要的业余爱好是给自己存一笔钱。

4 sock it to sb.【美】竭力对付某人；狠狠打击某人；给某人深刻印象
Right on, Joe, sock it to them! 乔，你说得对，尽力去说服他们吧。
They may let you off the first time, but the second time they'll sock it to you. 第一次他们可能放过你，可第二次就要对你不客气了。

soft

1 be soft on 爱上，钟情于；温和，宽厚
Joyce's been soft on Maggie for years. 乔伊斯多年来一直钟情于玛吉。

2 soft in the head 疯癫，昏头昏脑
Have you gone soft in the head? 你疯了吗？

soldier

play/come the old soldier 摆老资格；磨洋工；哄骗
Matthew enjoys playing the old soldier among his friends. 马修喜欢在朋友中间摆老资格。
You needn't try to come the old soldier over me. I'm not quite such a fool at that. 你甭想骗我，我在那方面没有那么傻。

some

1 and (then) some【美】还有别的，还不止这些；至少
Howard paid a thousand dollars and then some. 霍华德付了至少一千元。

2 some... 很不错的，出色的，真正的，了不起的

That's some apple. 那是个很好的苹果。
That was some speech you made! 你作的那次演讲真出色!
3 some...（常用于句首,含轻蔑、讽刺、厌烦之意）说不上,并不怎样,一点也不
Some pal you were, running away when I was in difficulties! 你算什么朋友,我遇到困难,你就溜了!
Some help you've been, I must say—you've just sat there and done nothing all afternoon! 你帮了什么忙? 我要说的是,你整个下午坐在那里什么也没做。

somebody

somebody up there loves/hates me 老天爷在帮我/罚我
Look at all the money I won/lost! I say somebody up there loves/hates me! 你看我赢/输了多少钱,我看一定是老天爷在帮我/罚我!

something

1 do something for/to 为……做事;改善,增强
Do something for somebody without expecting anything in return. 为某人做点什么事情,不期望获得任何回报。
We all want to do something for the Olympic Games. 我们都想为奥运会做点儿事。

2 make something of 【美】把……当作了不得的事;因……而争吵;利用……制造事端
When girls see another girl with a boy, they often try to make something of it. 姑娘们看到有谁跟一个小伙子在一起,常会无事生非地张扬一番。
Yes, I stole your girl, want to make something of it? 不错,我抢了你的女朋友,想为此打一架吗?

3 or something 大概（表示不同意或不完全相信）;或某种类似的东西
I thought jobs here were supposed to be well-paid or something. 我看人们认为这儿的工作报酬大概还不错吧。

4 quite/really something 不寻常的,值得注意的
The party was quite something. 那次社交聚会热闹极了。

5 something else 参见 else 2

6 something like 极为出色的,顶呱呱的;类似的,有点像

That's something like a rose. 真是一朵漂亮的玫瑰。

Three months' holiday a year? That's something like. 一年有三个月假期？真是太棒了。

Nick's something like his brother. 尼克像他的哥哥。

7 something tells me 我觉得，我怀疑

Something tells me she's lying. 我觉得她在撒谎。

8 there's something in 有点道理

There's something in what you say. 你说的有点道理。

son

1 son of a gun 小鬼，家伙，伙计（男子间亲热的称呼）；坏家伙，鬼东西

Come on, you old son of a gun, what have you been up to these last few years? 喂，老伙计，这些年你在干什么来着？

2 son of a sea cook 蠢货（海员骂人的话）

The captain called me the son of a sea cook, because I had made a blunder. 船长骂我是蠢货，因为我做错了事。

song

1 for a (mere)/an old song 非常便宜地，简直等于白送

I bought this painting for a song. 我以低价买了这幅画。

The buildings are going for a song. 房屋正在大贱卖。

2 give a song and dance 唠叨，空话，花言巧语，大篇谎话

Paul gave me a long song and dance about how busy he was. 保罗向我唠叨了一大通，说他如何忙得不可开交。

Every time Roger's late, he gives me a song and dance about oversleeping. 罗杰每次迟到，总要向我编一套如何睡过了头的谎话。

3 make a song and dance 小题大做，大肆宣扬

Her father made a great song and dance about her being home late. 她父亲对她回家太晚总是小题大做。

The Labour manifesto made a great song and dance about the mess the Conservatives had left. 工党的声明对保守党留下的烂摊子大肆渲染。

4 on (full) song 竭尽全力，鼓足劲头；处于良好的工作或竞技状态

The team was really on song today and won easily. 这个队今天竞技状态极佳，所以轻松取胜了。

soon

1 as soon as not 还是愿意

I would as soon stay here as not. 我还是愿意待在这儿。

2 no sooner said than done 说到做到,毫不延搁

Nicol asked her to get him a cup of wine. This was no sooner said than done. 尼科尔要她给他拿杯酒,话音刚落,酒就来了。

sort

1 and (all) that sort of thing 以及诸如此类的事情

2 he/she, etc. is not my sort 他/她等不合我的口味

3 in a sort of way 有一点儿,在某一方面

I like Jane in a sort of way, but she's too proud. 我有一点喜欢简,但是她太骄傲了。

The book is easier in a sort of way; it's also much shorter. 从某种意义上讲,这本书比较容易读,而且也短得多。

4 out of sorts 身体不适,心情不佳

I won't come out tonight; I'm feeling out of sorts. 今晚我不出来了,我有点不舒服。

A little group of old people were chanting the old favorites out of tune and out of unison but never out of sorts. 一小群老人唱着他们喜爱的老歌,虽然音走调,声不齐,但他们唱得很痛快。

5 sort of 有几分,有那么点,近似

Edison gave sort of a laugh. 爱迪生似乎笑了一下。

I won't tell you, it is sort of a secret. 我不告诉你,这事可以说是个秘密。

6 that's your sort 做得对,做得好,继续做下去

soul

1 be a good soul/there's a good soul 做个好人或好孩子(用在熟人或亲属之间,表示倚老卖老或轻蔑)

Be a good soul and leave me alone. 做个好孩子,让我清静一会儿。

2 never/not be able to call one's soul one's own 受人控制

You'd never have been able to call your soul your own if she'd married you. 假如她和你结了婚,你一定受她支配。

3 keep body and soul together 活命，生存

Tom doesn't like his job but he has to keep body and soul together somehow. 汤姆并不喜欢这份工作，但他总得设法活下去。

4 the life and soul 中心人物，最活跃有趣的人

Mr. Black was the life and soul of any place he happened to be in. 布莱克先生无论在哪儿都是最活跃、最风趣的人。

5 upon my soul（表示震惊或断言）天哪，凭良心说，真的，的的确确

Upon my soul, I had no idea how obstinate you are! 的的确确，我以前一点也不知道你竟如此固执。

sound

sound off 充分而直率地发表意见或抒发不满；大声斥责

On most matters Elizabeth is quite prepared to sound off without inhibition. 对大多数问题伊丽莎白都愿意毫无顾忌地直言。

If you don't agree with us, sound off! 如果你不同意我们的意见就直说好了。

soup

in the soup 在困境中，处于尴尬境地

We'll really be in the soup if the car won't start. 如果汽车发动不起来，我们可真要进退两难了。

spade

1 call a spade a spade 有啥说啥，直言不讳，实事求是

I believe in calling a spade a spade. 我赞成有啥说啥。

2 in spades【美】非常，极度；肯定地，明确地；坦率地，毫不留情地

Whether you realize it or not, you've got trouble in spades. 不管你是否意识到，你肯定是遇到麻烦了。

I was going to tell him off in spades. 我将毫不留情地数落他。

speak

1 so to speak/say 可以说，恕我直言，让我打个比喻

Therefore I think we must, so to speak, resort to more extreme measures. 因此，恕我直言，我认为我们必须采取更为激烈的措施。

This machine's, so to speak, the Rolls-Royce of computers. 这台机器可以说就是计算机里的劳斯莱斯。

2 speak for yourself 只讲你自己的，不要东拉西扯；这只是你的看法

"I think Catherine Cookson's books are the best I've ever read!" "Speak for yourself—I'm sticking to Rudyard Kipling!" "我认为凯瑟琳·库克森的书是我读过的最好的书。""这只是你的看法,我坚持认为最好的是鲁德亚德·吉卜林的书。"

3 speak with (one's) tongue in (one's) cheek 说话假惺惺

I feel sick of her. She always speaks with her tongue in her cheek. 我特别讨厌她,她说话总是假惺惺的。

speed

full speed/steam ahead 全速前进,全力以赴

I've got to finish writing this in a few days, so it's full steam ahead! 我必须在几天内写完这份材料,所以我得开足马力加油干!

Now we're out on the open seas—full speed ahead! 现在我们已到公海上了,全速前进!

spender

the last of the big spenders 你真会乱花钱,你可真大方(用于反义的嘲讽)

"This coat cost me all of £500!" "Ah—the last of the big spenders!" "这件大衣花了我五百英镑!""你可真舍得花钱!"

spirit

that's the (right) spirit 这才对头,这才应该,这才是好样的(用于鼓励)

"I'm absolutely certain I'll be completely vindicated." "That's the spirit!" "我百分之百地确信,我将获得彻底的昭雪。""你这样想才对!"

Keep it up! That's the spirit! 坚持到底,那才是好样的!

spit

1 spit it out 要说什么就大声说

What are you trying to say? Come on, spit it out. 你想要说什么? 来吧,爽爽快快地说吧!

Come on, spit it out, old chap—we're all friends here; feel free to say what's troubling you. 来吧，老伙计，痛痛快快说吧，我们大家都是朋友，你就把你的烦恼都说出来吧。

2 the dead/very spit of/the spit and image of 和……简直是一样的人

Tom is the spit and image of his father. 汤姆长得和他父亲一模一样。

splash

1 make a splash 引起轰动，惹人注目

The playwright made quite a splash on Broadway with his comedy. 那位剧作家的喜剧在百老汇引起很大的轰动。

2 splash out 大手大脚地花钱

We splashed out on a few luxuries. 我们大手大脚地花钱，买了几件奢侈品。

split

1 at full split 【美】以极高的速度，拼命地，飞快地

The boy was running towards the school at full split. 那男孩飞快地朝学校跑去。

2 run like split 飞奔

The dog ran like split across the lawn. 那条狗从草坪上飞奔而过。

3 split fair 说真话；告密，提供证据

Jenny will catch a plane to leave the city if I'd split fair. 如果我把事情挑明，珍妮就会搭上飞机离开。

4 split hairs 吹毛求疵，斤斤计较

I cannot split hairs on that burning query. 我不能对那个严重的问题说长道短。

David loves to split hairs. 戴维就爱做一些琐细的分析。

5 split the difference 折中，将差额各让一半；妥协

But anyway, they are second-hand furniture. Let's split the difference! 但不管怎么说，这些是二手家具，让我们折中一下吧！

spot

1 change one's spots 改变本性（常用于否定句或疑问句）

Unless Joe changes his spots, you are in for trouble. 除非乔改变本性，不然你就肯定要遭殃。

Laurie has been in and out of prison all his life. Can he ever change his spots? 劳里一生几进几出监狱,他可曾改变本性?

2 hit the high spots 【美】走马观花地游览;概述要点;做得过分,走极端
There's only half an hour left, so I'll just hit the high spots. 只剩半小时了,我就只概述一下要点。

3 hit/go to the spot 【美】(尤指食物和饮料)令人满意,切合需要
Mother's apple pie always hits the spot with the boys. 妈妈做的苹果馅饼总是最合男孩的口味。
Iced tea goes to the spot during the hot summer months. 在炎热的夏季,冰镇茶极受欢迎。

4 in a (bad/tight) spot 在困境中,在险境中
Now we're really in a spot. 这下我们可真是进退两难了。
That puts me in a bad spot. 那使我处境有点为难。

spread

1 spread/lay/put it on thick 参见 lay 3

2 spread oneself 努力,尽力,拼命讨好,大献殷勤;夸耀,吹嘘
Laurie had promised to spread himself in the preparation of the meal. 劳里已答应尽力准备好这顿饭。
Lindsay often spreads himself on his achievements. 林塞常常吹嘘自己的成就。

square

1 back at/to square one 回到起点,无进展
I'm back to square one with the work. 我的工作又得从头做起。
I've spent years writing this book, and now I've been told to write it all differently, so it's back to square one, I'm afraid. 我花了好几年时间写这本书,可现在又叫我重新改写。看来,我只得从头开始了。

2 on/upon the square 正直的,正当的
Lynd can be trusted to act on the square. 林德为人正派,可以信赖。
I'm not going to throw you over. I've always been on the square with you. 我并不打算抛弃你,我对你一向是真诚相待的。

3 square away/off 【美】准备动武,拉开架势;使平整,使整齐;使准备好
The wrestlers squared away for the first fall. 摔跤选手摆好架势,开始第

一局比赛。

Square that hat away! 把帽子戴正!

4 square oneself 弥补;挽回;要求宽恕;扯平;算账;报复

Lucia squared herself with her mother after their quarrel. 露西亚跟母亲吵架以后,向母亲道了歉。

Mark departed angrily, vowing to square himself before long. 马克愤愤而去,发誓不久定要报复。

5 a square peg in a round hole/a round peg in a square hole　参见 peg 1

6 square up (打斗时)摆好架势;妥善安排,解决

They squared up and began to engage a probing attack. 他们摆好打架的架势,并开始了试探性的攻击。

I have something to square up with you. 我有点事要和你商谈解决一下。

stab

1 a stab in the back 暗箭,诽谤;背叛行为

Such a vicious lie could be nothing but a stab in the back. 这种恶毒的谎言纯粹是暗箭伤人。

2 stab in the back 背后中伤,背叛

This kind of stabbing in the back gives journalism a bad name. 这种背后中伤给新闻业带来坏名声。

Maurice stabbed me in the back. 莫里斯在背后捅了我一刀。

stake

1 at stake 危如累卵;处于危险中

The Chinese nation has reached a point where its very existence is at stake. 中华民族到了生死存亡的关头。

We should explain to the students who have been involved in disturbances what is at stake. 学生闹事,我们要向他们讲清楚危害在哪里。

2 make/raise a/one's stake 【美】发财,赚钱

Lennie and I got to make a stake. 伦尼和我必须得攒点钱。

3 play for high/big stakes 大赌,豪赌,冒险

Disney is playing for high stakes. 迪斯尼这样做是冒了很大的风险的。

4 pull up stakes 【美】搬家,离开

I have decided to pull up stakes and go to live in Australia. 我已经决定搬

到澳大利亚去住。

stand

1 stand and deliver【古】站住，留下买路财（拦路强盗用语）

2 stand in with【俚】受……的喜爱；彼此友善；与……有勾搭，与……串通，合谋；联合

John stands in with the teacher. 约翰受到老师的喜爱。

The politicians stand in with the saloonkeepers. 那些政客与酒吧老板互相勾结，狼狈为奸。

3 stand pat 坚持，固守

Bill had made up his mind on the question and when his friends tried to change his mind he stood pat. 比尔对此问题已做了决定，当他的朋友企图改变他的心意时他坚持不变。

4 stand the guff【美】承受困难，忍受折磨

An athlete must learn to stand the guff. 运动员必须学会忍受磨炼。

5 stand up 失约；毁弃婚约

I thought you were going to stand me up again. 我以为你又要让我白等了。

6 stand/stick up for 奋战

You must stand up for your rights. 你一定要为维护自己的权利而战。

7 stand up with 作男女傧相；陪伴

Jim asked his brother to stand up with him. 吉姆请他弟弟做他的傧相。

8 stand/stick to one's guns/colors 坚持己见；坚守岗位；站稳立场

I tried to persuade the CEO to change his mind, but he stood to his guns. 我想劝公司首席执行官改变主意，可是，他怎样都不肯。

star

1 my stars（表示惊愕）哎呀

2 thank one's lucky stars 庆幸

You can thank your lucky stars you didn't fall in the hole. 你没掉到洞里去，真是走运。

You can thank your lucky stars your job's a lot easier than mine. 你真走运，你的工作比我的轻松得多。

start

1 start in 开始,动手;雇佣;开始批评、责备或训斥

It started in to rain. 开始下雨了。

The company started him in as a salesman. 公司一开始派他当推销员。

2 start on 与人吵架,找岔子;开始进行

Don't start on me. 别找我岔子。

stay

stay put 【美】留在原地,不离开;固定不动

Those kinds of people stay put in one job all their lives. 那种类型的人一辈子就从事一种工作,从不变动。

No, no, no. Both of you stay put, only need one of us to be stupid. 不,不,不。你们俩都别动,我们之中只要有一个傻大胆就行了。

steady

steady on 慢点;停下;小心;镇定下来,冷静下来,沉着一些

Steady on, old chap, there's no need to tell her everything about my past all at once! 别说了,老伙计,没有必要把我过去的事情马上全部告诉她。

Steady on, there's no need to lose your temper. 冷静冷静吧,用不着发脾气。

steam

1 let/blow off steam 发泄被压抑的感情,发泄怒气;松弛紧张的情绪;耗去多余的精力

Women were given a chance to let off steam at the meeting. 在会上妇女们有了一个出气发牢骚的机会。

We needed to let off a little steam after exams. 考试完了以后,我们要稍微放松一下。

2 run out of steam 没有动力,没有精力,筋疲力尽

The economy was running out of steam. 经济正在衰退。

His government seemed to be running out of steam. 他的政府看来摇摇欲坠了。

3 under one's own steam 靠自己的力量;自食其力

Now Grey could get about under his own steam. 现在格雷能自己走动了。

4 work off steam 通过体育活动或工作等消除怒气

Playing tennis is one of my favourite ways of working off steam. 打网球是我排遣心头怒气的最喜爱的方法之一。

step

1 mind/watch your step 走路小心；非常谨慎

Mind your step! The cat was sitting on the doorstep. 走路当心！那只猫在门口台阶上。

Watch your step and mind what you are saying. 谨言慎行。

2 step lively【美】快点上车或下车（售票员对乘客用语）；赶快加把劲，加大油门

Step lively, please. You're twenty minutes late already. 请快点。你已经晚了二十分钟了。

3 step on 粗暴对待，盛气凌人

The boss didn't care whether he stepped on anyone or not. 老板不在乎自己对别人是否粗暴无礼。

4 step on it/the gas 加快，赶快；猛踩油门

We will have to step on it if we don't want to be late. 如果我们不想迟到的话，一定得加快点。

I got into the taxi quickly, "Euston station, please, and step on it! The train goes in ten minutes." 我迅速钻进出租车说道："去尤斯顿车站，请开快点，火车十分钟后就要开了。"

5 step out【美】暂时离开，外出娱乐、赴约；退出，下台；对配偶不忠

Let's step out for a walk, shall we? 咱们出去走走，好吗？

I have to step out this evening. 今天晚上我得外出赴约。

6 step outside 有话咱们出去讲（向对手挑战）

Big Max was getting angry. "Would you care to step outside and repeat that?" he called out to Dave, who looked absolutely terrified. 大麦克斯勃然大怒，向戴夫喊道："你敢出去把你的话再说一遍吗？"而戴夫则已吓得面如土色了。

stew

1 be in a stew（因忧虑、愤怒等）心乱如麻，坐卧不安，焦急

I was in a stew over my job. 我为我的工作焦虑不安。

2 stew in one's own juice/grease 自作自受,自讨苦吃
You got caught by stealing those apples, and you can stew in your own juice. 你偷了那些苹果被抓住了,那是自作自受。

stick

1 be stuck on 迷恋;特别喜爱
Finn is really stuck on her new teacher. 芬恩实在喜欢他的新老师。

2 (be) stuck with 无法摆脱,无法解脱
They found themselves stuck with huge losses. 他们发现自己已经遭到了无法避免的巨大损失。
Will you help me with this mathematical problem? I'm stuck with it. 你能帮我解这道数学题吗? 我怎么也解不出来。

3 carry a big stick over 对……施行强权;对……严加控制
The trade unions were afraid that the government would carry a big stick over them. 工会担心政府会对他们采取强硬手段。

4 cut (one's) stick 逃走,溜掉;赶快跑开
The thief jumped into a car and cut his stick. 小偷跳上汽车逃走了。

5 get stuck in/into 抓紧干,加紧进行
Here's your dinner, get stuck in! 这是你的饭,快吃吧!

6 hop the stick 突然离开;死去
The professor hopped the stick all at once. 那个教授突然离开了。

7 jolly hockey sticks 快乐的曲棍球棒(表示对某件传统的或心想的事物感到高兴的心情)
"Term finishes in two weeks' time." "Ooh, jolly hockey sticks!" "还有两周就放假了。""啊,啊,快乐的曲棍球棒!"

8 more than one can shake a stick at【美】极多,不可胜数
I had more assignments for homework than I could shake a stick at. 我有很多很多的作业要做。

9 on the stick 抓紧,十分用心
If you are going to do it, you'd better get on the stick. 如果你打算做这件事,你最好抓紧些。

10 shake a stick at【美】关心,注意
The government's energy program shakes a stick at big consumers of

gasoline. 政府的能源计划关心的是用油大户。

There were just a few flakes, not enough snow to shake a stick at. 只不过飘了几片雪花,没下多少雪。

11 stick around 待在附近,留下

Stick around for a while, he will soon be back. 请等一会儿,他马上就回来。

12 stick down 放下;写下

You can stick the table down in a corner for the time being. 你可以把桌子暂时放在角落里。

Stick your name down here. 把你的名字写在这儿。

13 stick it on 索价过高;言过其实

The hotelkeepers stick it on during the busy season. 旅馆老板在旺季时漫天要价。

14 stick it out 容忍,忍受,经受,挺住

Much as he disliked the place, he thought he could stick it out one more year. 他虽然很不喜欢那个地方,但他想他还能坚持一年。

The 55 strikers stuck it out to the end. 有55名罢工者坚持到了最后。

15 stick one's neck/chin out 参见 chin 3

16 stick out 忍耐到底;坚持到底

Faulkner stuck the first term out and then left. 福克纳坚持念完了第一学期,然后离开了。

17 stick to it 坚持,不停地努力

If you know what you're doing is important and right, stick to it. 如果你知道你做的事是重要且正确的,那就要坚持下去。

18 stick/tend to one's knitting 别多管闲事

The trouble with Henry is that he is always telling other people what to do; he can't stick to his knitting. 亨利的缺点就是总是对别人指手画脚,爱多管闲事。

19 stick to one's/the ribs 参见 rib 3

20 stick up 持枪抢劫

Gallup was stuck up on the street. 盖洛普在街上遭到了抢劫。

21 stick up for 支持,拥护,为……辩护

Quit sticking up for Godwin! 别再护着戈德温了!

22 stick up to 抵抗，反抗；向……求婚

Hansom has *stuck up to* Isabel. 汉萨向伊莎贝尔求了婚。

23 stick with 继续做，不停止，不离开；欺骗；被迫做某事

Fred *stuck with* his homework until it was done. 弗雷德继续做功课，直到做完为止。

Practicing is tiresome, but *stick with* it and some day you will be a good pianist. 练习是很烦人的，但只要坚持下去，总有一天你会成为一个优秀的钢琴家。

24 that can shake a stick at 【美】可以比得上，可与……相媲美（常用于否定句）

I never set eyes on anything *that could shake a stick at* that picture. 我从来没有看到过一张画能够比得上它。

stink

1 create/kick up/make/raise a (big/real) stink about 为……大吵大闹；为……制造事端

If I lose my job, I'm certainly going to *raise a big stink about* it. 如果我丢了饭碗，我一定要大闹一场。

2 like stink 十分卖力地，拼命地

I've been working *like stink* since 5 o'clock this morning. 今天早上我从五点钟起一直卖力地干到现在。

stir

stir, stir 来吧，来吧（当企图挑起争论或制造麻烦时，边说边挥动双手，好像搅动一口大锅）

"Michael, what about you and Jane, then?" "*Stir, stir*! There she goes again!" "迈克尔，那么，你和简怎么办？""来吧，来吧，你看她又来了！"

stone

stone/stiffen the crows/stone me 参见 crow 4

stool

fall between two stools 两头落空

The book *fell between two stools*—the auther tried to make it suitable for both students and lay people. 这本书的作者想使它既适合学生,又适合一般读者,结果是两头落空。

stop

1　stop cold/dead 突然停止

When I saw Mary on the street, I was so surprised that I stopped dead. 我在街上看到玛丽时惊讶得突然站住不动了。

2　stop it 住手,停下,别这么干,阻止

Your teasing of the new typist has got beyond a joke and I advise you to stop it. 你对新打字员的取笑已经超出开玩笑的程度,我劝你立刻停止。

storm

1　bring a storm about one's ears 引起对……的强烈反感或愤怒

You'll be bringing a storm about your ears if you try to criticize their way of doing things. 你要是批评他们的做法,那你就捅了马蜂窝了。

2　a storm in a teacup 小事引起的轩然大波,小题大做

Mary won't be angry for long; its only a storm in a teacup. 玛丽不会生气很久的,不过是小题大做罢了。

3　brain storm 头脑风暴;灵机一动,集体研讨,心血来潮

I've just got a brain storm, let's talk about it. 我突然有了灵感,让我们讨论一下吧。

4　up a storm 极度地,丰富地;热烈地,热情地

Right now Evelina is cooking up a storm. 这时埃维莉娜正在起劲地烧饭做菜。

story

1　a likely story 怪事,真见鬼,哪有这样的事,太离奇了

"Hughes says he was at church on Sunday!" "A likely story—I bet he was playing football as usual!" "休斯说星期日他去教堂了!" "活见鬼,我敢打赌,他还跟往常一样在踢足球。"

2　(quite) another/a different story/a different kettle of fish 另一番情景;情况完全不同;另一个故事

Eddie can write French well, but speak it—that's quite another story—he's hopeless at that! 埃迪的法语写得很漂亮,但说就不行了,他对此已不

抱任何希望。
The room inside was a different story. 里面的房间则是另一番情景。

3 that's/it's the story of one's life 那就是……生活的经历或缩影
That's the third time this year a girl has chucked me—it's the story of my life! 这是今年第三次我被女友抛弃了,这就是我的生活经历。

4 to cut a long story short 长话短说
Stephen met Claire one night at a party. They saw each other the next Saturday at the club dance, and to cut a long story short, they got married last week! 斯蒂芬一天晚上在舞会上遇见了克莱尔,接着在下个星期六的俱乐部舞会上他们又见面了,长话短说吧,他们上星期结婚了。

stow

1 stow away 收藏
After New Year's day the Christmas decorations were stowed away until another season. 元旦以后圣诞节的装饰品都被收藏起来,留待下一个节假期用。

2 stow it 安静,住嘴

straight

1 straight from the horse's mouth 参见 mouth 11

2 straight from the shoulder 坦诚,坦白
John asked what he had done wrong. Bob told him straight from the shoulder. 约翰问鲍勃做错了什么事,鲍勃坦诚相告。

strain

don't strain yourself 别太紧张,慢慢来,别过度劳累
Don't strain yourself, will you? 慢慢来,好吗?

strange

1 it feels strange 这倒怪了
It feels strange to have a twin sister. 有个孪生姐妹感觉很奇怪。

2 strange to say 说来也怪
Strange to say, however, what everyone knows isn't true. 然而,说来奇怪,众所周知的事未必就是真的。

stranger

you are quite a stranger 好久不见了，你真是稀客

Hello, you're quite a stranger! Where have you been these past few weeks? 你好，好久不见了！这几个星期你到哪儿去了？

street

1 in Queer Street 陷入困境，为难，穷困，负债

A man must be in Queer Street indeed to take a risk like that. 只有穷极无聊的人才会冒这样的险。

2 not in the same street with/as 在能力方面差得多

As a scholar, he is not in the same street as his predecessor. 作为一个学者他远不能与他的前任相比。

3 put it on the street【美】泄露秘密

If you put it on the street, you'll be punished. 如果你泄露机密，你就会受到惩罚。

4 up/in one's street 符合……的能力，合……的口味，中……的意

The job was right up my street. 这工作正合我意。

strength

give me strength 上帝赐给我力量吧；真受不了；实在气不过（表示气愤、愤怒）

I have to watch 15 screaming children today? Oh, give me strength. 我今天得照看15个尖叫的孩子？噢，真受不了。

stride

1 get into one's stride 开始充满信心地工作，达到最佳竞技状态

Jane found the job difficult at first, but now she's really getting into her stride. 起初简觉得这工作很难，但现在已驾轻就熟了。

2 in stride 不影响正常活动地，泰然自若地

Other input costs have also crept up, including for iron ore and steel, but many companies are taking these, too, in stride. 其他生产投入成本也在上涨，比如铁矿石和钢铁价格，但许多公司对此也是从容应对。

3 make great/rapid strides 进展迅速，突飞猛进

They have made great strides towards self-sufficiency. 他们在自给自足方

面已取得了很大的进步。

4 **put sb. off his stride** 打乱某人的工作进程；使（某人）分心

strike

1 **have two strikes against one**【美】处于不利地位，处于严重情况
You succeed even though you had two strikes against you. 尽管在逆境中，你还是成功了。

2 **strike it rich** 发现富矿；突然走运，发横财
The farmer struck it rich when oil was found on his land. 那个农民的土地上发现了油矿，他一下子发财了。

3 **strike sb. dead if** 如果……就让某人不得好死
God will strike you dead if you tell lies. 如果撒谎，你会不得好死。

4 **strike me pink/strike a light** 真见鬼，真稀奇（表示惊讶、怀疑）
Strike me pink! So Andrew's finally passed his exam after all those attempts! 真稀奇！经过所有这些尝试，安德鲁就这样最终考试合格了。

string

1 **another/a second/an extra string to one's bow** 第二手准备，后备方案
As both a novelist and a university lecturer, Elizabeth has another string to her bow. 身兼小说家及大学讲师，伊丽莎白有第二手准备。

2 **have (got) sb. on a string** 操纵或支配某人
Funk's really got him on a string. 芬克真是牵着他的鼻子走。

3 **hold the purse strings** 掌握财权
Mother holds the purse strings in our family. 我们家是妈妈掌握财权。

4 **pull strings** 走后门
Jack pulled strings and got us a room at the crowded hotel. 杰克走后门在客满的旅馆里为我们找了一个房间。

5 **string along** 欺骗，愚弄；使不断追求或期待；忠实地跟随；完全相信
Gray will never marry her, he's just stringing her along. 格雷决不会和她结婚，他只不过吊她的胃口而已。
Mary was stringing John along for years but she didn't mean to marry him. 玛丽欺骗了约翰几年，但她并不想嫁给他。

6 **string out** 延长，延伸
They strung out their gossip for a long time. 他们长时间地闲扯拖延

时间。

7 string up 绞死,吊死;使紧张;使做好准备
Two of the rebel leaders were strung up. 两名为首的叛逆者被绞死了。
I saw clearly that Geoffrey strung up a little. 我看得很清楚,杰弗里有点紧张。

stroke

1 on the stroke 准时地,一分不差地
We pulled into the station on the stroke of six. 我们在时钟敲击六下时到站。

2 put sb. off his stroke 打乱某人工作或活动的进度;打扰某人,使某人激动
Some members of the audience tended to alter the questions. This clearly put Mr. Smith off his stroke. 一些听众老是变换问题,这无疑打乱了史密斯先生的思路。

strong

1 come/go it strong 显得夸张;做得过分
I know he doesn't like children, but I think he goes it a bit strong when he won't allow a child in his house. 我知道他不喜欢孩子,可是我认为他不让屋里有一个孩子,做得有点过分。
The newspaper's description of the accident was coming it a little strong. 报纸对这次事故的描写有点夸张。

2 come on strong 【美】十分招摇地吸引人;言行过分
Isabel knew she must not come on strong. She had chosen an outfit that was casual and yet had a touch of elegance. 伊莎贝尔明白自己不能招摇,于是挑选了一套既休闲又不失雅致的衣服。
Don't you think you came on a bit strong there? 你是否感到你在那一问题上过分了一点?

stuff

1 do one's stuff 干拿手的事,显身手;干分内的事
Do your stuff! You are the only one of us who speaks German. 露一手吧!你是我们中间唯一能讲德语的人。

2 get stuffed/stuff it/stuff you 滚开，去你的（表示厌恶、不愿、不信等）

I'm going to call you up this evening, so you can go and get stuffed! 我今天晚上会打电话给你，现在你给我走吧！

3 know one's stuff 精通业务，懂行

They answered all my questions correctly and without any pause for thought—they certainly know their stuff. 他们不假思索地正确地回答了我的全部问题，他们肯定精通业务。

4 not give a stuff 一点也不介意

Jimmy doesn't give a stuff about what the teacher said. 吉米对老师说的话一点儿也不介意。

5 on the stuff 吸毒成瘾

Isabel told me her son was on the stuff. 伊莎贝尔告诉我，她的儿子已吸毒成瘾。

6 strut one's stuff 炫耀自己的外表、服饰、本领等；卖弄自己的一套

Jeremy walked to the bus, loathing the loafers strutting their stuff in the street. 杰里米朝公共汽车走去，非常讨厌那些招摇过市的二流子。

7 stuff and nonsense 胡说八道

"Stuff and nonsense!" said Mr. Smith, "Don't try to make a fool of me." 史密斯先生说："胡说八道！你别想在我面前耍花招。"

8 that's the stuff/great stuff 这就对啦，好呀，这正对路，这正是所需要的

That's the stuff! Some more good hits like that and we'll beat them hollow! 干得好！像这样再给他们几个沉重的打击，我们就会彻底打垮他们。

9 the stuff to give'em/the troops 完全正确的做法

"I think we should just lay out a lot of cold food on the table and let people serve themselves!" "Excellent! That's the stuff to give'em." "我想我们就把许多冷菜放在桌子上，让大家自己吃吧！""好极了，这个办法很好！"

stuffing

1 knock/take the stuffing out of 挫败……的锐气，使……一蹶不振

Then I caught flu, which really knocked the stuffing out of me. 后来我得了流感，这场病真把我弄得元气大伤。

2 put stuffing into 增加……的力量；使……具有实质性的东西

Juliet really **puts the stuffing** back **into** those women. 朱丽叶真的使这些妇女重新增强了力量。

stump

1 **(go) on the stump**【美】作巡回政治演说；游说

Kennedy is very effective **on the stump**. 肯尼迪的演说很能打动人心。

2 **stir one's stumps** 拔脚就走，快走

Stir your stumps, or we'll leave without you. 快走，要不我们就丢下你自己走了。

3 **stump up** 不情愿地付出所需的钱；推出（with）

The Americans **stumped up with** *The Old Man and the Sea*. 美国人推出了《老人与海》。

4 **up a stump**【美】被难住，陷于困境

The problem got him **up a stump**. 这个问题把他难住了。

You're **up a stump**, ain't you? 你走投无路了吧，是不是？

style

1 **cramp one's style** 使……难以充分发挥；使……受到约束

The presence of anyone watching him practicing at the piano would **cramp his style**. 有人在旁边看他练钢琴，他就练不好。

I hope I did not **cramp your style**. 我希望我没有妨碍你。

2 **like/as if it's going out of style** 毫无节制地

Every Christmas people spend money **like it's going out of style**. 每逢圣诞节，人们花钱像流水。

3 **that's the style** 应该如此，做得对

"Is this the right way to do it?" "**That's the style**." "这样做对吗？""是该这样做。"

such

or some such 或诸如此类的

The doctor believed it might aid expiation or abreaction **or some such**. 医生认为这可能有助于精神补偿或精神发泄等诸如此类的疗效。

suck

1 **suck in** 欺骗,哄骗;吸进,吸收

Williams was sucked in and cheated of all his money by a little boy. 威廉姆斯上了一个小男孩的当,他所有的钱都被骗走了。

It's good for you to suck in fresh shore air. 呼吸清新的海滨空气对你有好处。

2 **what a suck/(yah-boo) sucks to you** 瞧你这副狼狈相;你真叫人讨厌(表示轻蔑、嘲笑、厌恶或失望)

"What a suck!" she said, tossing her head so her pigtails swung. "讨厌!" 她边说边把头一摆,两条辫子随着晃动起来。

I told auntie you didn't like the colour of my dress, but she said it was the nicest she'd ever seen, so yah-boo sucks to you! 我告诉婶婶说你不喜欢我这衣服的颜色,可她说这是她见到过的最好的颜色了。你看你多叫人讨厌!

sublime

from the sublime to the ridiculous 包罗万象,一应俱全;从崇高到荒诞,从一个极端到另一个极端(常用于对比两种截然不同的事物)

You had a Rolls-Royce, and now you've bought that old crock—that's going from the sublime to the ridiculous! 你有一部劳斯莱斯,现在又买了这辆老古董,真是一应俱全,什么都有了。

There is but one step from the sublime to the ridiculous. 可敬与可笑只有一步之遥。/真理与谬误只有一步之遥。

suffice

suffice it that/to say 简单地说,一言以蔽之

Suffice it that without leisure there is no liberty. 无闲暇何来自由——说这一句话就够了。

Suffice it to say, Isabel discovered she was pregnant, but had the baby and all is now well. 我只想说,伊莎贝尔发现自己怀孕了,但是生下了孩子,现在一切都好。

suit

suit oneself 随意,自便

Suit yourself—if you want to hang the picture upside-down, I don't mind! 随你的便,你就是把画倒着挂,我也不介意。

suppose

1 I don't suppose 我不知……能否……(礼貌地请求,希望得到肯定的答复)

"I don't suppose you could drive us into town, could you? We've got some shopping to do." "Yes, I think I could." "不知您能否带我们进城? 我们想去买点东西。""可以,我看没问题。"

2 I suppose 我猜想,我估计(礼貌地探听情况);我认为(口气委婉)

I suppose you'll not be staying to dinner, then, if you've got to be back soon? 我猜想如果你急于马上回去,就不打算在这儿吃饭了,是不是?
Being ill is just one of those things you have to put up with, I suppose. 依我看,疾病只是你被迫忍受的痛苦之一。

3 I suppose so 我看也是(勉强地表示同意)

"We ought to be going now!" "Yes, I suppose so." "我们现在该走了。""对,是该走了。"

4 suppose we 让我们(以祈使的口气建议)

Suppose we start(ed) tomorrow. 我们明天动身吧。(用过去时语气较委婉)
Suppose we go for a swim. 我们去游泳吧。

sure

1 (as) sure as death/a gun/fate/hell/guns/shooting/eggs are eggs/ferrets are ferrets/God made little apples/I stand here 毫无疑问,千真万确

Jenny will get me executed as sure as ferrets are ferrets. 珍妮会叫人把我处死的,肯定会的。
As sure as I'm standing here talking to you, I tell you I did see a flying saucer last night. 千真万确,就像我现在站在这里同你谈话一样,我告诉你,昨天晚上我真的看到了一个飞碟。

2 (and) that's for sure 确切的,肯定的,毫无疑问

Jimmy won't live much longer, and that's for sure. 吉米活不了多久了,这是肯定无疑的。

3 don't (you) be too sure 不要太自信,不要太自以为是

But don't you be too sure that you have me under your feet to be trampled on. 不要太自信,以为你能把我踩在脚下。

4 sure/right enough 果然,当真,必定,毫无疑问

We said things would turn out well, and sure enough they did. 我们说过情况会好转的,果然如此。

Dalton will come sure enough. 道尔顿一定会来。

5 to be sure 毫无疑问,当然;诚然,固然;必须承认;哎呀,真想不到

It's not the most beautiful car in the world, to be sure, but it's very economical, you know. 固然,这不是世界上最漂亮的小汽车,可它相当便宜。

And there Abraham was, to be sure! 那不是亚伯拉罕吗,真想不到!

6 well, I'm sure 哎呀,真想不到

Well, I'm sure! I didn't expect to see you here. 嘿,真没想到,我会在这儿见到你。

surely

1 surely to God/goodness 当然(表示不相信对方竟然不同意自己的话)

Surely to God that itself is reason enough to call the police. 事情本身就是叫警察的充分理由,这还有疑问吗?

2 surely you/you surely 想必你,你肯定(强调推断)

Surely you don't believe that! 你肯定不会相信那种话吧?

You know him, you surely? 想必你认识他吧?

surprise

you'd be surprised 情况并非你所想的那样(常用作反驳);你会很惊讶

You'd be surprised how many different birds and animals you can see there. 你会很惊讶竟然能在那里看到那么多种鸟类和动物。

sweat

1 by/in the sweat of one's brow/face 靠自己的辛勤劳动

John became a success entirely by the sweat of his brow. 约翰完全是靠自己的辛勤劳动取得成功的。

In the sweat of their face, the peasant couple sent all their children to university. 这对农民夫妇辛勤劳动,终于把几个孩子都送进了大学。

2 don't sweat it【美】别担心,不要郁闷

If you've planned to hit the zoo one afternoon but it's raining, don't sweat it, switch it out for something else. 如果你计划某一天下午去动物园但下雨了。不要郁闷,把它改成其他什么活动。

3 no sweat【美】毫不费力;不用担心

For those who know the trick it's no sweat. 对懂得诀窍的人来说,这一点也不难。

"Is it safe to go out at night here?" "Oh, no sweat." "这里夜间出去安全吗?""噢,非常安全。"

4 sweat blood 焦急万分,忧心忡忡;努力不懈

The engine of the airplane stopped and the pilot sweated blood as he glided to a safe landing. 飞机引擎突然停了,飞行员滑翔着做安全降落时急出了一身冷汗。

Jim sweated blood to finish his composition on time. 吉姆埋头苦干,准时写好了作文。

5 sweat it 为……担心;为……恼火

"What if they ask for my ID?" "Don't sweat it. They know me." "要是他们要我出示身份证怎么办?""别担心,他们认识我。"

6 sweat it out 做艰苦的锻炼;焦急地等待或忍受

Edmund's sweating it out in the gymnasium. 埃德蒙正在健身房里艰苦训练。

The men in the lifeboat just had to sweat it out until help came. 在救援到来之前,救生艇里的人们只能焦急地等待。

7 sweat out 在忍受或等待中度过;焦急地期待;勉强应付,吃力地完成或获得;艰苦地争取

Ellen sweated out a ten-year jail sentence. 埃伦熬过了十年徒刑。

Jim was sweating out the results of the exams. 吉姆在焦急地等待考试的结果。

sweet

1 be sweet on/upon 爱上,很喜欢

John is sweet on Alice. 约翰很爱爱丽丝。

2 keep sb. sweet 讨好,巴结(尤指用献殷勤、行贿等方式)

We're allowing the French engineers to use our computers, to keep them sweet in case we need their help later on. 我们允许那几个法国工程师用我们的电脑，尽量让他们满意，以防以后可能需要他们的帮助。

3 sweet talk 甜言蜜语；奉承

Sometimes a girl's better judgement is overcome by sweet talk. 有时女孩子的判断力会被甜言蜜语所欺骗。

Polly could sweet talk her father into anything. 波莉能用甜言蜜语哄得她父亲做任何事。

swing

1 get into the swing of 积极投入工作；对工作等开始熟悉；对……入门

Julia got into the swing of working after a vacation. 假期过后朱莉娅又积极投入工作。

You'll be able to do the job quite quickly when you get into the swing of it. 这项工作，只要你入门以后，就会干得很快的。

2 in full swing 正在全力地或十分热烈地进行中；正处于全盛时期

It began to rain when the garden party was in full swing. 游园会正开得起劲时，开始下起雨来。

The city's free market is in full swing. 这个城市的自由市场十分兴旺。

3 swing it on/across 跟……算账，向……报仇

4 swings and roundabouts/what you lose on the swings you gain on the roundabouts 失之东隅，收之桑榆；有得必有失

Higher earnings mean more tax, so it's all swings and roundabouts. 多挣钱就得多交税，有得有失。

system

all systems go 各系统（指火箭）准备就绪；一切正常

The royal couple have just arrived—so it's all systems go for the celebrations! 亲王夫妇已经到达，庆典可以开始！

T

tab

1 keep tabs/a tab/tag on 记录，监视，检查

Judith kept a tab on the expenses. 朱迪思把各项开支都记了账。

The foreman kept tab on the workmen. 工头监视着工人们。

2 pick up the tab 【美】代人付账，承担费用

Joyce picked up the whole tab for me. 乔伊斯代我付了所有的账。

Who's picking up the tab for the research? 谁来承担研究费用？

tack

1 get down to brass tacks/cases 参见 get 23

2 go sit on a tack 闭嘴走开，停止烦扰

Henry told Bill to go sit on a tack. 亨利叫比尔闭嘴走开。

3 spit tacks 【美】勃然大怒

I expected him to spit tacks over the injustice. 我料想他会被这种不公平的现象气得勃然大怒。

tag

keep a tag/tab on 参见 tab 1

take

1 have (got) what it takes 具备成功所需的一切条件（指素质、才能等）

If we didn't have what it took at the beginning we picked it up along the way. 如果说开始时我们还不具备成功的条件，随着一路做下来我们创造了这些条件。

2 take the bun 名列第一，得头奖；完全出人意料之外，了不起；超群出众（常作反语，用于讽刺或表示惊讶）

Mary took the bun in the singing contest. 玛丽在歌唱比赛中得了第一名。

3 it takes one to know one 你也好不到哪去

"Parry really is a fool.""It takes one to know one." "帕里真是个傻瓜。"

"你也不比他聪明。"

4 take a powder 逃走

All the gang had taken a powder when the cops arrived. 警察来时,那一帮人全跑了。

5 take a shine to/take kindly to 喜欢

Lamb took a shine to his new teacher the very first day. 第一天兰姆就喜欢上了他的新老师。

6 take down (a notch/peg) 挫其锐气,杀其威风;消停点儿,别得瑟

Bob thought he was a good wrestler, but Henry took him down. 鲍勃自认为是杰出的摔跤手,可亨利挫了他的锐气。

The team was feeling proud of its record, but last week the boys were taken down a peg by a bad defeat. 这支球队因自己的战绩而自高自大,但上星期的惨败挫了他们的锐气。

7 take for a ride 开车带走杀掉;戏弄,愚弄;吃哑巴亏;自讨没趣

The gang leader decided that the informer must be taken for a ride. 匪首决定把告密者绑架杀掉。

Poor Joe was taken for a ride. 可怜的乔被人骗了。

8 take it away 宣布演奏或演唱开始

From the thirteenth bar, take it away! 从第十三小节开始!

Take it away, Sam! 山姆,开始吧!

9 take it/things easy 参见 easy 7

10 take it into one's head/take a notion 灵机一动

The boy suddenly took it into his head to leave school and get a job. 这男孩突然决定要离校就业。

11 take it on the chin 参见 chin 4

12 take it or leave it 这是最低价,买不买随你

"I'll give you £100 for that desk!" "No! £200 is the price. Take it or leave it—I'm not bargaining with you!" "我出100英镑买那张桌子!""不行,定价200英镑,这是最低价,买不买随你。我不愿讨价还价!"

13 take it out on 泄愤,出气

The teacher was angry and took it out on the class. 老师生气时就拿学生出气。

14 take on 伤心;激动

Don't **take on** so! 不要这么悲伤!

Leonard **took on** terribly when his sister was so badly hurt. 见到妹妹伤得这么重,伦纳德伤心极了。

15 take oneself off 离开,滚开

Landon **has taken himself off**. 兰登已经离开了。

Take yourself off! 你给我滚开!

16 take stock in 有信心,相信,信任

They **took** little or no **stock in** the boy's story that he had lost the money. 他们不相信那小孩说的他丢了钱。

Do you **take** any **stock in** the gossip about Joan? 你相信有关琼的闲话吗?

17 take that 照打(边说边打)

Take that, you stupid boy! Will you never learn to respect your elders? 看我不打你这个笨蛋! 你就不学学怎样尊敬长辈吗?

18 take the cake 名列榜首;达到极限;最糟的;胆大妄为

Mr. Jones **takes the cake** as a storyteller. 琼斯先生讲故事,无人能超过他。

For being absent-minded, Mr. Smith **takes the cake**. 论健忘史密斯先生数第一。

19 take the bull by the horns 参见 bull 2

20 take the rap 承受处罚;背黑锅

Joe **took the** burglary **rap** for his brother and went to prison for two years. 乔为哥哥承担了盗窃罪,替他服刑两年。

21 take the starch out of 耗人精力,使人困倦;使泄气,使失去勇气或信心

The cross-country run **took** all **the starch out of** the boys. 参加越野赛跑的孩子们个个筋疲力尽。

22 take to the cleaners 洗劫,痛宰(指赌博);把……骗得精光

Watch out if you play poker with Joe; he will **take** you **to the cleaners**. 如果你跟乔玩扑克,你得当心他会把你宰个精光。

23 take to the woods 逃避,隐藏

When John saw the girls coming, he **took to the woods**. 约翰看到女孩子来了便躲开。

24 (the) deuce/devil take it 见鬼,糟了

Ah, **deuce take it**, to think of them imagining such a thing, the devils!

啊,见它的鬼,这是魔鬼才想得出的玩意儿!

25 you can take it from me/(you can) take my word for it 请相信我说的
You can take it from me; they're up to no good, I tell you—I've met their sort before! 请相信我,他们干尽了坏事。我告诉你,我可见过这号人。
Take my word for it, if he says he'll do something, then he won't break his promise. 请相信我,只要他说了要干什么事,就一定不会食言。

26 you can't take it with you 你总不能把钱财带进棺材里去
Perhaps the idea of "bigger is better" and "you can't take it with you" are now becoming outdated and outmoded ideologies—especially with the near collapse of worldwide financial structures. 也许,"越大就越好"和"今朝有酒今朝醉"之类的想法已经日渐过时——尤其是在全球金融结构近乎瓦解的情况下。

tale

1 tell its own tale 不言自明,不言而喻
What the teacher had said told its own tale. 老师所说的一切不言而喻。
The many crashes on the icy road tell their own tale. 路上结冰发生多起撞车事故,路面情况已不言而喻。

2 tell tales (out of school) 揭露隐私;搬弄是非,散布流言蜚语;撒谎
Do not tell tales out of school. 不要泄漏秘密。

3 thereby hangs a tale 其中大有文章,说来话长
When they built the new library in less than three months, not everyone was happy about the building methods they used, and thereby hangs a tale. 当他们在不到三个月的时间里建起了这座新图书馆时,并不是人人都对它的建筑方法感到满意。这事说来话长了。

talk

1 all talk and no cider 【美】空口白话,干打雷不下雨;小题大做,大惊小怪
2 know what one is talking about 是个行家,精于此道
3 now you are talking 这就对了,这才像话
"How much will you sell that car to me for?" "£600?" "No!" "£400?" "No!" "£200?" "Now you are talking—it's a deal!" "你那辆车卖给我要多少钱?" "600 英镑如何?" "不行!" "400 英镑呢?" "不行!" "200 英镑吧?" "这才像话,咱们一言为定!"

4 talk a dog's/donkey's/horse's hind leg off/talk one's head off/talk the hind leg off a dog/donkey/horse/talk the bark off a tree 参见 head 41

5 talk about/of 说到……可真不得了（用于加强语气，表示惊讶、讥讽等）
Talk about pride—he's the most big-headed man I've ever met! 说到骄傲自大，他是我见过的最自负的人。
Talk of English comforts! It's a national delusion. 说什么英国式的舒适享受，只不过是英国人自欺欺人罢了。

6 talk back 顶嘴
Don't you dare talk back to me like that! 不许你这样放肆地跟我顶嘴！

7 talk big 吹牛，夸耀
Felton talks big about his pitching, but he hasn't won a game. 费尔顿自夸他投球如何棒，但他从未赢过一场球。

8 talk shop 参见 shop 3

9 talk through/out of one's hat/talk wet 参见 hat 14

10 talk turkey 谈正事，说老实话；坦白交谈
Let's talk turkey about the bus trip. 让我们谈点乘汽车旅行的事吧。

11 you can talk/look who's talking/you can't talk 不用担心，你干得了；亏你有脸说别人
"I'm going to stay in bed late tomorrow." "You can talk—I've got to be up at six to go to work." "明天早上我打算睡个懒觉。""你倒舒服，可我六点钟就得起床去上班！"

tan

tan one's hide for doing/the hide off sb. 责打某人
Bob's father tanned his hide for staying out too late. 鲍勃的父亲因为他外出晚归而责打他。

taste

1 there's no accounting for tastes 人各有所好

2 to one's taste 合……的口味；称……的心
This dish is to his taste. 这道菜合他的口味。

3 to the king's/queen's taste 好极了，无可挑剔，尽善尽美
The rooms in their new home were painted and decorated to the king's taste. 他们新居的每个房间都装饰得尽善尽美。

tea

1 a/one's cup/dish of tea 参见 cup 2

2 for all the tea in China 无论如何(常用于否定句)

I wouldn't go back to that job for all the tea in China! 我无论如何不会回去干那个工作了!

3 tea and sympathy 对不幸者的同情与安慰

4 take tea with sb. 与某人打交道;与某人狭路相逢

teach

that/I will teach sb. to do sth. 那/我会教训某人不要干某事

I will teach him to meddle in my affairs. 我要让他知道别干涉我的事。

I'll teach you to spoil our good name. 如果你败坏我的好名声,我就要对你不客气了。

tear

1 be torn between 左右为难

Fowler was torn between staying and leaving. 是去是留福勒左右为难。

2 tear down 【美】惩罚,批评;拆卸,拆毁

The old cinema was torn down and replaced by a restaurant. 老电影院被拆掉,取而代之的是一个饭店。

3 that's torn it 计划被破坏了

It's raining! That's torn it! We were hoping for good weather for the fete! 下雨了,我们的计划落空了。我们原来盼望好天气办游园会。

That's really torn it now! We'll never beat the other side now for they know our secret. 现在希望真的破灭了,对方知道了我们的秘密,我们再也别想打败他们了。

4 crocodile tears 鳄鱼的眼泪,假慈悲

They are only crying crocodile tears at the old man's funeral. 他们在那老人葬礼上的哭是虚情假意的。

tee

1 tee off 责骂,猛烈抨击,使生气;开始;发球

They teed off the fund-raising campaign with a dinner. 他们以宴会形式开始募捐活动。

Giles teed off on his son for wrecking the car. 贾尔斯因儿子损坏了那辆车而责骂他。

2 tee up 安排,准备

Has it all been teed up? 一切都准备好了吗?

tell

1 do tell 快告诉我;不见得吧,绝不会吧,真有这事

The boy after hearing the story through, exclaimed "Do tell!" 孩子听完这事后,叫道:"真有这事呀!"

2 don't tell me/tell me another/never tell me 我不信,不至于吧,不见得吧,哪有这种事,别瞎说(表示惊讶或惊恐)

Don't tell me it's too late! 还不至于太晚吧!

"Don't tell me you've heard the news already!" "Yes, Marcia's expecting a baby!" "你真的听说这个消息啦?" "不错,马西娅怀孕了!"

3 I (can) tell you/let me tell you 我可以肯定地说,确实

It's boiling hot outside, I can tell you! 外面热得要命,真的!

I can tell you it's all written down. 我敢说这都记下了。

4 I can't tell you 由于高兴而不知所措

I can't tell you what it means to have company; I got so lonely here all by myself, you see. 我觉得一个人有了伙伴该有多么快乐,可是你看现在我孤孤单单地一个人在这里多么寂寞。

5 I'll tell you what 你听着,让我告诉你

I'll tell you what, I'm going to be there early and help you out. 这样吧,我会早点到,帮你一把。

6 I'm not telling/saying 我不告诉你

"Where were you last night?" "I'm not telling!" "昨晚你去哪了?" "我不告诉你。"

7 I'm telling you 听我说,我说的没错

I'm telling you, he doesn't always do what he promises. 我说的不会错,他并不总是信守承诺。

8 tell a thing or two 告知一二,简单说明;责备

I'll tell him a thing or two that will make him change his mind. 我只要简单地告诉他一些实情,他就会改变主意。

9 tell it like it is【美】说实话

Thank you for being honest, for telling it like it is. 谢谢你这样坦诚地实言相告。

10 tell it/that to the marines/horse/Sweeney 参见 marine

11 tell sb. where to get off/head in【美】生气地对某人说话；使某人碰一鼻子灰；斥责某人，痛骂某人

12 that would be telling 我不告诉你（为了保密）

"Who were you with last night?" "Ah! That would be telling!" "昨晚你和谁在一起？""啊，这是秘密！"

13 you can't tell sb. anything 你不能告诉某人；你不必告诉某人

You can't tell him anything. The moment he hears some bit of gossip, it's all round the town! 你什么也不能对他讲，只要他听到一点流言蜚语，他就会立刻把谣言传遍全城。

14 you never can tell 很难说，没法预料

15 you tell me 我不知道

"How can we possibly get through this week with just this amount of money?" "You tell me." "这一点钱我们这一周怎么够用？""你说呢！"

16 you're telling me 还要你告诉我，我早就知道了

"It's raining outside." "You're telling me—I've been out to get the paper and I'm absolutely soaked!" "现在外面在下雨。""我知道，刚才我出去拿报纸，浑身都淋湿了！"

ten

ten to one 十有八九

Ten to one it will rain tomorrow. 十有八九明天会下雨。

It's ten to one that Barton will be late. 巴顿十有八九会迟到。

thank

1 I thank you (not) to 请你……（较严肃、正式地）

I thank you not to walk on the grass. 请你不要在草坪上走。

2 I'll thank you to 请你……（加强命令、要求等的语气）

I'll thank you to mind your own business! 请你别管闲事！

3 thank God/goodness/heaven(s) 参见 god 17

4 thank one's lucky stars 真走运，幸运之至

You can thank your lucky stars you didn't fall in the hole. 你没掉进洞里，真走运！

5 thank you ever so much/many thanks/thanks a lot/thank you very much/thanking you 真多谢你了

6 thank you for nothing 参见 nothing 14

7 won't thank you for 因……必定会对你发脾气

Henry won't thank you for damaging his new car. 你损坏了亨利的新车，他必定对你非常生气。

that

1 that it is/was/it is that 正是这样

"It was a bright, crisp winter last year, wasn't it?" "Yes, that it was!" "去冬天气晴朗，空气清新，是吗？""正是这样。"

"It's cold out, isn't it?" "It is that!" "外面很冷，是吧？""是的，很冷。"

2 that'll be the day 参见 day 9

3 that's a dear/(good) boy/girl 这才乖呢；这才是好孩子

That's a good boy/girl! 这才是好孩子！

4 that's about it 就这些，到此为止

Well, that's about it for tonight, folks. We'll see you same channel same time, next week! 好，朋友们，今晚的节目到此为止。下周同一频道同一时间再见！

5 that's all (there is to it) 情况就是这样；只是，仅仅（用于结尾，表示强调）

If we've not got any money, we won't be able to afford a holiday, that's all. 如果我们没有钱，我们就没法度假，情况就是这样。

6 that's all very fine/well 【讽】好极了，太妙了

7 that's as maybe 那还不一定

"When I'm at college next year…!" "That's as maybe, my girl! you've not passed your exams yet." "明年我升了大学……""那还不一定呢，我的女儿，你现在还没有通过考试呢。"

8 that's how it is 情况就是这样，事实如此

My job's in Birmingham, and I have to travel up there every day—that's how it is at the moment. 我的工作在伯明翰，所以我只好每天乘车去上班。目前情况就是这样。

9　that's it 就是这个问题，正是这样；就这样，干得好；真讨厌，真糟糕

That's it! I'm fed up with you children breaking things! You can go straight to bed! 好了，够了，真烦死人，你们这些孩子把东西都弄坏了！你们都给我睡觉去！

Well, that's it then! If we're beaten as badly as that in every match this season, we'll never get promoted in the league! 坏了，如果这个赛季我们每场都输得那么惨的话，我们就别想在协会里升级了！

10　that's that 就是这样，如此而已，到此结束

I've told you before, I won't go, and that's that! 我以前告诉过你，我不去。就是这样！

It was a policy, and that was that. 那是政策，没什么多讲的。

11　that's what it is/was 这就是……的原因

"That cab driver didn't look very happy!" "You drove straight out in front of him at the last set of traffic lights, that's what it was." "那出租车司机看上去很不高兴。""刚才在那个交通岗前你一下子超过了他，所以他才不高兴。"

there

1　(be) all there 头脑正常（常用于否定句、疑问句）；警觉的，机敏的

Do you think Charley is all there? 你认为查利神志正常吗？

Jonah was sane enough, hard as nails, very much all there. 乔纳头脑相当清醒，冷酷无情又非常机警。

2　have been there before/lived there some years 早就知道了，领略过此中甘苦

You can do it because you have been there before, and you will achieve success. 你们能够做到，因为你们领略过此中甘苦，所以你们会获得成功。

3　so there 这是最后的决定，再没有商量的余地；事情就是这样

You can't have any more, so there! 你不能再要了，没有商量的余地！

You can stop boasting—I've beaten you now, so there! 你别吹牛啦，现在我打败了你，事情就是这样！

4　there it is 这就是困难或麻烦所在；事情就是这样

There it is, I'm afraid, the firm's run out of money, so we've got no choice but to make some of workers redundant. 恐怕问题就在这里，公司已经没钱了，所以我们除了辞退一些工人以外别无选择。

5 there, there/there now 好了，好了

6 there or thereabouts 大约，差不多

7 there you are 给你，这是你要的东西；你瞧，我说对了吧；完了，事情办好了；目的达到了；原来你在这儿；你这才来

There you are, sir, your shoes, mended as you asked. 给你，先生，您的鞋已经修好了。

We've been looking for you everywhere. There you are. 我们到处找你，原来你在这儿。

8 there's... ……怎么样（提出建议）

"Where else could we go?" "There's always London—I'd quite like to go round some of the museums again." "我们还可以到哪儿去玩？""伦敦怎么样，我很想再去那里参观一些博物馆。"

9 there's/that's a... 真是好样的

You eat all your cabbage now, there's a good boy! 你把卷心菜都吃了，真是个好孩子！

10 there's/that's... for you 真是没得说的

I arrived at the hotel, and a porter took my cases upstairs, someone ran my bath, and dinner was brought to my room—now, there's service for you! 我一进饭店，一个搬运工就把我的行李送上楼去，有人照料我洗澡，午饭送到房间里来。你看，这儿的服务真是好得没说的！

thick

1 a bit thick/a little too thick 太过分，令人受不了

I think it a bit thick to do it that way. 我认为那样做太过分了。

2 as thick as thieves 非常亲密，非常友好

The two classmates are as thick as thieves. 这两个同学非常亲密。

3 through thick and thin 不顾艰难险阻，愿赴汤蹈火；在任何情况下

We'll stand by you through thick and thin. 在任何艰难的情况下我们都将始终支持你。

They were friends through thick and thin. 他们是同甘共苦的朋友。

thin

that's too thin 难以置信，容易识破

And so plainly, Newman was lying. His story was *too thin*. 这样说来纽曼显然在撒谎。他的谎言太拙劣了。

thing

1 a soft thing 工作轻松，报酬优厚；易赚钱的买卖；有利的事

2 a thing or two 知识，经验；责备，警告，教训

I love my job. I could tell you *a thing or two*. 我热爱我的工作，我可以给你谈谈我的经验。

If Jim does it again, I'll tell him *a thing or two*. 如果吉姆下次再犯，我可要教训教训他了。

3 and things 等等，之类

"You can't compromise any health care medical records *and things* like that," he said. "你不能在任何健康关怀医疗记录和那一类的事情上妥协，"他说。

4 any old thing 什么都可以

Writing *any old thing* is always a lot easier than thinking first about what it is you are trying to say. 与先想清楚你到底想表达什么相比，草草写下陈词滥调总是要简单得多。

5 as things go 在目前情况下，就一般情况而言；照习惯来说

As things go over there, Olenski's acted generously: he might have turned her out without a penny. 按那边的情形，奥兰斯基做得已经很慷慨了：他本来可以一个铜板都不给就把她撵走的。

6 do one's (own) thing 做自己最爱做的事；按自己的意愿行事

Sometimes you don't have to care about what the others say, just go ahead and *do your own thing*. 有时你不必听别人说三道四，只管按自己的意愿做就是了。

7 first things first 重要的事先做

You must go and finish off your work, before you can go out to play. *First things first*! 你应该先做完作业再出去玩，重要的事先做嘛！

8 for one thing..., and for another... 一则……，再则……

"Why can't I get a motorbike?" "*For one thing*, you're too young, and for another, you're not sensible enough yet." "为什么我不能有一辆摩托车?" "一则你太小,再则你还不太懂事。"

9 have a thing about 有一种病态的或强烈的爱好、厌恶、惧怕等;抱有偏见

I have a thing about fingernails scratching the blackboard. 我很讨厌指甲刮黑板的声音。

10 have a thing/an affair with 与……有染

The black sheep of the family has a thing with the widow. 那个败家子跟那个风流寡妇有一腿。

11 it's a good thing 参见 good 12

12 just one of those things 命中注定的事,不可避免的事,必须接受或承认的事

Being made redundant is just one of those things these days, I suppose. 我看,现在被辞退已是不可避免的了。

13 just/quite the thing/the right/very thing 正好,正需要,正该这样;很时髦

The cooling taste of mint may sound like just the thing after a heavy meal, but it could spell trouble. 薄荷糖的清凉味听起来可能只像是一顿丰盛的膳食之后的东西,但是它可能意味着麻烦。

14 kind/sort of thing 大概,可能

How long did it go on, kind of thing? 那件事大概进行了多久?

It was a big car, sort of thing, a Cadillac, perhaps. 那是一种大型轿车,大概是一辆凯迪拉克。

15 let things go hang/let things slide/rip 随它去,听其自然;不关心

We can't let things go hang. 我们不能任其发展。

16 make a good thing of 从……中得益或获利

The old heavy smoker made a good thing of the transaction. 那个老烟枪从这笔交易中赚了一大笔钱。

17 make a thing of 把……作为争论点;对……小题大作;认为……不得了;从……中获得好处

Don't make a thing of it! 别当傻瓜,别做傻事。

Don't let negativity bring you down. Make it a thing of the past and see how positive life can be! 不要让消极情绪打倒你,想想过去曾有过的成功,你就会意识到,你的生活是积极向上的!

18 make things hum 搞得很热闹,搞得有声有色,使朝气蓬勃

The new manager soon made things hum. 这位新经理不久便使一切都活跃起来了。

19 no such thing 没有的事;完全不对

But there is no such thing. 但是没有这样的事情。

20 not quite the thing 感到不适,身体不太好

I am not quite the thing this morning. 今早身体不大舒服。

21 of all things 偏偏,真没想到,怎么搞的(表示惊讶、愤慨)

Well, of all things, what are you doing here? 哎呀,真是,你在这儿搞什么名堂?

Hansen tried to do, of all things, that job. 汉森偏偏想要做那份工作。

Jackson blushed, of all things. 杰克逊竟然脸都红了。

22 old thing 老朋友,老兄,老伙计

I say, old thing, what a funny hat you're wearing today! 我说老伙计,你今天戴的这顶帽子真可笑!

23 out of things 置身事外;闷闷不乐

24 see things 产生幻觉

Oh, you're seeing things. 啊,你见鬼了。

25 sure thing【美】当然,一定,没问题

"Can you come round tonight?" "Sure thing! I'll be with you at six." "今晚你能来玩吗?""当然可以! 我六点钟来。"

26 the thing is 问题是;需要考虑的是;最重要的是

The thing is, can we finish the work in time. 问题是我们能不能按时完成这项工作。

The thing is to seek truth from facts. 最要紧的是实事求是。

think

1 come to think of it 想起来了;的确,真的

Come to think of it, I should write my daughter today. 想起来了,我今天该给女儿写信。

2 I don't think 我却不相信,靠不住

Everyone says Davy is honest—Honest, I don't think! 大家都说戴维诚实。诚实! 我才不相信呢。

You are a model of tact, I don't think. 你是足智多谋的代表人物,我看不见得。

3　I should have thought 我还以为……(表示惊讶)

Isn't he here yet? I should have thought he'd be on time for his own wedding! 他还没来呀? 我还以为他总该按时出席自己的婚礼呢。

4　I should think 当然,的确如此

"He's very proud of his first book!" "I should think so, the years it's taken for him to write it!" "他为他的第一本书而自豪。""当然喽,为写这本书他花了好几年时间。"

Hot—I should jolly well think it was—it was baking in there! 好热! 一点不错,我看在那儿人都会被烤干的。

5　I thought as much 果然不出我所料(常指预见坏事)

Did you have difficulty finding our house? I thought as much, since you were so late. 我们的房子很不好找吧? 果然不出我所料,你这么晚才来。

6　(just) think of it/to think of it 简直想不到

7　only think 你想想看;真想不到

8　that's what you think 你想得倒美(带轻蔑口气)

"When I get my extra money back from the tax people, I'm going to spend it on a new dress!" "That's what you think—I'm keeping it to pay for the repairs to the car!" "要是我从纳税人那里得到这笔额外收入,我打算用它买套新衣服!""你想得倒美! 我得用它付修车费!"

9　what do you think 你知道吗,你猜怎么着(向人介绍令人惊讶的事)

What do you think? I've promoted! 你知道吗? 我获得晋升了!

10　think nothing of it 不足挂齿,不用客气

"Thank you very much for your help." "Think nothing of it." "多谢你帮忙。""不用客气。"

11　who do you/does he, etc. think you are/he is, etc. 你/他等以为你/他等是什么人;你/他等以为你/他等很了不起吗

Just look at her, dressed like that! Who does she think she is? 瞧瞧她那副模样,那身穿戴! 她真不知道自己是谁了呢!

12　you can't think 你简直想不到,你简直不能想象

this

this is it/that's the thing 是这样,说得对;就是这话;这是你期待已久的;这是关键时刻

This is it, the finest vase of its kind in the country. 请看,这就是国内同类产品中最精致的花瓶!

"Well, *this is it*! It's now or never!" I thought as I went into the interview room. "好啦,这是关键时刻,成败在此一举!"我边想边走进面试的房间。

thought

1 it's a thought 这是值得考虑的意见

2 perish the thought 死了心吧;但愿不是这样(指令人不愉快或不幸的事)

Sally's not back yet. If something should have happened to her, and *perish the thought*, you'll be to blame for not looking after her properly, you know. 萨莉还没回来,但愿她没出事才好。要是她出了事,你就会为没照顾好她而受到责备,你知道吗?

throat

1 cut one's own throat 断送自己的前途;自取灭亡

Ellen *cut his own throat* by his carelessness. 埃伦因粗心大意而断送了自己的前途。

2 jump down one's throat 猛烈批评,严厉训斥,突然猛烈攻击

The ecologists will *jump down our throats* if we kill an endangered species for sport. 如果我们杀死一只濒临灭绝的动物取乐,生态学家就会猛烈抨击我们。

3 shove/ram down one's throat/cram/ram/thrust sth. down one's throat 强迫……接受意见

They *rammed* a pro-company contract *down the union's throat*. 他们强迫工会接受有利于资方的合同。

throw

1 throw in the sponge/towel/up the sponge 认输,投降;承认失败

When Horold saw his arguments were not being accepted, he *threw in the towel* and left. 哈罗德看到自己的意见不被接受,就认输离开了。

There was no other way out—he had to *throw up the sponge*. 他没别的办

法,只好投降!

Isn't it too early to throw in the towel? We may still be able to finish it in time. 现在就放弃,不是太早了么? 我们或许还可以及时完成任务的。

2 throw/fling oneself at someone's head 参见 fling 1

3 throw/toss one's hat in the ring 宣布竞选,成为候选人

Bill threw his hat in the ring for class president. 比尔宣布竞选班长。

4 throw one's weight around/about 专横跋扈,仗势欺人,耀武扬威,滥用职权

I'm not going to have him throwing his weight about with me. 我不会让他对我滥用职权。

5 throw the book at 参见 book 16

6 throw up 呕吐;离去

Dennis took the medicine but threw it up a minute later. 丹尼斯吃了药,但一分钟后就吐了出来。

thumb

1 be/turn thumbs down (on) 反对,抵制,禁止

Everybody was thumbs down on the suggestion. 大家都反对这个建议。

2 be/turn thumbs up (on) 赞成,满意,称赞

They unanimously turned their thumbs up on the plan. 他们一致赞成这个计划。

3 twiddle/twirl one's thumbs 闲着无事,无所事事

What do you expect me to do all day—just sit around, twiddling my thumbs? 你想叫我成天干什么? 难道就这样到处闲逛,无所事事?

ticket

1 not (quite) the ticket 不合适,不对路,不时髦,不合要求

2 get one's (walking) ticket 【口】被辞退,遭解雇

The manager got his ticket yesterday. 那个经理昨天被解雇了。

3 give sb. his walking ticket 【口】叫某人卷铺盖,叫某人滚蛋,解雇某人,炒鱿鱼

The boss gave the manager his walking ticket yesterday. 老板昨天把那个经理解雇了。

4 that's the ticket 正合适,正对路,正时髦,正合要求

"All packed up and ready to go?" "That's the ticket." "行李都收拾好了，可以走了吧？""对了。"

5 what's the ticket 你打算怎么办，究竟怎么办
6 work one's ticket【口】为逃避工作装病（找其他借口）；谋求退役
7 write one's own ticket【口】自己制订计划；自行决定条件；自己规划前程

Although many of people in IT field are very young, they have been able to write their own tickets in their business. 虽然在IT业的许多人都很年轻，但他们已经能够在他们的领域自定身价了。

tickle

be tickled pink/to death 很喜欢
Evelyn was tickled pink by the gift. 那件礼物让伊夫琳高兴极了。

time

1 all in good time 来得及，快了，别急

"Can you give me back the money and the books I lent you?" "All in good time!" "你能把借我的钱和书都还我吗？""快了，别急嘛！"

2 any time 不用说谢，不用客气，随时为您效劳

"Thanks for a lovely evening!" "Any time! It was very nice to see you again and have a good chat!" "谢谢你今晚的热情招待！""不用客气，真高兴我们又见面了，我们聊得很畅快！"

3 do (one's) time 服刑

MacDonald admits his crimes openly, and is not afraid to do time for them. 麦克唐纳公开承认了自己的罪行，也不怕为此而坐牢。

4 every time 当然，毫无例外地，毫不犹豫地

You can rely on Gilbert every time. 你可以毫不迟疑地信赖吉尔伯特。
"Will you do it for Isabel?" "Every time." "这事你肯替伊莎贝尔做吗？""当然。"

5 give sb. the time of day 理睬某人（常用于否定句）

Foster wouldn't give me the time of day. 福斯特不愿意理我。

6 half the time 经常，几乎总是

Garcia says he's busy—but he's reading stories half the time. 加西亚说他很忙，可是他几乎总是在看故事书。

7　have a thin time 遇到不愉快的事,感到烦恼

Unemployed workers have a thin time. 失业工人度日如年。

8　have no time for 不喜欢,讨厌

I have no time for idlers. 我讨厌游手好闲的人。

9　in jig time 【美】很快,马上

I guarantee you'll have a job in jig time. 我保证你马上就能找到工作。

10　it beats my time 真叫我莫名其妙,真出乎意料

11　(it's) about time, too 终于到时候了;终于盼来了

Good—I can see the bus coming—and about time, too! 太好了,我看见汽车开过来了,终于等来了!

12　make time with 【美】与(异性)相爱,爱情在顺利地进行;与(异性)私通,勾引(异性)

The man was trying to make time with the waitress in the restaurant. 那个男人正在勾引餐馆的女招待。

13　nine times out of ten 十之八九,几乎总是

Nine times out of ten, Oscar will be using the phone. 十之八九,奥斯卡将使用这部电话。

14　no time 【美口】一会儿;没有时间

This is no time for you to do that. 这可不是你做那事的时候。

Get on with the work—this is no time to sit back. 好好干活,现在可不是坐吃山空的时候。

15　no time to swap knives 【美】没工夫改变计划、策略,来不及改弦更张

I have no time to swap knives. 我没工夫改变计划。

16　now's the time ……时候到了

Whether you're just entering college or preparing for graduation, now's the time to start thinking about your career. 不论你是刚进入大学还是就要毕业了,现在是该考虑职业生涯的时候了。

17　off time 关机时间;不合时宜的,不恰当的

Sorry, I spoke you some off time words. 对不起,我对你说了一些不合时宜的话。

18　of the time 当代的,当今的;当时的

He was among the first to question the received wisdom of the time. 他是那个时代首先质疑当时被普遍认可的处世之道的人之一。

19 pass the time of day with 与……打招呼，与……寒暄

People who live in towns are often too busy to pass the time of day with each other. 在城里生活的人往往忙碌得连寒暄都顾不上。

20 (so) that's the time of day 原来如此；就是这样；这样就好

Steady, sir, steady! That's the time of day! 站稳了，先生，站稳了。这样就行！

21 take one's time 不着急，不慌不忙

You can take your time about it. 这事你慢慢地做好了。

22 take sb. all his time 费大劲

It took Tom all his time to keep his temper. 汤姆好不容易才按捺住性子。

23 there is a time for everything 在一定的时候做一定的事，适时做事

There is a time for everything, and a certain amount of play-acting may be best for the first 4 minutes of contact with strangers. 凡事都要把握时机，在与陌生人接触的头四分钟，适度的做作也许最合适。

24 there's always (a) next time 机会总会有的

25 the time of one's life 一生中最难忘的、特别愉快、特别激动的一段时间

I suppose the four years in the university is the time of one's life, at least for me. 我想大学的四年时光可能是人一生中最美好的，至少对我来说是这样。

tip

1 at the tips of one's fingers 手头上的，随时可用的，精通

The scientist has Sanskrit at the tips of his fingers. 那个科学家精通梵文。

2 on/at the tip of one's tongue 就在嘴边的，差点说出口；差点想起来的

His name's on the tip of my tongue—ah, yes, Pressworth, that was it. 我一时想不起他的名字了。啊，对了，普雷斯沃思，是这个名字。

The words are on the tip of my tongue, but I don't quite know how to put what I want to say. 话到嘴边我突然忍住了。我真不知道如何表达我想说的话。

3 tip sb. off 向某人透露消息；暗中串通某人

Apparently the gang had been tipped off. 显然有人给那伙匪徒通风报信了。

4 tip the scales 称重量；具有决定性影响

Personality, talent, kindness, and maybe even quirkiness, may tip the scales. 人格、才艺、亲和力,甚至于奇谋诡诈的手段,都有可能成为加重分量的砝码。

toffee

can't do sth. for toffee 完全不会干
Hodge can't sing for toffee. 霍奇根本不会唱歌。

tomorrow

like there is/as if there were no tomorrow 不顾一切地
Harold was eating like there's no tomorrow. 哈罗德不顾一切地狼吞虎咽起来。

tongue

1 bite one's tongue off 后悔讲过的话,懊悔自己说过的话
I could bite my tongue off whenever I think of what I had said that day. 一想到那天说的话我就后悔得要死。

2 bite one's tongue/lip(s) 参见 lip 1

tooth

1 a kick in the teeth 非难,责备,侮辱;挫折,重大失败
Mary worked hard to clean up John's room, but all she got for her trouble was a kick in the teeth. 玛丽辛辛苦苦把约翰的房间打扫干净,不料她所得到的却是一番侮辱。
Not being accepted by colleges is surely a kick in the teeth for an excellent student like Kate. 对像凯特这样优秀的学生来说,不被大学录取肯定是一个重大打击。

2 to the teeth 完全地,充分地
Daddy and mummy fought a war to the teeth. 爸爸和妈妈大吵了一架。

3 tooth and nail/claw 竭尽全力地,猛烈地
They will fight tooth and nail for the right to vote. 他们将竭尽全力为争取选举权而斗争。

top

1 blow one's top 怒发冲冠,发脾气,气急败坏,大发雷霆

Don't blow your top when one or two people think it's smart to point out your faults and failings in a negative way. 当某些居心不良的人以负面的形式指出你的错误与失败时,千万别发脾气。

2 off one's top 神经失常,疯癫;心烦意乱
The football player was off his top. 那个足球运动员神经失常了。

3 off the top of one's head 【美】不假思索地,即兴地
I don't know the exact number of people who have been invited, but off the top of my head I should think there will be about forty. 我不知道被邀请者的确切人数,但不用思索,我认为会有 40 人左右。

4 on (the) top of (all) that 加之,此外
Hill broke his leg, and on top of that caught smallpox. 希尔摔断了腿,不幸又染上了天花。

5 on top of the world 非常幸福或成功;心满意足;声名显赫;处于最佳地位
Everything was working smoothly and I felt on top of the world. 一切都很顺利,我感到非常满意。

6 the top of the morning (to you) 早上好

7 to top it all (off) 加之,更有甚者;最糟的是;最后
It was raining, the bus was late, and, to top it all, John had no coat. 天下着雨,公共汽车晚点,更糟的是,约翰没有雨衣。

toss

toss off 一气喝干,一气干完;毫不费劲地做出
Hoover tossed off a glass of beer. 胡佛一口气喝完一杯啤酒。
Hughes tossed the article off in half an hour. 休斯在半个小时内一气呵成地把文章写好了。

tower

tower of ivory/ivory tower 象牙塔,世外桃源
With the fast development of higher education today, universities are no longer traditional "tower of ivory". 在高等教育迅猛发展的今天,高校不再是传统的"象牙塔"。

track

1 in one's tracks 【美】就地，当场；立刻

The horse fell dead in his tracks. 那匹马当场倒毙。

2 jump the track 【美】出轨；步入歧途；突然改变话题；心不在焉，胡思乱想

Parents must keep a strict hand over the children. Otherwise they may jump the track. 父母必须严格管教子女，否则他们也许会走错方向，偏离轨道。

3 make tracks 【美】匆匆离开，赶快走；进展迅速

Man, it's time we made tracks. 伙计，咱们得赶快走。

trade

trade on/upon 利用

You must never trade on his reputation. 你千万不要利用他的名声。

You trade on our relationship to do this. 你利用我们的关系来干这种事。

trap

1 keep one's trap shut 闭口不言

2 open one's trap 开口说话

When Jenny opens her trap, she has an accent that is American. 珍妮一说话就带有美国口音。

3 shut your trap 住嘴

"Shut your trap," said Harris. "You'll do us all in." "住嘴，"哈里斯说。"你要连累我们大伙儿呀。"

4 understand trap 精明，慎重

George does not understand trap but he know love. 乔治不聪明但是他知道爱是什么。

tree

1 bark up the wrong tree 枉费气力，找错目标；错怪了人；捕风捉影

I may be barking up the wrong tree in the neck of the woods. 我在那一带寻找也许是白费力气。

If Edmund thinks he can fool me, he's barking up the wrong tree. 假如埃德蒙认为他能愚弄我，那他找错目标了。

2　(be) up a (gum) tree 进退两难；陷入困境；走投无路

I had her in my power—up a tree, as the Americans say. 我把她牢牢控制住了，就像美国人说的我让她陷入困境。

And we are really up a gum tree to find a way out. 我们的确是处境艰难，找不到出路。

3　be out of one's tree 傻极了；发疯；在异地

"I don't want to live here." "Then you must be out of your tree." "我不想住在这儿。""那你可傻极了。"

4　can't see the woods/forest for the trees 只见树木，不见森林；以偏概全；因小失大，缺乏远见

Teachers sometimes notice language errors and do not see the good ideas in a composition, they can't see the woods for the trees. 老师批改作文，时常只注意语病，不看全文主旨，往往因小失大。

5　grow on trees 极易得到，伸手可得

Money doesn't grow on trees. 金钱来之不易。

6　pull up trees 获得巨大成就

The new manager doesn't seem the kind of person who'll pull up trees. 这位新经理看上去不像是有颇多建树的人。

trick

1　a trick/the tricks of the trade 生意花招；获胜的窍门

Frances has only been with us a month so she's still learning the tricks of the trade. 弗朗西丝到我们这里才一个月，还正在学习行内诀窍。

2　a trick worth two of that 更好的办法，更妙的策略

I know a trick worth two of that. 我有更好的办法。

3　be at one's tricks 作弄人

Nature is at her tricks again. 造化又在作弄人。

4　be up to one's tricks 恶作剧，调皮捣蛋；耍花招，惯用的伎俩

Eden is up to his tricks the minute my back's turned. 我一转身，艾登就在我背后调皮捣蛋。

5　do/work/turn the trick/take a trick 有效；能达到目的

I need a piece of paper. This old envelope will do the trick. 我需要一张纸，这个旧信封正合用。

6 for my next trick 【谑】看我再来一次（做某事失败后为掩饰难堪而说的话）

7 how's tricks 你好吗（用于问候）

8 never/not miss a trick 不失时机地利用；对发生的事无所不晓

Freeman's a very clever man and never misses a trick in improving his business. 弗里曼是个聪明能干的人，总是不失时机地利用有利条件去发展业务。

Isabel never seems to miss a trick. 伊莎贝尔对发生的事好像无所不晓。

9 none of your tricks 别耍花招，不上你的鬼当

None of your tricks with me! 我不会再上你的当了。

10 play/put/pull a trick on sb./play/serve sb. a trick/tricks 对某人耍手段；和某人开玩笑

Jeremy's played a mean trick on me. 杰里米对我使用了卑劣手段。

My memory plays me odd tricks. 我的记忆力不行了，常常和我开玩笑。

trouble

1 ask for/look for/seek trouble 自找苦吃

It's asking for trouble to associate with him. 跟他来往是自找麻烦。

2 be more trouble than a cartload of monkeys 极其烦心；极为讨厌

My three grandchildren are more trouble than a cartload of monkeys. 我的三个孙子非常顽皮、淘气。

3 borrow trouble 自找麻烦，自寻烦恼

If we acquiesce, we'll borrowing trouble for the future. 假如我们默许，日后将平添麻烦。

Forget about it; why borrow trouble? 忘了它吧，何苦自寻烦恼？

4 meet trouble 杞人忧天，自寻烦恼；遇到问题

Mike and Cindy meet trouble again. 麦克和辛迪又遇到麻烦了。

5 no trouble at all 不麻烦，没什么，很容易，不费事

No trouble at all. Just hope you get well quick. 没有什么问题，希望你早日康复。

true

1 as true as steel/flint/touch 极其忠实的，非常可靠的；千真万确的

Joyce is one of my old friends and is as true as steel what ever happens. 乔

伊斯是我的一个老朋友,无论发生什么事,他都是忠实可靠的。

2 it is true 的确,真的

I wonder if it is true. 我怀疑这是不是真的。

3 it just isn't true 真的(强调和加强语气)

I'm so happy, it just isn't true! 我多么高兴啊,千真万确!

It just isn't true how much work I've got to do this weekend! 我这个周末要做的事多得很,一点不假!

4 too true 完全正确

Many buyers of their repackaged loans, therefore, assumed an implicit federal government guarantee—an assumption, as we now know, that was all too true. 许多买家重新贷款是假设政府暗示担保,我们知道,这种假设是非常正确的。

5 true as I stand here 绝对真实,一点不假

trump

turn up trumps 意外的友善,意外的帮助,意外的成功;结果令人满意

My uncle turned up trumps and lent me money to go on holiday. 我叔叔竟然很好说话,借钱给我外出度假。

trust

trust you/him, etc. to 你/他等果然干出某些蠢事

Trust you to open your big month and let out the secret! 你果然开口泄露了秘密!

truth

to tell (you) the truth/truth to tell 老实说,说实话

To tell (you) the truth, I don't agree with what you said. 给你说实话,我不同意你说的话。

try

1 try it on with 对……粗野无礼;向……行骗

Frances slapped his face because he tried it on with her. 弗朗西丝打了他耳光,因为他对她行为粗野。

Flower tried it on with the bank clerk and was caught. 弗劳尔向银行职员

行骗被逮住了。

2 try on 愚弄；耍花招

It's no use trying on your tricks with me. 你对我们耍花招是没用的。

tube

be/go down the tube(s) 完蛋，不行了

The whole thing will go down the tube. 一切都将完蛋。

tuck

1 nip and tuck 势均力敌；苦战到底

The game was nip and tuck until the last minute. 比赛结束前双方势均力敌。

2 tuck in/into 狼吞虎咽

We tucked in as much as we desired. 我们尽情吃喝。

turkey

talk (old) turkey/say turkey 【美】坦率认真地谈；谈愉快的事；说老实话

Let's talk turkey about what really happened. 让我们坦率认真地谈谈实际发生的事吧。

turn

1 give sb. (quite) a turn 使某人大吃一惊

Why, Polly! You! What a turn you've given me! Who'd have thought it? 哎呀，波莉，是你呀！你把我吓了一跳，谁想到是你呀？

2 turn it in 住嘴，别干了；别说了

3 turn one's head 晕头转向；得意忘形

Winning the class election turned his head. 班上选举胜利使他得意忘形。

4 turn one's stomach 倒胃口，令人不舒服

The smell of the food turned the pregnant woman's stomach. 食物的气味令那个怀孕的女人倒胃口。

5 turn tail 逃跑，躲开

After the crash, the vehicle turned tail and ran. 撞车后，肇事车辆掉头就跑。

6 turn the trick 如愿以偿

Jerry wanted to win both the swimming and driving contests, but he couldn't quite turn the trick. 杰里想同时赢得游泳和跳水比赛,但未能如愿。

7 turn up one's toes 【俚】死亡,翘辫子

8 turn the scale 扭转局势

We can only turn the scale by supporting domestic famous brands strongly, to make them step into international market and accepted by them. 只有大力扶持国内知名品牌,使之走向国际市场并得到认可,才能扭转这一局面。

turn-up

a turn-up for the book(s) 意想不到的事

It was quite a turn-up for the book when I was offered the job. 我被录用做这工作,实在是意想不到的事。

tut

tut, tut 啧,啧(表示不赞成、指责、轻蔑等)

Tut, tut, Perry! I'm surprised at your behaving like that! I'd have thought you'd have known better. 啧,啧!佩里,你这种表现真叫我吃惊!我还以为你更明白事理呢。

twaddle

talk twaddle 说些不三不四的话

I can talk the most superb twaddle for six hours by the clock, watch in hand. 我还可以一连六个钟头天花乱坠地大谈一通。

two

1 in twos 立刻,一下子

The business was over in twos. 事情很快就办完了。

2 put two and two together 综合起来判断,根据事实推断

Putting two and two together, I felt that I could not have been far wrong. 总的来说,我感到我自己是错不到哪儿去的。

3 that makes two of us 对我同样适用,我也有同感

That makes two of us! She's a low-pitched actress. 我也有同感,她是个低

调的演员。

4 two can play at that game 这一套你会我也会（表示要报复）

"I'll have you both licked when I get out, that I will," rejoined the boy, beginning to snivel. "Two can play at that game, mind you," said Tom. "等我走出学校,我要叫人把你们俩狠狠揍一顿,我一定会的,"那孩子回答道,开始哭鼻子。"你叫人,我们也会叫人,你不要忘记,"汤姆说。

I discovered that my husband was having an affair—well, two can play at that game! 我发现我丈夫有风流韵事——好了,那一套不只他会,我也会!

5 two (for) a penny 多得很；很便宜

Small houses are very expensive there, but in here they are two a penny. 小型住宅在那儿很贵,可这里很便宜。

twopence

want twopence in the shilling 傻里傻气,疯疯癫癫,脑子不灵,精神失常

under

1 under one's belt 入肚；在经验记忆之中；成功地取得；努力以取得
Jim has to get a lot of algebra under his belt before the examination. 吉姆在考试前不得不加紧复习代数。

2 under one's nose 当……的面，公然，在眼皮底下，在鼻子底下
My classmates get the answers to the homework problems from books and former students, and they copy one another's homework in class, right under the professor's nose! 我的同学做作业不会时就从书上或是从学过这门课的同学那里抄答案。在班里，他们就在教授的眼皮底下相互抄作业！

3 under one's own steam 自食其力，独自地，凭自己的努力
My daughter has a degree in computer science, so I used to call her whenever I had questions. Last month, I took a course at the community college on computers. Now I can operate under my own steam. 我的女儿获得过计算机科学的学位，所以以前我一有问题就打电话问她。上个月，我在社区大学里上了一门电脑课。现在我可以靠自己来操作电脑了。

4 under the counter 私下买卖，违法的；走后门，偷偷地
The government's consumer watchdog accuses them of hoarding and speculation, complaining that they are selling under the counter to restaurants at a higher price. 政府的消费者监督机构指责他们囤积居奇，抱怨说他们正在暗地里以更高价格向饭店销售。

understand

now, understand me 喂，听着（表示警告或威胁）

up

1 up a stump【美俚】束手无策，处境尴尬，绊住，阻塞；弄糟
The philosophy teaching has been located up a stump by the inertial effect of the examination education in our college and university in actuality. 在

应试教育的惯性作用下,高校哲学教学在现实中处于尴尬地位。

2 up against it【美】面临困难

The Smith family is up against it because Mr. Smith cannot find a job. 史密斯先生找不到工作,他的家庭生活窘迫。

You'll be up against it if you don't pass the test. 如果你测验不及格,你的日子就会不好过。

3 up front 开诚布公,预先,坦率地,直截了当地

They think specifying everything up front and not deviating from the specification will ensure this. 他们认为预先说明每项事情并且不背离规范就能确保这一点。

4 up the creek 无计可施;动弹不得

I'll be up the creek if I don't pass this history test. 如果历史考试不及格,我真是无计可施了。

5 uptight about 忧虑,烦心,焦急

Why are you so uptight about getting that job? 你为什么急于得到那份工作?

6 up to par/scratch/snuff/up to the mark 参见 scratch 5

7 up to the/one's chin/ears/elbows/eyes/knees in 参见 chin 5

8 up with 支持(作为口号)

Up with the revolution! Up with the workers! 支持革命! 支持工人们的行动!

9 up with you 起床,起来

Up with you, Tom. It's time to go to school. 汤姆,起床了,上学的时间到了。

10 up yours 去你的

The car park attendant told Andrew, "You can't park here!" But he called back, "Up yours!" and drove in. 停车场的管理员对安德鲁说:"这儿不能停车!"安德鲁吼道:"去你的!"仍然把车开了进来。

11 what are you up to 你打的什么主意,你要干什么

Hi, Cathy. What are you up to this weekend? 你好,凯茜。你这个周末做什么?

12 what's up 怎么啦,什么事

You look upset. What's up? 你看起来很不安。怎么了?

upset

upset the/one's applecart 破坏计划，摧毁美梦
Her refusal to help quite upset the applecart. 她不肯帮忙，计划也就落空了。

use

1 have no use for 不喜欢，不能忍受；不需要，用不着
Bosses have no use for people who complain all day. 老板们不喜欢整天抱怨的人。

2 no earthly use 完全没用
That bike has no earthly use for the old man. 那辆自行车对这个老人完全没有用处。

3 use one's brain(s)/head/wits/bean/noodle/noggin/loaf 动脑筋，好好想想
The teacher often advises children to use their brains. 那个老师经常让孩子们多动脑筋。

4 use up 筋疲力尽
After rowing the boat across the lake, Robert was used up. 划船过湖以后，罗伯特筋疲力尽了。

5 what's the use of 有什么用处，有什么了不起
What's the use of her braying out such words? 她粗声粗气地说这种话有什么用呢？

usual

the/one's usual 通常饮用或食用的
"The usual please, love." "Right, beans and chips coming up!" "照往常的来一份，伙计。""好嘞，青豆炸土豆条来啦！"

very

1 cannot very well do sth. 不能做某事（表示委婉地拒绝）

I cannot very well drag him out of the meeting, can I? 我又不好把他从会场里拉出来，是吧？

2 very good（客气地同意）好吧，是，遵命

Very good, we'll go for a walk. 好吧，咱们去散散步。

"Bring the man in, sergeant." "Very good, sir." "把那个男子带进来，警官。""是，长官。"

3 very well（表示勉强同意）那好吧

Oh, very well, but I still think that I'm right. 嗯，那好吧，不过我仍然认为我是对的。

vest

1 close to the vest 谨慎小心，避免冒险

At meetings, the Japanese play close to the vest. 会谈时，日本人谨慎小心，从不冒险。

2 pull down one's vest【美】循规蹈矩；冷静，镇定

visit

1 pop visit 短暂的访问

I'll pop visit to Paris next week. 下周我将去巴黎做个短暂的访问。

2 visit with【美】访问，在……逗留；闲谈

Elizabeth will come down and visit with you for a few months. 伊丽莎白会来你这儿做客，住上几个月。

Edward loves visiting with his neighbour and having a good gossip. 爱德华喜欢找邻居聊天，说人家的闲话。

VOW

vow and declare 断言,肯定地说;郑重宣告,郑重声明
Why, I vow and declare! That's your husband, my dear. 啊!亲爱的,我断言那就是你丈夫!

wade

1 wade in 介入，插手，干预；猛烈攻击；精力充沛地工作

The house was a mess after the party, but mother waded in and soon had it clean again. 宴会后屋子很凌乱，但是经过母亲一番整理，屋子很快恢复了整洁。

2 wade into 猛烈攻击；精力充沛地工作

The police waded into the crowd with their clubs swinging. 警察挥舞警棍殴打人群。

wag

beards/chins/jaws/tongues are wagging 人们说闲话，议论纷纷

Ellis meant to have the child. If tongues are wagging, let them! 艾利斯一定要那个孩子。如果人们说闲话，让他们说好了！

wagon

1 fix one's/little red wagon 【美】揍人；报复；使……完蛋

Stop that right away or I'll fix your wagon! 住手，否则看我揍你！

2 hitch one's wagon to a star 【美】有雄心壮志；好高骛远；痴心妄想

John hitched his wagon to a star and decided to try to become president. 约翰野心勃勃想当总统。

wait

1 I can hardly wait 我简直等不了了，来就来吧（作为回答表示说话人并非真心期待某事）

"Mother's coming down from Glasgow next week to stay with us." "I can hardly wait!" "母亲下周要从格拉斯哥来同我们住一起。""来就来吧！"

2 I can't wait 我迫不及待地盼望

I can't wait to see her face when she opens her present. 在她打开她的礼物时，我迫不及待地看她脸上的表情。

3 just you wait/wait and see（表示威胁）等着吧，等着瞧
Just you wait—I'll get you back for this! 你等着瞧吧，我要你偿还这一切！
Just you wait till your father comes home! 等你父亲回来跟你算账！

4 wait for it 等着瞧吧，别慌，别忙，听着；且听我说
"What about the profits?" "Wait for it! I will explain that later." "利润怎么样？""别急，我一会儿再解释。"

walk

1 take a walk【美】快走；走开；出去走走，去散步

2 walk/step all over 轻蔑地对待，盛气凌人地对待；轻易地击败；统治、利用或作践……
Are you going to let that old banker walk all over you? 你要让那个老银行家盛气凌人地对待你吗？
Jones simply walked all over Brown in billiards. 在台球比赛中琼斯不费吹灰之力赢了布朗。

3 walk away/off 带走；偷走，拐走；在竞赛中轻易获胜
Someone has walked off with my umbrella. 有人把我的雨伞带走了。

4 walk away from 远远超过；轻易胜过；平安离开
My horse just walked away from all the others in that race. 在那次比赛中我的马遥遥领先所有的马。

5 walk down 通过散步消除；通过散步消化；在步行速度和距离上胜过
The patient wanted to walk down these poison. 病人想通过散步消除这些毒素。

6 walk into 猛烈攻击，痛斥，严厉批评；大口吞咽；轻易获得工作
The boss walked into Peter for being so careless. 老板痛骂彼得太粗心。
Can you see the little fellow walking into the pie? 你能看到那个正贪婪吃馅饼的小家伙吗？

7 walk on air 快乐，兴奋
Sue has been walking on air since she won the prize. 苏获奖后一直兴奋不已。

8 walk out on 抛弃，离开，不顾，不履行协议
Gill walked out on him on account of his laziness. 吉尔因他懒惰而离开了他。

9 walk out with 追求，与……恋爱

The cook is walking out with one of the tradesmen. 女厨师正同一个商人谈恋爱。

10 walk tall 趾高气扬，昂首阔步

Gunter had survived a dozen exploits, and now he walked tall in the camps. 冈特立功十余次而生还，因而在军营里趾高气扬。

11 walk the plank 被迫辞职

When a new owner bought the store, the manager had to walk the plank. 新老板买下了这个商店，经理被迫辞职。

12 win in a walk 轻易取胜

If there had been an election, he would have won in a walk. 如果当时举行选举的话，他本会轻易取胜的。

13 walk Spanish【美】小心翼翼地走路；被解雇；被罢免，被驱逐

John is walked Spanish by his company. 约翰被公司解雇了。

want

you want to/you ought to/you should 你应当……（要求对方特别注意或提出警告、批评等）

You want to look where you're going, young man! 你应当看看你走到哪去了，年轻人！

wash

1 come out in the wash 一切早晚都会解决的；一切都会真相大白

There are still a number of things unexplained but they will all come out in the wash. 仍有一些事情没有得到解释，但最终会真相大白的。

There's no need to worry, it'll all come out in the wash. 不必担心，问题会圆满解决的。

2 wash out 使衰弱；结束；毁坏；取消；放弃；使退学；被淘汰

I feel washed out. I shall stop working. 我觉得太累了，我要歇工休息。

Harry washed out after one semester. 哈里念了一学期就退学了。

3 wash one's hands of 洗手不干；撒手不管

We washed our hands of politics long ago. 很久以前，我们就不过问政治了。

I will wash my hands of gambling. 我以后再也不赌博了。

watch

1 watch it 小心

You'd better watch it. If you get into trouble again, you'll be expelled. 你最好小心点。假如你再惹麻烦,你就会被开除。

2 watch one's dust/smoke 参见 dust 6

3 watch oneself 注意,留神,谨慎,自我克制

Spring is the most dangerous time of year, you have got to watch yourself. 春天是一年中最危险的季节,你得注意。

4 watch out【美】密切注意,戒备,提防,小心

Special troops will be garrisoned all along the coast to watch out for enemy airplanes. 沿海都要驻扎特别部队以监视敌机。

Watch out! There's a car coming! 小心,有车子开过来!

water

1 above (the) water 摆脱麻烦或困境;摆脱债务

To stay above water, many businesses have already been forced to take desperate measures. 为了不陷入困境,许多企业已被迫采取非常措施。

2 be in/get into deep water(s) 招致麻烦,陷入困境

3 be in/get into hot water 陷入困境或烦恼

You'll get into hot water if you take apples from Mr. Scott's tree. 你如果从斯科特先生的树上摘苹果,会招来麻烦的。

4 live/be in low water 经济困难,手头拮据

With employment difficulty, demobilized soldiers have been ranked among weak colonies of our society and some of retired officers live in low water. 由于就业困难,部分退役军官生活拮据,退役士兵则被列入社会弱势群体的行列。

5 be in rough/trouble water 处于困境,灾难重重

6 be in smooth water 事事如意,顺境

This year things are going better and we are in smooth water. 今年我们一切顺利,日子过得不错。

7 come hell or high water 无论如何,只许成功不许失败

The soldier is determined to finish the task come hell or high water. 那个战士决心无论如何都要完成任务。

8　hold water 经得起考验；符合逻辑；可靠；有效

The theory may hold water. 这理论可能行得通。

The argument holds no water. 这个论点站不住脚。

9　pour/throw cold water on 向……泼冷水，使泄气，使沮丧

You should not throw cold water on the student. He is already losing heart. 你不该对那个学生泼冷水，他已经丧失信心了。

10　pour oil on the troubled water(s) 劝架，说和，平息风波；调解争端

The groups were nearing a bitter quarrel until the leader poured oil on the troubled waters. 两组人正要大吵大闹时被领导劝开了。

wave

make waves　参见 make 28

way

1　in a bad way　参见 bad 4

2　in a great way【英口】很激动，狂躁不安

The dog seemed to be in a great way. 那只狗看起来狂躁不安的样子。

3　on your way 走开

"On your way!" he shouted to the boys. 他向那些孩子吼道："走开！"

4　every which way【美】四面八方；混乱的

Her short-cut hair was all every which way. 她那剪得短短的头发乱得一团糟。

5　get that way【美】处境不佳，尴尬

How did you get that way? 你怎么这么尴尬？

6　go a long/great/good way 叫人受不了

A little of his company goes a long way. 跟他在一起不一会儿就受不了了。

7　go all the way with 与……意见完全一致

I agree with much of what you say, but I can't go all the way with you. 在许多方面我都同意你说的，但还不能完全同意。

8　in a sort of way 有点，有几分，在某点上，在某种意义上

9　in the worst way 极其，非常

Jonathan wanted to be a footballer in the worst way. 乔纳森渴望成为一个足球运动员。

10　no way 决不；不可能

"Will you lent me £50?" "No way, you didn't pay me back the last time I lent you some, so I'm not giving you any more now!" "你能借给我50英镑吗？""不行，上次我借给你的钱你还没还，现在我不会再借给你了！"

No way will I give you that money. 那钱我无论如何不会给你。

11　on the way out 行将过时；行将消失或失败、灭亡

That type of dress is on the way out. 那种服装式样已经快过时了。

12　six ways to/for Sunday 【美】在许多方面；彻底，完全

I was deceived six ways to Sunday. 我彻底受骗了。

13　there is/are no two ways about it 别无他法；毫无疑问

There's no two ways about it—I'm afraid we shall have to follow the rules. 别无他法，我看我们只有服从规则。

14　there is no way 没有可能

There is no way for you to reach her. 你没办法找到她。

15　way out 出口，解决方法，解决之道，摆脱困境的办法

The way out of our dilemma is to tunnel fearlessly through until we reach daylight. 我们离开困局的出路就是勇敢穿过隧道，直到我们到达光明的出口。

wear

1　wear out one's welcome 不受欢迎

This hot weather has worn out its welcome with us. 我们不喜欢这种闷热的天气。

2　wear the breeches/trousers/pants （女子）具有坚强性格，当家掌权

It is Mrs. Smith, not Mr. Smith, who wears the breeches in that family. 在家里当家的不是史密斯先生，而是史密斯太太。

3　wear well 令人满意；经久耐用；不见老

Katharine may be seventy, but she's worn well. 凯瑟琳大概有七十岁了，可并不见老。

weather

1　lovely weather for ducks 正在下雨；这种天气至少鸭子喜欢（下雨时的调侃语）

You're lucky it's sunny in Scotland; it's lovely weather for ducks down here. 苏格兰是晴天,你们真幸运,而南部却在下雨。

2 under the weather 不舒服,不高兴;经济困难

Robert was feeling a bit under the weather as he'd not had much sleep for several nights. 罗伯特感到有点不舒服,他已有好几个晚上没有睡好觉了。

weight

1 throw one's weight about/around 作威作福,狂妄自大,耀武扬威,仗势欺人

Bob was stronger than other boys, and he threw his weight about. 鲍勃仗着自己身强力壮,老是欺负别的孩子。

2 worth one's weight in gold 非常宝贵;很有经验

Judd's worth his weight in gold—I don't know anyone who's more reliable. 贾德是个宝贵的人才,我还没见过比他更值得信赖的人。

welcome

you are welcome 欢迎;别客气;请自便

"Thanks for your help!" "You're welcome!" "谢谢你的帮助!""别客气!"

well

1 all well and good 好吧,行(有时表示心平气和地接受决定);也好,也行(有时表示讥讽或不无勉强地赞同)

If Maggie offers me some work, all well and good, if not I don't mind much. 如果玛吉再分给我一些工作,也行;如果不分给我,我也不介意。

2 it's all very well/it's all right 好倒是好;固然不错(表示不满、讥讽等)

It's all very well to say that, but what can I do? 你说得倒好,可是我有什么办法?

3 jolly well 实在,的确,一定,最好

4 just as well 幸好,正好;不妨;不必遗憾

"We were too late for the concert!" "Just as well—it wasn't very good anyway." "听音乐会我们来得太晚了!""幸好这个音乐会不怎么样。"

It would be just as well to telephone them before we arrive. 我们不妨在到达前给他们打个电话。

5 oh well 好吧,算了吧(表示不无勉强地接受)

Oh well, I shouldn't grumble, I suppose this is the first time something like this has happened. 好吧,我不该发牢骚。我想这是第一次发生这样的事吧。

6 very well 好吧(表示同意或接受,有时也表示不同意)
"Please be home early tonight—I want to wash your hair." "Very well, mother!" "今晚早点回来,我要给你洗头。""好吧,母亲。"

7 well, well 啊呀呀(表示惊讶)
Well, well, who'd have thought those two would end up getting married? 啊呀呀,谁想到他俩到底还是结婚了。

wet

1 be all wet 【美】完全搞错了;毫无价值;瞎扯,胡说
You are all wet if you think I'm giving up that easy. 如果你认为我那么轻易认输,那你就大错特错了。

2 wet behind the ears 参见 ear 10

whack

1 at a/one whack/single sitting/stroke 一鼓作气地,一气呵成地,一口气
I read the book at a whack. 我坐着一口气将这本书读完了。

2 get/have/take one's whack 大喝一顿,饱餐一顿;获得充分的一份
The young man had his whack in the party. 那个小伙子在聚会上饱餐了一顿。

3 have/take a whack at 【美】照……猛击一下,用力攻击;尝试
The little boy tried to take a whack at me! 那个小男孩儿居然想打我!
Let me take a whack at it. I think I can fix it. 让我来试试看,我想我能修理它。

4 in whack 【美】有条不紊;情况良好,情况正常
Mark is in fine whack. 马克情况不错。

5 it's/that's a whack 【美】一言为定
"I'll stay if you will." "Good—that's a whack." "你要是留下的话,我就不回去。""好,一言为定。"

6 out of whack 【美】不正常,有毛病
If you do not have the time, your priorities are out of whack. 如果你没有时间,那是你把不该放在优先位置上的事情放错了地方。

7 whack out 起劲地干完；使……输得精光

Abraham can whack out a short story every week. 亚伯拉罕每星期能写出一篇短篇小说。

8 whack up 起劲地干完；分享，分配；增加

The robbers decided to whack up the profits from the robbery. 盗贼们决定分赃。

They are discussing how to whack up the profits. 他们在讨论怎样分红利。

whale

1 very like a whale 【讽】你讲得多对啊，当然是这样

Ay, what you have said is very like a whale. 对，你说的话真对。

2 whale away 击打，痛揍，猛击；抨击

The boxer is whaling away at his opponent with both fists. 拳击手挥动双拳猛击对手。

Mary has been whaling away on the typewriter for an hour. 玛丽不停地打了一小时的字。

what

1 and what not 以及其他东西；诸如此类；等等

Grace called me fool and what not. 格雷斯骂我是傻瓜，还骂我这一类的许多话。

2 I'll/I tell you what 我的主张、意见、建议是；你听我说

3 for what I can tell/know 据我所知，据我了解

For what I can tell, Tom won't come to attend the meeting. 据我所知，汤姆不会来参加会议。

4 give sb. what for 严厉惩罚某人，申斥某人；痛揍某人

If Harold has any of his insolence to me next time, I'll give him what for. 如果哈罗德下次对我无礼，我要狠狠教训他。

5 or what/whatever （用于句末）还是别的什么

I've not seen her recently—I don't know whether she's moved away, whether I've upset her, or what. 最近我一直没见到过她，不知是她搬走了呢，还是我得罪了她，或者还有什么别的原因。

6 so what/what of/about it 那又怎么样呢，那有什么关系，那有什么法子，

那有什么了不起的

"Madge doesn't like you?" "So what?" "马奇不喜欢你?" "那又怎么样呢?"

7 what about 参见 about 2

8 what can I do for you 我能为你做什么吗

My pleasure. What can I do for you? 很高兴为您服务,我能帮您做什么?

9 what do you say ……你说怎么样(提出建议)

What do you say we have a rest? 休息一下,你看怎么样?

10 what good/use is it 它能派什么用场,它有什么用

What good is it unless I can use it to help solve my daily problems, large or small? 如果它不能帮我解决日常生活中大大小小的问题,那它有什么用呢?

11 what have you 等等,任何你想要的

The store sells big ones, small ones, medium ones or what have you. 店里有大、中、小的任何你想要的尺寸,供你挑选。

12 what if 如果……将会怎样;即使……又有什么关系

What if we bought a new carpet—would it make any difference to the room? 如果我们买一条新地毯的话,情况会怎么样? 它会使这房间改变样子吗?

13 what is it (now) 你想要什么,你想干什么

"Herby, are you in there?" "What is it? I'm busy." "赫尔拜,你在那里吗?" "你要干什么,我忙着呢!"

14 what is it to you 你为什么对这感兴趣

"How old are you?" "Why do you want to know? What is it to you?" "你多大年纪?" "你问这干什么? 你为什么对这感兴趣?"

15 what it takes 取得成功的必要条件(如雄心、才智、金钱、美貌等)

Given your experience in the business, could you share with me on what it takes to be successful in this profession? 根据您个人的经验,您是否可以和我分享一下您在这个领域中获得成功的心得?

16 what next 参见 next 4

17 what of 情况如何

"What of the planes?" "Returned to their bases." "那些飞机怎么样了?" "都回基地了。"

18 what with 因为,由于,考虑到

We've had awful weather this year, what with all the snow and heavy frosts. 今年我们这儿天气很恶劣，又是大雪，又是霜冻。

19 what's all this 情况怎么样，出了什么事

What's all this, boys? Why aren't you paying attention and listening? 怎么啦，孩子们？你们为什么不注意听讲？

20 what's the (big) idea 居心何在，想干什么，怎敢如此

What's the idea of coming in here after I told you not to? 我叫你别来，你怎敢再来？

You're spreading false rumors about me, what's the big idea? 你散布我的谣言居心何在？

21 what's up/cooking/doing 怎么啦，干什么，出了什么事

What's up? What's everyone looking at? 怎么啦，大家都在看什么？

22 what's what 事情的真相或究竟、诀窍等

When it comes to cooking, Jenny knows what's what. 谈到烹饪，珍妮是内行。

23 what's with/what's up with/what's by 怎么啦，什么事；近况如何；有何消息

Mary looks worried, what's with her? 玛丽面有愁容，她怎么啦？

I'm fine. What's with you? 我很好，你近来怎么样？

24 what's yours 你想喝点什么

"What's yours, Nick?" "Gin and tonic, please." "你想喝点什么，尼克？" "请来点奎宁杜松子酒。"

wheel

a third wheel 电灯泡

"Can we have a minute alone?" "Sure, I don't want to be a third wheel." "让我们单独待一会儿，好吗？""当然，我可不想当电灯泡。"

where

1 where it is 关键所在，实情所在

Julia doesn't want to go, that where it is. 朱莉娅不愿去，问题就在这里。

2 where it's at 【美】使人大感兴趣或大为激动的地方；根本性的事物

If you're interested in good food, Paris is where it's at. 如果你对美食感兴趣，巴黎是个好去处。

Education is where it's at. 教育是关键所在。

whether

whether or no/not 无论如何，在任何情况下
Kelsen threatens to go, whether or no. 凯尔森威胁说他无论如何都要走。

while

1 make it worth one's while 酬谢……；贿赂……
How much will you give me to make it worth my while to do it? 我做这事你将怎样酬谢我？
2 while you are about it 顺便，在你做这事的同时
While you are about it, top me with a gallon or so of unleaded. 请你现在顺便给我加一加仑左右的无铅汽油把油箱灌满。
3 worth one's while 值得……花时间、精力等
It will be worth your while to go and see him. 你去看看他是值得的。

whistle

1 let sb. go whistle 使某人失望；不顾某人的意愿；无礼地拒绝某人，赶走某人
2 pay (dear) for one's whistle 得不偿失，高价买小东西
If a man likes to do it, he must pay for his whistle. 如果有人喜欢做这事，他就会得不偿失。
3 whistle for 得不到，空指望
If you want a house in this village, you'll have to whistle for it. 如果你想在这个村子里弄一幢房子，那你是在白日做梦。
4 whistle in the dark 为自己壮胆；故作镇静
When Harriman was on the way home at midnight, he sang songs and coughed to whistle in the dark. 哈里曼半夜回家时，为了壮胆，他不是唱歌，就是咳嗽。
5 in less than a pig's whistle 立刻，马上
We shall graduate in less than a pig's whistle. 我们马上就要毕业了。

white

a white elephant 累赘，昂贵而又无用的东西

Each holiday for me seemed like *a white elephant*, a thing which can't make people excited. 每一个节日对我来说如同鸡肋,令人提不起劲。

whoop

whoop it/things up 欢闹,狂欢,庆祝;大事宣扬

The team *whooped it up* after winning the game. 该队在获胜后欢呼雀跃。

wick

1 get on one's wick 激怒……

Parades and bullshit *get on his wick*. 游行和说大话常使他极为恼怒。

2 turn the wick up 启动发动机,加速;把灯芯调高

The light is getting weaker. *Turn the wick up*, please. 光线越来越暗,你去挑挑灯芯吧。

3 turn the wich down 关闭发动机,减速;把灯芯调低

will

1 if you will 如果你喜欢的话,如果你允许的话

If you will undertake the affair, I shall be very grateful. 要是你愿意承办这件事,我将不胜感激。

2 will he, nill he 不管他愿意不愿意,无选择余地

Jackson must bear the consequences of his improvident action *will he, nill he*. 不管杰克逊愿意不愿意,他必须对自己挥霍浪费所造成的后果负责。

win

1 you can't win 不管你做什么都将被认为一无是处(表示恼怒)

Paradoxically the struggle for autonomy is one *you can't win* on your own. 很矛盾的是,为争取人身自由而进行的斗争是你无法独自去赢得的。

2 you can't win them all 你不可能事事成功,你不可能一直走运(表示安慰)

We spent years for a by-pass. Now it's been built, you hear the heavy lorries driving by so fast that it's as noisy as ever. *You can't win them all*, can you? 我们花了几年时间修一条便道,现在建成了。可是你听那些载重汽车跑得多快,现在比过去更加喧闹了。唉,没法子,事无两全嘛!

3 win in a walk/breeze 轻易获胜

Our team won the game in a breeze. 我们队轻易赢得比赛。

4 win hands down 轻易取胜，毫不费劲地跑赢

Early on Bush had such a healthy lead, some experts were predicting he would win hands down in November. 刚开始时布什稳稳地处于领先地位，以至于某些专家当时预计他11月份不费吹灰之力就能获胜。

wind

1 burn the wind 【美口】奔驰，飞速前进，飞快地跑

The car was burning the wind along the road. 那辆轿车正沿着马路向前奔驰。

2 put/get the wind up 使……感到害怕；害怕，吓坏了

The noise put the wind up me. 那声音真使我害怕。

3 raise the wind 筹款；制造混乱，兴风作浪

You can raise the wind by selling your stamp collection. 你把你收集的邮票卖掉就可以筹到钱了。

4 sits the wind there 情况是这样的吗，事情的动向是那样吗

"Sits the wind there?" the teacher asked. "情况是这样的吗？"老师问道。

5 slip one's wind/breath 咽气，断气，死

The horse has just slipped its wind. 那匹马刚刚断气。

6 there's something in the wind 好像要发生什么事

A gunshot echoed in the woods and broke the dead silence in the morning. "There's something in the wind," I thought. 枪声在林间回荡，打破了清晨的沉寂。"发生什么事了吧？"我思忖着。

7 what (good) wind brings/blows you here 什么风把你吹来的

"What good wind brings you here?" "Not an ill wind." "什么风把你吹来的？""肯定不是恶风。"

8 in the wind 即将发生；在进行

Yes, Knox is in the wind. You need to know that targeting the Nigerians was the right thing to do. 对，还是没有抓到诺克斯。但是你们要明白追捕尼日利亚人才是正事。

9 what's in the wind 有什么风声，要发生什么事

wipe

1 wipe off 抹掉，消灭；还清债务；杀死，谋杀

The man in black threatens that he will wipe his father off. 那个穿黑衣服的人扬言要杀他的父亲。

They hope he will wipe off all their debt. 他们希望他把他们欠的债一笔勾销。

2 wipe out 除去,消灭,毁灭,勾销债务;干掉

The earthquake wiped out the town. 这场地震毁了全城。

wire

1 down to the wire【美】直到最后,最后关头

Obviously a final match like this coming down to the wire, you can't get anything better than that. 显然在这样一场决赛的最后关头获胜,我们不可能做得比这更好了。

2 get/have one's wires crossed 发生误会

If you think there's a meeting today, you really have your wires crossed; it's not till next month. 如果你以为今天开会,那你就弄错了,下个月才开会。

3 under the wire【美】及时赶上或完成,在最后期限前

I finished my assignment just under the wire. 我恰好在最后期限之前完成了我的任务。

4 wire in 拼命苦干;给……接上电源线

It's raining! Wire in, everybody! 要下雨了! 大家加油干啊!

wise

1 get wise【美】发觉,明白;变得傲慢无礼,放肆

I hope you'll get wise and learn to keep your mouth shut. 我希望你学乖些,不要声张。

Don't get wise with me, young man! 别跟我放肆,年轻人!

2 put sb. wise 使某人了解,使某人知道

Lawrence put me wise about official life abroad. 劳伦斯让我了解一些国外的官场生活。

3 wise after the event/behind 事后诸葛亮,马后炮

But we're always wise after the event. That's not much good to me now. 但我们总是事后诸葛亮,这对我可不是什么好事。

4 wise up 恍然大悟,知道底细

Joe immediately quit his job when he wised up to what really going on. 乔在知道底细后立即辞职不干了。

5 as wise as Solomon 非常聪明，像所罗门一样聪明

Yet we will never be as wise as Solomon, the wisest man who ever lived. 但是我们永远都不可能像所罗门那么聪明，因为所罗门王是迄今为止最聪明睿智的人。

with

1 be with 理解……讲的话

"Are you still with me?" "Sorry, I'm not quite with you." "我的话你还能听懂吗？""对不起，我不太听得懂。"

2 with bells on 满怀热情的；非常愿意

"Will you come to the party?" "I'll be there with bells on." "你愿意参加这个晚会吗？""高兴之至。"

woe

1 woe be to 愿……遭殃

Woe be to him who chances to be there! 谁碰上了，就该谁倒霉！

2 woe betide 倒霉，遭殃（表示威胁）

Woe betide you if you arrive late. 你如果迟到，你就要倒霉了。

3 woe is me 我好苦啊，我真不幸

By the way, this is not a woe-is-me story, but rather an honest account of my experience and I am not alone with a story like this. 顺便说一下，这不是一个"我最倒霉"的故事，而是我亲身经历的事，像我这样有同样经历的人并不只有我一个。

4 woe worth 真该诅咒

Woe worth the day! 今天真倒霉！

wolf

a wolf in sheep's clothing 披着羊皮的狼；伪君子

Beware of the new manager. He seems polite, but he's a wolf in sheep's clothing. 当心这位新经理。他看似很有礼貌，却可能是笑里藏刀的那种人。

wonder

1 for a wonder 真奇怪,意想不到

You are punctual for a wonder. 真没想到,你居然这么准时。

2 I shouldn't wonder 我不会感到奇怪

James will have left that job now, I shouldn't wonder. 詹姆斯将离开那份工作,我并不感到奇怪。

3 it's a wonder (that) 真奇怪

It's a wonder you're still living here after all these years! 真奇怪,过了这么些年了你还住在这儿!

4 (it's) no/little/small wonder 难怪

No wonder Jack couldn't come dancing with us; he has broken his leg, after all. 难怪杰克不能来跳舞了,他跌断了腿。

5 the wonder is 奇怪的是

The wonder is Lily remembered my name! 奇怪的是,莉莉居然还记得我的名字!

6 wonders will never cease 真是怪事

"I've done the washing-up, Mum!" "Wonders will never cease!" "妈妈,我把餐具洗完了。""啊,真有这样的事!"

wood

1 knock (on)/touch wood 用手碰木头,迷信认为可以避邪

Touch wood, I'm back to normal. 真是走运,我又恢复了正常。

2 out of the wood(s) 【美口】脱离险境或困境

Mary nearly died during the operation, and she is not out of the woods. 玛丽在做手术时几乎死去,现在还没脱离危险。

Don't shout/halloo/cry halloo till you are out of the wood. 未离险境,先别高兴。

3 saw wood 【美】一心干活,不管别人的事;睡觉,打鼾;(在政治上)采取消极态度

I bet you will never fall asleep when he begins to saw wood. 我敢打赌他一旦打起鼾来你就别再想睡着了。

4 take to the woods 逃脱;逃避责任;躲起来,跑开

As the enemy advance continued, the townspeople would take to the woods carrying all their belongings. 敌人还在继续前进,市民们将携带行李物品躲起来。

wool

1 keep your wool on 冷静点,别生气

2 lose one's wool【口】发怒,生气

The fellow often *loses his wool*. 那家伙老是发脾气。

3 much cry and little wool/more cry than wool 参见 cry 5

word

1 (could I have) a word in your ear 可以和你私下谈谈吗,可以和你说个悄悄话吗

A word in your ear, John? It's about those new contracts we mentioned. 约翰,能单独和你谈一下吗? 是有关我们刚签订的那些新合同的事。

2 eat/swallow one's words 被迫收回前言,承认错误

They told him he would never succeed at anything, but he made them *eat their words*. 他们对他说,他什么事也做不成,但他却使他们承认自己说错了话。

3 famous last words 别耍贫嘴,别瞎吹(表示嘲弄、警告、不信任)

"I'll be back in half an hour!" "*Famous last words*—you've said that before and you've been gone all morning!" "半个小时后我就回来!" "净瞎吹! 你曾说过这话,可一跑就是一个上午不见人影。"

4 from the word go【美】从头;始终,彻头彻尾

We turn out the whole thing—clean *from the word go*—in our factory. 所有的制造程序从头到尾都是在我们工厂里完成的。

5 get a word in edgeways/edgewise 参见 get 6

6 hang on/upon one's words/every word 认真地听……的话

Anna *hangs on every word of her history teacher* and take very careful notes. 安娜认真地听历史老师讲的每一句话,并仔细地做笔记。

7 in a/one word 一句话,总而言之;简单说来

In a word, they can do everything they like with money. 总之,他们用金钱能做到他们喜欢做的一切。

8 in a few words 总之;简单说来

Let us condense, *in a few words*, a part of what we have just written. The only social peril is darkness. 让我们把刚才所说的一部分用几个字概括起来就是，社会的唯一危害是黑暗。

9　in other words 换句话说

In other words, you may not be sure what to do next in this predicament. 换句话说，你可能并不知道你在这种困境中接下来要做什么。

10　in so many words 一字不差地说，清清楚楚地说，毫不含糊地说，直截了当地说

Let us suppose that you are fortunate and can describe to your own satisfaction in so many words the exact meaning of your chosen theme. 让我们设想，你很幸运，能够清清楚楚地描述你自己选择的主题。

11　isn't the word for it 不准确

Unkind isn't the word for it! He treats the animals appallingly! 岂止是"不好"！他对待动物是太不像话了！

12　mark my words 记住我的话；听我说

Mark my words, he'll let you down. He's worked for me in the past, so I know he's not very reliable. 记住我的话，他会让你失望的。他以前为我工作，所以我知道他靠不住。

13　my word 哎呀

My word, Laura! You do look stunning! 哎呀，劳拉，你看上去真漂亮啊！

14　not a word 别说出去

Here comes Mum, so remember, not a word about her birthday present! 妈妈来了，记住了，别对她说礼物的事！

15　not another word 别再说了

So that's settled then, is it? Now, not another word about it! 这事就这么定了。现在再也别提它了！

16　not in so many words 不十分明确；不十分确切

We weren't invited in so many words, but Nora certainly told us she was having a party. 我们没有明确地被邀请，但诺拉已经肯定地告诉我们她要举办一个晚会。

17　one more word out of 安静，如不安静就要受惩罚（表示威胁或警告）

One more word out of you, and I won't let you go on the trip. 安静，否则我就不让你们去旅行。

18　say the word 吩咐一下，表示一下

Say the word and it'll be done. 只要你吩咐一声,这事马上就办好。

19 sharp's the word 快点

Sharp's the word! We've got to go in a minute—come on and get ready! 快点！我们马上就出发。快做好准备！

20 take one's word for it 相信……的话

I take your word for it that you never said such a thing. 我相信你从未说过这样的话。

21 take the words out of one's mouth 先讲出……要说的话

I was about to say that. You've taken the word out of my mouth. 我正要这么说,你倒先把它说出来了。

22 true to one's word/keep/hold one's word 遵守诺言

You must keep your word even if you should lose by it. 即使守信用会吃亏,你也必须遵守诺言。

23 upon my word 说实在话；我保证；一点不假

"Are you serious?" "Upon my word I am." "这话当真？" "我向你保证,一点不假。"

24 what's the good word 有什么好消息,近来好吗（熟人间打招呼）

You are so glad today. What's the good word? 你今天特别高兴,有什么好消息？

25 words fail me 说不出话来（由于激动、惊讶、高兴、生气等）

You say you spent £1,000 on that car! Words fail me! What a fool you are! 你说你买那车花了一千英镑,天哪,叫我说什么好呢！你真是个大傻瓜！

work

1 all in a/the day's work 习以为常,不足为奇

To anyone working in a hotel, angry complains from guests are all in a day's work. 对在酒店里工作的人来说,客人们怒气冲冲地提意见是家常便饭。

2 get the works 【美】吃苦头,受折磨,遭惩罚；被杀害

You are going to get the works if you ever come back again. 如果你再回来,就给你一点厉害。

3 give sb. the works 【美】给某人吃苦头,折磨、惩罚或杀害某人；给某人

全套待遇；对某人和盘托出

I'll give you the works if you ever come back again. 如果你再回来，我就给你一点厉害瞧瞧。

4 give sth. the works 对某物进行全盘处理；使某物大为改观

We're giving our house the works—we're painting the whole place and putting in new furniture. 我们要把屋子全面装修一番，要全部油漆一遍，再放进新的家具。

5 gum/bung up the works【美】毁坏，搞糟，搞乱

I think we better leave Joe out of our first meeting with this new customer. Joe means well, but I'm afraid he'll say something stupid and really gum up the works for us. 我想我们和这位新顾客举行第一次会议的时候乔最好不要在场。乔用意不坏，只是我怕他会说出些不恰当的蠢话把我们的事情搞砸了。

6 have one's work cut out 面临艰巨的任务；十分忙碌

We'll have our work cut out to finish on time. 我们要按时完成任务，是够艰巨的。

7 it won't work 那不行，你没用

If you're restarting, but it won't work, check this panel to see if its actually able to start. 如果你要重新启动，但它启动不了，检查一下仪表板，看看它是否真正能够启动。

8 make short/quick work of 迅速干掉，迅速解决

The children made short work of the cakes. 孩子们把蛋糕一下子吃光了。

9 shoot the works 参见 shoot 9

10 work over 殴打，伤害

The gang worked him over. 这帮歹徒把他毒打了一顿。

11 work like a Trojan/dog 勇敢拼搏，工作勤奋

Edward worked like a Trojan, and yet failed to get the project through. 爱德华埋头苦干，但企划案还是没能通过。

world

1 all's right with the world 一切都很好，一切令人满意

God's in his heaven, all's right with the world. 神在天堂司宇宙，世间一切皆太平。

2 be broke to the world 参见 broke 1

3 come/go down in the world 落魄；衰落，倒退

Poor old George has come down in the world since his business failed. 可怜的老乔治自从他的生意失败以后就落魄了。

These people would ask for insult and come down in the world for heavy debt. 这种人多半会自取其辱，最后栽在债台高筑的漩涡之中。

4 come/get/go up in the world 发迹，兴盛，飞黄腾达

Mr. Rubin came up in the world because he had the talent for making money. 卢宾先生成功了，因为他有赚钱的才能。

Smith has got up in the world. 史密斯已经飞黄腾达了。

5 how goes the world with you/how is the world treating/using you 近况如何，日子过得怎样

How goes the world with you? 你近况如何？

6 how the world goes/wags 情况怎样

7 in the world 究竟，到底

Who are you in the world? 你到底是谁呀？

8 it's a small world 这世界真小

When I was introduced to the new boss I realized that we'd both been to the same school. It's a small world. 当我被介绍给新上司时，我发现我们俩曾在同一所学校上过学。这世界真小。

9 let the world wag (as it will) 听其自然，任凭时事变迁

Let the world wag as it will. 听其自然。

10 on top of the world 非常高兴

I'm feeling on top of the world today—I've just heard I've passed all my exams! 今天我高兴极了，因为我听说我的全部考试都通过了。

11 out of this/the world【美】非凡的，极好的，十全十美的；脱离实际的，不合理的

I think the flavor of fresh strawberries is out of this world. 我认为新鲜草莓的味道鲜美无比。

12 set the world on fire 非常成功，大出风头

His invention set the world on fire. 他的发明大获成功。

13 tell the world【美】公开讲，断言

With the help of social media, they tell the world exactly what to expect.

通过社会媒体的帮助,他们告诉全世界这里将会发生什么。

14 the world is good enough to eat 这世界真甜美

15 the world is one's oyster 世界属于……

When John won the scholarship, he felt the world was his oyster. 约翰获得了奖学金,觉得仿佛这世界就是他的。

16 think the world of 非常看重,钦佩;喜爱

John thinks the world of his Dad. 约翰极为敬佩他的父亲。

17 to the world【俚】完全地,极度地

William is a fool to the world. 威廉是个地道的傻瓜。

18 would give the world/worlds 非常乐意

My brother's going to China this week. I'd give the world to be going with him. 我哥哥本周要去中国,我真想和他一起去。

worry

1 I should worry 我一点也不在乎(反语)

"But it's a serious matter for you." "Serious my foot. Why should I worry?" "这件事对你来说很重要!" "什么大事,去你的吧!我担心什么?"

2 not to worry 不必担心

"I've lost my ticket." "Well, not to worry, we can pay when we get to London." "我的机票丢失了。" "别担心,到了伦敦再补票吧。"

3 worry along/through 克服困难前进;应付过去;熬下去

Jane must try to worry along without him. 没有他,简也要设法应付过去。

4 you should worry【谑】你当然不必担心

You should worry with a salary like that coming in every month! You don't know how lucky you are! 你当然不必为每月的工资担心啦!你是身在福中不知福!

worse

things could be worse 还可以,还好(回答别人询问近况、身体等)

"How are you, Jim?" "Things could be worse. Thanks." "吉姆,近来怎么样?" "还好,谢谢。"

worst

if the worst comes to the worst 如果最坏的事情发生;到了一筹莫展之时;

万不得已时
If the worst comes to the worst, we can go by bus tomorrow. 如果没有更好的办法,我们明天就搭公共汽车去。

worth

1 for all one is worth【美】尽力,拼命
William ran for all he was worth to catch the bus. 威廉拼命跑去赶公共汽车。

2 for what/all it is worth 不论真伪,不论好坏,不论对否
You may accept it for what it's worth. 不论此说是真是假,你姑妄听之好了。

3 not worth a bean 不值一文,毫无价值,毫无用处
This old bank note does not worth a bean now. 这张旧纸币现在已经一文不值了!

4 worth it 值得的,值得信赖的;有用的
They are expensive, but they are worth it. 那些东西很贵,但划得来。
Don't lock the door; it isn't worth it. 门别锁了,用不着。

wrap

1 be wrapped up in 专心致志于;对……倾注全部注意或爱慕;与……有关;全靠
Malory's wrapped up in his studies. 马洛里专心致志地学习。
Your future is not entirely wrapped up in your passing this examination. 你的未来并不完全取决于你是否通过这场考试。

2 wrap around/round 包裹;使吃,使喝,使撞上
The cool air seemed to wrap around my body. 冰冷的空气一下包裹住了我的身体。

3 wrap up 完成,结束;赢得比赛;总结;严重损坏
Let's wrap up the job and go home. 让我们干完活回家去。
They wrapped up the baseball game in the seventh innings. 棒球打到第七局时他们赢了。

write

1 could I have that in writing【谑】我可以载入史册喽(幽默地回答别人的

奉承话)

"We've always found you to be a man of most remarkable abilities!" "Could I have that in writing!" "我们始终认为你是一个具有超人才干的人才!""那我可以载入史册喽!"

2 nothing to write home about 参见 home 6

wrong

1 be wrong in the/one's head 疯狂,疯癫

You must be wrong in the head if you believe that. 你相信那件事可就太疯狂了。

2 get in wrong with【美】令人讨厌

Michael is forever getting in wrong with the people next door. 迈克尔老是惹得邻居讨厌。

3 get sb./sth. wrong 误解/曲解某人/某事

Don't get me wrong. 不要误会我。

Y

year

in the year dot/one【英口】很久很久以前

If people ever dressed like that, it must have been *in the year dot*. 即使有人那样穿戴,那也是很久很久以前的事了。

yes

yes and no 也是也不是,也好也不好,也行也不行

"Have you made up your mind whether to go?" "*Yes and no.*" "你下决心要去吗?""想去又不想去。"

you

1 for you 就是这样,真是这样(用于句末加强语气)

There's a fine rose *for you*! 真是一朵好玫瑰!

Nancy changed her mind going. That's a girl *for you*. 南希改变主意不去了,女孩子就是这样。

2 to you 你应当叫,你不妨说,通常说法

Not John, if you don't mind—Mr. Smith *to you*. 对不起,不要叫他约翰,你该叫他史密斯先生。

3 you don't say 我不信,真的吗(表示惊奇)

Your ring is a real diamond? *You don't say*! 你的戒指真是钻石的?我不信!

4 you said it/you can say that again 完全同意

"That sure was a good show." "*You said it*!" "那真是一场很好的表演。""我完全同意!"

5 you tell'em 对呀,干得好(表示同意或鼓励)

The speaker said his party would win the election and the crowd shouted "*You tell'em*!" 演讲人说他的党会赢得选举,听众高呼"干得好,干得好!"

6 you're another 你也一样嘛(用于争执时还嘴)

I must say that I have never heard, from any Western pacifist, an honest answer to this question, though I have heard plenty of evasions, usually of the "you're another" type. 我必须说,我没有听到任何一位西方和平主义者对这个问题的诚实回答,尽管我听到大量的借口,一般都是"你也一样嘛"之类的话。

yourself

be yourself 你得镇静一点,别慌张;你得振作起来;恢复健康

You don't seem to be yourself today, Jim. 吉姆,你今天好像有些不自在。Don't act sophisticated, just be yourself. 不要做出老于世故的样子,自然点儿。

参考文献

[1] 薄冰,王福祯.英语惯用法词典[M].北京:商务印书馆国际有限公司,2009.
[2] 费致德.现代英语惯用法词典[M].北京:商务印书馆,1981.
[3] 葛传椝.葛传椝英语惯用法词典[M].上海:上海译文出版社,2012.
[4] 荷恩毕.英语句型和惯用法[M].3版.刘贤彬,蔡丕杰,译.北京:商务印书馆,1981.
[5] 高凌,包天仁.新编大学英语动词用法词典[M].北京:世界图书出版公司,2000.
[6] 胡宛如.实用汉英英汉近义词辨析词典[M].北京:北京出版社,2005.
[7] 黄勇民.现代英语惯用法词典[M].上海:复旦大学出版社,2006.
[8] 斯旺.英语用法指南[M].庄绎传,郑荣成,等译.北京:外语教学与研究出版社,2000.
[9] 王福祯.新编英语惯用法词典[M].上海:上海远东出版社,2001.
[10] 王琼,徐达山.当代英语惯用法词典[M].北京:北京科学技术出版社,2004.
[11] 赵朝勇.英语习语——"源"来如此[M].上海:华东理工大学出版社,2010.
[12] 赵振才.英语常见问题解答大词典[M].哈尔滨:黑龙江人民出版社,1998.